Microsoft Azure Architect Technologies Study Companion

Hands-on Preparation and Practice for Exam AZ-300 and AZ-303

Rahul Sahay

Foreword by Mrinal Pandya

Apress®

Microsoft Azure Architect Technologies Study Companion: Hands-on Preparation and Practice for Exam AZ-300 and AZ-303

Rahul Sahay
Bangalore, India

ISBN-13 (pbk): 978-1-4842-6199-6
https://doi.org/10.1007/978-1-4842-6200-9

ISBN-13 (electronic): 978-1-4842-6200-9

Managing Director, Apress Media LLC: Welmoed Spahr
Acquisitions Editor: Smriti Srivastava
Development Editor: Laura Berendson
Coordinating Editor: Shrikant Vishwakarma

Cover designed by eStudioCalamar

Cover image designed by Freepik (www.freepik.com)

Distributed to the book trade worldwide by Springer Science+Business Media New York, 233 Spring Street, 6th Floor, New York, NY 10013. Phone 1-800-SPRINGER, fax (201) 348-4505, e-mail orders-ny@springer-sbm.com, or visit www.springeronline.com. Apress Media, LLC is a California LLC and the sole member (owner) is Springer Science + Business Media Finance Inc (SSBM Finance Inc). SSBM Finance Inc is a **Delaware** corporation.

For information on translations, please e-mail booktranslations@springernature.com; for reprint, paperback, or audio rights, please e-mail bookpermissions@springernature.com.

Apress titles may be purchased in bulk for academic, corporate, or promotional use. eBook versions and licenses are also available for most titles. For more information, reference our Print and eBook Bulk Sales web page at www.apress.com/bulk-sales.

Any source code or other supplementary material referenced by the author in this book is available to readers on GitHub via the book's product page, located at www.apress.com/978-1-4842-6199-6. For more detailed information, please visit www.apress.com/source-code.

Printed on acid-free paper

To my parents; to my wife, Nivedita; and to my son, Shivansh.
Without their support, this book would not have been
completed on time.

I would also like to dedicate this book to the readers,
who have expressed interest in learning Azure and have shown
trust in me by choosing this book to do it.

Table of Contents

About the Author

Rahul Sahay is a Microsoft MVP specializing in web technologies and currently is a software development engineer at Kongsberg Digital. He has been working in various aspects of the software development life cycle for 11+ years, focusing on web stack development. He has developed a range software, from client applications to web services to websites. Rahul is well-versed in C#, ASP.NET, .NET Core, Angular, microservices, Azure, Kubernetes, Docker, DevOps, Power BI, etc. He is also involved in designing application architecture from scratch. He spends most of his time writing platform-agnostic and cloud-agnostic code.

About the Technical Reviewer

Vidya Vrat Agarwal is a software architect, author, blogger, Microsoft MVP, C# Corner MVP, speaker, and mentor. He is a TOGAF-certified architect and a certified scrum master (CSM). He is currently working as a principal architect at T-Mobile US. He started working on Microsoft .NET with its first beta release. Vidya is passionate about people, process, and technology and loves to contribute to the .NET community. He lives in Redmond, Washington, with wife, Rupali; two daughters, Pearly and Arshika; and a girl puppy, Angel.

Foreword

Since the advent of cloud computing, there have been continuous improvements and additions to the cloud services offered by providers. Microsoft Azure is on the forefront by continuously expanding its set of services and helping organizations meet their business challenges.

Microsoft Azure gives businesses the freedom to develop and deploy their solutions on an ever-expanding global network, while allowing them to use the tools and frameworks of their own choice. In addition, continuous innovation by Microsoft not only supports an organization's product development needs today but also assures support for their product visions of the future.

This book was written for professionals who want to design robust solutions using Microsoft Azure for their businesses and products. It will help solution architects translate their business requirements into a cloud solution that not only uses the power of cloud computing on Microsoft Azure but also assures them that their products are scalable and reliable. With the help of this book, I believe that solution architects will be able to master the best cutting-edge technologies on the cloud and will be able to build solutions for tomorrow.

Mrinal Pandya
Department Manager
Kongsberg Digital
Bangalore, India

Acknowledgments

I would like to thank Apress for distributing this top-notch Azure book. Your group's support for completing the book was truly commendable. Also, I would like to express gratitude to Mrinal Pandya, my supervisor, for writing the foreword for the book. Finally, my gratitude goes to Vidya Vrat Agarwal for giving his time to review the book.

Introduction

This book covers the material you need to know to take and pass the AZ-300 exam, Architecting Microsoft Azure Solutions. Yet, the goal of this book is not to just prepare you to take the exam; rather, it is to help you become an Azure expert by being able to plan even the most complex design.

As you progress through the chapters of the book, you will see complex scenarios and learn how to execute the equivalent solutions in Azure.

Note that the AZ-300 program will eventually be renamed AZ-303. For more updates, visit https://docs.microsoft.com/en-us/learn/certifications/exams/az-300.

CHAPTER 1

Setting Expectations

In this chapter, we will get started with the prerequisites that are required to prepare for the Architecting Microsoft Azure Solutions certification exam. At the end of the book, you will find exercises (Chapter 22) you can complete to prepare for the lab assignments on the exam, and you will find practice questions (Chapter 23) to serve as a mock exam. It doesn't matter whether you are beginner or already have a few years of experience with Azure. There are a few things to note about this book:

- This book provides the content you will need to prepare for the AZ-300 certification exam.

- It is not an easy task to prepare for certification. Even if you have previous experience with Azure, you will need practice.

- Hands-on exercises are provided from a certification perspective.

- Even if you don't want a certification, you will learn many important concepts.

- By the time you finish the book, you will have a broad understanding of each concept and expert knowledge in some areas.

What Is Azure?

Azure, which is Microsoft's cloud offering, is a pay-as-you-go computing platform with tons of services. Azure is an ever-expanding set of cloud services to enable organizations to meet their business challenges. It offers the opportunity to build, manage, and deploy applications on a massive, global network utilizing your favorite tools and frameworks. You can find more details about Azure at https://azure.microsoft.com/en-in/overview/what-is-azure/.

© Rahul Sahay 2020
R. Sahay, *Microsoft Azure Architect Technologies Study Companion*,
https://doi.org/10.1007/978-1-4842-6200-9_1

What Is Cloud Computing?

Cloud computing is the delivery of computing services—including servers, storage, databases, etc.—over the Internet ("the cloud") to offer faster innovation, flexible resources, and economies of scale. You pay only for the cloud services you use, which helps you lower your operating costs, run your infrastructure more efficiently, and scale as your business needs change. The following are the top benefits of cloud computing:

- Cost
- Speed
- Global scale
- Productivity
- Performance
- Reliability
- Security
- And many more, which we will cover in depth in this book

Types of Cloud Computing

There are three types of cloud computing available on the market: public, private, and hybrid. Before getting started, you should know which offering suits you or your company best.

Public

In simple terms, according to Microsoft, "Public clouds are the most common way of deploying cloud computing. The cloud resources (like servers and storage) are owned and operated by a third-party cloud service provider and delivered over the Internet. Azure is an example of a public cloud. With a public cloud, all hardware, software, and other supporting infrastructure is owned and managed by the cloud provider. In a public cloud, you share the same hardware, storage, and network devices with other organizations or cloud tenants."

These are a few high-level advantages of a public cloud:

- Lower costs—no need to purchase hardware or software, and you pay only for the service you use.

- No maintenance—your service provider provides the maintenance.

- Near-unlimited scalability—on-demand resources are available to meet your business needs.

- High reliability—a vast network of servers ensures against failure.

Private

A private cloud consists of computing resources used exclusively by one business or organization. The private cloud can be physically located at your organization's on-site data center, or it can be hosted by a third-party service provider. But in a private cloud, the services and infrastructure are always maintained on a private network, and the hardware and software are dedicated solely to your organization. In this way, a private cloud can make it easier for an organization to customize its resources to meet specific IT requirements. Private clouds are often used by government agencies, financial institutions, or any other mid- to large-size organization with business-critical operations seeking enhanced control over their environment.

The following are advantages of private clouds:

- More flexibility—your organization can customize its cloud environment to meet specific business needs.

- Improved security—resources are not shared with others, so higher levels of control and security are possible.

- High scalability—private clouds still afford the scalability and efficiency of a public cloud.

- More flexibility—the Azure stack can be downloaded into private data centers, which means your own private data center will be boosted by Azure's private cloud.

Hybrid

Often referred to as "the best of both worlds," hybrid clouds combine on-premises infrastructure, or private clouds, with public clouds so organizations can reap the advantages of both. In a hybrid cloud, data and applications can move between private and public clouds for greater flexibility and more deployment options. For instance, you can use the public cloud for high-volume, lower-security needs such as web-based email and then use the private cloud (or other on-premises infrastructure) for sensitive, business-critical operations such as financial reporting. In a hybrid cloud, "cloud bursting" is also an option.

The following are advantages of hybrid clouds:

- Control—your organization can maintain a private infrastructure for sensitive assets.

- Flexibility—you can take advantage of additional resources in the public cloud when you need them.

- Cost-effectiveness—with the ability to scale to the public cloud, you pay for extra computing power only when needed.

- Ease—transitioning to the cloud doesn't have to be overwhelming because you can migrate gradually, phasing in workloads over time.

Types of Cloud Services

Most cloud computing is categorized into four broad categories.

Infrastructure as a service (IaaS) is where you rent the IT infrastructure—servers and virtual machines (VMs), storage, networks, etc.—from a cloud provider on a pay-as-you-go basis.

Platform as a service (PaaS) refers to cloud computing services that supply an on-demand environment for developing, testing, delivering, and managing software applications. PaaS is designed to make it easier for developers to quickly create web or mobile apps, without worrying about setting up or managing the underlying infrastructure.

Software as a service (SaaS) is a method for delivering software applications over the Internet, on demand and typically on a subscription basis. With SaaS, cloud providers host and manage the software application and underlying infrastructure, and they also handle any maintenance, such as software upgrades and security patching.

Serverless computing focuses on building app functionality without spending time continually managing the servers and infrastructure required. The cloud provider handles the setup, capacity planning, and server management for you. Serverless architectures are highly scalable and event-driven.

These are the high-level classification of categories. All these categories are explained in more detail in the coming chapters.

Azure Free Account

To get started, you need either a subscription or a free account. You can visit `https://azure.microsoft.com/en-us/free/` to sign up and get a free credit worth $200 for one month. Check the website for the most up-to-date list of free offerings.

Setting the Budget

It's always good practice to stay within your budget. Hence, the first thing we are going to do is set up a budget. (If you are using free account, then you don't have to worry about this.) If you have a subscription for Visual Studio, a pay-as-you-go account, or any other subscription, then go to the home page at `https://portal.azure.com`, as shown in Figure 1-1.

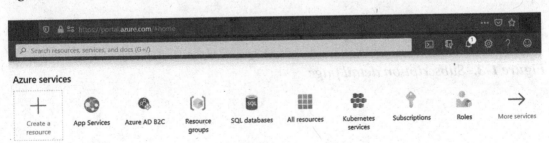

Figure 1-1. *Azure home page*

Click Subscriptions, as shown in Figure 1-1. This will bring up the screen in Figure 1-2.

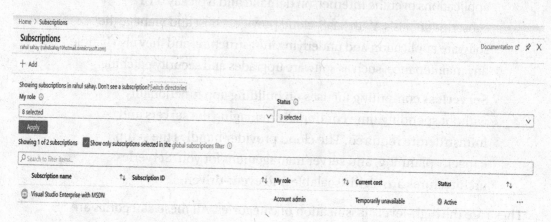

Figure 1-2. *Subscriptions page*

Figure 1-2 shows my subscription, where I have purposely masked the subscription ID. You can click the ID and rename it, as shown in Figure 1-3.

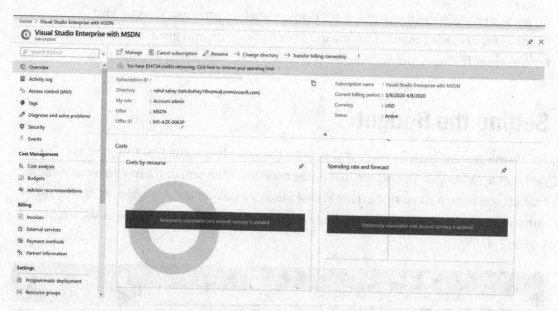

Figure 1-3. *Subscription detail page*

Currently, you won't see anything here as you haven't set up anything so far. But, when I click "Costs by resource," the screen in Figure 1-4 appears.

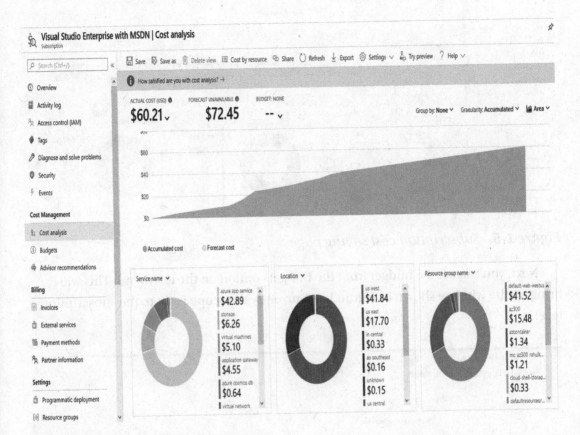

Figure 1-4. *Subscription cost page*

Save the costs, and you'll see the screen in Figure 1-5.

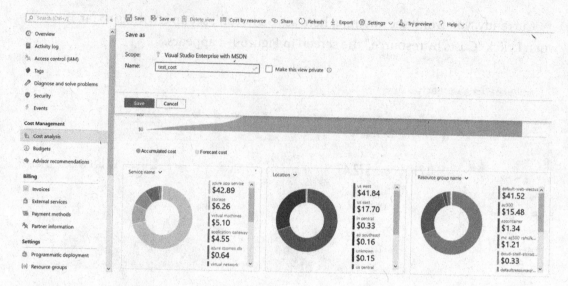

Figure 1-5. *Subscription cost saving page*

Next, you can set the budget from the Budgets option on the left menu. This will
bring up the window shown in Figure 1-6. Currently the scope is set to the subscription
level.

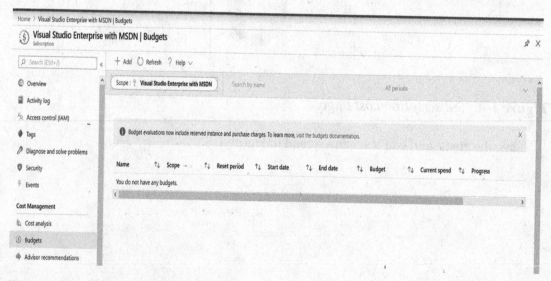

Figure 1-6. *Subscription level page*

You can also set the budget at the minute level, such as the resource group level or even the resource, as shown in Figure 1-7.

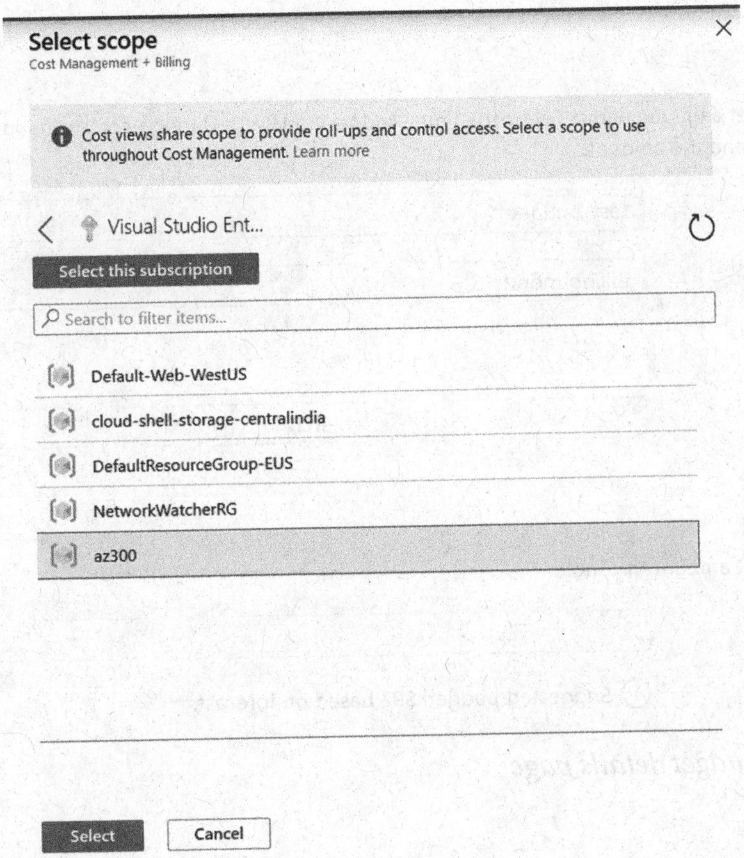

Select scope
Cost Management + Billing   ×

ℹ️ Cost views share scope to provide roll-ups and control access. Select a scope to use throughout Cost Management. Learn more

< 🔑 Visual Studio Ent...   ↻

Select this subscription

🔍 Search to filter items...

[⬡] Default-Web-WestUS

[⬡] cloud-shell-storage-centralindia

[⬡] DefaultResourceGroup-EUS

[⬡] NetworkWatcherRG

[⬡] az300

Select   Cancel

Figure 1-7. Scope level page

I am fine with the subscription level; hence, I will cancel this and continue with the subscription level. I am adding the new budget details shown in Figure 1-8 and Figure 1-9.

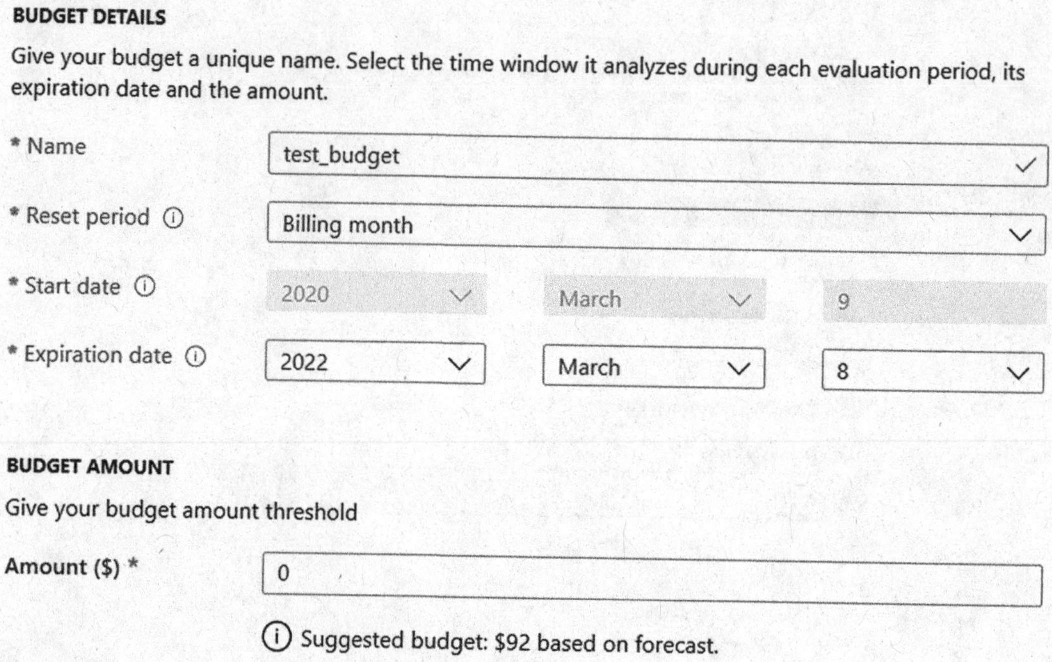

BUDGET DETAILS

Give your budget a unique name. Select the time window it analyzes during each evaluation period, its expiration date and the amount.

* Name	test_budget		✓
* Reset period ⓘ	Billing month		⌄
* Start date ⓘ	2020 ⌄	March ⌄	9
* Expiration date ⓘ	2022 ⌄	March ⌄	8 ⌄

BUDGET AMOUNT

Give your budget amount threshold

Amount ($) *	0

ⓘ Suggested budget: $92 based on forecast.

Figure 1-8. *Budget details page*

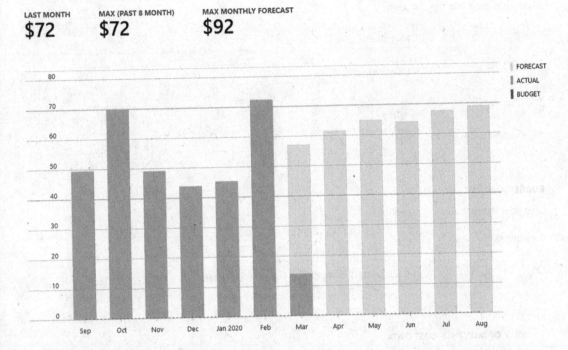

VIEW OF MONTHLY COST DATA
Sep 2019 - Aug 2020

LAST MONTH	MAX (PAST 8 MONTH)	MAX MONTHLY FORECAST
$72	**$72**	**$92**

Figure 1-9. Budget details, continued

This screen gives a clear picture of my past spending and forecasts my future spending. I can go ahead and put $92 as my budget or I can increase it a little bit, as shown in Figure 1-10.

11

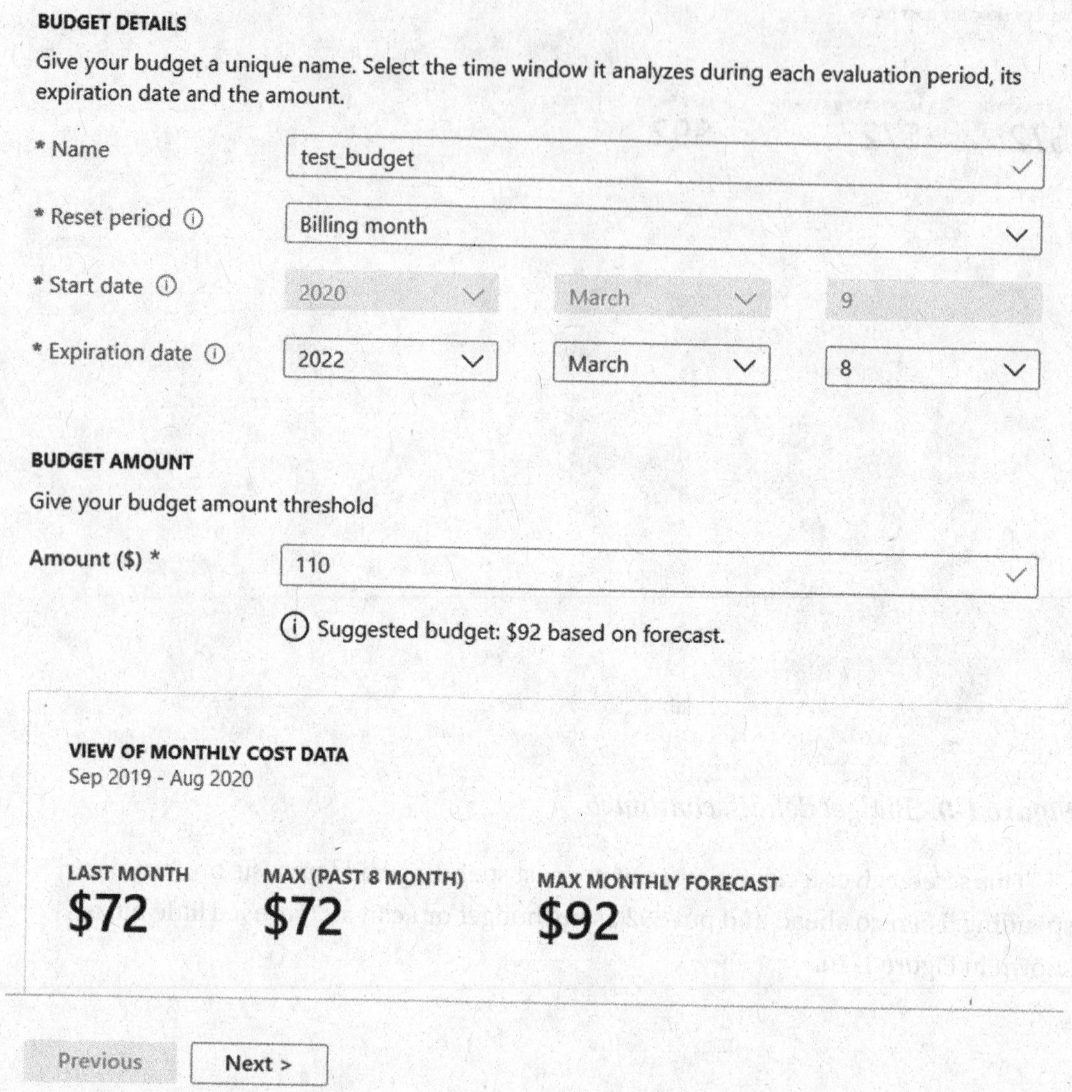

BUDGET DETAILS

Give your budget a unique name. Select the time window it analyzes during each evaluation period, its expiration date and the amount.

* Name

test_budget ✓

* Reset period ⓘ

Billing month ⌄

* Start date ⓘ

2020 ⌄   March ⌄   9

* Expiration date ⓘ

2022 ⌄   March ⌄   8 ⌄

BUDGET AMOUNT

Give your budget amount threshold

Amount ($) *

110 ✓

ⓘ Suggested budget: $92 based on forecast.

VIEW OF MONTHLY COST DATA
Sep 2019 - Aug 2020

LAST MONTH
$72

MAX (PAST 8 MONTH)
$72

MAX MONTHLY FORECAST
$92

Previous   Next >

Figure 1-10. *Budget amount page*

Click the Next button. This will take you to the screen shown in Figure 1-11.

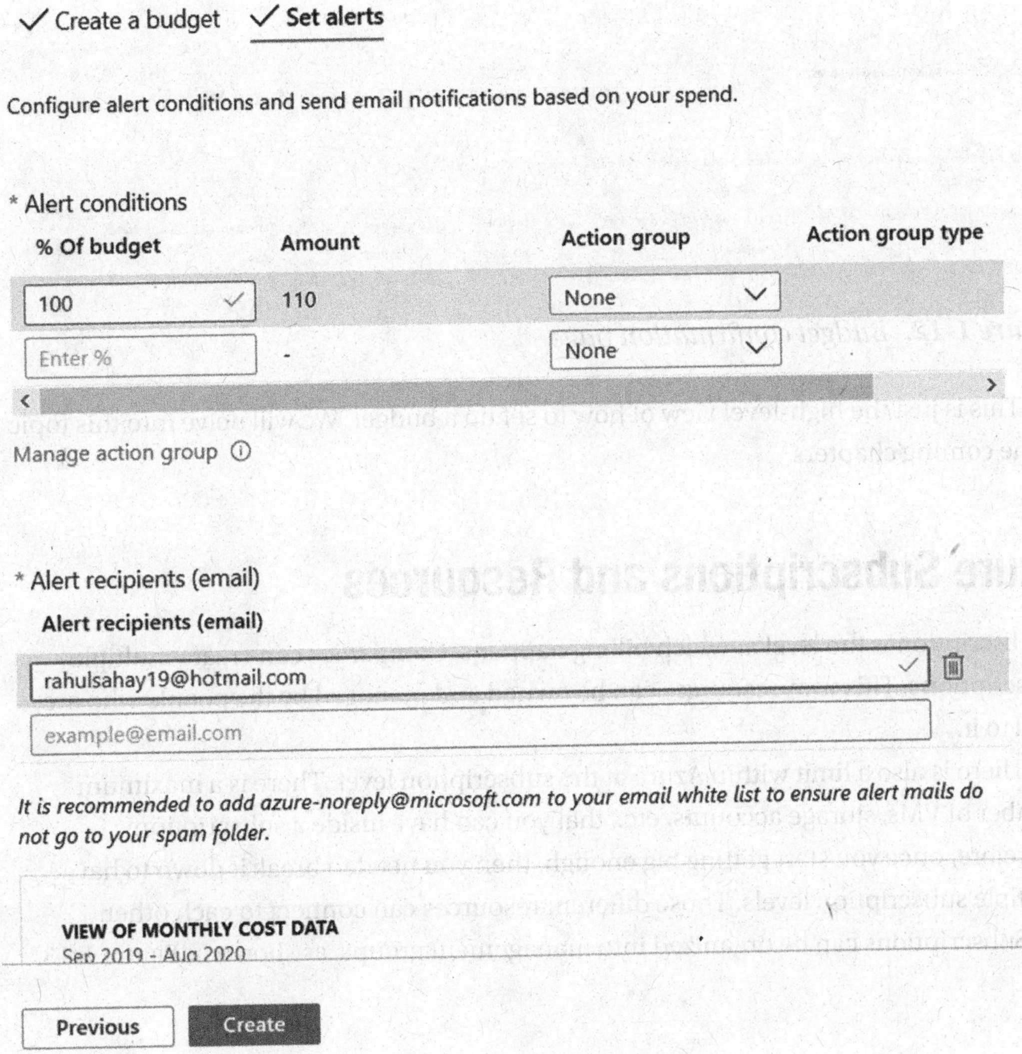

✓ Create a budget   ✓ **Set alerts**

Configure alert conditions and send email notifications based on your spend.

* Alert conditions

% Of budget	Amount	Action group	Action group type
100 ✓	110	None ⌄	
Enter %	-	None ⌄	

< _____ >

Manage action group ⓘ

* Alert recipients (email)

Alert recipients (email)

| rahulsahay19@hotmail.com ✓ | 🗑 |

| example@email.com | |

It is recommended to add azure-noreply@microsoft.com to your email white list to ensure alert mails do not go to your spam folder.

VIEW OF MONTHLY COST DATA
Sep 2019 - Aug 2020

| Previous | Create |

Figure 1-11. *Budget alert condition page*

You can set up an alert condition here so that when 100 percent of this budget hits, you will get an email notification. Upon creation, it will look like the screen in Figure 1-12.

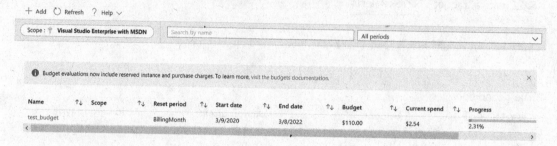

Figure 1-12. *Budget confirmation page*

This is just the high-level view of how to set up a budget. We will delve into this topic in the coming chapters.

Azure Subscriptions and Resources

A subscription is the level at which billing happens. Companies can create multiple subscriptions. This way, resources can be owned and managed by the people who are local to it.

There is also a limit within Azure at the subscription level. There is a maximum number of VMs, storage accounts, etc., that you can have inside a subscription. Therefore, once you start getting big enough, then you need to break it down to have multiple subscription levels. Those different resources can connect to each other.

Subscriptions can be organized into management groups, as shown in Figure 1-13.

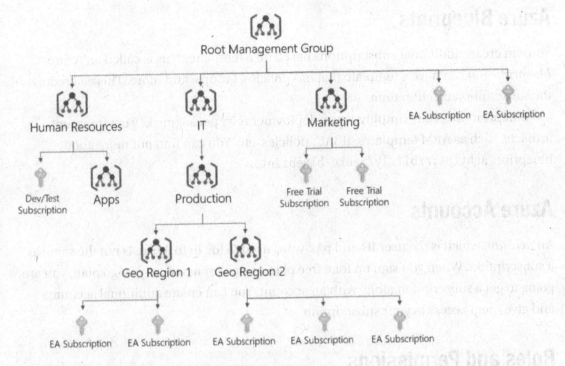

Figure 1-13. *Root management group page*

Azure Subscription Options

There are three subscription options in Azure.

- Enterprise agreement

- Pay-as-you-go option

- Free plan

The enterprise agreement is one of the most common ways for large companies to use Azure. For example, you can negotiate that you want 100 VMs as part of your contract.

Individuals can explore the pay-as-you-go option. No is agreement required.

You can also buy from a Microsoft partner. For example, if a Microsoft partner is developing a custom solution on top of Azure, you can buy from them.

Azure Blueprints

You can create additional subscriptions based on a template. This is called an Azure *blueprint*. You can have a template that has policies, groups, and more. This will reduce the subscription creation time.

Blueprints basically simplify Azure deployments by packaging key environment artifacts, such as ARM templates, RBAC, policies, etc. You can find out more about blueprints at `https://bit.ly/azure-blueprints`.

Azure Accounts

An *account*, which is the user ID and password used to log in to Azure is not the same as a subscription. When you sign up for a free plan or sign for a pay-as-you-go plan, you are going to get a subscription along with an account. You can create additional accounts and give them access to your subscription.

Roles and Permissions

Not everyone is going to have the same permission. There are many roles such as owner, contributor, and many other levels down to the reader level. You can set permissions at very granular level.

Azure Policy

You probably don't want anyone to come and create a VM with 16 or more CPUs. Therefore, you can create a policy and enforce it on all VM creation or an entire resource group or entire account.

Subscriptions with Resources

Figure 1-14 explains how subscriptions relate to resources.

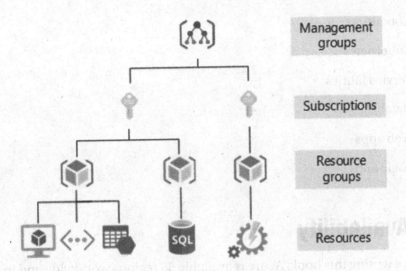

Figure 1-14. Group hierarchy page

A resource group (RG) is like a file structure or file group. Here, resources belong to one and only one RG.

Permissions and Reporting

The good thing about resource groups that they become a boundary for certain permissions and reporting. You can delete the resources easily. You can create resource groups that represent projects, groups of people, etc.

Tagging

Azure uses a tagging metaphor. Therefore, beyond RGs, you can also set tags on resources such as billing, production, staging, etc.

Azure Services

The following are the services that Azure provides. In the coming chapters, you will learn about these services in detail with complete Azure lab examples.

- Virtual machines

- Azure functions

17

- Containers

- Kubernetes

- Service fabrics

- Databases

- Web apps

- Logic apps

Azure Availability

At the time of writing this book, Azure is available 58 regions worldwide and in 140 countries, as shown in Figure 1-15.

Figure 1-15. *Azure availability page*

Not all regions are available to all customers. For example, the US government has three individual clouds that are meant for the US government only. Likewise, Germany has its own clouds only for German citizens. There are other restricted regions as well.

CHAPTER 2

Virtual Machines

A *virtual machine* is a computer file, aka image, that behaves like an actual computer. In other words, it's a way to create a computer within a computer. It runs in a window, much like any other program, giving the end user the same experience on a virtual machine as they would have on an actual machine. The virtual machine is isolated from the OS, meaning that the software inside a virtual machine cannot tamper with anything on the host machine. This makes it an ideal platform for testing any software beta releases. Here are a few salient points about VMs:

- Virtual machines are one of three pillars of cloud computing's infrastructure as a service. (The other two are storage and networking.)

- You can install anything on a VM.

- You can use a virtual machine and then shut it down. You will be charged only for that usage period.

- Based on your needs, you can choose from different combinations of settings. Azure provides more than 120 combinations of settings for creating VMs.

Based on the instance size, billing will differ. The 120+ types are categorized under Instance Types. Here are the categories:

General Purpose—balanced VMs. This is the description according to Microsoft: "Balanced CPU-to-memory ratio. Ideal for testing and development, small to medium databases, and low to medium traffic web servers."

- D Series

- A Series (noncritical)

- B Series (economical)

- DC Series (preview, confidential computing)

19

Compute Optimized—double the CPU cores. This is the description according to Microsoft: "High CPU-to-memory ratio. Good for medium traffic web servers, network appliances, batch processes, and application servers."

- F Series

Memory Optimized—double the memory. This is the description according to Microsoft: "High memory-to-core ratio. Great for relational database servers, medium to large caches, and in-memory analytics."

- E Series

- D11-15

- G Series (includes powerful CPU for database workloads)

- M Series (certified for SAP HANA, up to 416 cores + 12 TB memory)

Storage Optimized—double the local storage. This is the description according to Microsoft: "High disk throughput and IO. Ideal for Big Data, SQL, and NoSQL databases."

- L Series

GPU—Access to a graphics processing unit. This is the description according to Microsoft: "Specialized virtual machines targeted for heavy graphic rendering and video editing available with single or multiple GPUs."

- N Series (including NC, NV, ND)

High-Performance Compute—fastest everything. This is the description according to Microsoft: "Our fastest and most powerful CPU virtual machines with optional high-throughput network interfaces (RDMA)."

- H Series (incl HB and HC)

Creating a VM

This section covers how to create a VM, which is pretty straightforward. To start, click "Virtual machines" and then Create, as shown in Figure 2-1. You will then see the screen in Figure 2-2.

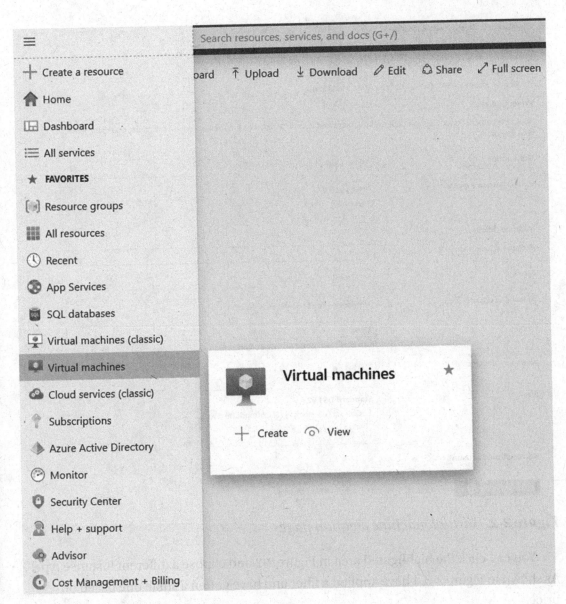

Figure 2-1. *Getting started creating a VM*

Dashboard > Create a virtual machine

Create a virtual machine

customization.

Looking for classic VMs?   Create VM from Azure Marketplace

Project details

Select the subscription to manage deployed resources and costs. Use resource groups like folders to organize and manage all your resources.

Subscription * ⓘ

| Visual Studio Enterprise with MSDN | ∨ |

Resource group * ⓘ

| (New) az300 | ∨ |

Create new

Instance details

Virtual machine name * ⓘ

| aznewvm | ✓ |

Region * ⓘ

| (Asia Pacific) Central India | ∨ |

Availability options ⓘ

| No infrastructure redundancy required | ∨ |

Image * ⓘ

| Windows Server 2016 Datacenter | ∨ |

Browse all public and private images

Azure Spot instance ⓘ

○ Yes ● No

Size * ⓘ

> **Standard DS1 v2**
> 1 vcpu, 3.5 GiB memory ($62.50/month)
> Change size

Administrator account

[Review + create]   [< Previous]   [Next : Disks >]

Figure 2-2. *Virtual machine creation page*

You can click the highlighted area in Figure 2-2 and choose a different instance type. As shown in Figure 2-3, I have applied a filter and have gotten a small one based on price.

Select a VM size
Browse available virtual machine sizes and their features

| Search by VM size... | | Clear all filters | | | | | | | |

Size : **Small (0-6)** ⊗   Generation : **2 selected** ⊗   Family : **General purpose** ⊗   Premium disk : **Supported** ⊗   vCPUs : **1-4** ⊗   ⊹ Add filter

Showing 11 of 178 VM sizes. | Subscription: Visual Studio Enterprise with MSDN | Region: Central India | Current size: Standard_DS1_v2

VM Si...↑↓	Offering ↑↓	Family ↑↓	vCP...↑↓	RAM (...↑↓	Data disks ↑↓	Max IOPS ↑↓	Temporary stora...↑↓	Premium disk s... ↑↓	Cost/month (est...↑↓
DS1_v2	Standard	General purpose	1	3.5	4	3200	7	Yes	$62.50
DS2_v2	Standard	General purpose	2	7	8	6400	14	Yes	$125.74
DS3_v2	Standard	General purpose	4	14	16	12800	28	Yes	$250.73
B1ls ⓘ	Standard	General purpose	1	0.5	2	160	4	Yes	$4.17
B1ms ⓘ	Standard	General purpose	1	2	2	640	4	Yes	$16.67
B1s ⓘ	Standard	General purpose	1	1	2	320	4	Yes	$8.33
B2ms ⓘ	Standard	General purpose	2	8	4	1920	16	Yes	$66.66
B2s ⓘ	Standard	General purpose	2	4	4	1280	8	Yes	$33.33
B4ms ⓘ	Standard	General purpose	4	16	8	2880	32	Yes	$133.18
D2s_v3 ⓘ	Standard	General purpose	2	8	4	3200	16	Yes	$78.12
D4s_v3 ⓘ	Standard	General purpose	4	16	8	6400	32	Yes	$156.24

Figure 2-3. *Virtual machine size page*

However, offerings and costs differ from region to region. If I select East US, for example, I may get more options for a lower cost, as shown in Figure 2-4.

Select a VM size
Browse available virtual machine sizes and their features

| Search by VM size... | | Clear all filters | | | | | | | |

Size : **Small (0-6)** ⊗   Generation : **2 selected** ⊗   Family : **General purpose** ⊗   Premium disk : **Supported** ⊗   vCPUs : **1-4** ⊗   ⊹ Add filter

Showing 13 of 258 VM sizes. | Subscription: Visual Studio Enterprise with MSDN | Region: East US | Current size: Standard_DS1_v2

VM Si...↑↓	Offering ↑↓	Family ↑↓	vCP...↑↓	RAM (...↑↓	Data disks ↑↓	Max IOPS ↑↓	Temporary stora...↑↓	Premium disk s... ↑↓	Cost/month (est...↑↓
B1ls	Standard	General purpose	1	0.5	2	160	4	Yes	$3.87
B1ms	Standard	General purpose	1	2	2	640	4	Yes	$15.40
B1s	Standard	General purpose	1	1	2	320	4	Yes	$7.74
B2ms	Standard	General purpose	2	8	4	1920	16	Yes	$61.90
B2s	Standard	General purpose	2	4	4	1280	8	Yes	$30.95
B4ms	Standard	General purpose	4	16	8	2880	32	Yes	$123.50
D2s_v3	Standard	General purpose	2	8	4	3200	16	Yes	$71.42
D4s_v3	Standard	General purpose	4	16	8	6400	32	Yes	$142.85
DS1_v2	Standard	General purpose	1	3.5	4	3200	7	Yes	$54.31
DS2_v2	Standard	General purpose	2	7	8	6400	14	Yes	$108.62
DS3_v2	Standard	General purpose	4	14	16	12800	28	Yes	$217.99
D2as_v4 ⓘ	Standard	General purpose	2	8	4	3200	16	Yes	$71.42
D4as_v4 ⓘ	Standard	General purpose	4	16	8	6400	32	Yes	$142.85

Figure 2-4. *Virtual machine cost page*

As you can see, the price is lower for this region.

In addition to RDP, I have enabled ports 80 and 443 (see Figure 2-5). This is a good option for web developers. Port 443 enables developers to use Secure Socket Layer (SSL) features.

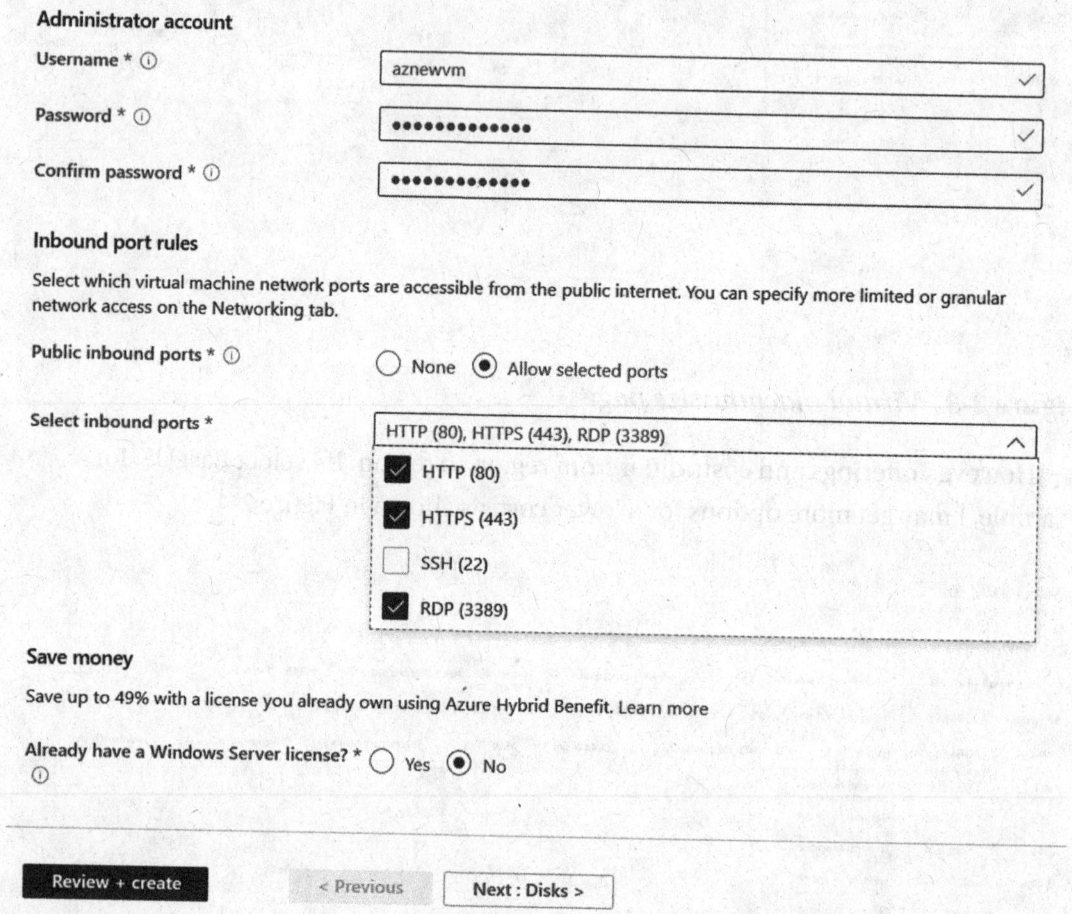

Administrator account

Username * ⓘ

> aznewvm ✓

Password * ⓘ

> •••••••••••••• ✓

Confirm password * ⓘ

> •••••••••••••• ✓

Inbound port rules

Select which virtual machine network ports are accessible from the public internet. You can specify more limited or granular network access on the Networking tab.

Public inbound ports * ⓘ   ○ None ◉ Allow selected ports

Select inbound ports *

> HTTP (80), HTTPS (443), RDP (3389) ∧
>
> ☑ HTTP (80)
>
> ☑ HTTPS (443)
>
> ☐ SSH (22)
>
> ☑ RDP (3389)

Save money

Save up to 49% with a license you already own using Azure Hybrid Benefit. Learn more

Already have a Windows Server license? * ⓘ ○ Yes ◉ No

[Review + create]   [< Previous]   [Next : Disks >]

Figure 2-5. *Virtual machine ports page*

If you already have a Windows server license, then you can apply that as well, and the pricing will drop further. On the next page, you will see the Show Disks option. If you want additional disks, you can choose from the options, as shown in Figure 2-6. These are selected by default.

Basics	Disks	Networking	Management	Advanced	Tags	Review + create

Azure VMs have one operating system disk and a temporary disk for short-term storage. You can attach additional data disks. The size of the VM determines the type of storage you can use and the number of data disks allowed. Learn more

Disk options

OS disk type * ⓘ

Premium SSD	⌄

Enable Ultra Disk compatibility ⓘ   ◯ Yes ◉ No

Ultra Disk compatibility is not available for this VM size and location.

Data disks

You can add and configure additional data disks for your virtual machine or attach existing disks. This VM also comes with a temporary disk.

LUN	Name	Size (GiB)	Disk type	Host caching

Create and attach a new disk   Attach an existing disk

⌄ **Advanced**

Review + create		< Previous	Next : Networking >

Figure 2-6. *Virtual machine disks page*

The process is similar for networking, management, and other configuration items. You can also click "Review + create" to go with the default options. See Figure 2-7.

Basics	Disks	Networking	Management	Advanced	Tags	Review + create

Define network connectivity for your virtual machine by configuring network interface card (NIC) settings. You can control ports, inbound and outbound connectivity with security group rules, or place behind an existing load balancing solution.
Learn more

Network interface

When creating a virtual machine, a network interface will be created for you.

Virtual network * ⓘ

(new) az300-vnet   ⌄
Create new

Subnet * ⓘ

(new) default (10.0.0.0/24)   ⌄

Public IP ⓘ

(new) aznewvm-ip   ⌄
Create new

NIC network security group ⓘ   ◯ None ⦿ Basic ◯ Advanced

Public inbound ports * ⓘ   ◯ None ⦿ Allow selected ports

Select inbound ports *

HTTP (80), HTTPS (443), RDP (3389)   ⌄

> ⚠ **This will allow all IP addresses to access your virtual machine.** This is only recommended for testing. Use the Advanced controls in the Networking tab to create rules to limit inbound traffic to known IP addresses.

Review + create		< Previous	Next : Management >

Figure 2-7. *Virtual machine networking page*

Accelerated networking is when two machines running on the same network are able to talk to each other. It is not supported for the size of virtual machine that I chose, but it works much faster than standard networking. See Figure 2-8.

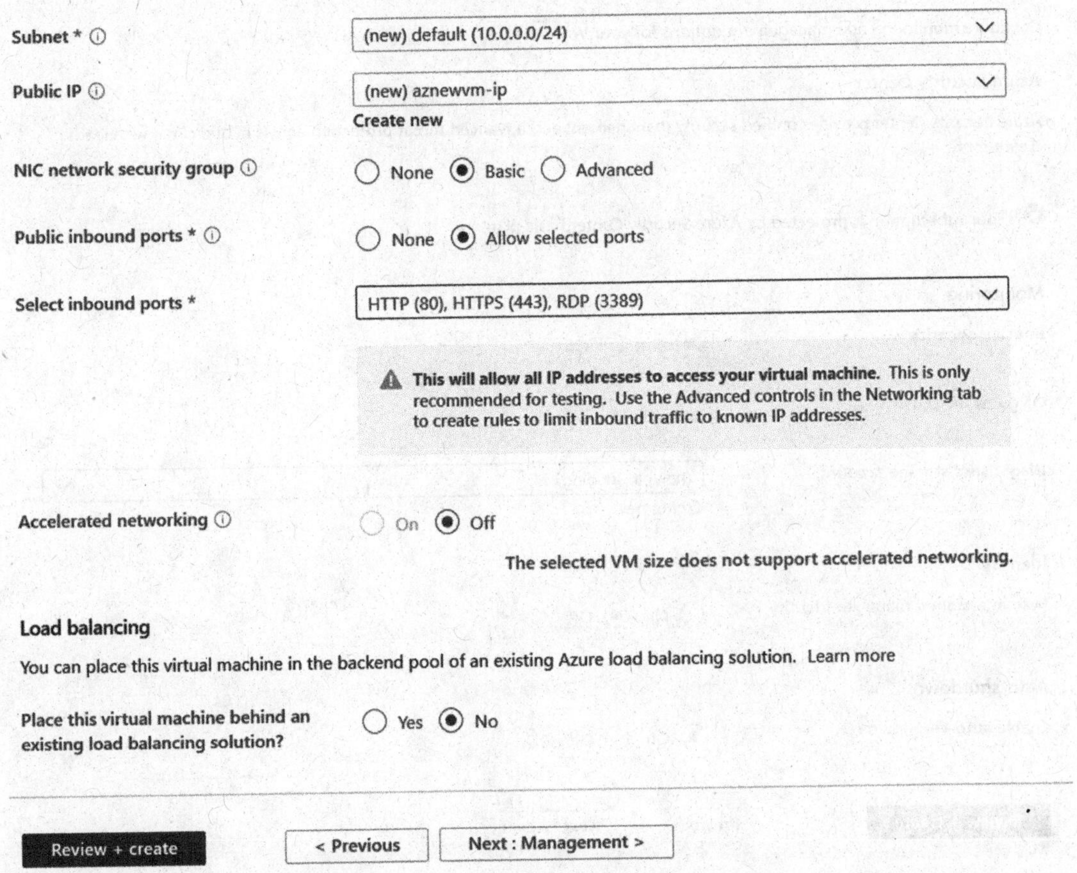

Subnet * ⓘ	(new) default (10.0.0.0/24) ⌄
Public IP ⓘ	(new) aznewvm-ip ⌄
	Create new
NIC network security group ⓘ	○ None ◉ Basic ○ Advanced
Public inbound ports * ⓘ	○ None ◉ Allow selected ports
Select inbound ports *	HTTP (80), HTTPS (443), RDP (3389) ⌄

⚠ **This will allow all IP addresses to access your virtual machine.** This is only recommended for testing. Use the Advanced controls in the Networking tab to create rules to limit inbound traffic to known IP addresses.

Accelerated networking ⓘ	○ On ◉ Off
	The selected VM size does not support accelerated networking.

Load balancing

You can place this virtual machine in the backend pool of an existing Azure load balancing solution. Learn more

Place this virtual machine behind an existing load balancing solution?	○ Yes ◉ No

[Review + create]   [< Previous] [Next : Management >]

Figure 2-8. *Virtual machine accelerated networking option*

We will discuss load balancing in another chapter. On the management page, you will get the options shown in Figure 2-9.

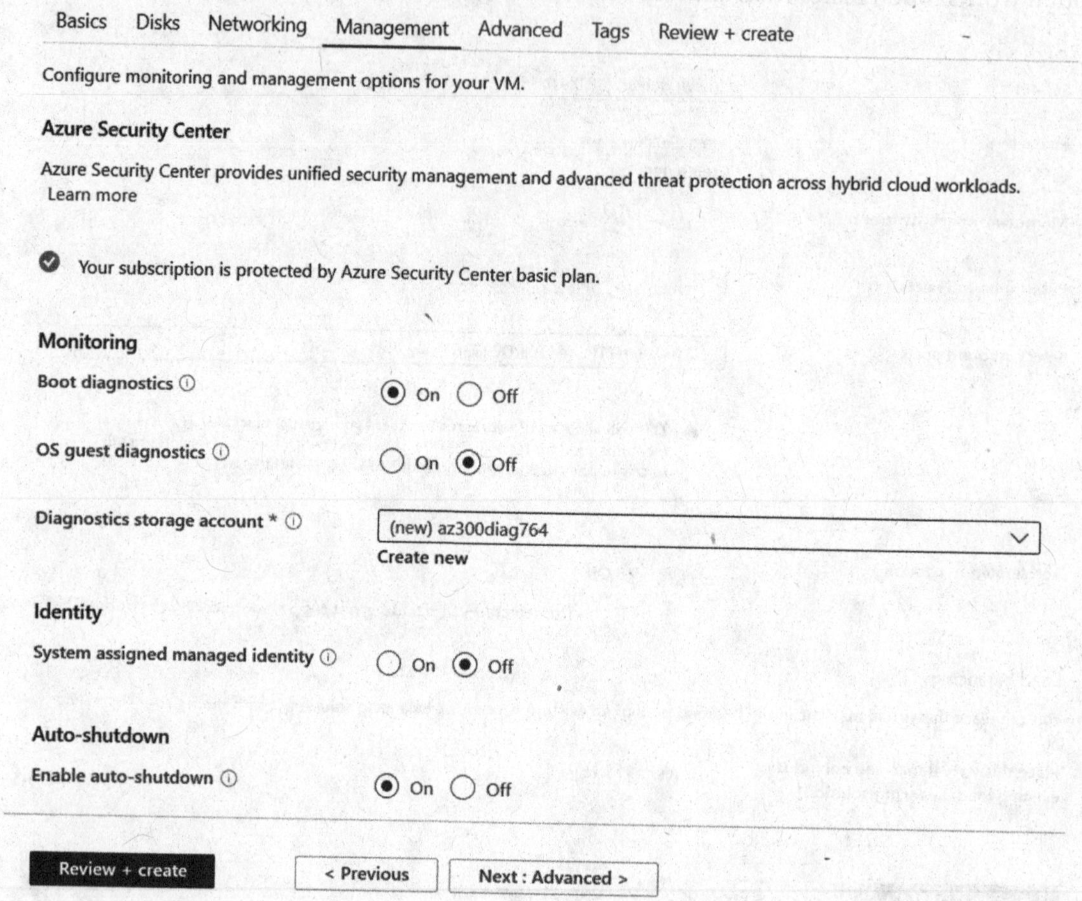

Basics   Disks   Networking   **Management**   Advanced   Tags   Review + create   _

Configure monitoring and management options for your VM.

Azure Security Center

Azure Security Center provides unified security management and advanced threat protection across hybrid cloud workloads. Learn more

✓   Your subscription is protected by Azure Security Center basic plan.

Monitoring

Boot diagnostics ⓘ   ● On   ○ Off

OS guest diagnostics ⓘ   ○ On   ● Off

Diagnostics storage account * ⓘ   (new) az300diag764   ⌄
                                     Create new

Identity

System assigned managed identity ⓘ   ○ On   ● Off

Auto-shutdown

Enable auto-shutdown ⓘ   ● On   ○ Off

| Review + create | < Previous | Next : Advanced > |

Figure 2-9. *Virtual machine management page*

If you want to set up diagnostics or any additional identity management, you can set it up on the management page. This will enable you to grant role-based access.

You can also set when you want the machine to shut down and configure whether you want a backup of your machine, as shown in Figure 2-10.

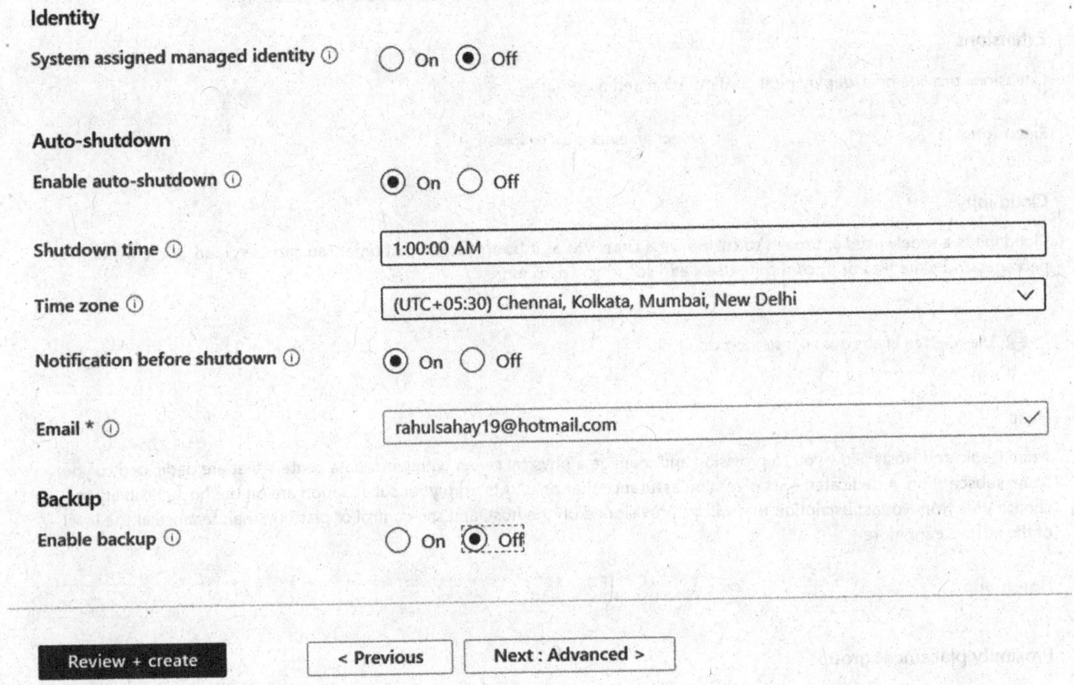

Identity

System assigned managed identity ⓘ   ◯ On ⦿ Off

Auto-shutdown

Enable auto-shutdown ⓘ   ⦿ On ◯ Off

Shutdown time ⓘ | 1:00:00 AM |

Time zone ⓘ | (UTC+05:30) Chennai, Kolkata, Mumbai, New Delhi   ⌄ |

Notification before shutdown ⓘ   ⦿ On ◯ Off

Email * ⓘ | rahulsahay19@hotmail.com   ✓ |

Backup

Enable backup ⓘ   ◯ On ⦿ Off

| Review + create | | < Previous | | Next : Advanced > |

Figure 2-10. *Virtual machine backup page*

Next, you will see advanced settings for any kind of post-installation steps such as antivirus installation, configuration management, etc. (see Figure 2-11).

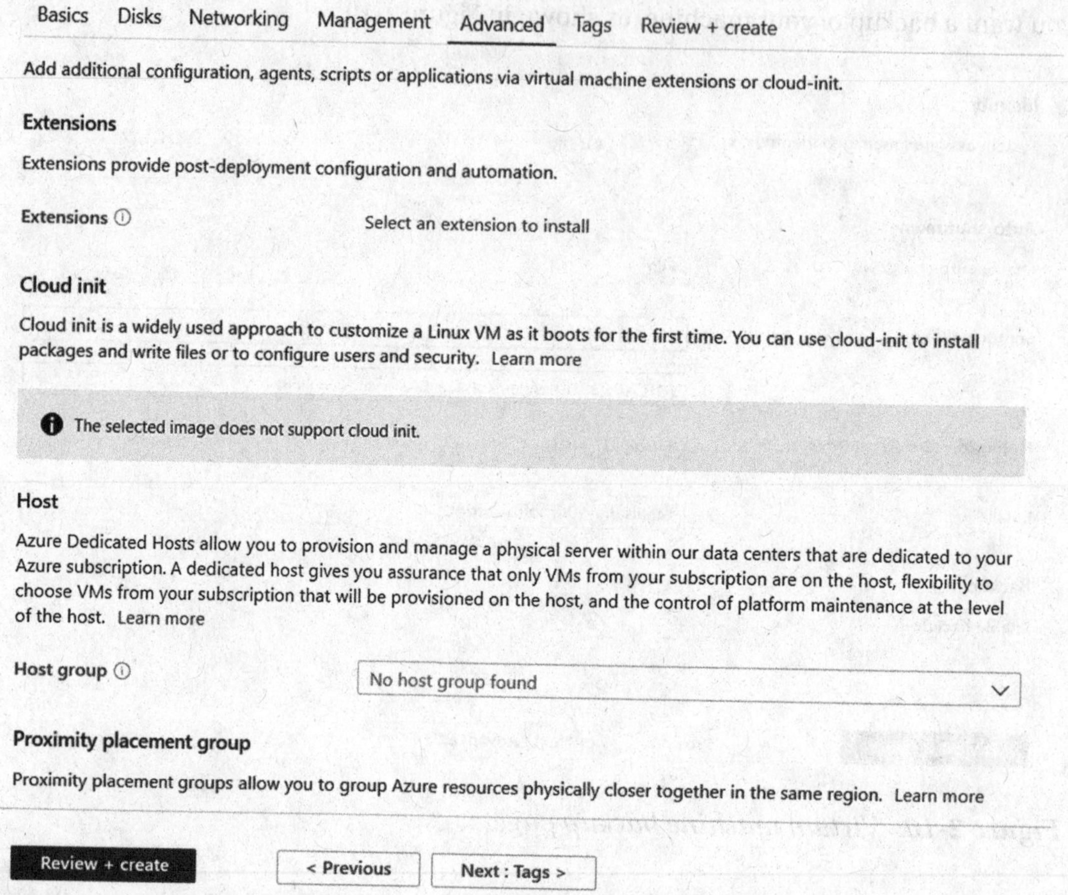

Basics   Disks   Networking   Management   **Advanced**   Tags   Review + create

Add additional configuration, agents, scripts or applications via virtual machine extensions or cloud-init.

Extensions

Extensions provide post-deployment configuration and automation.

Extensions ⓘ   Select an extension to install

Cloud init

Cloud init is a widely used approach to customize a Linux VM as it boots for the first time. You can use cloud-init to install packages and write files or to configure users and security. Learn more

> ⓘ The selected image does not support cloud init.

Host

Azure Dedicated Hosts allow you to provision and manage a physical server within our data centers that are dedicated to your Azure subscription. A dedicated host gives you assurance that only VMs from your subscription are on the host, flexibility to choose VMs from your subscription that will be provisioned on the host, and the control of platform maintenance at the level of the host. Learn more

Host group ⓘ | No host group found   ⌄ |

Proximity placement group

Proximity placement groups allow you to group Azure resources physically closer together in the same region. Learn more

[Review + create]   [< Previous]   [Next : Tags >]

Figure 2-11. *Virtual machine advanced page*

Next comes tagging, where you can set up the tags, as shown in Figure 2-12. Azure will automatically pick and tag items associated with a VM. Tagging is one of the cleanest ways to segregate resources such as which resource belongs to which category.

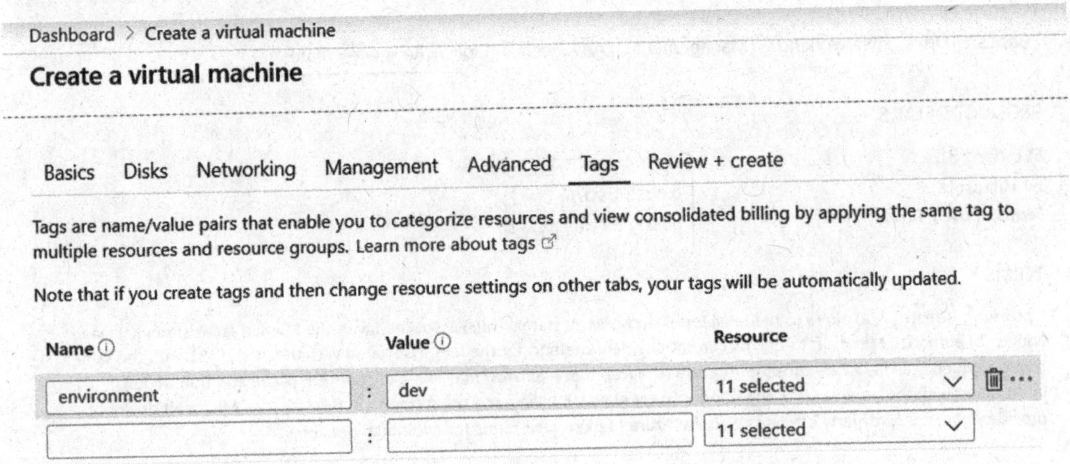

Dashboard > Create a virtual machine

Create a virtual machine

Basics   Disks   Networking   Management   Advanced   Tags   Review + create

Tags are name/value pairs that enable you to categorize resources and view consolidated billing by applying the same tag to multiple resources and resource groups. Learn more about tags ⬀

Note that if you create tags and then change resource settings on other tabs, your tags will be automatically updated.

Name ⓘ		Value ⓘ	Resource		
environment	:	dev	11 selected	⌄	🗑 ⋯
	:		11 selected	⌄	

Figure 2-12.   Virtual machine tags page

Last but not the least, you will see the lovely summary page, as shown in Figure 2-13.

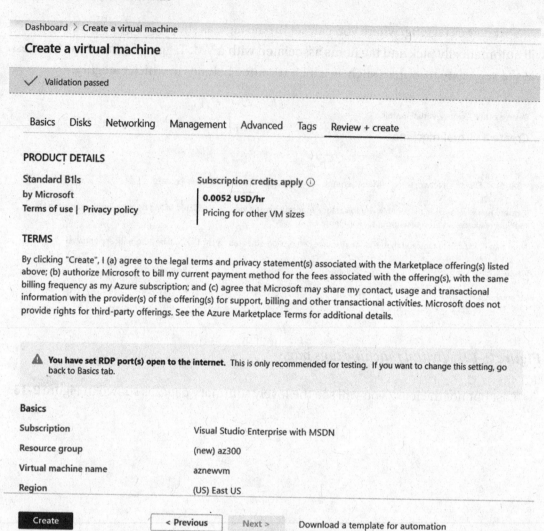

Figure 2-13.   Virtual machine review page

Once you're done with all the settings, you can click the Create button. See Figure 2-14.

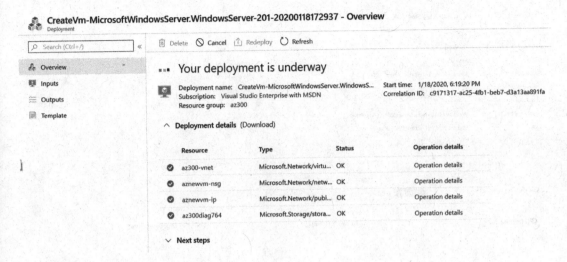

Figure 2-14. Deployment page

This is going to take some time. You can see that deployment is happening in real time. Once it's done, you will see a screen like the one shown in Figure 2-15.

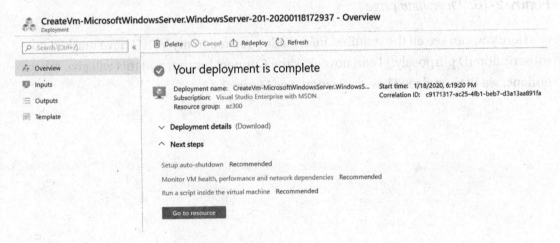

Figure 2-15. Deployment status page

Now you can simply click "Go to resource," which will bring up the screen shown in Figure 2-16.

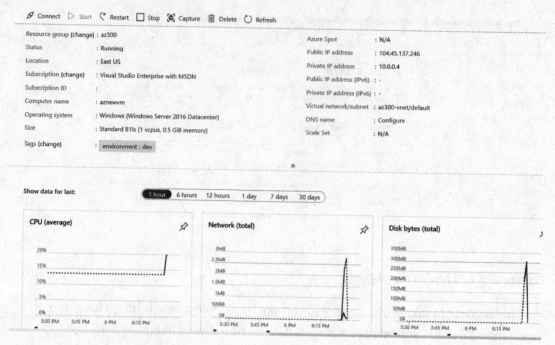

Figure 2-16. *Overview page*

Here you can see all the required information related to my VM. (I have masked my subscription ID purposely.) I can now click the Connect button, and this will give me two options: via RDP or via SSH or via Bastion. See Figure 2-17.

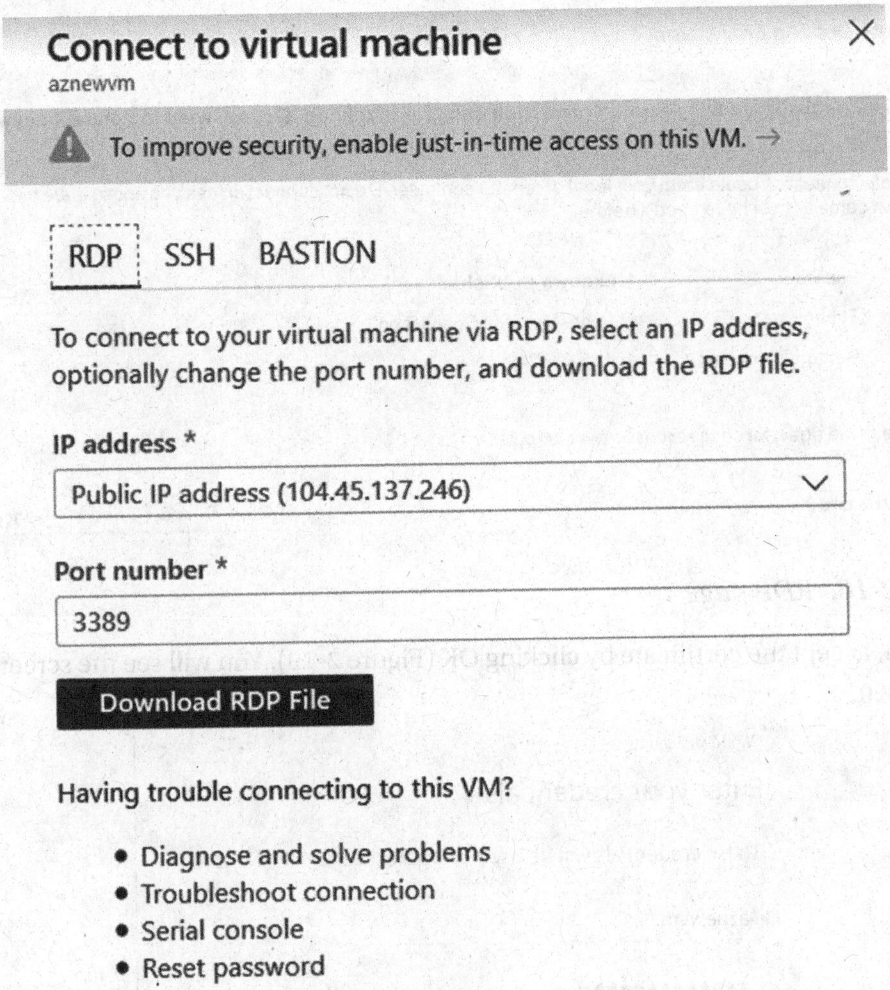

Connect to virtual machine ✕
aznewvm

> ⚠ To improve security, enable just-in-time access on this VM. →

___RDP___ SSH BASTION

To connect to your virtual machine via RDP, select an IP address, optionally change the port number, and download the RDP file.

IP address *

Public IP address (104.45.137.246) ⌄

Port number *

3389

Download RDP File

Having trouble connecting to this VM?

- Diagnose and solve problems
- Troubleshoot connection
- Serial console
- Reset password

Figure 2-17. Virtual machine connect page

Bastion is the new addition here. Using a Bastion host can help limit threats such as port scanning and other types of malware targeting your VMs. We will talk about Bastion hosts later in the "Setting Up a Bastion Host" section. You can download the RDP file and then connect via RDP to the VM, as shown in Figure 2-18.

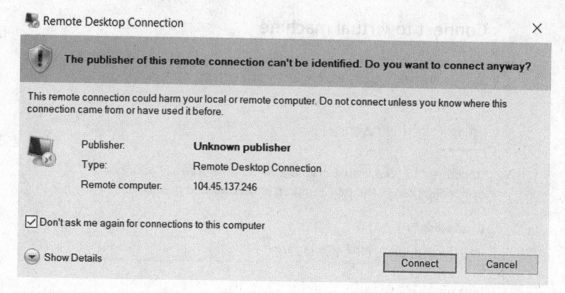

Figure 2-18. *RDP page*

Then, accept the certificate by clicking OK (Figure 2-19). You will see the screen in Figure 2-20.

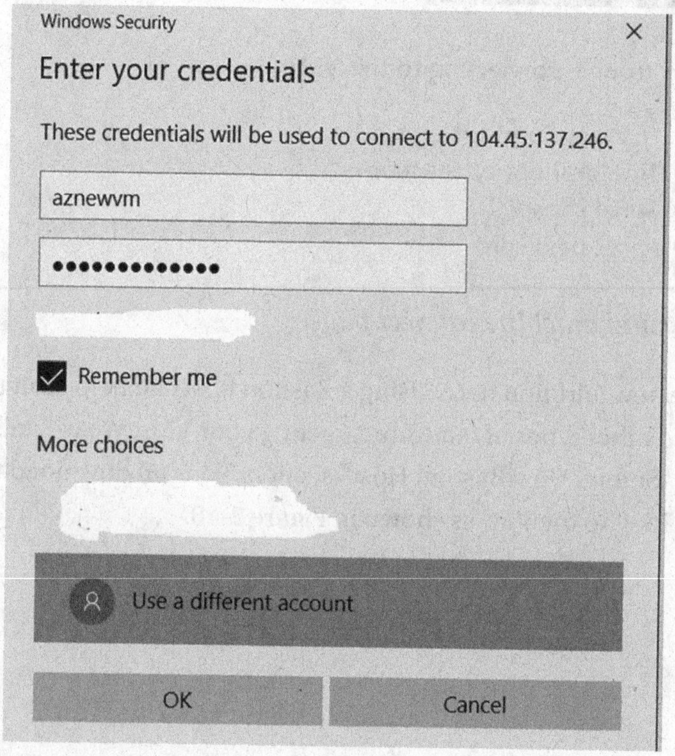

Figure 2-19. *RDP credentials page*

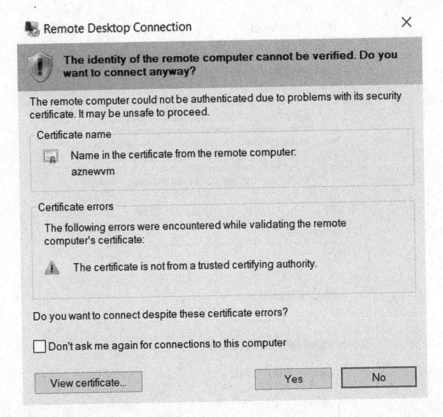

Figure 2-20. RDP certificate page

This will bring you to your new VM. Connecting will take a few minutes the first time as Azure will be configuring a bunch of services under the hood. Now, let's say you want to delete the VM. You can do that at the resource group (RG) level, as shown in Figure 2-21.

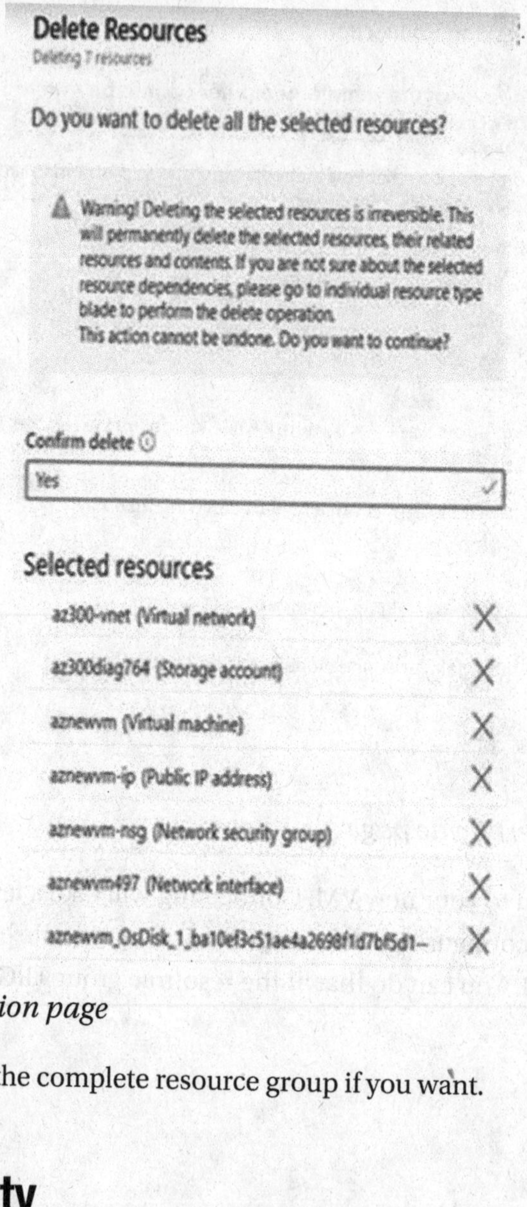

Delete Resources
Deleting 7 resources

Do you want to delete all the selected resources?

⚠ Warning! Deleting the selected resources is irreversible. This
will permanently delete the selected resources, their related
resources and contents. If you are not sure about the selected
resource dependencies, please go to individual resource type
blade to perform the delete operation.
This action cannot be undone. Do you want to continue?

Confirm delete ⓘ

| Yes | ✓ |

Selected resources

az300-vnet (Virtual network)	X
az300diag764 (Storage account)	X
aznewvm (Virtual machine)	X
aznewvm-ip (Public IP address)	X
aznewvm-nsg (Network security group)	X
aznewvm497 (Network interface)	X
aznewvm_OsDisk_1_ba10ef3c51ae4a2698f1d7bf5d1–	X

Figure 2-21. *RG deletion page*

You can also delete the complete resource group if you want.

High Availability

You can set up high availability at the time of VM creation, as shown in Figure 2-22.

Basics   Disks   Networking   Management   Advanced   Tags   Review + create

Create a virtual machine that runs Linux or Windows. Select an image from Azure marketplace or use your own customized image.
Complete the Basics tab then Review + create to provision a virtual machine with default parameters or review each tab for full customization.
Looking for classic VMs?   Create VM from Azure Marketplace

Project details

Select the subscription to manage deployed resources and costs. Use resource groups like folders to organize and manage all your resources.

Subscription * ⓘ

| Visual Studio Enterprise with MSDN ⌄ |

 ⌐ Resource group * ⓘ

| az300 ⌄ |

Create new

Instance details

Virtual machine name * ⓘ

| azvm ✓ |

Region * ⓘ

| (US) East US ⌄ |

Availability options ⓘ

| No infrastructure redundancy required ⌃ |

| No infrastructure redundancy required |
| Availability zone |
| Virtual machine scale set (preview) |
| Availability set |

Image * ⓘ

Azure Spot instance ⓘ

| Review + create | | < Previous | | Next : Disks > |

Figure 2-22.   High availability page

With the availability set, you are indicating to Azure that this VM will be part of the availability set group. See Figure 2-23.

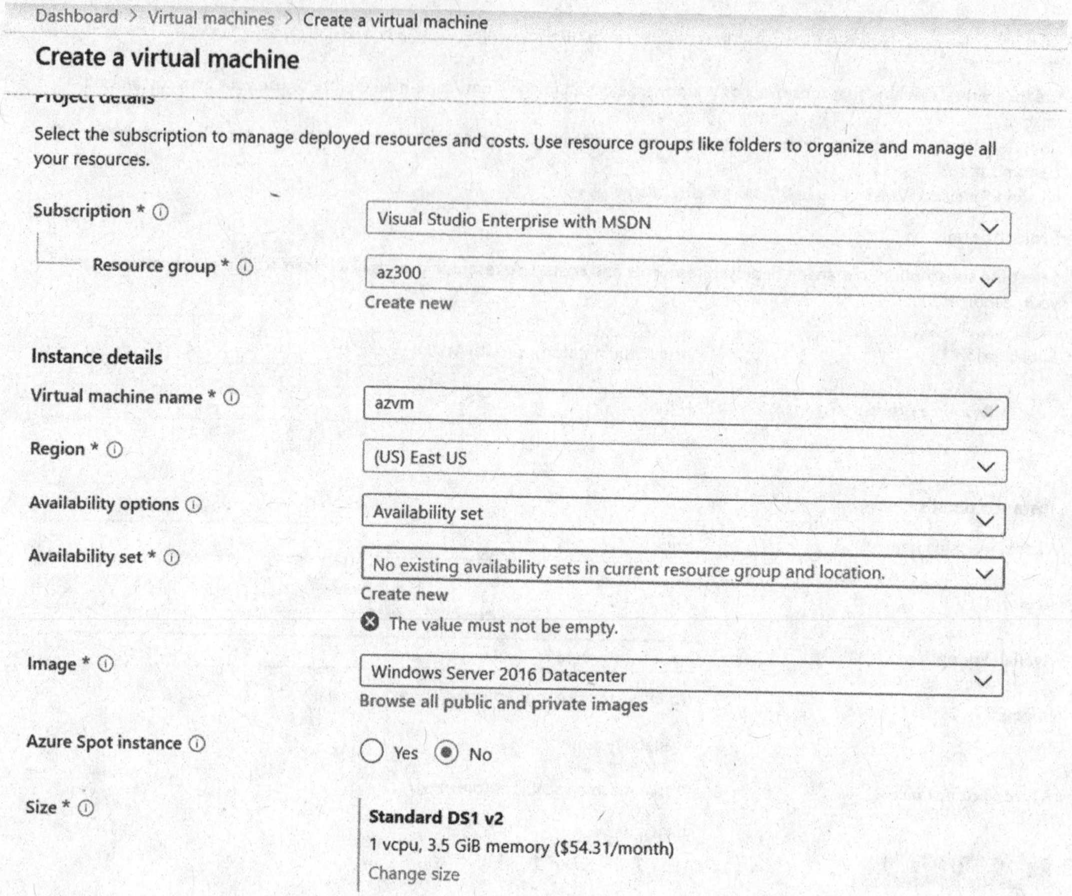

Dashboard > Virtual machines > Create a virtual machine

Create a virtual machine

Project details

Select the subscription to manage deployed resources and costs. Use resource groups like folders to organize and manage all your resources.

Subscription * ⓘ

> Visual Studio Enterprise with MSDN ⌄

└─── Resource group * ⓘ

> az300 ⌄
> Create new

Instance details

Virtual machine name * ⓘ

> azvm ✓

Region * ⓘ

> (US) East US ⌄

Availability options ⓘ

> Availability set ⌄

Availability set * ⓘ

> No existing availability sets in current resource group and location. ⌄
> Create new
> ✖ The value must not be empty.

Image * ⓘ

> Windows Server 2016 Datacenter ⌄
> Browse all public and private images

Azure Spot instance ⓘ

○ Yes ⦿ No

Size * ⓘ

Standard DS1 v2
1 vcpu, 3.5 GiB memory ($54.31/month)
Change size

Figure 2-23. *Setting up an availability set*

This is how you specify that your VM must be part of this group. Now, Microsoft is going to distribute this VM across multiple hardware servers across multiple services in a rack in order to provide you two benefits.

- **Fault domains**: One benefit is called *fault domains*. A fault domain is a physical unexpected point of failure within the Azure network. So, let's say you have two VMs not in an availability set and by some chance both of these VMs are running on the same physical computer within Azure. And if something happens to this computer, let's say a hardware failure or a power supply problem, then both of the VMs will go down as the network goes down. Therefore, if you have your machine across two or more fault domains, that means your VMs will be distributed across different physical sets of hardware. This reduces the likelihood of any kind of failure. You can choose from one to three fault domains. See Figure 2-24.

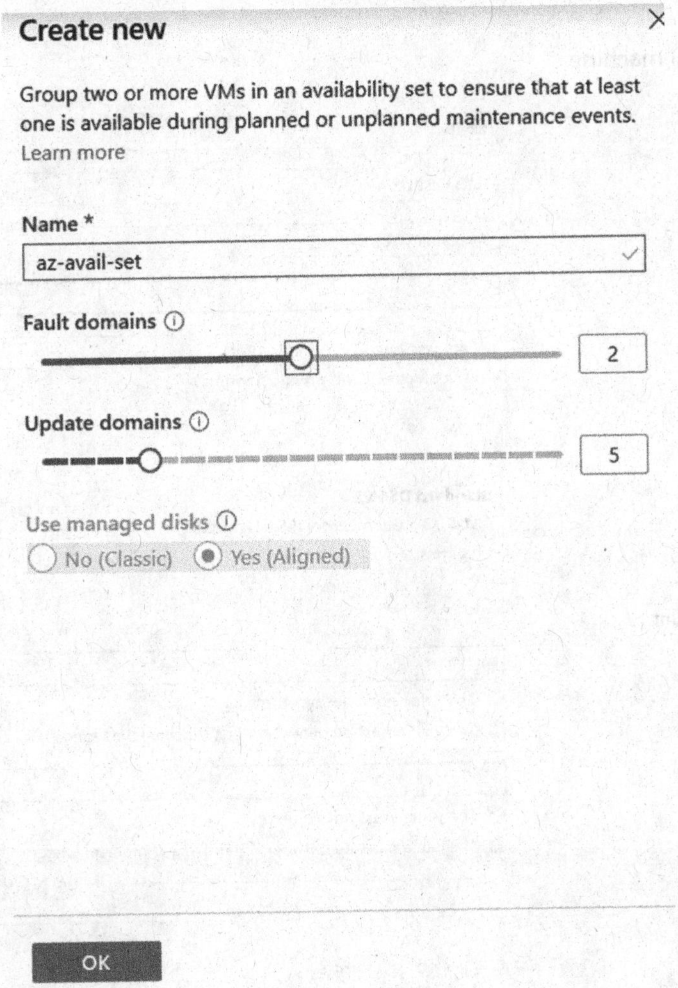

Figure 2-24. *Fault domain page*

- **Update domains**: Update domains are much more flexible. You can choose between 1 to 20. This allows you to schedule rollouts for Windows and Azure fixes. So, let's say Microsoft releases a new update for the software; it will update the machines one at a time. No two occurrences will be happening parallelly. Therefore, these machines can be rebooted for software updates or patches.

Availability Zone

You also have an option to select an availability zone from the drop-down, as shown in Figure 2-25.

Create a virtual machine

Virtual machine name * ⓘ	azvm ✓
Region * ⓘ	(US) East US ∨
Availability options ⓘ	Availability zone ∨
Availability zone * ⓘ	1 ∨
Image * ⓘ	Windows Server 2016 Datacenter ∨
	Browse all public and private images
Azure Spot instance ⓘ	◯ Yes ◉ No
Size * ⓘ	**Standard DS1 v2**
	1 vcpu, 3.5 GiB memory ($54.31/month)
	Change size

Administrator account

Username * ⓘ	
	❌ The value must not be empty.
	❌ The value must be between 1 and 20 characters long.
Password * ⓘ	
	❌ The value must not be empty.
	❌ The value must be between 12 and 123 characters long.
Confirm password * ⓘ	

[Review + create]   [< Previous]   [Next : Disks >]

Figure 2-25. *Selecting an availability zone*

The cool thing about this is that Microsoft has given us the option of deploying our VMs into specific data centers within this region. If we are in the eastern United States, we can deploy our VM to a physical location in that region, either in building 1, 2, or 3.

One thing to note here is that availability sets and availability zones don't provide load balancing. Therefore, you need to create load balancers explicitly for the traffic to be evenly distributed. Microsoft calls this type of setup a *service line agreement* (SLA).

Virtual Machine Scale Set

Now, there is another option you can set up with the availability options, and that is called a virtual machine scale set (VMSS). Microsoft Azure VMSSs are groups of individual virtual machines within the Microsoft Azure public cloud that information technology (IT) administrators can configure and manage as a single unit. VMSSs allow us to create VMs that are scalable from 1 to 100 or even to 1,000 VMs in a single scale set.

Azure virtual machine scale sets let you create and manage a group of identical, load-balanced VMs. The number of VM instances can automatically increase or decrease in response to demand or a defined schedule. Scale sets provide high availability to your applications and allow you to centrally manage, configure, and update a large number of VMs. You can see an example of creating a VM with the VMSS option in Figure 2-26 and Figure 2-27.

Create a virtual machine

Virtual machine name * ⓘ	azvm ✓
Region * ⓘ	(US) East US ⌄
Availability options ⓘ	Virtual machine scale set (preview) ⌄
Virtual machine scale set (preview) * ⓘ	No applicable scale sets in the current resource group and region. ⌃ Create new
Image * ⓘ	Windows Server 2016 Datacenter ⌄ Browse all public and private images
Azure Spot instance ⓘ	◯ Yes ⦿ No
Size * ⓘ	**Standard DS1 v2** 1 vcpu, 3.5 GiB memory ($54.31/month) Change size

Administrator account

Username * ⓘ	
	✖ The value must not be empty. ✖ The value must be between 1 and 20 characters long.
Password * ⓘ	
	✖ The value must not be empty. ✖ The value must be between 12 and 123 characters long.

[Review + create]   < Previous   [Next : Disks >]

Figure 2-26. *Creating a scale set*

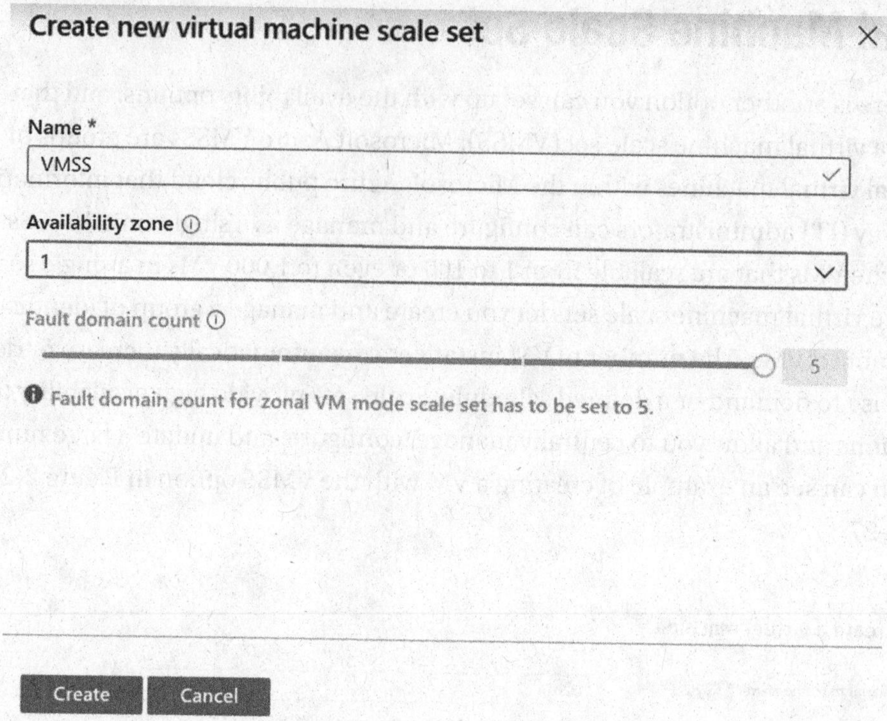

Create new virtual machine scale set   ✕

Name *

VMSS   ✓

Availability zone ⓘ

1   ⌄

Fault domain count ⓘ

───○   5

ⓘ Fault domain count for zonal VM mode scale set has to be set to 5.

Create   Cancel

Figure 2-27. *Creating a scale set, continued*

This is one way of doing this wherein we are deploying our single virtual machine at build time to the VMSS. However, a VMSS follows a different workflow altogether. You can just search for *VMSS*, as shown in Figure 2-28, to learn more about them.

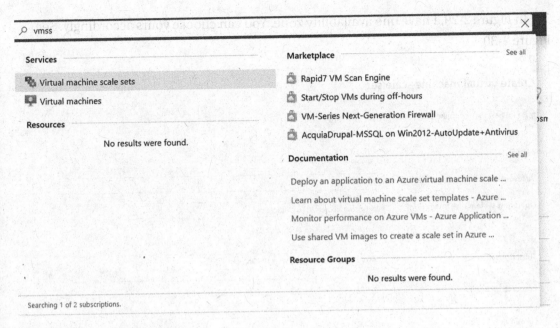

Figure 2-28. *VMSS service*

Upon clicking xxx , you will see the screen in Figure 2-29.

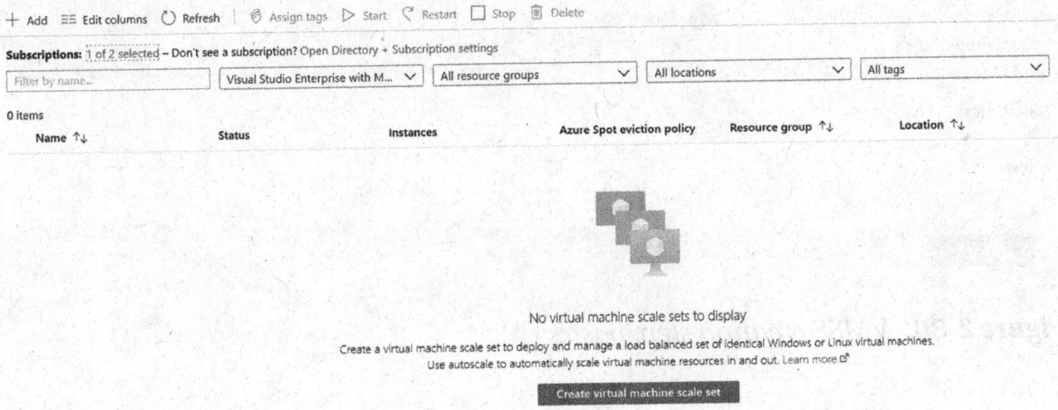

Figure 2-29. *VMSS creation page*

In Figure 2-29, I have one availability zone. You can choose yours accordingly. See Figure 2-30.

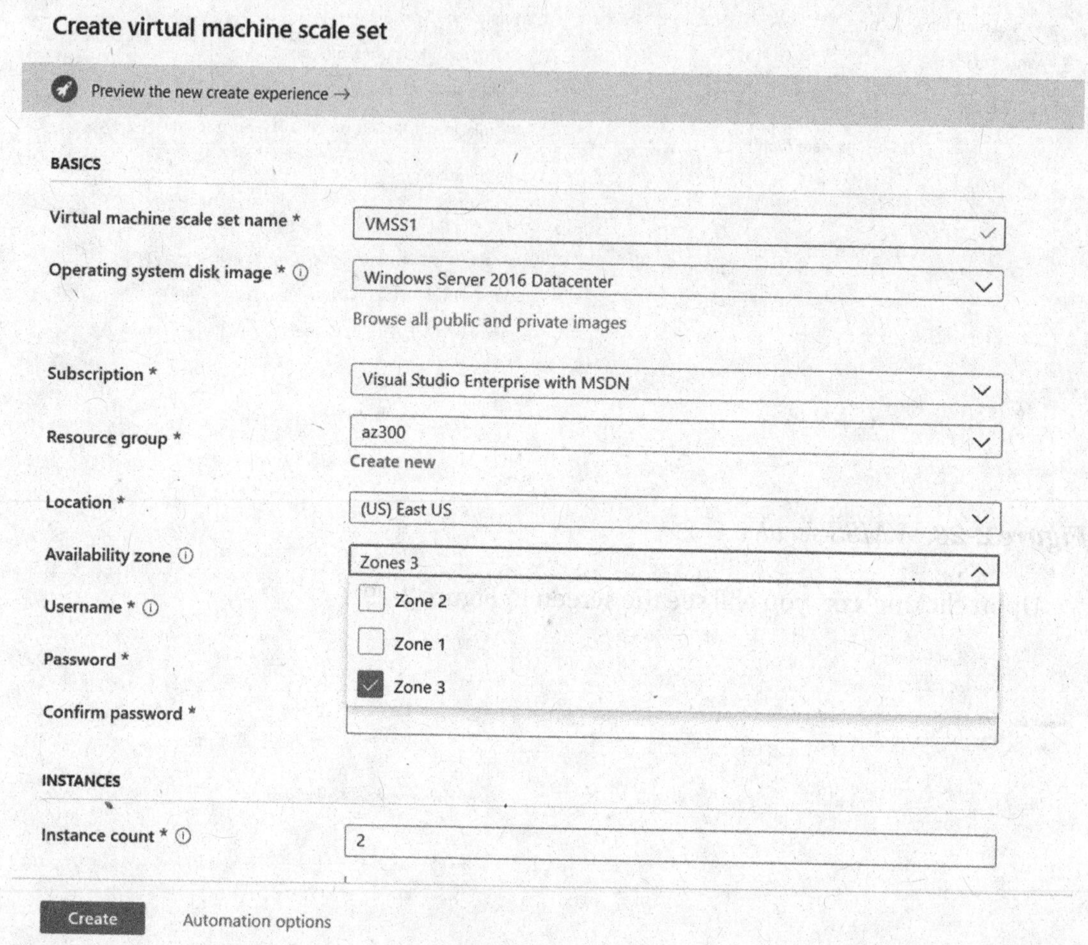

Create virtual machine scale set

Preview the new create experience →

BASICS

Virtual machine scale set name *	VMSS1 ✓
Operating system disk image * ⓘ	Windows Server 2016 Datacenter ⌄
	Browse all public and private images
Subscription *	Visual Studio Enterprise with MSDN ⌄
Resource group *	az300 ⌄
	Create new
Location *	(US) East US ⌄
Availability zone ⓘ	Zones 3 ⌃
	☐ Zone 2
Username * ⓘ	☐ Zone 1
Password *	☑ Zone 3
Confirm password *	

INSTANCES

Instance count * ⓘ	2

[Create]   Automation options

Figure 2-30. VMSS creation step, basics

You need to create a username and password, and you need to choose an instance count. The count can be from 0 to 1000. I have chosen 5 in Figure 2-31.

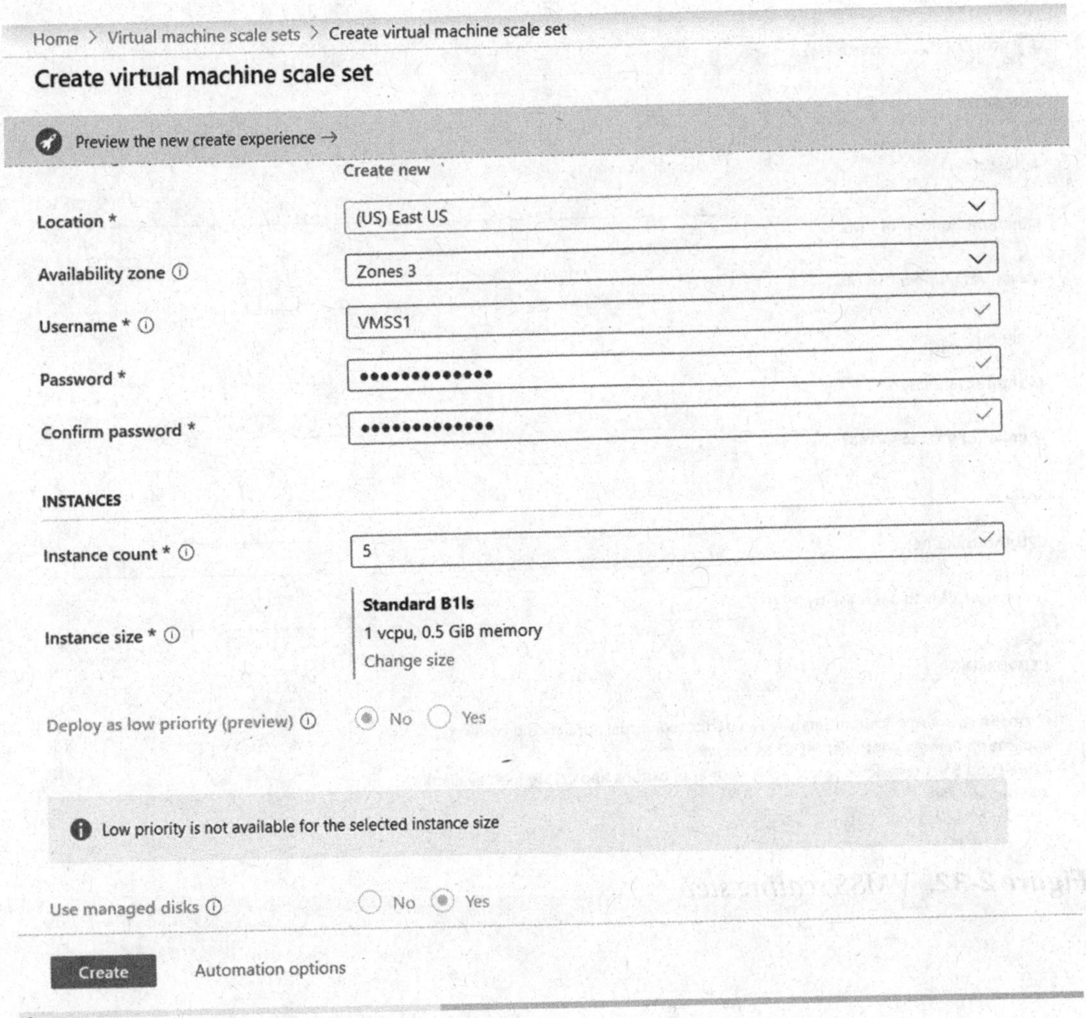

Home > Virtual machine scale sets > Create virtual machine scale set

Create virtual machine scale set

🧭 Preview the new create experience →

Create new

Location *	(US) East US
Availability zone ⓘ	Zones 3
Username * ⓘ	VMSS1
Password *	••••••••••••••
Confirm password *	••••••••••••••

INSTANCES

Instance count * ⓘ   5

Instance size * ⓘ   **Standard B1ls**
1 vcpu, 0.5 GiB memory
Change size

Deploy as low priority (preview) ⓘ   ◉ No ◯ Yes

ℹ Low priority is not available for the selected instance size

Use managed disks ⓘ   ◯ No ◉ Yes

Create   Automation options

Figure 2-31. Choosing an instance count

Now, let's look at the scaling factor. See Figure 2-32.

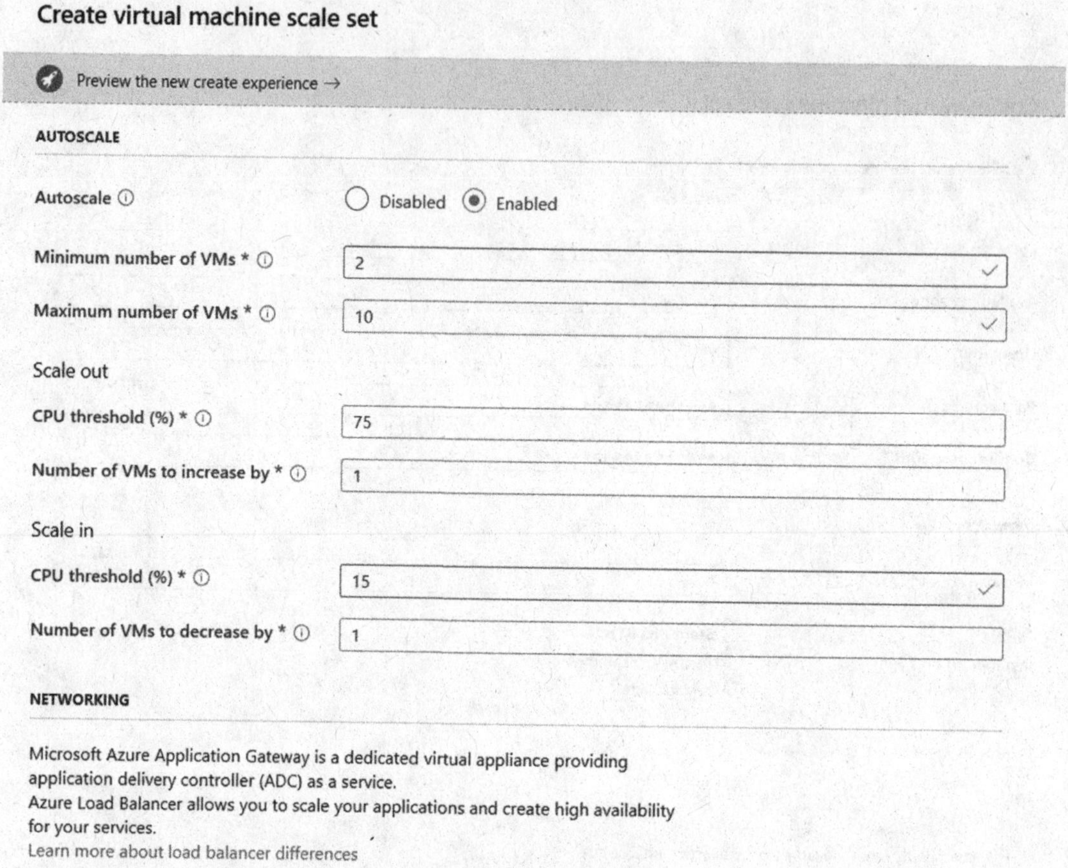

Create virtual machine scale set

Preview the new create experience →

AUTOSCALE

Autoscale ⓘ	○ Disabled ● Enabled

Minimum number of VMs * ⓘ

> 2 ✓

Maximum number of VMs * ⓘ

> 10 ✓

Scale out

CPU threshold (%) * ⓘ

> 75

Number of VMs to increase by * ⓘ

> 1

Scale in

CPU threshold (%) * ⓘ

> 15 ✓

Number of VMs to decrease by * ⓘ

> 1

NETWORKING

Microsoft Azure Application Gateway is a dedicated virtual appliance providing
application delivery controller (ADC) as a service.
Azure Load Balancer allows you to scale your applications and create high availability
for your services.
Learn more about load balancer differences

Figure 2-32. *VMSS scaling step*

Here I am setting the maximum number of VMs to 10 and the minimum number to 2. This means if my CPU goes up by 75%, one more VM is created, and if it goes down by 15%, one more VM is scaled in. Therefore, the scale set has to be load balanced, which means either it can use an application gateway, which is the default, or it can use a load balancer. See Figure 2-33.

Create virtual machine scale set

🔵 Preview the new create experience →

NETWORKING

Microsoft Azure Application Gateway is a dedicated virtual appliance providing application delivery controller (ADC) as a service.
Azure Load Balancer allows you to scale your applications and create high availability for your services.
Learn more about load balancer differences

Resources	Optimal for	Supported Protocols	SSL offloading	RDP to instance
Application Gateway	Web-based traffic	HTTP/HTTPS/WebSoc...	Supported	Not supported
Load balancer	Stream-based traffic	Any	Not supported	Supported

Choose Load balancing options	⦿ Application Gateway ◯ Load balancer ◯ None
Application Gateway * ⓘ	No available application gateways in the selected subscription and location ⌄
Virtual network	
Subnet ⓘ	No application gateway selected ⌄
Public IP address per instance ⓘ	◯ On ⦿ Off
Accelerated networking ⓘ	◯ On ⦿ Off

[Create]   Automation options

Figure 2-33. *VMSS load balancing step*

An application gateway is used for any kind of web-related traffic, and a load balancer is basically for anything. Let's go ahead and create a VMSS using a load balancer. See Figure 2-34.

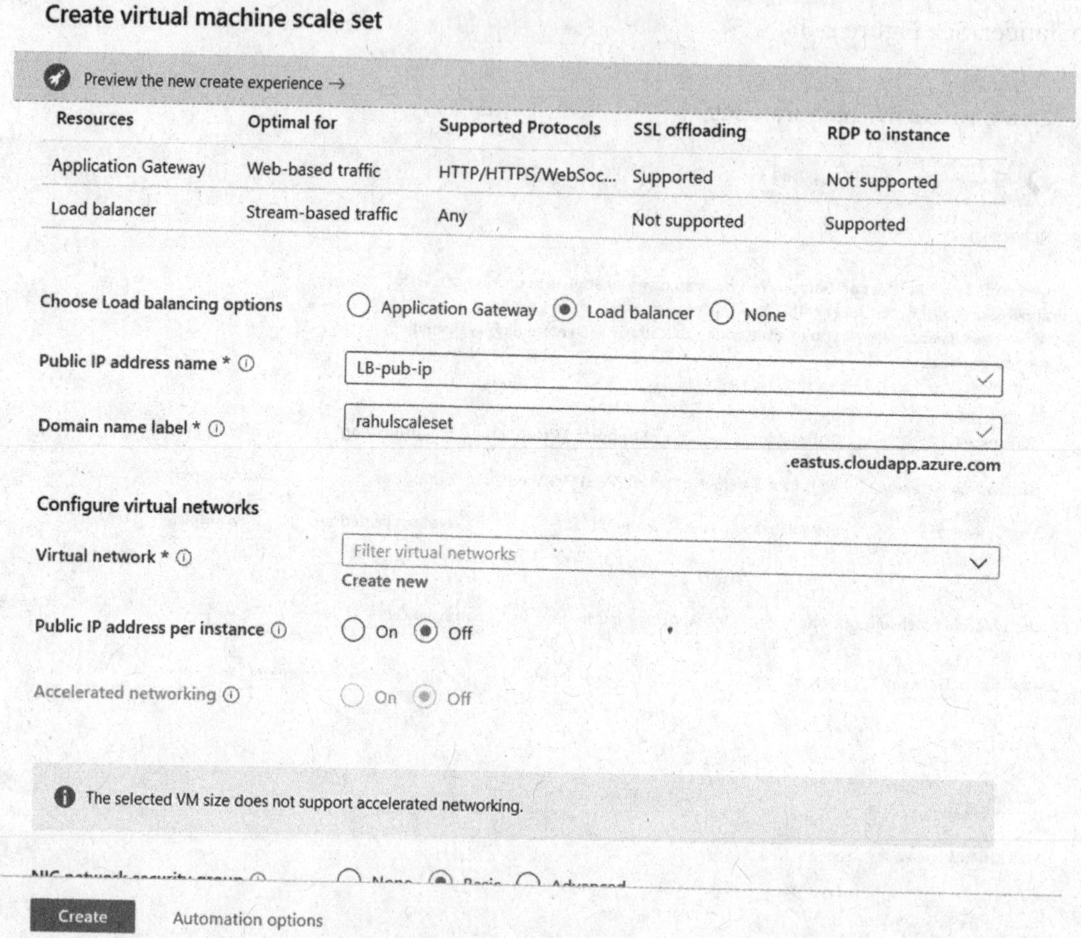

Create virtual machine scale set

> 🧭 Preview the new create experience →

Resources	Optimal for	Supported Protocols	SSL offloading	RDP to instance
Application Gateway	Web-based traffic	HTTP/HTTPS/WebSoc...	Supported	Not supported
Load balancer	Stream-based traffic	Any	Not supported	Supported

Choose Load balancing options   ○ Application Gateway ● Load balancer ○ None

Public IP address name * ⓘ   `LB-pub-ip` ✓

Domain name label * ⓘ   `rahulscaleset` ✓

.eastus.cloudapp.azure.com

Configure virtual networks

Virtual network * ⓘ   `Filter virtual networks` ⌄
                          Create new

Public IP address per instance ⓘ   ○ On ● Off

Accelerated networking ⓘ   ○ On ● Off

> ⓘ The selected VM size does not support accelerated networking.

NIC network security group ⓘ   ○ None ● Basic ○ Advanced

[Create]   Automation options

Figure 2-34. *VMSS load balancing settings*

Now, I need to create a virtual network, as shown in Figure 2-35 and Figure 2-36.

Create virtual network   ✕

The Microsoft Azure Virtual Network service enables Azure resources to securely communicate with each other in a virtual network which is a logical isolation of the Azure cloud dedicated to your subscription. You can connect virtual networks to other virtual networks, or your on-premises network. Learn more

Name *   MyVN   ✓

Address space

The virtual network's address space, specified as one or more address prefixes in CIDR notation (e.g. 192.168.1.0/24).

☑	Address range	Addresses	Overlap		
☑	10.0.0.0/16	10.0.0.0 - 10.0.255.255 (65536 addresses)	None	🗑	...
		(0 Addresses)	None		

Subnets

The subnet's address range in CIDR notation. It must be contained by the address space of the virtual network.

☑	Subnet name	Address range	Addresses		
☑	default	10.0.0.0/24	10.0.0.0 - 10.0.0.255 (256 addresses)	🗑	...
			(0 Addresses)		

| OK | Discard |

Figure 2-35. *Setting up a VMSS virtual network*

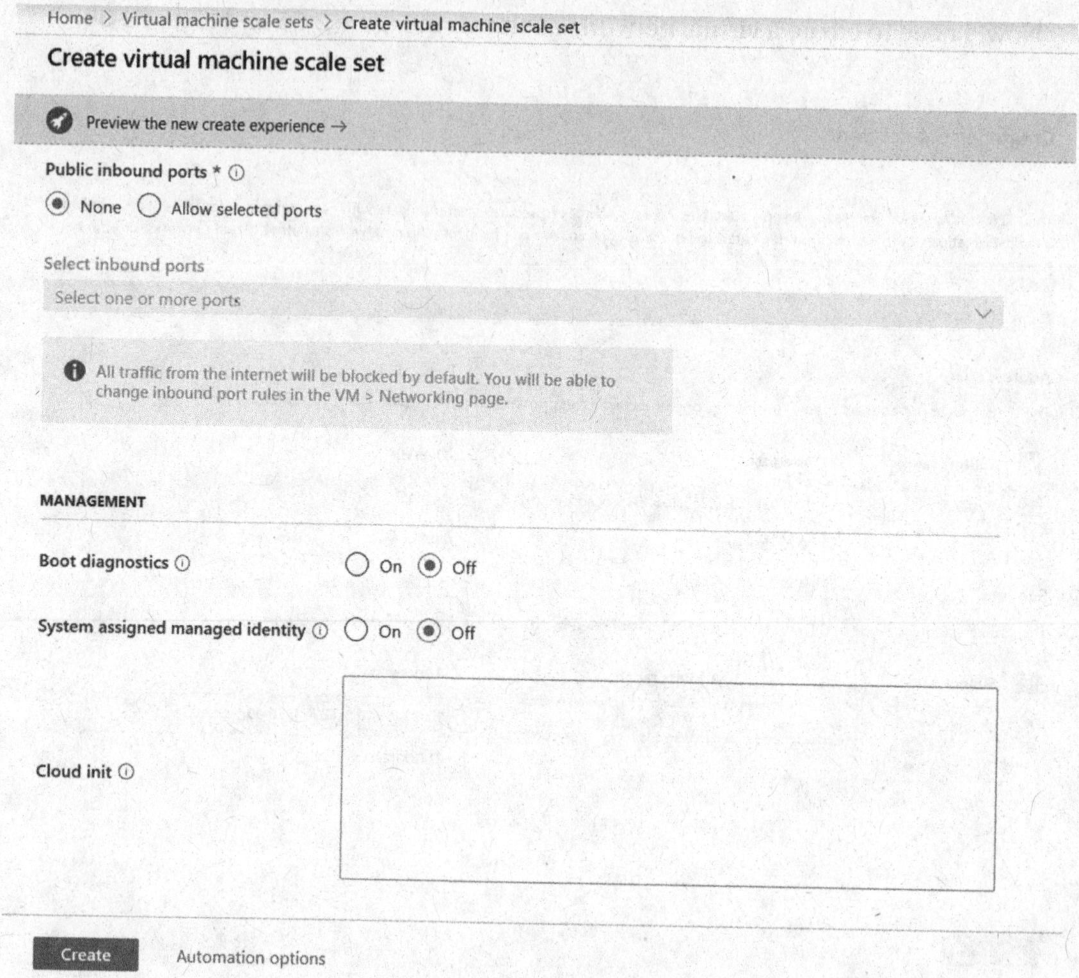

Home > Virtual machine scale sets > Create virtual machine scale set

Create virtual machine scale set

Preview the new create experience →

Public inbound ports * ⓘ

◉ None   ○ Allow selected ports

Select inbound ports

Select one or more ports   ⌄

ⓘ All traffic from the internet will be blocked by default. You will be able to
change inbound port rules in the VM > Networking page.

MANAGEMENT

Boot diagnostics ⓘ   ○ On ◉ Off

System assigned managed identity ⓘ ○ On ◉ Off

Cloud init ⓘ

Create   Automation options

Figure 2-36. Setting up the VMSS management

Click the Create button. You can see in real time how things are deployed, as shown
in Figure 2-37.

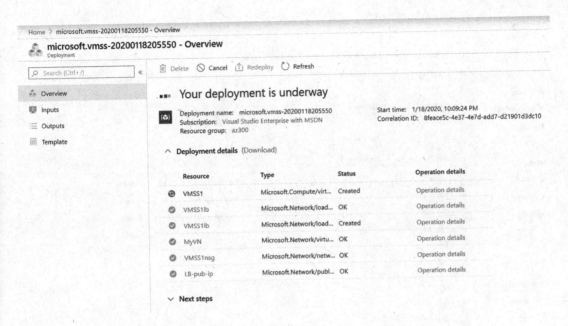

Figure 2-37. *Deploying a VMSS*

Once the deployment is complete, you can navigate to the VMSS, as shown in Figure 2-38.

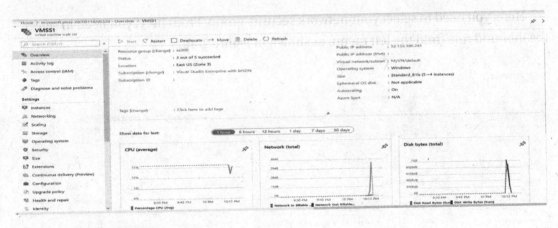

Figure 2-38. *VMSS overview page*

You need to configure the VM's inbound port rules for RDP access. For that, go to the resource group where you created a VMSS. In this case, it's az300. See Figure 2-39.

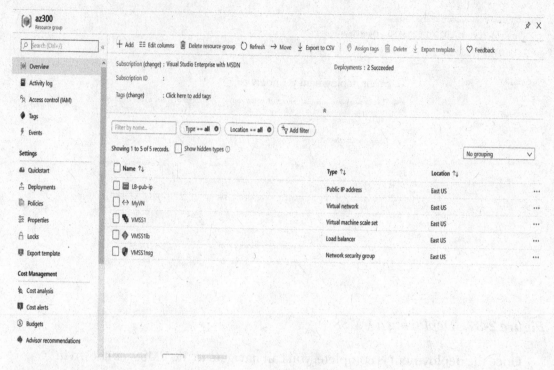

Figure 2-39. *Configuring the VM's inbound port rules*

Here, you need to select your network security group. From here, you need to select the inbound rule from the left menu, as shown in Figure 2-40.

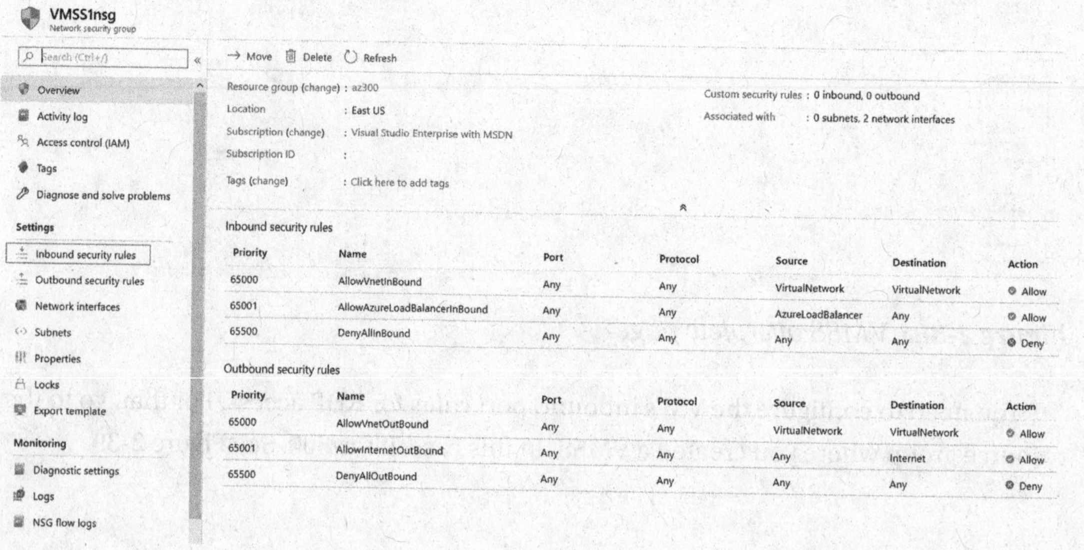

Figure 2-40. *VMSS security page*

Now, add the rules accordingly. See Figure 2-41 and Figure 2-42.

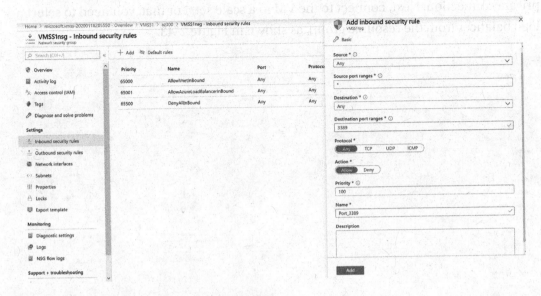

Figure 2-41. *VMSS security creation page*

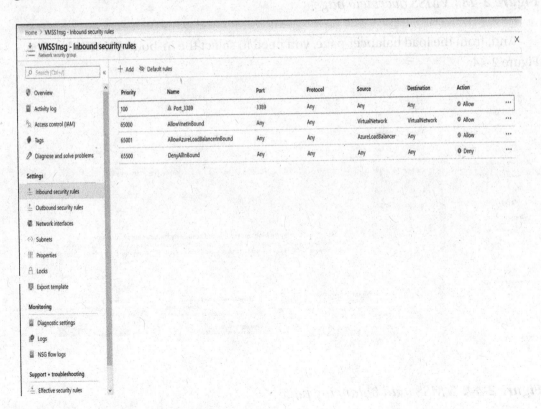

Figure 2-42. *VMSS security rules page*

An exclamation mark means this is just for testing. For production, use a VPN or private connection. Next, connect to the VM in a scale set. For that, you need to select a load balancer from the resource group, as shown in Figure 2-43.

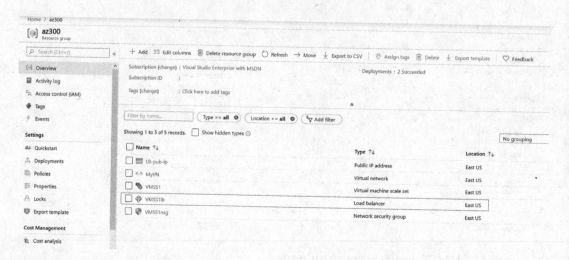

Figure 2-43. *VMSS overview page*

And, from the load balancer page, you need to select the in-bound NAT rules. See Figure 2-44.

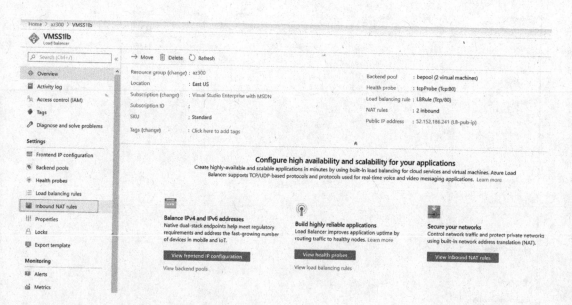

Figure 2-44. *VMSS load balancing page*

The rules will look like Figure 2-45.

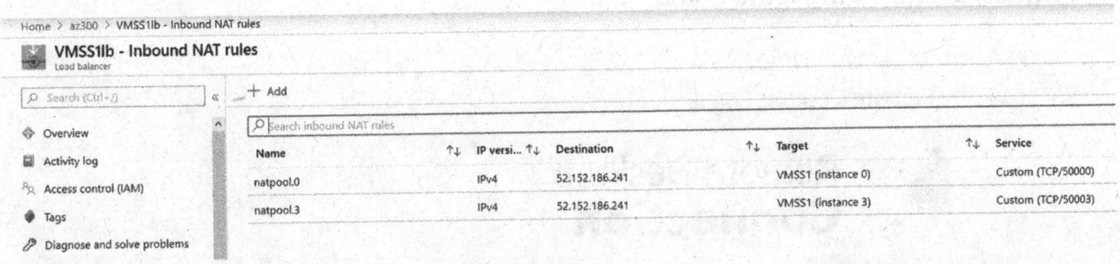

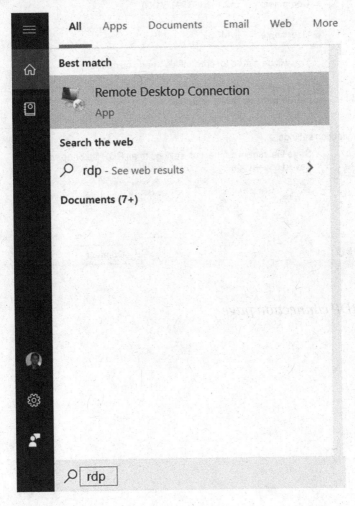

Figure 2-45. *VMSS inbound NAT rule page*

Now you can RDP to 52.152.186.241:50000 or 52.152.186.241:50003. You can type **rdp** in the search bar, as shown in Figure 2-46.

Figure 2-46. *RDP connection page*

Then enter the required address, as shown in Figure 2-47. You'll be asked for your credentials, as shown in Figure 2-48.

Figure 2-47. *RDP connection page*

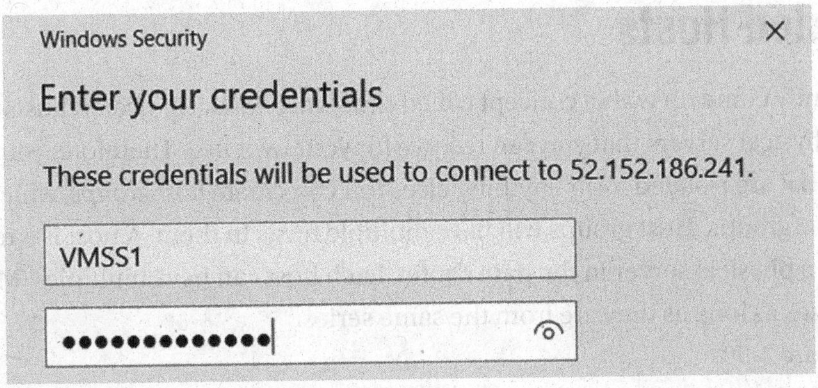

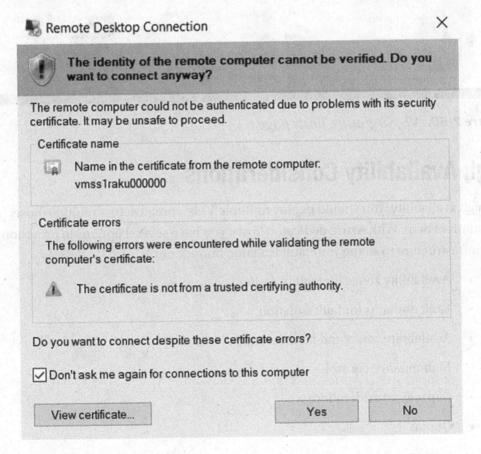

Figure 2-48. *RDP credentials page*

Next, accept the certificate, as shown in Figure 2-49.

Figure 2-49. *VMSS certificate page*

Dedicated Hosts

Azure recently come up with a concept called *dedicated hosts*. Dedicated hosts are basically physical servers that you can reserve for your own use. Therefore, you can have VMs that are isolated from anything else. You can create *host groups*, which are like resource groups. Host groups will have multiple hosts in them. A host is a resource mapped to a physical server in the data center. Each host can have multiple VMs of different sizes as long as they are from the same series.

See Figure 2-50.

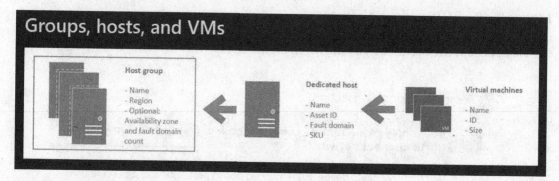

Figure 2-50. *VMSS groups, hosts page*

High Availability Considerations

For high availability, you should deploy multiple VMs, spread across multiple hosts (a minimum of two). With Azure dedicated hosts, you have several options to provision your infrastructure to shape your fault isolation boundaries.

- Availability zones for fault isolation
- Fault domains for fault isolation
- Availability zones and fault domains
- Maintenance control
- Capacity considerations
- Quotas
- Pricing
- VM families and hardware generations

For more information regarding dedicated hosts, refer to `https://bit.ly/Azure-Dedicated-Hosts`. Basically, dedicated hosts guarantee that you won't be affected because of any other Azure customers.

Creating a Host Group

A host group is a new type of resource that represents a collection of dedicated hosts. Having said that, let's get started. Search for *Host Groups* in the Azure portal. See Figure 2-51.

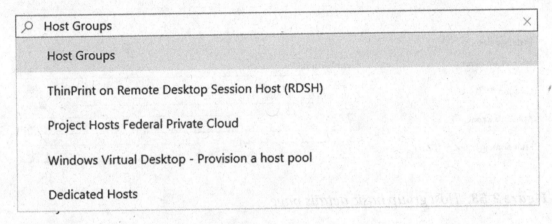

Figure 2-51. *Host Groups search page*

Click it to bring up the screen shown in Figure 2-52.

Figure 2-52. *Host Groups page*

Click the Create button and enter your details, as shown in Figure 2-53.

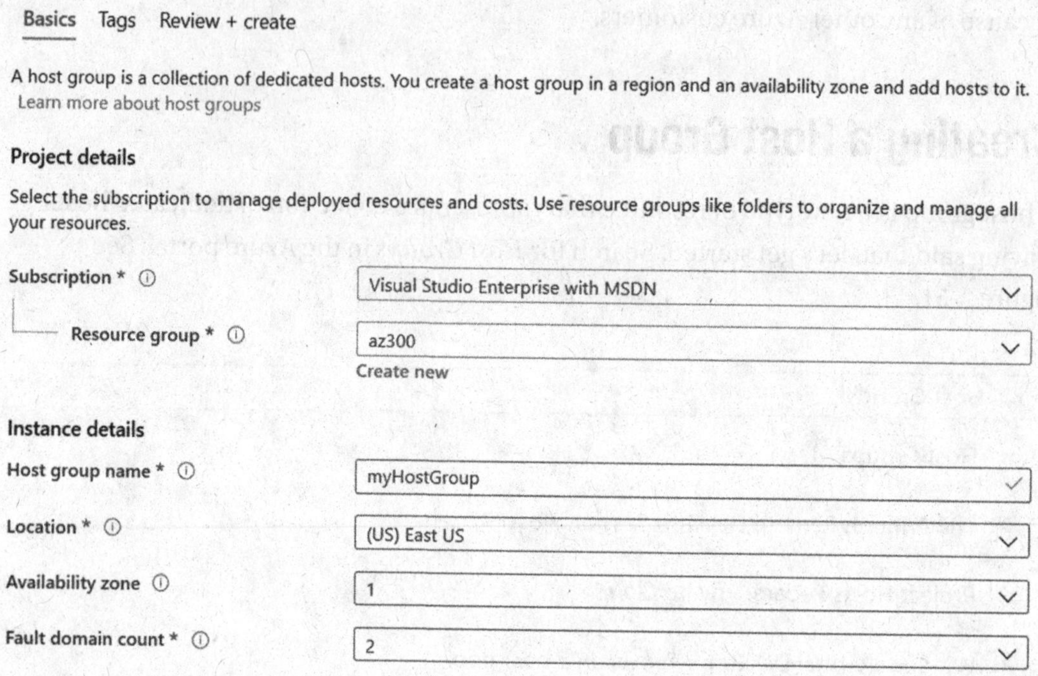

Basics   Tags   Review + create

A host group is a collection of dedicated hosts. You create a host group in a region and an availability zone and add hosts to it.
Learn more about host groups

Project details

Select the subscription to manage deployed resources and costs. Use resource groups like folders to organize and manage all your resources.

Subscription * ⓘ
> Visual Studio Enterprise with MSDN

> Resource group * ⓘ
> > az300
> > Create new

Instance details

Host group name * ⓘ
> myHostGroup

Location * ⓘ
> (US) East US

Availability zone ⓘ
> 1

Fault domain count * ⓘ
> 2

Figure 2-53. *Host group basic details page*

I have chosen 1 as the availability zone and 2 as the fault domain count. Next provide the tags. See Figure 2-54.

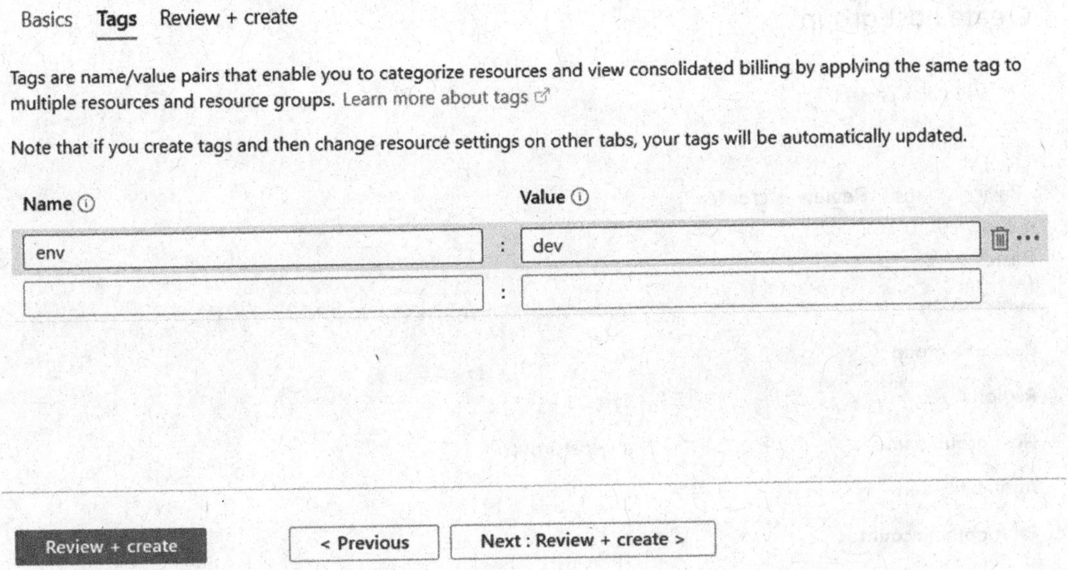

Basics   **Tags**   Review + create

Tags are name/value pairs that enable you to categorize resources and view consolidated billing by applying the same tag to multiple resources and resource groups. Learn more about tags ⌕

Note that if you create tags and then change resource settings on other tabs, your tags will be automatically updated.

Name ⓘ		Value ⓘ	
env	:	dev	🗑 ⋯
	:		

[Review + create]   [< Previous]   [Next : Review + create >]

Figure 2-54. *Host groups tag page*

Finally, you'll see the "Review + create" screen, as shown in Figure 2-55.

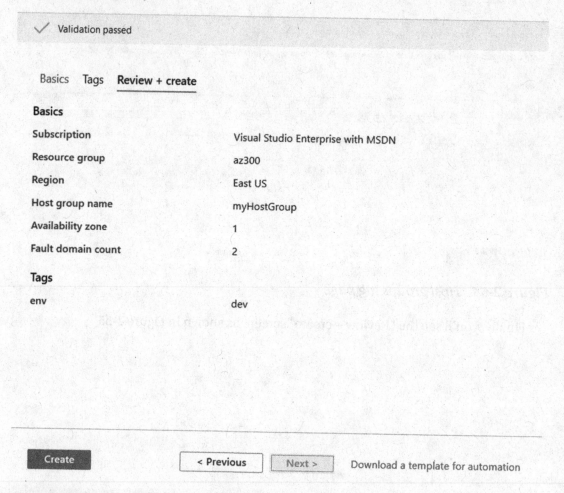

Create host group

✓ Validation passed

Basics   Tags   **Review + create**

Basics

Subscription	Visual Studio Enterprise with MSDN
Resource group	az300
Region	East US
Host group name	myHostGroup
Availability zone	1
Fault domain count	2

Tags

env	dev

Create   < Previous   Next >   Download a template for automation

Figure 2-55. *Host group's Review + create screen*

Next click the Create button. It will take a couple of minutes to provision the resource. Upon successful creation, you'll see the page shown in Figure 2-56.

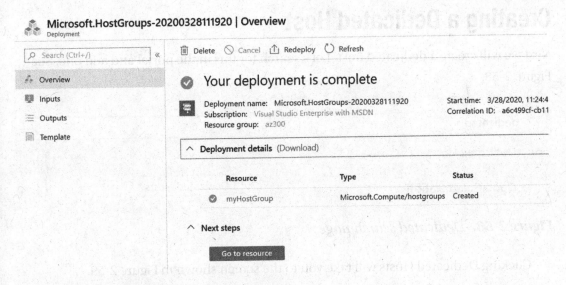

Figure 2-56. *Host group deployment page*

Once you click a resource, you will get to an overview page. See Figure 2-57.

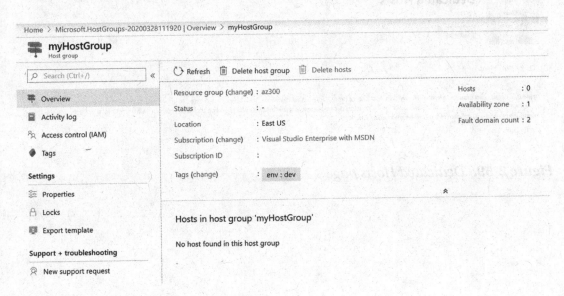

Figure 2-57. *VMSS groups, hosts page*

Creating a Dedicated Host

Next we will create a dedicated host. Let's search for this in the portal and add one. See Figure 2-58.

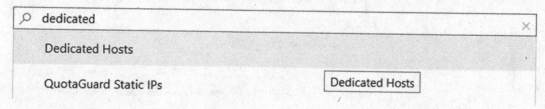

Figure 2-58. *Dedicated search page*

Clicking Dedicated Hosts will take you to the screen shown in Figure 2-59.

Figure 2-59. *Dedicated Hosts page*

Click Create and provide the information shown in Figure 2-60.

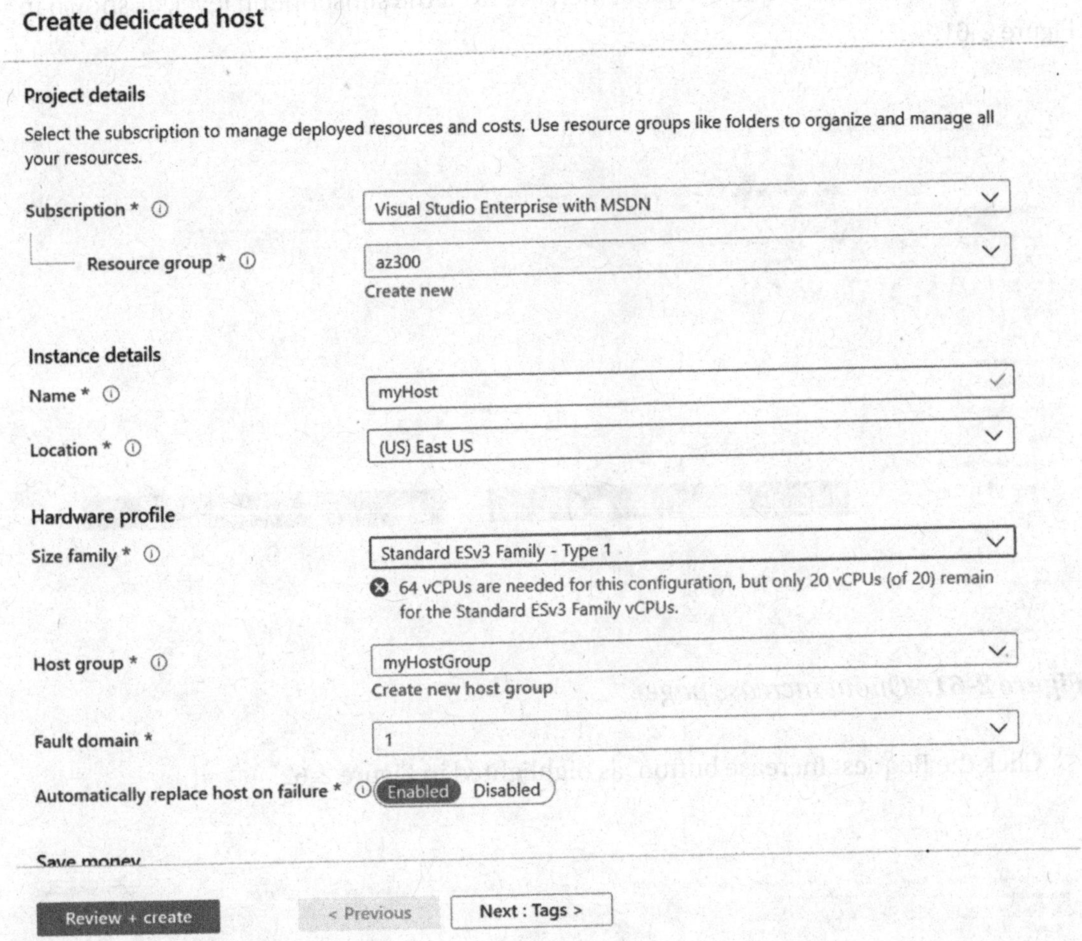

Create dedicated host

Project details

Select the subscription to manage deployed resources and costs. Use resource groups like folders to organize and manage all your resources.

Subscription * ⓘ

Visual Studio Enterprise with MSDN ⌄

└─ Resource group * ⓘ

az300 ⌄
Create new

Instance details

Name * ⓘ

myHost ✓

Location * ⓘ

(US) East US ⌄

Hardware profile

Size family * ⓘ

Standard ESv3 Family - Type 1 ⌄

❌ 64 vCPUs are needed for this configuration, but only 20 vCPUs (of 20) remain for the Standard ESv3 Family vCPUs.

Host group * ⓘ

myHostGroup ⌄
Create new host group

Fault domain *

1 ⌄

Automatically replace host on failure * ⓘ (Enabled   Disabled)

Save money

[Review + create]   [< Previous]   [Next : Tags >]

Figure 2-60. *Dedicated host creation page*

Requesting a Quota Increase

If you need to, you can request a quota increase from the subscription level, as shown in Figure 2-61.

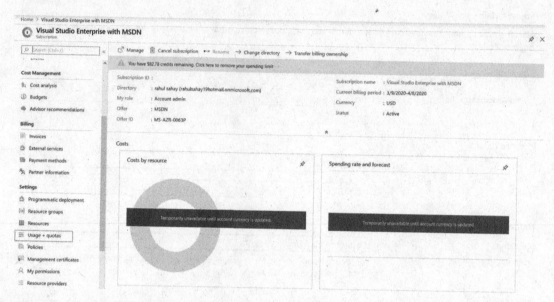

Figure 2-61. *Quota increase page*

Click the Request Increase button, as highlighted in Figure 2-62.

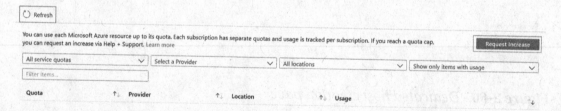

Figure 2-62. *Request Increase button*

Next select "Azure services," as shown in Figure 2-63. Then fill in the details, as shown in Figure 2-64.

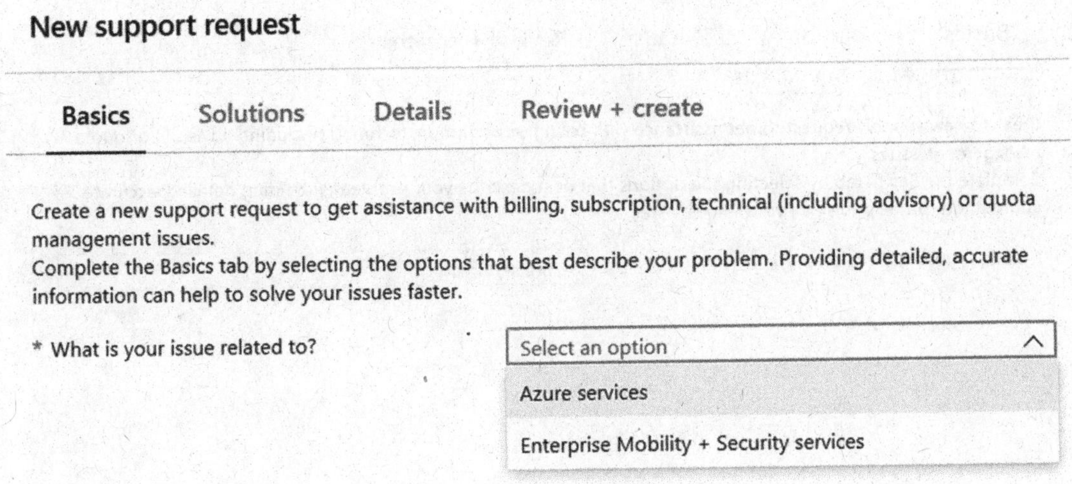

New support request

| Basics | Solutions | Details | Review + create |

Create a new support request to get assistance with billing, subscription, technical (including advisory) or quota management issues.
Complete the Basics tab by selecting the options that best describe your problem. Providing detailed, accurate information can help to solve your issues faster.

* What is your issue related to?   Select an option   ∧

Azure services

Enterprise Mobility + Security services

Figure 2-63. *Going to the support request page*

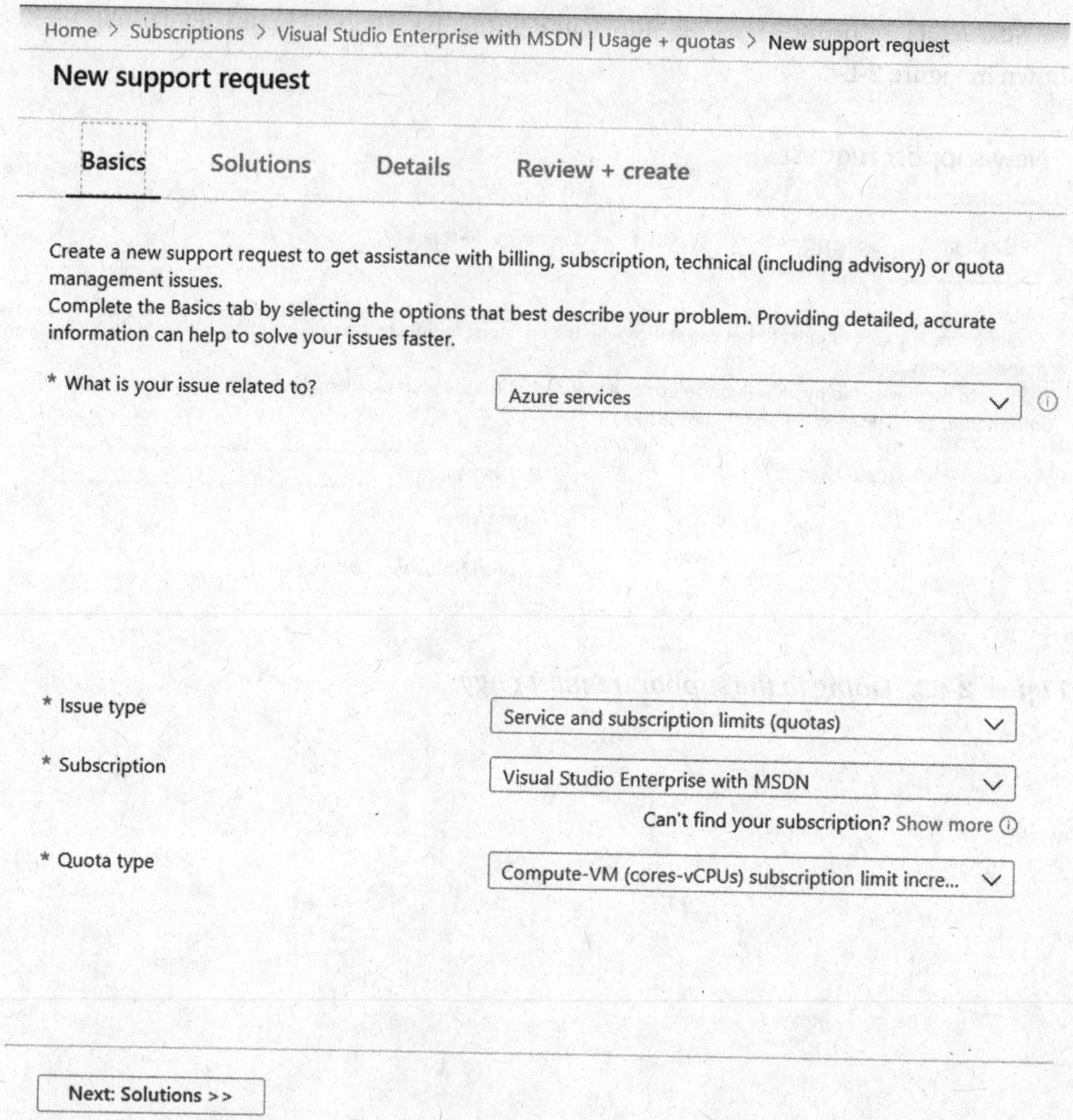

Home > Subscriptions > Visual Studio Enterprise with MSDN | Usage + quotas > New support request

New support request

Basics   Solutions   Details   Review + create

Create a new support request to get assistance with billing, subscription, technical (including advisory) or quota management issues.

Complete the Basics tab by selecting the options that best describe your problem. Providing detailed, accurate information can help to solve your issues faster.

* What is your issue related to?

| Azure services | ⌄ | ⓘ |

* Issue type

| Service and subscription limits (quotas) | ⌄ |

* Subscription

| Visual Studio Enterprise with MSDN | ⌄ |

Can't find your subscription? Show more ⓘ

* Quota type

| Compute-VM (cores-vCPUs) subscription limit incre... | ⌄ |

Next: Solutions >>

Figure 2-64. *Support request basic page*

Then provide the required details, as shown in Figure 2-65.

New support request

Basics   Solutions   **Details**   Review + create

Information provided on this tab will be used to further assess your issue and help the support engineer troubleshoot the problem. Verify the contact information before moving to the Review + Create.

⚠ Our support team is currently handling a high volume of cases. You may experience longer than expected response time. Please be assured that your request will be handled as soon as possible. We are committed to providing excellent customer service and support and we are working hard to meet increased demand.

PROBLEM DETAILS

Additional information is required to promptly process your request for a quota increase.

* Request details

Provide details for the request
Enter details

SUPPORT METHOD

Support plan

Azure Support Plan - Developer

* Severity

C - Minimal impact   ∨

* Preferred contact method

○ Contact me later   ○ Call me later

✉   ☎

Email   Phone

<< Previous: Basics   Next: Review + create >>

Figure 2-65. *Support request details page*

Next, click "Enter details" and enter the information shown in Figure 2-66.

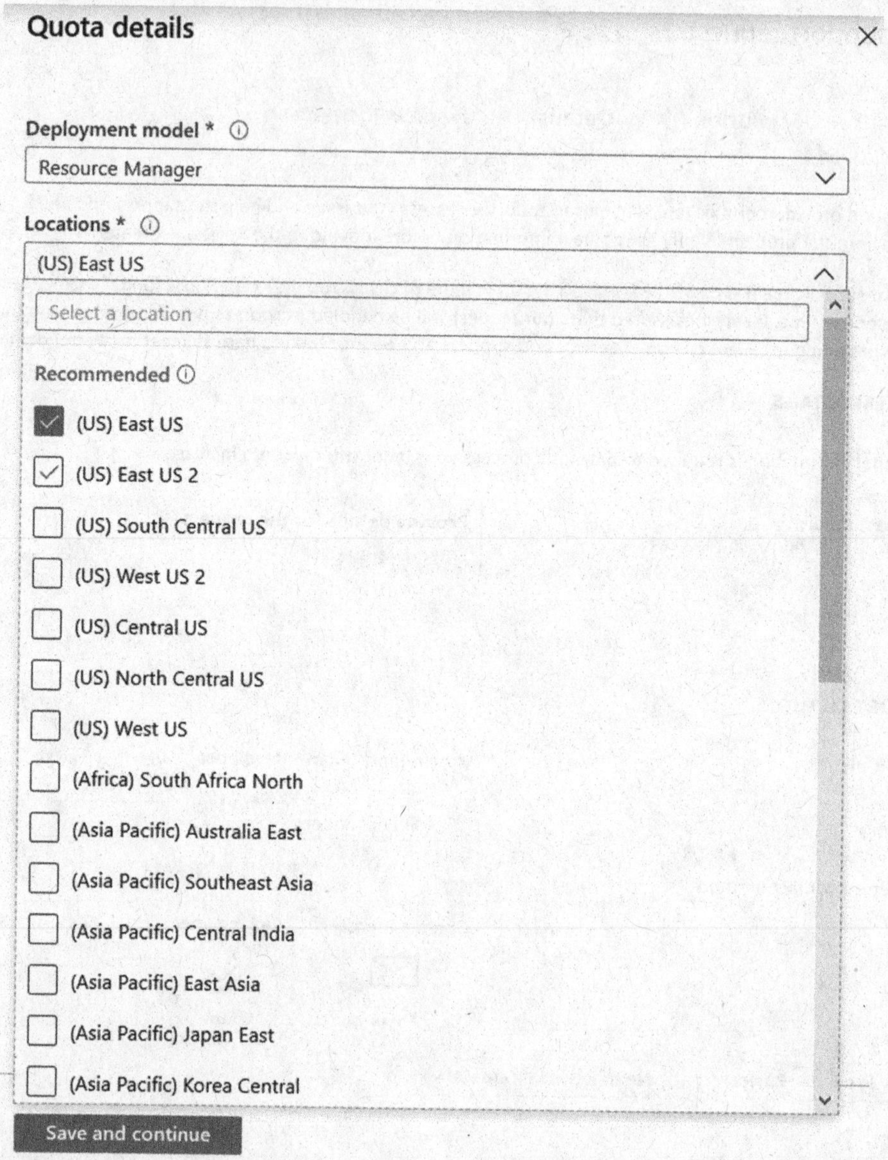

Figure 2-66. *Quota details*

Click "Save and continue" and provide the VM and spot VM details. See Figure 2-67.

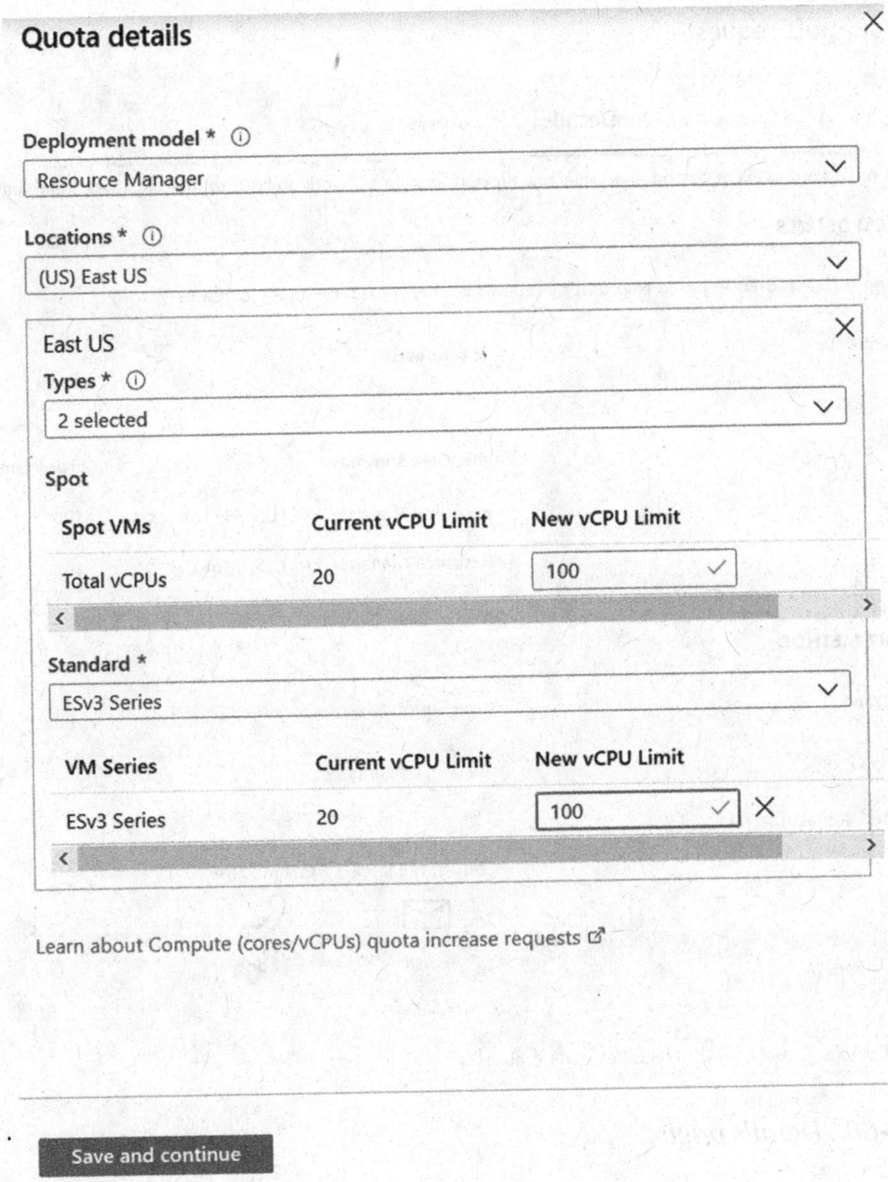

Quota details   ✕

Deployment model * ⓘ

| Resource Manager | ⌄ |

Locations * ⓘ

| (US) East US | ⌄ |

East US   ✕

Types * ⓘ

| 2 selected | ⌄ |

Spot

Spot VMs	Current vCPU Limit	New vCPU Limit
Total vCPUs	20	100 ✓

‹   ›

Standard *

| ESv3 Series | ⌄ |

VM Series	Current vCPU Limit	New vCPU Limit
ESv3 Series	20	100 ✓ ✕

‹   ›

Learn about Compute (cores/vCPUs) quota increase requests ☐

Save and continue

Figure 2-67. VM and spot VM details

Then you will see the screen in Figure 2-68.

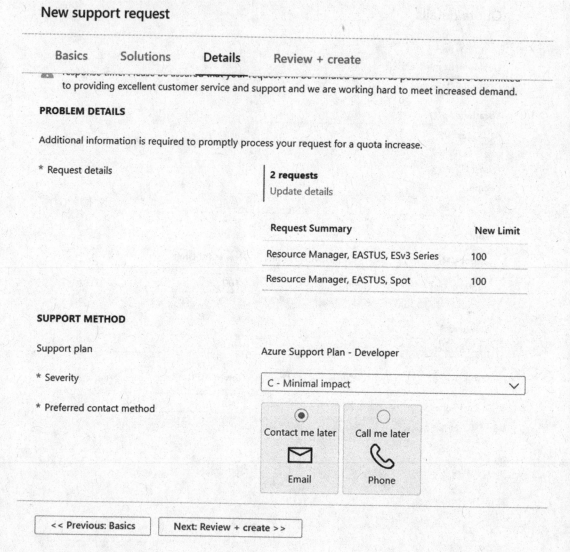

New support request

Basics	Solutions	**Details**	Review + create

to providing excellent customer service and support and we are working hard to meet increased demand.

PROBLEM DETAILS

Additional information is required to promptly process your request for a quota increase.

* Request details

2 requests
Update details

Request Summary	New Limit
Resource Manager, EASTUS, ESv3 Series	100
Resource Manager, EASTUS, Spot	100

SUPPORT METHOD

Support plan   Azure Support Plan - Developer

* Severity   C - Minimal impact ⌄

* Preferred contact method

● Contact me later	○ Call me later
✉ Email	📞 Phone

`<< Previous: Basics`   `Next: Review + create >>`

Figure 2-68. *Details page*

You also need to provide the contact details in the form and your preferred contact method. Next you will go to the review screen. See Figure 2-69.

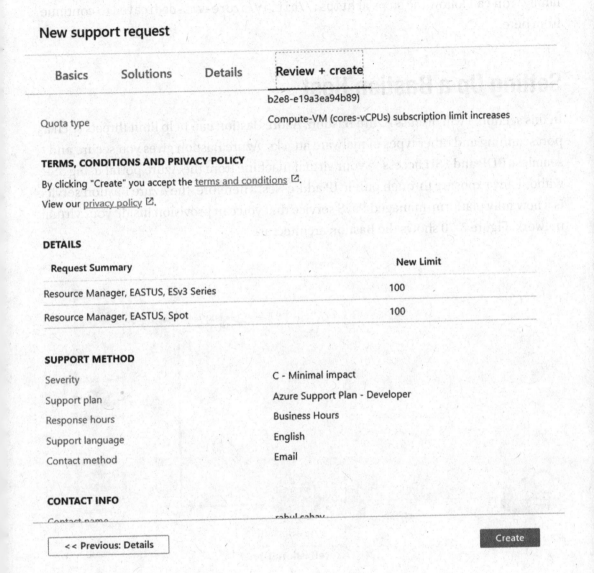

New support request

Basics	Solutions	Details	Review + create

b2e8-e19a3ea94b89)

Quota type   Compute-VM (cores-vCPUs) subscription limit increases

TERMS, CONDITIONS AND PRIVACY POLICY

By clicking "Create" you accept the terms and conditions ⤢.

View our privacy policy ⤢.

DETAILS

Request Summary	New Limit
Resource Manager, EASTUS, ESv3 Series	100
Resource Manager, EASTUS, Spot	100

SUPPORT METHOD

Severity	C - Minimal impact
Support plan	Azure Support Plan - Developer
Response hours	Business Hours
Support language	English
Contact method	Email

CONTACT INFO

Contact name   rahul sahay

| << Previous: Details | | Create |

Figure 2-69. *Review screen*

Upon successful creation, you will receive an email with the resolution time. Once the requested quota is allocated, then you can create a dedicated host with the required family. You can follow the steps at `https://bit.ly/azure-vms-dedicated` to continue from here.

Setting Up a Bastion Host

In this section, I will discuss Azure Bastion. Azure Bastion can help limit threats such as port scanning and other types of malware attacks. Azure Bastion gives you secure and seamless RDP and SSH access to your virtual machine from the Azure portal using SSL without any exposure through public IP addresses. Therefore, the Azure Bastion service is a new fully platform-managed PaaS service that you can provision inside your virtual network. Figure 2-70 shows the Bastion architecture.

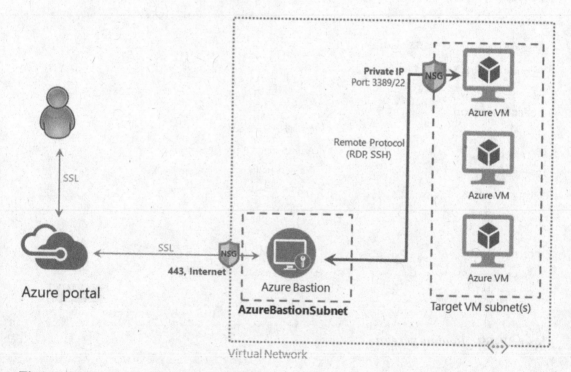

Figure 2-70. Bastion architecture page

One thing to note here is that Bastion deployment is per a virtual network, not per subscription/account or virtual machine. Once you provision an Azure Bastion service in your virtual network, the RDP/SSH experience is available to all your VMs in the same virtual network. Having said that, let's create a virtual network for Bastion. See Figure 2-71.

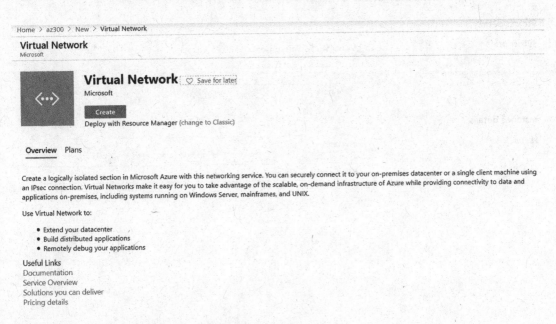

Figure 2-71. *Virtual network creation page*

I am providing the details shown in Figure 2-72.

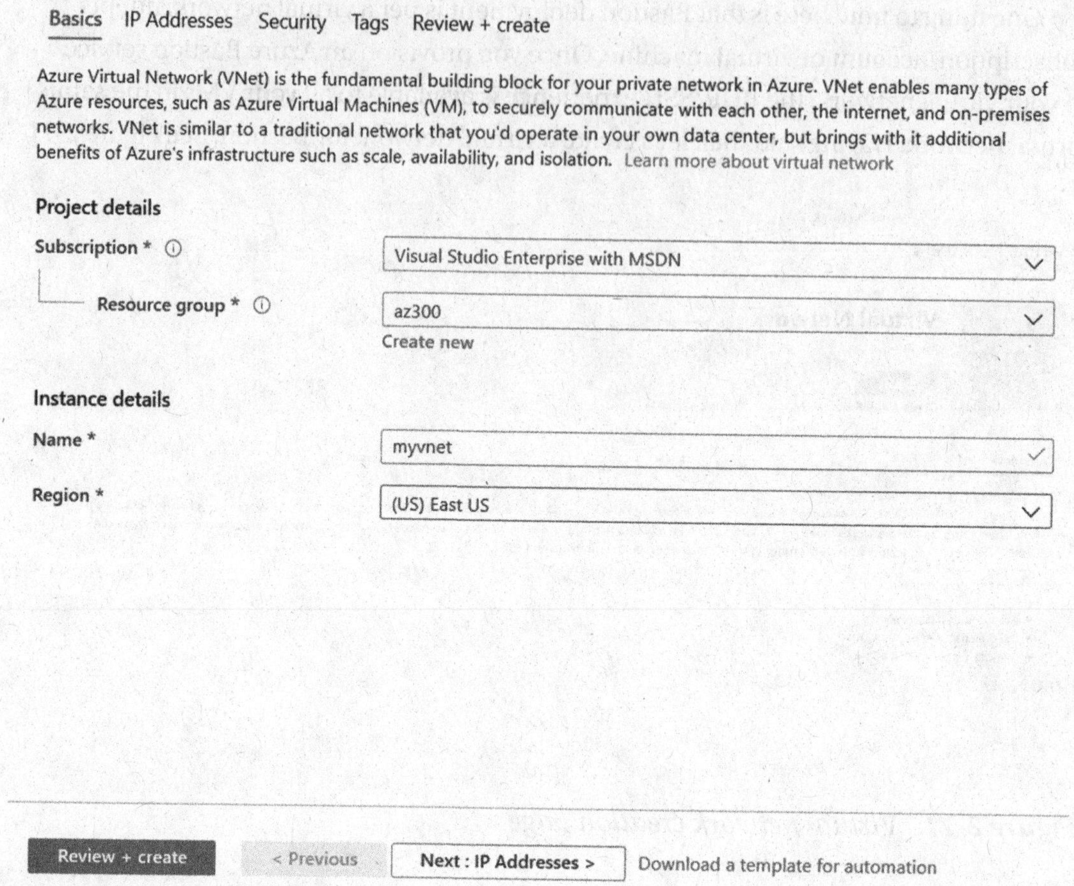

Basics   IP Addresses   Security   Tags   Review + create

Azure Virtual Network (VNet) is the fundamental building block for your private network in Azure. VNet enables many types of Azure resources, such as Azure Virtual Machines (VM), to securely communicate with each other, the internet, and on-premises networks. VNet is similar to a traditional network that you'd operate in your own data center, but brings with it additional benefits of Azure's infrastructure such as scale, availability, and isolation. Learn more about virtual network

Project details

Subscription * ⓘ

| Visual Studio Enterprise with MSDN | ⌄ |

Resource group * ⓘ

| az300 | ⌄ |
Create new

Instance details

Name *

| myvnet | ✓ |

Region *

| (US) East US | ⌄ |

Review + create   < Previous   **Next : IP Addresses >**   Download a template for automation

Figure 2-72. *Virtual network basics*

Next comes the IP address. I am just keeping everything at the defaults for now. I will create a different subnet later. See Figure 2-73.

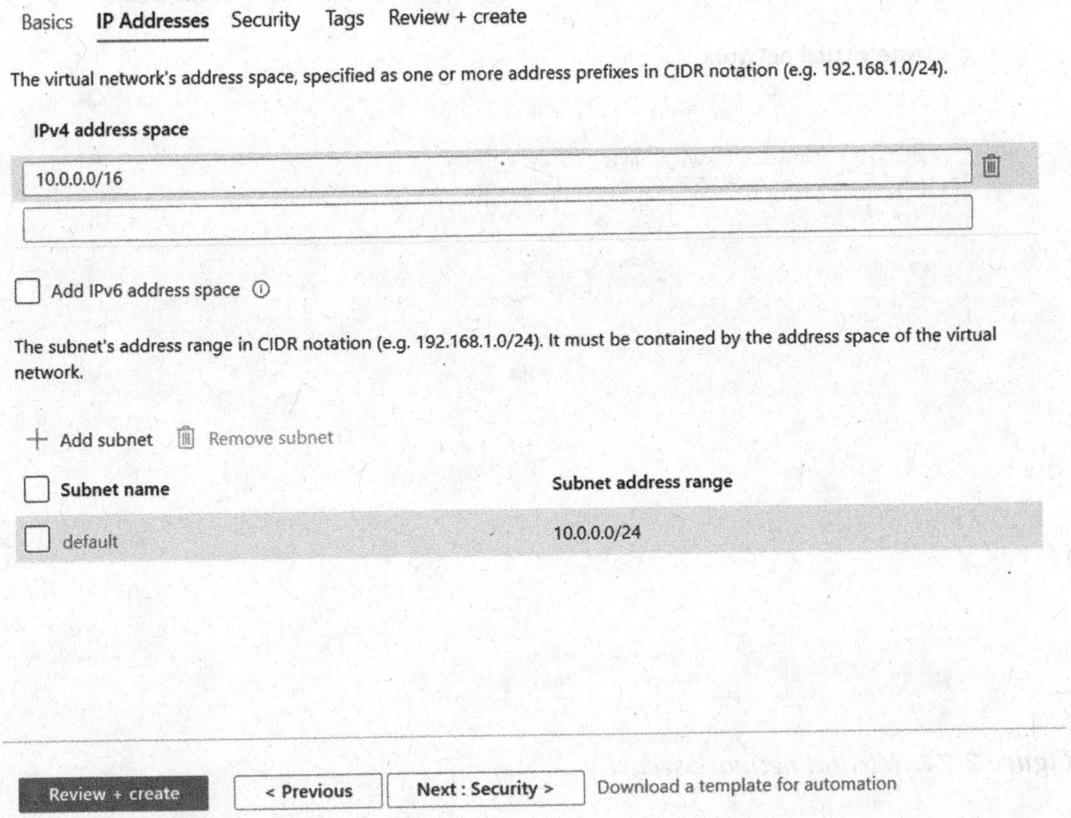

Basics   **IP Addresses**   Security   Tags   Review + create

The virtual network's address space, specified as one or more address prefixes in CIDR notation (e.g. 192.168.1.0/24).

IPv4 address space

10.0.0.0/16	🗑

☐ Add IPv6 address space ⓘ

The subnet's address range in CIDR notation (e.g. 192.168.1.0/24). It must be contained by the address space of the virtual network.

╋ Add subnet   🗑 Remove subnet

☐ Subnet name	Subnet address range
☐ default	10.0.0.0/24

Review + create		< Previous	Next : Security >	Download a template for automation

Figure 2-73. *Virtual network IP*

Next comes security. See Figure 2-74.

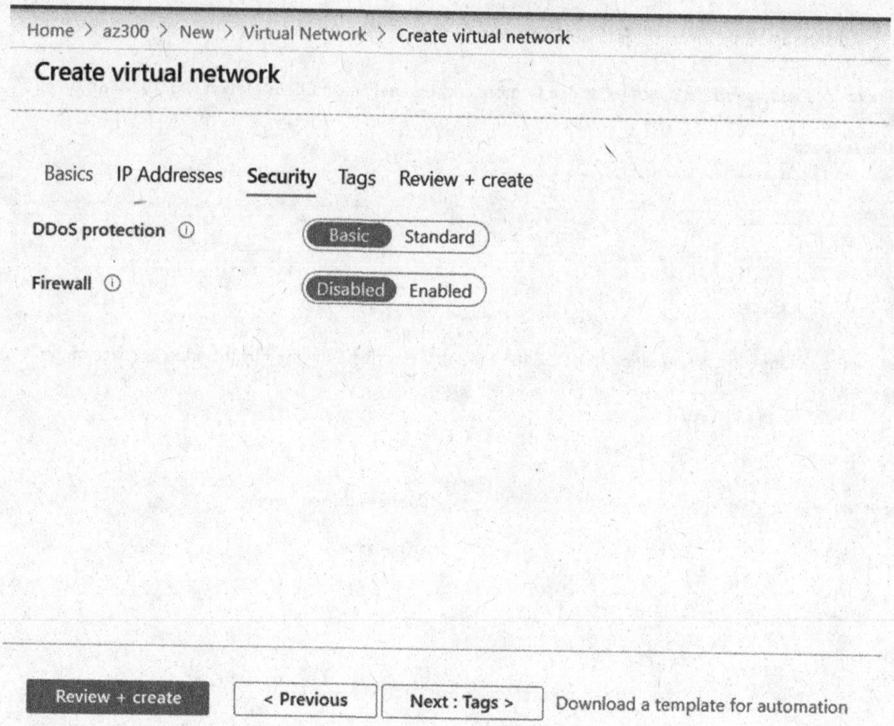

Home > az300 > New > Virtual Network > Create virtual network

Create virtual network

Basics   IP Addresses   **Security**   Tags   Review + create

DDoS protection ⓘ   (Basic) Standard

Firewall ⓘ   (Disabled) Enabled

[Review + create]   [< Previous]   [Next : Tags >]   Download a template for automation

Figure 2-74. *Virtual network security*

Next, I will provide tags. See Figure 2-75.

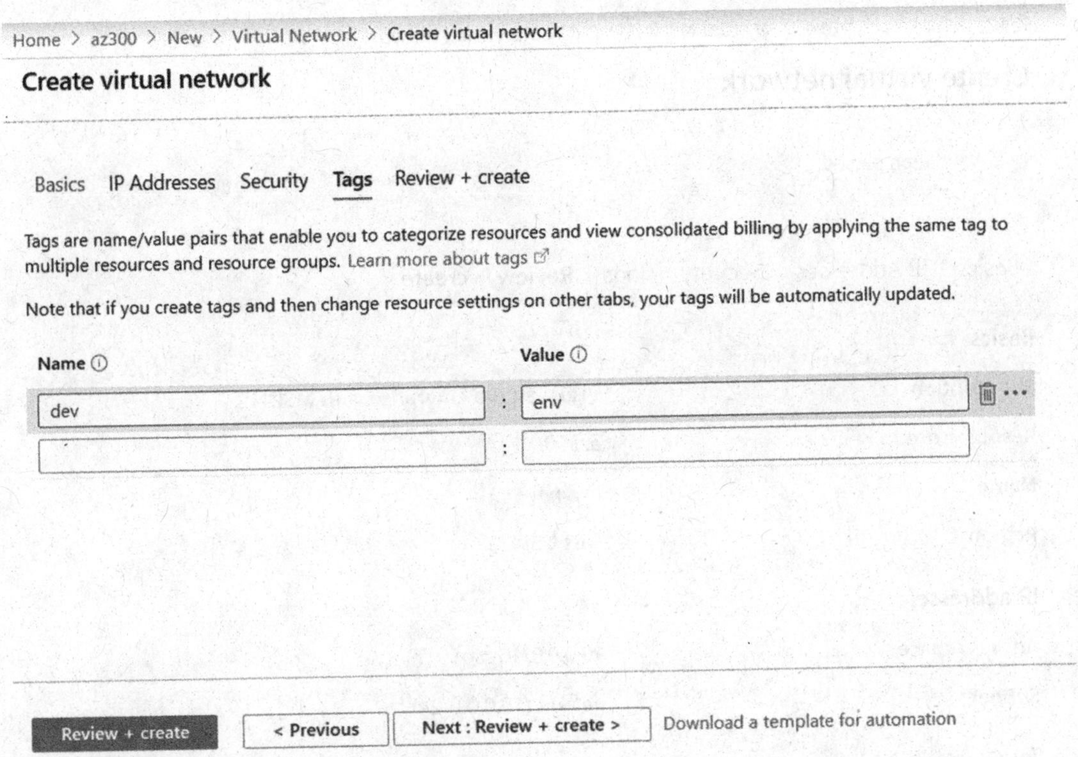

Home > az300 > New > Virtual Network > Create virtual network

Create virtual network

Basics   IP Addresses   Security   **Tags**   Review + create

Tags are name/value pairs that enable you to categorize resources and view consolidated billing by applying the same tag to multiple resources and resource groups. Learn more about tags ☐

Note that if you create tags and then change resource settings on other tabs, your tags will be automatically updated.

Name ⓘ		Value ⓘ	
dev	:	env	🗑 ⋯
	:		

Review + create		< Previous	Next : Review + create >	Download a template for automation

Figure 2-75. Virtual network tags

Finally, you'll see the review screen. See Figure 2-76.

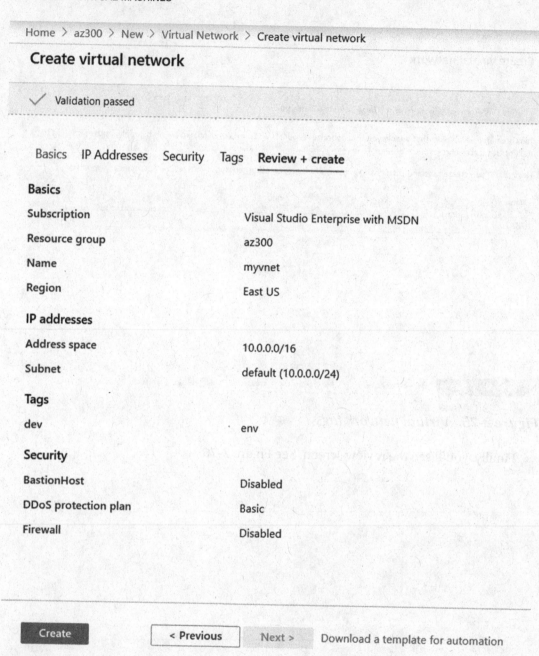

Figure 2-76. *Virtual network review screen*

Upon successful creation, you will see the screen in Figure 2-77.

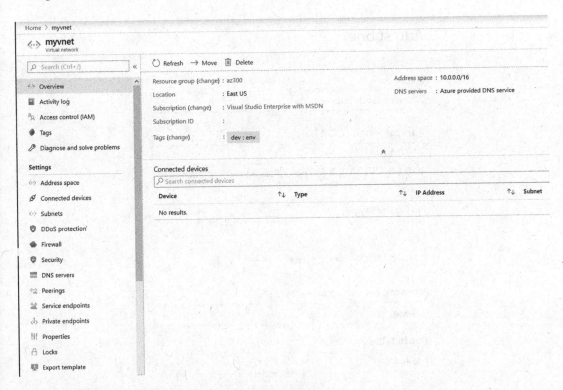

Figure 2-77. *Virtual network overview screen*

Click the Subnets section in the left menu under Settings. This will take you to the screen shown in Figure 2-78.

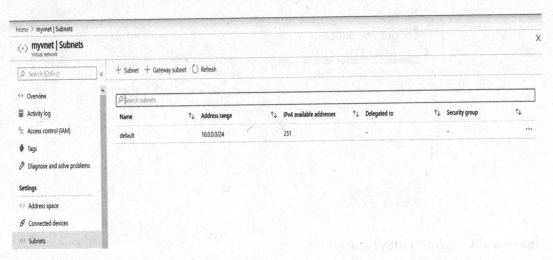

Figure 2-78. *Subnets overview screen*

I will now click Subnet and provide the information shown in Figure 2-79.

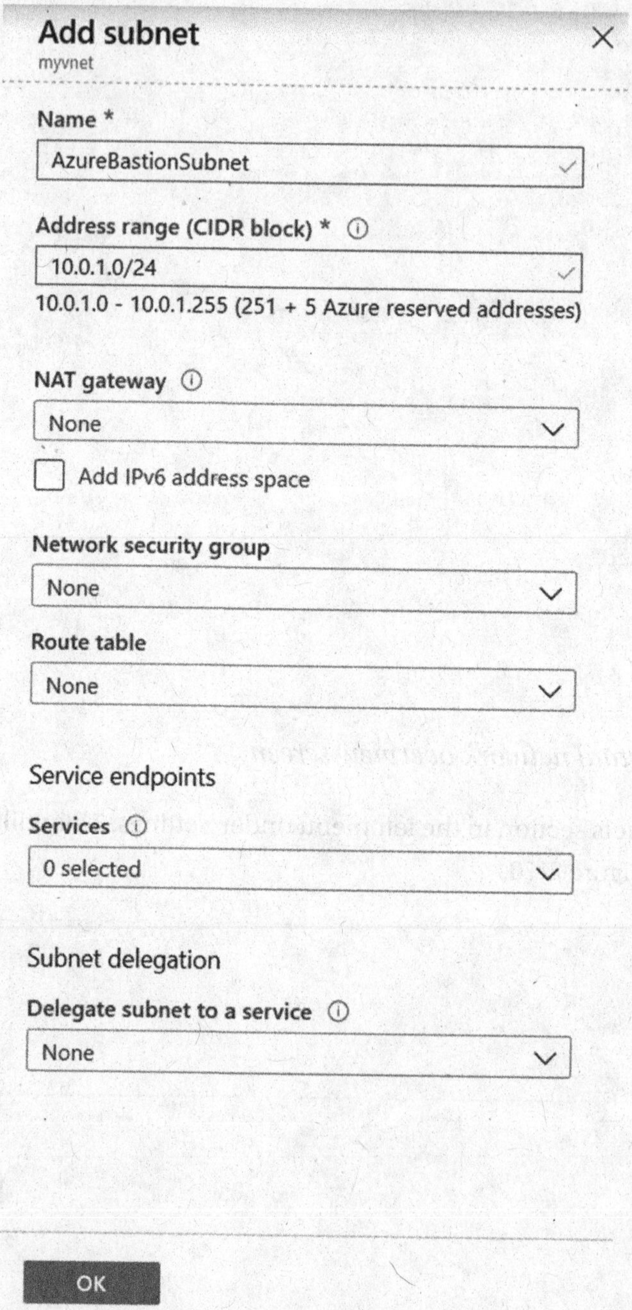

Add subnet   ✕
myvnet

Name *

AzureBastionSubnet   ✓

Address range (CIDR block) *   ⓘ

10.0.1.0/24   ✓

10.0.1.0 - 10.0.1.255 (251 + 5 Azure reserved addresses)

NAT gateway   ⓘ

None   ⌄

☐ Add IPv6 address space

Network security group

None   ⌄

Route table

None   ⌄

Service endpoints

Services   ⓘ

0 selected   ⌄

Subnet delegation

Delegate subnet to a service   ⓘ

None   ⌄

OK

Figure 2-79. *Subnets overview screen*

One point to note here that we need to create a subnet with the name AzureBastionSubnet, and the address range must be at least /27. Therefore, the virtual network should have at least two subnets: one for VM and the other one for Bastion. Upon successful creation, it should look like Figure 2-80.

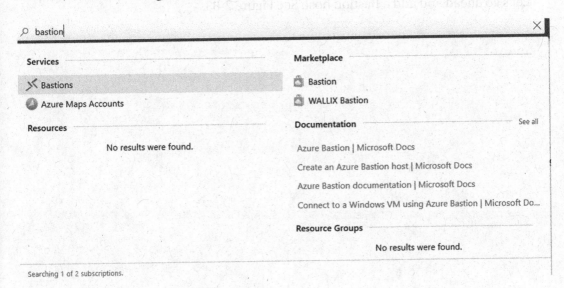

Figure 2-80. *Subnets screen*

Let's go ahead and create a Azure Bastion host now. Let's search for *bastion* in the services, as shown in Figure 2-81.

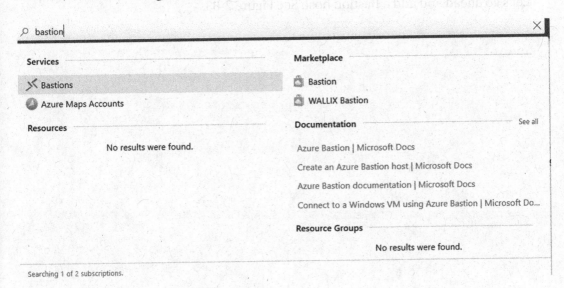

Figure 2-81. *Bastion search screen*

Clicking Bastion will take us to the screen shown in Figure 2-82.

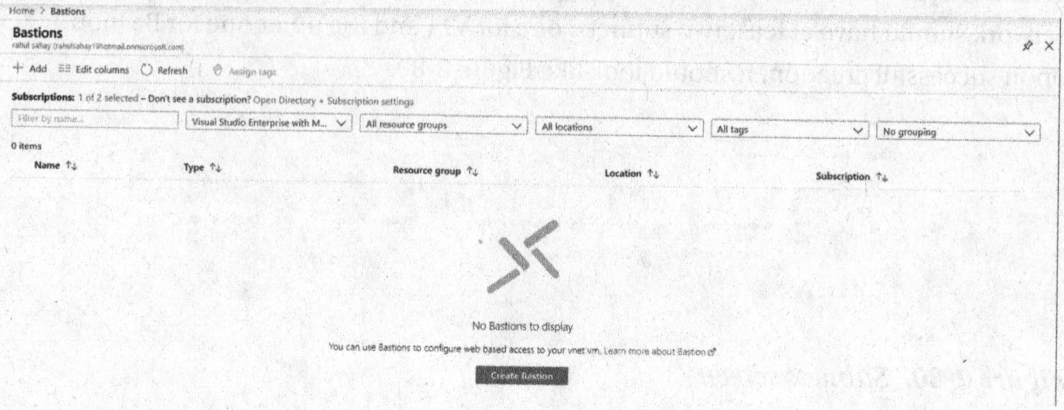

Figure 2-82. *Bastion screen*

Let's go ahead and add a Bastion host. See Figure 2-83.

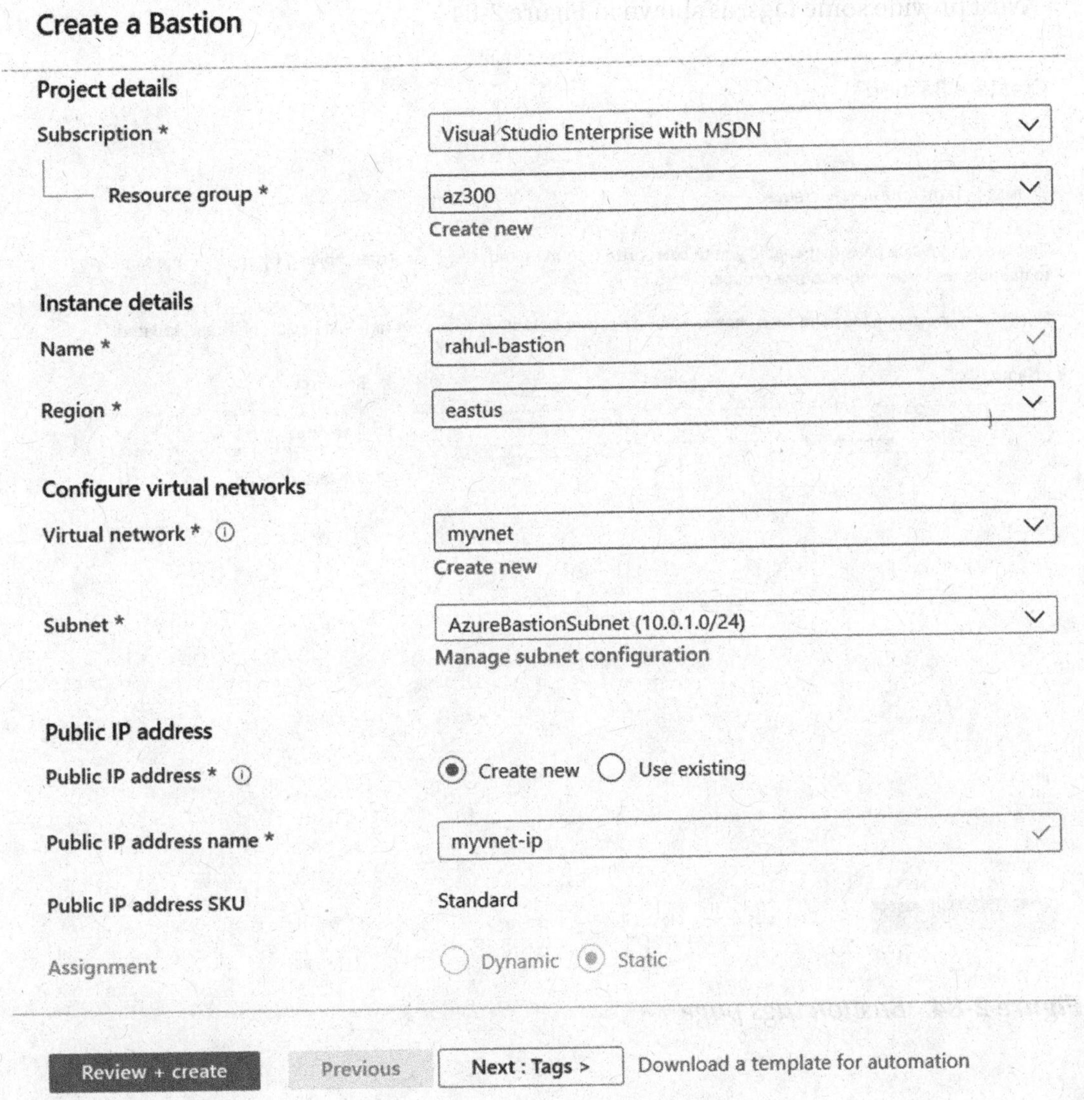

Create a Bastion

Project details

Subscription *

| Visual Studio Enterprise with MSDN | ∨ |

Resource group *

| az300 | ∨ |

Create new

Instance details

Name *

| rahul-bastion | ✓ |

Region *

| eastus | ∨ |

Configure virtual networks

Virtual network * ⓘ

| myvnet | ∨ |

Create new

Subnet *

| AzureBastionSubnet (10.0.1.0/24) | ∨ |

Manage subnet configuration

Public IP address

Public IP address * ⓘ   ⦿ Create new   ○ Use existing

Public IP address name *

| myvnet-ip | ✓ |

Public IP address SKU   Standard

Assignment   ○ Dynamic ⦿ Static

| Review + create | Previous | Next : Tags > | Download a template for automation

Figure 2-83. *Bastion creation page*

Next provide some tags, as shown in Figure 2-84.

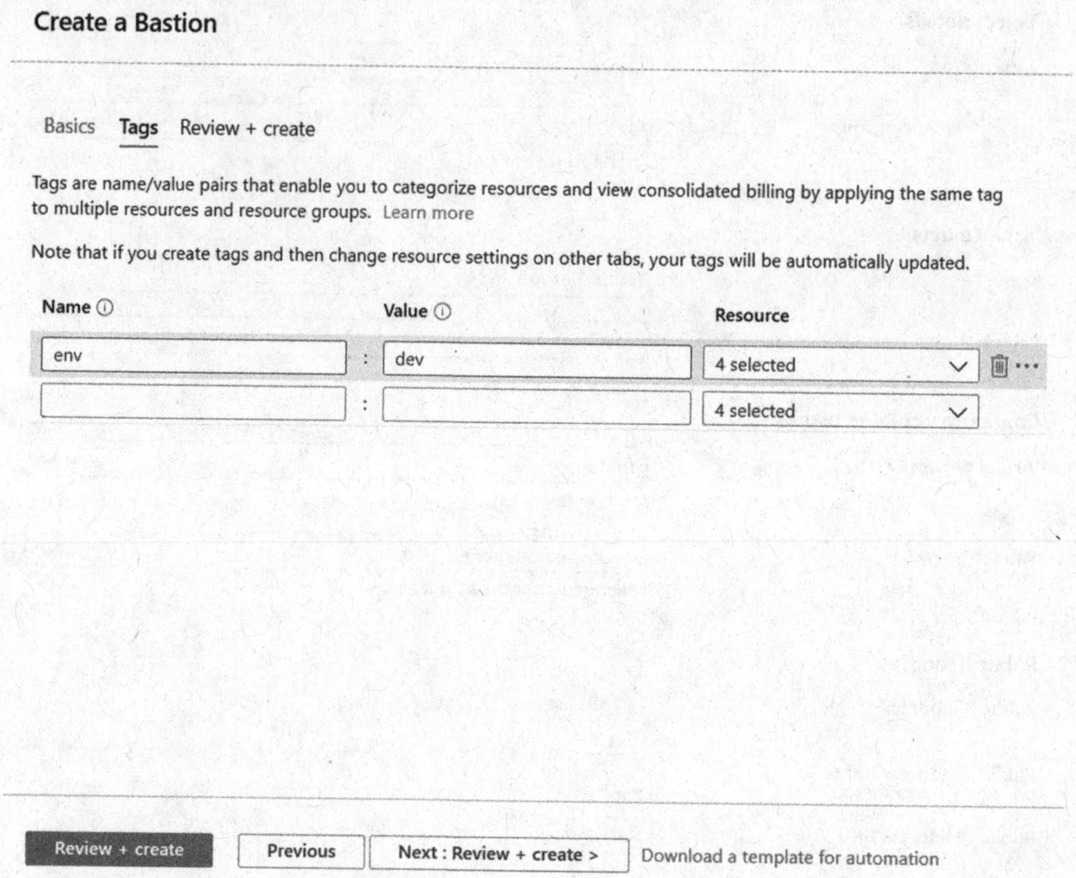

Create a Bastion

Basics   **Tags**   Review + create

Tags are name/value pairs that enable you to categorize resources and view consolidated billing by applying the same tag to multiple resources and resource groups. Learn more

Note that if you create tags and then change resource settings on other tabs, your tags will be automatically updated.

Name ⓘ		Value ⓘ		Resource	
env	:	dev		4 selected ∨	🗑 •••
	:			4 selected ∨	

| Review + create | | Previous | | Next : Review + create > | | Download a template for automation |

Figure 2-84. *Bastion tags page*

Finally, you'll see the review screen. See Figure 2-85.

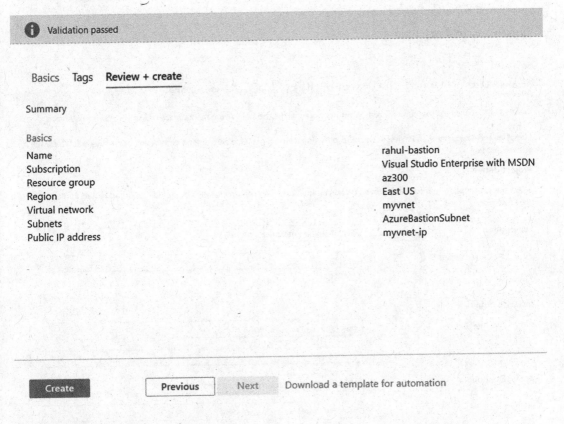

Create a Bastion

Validation passed

Basics   Tags   **Review + create**

Summary

Basics

Name	rahul-bastion
Subscription	Visual Studio Enterprise with MSDN
Resource group	az300
Region	East US
Virtual network	myvnet
Subnets	AzureBastionSubnet
Public IP address	myvnet-ip

Create   Previous   Next   Download a template for automation

Figure 2-85. *Bastion review page*

Upon successful creation of the host, it will appear, as shown in Figure 2-86.

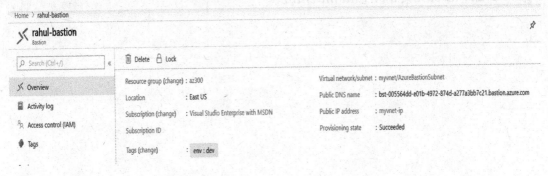

Home > rahul-bastion

rahul-bastion
Bastion

Delete   Lock

Search (Ctrl+/)

Overview   Resource group (change) : az300   Virtual network/subnet : myvnet/AzureBastionSubnet

Activity log   Location   : East US   Public DNS name   : bst-005564dd-e01b-4972-874d-a277a3bb7c21.bastion.azure.com

Access control (IAM)   Subscription (change) : Visual Studio Enterprise with MSDN   Public IP address : myvnet-ip

Tags   Subscription ID   Provisioning state : Succeeded

                        Tags (change)   : env : dev

Figure 2-86. *Bastion overview page*

I will now go ahead and create a virtual machine under this network so that I can connect with the Bastion host. See Figure 2-87 and Figure 2-88.

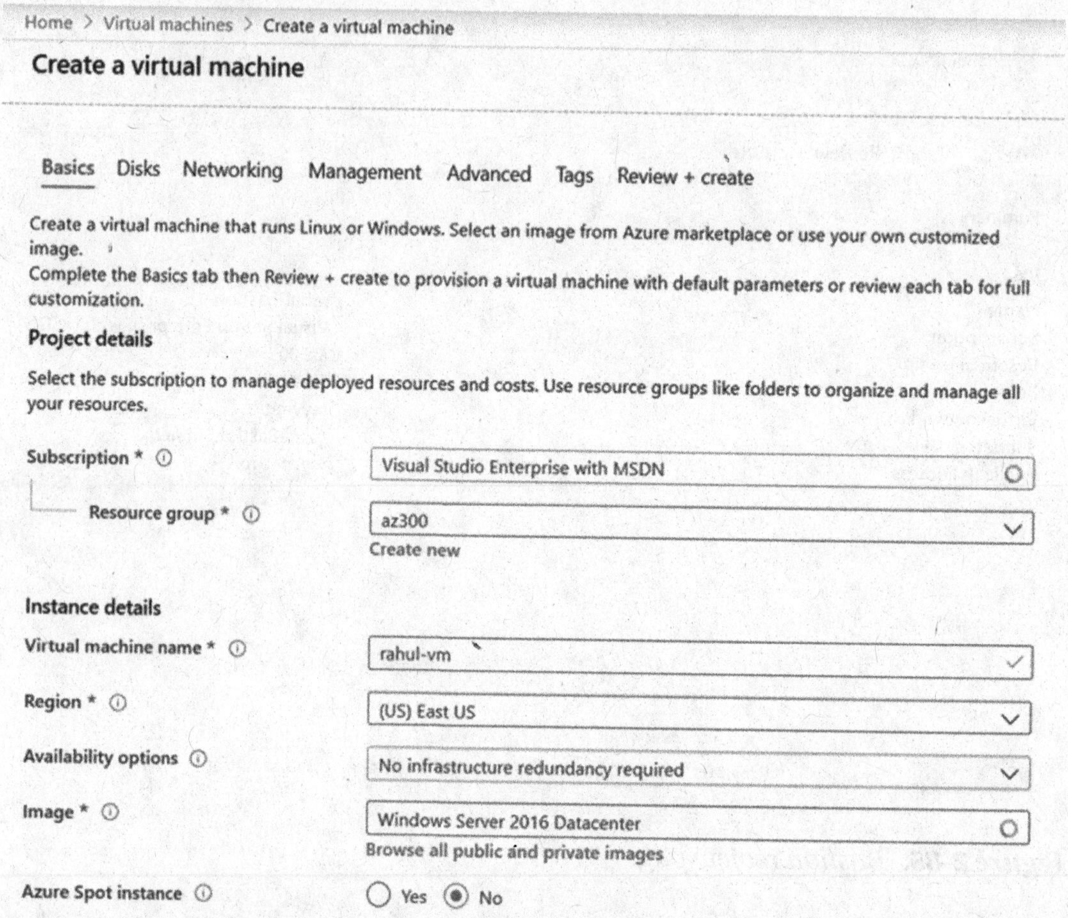

Home > Virtual machines > Create a virtual machine

Create a virtual machine

Basics   Disks   Networking   Management   Advanced   Tags   Review + create

Create a virtual machine that runs Linux or Windows. Select an image from Azure marketplace or use your own customized image.
Complete the Basics tab then Review + create to provision a virtual machine with default parameters or review each tab for full customization.

Project details

Select the subscription to manage deployed resources and costs. Use resource groups like folders to organize and manage all your resources.

Subscription * ⓘ | Visual Studio Enterprise with MSDN   ○ |

　　　└─ Resource group * ⓘ | az300   ∨ |
                              Create new

Instance details

Virtual machine name * ⓘ | rahul-vm   ✓ |

Region * ⓘ | (US) East US   ∨ |

Availability options ⓘ | No infrastructure redundancy required   ∨ |

Image * ⓘ | Windows Server 2016 Datacenter   ○ |
                              Browse all public and private images

Azure Spot instance ⓘ   ○ Yes   ⊙ No

Figure 2-87. *Creating a virtual machine*

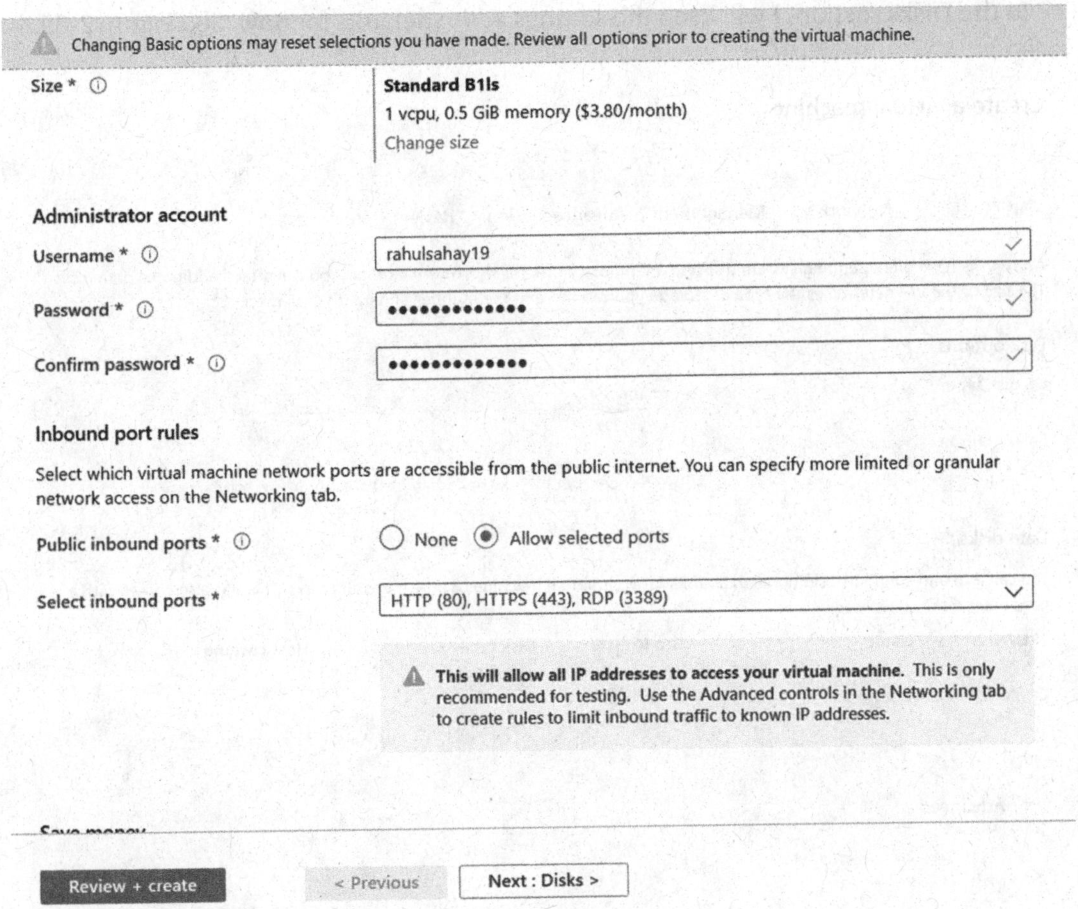

⚠ Changing Basic options may reset selections you have made. Review all options prior to creating the virtual machine.

Size * ⓘ   **Standard B1ls**
                                             1 vcpu, 0.5 GiB memory ($3.80/month)
                                             Change size

Administrator account

Username * ⓘ   rahulsahay19   ✓

Password * ⓘ   ●●●●●●●●●●●●●   ✓

Confirm password * ⓘ   ●●●●●●●●●●●●●   ✓

Inbound port rules

Select which virtual machine network ports are accessible from the public internet. You can specify more limited or granular network access on the Networking tab.

Public inbound ports * ⓘ   ○ None   ⦿ Allow selected ports

Select inbound ports *   HTTP (80), HTTPS (443), RDP (3389)   ⌄

                                   ⚠ **This will allow all IP addresses to access your virtual machine.** This is only
                                      recommended for testing. Use the Advanced controls in the Networking tab
                                      to create rules to limit inbound traffic to known IP addresses.

Save money

[Review + create]   [< Previous]   [Next : Disks >]

Figure 2-88. *Giving the details of the virtual machine*

In the Disks section, I will keep the settings at the defaults for now. See Figure 2-89.

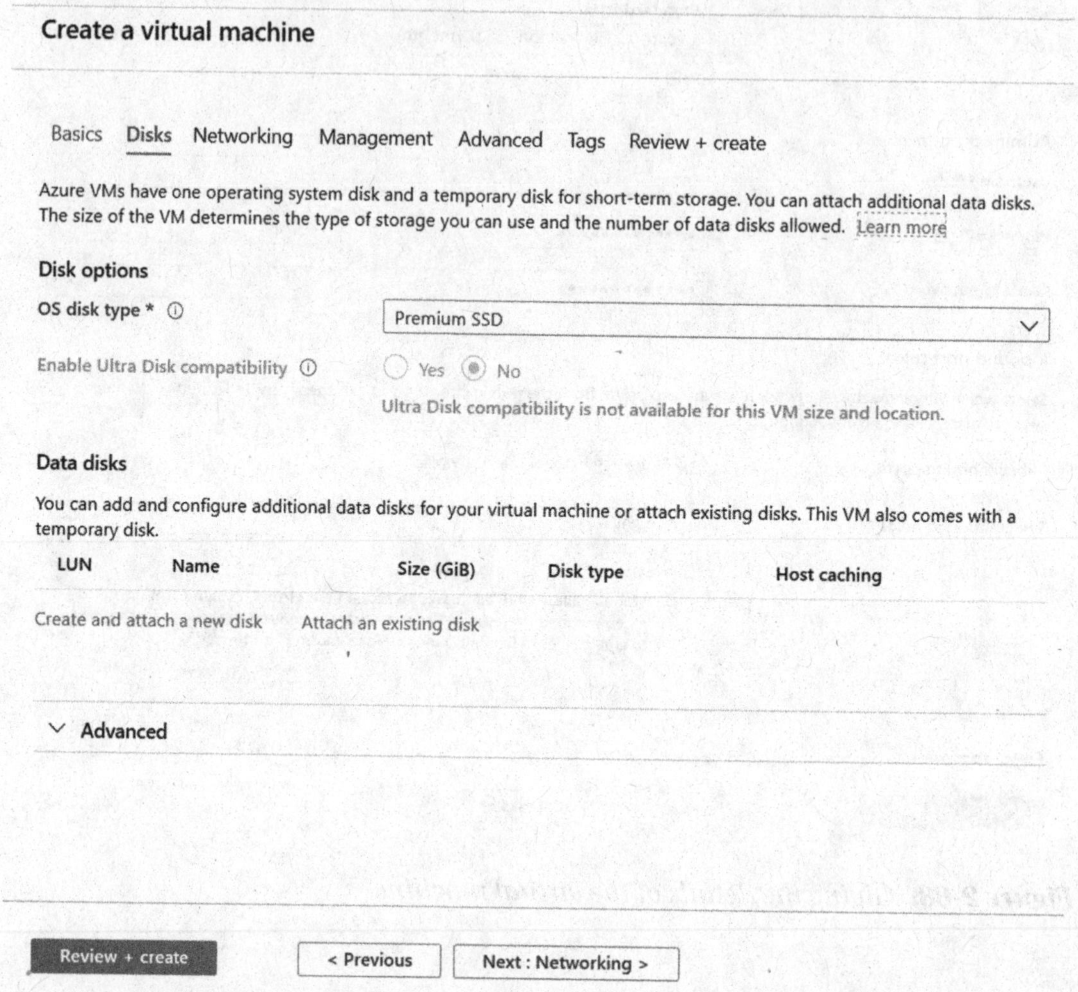

Create a virtual machine

Basics   **Disks**   Networking   Management   Advanced   Tags   Review + create

Azure VMs have one operating system disk and a temporary disk for short-term storage. You can attach additional data disks. The size of the VM determines the type of storage you can use and the number of data disks allowed. Learn more

Disk options

OS disk type * ⓘ

| Premium SSD | ⌄ |

Enable Ultra Disk compatibility ⓘ   ○ Yes   ● No

Ultra Disk compatibility is not available for this VM size and location.

Data disks

You can add and configure additional data disks for your virtual machine or attach existing disks. This VM also comes with a temporary disk.

LUN	Name	Size (GiB)	Disk type	Host caching

Create and attach a new disk   Attach an existing disk

⌄ **Advanced**

[Review + create]   [< Previous]   [Next : Networking >]

Figure 2-89. *Bastion disks page*

Under Networking, I will make sure that I connect to myvnet. See Figure 2-90.

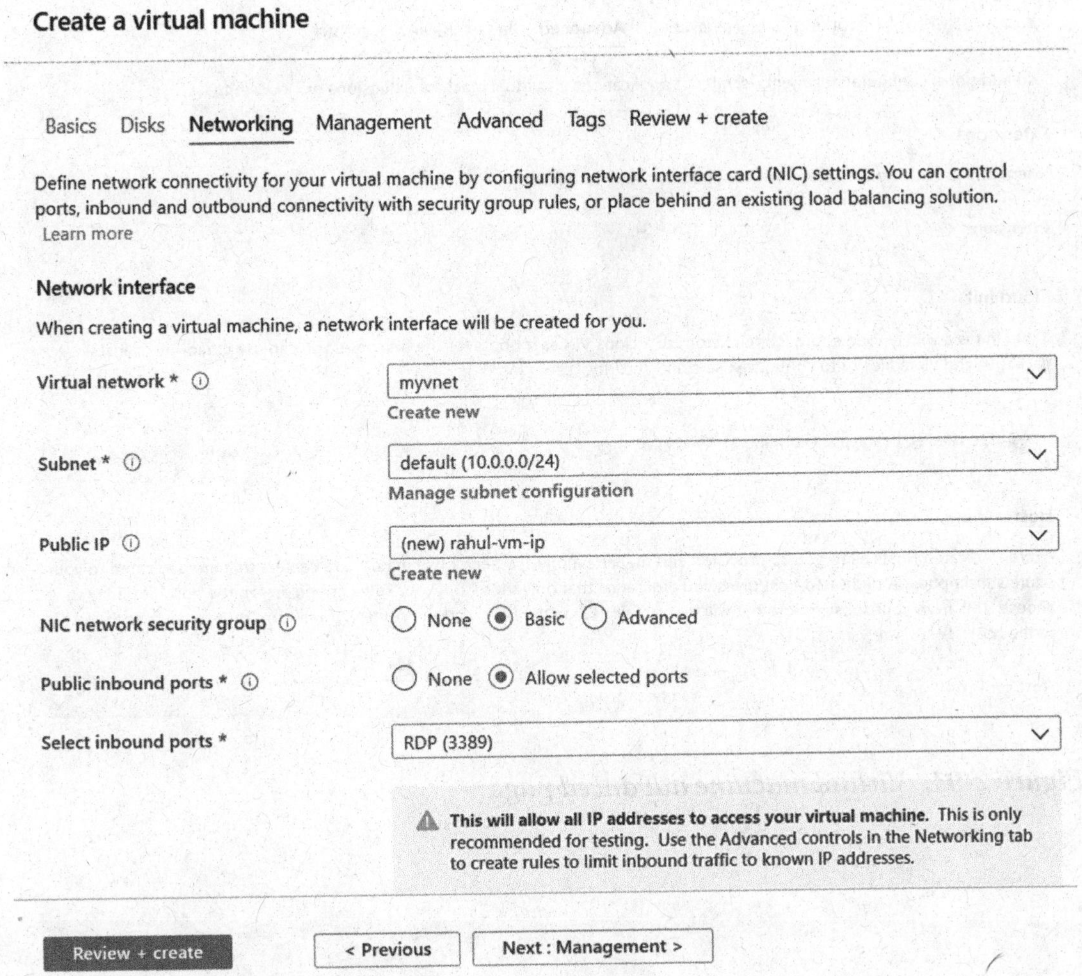

Create a virtual machine

Basics   Disks   **Networking**   Management   Advanced   Tags   Review + create

Define network connectivity for your virtual machine by configuring network interface card (NIC) settings. You can control ports, inbound and outbound connectivity with security group rules, or place behind an existing load balancing solution. Learn more

Network interface

When creating a virtual machine, a network interface will be created for you.

Virtual network * ⓘ	myvnet ⌄
	Create new
Subnet * ⓘ	default (10.0.0.0/24) ⌄
	Manage subnet configuration
Public IP ⓘ	(new) rahul-vm-ip ⌄
	Create new
NIC network security group ⓘ	○ None ⦿ Basic ○ Advanced
Public inbound ports * ⓘ	○ None ⦿ Allow selected ports
Select inbound ports *	RDP (3389) ⌄

⚠ **This will allow all IP addresses to access your virtual machine.** This is only recommended for testing. Use the Advanced controls in the Networking tab to create rules to limit inbound traffic to known IP addresses.

Review + create   < Previous   Next : Management >

Figure 2-90. *Virtual machine networking page*

For the other settings, I will keep the defaults, as shown in Figure 2-91 and Figure 2-92.

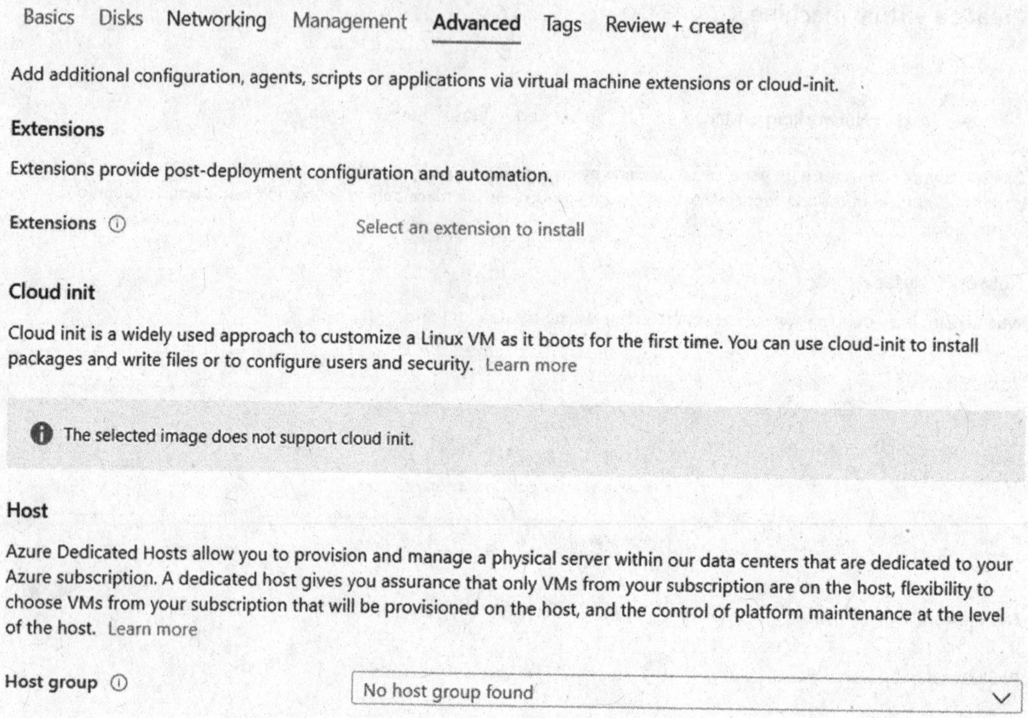

Basics   Disks   Networking   Management   **Advanced**   Tags   Review + create

Add additional configuration, agents, scripts or applications via virtual machine extensions or cloud-init.

Extensions

Extensions provide post-deployment configuration and automation.

Extensions ⓘ   Select an extension to install

Cloud init

Cloud init is a widely used approach to customize a Linux VM as it boots for the first time. You can use cloud-init to install packages and write files or to configure users and security. Learn more

> ⓘ The selected image does not support cloud init.

Host

Azure Dedicated Hosts allow you to provision and manage a physical server within our data centers that are dedicated to your Azure subscription. A dedicated host gives you assurance that only VMs from your subscription are on the host, flexibility to choose VMs from your subscription that will be provisioned on the host, and the control of platform maintenance at the level of the host. Learn more

Host group ⓘ   No host group found   ∨

Figure 2-91. Virtual machine advanced page

ℹ The selected image does not support cloud init.

Host

Azure Dedicated Hosts allow you to provision and manage a physical server within our data centers that are dedicated to your Azure subscription. A dedicated host gives you assurance that only VMs from your subscription are on the host, flexibility to choose VMs from your subscription that will be provisioned on the host, and the control of platform maintenance at the level of the host. Learn more

Host group ⓘ

No host group found   ⌄

Proximity placement group

Proximity placement groups allow you to group Azure resources physically closer together in the same region. Learn more

Proximity placement group ⓘ

No proximity placement groups found   ⌄

VM generation

Generation 2 VMs support features such as UEFI-based boot architecture, increased memory and OS disk size limits, Intel® Software Guard Extensions (SGX), and virtual persistent memory (vPMEM).

VM generation ⓘ   ◉ Gen 1   ○ Gen 2

ℹ Generation 2 VMs do not yet support some Azure platform features, including Azure Disk Encryption.

Review + create   < Previous   Next : Tags >

Figure 2-92. *Virtual machine advanced page, continued*

Next, I will provide tags, as shown in Figure 2-93.

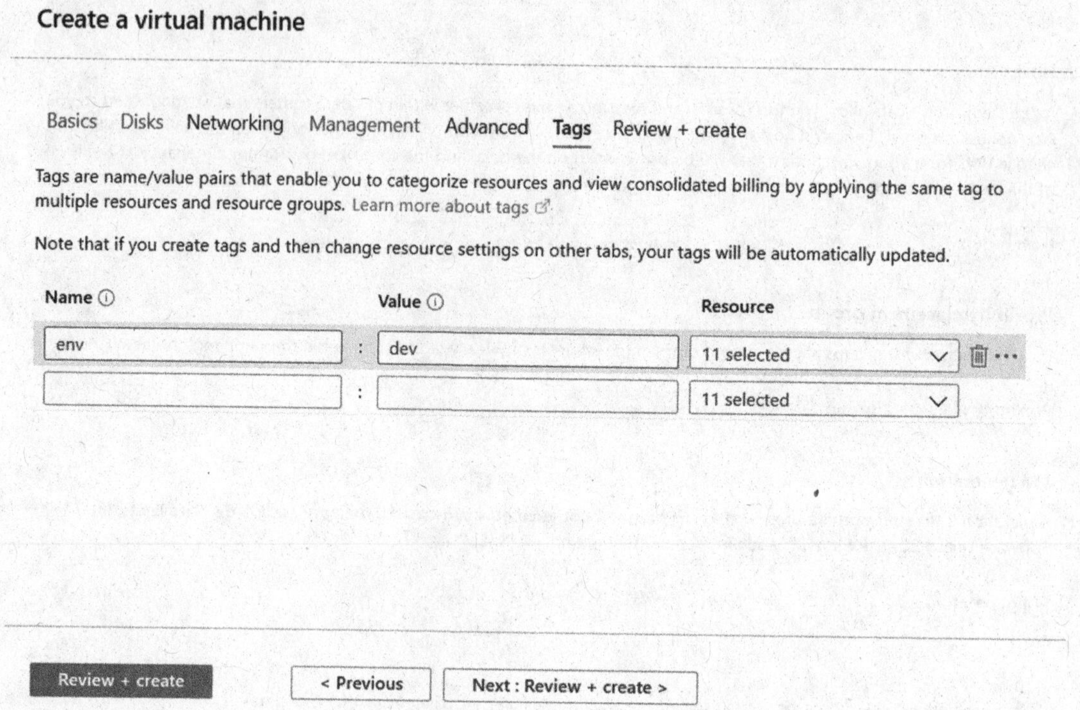

Create a virtual machine

Basics   Disks   Networking   Management   Advanced   **Tags**   Review + create

Tags are name/value pairs that enable you to categorize resources and view consolidated billing by applying the same tag to multiple resources and resource groups. Learn more about tags ⬀

Note that if you create tags and then change resource settings on other tabs, your tags will be automatically updated.

Name ⓘ		Value ⓘ	Resource		
env	:	dev	11 selected	⌄	🗑 •••
	:		11 selected	⌄	

Review + create		< Previous	Next : Review + create >

Figure 2-93. *Virtual machine tags page*

Finally, you'll see the "Review + create" screen, as shown in Figure 2-94.

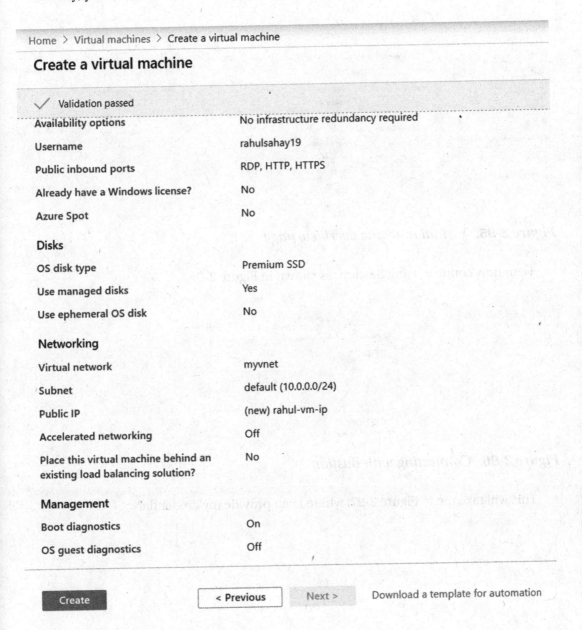

Figure 2-94. Virtual machine review page

Upon successful creation, you will be taken to the screen shown in Figure 2-95.

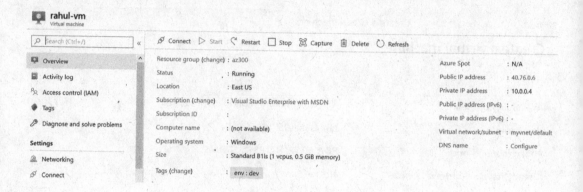

Figure 2-95. *Virtual machine overview page*

I can now connect using Bastion, as shown in Figure 2-96.

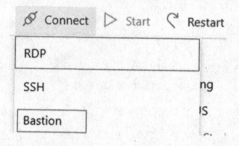

Figure 2-96. *Connecting with Bastion*

This will take me to Figure 2-97, where I can provide my credentials.

⚠ To improve security, enable just-in-time access on this VM. →

RDP   SSH   **BASTION**

Connect with Bastion

To connect to your virtual machine over the web, enter login credentials and click connect (opens a new browser window).

☑ Open in new window

Username * ⓘ

| rahulsahay19 | ✓ |

Password * ⓘ

| •••••••••••••• | ✓ |

Connect

Figure 2-97. *Virtual machine Bastion page*

After clicking Connect, you will see the screen in Figure 2-98.

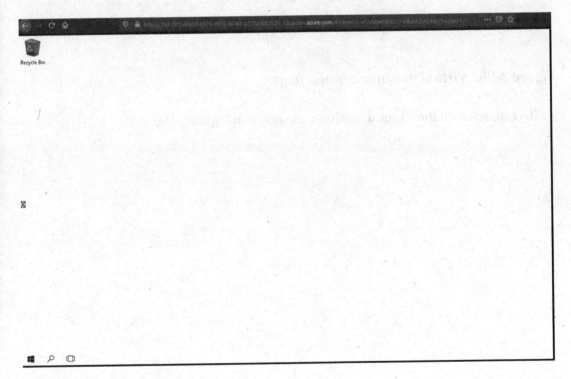

Figure 2-98. *Virtual machine*

Here, the VM gets opened in another window and is pretty fast and secure. One thing to note is that I resized the VM size to a B2 instance. You may try with another instance if the B1 instance is crashing intermittently.

Similarly, I have created another VM. This time I created a Ubuntu VM on the same virtual network and connected via Bastion, as shown in Figure 2-99.

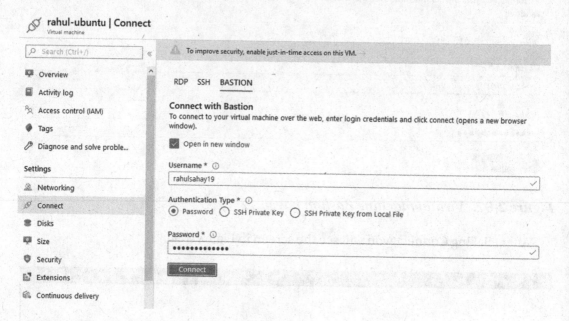

Figure 2-99. *Virtual machine connect page*

It connected on the Ubuntu machine, as shown in Figure 2-100.

```
←  →  C  ⌂              ⓪  🔒  https://bst-005564dd-e01b-4972-874d-a277a3bb7c21-1.bastion.azure.com/#/client/cmFod

Welcome to Ubuntu 18.04.4 LTS (GNU/Linux 5.0.0-1032-azure x86_64)

 * Documentation:  https://help.ubuntu.com
 * Management:     https://landscape.canonical.com
 * Support:        https://ubuntu.com/advantage

  System information as of Thu Mar 19 20:48:23 UTC 2020

  System load:  0.73              Processes:             135
  Usage of /:   4.0% of 28.90GB   Users logged in:       0
  Memory usage: 4%                IP address for eth0: 10.0.0.5
  Swap usage:   0%

) packages can be updated.
) updates are security updates.


The programs included with the Ubuntu system are free software;
the exact distribution terms for each program are described in the
individual files in /usr/share/doc/*/copyright.

Ubuntu comes with ABSOLUTELY NO WARRANTY, to the extent permitted by
applicable law.

To run a command as administrator (user "root"), use "sudo <command>".
See "man sudo_root" for details.

rahulsahay19@rahul-ubuntu:~$ █
```

Figure 2-100. Virtual machine Ubuntu version

CHAPTER 3

ARM Templates

In this chapter, we will discuss how to automate the deployment of virtual machines. Within Microsoft Azure, automation is usually done using Azure Resource Manager (ARM) templates, which is the modern way of deploying resources into Azure. The opposite of ARM is Azure Service Manager (ASM), which is a classic deployment model that we don't use anymore.

Let's start the process of deploying a virtual machine. Normally, whenever we deploy any VM, its deployment page looks like Figure 3-1.

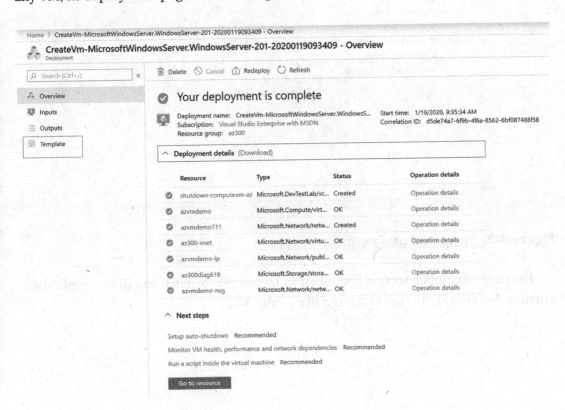

Figure 3-1. *Deployment page*

© Rahul Sahay 2020
R. Sahay, *Microsoft Azure Architect Technologies Study Companion*,
https://doi.org/10.1007/978-1-4842-6200-9_3

On the left side, you can see a Template section. When you click Template, it will present the UI shown in Figure 3-2. The screen lists two categories.

1) Templates

2) Parameter files

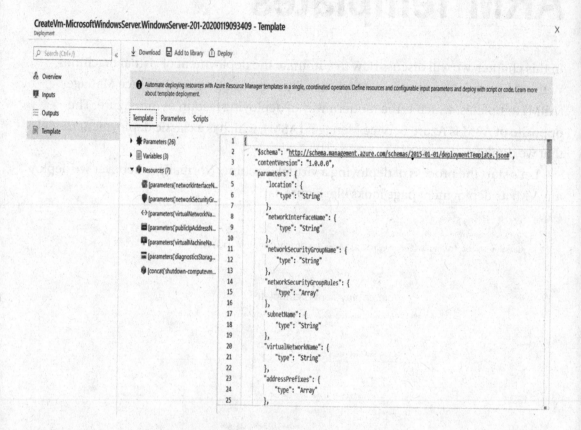

Figure 3-2. Templates and parameter files

Earlier the Template section contained CLI, PowerShell, .NET, and Ruby scripts also. But now there is a Scripts tab that looks like Figure 3-3.

Figure 3-3. *Scripts tab*

Download the template by clicking the Download button at the top. In the downloaded template, you can see a parameters file and a template file, as shown in Figure 3-4.

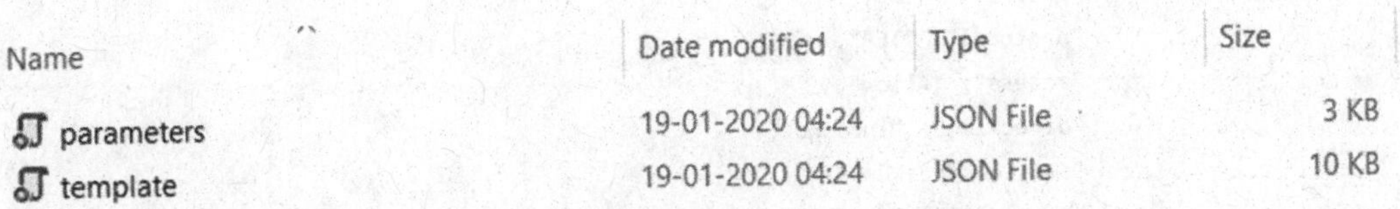

Name	Date modified	Type	Size
parameters	19-01-2020 04:24	JSON File	3 KB
template	19-01-2020 04:24	JSON File	10 KB

Figure 3-4. *Parameters and template files*

The parameters JSON file looks like Figure 3-5.

```
{
    "$schema": "https://schema.management.azure.com/schemas/2015-01-01/deploymentParameters.json#",
    "contentVersion": "1.0.0.0",
    "parameters": {
        "location": {
            "value": "eastus"
        },
        "networkInterfaceName": {
            "value": "azvmdemo711"
        },
        "networkSecurityGroupName": {
            "value": "azvmdemo-nsg"
        },
        "networkSecurityGroupRules": {
            "value": [
                {
                    "name": "RDP",
                    "properties": {
                        "priority": 300,
                        "protocol": "TCP",
                        "access": "Allow",
                        "direction": "Inbound",
                        "sourceAddressPrefix": "*",
                        "sourcePortRange": "*",
                        "destinationAddressPrefix": "*",
                        "destinationPortRange": "3389"
                    }
                }
            ]
        },
        "subnetName": {
            "value": "default"
        },
        "virtualNetworkName": {
            "value": "az300-vnet"
        },
```

Figure 3-5. *Parameters JSON file*

For the complete file, you can check out `https://bit.ly/Azure-params`.
The template file looks like Figure 3-6.

```json
{
    "$schema": "http://schema.management.azure.com/schemas/2015-01-01/deploymentTemplate.json#",
    "contentVersion": "1.0.0.0",
    "parameters": {
        "location": {
            "type": "String"
        },
        "networkInterfaceName": {
            "type": "String"
        },
        "networkSecurityGroupName": {
            "type": "String"
        },
        "networkSecurityGroupRules": {
            "type": "Array"
        },
        "subnetName": {
            "type": "String"
        },
        "virtualNetworkName": {
            "type": "String"
        },
        "addressPrefixes": {
            "type": "Array"
        },
        "subnets": {
            "type": "Array"
        },
        "publicIpAddressName": {
            "type": "String"
        },
```

Figure 3-6. *Template file*

For the complete reference, you can visit `https://bit.ly/azure-templates`.

The `templates.json` file starts with a schema at the top of the file. Then, it has various parameters in it, which we will eventually use to modify the template. Variables are similar to parameters; the only difference is that they are computed fields.

The key section here is the resources section. This is where all the resources within this deployment get defined. The last section is the output. This ARM template is going to return the admin's username as its output.

In the case of parameters, there will be one parameter for each of the parameters defined by the template. The template has one `location` parameter that is a string, and in the parameters file, the location is set to `EastUS`. These values come from how we initially created the VM in the UI. In other words, Azure has grabbed all the values as part of the template.

Now, let's look an example of a network interface card (see Figure 3-7).

```
{
    "type": "Microsoft.Network/networkInterfaces",
    "apiVersion": "2019-07-01",
    "name": "[parameters('networkInterfaceName')]",
    "location": "[parameters('location')]",
    "dependsOn": [
        "[concat('Microsoft.Network/networkSecurityGroups/', parameters('networkSecurityGroupName'))]",
        "[concat('Microsoft.Network/virtualNetworks/', parameters('virtualNetworkName'))]",
        "[concat('Microsoft.Network/publicIpAddresses/', parameters('publicIpAddressName'))]"
    ],
    "tags": {
        "demo": "azure"
    },
    "properties": {
        "ipConfigurations": [
            {
                "name": "ipconfig1",
                "properties": {
                    "subnet": {
                        "id": "[variables('subnetRef')]"
                    },
                    "privateIPAllocationMethod": "Dynamic",
                    "publicIpAddress": {
                        "id": "[resourceId(resourceGroup().name, 'Microsoft.Network/publicIpAddresses', parameters('publicIpAddressName
                    }
                }
            }
        ],
        "networkSecurityGroup": {
            "id": "[variables('nsgId')]"
        }
    }
}
```

Figure 3-7. *Network interface file*

The file starts with the type `Microsoft.Network/networkInterfaces`. This is the network interface resource.

- It takes the name of the card from the parameters section.

- It has some pretty static code for the API version.

- The location is the same as we passed in the parameters.

- Similarly, we have applied tags.

- The network interface card has this IP address, which is being set up in the next property under `ipconfig`.

- The file also specifies the network security group as `nsgId`.

- Finally, the file depends on the following:

  - `networkSecurityGroupName`

  - `virtualNetworkName`

  - `publicIpAddressName` (hence, the previously listed dependencies need to be created first)

Figure 3-8 shows the list of dependencies.

```
{
                "type": "Microsoft.Network/networkSecurityGroups",
                "apiVersion": "2019-02-01",
                "name": "[parameters('networkSecurityGroupName')]",
                "location": "[parameters('location')]",
                "tags": {
                    "demo": "azure"
                },
                "properties": {
                    "securityRules": "[parameters('networkSecurityGroupRules')]"
                }
        },
        {

            "type": "Microsoft.Network/virtualNetworks",
            "apiVersion": "2019-04-01",
            "name": "[parameters('virtualNetworkName')]",
            "location": "[parameters('location')]",
            "tags": {
                "demo": "azure"
            },
            "properties": {
                "addressSpace": {
                    "addressPrefixes": "[parameters('addressPrefixes')]"
                },
                "subnets": "[parameters('subnets')]"
            }
        },
        {

            "type": "Microsoft.Network/publicIpAddresses",
            "apiVersion": "2019-02-01",
            "name": "[parameters('publicIpAddressName')]",
            "location": "[parameters('location')]",
            "tags": {
                "demo": "azure"
            },
            "sku": {
                "name": "[parameters('publicIpAddressSku')]"
            },
            "properties": {
                "publicIpAllocationMethod": "[parameters('publicIpAddressType')]"
            }
```

Figure 3-8.   *Dependencies file*

Creating a VM with an ARM Template

Creating a VM with an ARM template is a complex task. In this case, the network interface card, its dependencies, and other things have to be created first.

Let's start with the bare minimum of changes. Therefore, I will start with network interface card and give it a new name of rahulnic123. I am going to keep the same network security group, and we will launch in the same virtual network. However, it's going to need a new public IP address, for example, azvmdemo2-ip. So, change the name of the VM to azvmdemo2. Leave the other settings the same. I have modified the parameters file accordingly.

Azure will consider this template as the baseline template as we haven't changed anything in the template, and then it can deploy the same template again and again with the changed parameter values. This is known as *desired state configuration* (DSC).

Hence, we can take these files, have them in our source control, and then we can just do versioning on top of it. This is also known as *infrastructure as a service*.

Deploying a VM

Let's go ahead and deploy the VM. In the Templates section, click the Add button, as shown in Figure 3-9.

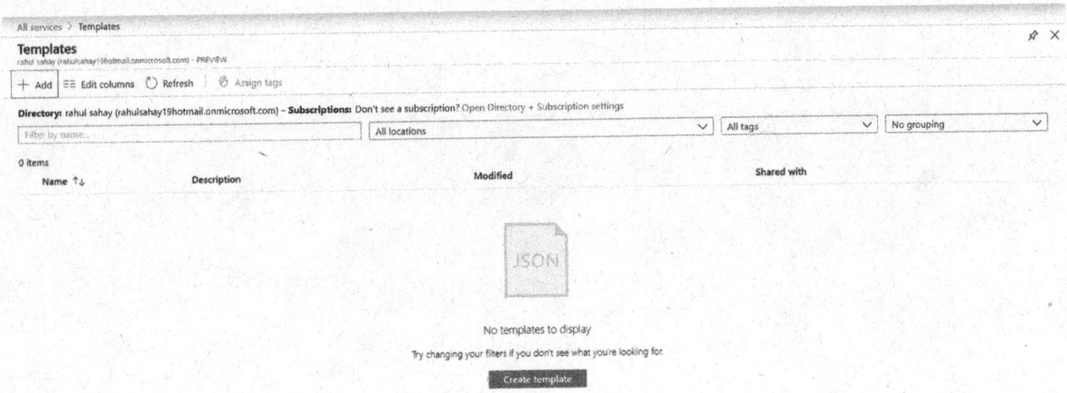

Figure 3-9. Template file

Now enter the details, as shown in Figure 3-10.

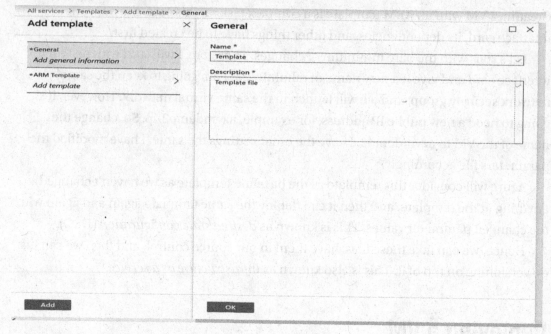

Figure 3-10. *Adding a template file*

Click OK and then select the ARM template. See Figure 3-11.

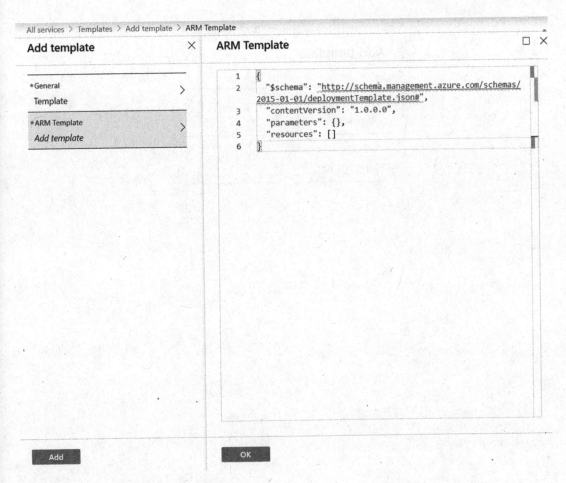

Figure 3-11. *ARM template*

Drop your ARM template from the machine and click the Add button, as shown in Figure 3-12.

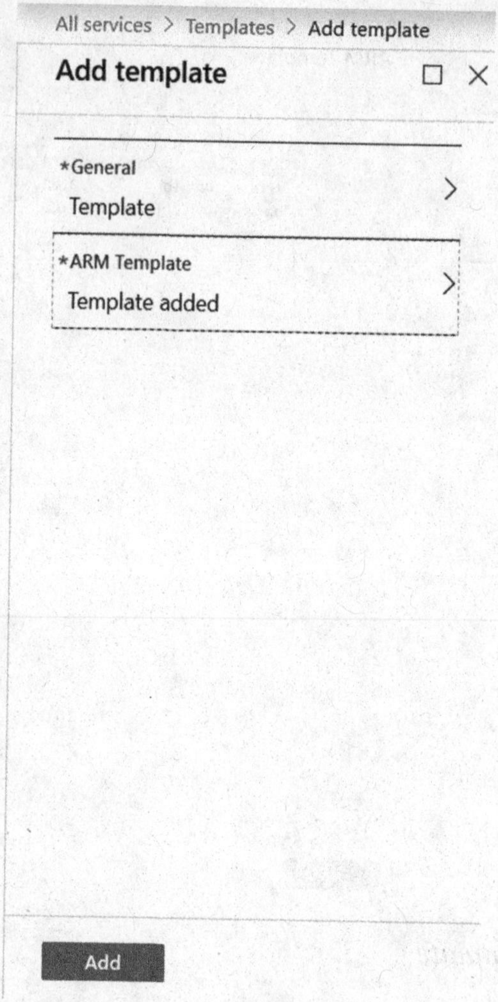

All services > Templates > Add template

Add template   □ ✕

⋆General
Template   >

⋆ARM Template
Template added   >

Add

Figure 3-12. *Adding a template*

This will drop a template file, as shown in Figure 3-13.

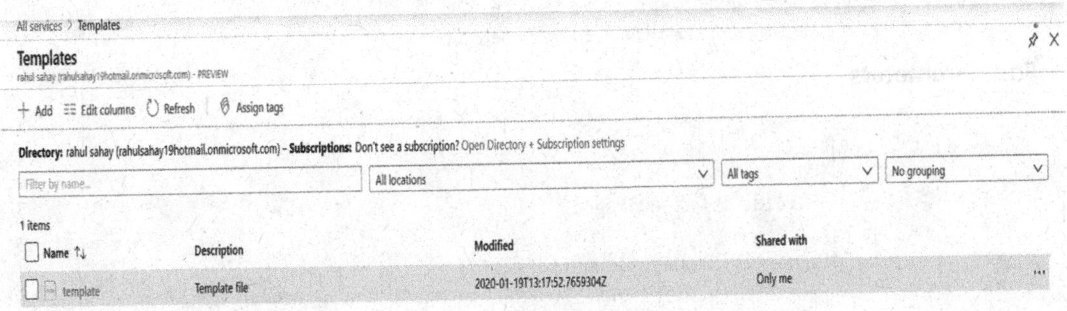

Figure 3-13. *New template in the Templates section*

Now click Deploy, as shown in Figure 3-14.

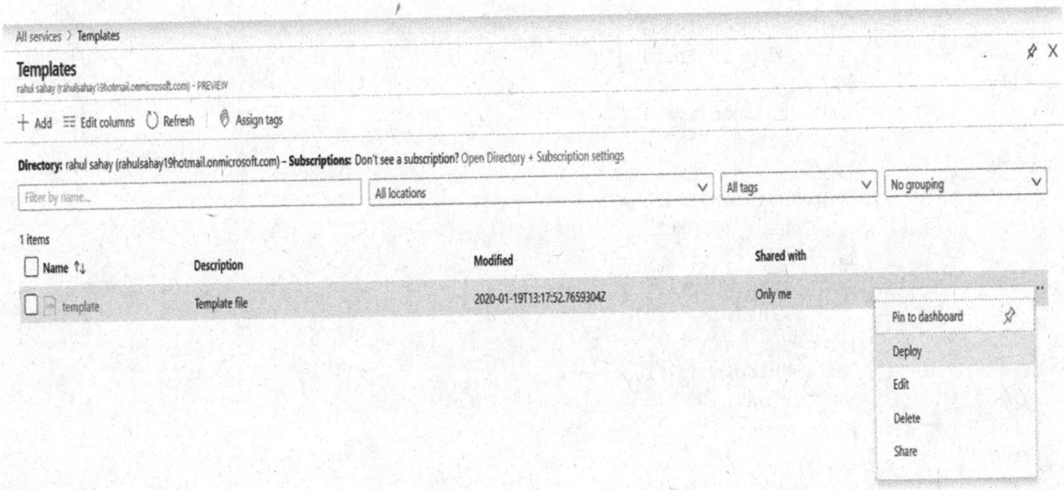

Figure 3-14. *Deploying an ARM template*

This will bring up Figure 3-15. Here, I can choose to enter all the details manually or upload the parameters file, which we modified already.

All services > Templates > Custom deployment > Edit parameters

Edit parameters

↑ Load file   ↓ Download

```
 80                      "value": "az300diag619"
 81              },
 82              "diagnosticsStorageAccountId": {
 83                      "value": "Microsoft.Storage/storageAccounts/az300diag619"
 84              },
 85              "diagnosticsStorageAccountType": {
 86                      "value": "Standard_LRS"
 87              },
 88              "diagnosticsStorageAccountKind": {
 89                      "value": "Storage"
 90              },
 91              "autoShutdownStatus": {
 92                      "value": "Enabled"
 93              },
 94              "autoShutdownTime": {
 95                      "value": "19:00"
 96              },
 97              "autoShutdownTimeZone": {
 98                      "value": "UTC"
 99              },
100              "autoShutdownNotificationStatus": {
101                      "value": "Disabled"
102              },
103              "autoShutdownNotificationLocale": {
104                      "value": "en"
105              }
106          }
107      }
```

Save   Discard

Figure 3-15. *Editing parameters*

Now, click Save. See Figure 3-16.

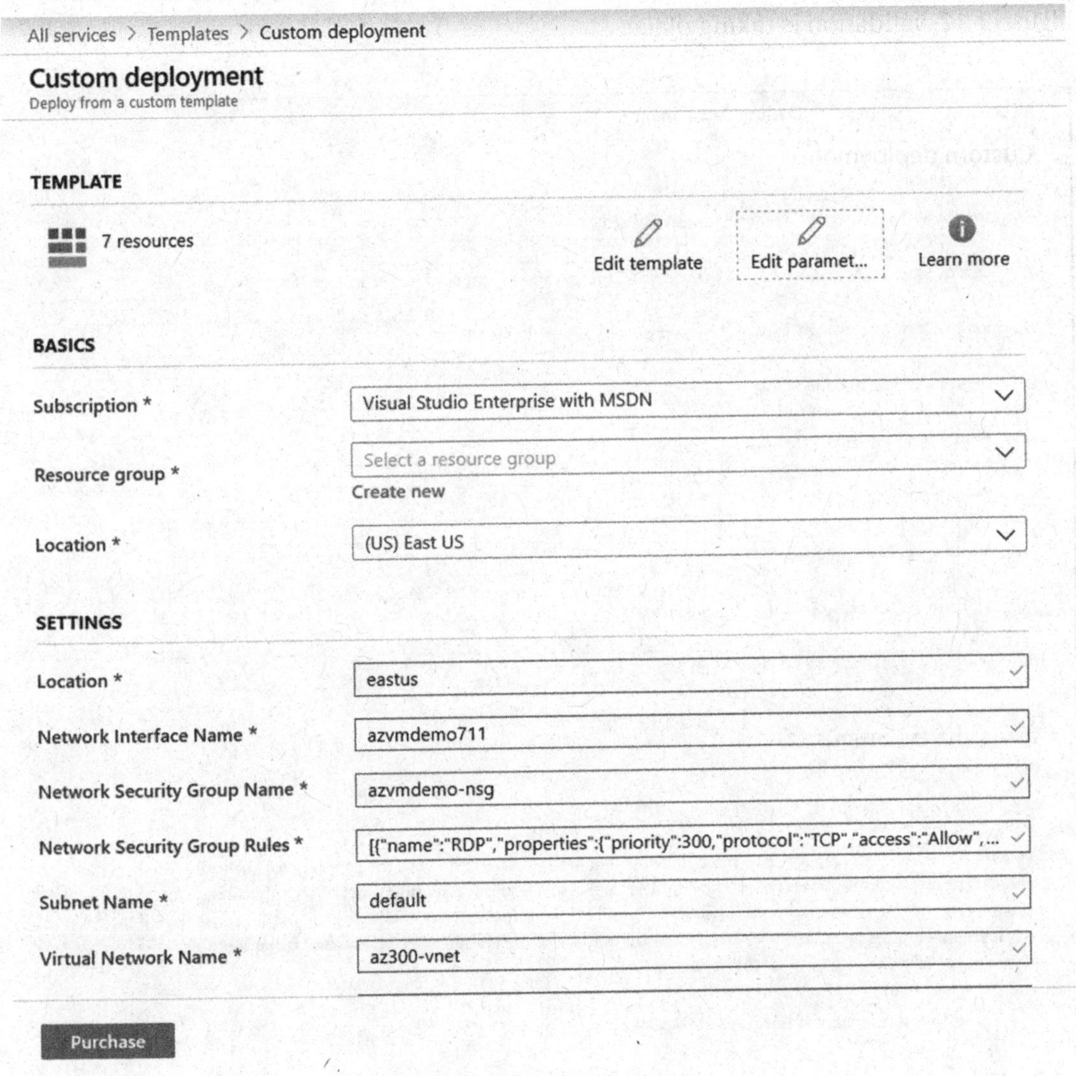

All services > Templates > Custom deployment

Custom deployment
Deploy from a custom template

TEMPLATE

▦ 7 resources

✏ Edit template   ✏ Edit paramet...   ⓘ Learn more

BASICS

Subscription *	Visual Studio Enterprise with MSDN	⌄
Resource group *	Select a resource group	⌄
	Create new	
Location *	(US) East US	⌄

SETTINGS

Location *	eastus	✓
Network Interface Name *	azvmdemo711	✓
Network Security Group Name *	azvmdemo-nsg	✓
Network Security Group Rules *	[{"name":"RDP","properties":{"priority":300,"protocol":"TCP","access":"Allow",...	✓
Subnet Name *	default	✓
Virtual Network Name *	az300-vnet	✓

Purchase

Figure 3-16. Custom deployment

You can see that almost all the parameters have been uploaded. You need to fill in the resource group and password and then click Purchase. Here, as you can see in Figure 3-17, validation is taking place.

All services > Templates > Custom deployment

Custom deployment
Deploy from a custom template

Diagnostics Storage Account Name *	az300diag619
Diagnostics Storage Account Id *	Microsoft.Storage/storageAccounts/az300diag619
Diagnostics Storage Account Type *	Standard_LRS
Diagnostics Storage Account Kind *	Storage
Auto Shutdown Status *	Enabled
Auto Shutdown Time *	19:00
Auto Shutdown Time Zone *	UTC
Auto Shutdown Notification Status *	Disabled
Auto Shutdown Notification Locale *	en

TERMS AND CONDITIONS

Azure Marketplace Terms | Azure Marketplace

By clicking "Purchase," I (a) agree to the applicable legal terms associated with the offering; (b) authorize Microsoft to charge or bill my current payment method for the fees associated the offering(s), including applicable taxes, with the same billing frequency as my Azure subscription, until I discontinue use of the offering(s); and (c) agree that, if the deployment involves 3rd party offerings, Microsoft may share my contact information and other details of such deployment with the publisher of that offering.

☑ I agree to the terms and conditions stated above

Validating... ○

Figure 3-17. Template validation

Then of course fill in the deployments page as usual, as shown in Figure 3-18.

⋯ Your deployment is underway

Deployment name: rahulsahay19_hotmail.com.template   Start time: 1/19/2020, 7:15:40 PM
Subscription: Visual Studio Enterprise with MSDN   Correlation ID: 691f7c6b-3d48-4f9a-8bac-2110ec7dbbb0
Resource group: az300

∧ **Deployment details** (Download)

Resource	Type	Status	Operation details
✓ rahulnic123	Microsoft.Network/netw...	Created	Operation details
✓ azvmdemo2-ip	Microsoft.Network/publ...	OK	Operation details
⊜ az300diag619	Microsoft.Storage/stora...	Accepted	Operation details
✓ azvmdemo-nsg	Microsoft.Network/netw...	OK	Operation details
✓ az300-vnet	Microsoft.Network/virtu...	OK	Operation details

∨ **Next steps**

Figure 3-18. *Deployment in progress*

Finally, the deployment is complete, as shown in Figure 3-19.

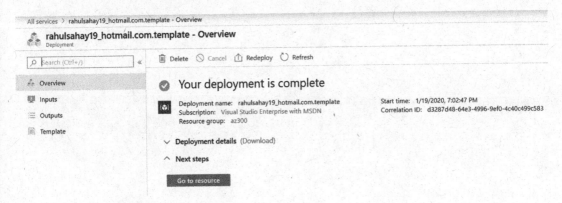

Figure 3-19. *Deployment complete*

One thing to note here is that ARM templates can be used for almost any resource. They're not limited to VMs only.

CHAPTER 4

Virtual Machine Encryption

Virtual machine encryption is a robust feature that keeps VMs safe and secure from any unauthorized access. Disks can be encrypted by using the cryptographic keys that are secured in Azure Key Vault, which uses FIPS 140-2 level 2 standards. The cryptographic keys are used to encrypt and decrypt the virtual disks attached to your VM.

Files in Azure storage accounts are by default encrypted using secure storage encryption. But, once you are able to see the storage with a .vhd account, it is not encrypted.

You can use BitLocker to encrypt virtual disks within Azure. The cryptography key for BitLocker will be stored in Azure Key Vault. Therefore, the first thing we need to create is a key vault in Azure. I will explain the Azure Key Vault service in detail in Chapter 19. For now, just follow the workflow shown in this chapter. Figure 4-1 shows the "Create key vault" page.

© Rahul Sahay 2020
R. Sahay, *Microsoft Azure Architect Technologies Study Companion*,
https://doi.org/10.1007/978-1-4842-6200-9_4

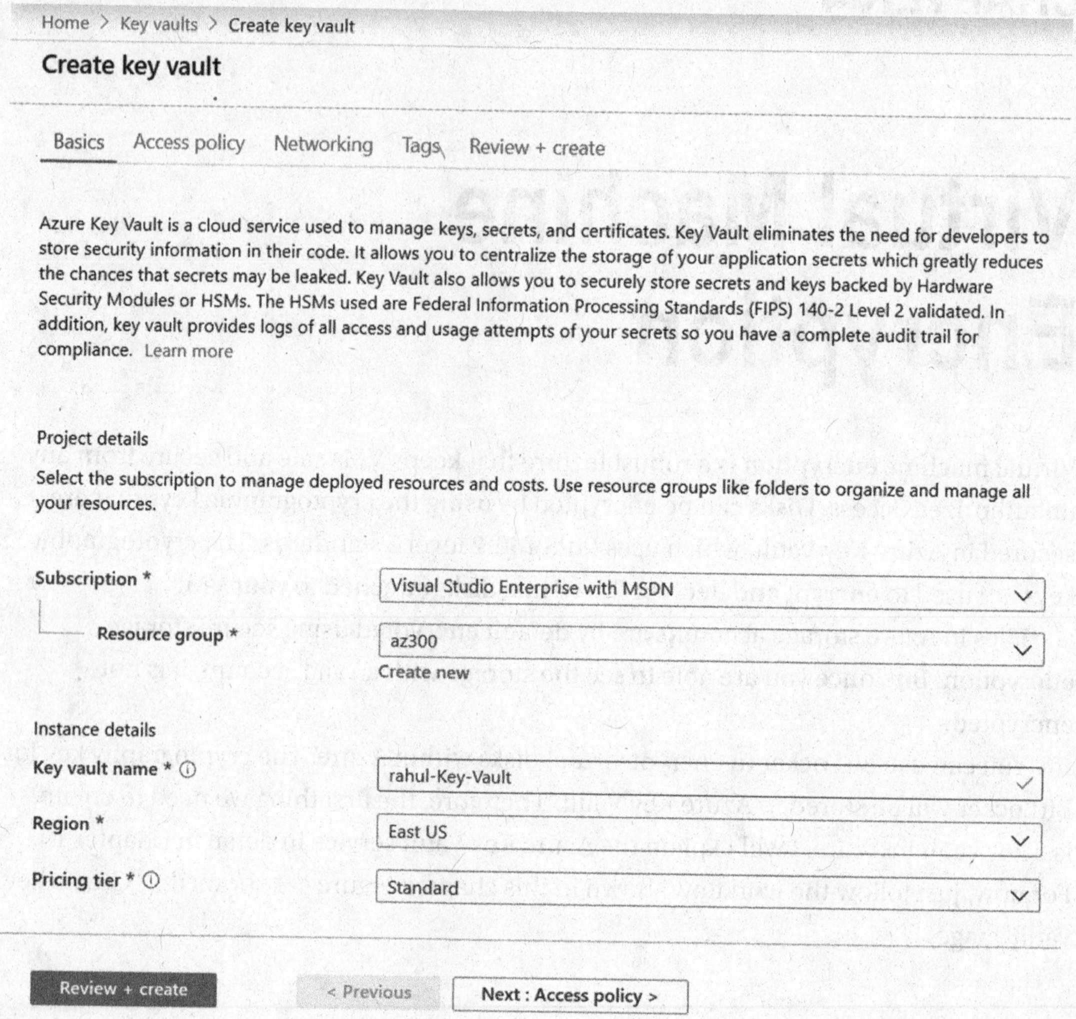

Home > Key vaults > Create key vault

Create key vault

Basics   Access policy   Networking   Tags   Review + create

Azure Key Vault is a cloud service used to manage keys, secrets, and certificates. Key Vault eliminates the need for developers to store security information in their code. It allows you to centralize the storage of your application secrets which greatly reduces the chances that secrets may be leaked. Key Vault also allows you to securely store secrets and keys backed by Hardware Security Modules or HSMs. The HSMs used are Federal Information Processing Standards (FIPS) 140-2 Level 2 validated. In addition, key vault provides logs of all access and usage attempts of your secrets so you have a complete audit trail for compliance. Learn more

Project details

Select the subscription to manage deployed resources and costs. Use resource groups like folders to organize and manage all your resources.

Subscription *   Visual Studio Enterprise with MSDN   ⌄

        Resource group *   az300   ⌄
                                  Create new

Instance details

Key vault name * ⓘ   rahul-Key-Vault   ✓

Region *   East US   ⌄

Pricing tier * ⓘ   Standard   ⌄

[Review + create]   [< Previous]   [Next : Access policy >]

Figure 4-1. *Creating a key vault*

Creating a Key Vault

While creating a key vault, make sure to select the checkbox for virtual machine encryption. I checked all of the options, as shown in Figure 4-2.

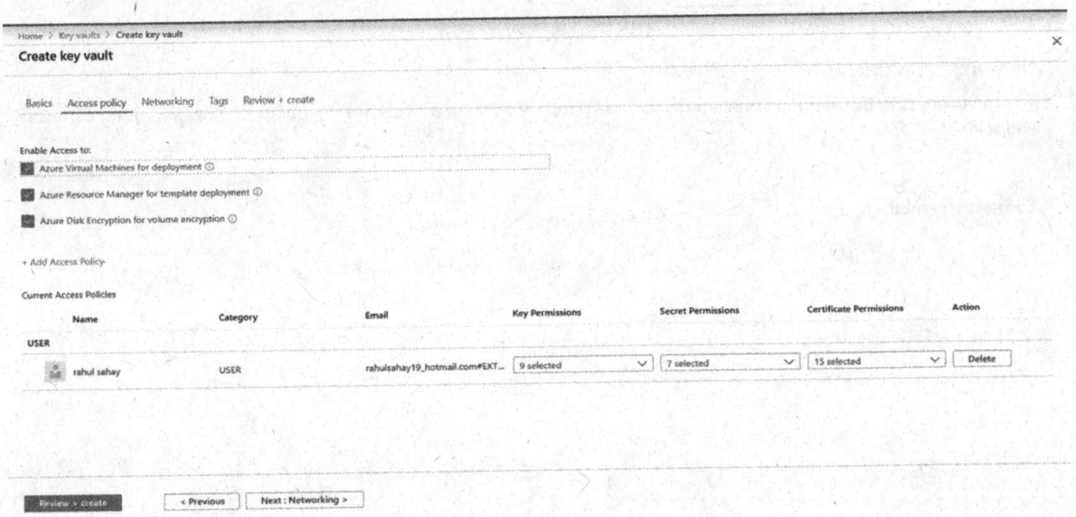

Figure 4-2. *Access policy page*

Next, click Next: Networking. Allow public networks, as shown in Figure 4-3.

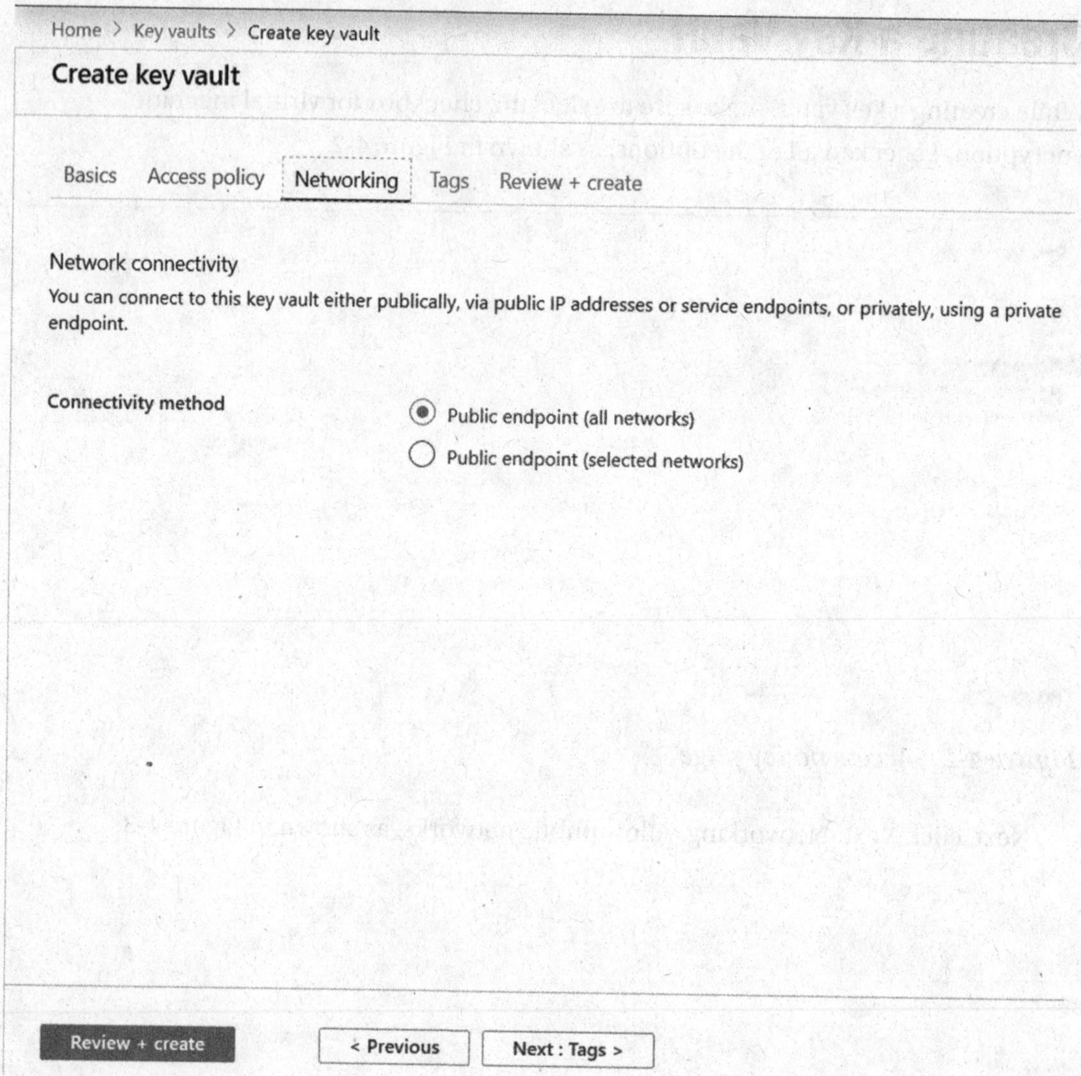

Home > Key vaults > Create key vault

Create key vault

Basics   Access policy   Networking   Tags   Review + create

Network connectivity

You can connect to this key vault either publically, via public IP addresses or service endpoints, or privately, using a private endpoint.

Connectivity method

◉ Public endpoint (all networks)

◯ Public endpoint (selected networks)

Review + create   < Previous   Next : Tags >

Figure 4-3. *Networking page*

Next, you need to provide some tags, as shown in Figure 4-4.

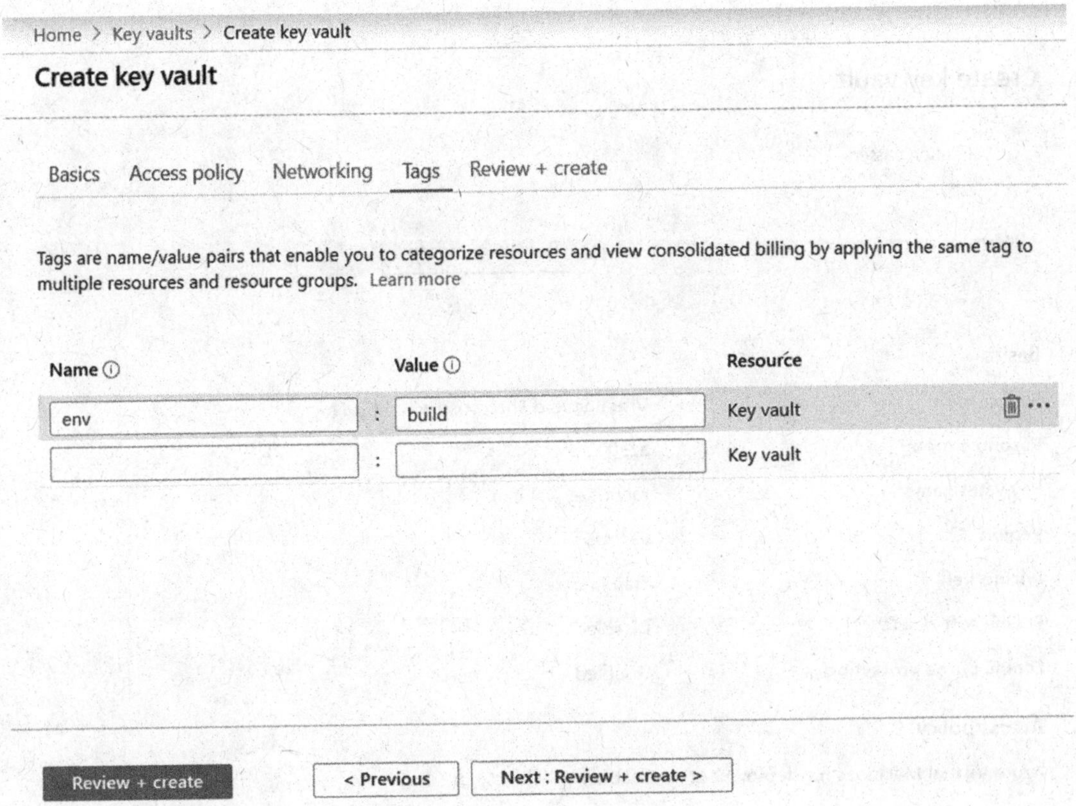

Home > Key vaults > **Create key vault**

Create key vault

Basics   Access policy   Networking   Tags   Review + create

Tags are name/value pairs that enable you to categorize resources and view consolidated billing by applying the same tag to multiple resources and resource groups. Learn more

Name ⓘ		Value ⓘ	Resource	
env	:	build	Key vault	🗑 •••
	:		Key vault	

Review + create		< Previous	Next : Review + create >

Figure 4-4. Tags page

Finally, you will see the review screen, as shown in Figure 4-5.

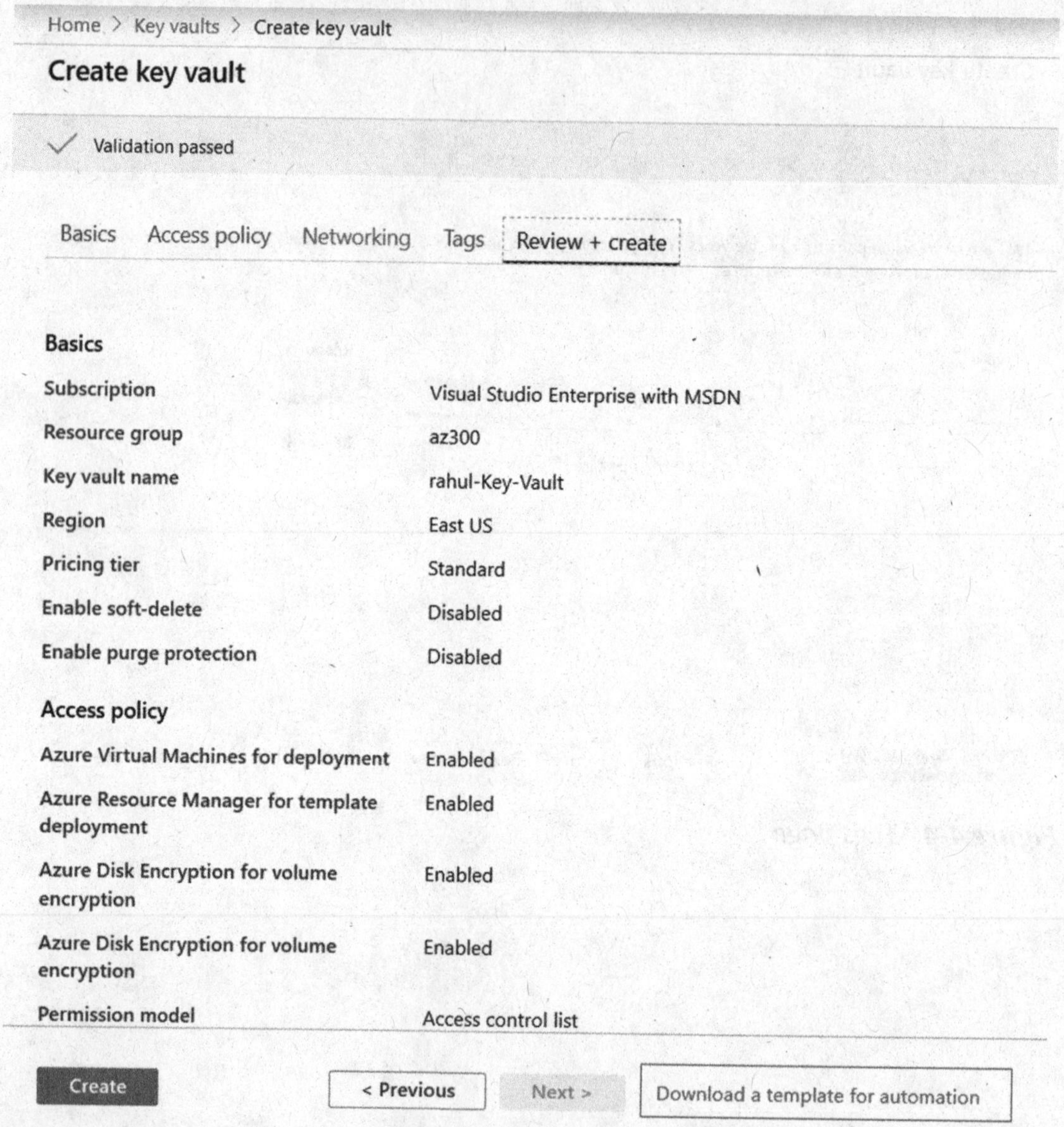

Home > Key vaults > Create key vault

Create key vault

✓ Validation passed

Basics   Access policy   Networking   Tags   Review + create

Basics

Subscription	Visual Studio Enterprise with MSDN
Resource group	az300
Key vault name	rahul-Key-Vault
Region	East US
Pricing tier	Standard
Enable soft-delete	Disabled
Enable purge protection	Disabled

Access policy

Azure Virtual Machines for deployment	Enabled
Azure Resource Manager for template deployment	Enabled
Azure Disk Encryption for volume encryption	Enabled
Azure Disk Encryption for volume encryption	Enabled
Permission model	Access control list

Create   < Previous   Next >   Download a template for automation

Figure 4-5. Review page

You can also automate your vaults. I have highlighted the relevant option in Figure 4-5. Upon the vault has been successfully created, you will land on the Overview page, as shown in Figure 4-6.

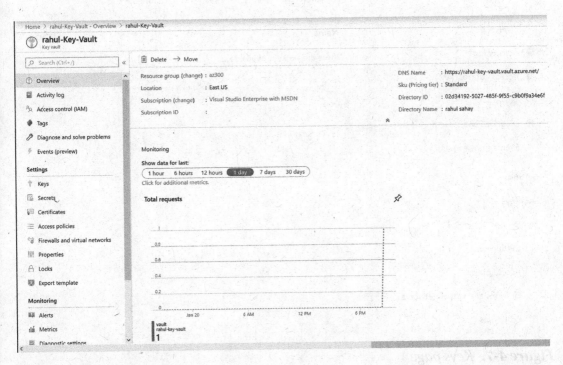

Figure 4-6. Overview page

If you followed the steps so far, you have created your key vault. Keep in mind that to encrypt a VM, your key vault and VM should be in the same region.

Creating Keys

Let's go ahead and click the Keys link in the left menu. This will bring up the screen shown in Figure 4-7.

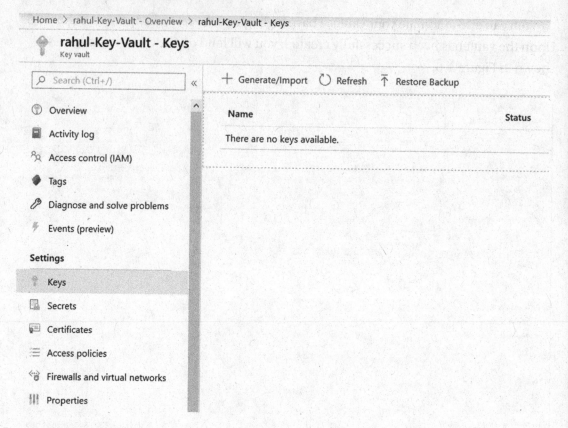

Figure 4-7. *Keys page*

Click the Generate/Import button. This will bring up the screen shown in Figure 4-8.

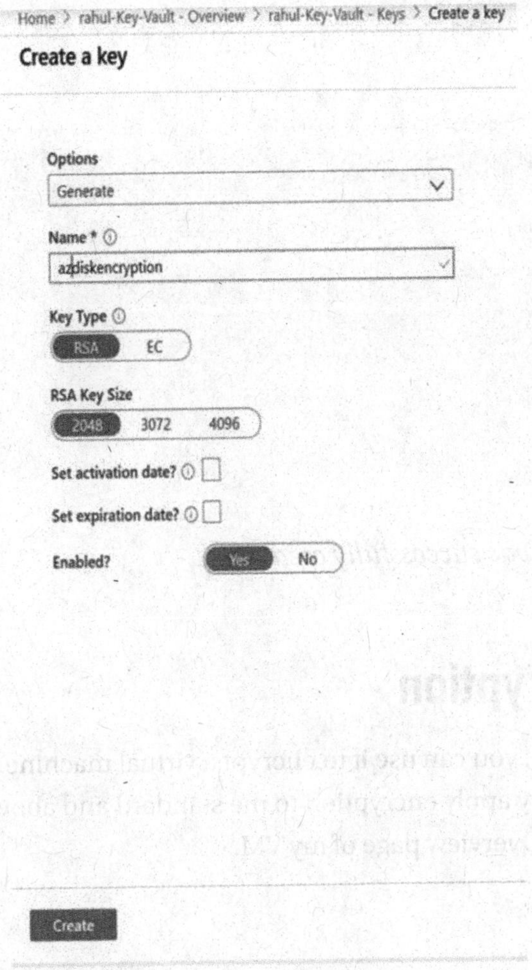

Home > rahul-Key-Vault - Overview > rahul-Key-Vault - Keys > Create a key

Create a key

Options

Generate ⌄

Name * ⓘ

azdiskencryption ⌄

Key Type ⓘ

RSA   EC

RSA Key Size

2048   3072   4096

Set activation date? ⓘ ☐

Set expiration date? ⓘ ☐

Enabled?   Yes   No

Create

Figure 4-8. Key creation page

Here, I have just used all the default values, as shown in Figure 4-9.

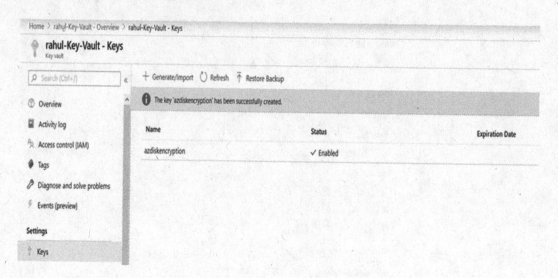

Figure 4-9. *The key was successfully created*

Enabling Encryption

Once the key is created, you can use it to encrypt a virtual machine. One point to note here is that you can only apply encryption to the standard and above, meaning DS1. Figure 4-10 shows the Overview page of my VM.

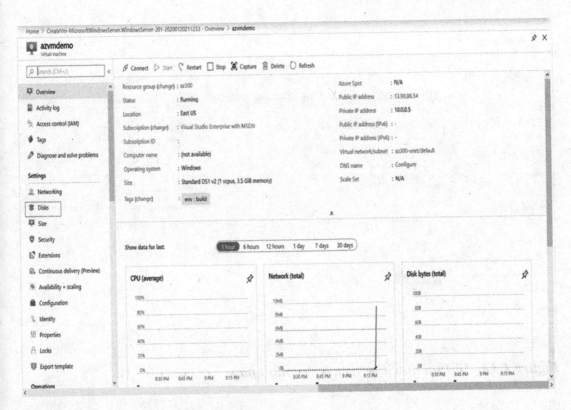

Figure 4-10. *Virtual machine page*

Currently, this VM is not encrypted. Now, you can click Disks, as highlighted in Figure 4-10. You'll see the screen shown in Figure 4-11.

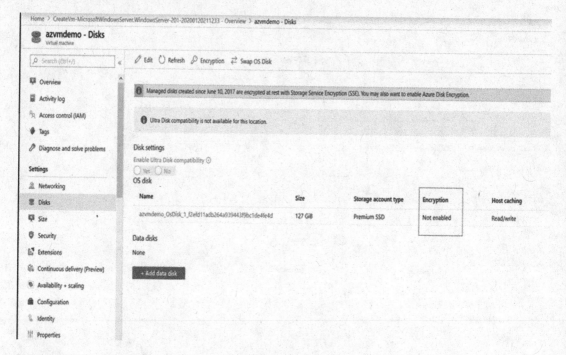

Figure 4-11. *Virtual machine disk encryption page*

You can see in Figure 4-11 that encryption is not enabled. To enable encryption on this disk, you can do it either with UI or with PowerShell. Let's do it in the UI.

Encrypting an OS Disk

As shown in Figure 4-12, I am going to encrypt an OS disk. You can encrypt both OS and data disks if you want. But for data, you need to mount the data disk before encrypting. Fill in the settings, as shown in Figure 4-13.

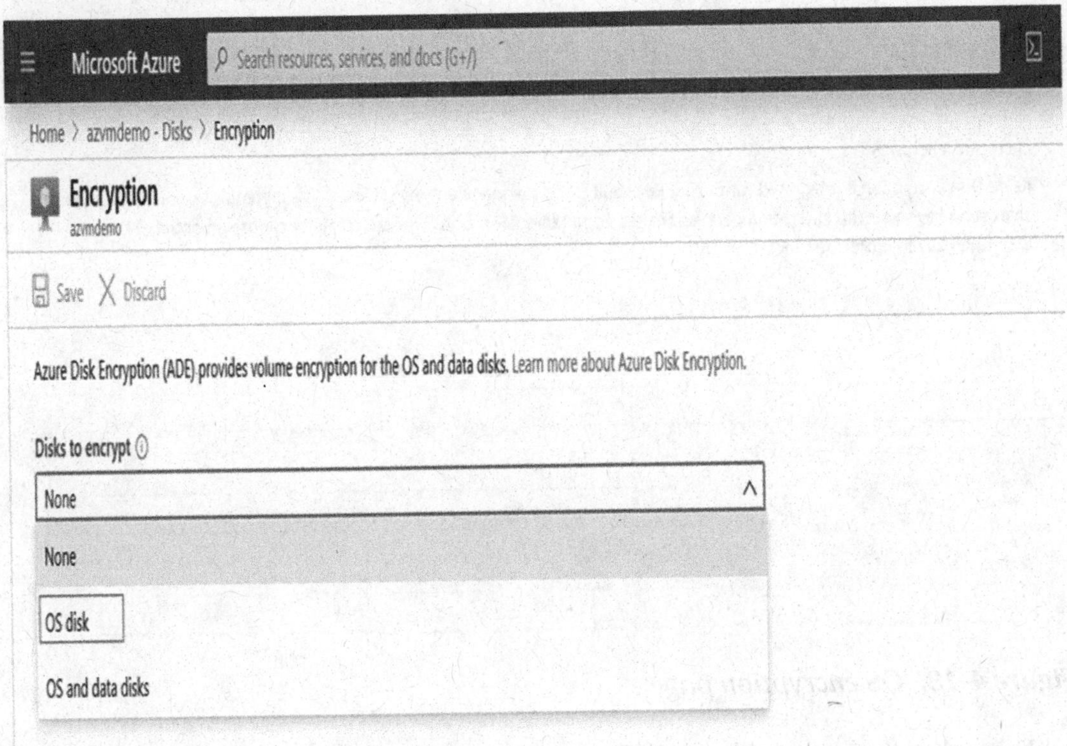

Figure 4-12. *Encryption page*

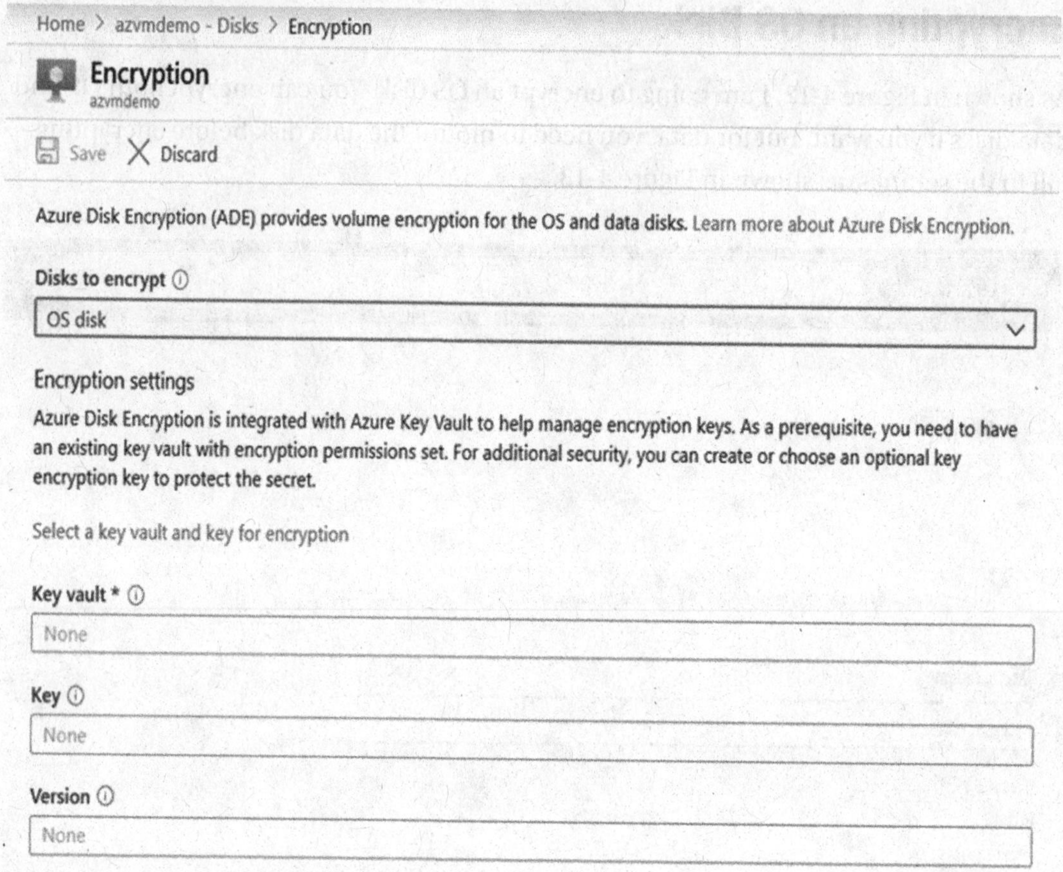

Figure 4-13. *OS encryption page*

Next select the vault, as shown in Figure 4-14 and Figure 4-15.

Home > azvmdemo - Disks > Encryption > Select key from Azure Key Vault

Select key from Azure Key Vault

Key vault *	rahul-Key-Vault	∨
	Create new	
Key	azdiskencryption	∨
	Create new	
Version ⓘ	e17e234e85164f288ecc1b1517b6d12e	∨
	Create new	

Select

Figure 4-14. *Azure key vault page*

Home > azvmdemo - Disks > Encryption

Encryption
azvmdemo

🖫 Save   ✕ Discard

Azure Disk Encryption (ADE) provides volume encryption for the OS and data disks. Learn more about Azure Disk Encryption.

Disks to encrypt ⓘ

| OS disk | ∨ |

Encryption settings

Azure Disk Encryption is integrated with Azure Key Vault to help manage encryption keys. As a prerequisite, you need to have an existing key vault with encryption permissions set. For additional security, you can create or choose an optional key encryption key to protect the secret.

Select a key vault and key for encryption

Key vault * ⓘ –

| /subscriptions/   /resourceGroups/az300/providers/Microsoft.KeyVault/vaults/rahu ✕ |

Key ⓘ

| azdiskencryption |

Version ⓘ

| e17e234e85164f288ecc1b1517b6d12e |

Figure 4-15. *Key vault encryption page*

135

Click Yes, as shown in Figure 4-16, and continue.

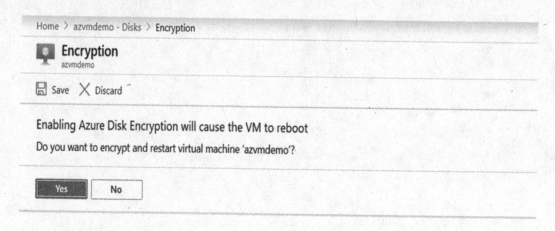

Figure 4-16. *Encryption confirmation page*

In the notification center, you can see that it's enabling encryption, as shown in Figure 4-17.

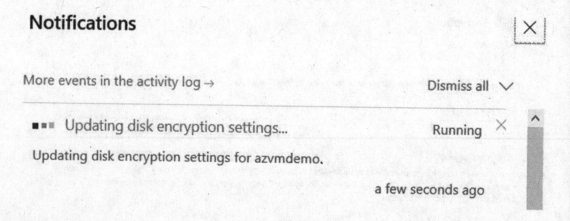

Figure 4-17. *Notifications page*

Either the disk will be encrypted or you will get an error. If you get an error, you can try encrypting the disk with a PowerShell script.

Enabling Encryption Using PowerShell

To enable encryption with PowerShell, open the cloud shell that is embedded in the Azure portal. If you are configuring PowerShell for the first time, you need to mount storage for that, as shown in Figure 4-18.

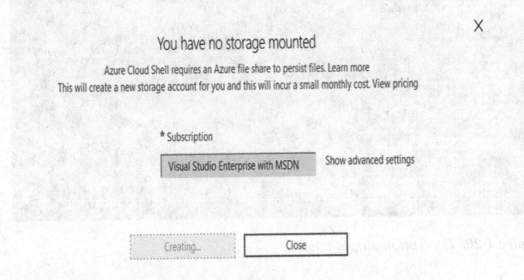

Figure 4-18. Encryption with PowerShell

For a quick reference, you can visit https://bit.ly/azure-encrypt.

I have modified the command with my key vault and resource group with the following code, as shown in Figure 4-19:

```
az vm encryption enable -g "az300" --name "azvmdemo" --disk-encryption-keyvault "rahul-Key-Vault"
```

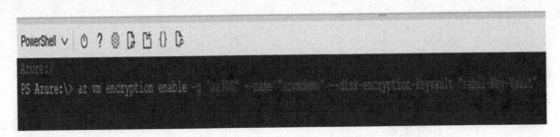

Figure 4-19. Encryption demo

To get the confirmation, execute `az vm show --name "azvmdemo" -g "az300"`. This will display `"EncryptionOperation": "EnableEncryption"`, as shown in Figure 4-20.

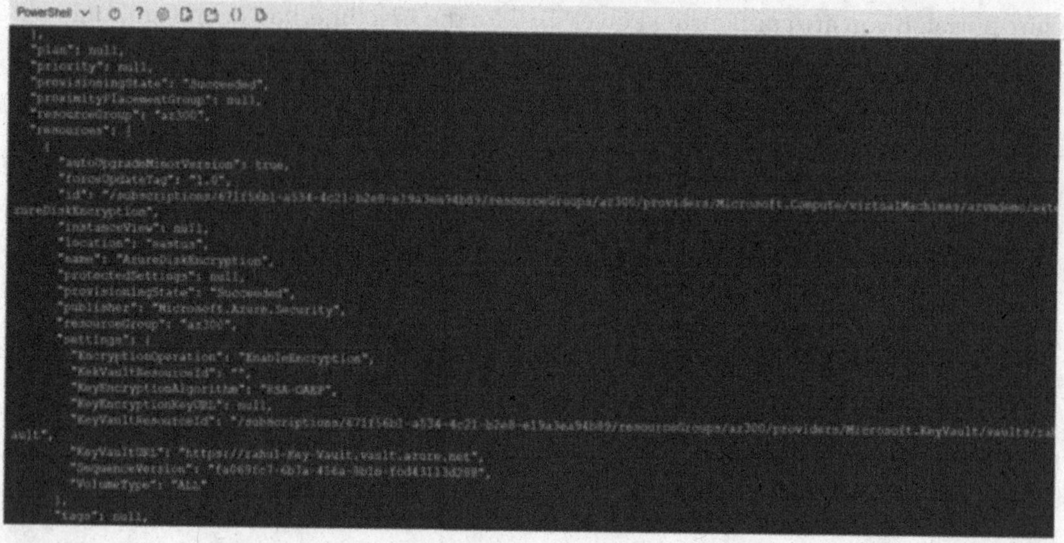

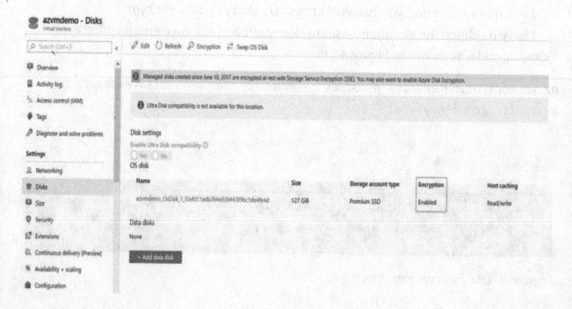

Figure 4-20.   Encryption output page

This means that the VM was successfully encrypted. We can verify this from the UI, as shown in Figure 4-21.

Figure 4-21.   VM disk encryption result

CHAPTER 5

Azure Monitoring

Azure Monitor helps you understand how your applications are performing and proactively identifies issues. It maximizes the availability and performance of your applications and services by delivering end-to-end solutions for collecting, analyzing, and acting on telemetry from the cloud and the on-premises environment. You can do a variety of things with Azure Monitor, such as the following:

- Detect and diagnose issues across applications and dependencies with Application Insights

- Correlate infrastructure issues with Azure Monitor for VMs and Azure Monitor for Containers

- Drill into your monitoring data with Azure Log Analytics for troubleshooting and deep diagnostics

- Support operations at scale with smart alerts and automated actions

- Create visualizations with Azure dashboards and workbooks

Opening Azure Monitor

If you search for *Monitor* and look under Services, you'll find Azure Monitor, as shown in Figure 5-1.

© Rahul Sahay 2020
R. Sahay, *Microsoft Azure Architect Technologies Study Companion*,
https://doi.org/10.1007/978-1-4842-6200-9_5

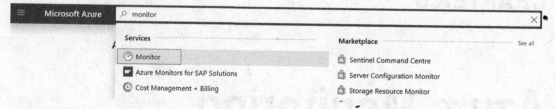

Figure 5-1. *Monitor search screen*

Click Monitor. This will bring up the screen shown in Figure 5-2.

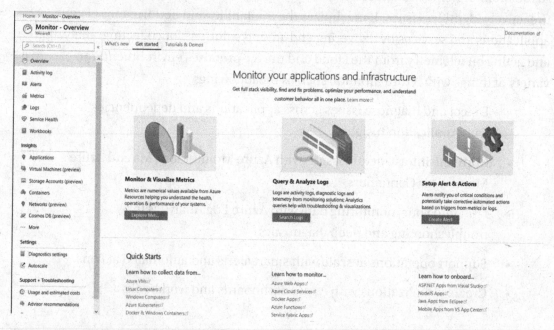

Figure 5-2. *Monitor overview screen*

Azure Monitor is a relatively new dashboard for all your monitoring activities across multiple applications or infrastructure. It's very diverse, but everything is gathered into the dashboard for you. This means you can set up metrics at the resource group level or at the individual resource level. If you click the "Diagnostics settings" link, you will see all the resources, as shown in Figure 5-3.

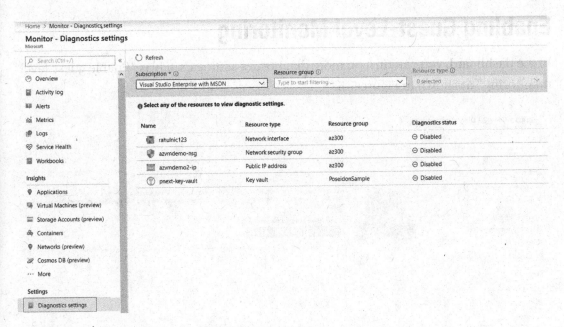

Figure 5-3. *Monitor diagnostics screen*

Now, let's look at the VM level, as shown in Figure 5-4.

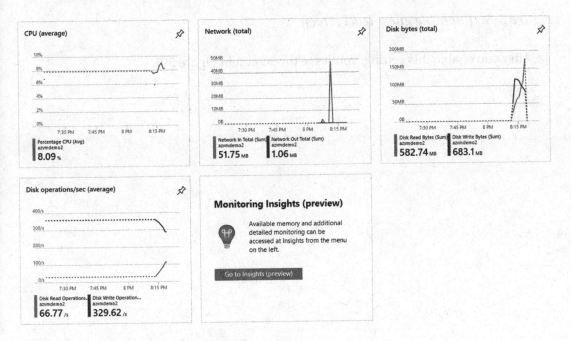

Figure 5-4. *Virtual machine monitor screen*

Here, you can see that some diagnostics have already been enabled.

Enabling Guest-Level Monitoring

In the dashboard, you can turn on more diagnostics settings, such as "Enable guest-level monitoring," as shown in Figure 5-5.

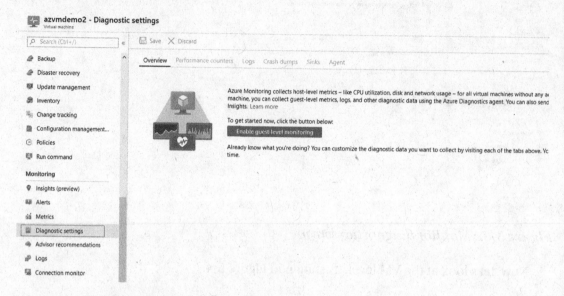

Figure 5-5. *Enabling guest-level screen*

After you enable this setting, you'll see the screen in Figure 5-6.

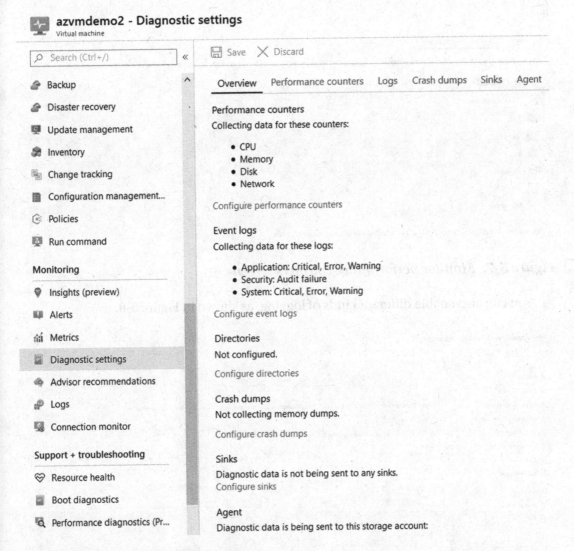

Figure 5-6. *VM diagnostics settings*

Here, you can see that all the potential counters are listed. Let's switch to the "Performance counters" tab, as shown in Figure 5-7, where you can enable additional counters.

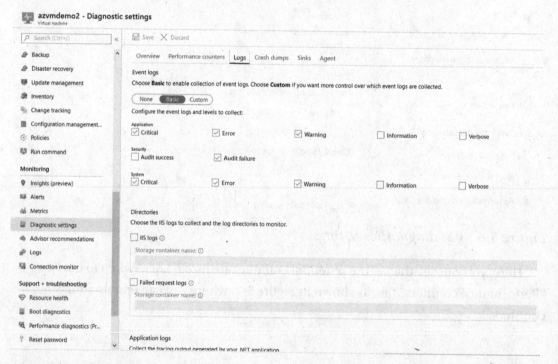

Figure 5-7. *Monitor performance counters screen*

You can also enable different kinds of logging, as shown in Figure 5-8.

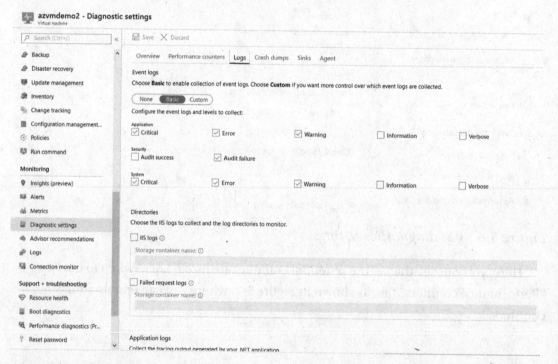

Figure 5-8. *Monitor logs*

Likewise, you can enable crash dumps and sinks, as shown in Figure 5-9.

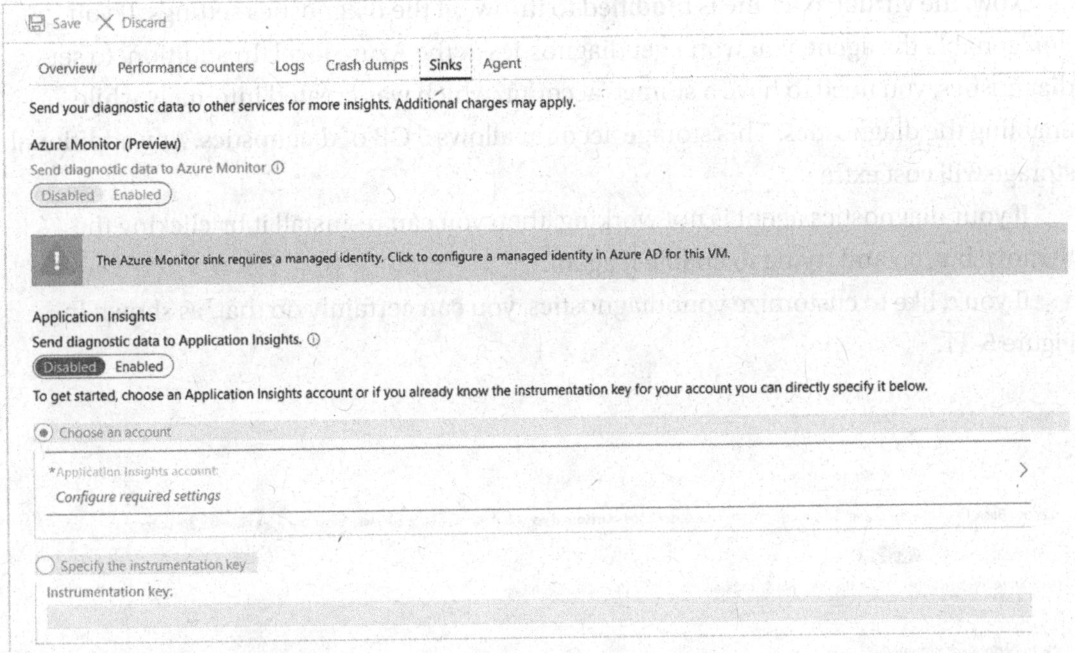

Save   X Discard

Overview   Performance counters   Logs   Crash dumps   **Sinks**   Agent

Send your diagnostic data to other services for more insights. Additional charges may apply.

Azure Monitor (Preview)

Send diagnostic data to Azure Monitor ⓘ

Disabled   Enabled

⚠   The Azure Monitor sink requires a managed identity. Click to configure a managed identity in Azure AD for this VM.

Application Insights

Send diagnostic data to Application Insights. ⓘ

Disabled   Enabled

To get started, choose an Application Insights account or if you already know the instrumentation key for your account you can directly specify it below.

⦿ Choose an account

*Application Insights account:
Configure required settings   >

○ Specify the instrumentation key

Instrumentation key:

Figure 5-9. *Sinks screen*

Last but not the least, you can use an agent, as shown in Figure 5-10.

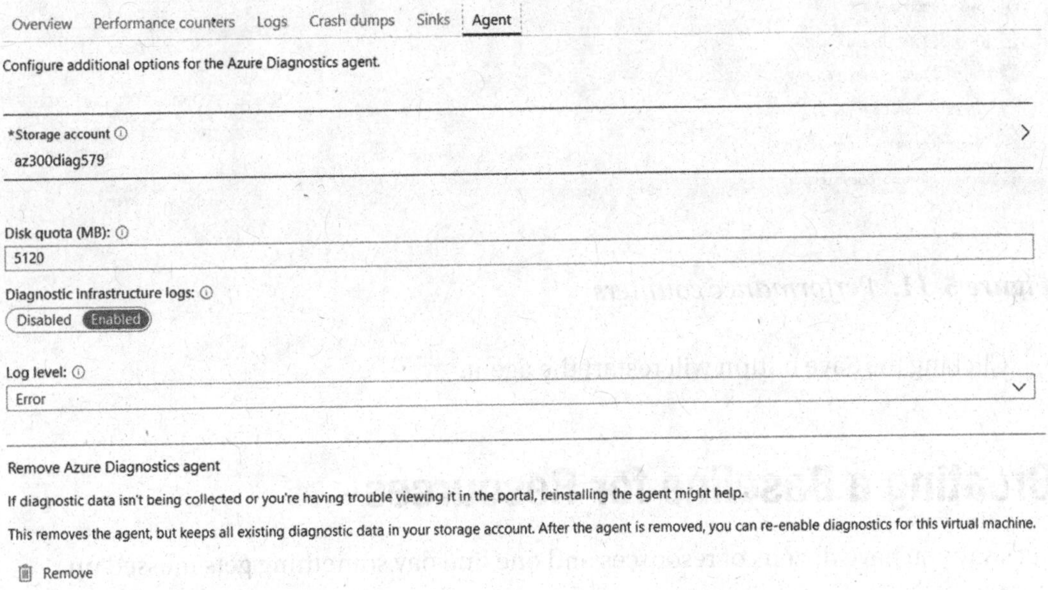

Overview   Performance counters   Logs   Crash dumps   Sinks   **Agent**

Configure additional options for the Azure Diagnostics agent.

*Storage account ⓘ   >
az300diag579

Disk quota (MB): ⓘ
5120

Diagnostic infrastructure logs: ⓘ
Disabled   Enabled

Log level: ⓘ
Error   ⌄

Remove Azure Diagnostics agent

If diagnostic data isn't being collected or you're having trouble viewing it in the portal, reinstalling the agent might help.

This removes the agent, but keeps all existing diagnostic data in your storage account. After the agent is removed, you can re-enable diagnostics for this virtual machine.

🗑 Remove

Figure 5-10. *Agent screen*

Now, the virtual machine is modified to throw off the diagnostics settings. If you don't enable the agent, you won't get diagnostics at the Azure level. In addition, to set diagnostics, you need to have a storage account, which was created internally while enabling the diagnostics. This storage account allows 5 GB of diagnostics. Any additional storage will cost extra.

If your diagnostics agent is not working, then you can re-install it by clicking the Remove button and trying to enable it again.

If you'd like to customize your diagnostics, you can certainly do that, as shown in Figure 5-11.

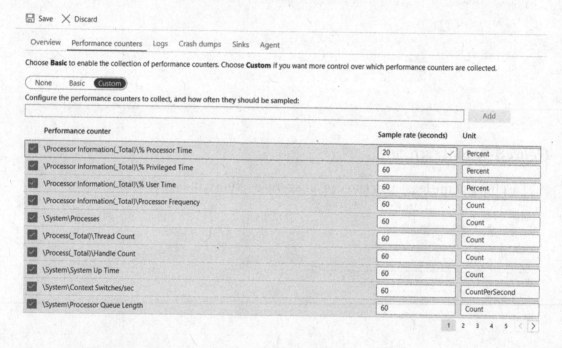

Figure 5-11. *Performance counters*

Clicking the Save button will restart the agent.

Creating a Baseline for Resources

Let's say you have dozens of resources and one fine day something gets messed up and all the resources are wiped out for some reason. How will you recover from that situation? The concept of a *baseline* is that each resource should be stored as a script or as a template in ARM. For example, if you have all the resources stored as ARM templates in Git, then that is considered your baseline.

Click Deployments, as shown in Figure 5-12, to configure a baseline.

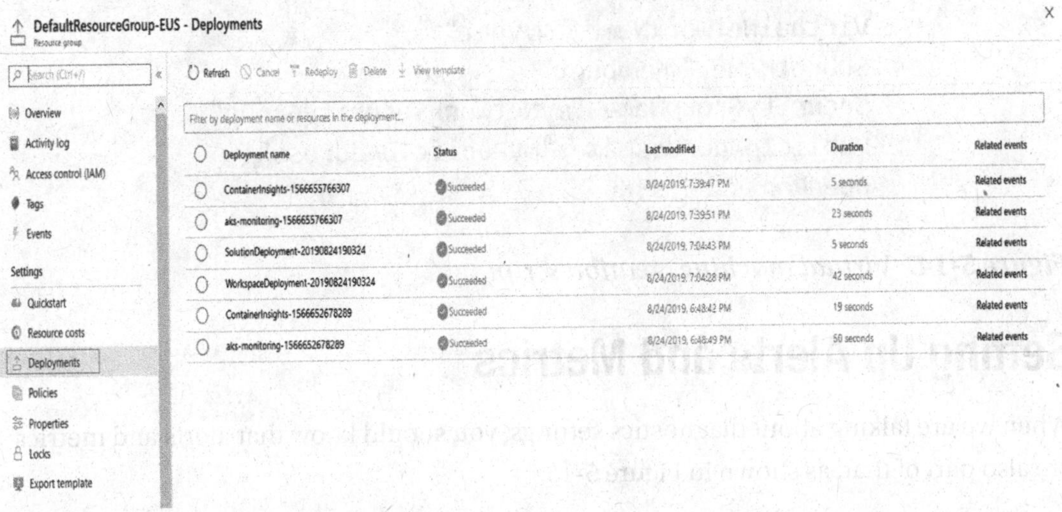

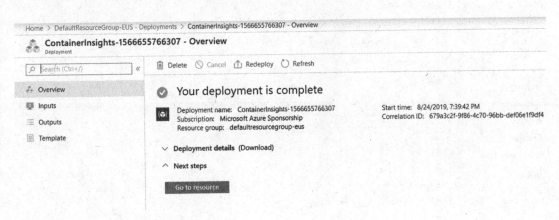

Figure 5-12. Default resource group

Go to an individual deployment, as shown in Figure 5-13.

Figure 5-13. Container insights

You can either click the Redeploy option or download the ARM template from the Templates section. Another way to create a baseline is via a PowerShell script. But, Microsoft doesn't generate a PowerShell script from this environment; rather, you can refer to the samples available in the Microsoft documentation to build your own and then push the script to Git using https://bit.ly/azure-vm-pwsh. Figure 5-14 shows an example script.

```
New-AzVm `
-ResourceGroupName "myResourceGroup" `
-Name "myVM" `
-Location "East US" `
-VirtualNetworkName "myVnet" `
-SubnetName "mySubnet" `
-SecurityGroupName "myNetworkSecurityGroup" `
-PublicIpAddressName "myPublicIpAddress" `
-OpenPorts 80,3389
```

***Figure 5-14.** Virtual machine creation script*

Setting Up Alerts and Metrics

When we are talking about diagnostics settings, you should know that alerts and metrics are also part of that, as shown in Figure 5-15.

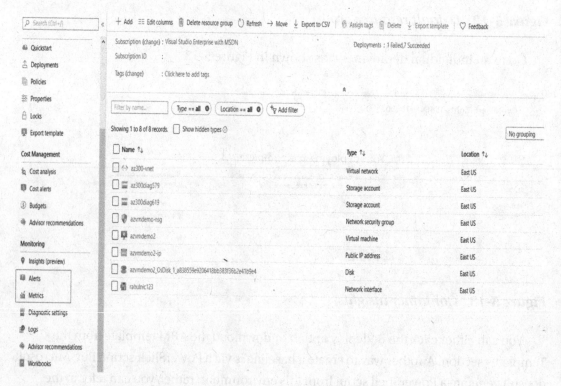

***Figure 5-15.** Alerts and metrics*

Creating an Alert

Let's go ahead and click Alerts. This will bring up the screen shown in Figure 5-16.

All is good! You have no alerts.

Getting your alert rules ....

Figure 5-16. *Alert creation screen*

You can set up an alert as shown in Figure 5-17. It's pretty straightforward.

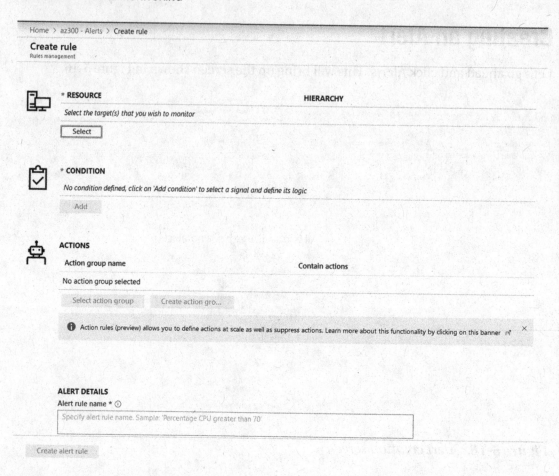

Figure 5-17. *New alert rule*

Here, I will first select a resource, as shown in Figure 5-18. Figure 5-19 shows the screen for the resource selected.

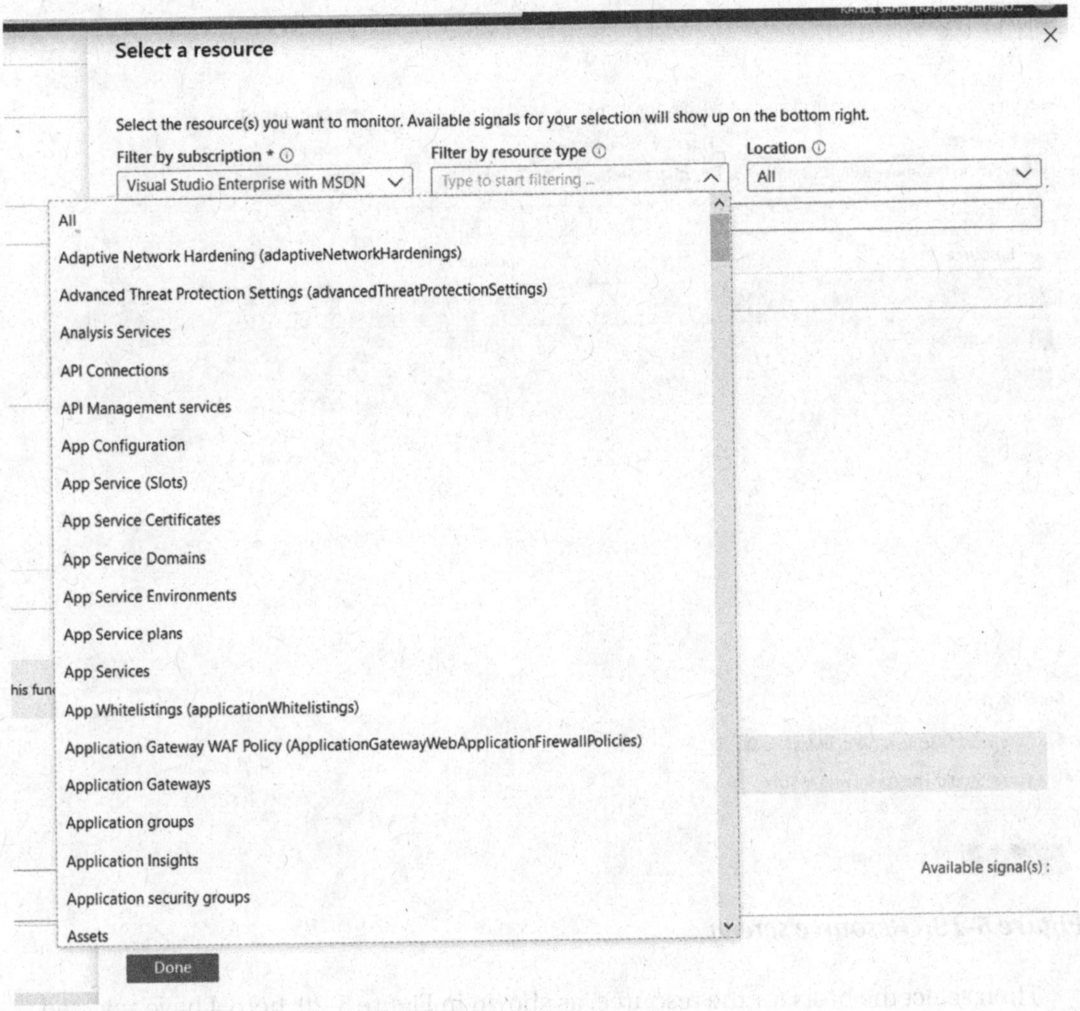

Select a resource   ×

Select the resource(s) you want to monitor. Available signals for your selection will show up on the bottom right.

Filter by subscription * ⓘ	Filter by resource type ⓘ	Location ⓘ
Visual Studio Enterprise with MSDN ∨	Type to start filtering ... ∧	All ∨

All

Adaptive Network Hardening (adaptiveNetworkHardenings)

Advanced Threat Protection Settings (advancedThreatProtectionSettings)

Analysis Services

API Connections

API Management services

App Configuration

App Service (Slots)

App Service Certificates

App Service Domains

App Service Environments

App Service plans

App Services

App Whitelistings (applicationWhitelistings)

Application Gateway WAF Policy (ApplicationGatewayWebApplicationFirewallPolicies)

Application Gateways

Application groups

Application Insights

Application security groups

Assets

Available signal(s) :

Done

Figure 5-18. *Resource selection screen*

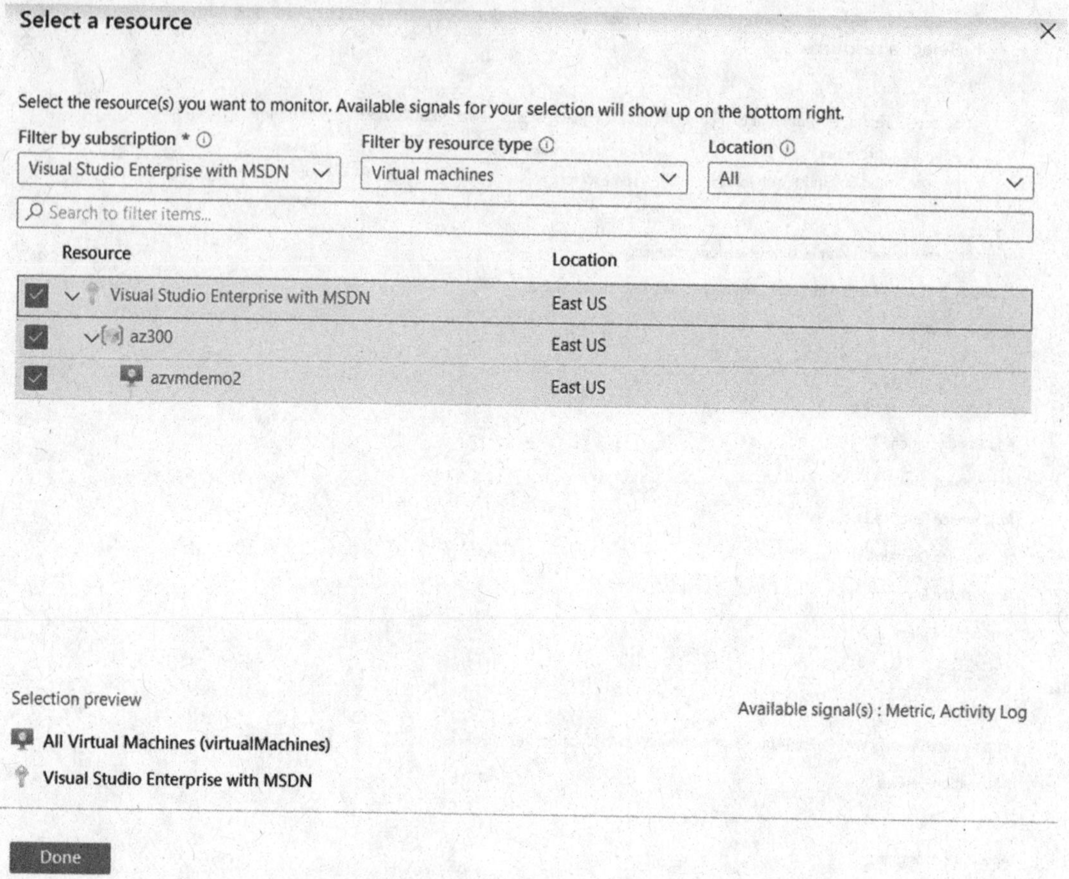

Select a resource   ✕

Select the resource(s) you want to monitor. Available signals for your selection will show up on the bottom right.

Filter by subscription * ⓘ	Filter by resource type ⓘ	Location ⓘ
Visual Studio Enterprise with MSDN ∨	Virtual machines ∨	All ∨

🔍 Search to filter items...

Resource	Location
☑ ∨ ⬤ Visual Studio Enterprise with MSDN	East US
☑ ∨[⬛] az300	East US
☑ 🖥 azvmdemo2	East US

Selection preview   Available signal(s) : Metric, Activity Log

🖥 All Virtual Machines (virtualMachines)

🔑 Visual Studio Enterprise with MSDN

[Done]

Figure 5-19. *Resource screen*

Then select the basis for the resource, as shown in Figure 5-20; here, I have selected CPU. Then you can configure the signal, as shown in Figure 5-21 and Figure 5-22.

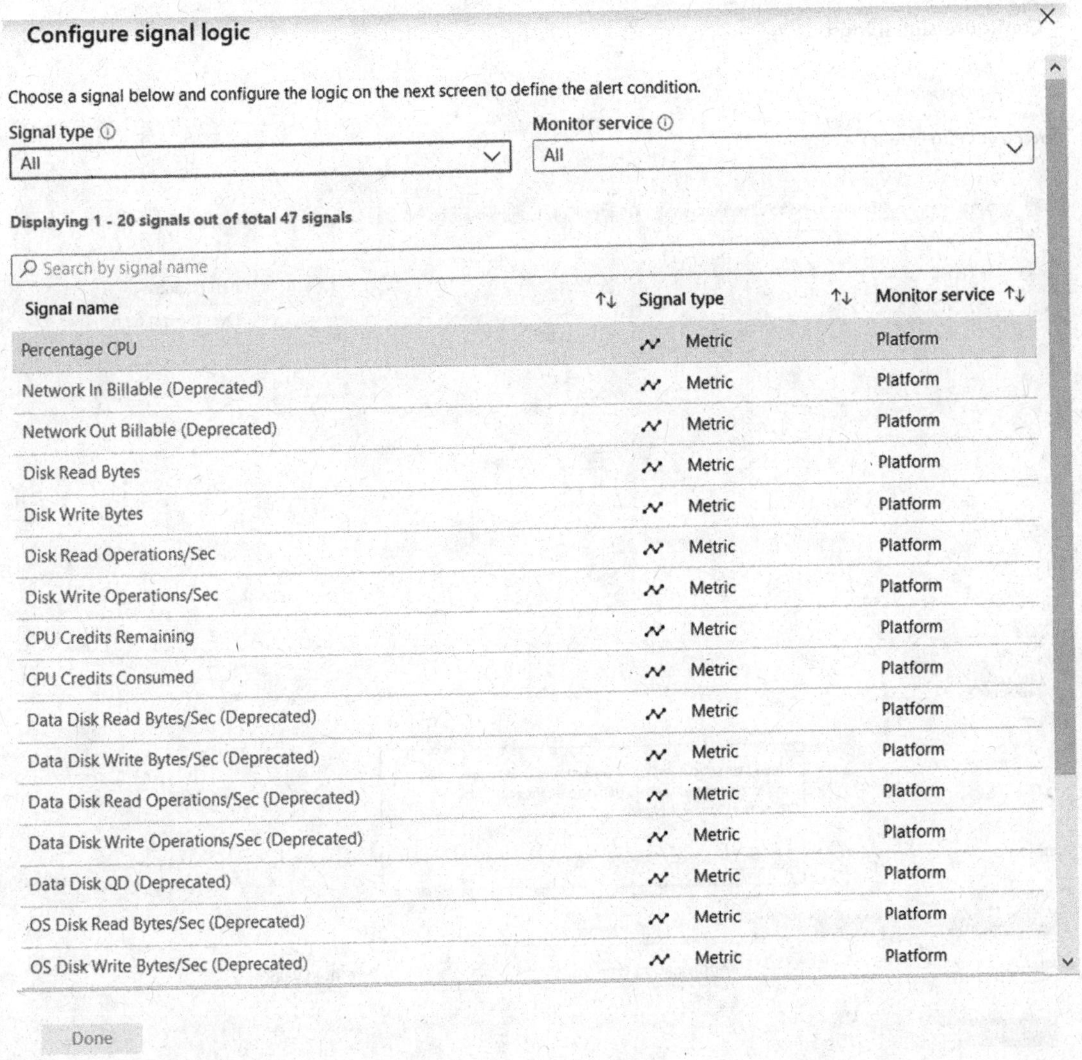

Configure signal logic   ✕

Choose a signal below and configure the logic on the next screen to define the alert condition.

Signal type ⓘ   Monitor service ⓘ

| All ∨ | All ∨ |

Displaying 1 - 20 signals out of total 47 signals

🔍 Search by signal name

Signal name ↑↓		Signal type ↑↓	Monitor service ↑↓
Percentage CPU	∿	Metric	Platform
Network In Billable (Deprecated)	∿	Metric	Platform
Network Out Billable (Deprecated)	∿	Metric	Platform
Disk Read Bytes	∿	Metric	Platform
Disk Write Bytes	∿	Metric	Platform
Disk Read Operations/Sec	∿	Metric	Platform
Disk Write Operations/Sec	∿	Metric	Platform
CPU Credits Remaining	∿	Metric	Platform
CPU Credits Consumed	∿	Metric	Platform
Data Disk Read Bytes/Sec (Deprecated)	∿	Metric	Platform
Data Disk Write Bytes/Sec (Deprecated)	∿	Metric	Platform
Data Disk Read Operations/Sec (Deprecated)	∿	Metric	Platform
Data Disk Write Operations/Sec (Deprecated)	∿	Metric	Platform
Data Disk QD (Deprecated)	∿	Metric	Platform
OS Disk Read Bytes/Sec (Deprecated)	∿	Metric	Platform
OS Disk Write Bytes/Sec (Deprecated)	∿	Metric	Platform

Done

Figure 5-20. *Signal logic screen*

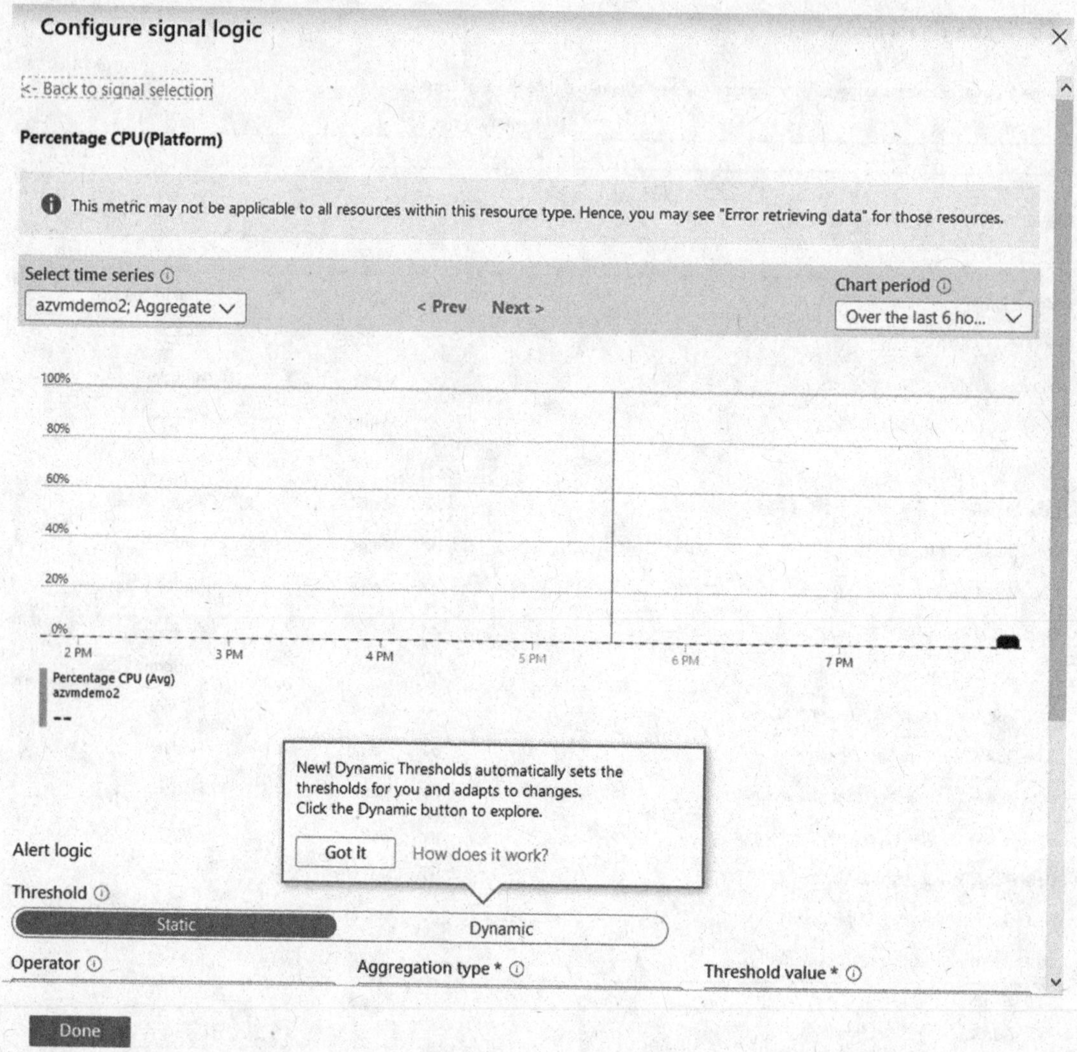

Figure 5-21. *Configuring the signal logic*

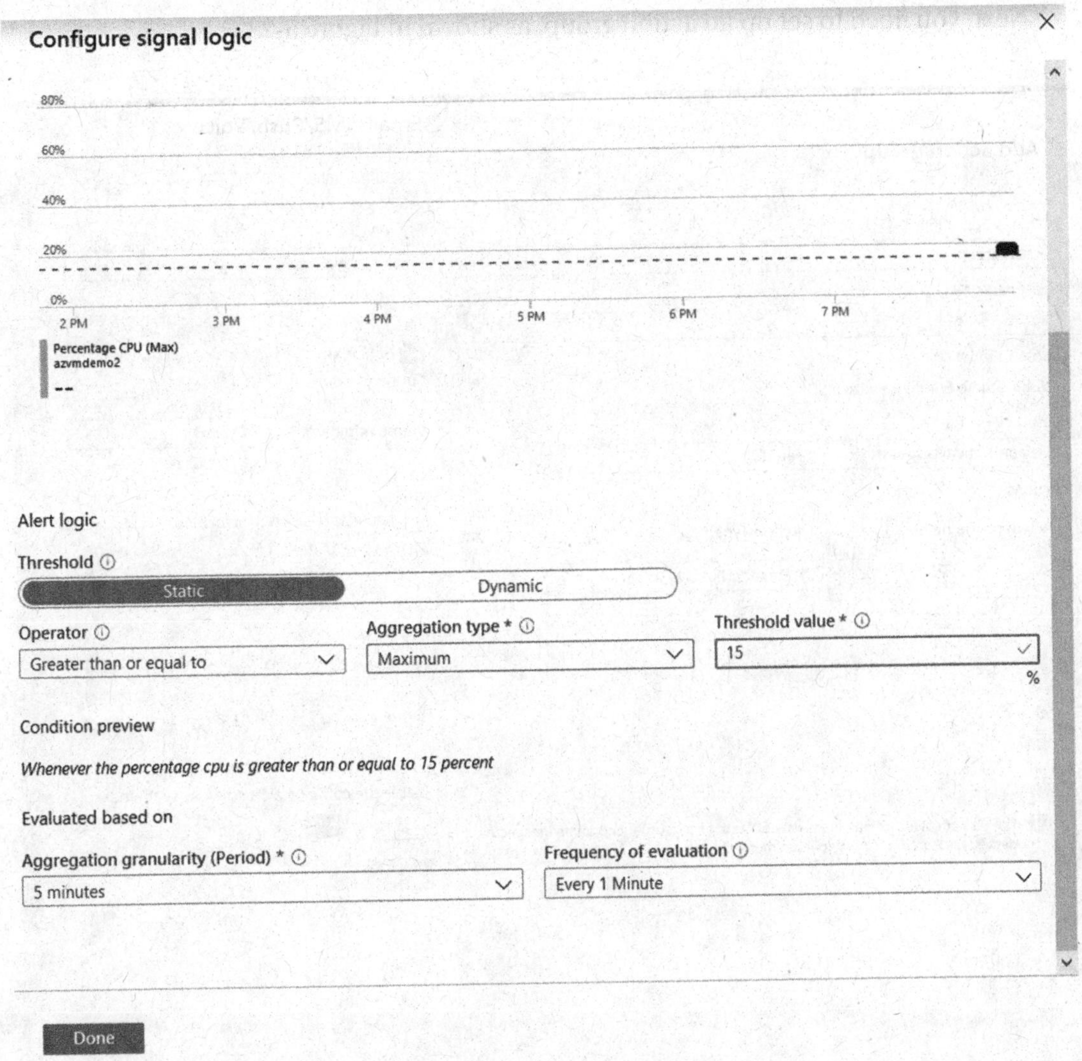

Configure signal logic   ✕

Alert logic

Threshold ⓘ

| Static | Dynamic |

Operator ⓘ

Greater than or equal to   ∨

Aggregation type * ⓘ

Maximum   ∨

Threshold value * ⓘ

15   ✓
                                                              %

Condition preview

Whenever the percentage cpu is greater than or equal to 15 percent

Evaluated based on

Aggregation granularity (Period) * ⓘ

5 minutes   ∨

Frequency of evaluation ⓘ

Every 1 Minute   ∨

Done

Figure 5-22. *Configuring the signal logic, continued*

Next, you need to set up an action group, as shown in Figure 5-23.

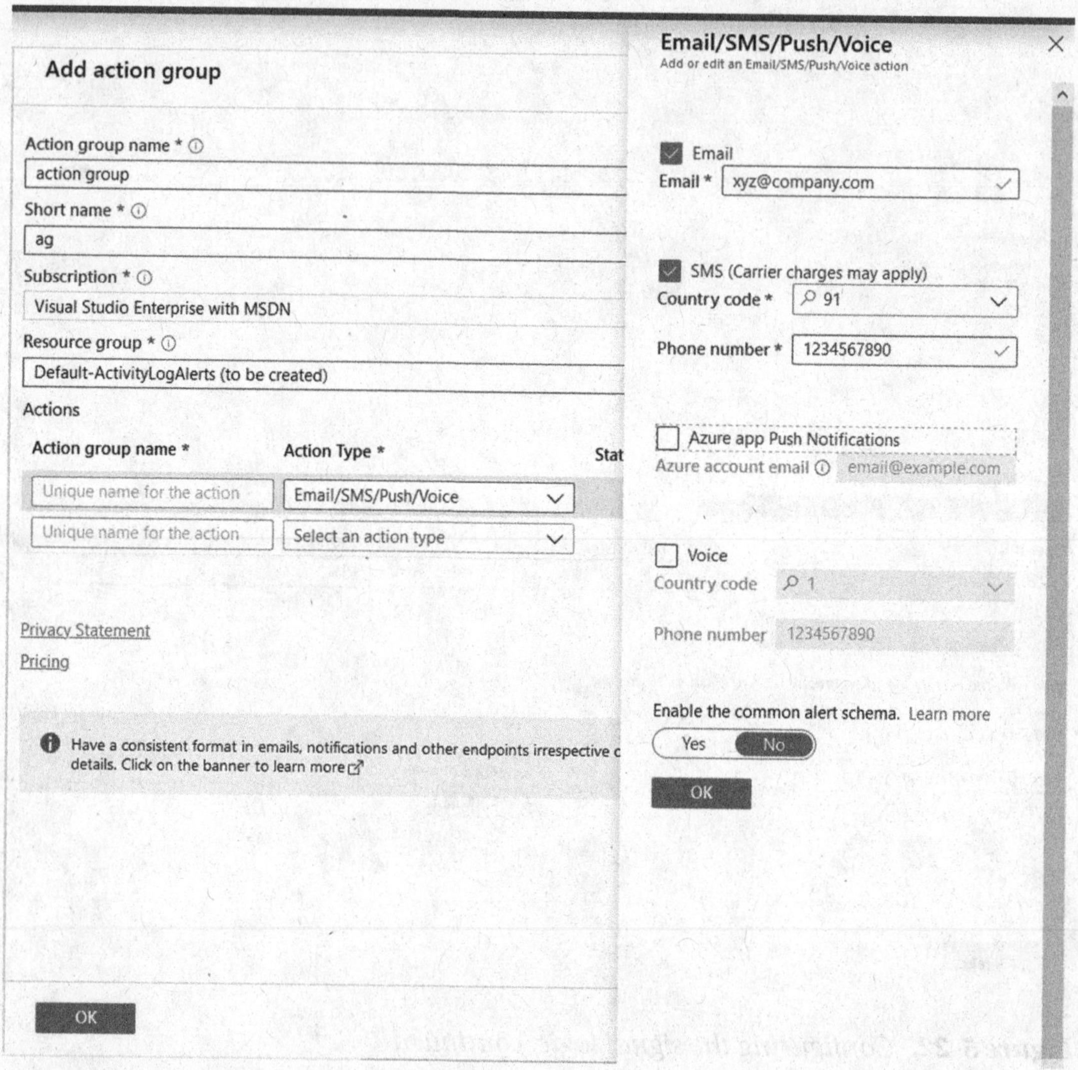

Figure 5-23. *Adding an action group*

Here, you can enable Azure push notifications so that the owner will get the alerts.

Understanding Metrics

Alerts are basically notifications that get fired when they meet some criteria. You can set up metrics that should be consistently watched on a resource. Let's click the Metrics menu, which takes you to the screen shown in Figure 5-24.

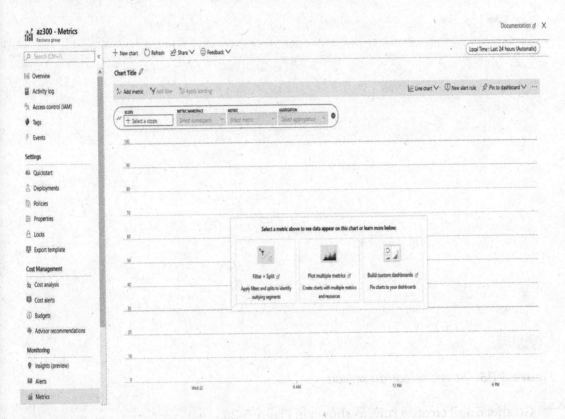

Figure 5-24. Metrics screen

Setting Up a Metric

Let's set up a metric for a VM. Select the scope from the drop-down, as shown in Figure 5-25.

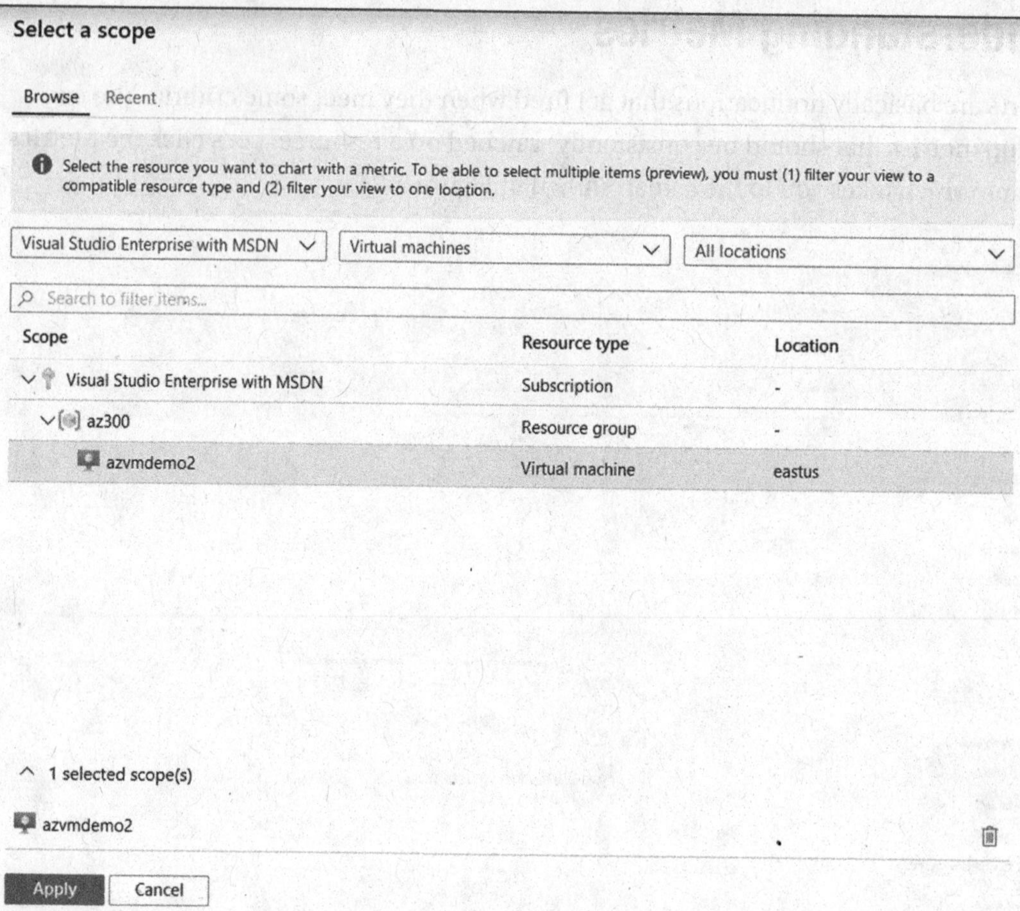

Figure 5-25. *Scope selection screen*

Go ahead and create a rule, as shown in Figure 5-26.

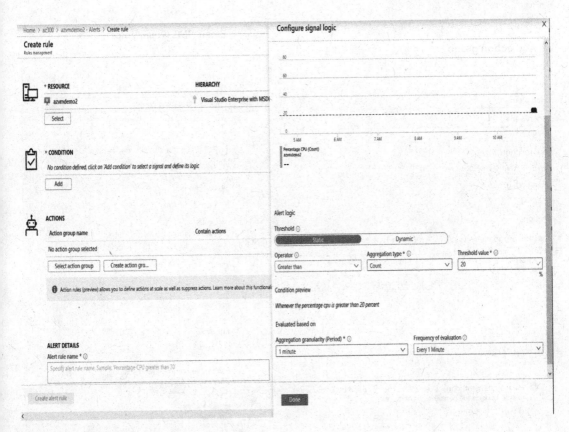

Figure 5-26. *Rule creation screen*

Select the proper action group, as shown in Figure 5-27.

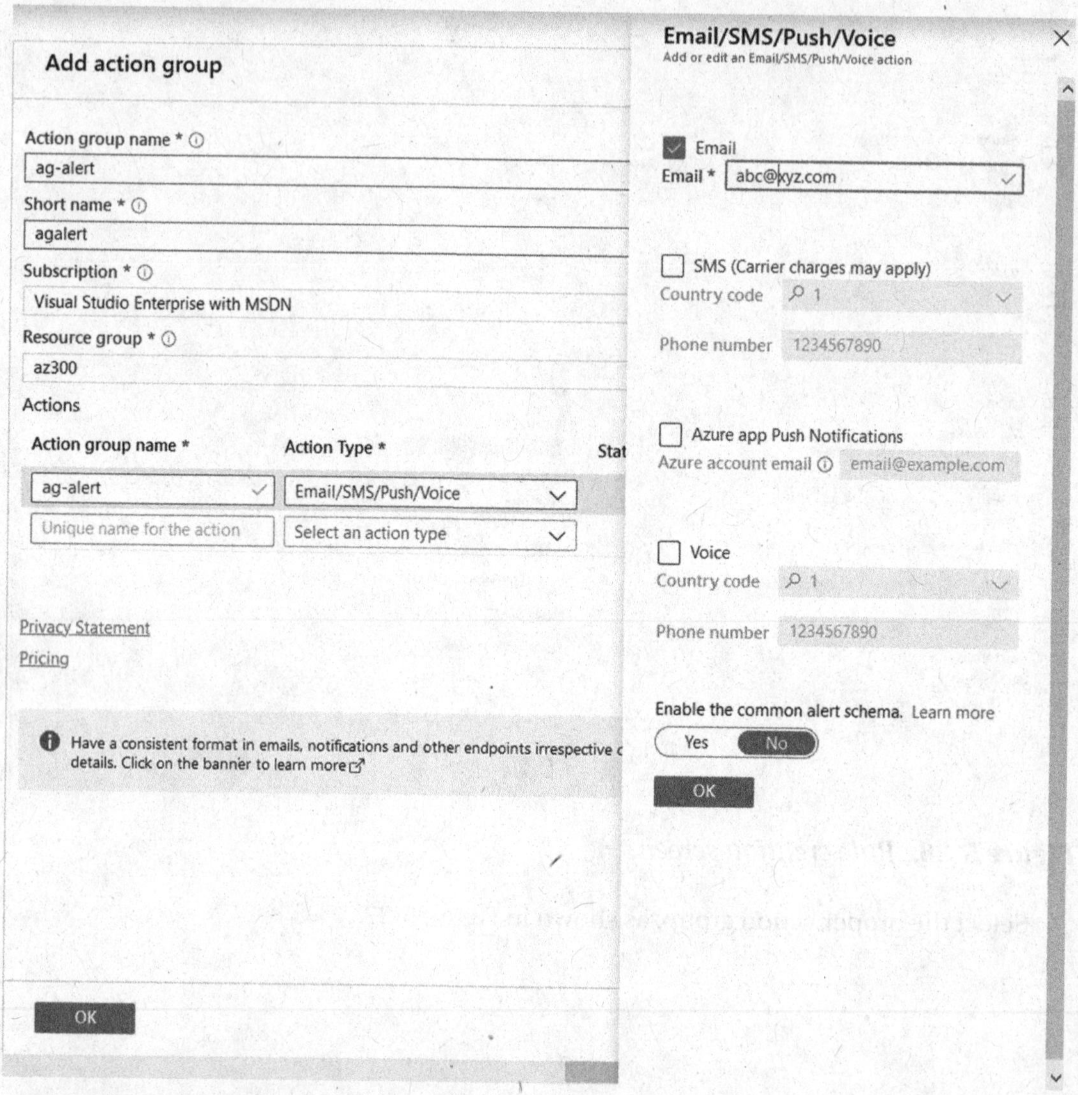

Figure 5-27. *Adding an action group*

Here, I will be creating one Sev 1 alert as this is related to the CPU. You can choose accordingly based on your needs and assign a proper severity to it, as shown in Figure 5-28.

Home > az300 > azvmdemo2 - Alerts > Create rule

Create rule
Rules management

ACTIONS

Action group name	Contain actions	
ag-alert	1 Email	🗑

[Select action group] [Create action gro...]

ℹ Action rules (preview) allows you to define actions at scale as well as suppress actions. Learn more about this functionality by clicking on this banner ⧉   ✕

ALERT DETAILS
Alert rule name * ⓘ

CPU Running High

Description

CPU Running High

Severity * ⓘ
Sev 1 ⌄

Enable rule upon creation
[Yes] No

ℹ It can take up to 10 minutes for a metric alert rule to become active.

[Create alert rule]

Figure 5-28. Action creation

Now, when you click "Create alert rule," you will see the screen shown in Figure 5-29.

Rules
Rules management   ✕

\+ New alert rule   ☰ Edit columns   🔗 Manage action groups   ☐ View classic alerts   ↻ Refresh | ▷ Enable   ☐ Disable   🗑 Delete

Don't see a subscription? Open Directory + Subscription settings

Subscription * ⓘ	Resource group * ⓘ	Resource type ⓘ	Resource ⓘ	Signal type ⓘ	Status ⓘ
Visual Studio Enterprise with MSDN ⌄	az300 ⌄	0 selected ⌄	azvmdemo2 ⌄	All sources ⌄	Enabled ⌄

Selected subscriptions > az300 > azvmdemo2

Displaying 1 - 1 rules out of total 1 rules

🔍 Search alert rules based on rule name and condition...

Name	↑↓	Condition	↑↓	Status	Target resource	↑↓	Target Resource Type	↑↓	Signal type	↑↓
☐ CPU Running High		Percentage CPU GreaterThan 20		⊘ Enabled	azvmdemo2		Virtual machines		Metrics	

Figure 5-29. Rules screen

Managing Actions

You can also manage action groups, as shown in Figure 5-30.

Figure 5-30. *Actions overview screen*

When you click "Manage actions," you will see the screen in Figure 5-31.

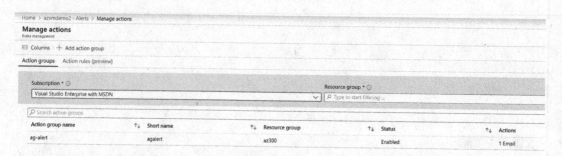

Figure 5-31. *"Manage actions" screen*

From here, you can edit an existing action or create a new one, as shown in Figure 5-32.

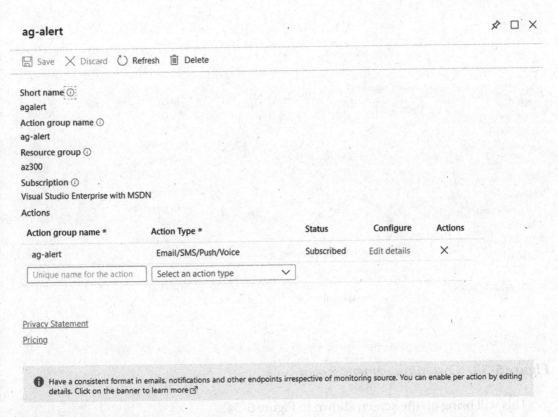

Figure 5-32. *Alert screen*

Managing Costs

Select the cost management for all services, as shown in Figure 5-33.

Figure 5-33. *Cost management screen*

This will bring up the screen shown in Figure 5-34.

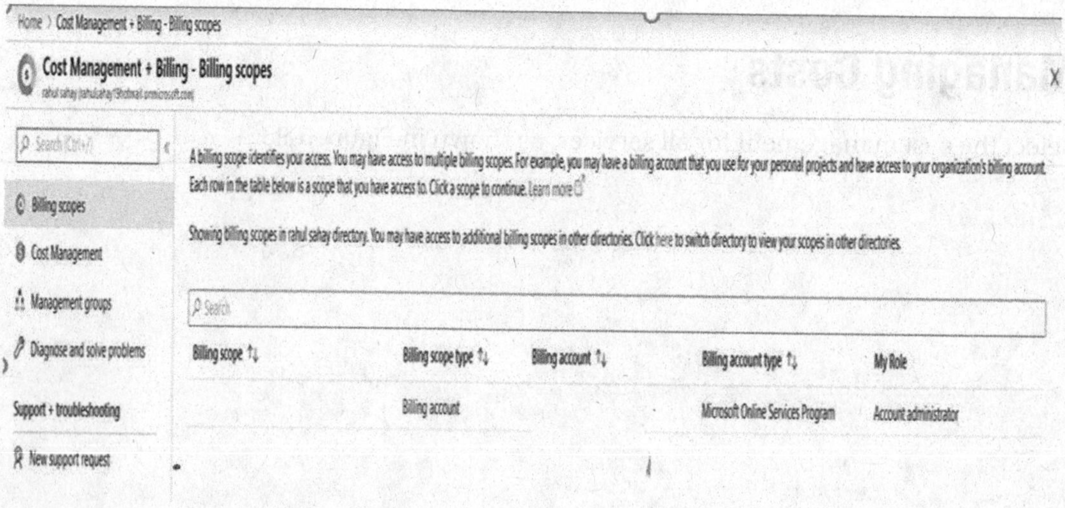

Figure 5-34. *Cost management screen*

I have masked my email address here. Next, click Cost Management in the left panel. This takes you to an overview screen, as shown in Figure 5-35.

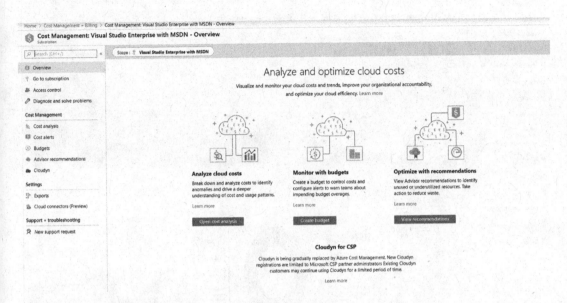

Figure 5-35. *Cost management overview screen*

You can now go ahead and click "Open cost analysis." This will bring up the screen shown in Figure 5-36.

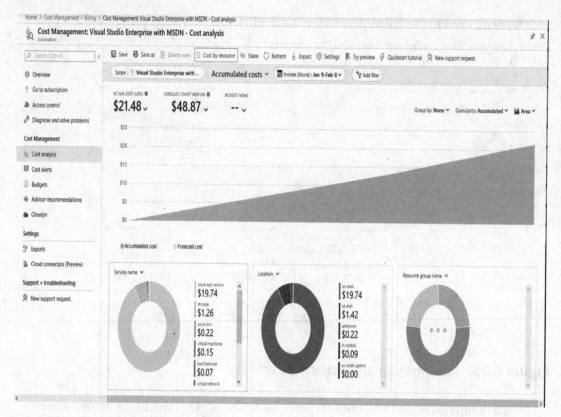

Figure 5-36. *Cost analysis screen*

This is a high-level chart; if you want to get more detailed information, then you can click "Cost by resource" as highlighted. This will take you to the screen shown in Figure 5-37.

Home > Cost Management + Billing > Cost Management: Visual Studio Enterprise with MSDN - Cost analysis

Cost Management: Visual Studio Enterprise with MSDN - Cost analysis
Subscription

Search (Ctrl+/)

Save | Save as | Delete view | Cost by resource | Share | Refresh | Export | Settings | Try preview | Quickstart tutorial | New support request

- Overview
- Go to subscription
- Access control
- Diagnose and solve problems

Cost Management
- Cost analysis
- Cost alerts
- Budgets
- Advisor recommendations
- Cloudyn

Settings
- Exports
- Cloud connectors (Preview)

Support + troubleshooting
- New support request

Scope : Visual Studio Enterprise with ... | Cost by resource ∨ | Invoice (Azure) : Jan 9 - Feb 8 ∨ | Add filter

ACTUAL COST (USD) | FORECAST: CHART VIEW ON | BUDGET: NONE
$21.48 ∨ | $48.87 ∨ | -- ∨

Group by: Resource ∨   Granularity: None ∨   Table ∨

Filter items   27 rows

Resource	Resource type	Location	Resource group name	Tags	Cost ↓
default1	App Service plan	us west	default-web-westus	Not applicable	$19.74
azvmdemo2_osdisk_1_a838559w92...	Disk	us east	az300	demo:azure	$0.72
azvmdemo_osdisk_1_b31db9a9eefb...	Disk	us east	az300	demo:azure	$0.26
sampledevs.com	DNS zone	unknown	poseidonsample	Not applicable	$0.22
csg671i56b1a534s4c21xb2e	Storage account	in central	cloud-shell-storage-centralindia	ms-resource-usage:azure-cloud-shell	$0.09
azvmdemo	Virtual machine	us east	az300	demo:azure, env:build	$0.09
vmss1lb	Load balancer	us east	az300	Not applicable	$0.07
vmss1_vmss1_0_osdisk_1_c607b38...	Disk	us east	az300	Not applicable	$0.05
vmss1_vmss1_3_osdisk_1_5df901c9...	Disk	us east	az300	Not applicable	$0.05
vmss1	Virtual machine scale set	us east	az300	Not applicable	$0.03
azvmdemo2	Virtual machine	us east	az300	demo:azure	$0.03
aznewvm_osdisk_1_ba10ef3c51ae4a...	Disk	us east	az300	environment:dev	$0.03
azvmdemo_osdisk_1_f2efd11adb26...	Disk	us east	az300	env:build	$0.03
azvmdemo2_osdisk_1_4e3ce0ec6d5...	Disk	us east	az300	demo:azure	$0.03
azvmdemo2-ip	Public IP address	us east	az300	demo:azure	$0.02
azvmdemo-ip	Public IP address	us east	az300	demo:azure, env:build	$0.02
aznewvm	Virtual machine	us east	az300	environment:dev	<$0.01

Figure 5-37. *Cost by resource*

CHAPTER 6

Azure Recommendations

Azure Advisor is your free, personalized guide to Azure best practices. This tool quickly and easily optimizes your Azure deployments. It analyzes your configuration and usage telemetry and offers personalized, actionable recommendations to help you optimize your Azure resources for high availability, security, performance, cost, etc.

Creating a Recommendation

When you click "Advisor recommendations" under Cost Management, you'll see the screen shown in Figure 6-1.

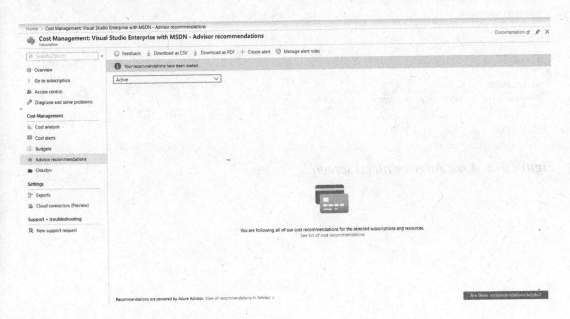

Figure 6-1. *Cost management screen*

© Rahul Sahay 2020
R. Sahay, *Microsoft Azure Architect Technologies Study Companion,*
https://doi.org/10.1007/978-1-4842-6200-9_6

Here, you can create a rule like the ones you have created in previous chapters, as shown in Figure 6-2 and in Figure 6-3.

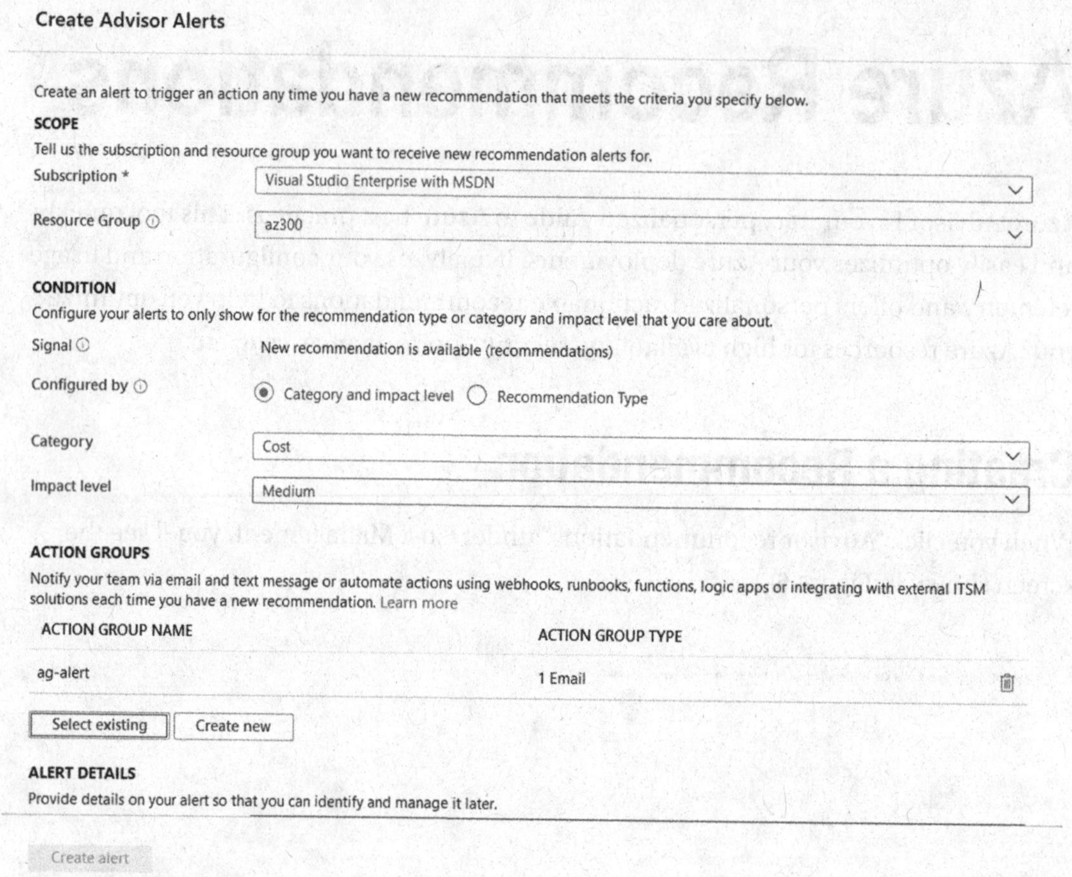

Create Advisor Alerts

Create an alert to trigger an action any time you have a new recommendation that meets the criteria you specify below.

SCOPE

Tell us the subscription and resource group you want to receive new recommendation alerts for.

Subscription * | Visual Studio Enterprise with MSDN

Resource Group ⓘ | az300

CONDITION

Configure your alerts to only show for the recommendation type or category and impact level that you care about.

Signal ⓘ | New recommendation is available (recommendations)

Configured by ⓘ | ⦿ Category and impact level ◯ Recommendation Type

Category | Cost

Impact level | Medium

ACTION GROUPS

Notify your team via email and text message or automate actions using webhooks, runbooks, functions, logic apps or integrating with external ITSM solutions each time you have a new recommendation. Learn more

ACTION GROUP NAME	ACTION GROUP TYPE	
ag-alert	1 Email	🗑

[Select existing] [Create new]

ALERT DETAILS

Provide details on your alert so that you can identify and manage it later.

[Create alert]

Figure 6-2. *Cost Advisor alerts screen*

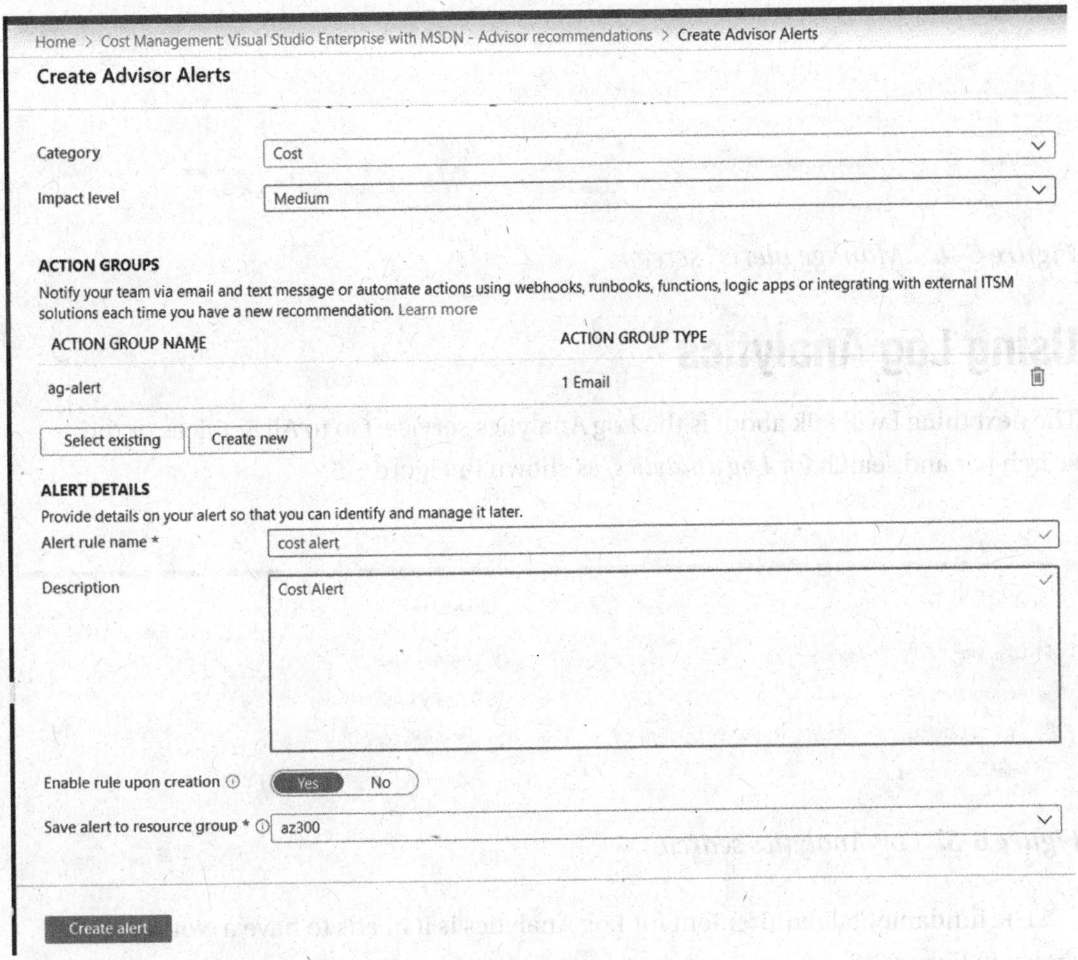

Home > Cost Management: Visual Studio Enterprise with MSDN - Advisor recommendations > **Create Advisor Alerts**

Create Advisor Alerts

Category   Cost   ∨

Impact level   Medium   ∨

ACTION GROUPS

Notify your team via email and text message or automate actions using webhooks, runbooks, functions, logic apps or integrating with external ITSM solutions each time you have a new recommendation. Learn more

ACTION GROUP NAME   ACTION GROUP TYPE

ag-alert   1 Email   🗑

[Select existing]   [Create new]

ALERT DETAILS

Provide details on your alert so that you can identify and manage it later.

Alert rule name *   cost alert   ✓

Description   Cost Alert   ✓

Enable rule upon creation ⓘ   (Yes   No)

Save alert to resource group * ⓘ   az300   ∨

[Create alert]

Figure 6-3. *Cost Advisor alerts configuration*

Once the rule has been created, Azure will show a notification. Click "Manage alerts," and you will see the screen shown in Figure 6-4.

Figure 6-4. *"Manage alerts" screen*

Using Log Analytics

The next thing I will talk about is the Log Analytics service. Go to All Services or the search bar and search for *Log analytics,* as shown in Figure 6-5.

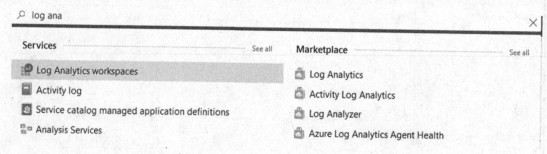

Figure 6-5. *Log Analytics search*

The fundamental requirement for Log Analytics is it needs to have a workspace, as shown in Figure 6-6.

Figure 6-6. *Log Analytics workspace list*

This is just the storage account or container that you set for the logs to get in. Here, you can configure the workspace data sources, as highlighted in Figure 6-7 and Figure 6-8.

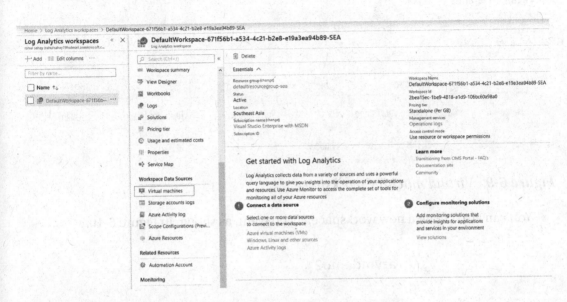

Figure 6-7. *Log Analytics workspace*

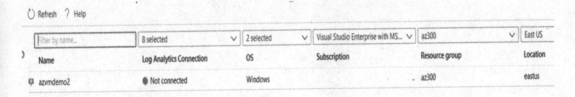

Figure 6-8. *Log Analytics connection*

First the screen will show that the VM is not connected; select the VM and click the Connect button, as shown in Figure 6-9.

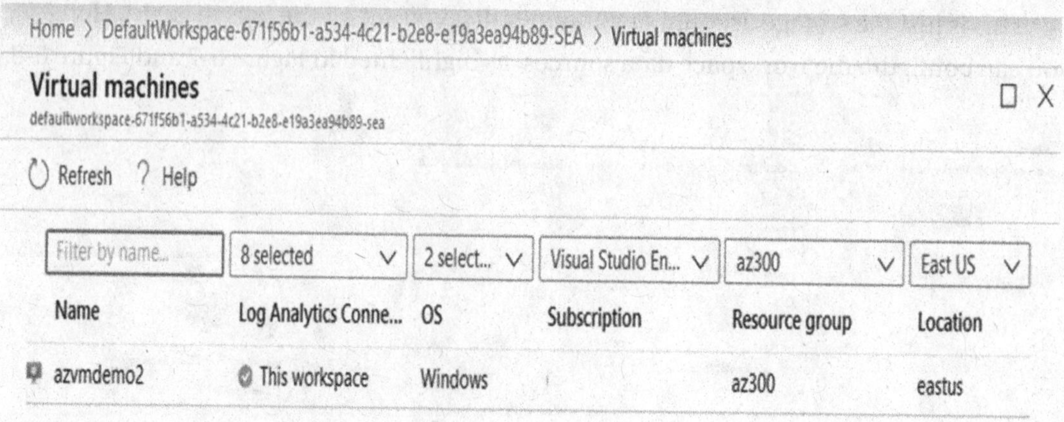

Home > DefaultWorkspace-671f56b1-a534-4c21-b2e8-e19a3ea94b89-SEA > Virtual machines

Virtual machines
defaultworkspace-671f56b1-a534-4c21-b2e8-e19a3ea94b89-sea   ☐ X

◯ Refresh   ? Help

Filter by name...	8 selected ∨	2 select... ∨	Visual Studio En... ∨	az300 ∨	East US ∨
Name	Log Analytics Conne...	OS	Subscription	Resource group	Location
🖥 azvmdemo2	⊘ This workspace	Windows		az300	eastus

Figure 6-9. *Virtual machine workspace*

You can also create a new workspace, if you want, as shown in Figure 6-10.

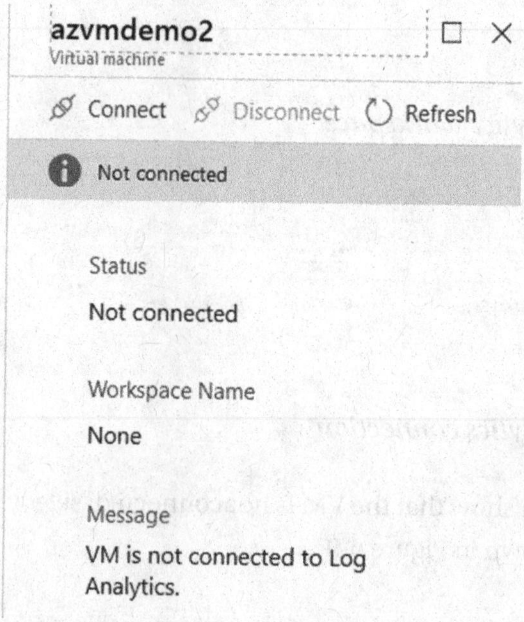

azvmdemo2   ☐ X
Virtual machine

🖉 Connect   ♊ Disconnect   ◯ Refresh

ℹ   Not connected

Status

Not connected

Workspace Name

None

Message

VM is not connected to Log
Analytics.

Figure 6-10. *New workspace*

Now all the logs for that virtual machine will be logged in this workspace, which is searchable. Similarly, you can enable activities for storage accounts. You can also track activity via an activity log at the Azure account level. Figure 6-11 shows Azure Resources.

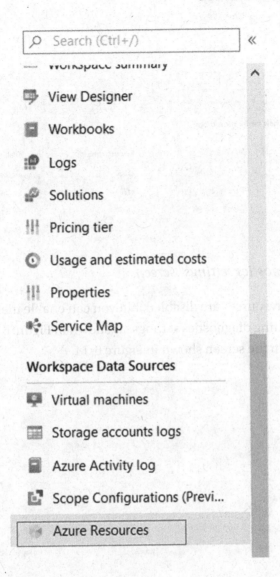

Figure 6-11. *Azure Resources menu item*

Here, you can click Azure Resources to see the eligible resources, as shown in Figure 6-12.

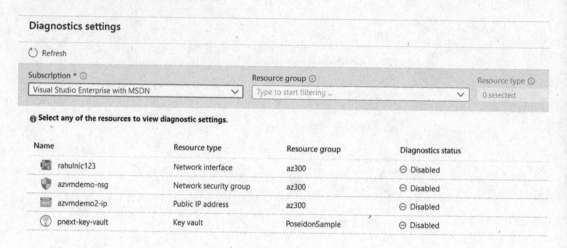

Figure 6-12. *"Diagnostics settings" screen*

Currently, all the resources are disabled, but you can enable them in the same way as you did when selecting diagnostics settings, as shown in Figure 6-13. Let's add a new diagnostic setting from the screen shown in Figure 6-14.

Diagnostics settings

◯ Refresh

Subscription * ⓘ	Resource group ⓘ	Resource type ⓘ	Resource ⓘ
Visual Studio Enterprise with MSDN ⌄	az300 ⌄	Network interfaces ⌄	rahulnic123

Visual Studio Enterprise with MSDN 〉 az300 〉 rahulnic123

Diagnostics settings

Name	Storage account	Event hub	Log Analytics workspace	Edit setting
No diagnostic settings defined				

+ Add diagnostic setting

Click 'Add Diagnostic setting' above to configure the collection of the following data:

• AllMetrics

Figure 6-13. *Diagnostics settings screen*

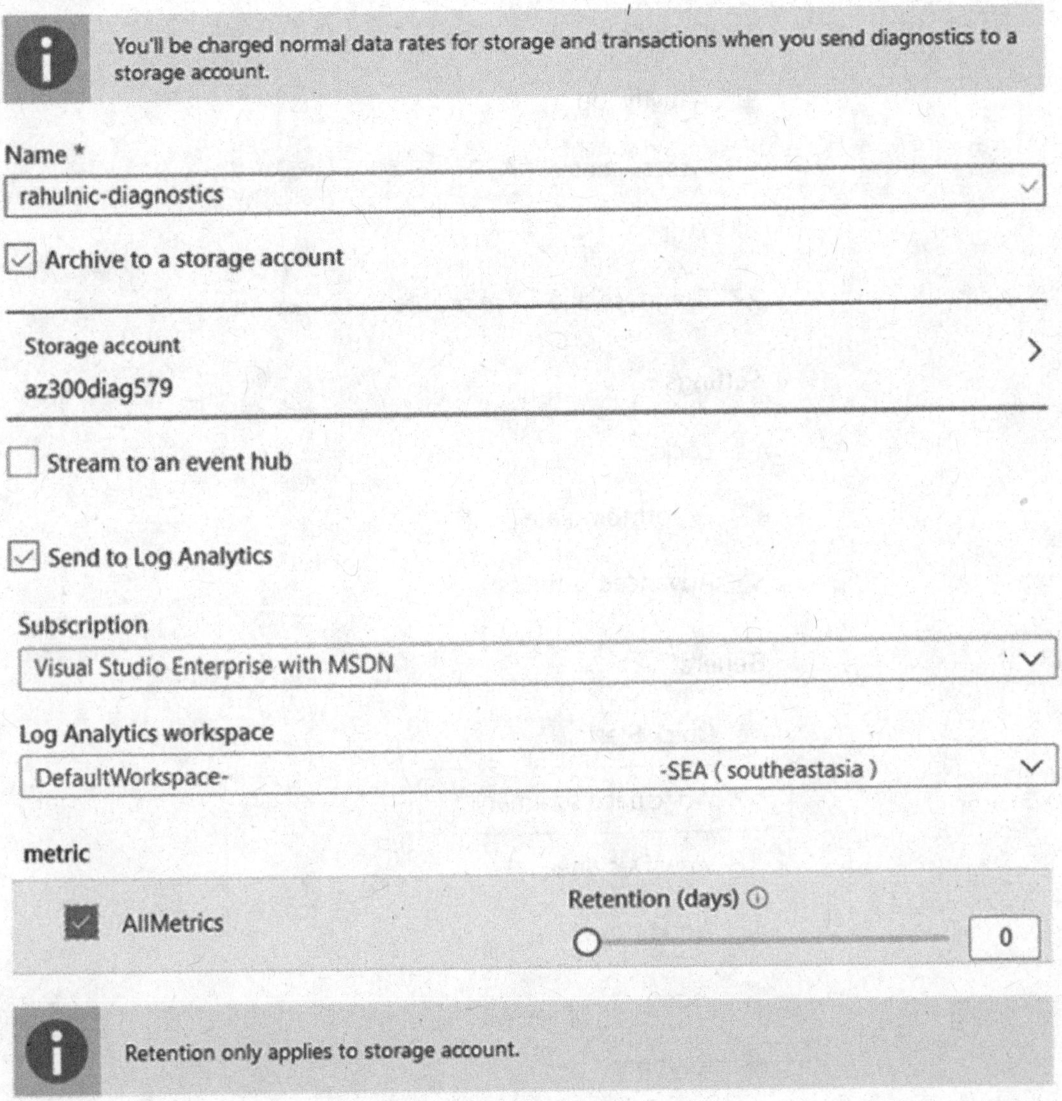

You'll be charged normal data rates for storage and transactions when you send diagnostics to a storage account.

Name *

rahulnic-diagnostics

☑ Archive to a storage account

Storage account

az300diag579

☐ Stream to an event hub

☑ Send to Log Analytics

Subscription

Visual Studio Enterprise with MSDN

Log Analytics workspace

DefaultWorkspace-   -SEA (southeastasia)

metric

| ☑ AllMetrics | Retention (days) ⓘ | 0 |

Retention only applies to storage account.

Figure 6-14. *Creating a diagnostics setting*

Figure 6-15 shows the "Workspace summary" menu item.

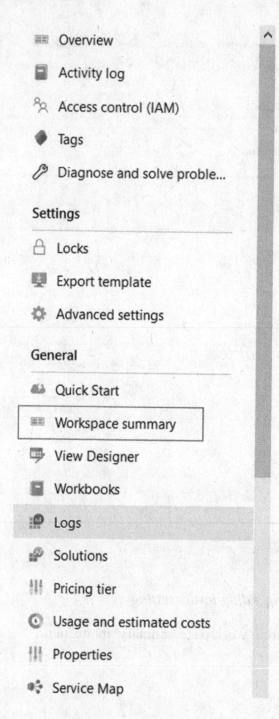

Figure 6-15. *"Workspace summary" menu item*

After you click "Workspace summary," you can see that you have many activities to search for. If you click Logs, you will see the screen in Figure 6-16.

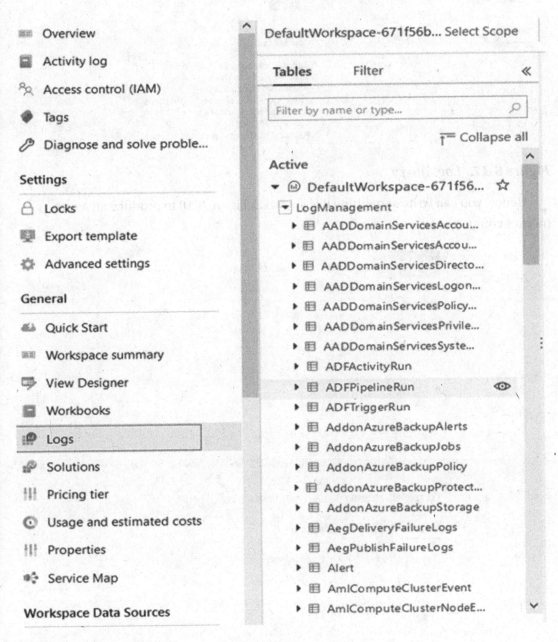

Figure 6-16. *Logs search*

This is the place where you can query the logs, and you can save a query for later use as well. A query also has intelligence baked in, as shown in Figure 6-17.

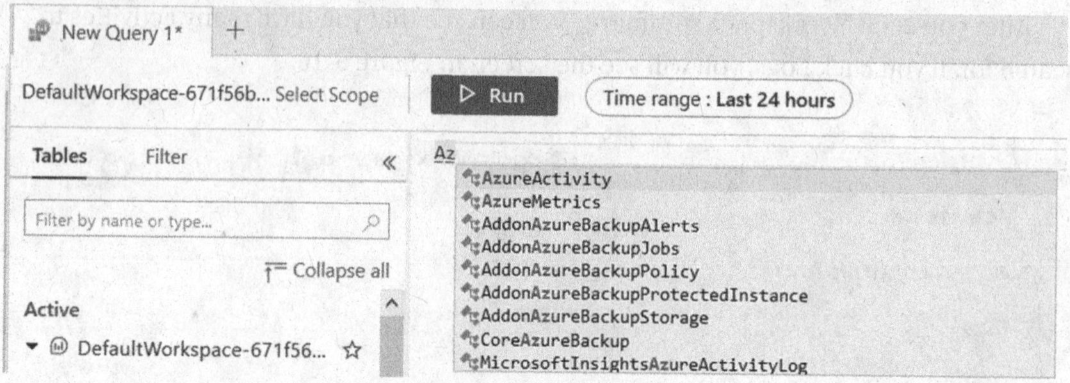

Figure 6-17. *Logs query*

Hence, you can write something like shown in Figure 6-18 to produce an Azure metrics count.

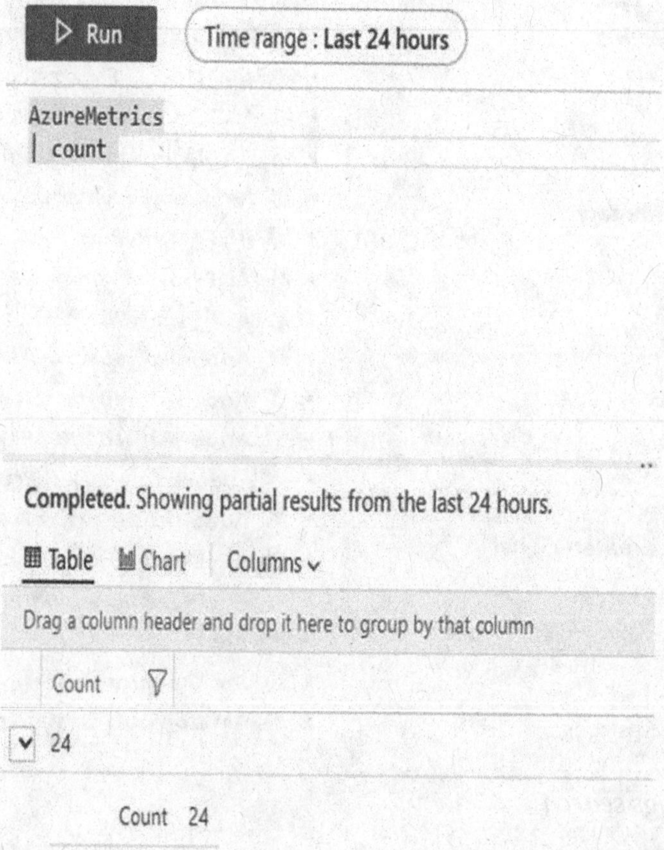

Figure 6-18. *Log Analytics search*

On the left side, you can see the Filter tab, as shown in Figure 6-19.

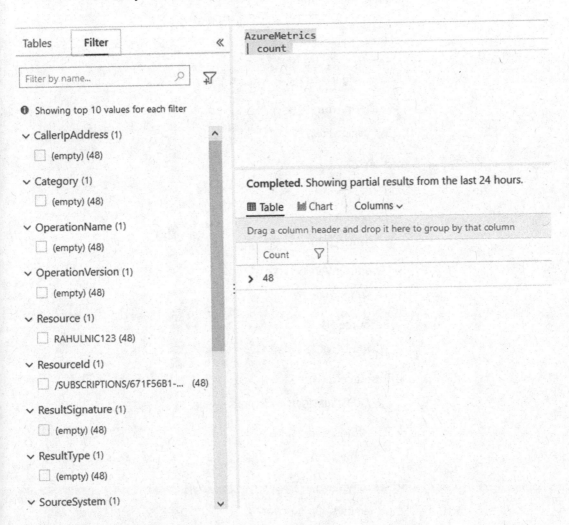

Figure 6-19. *Logs filter*

Select the filter and click Apply & Run, as shown in Figure 6-20. This will display results, as shown in Figure 6-21.

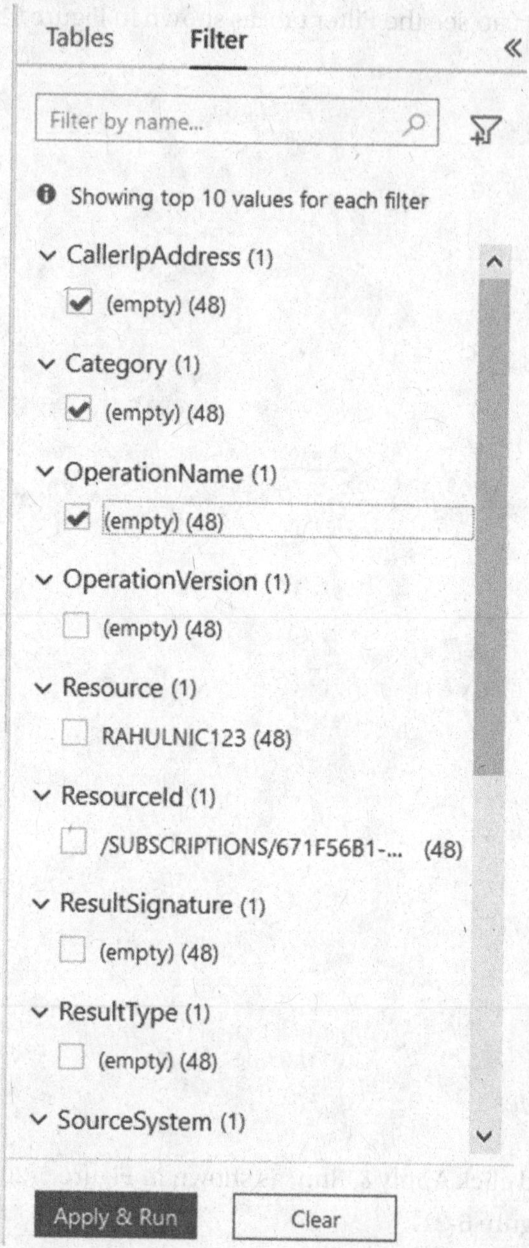

Figure 6-20. *Logs filtering applied*

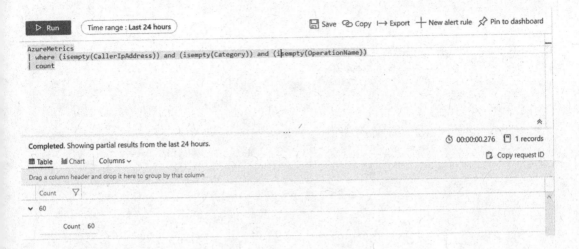

Figure 6-21. *Logs filtering result*

You can also set an alert rule on this filter to alert you if something goes wrong. This is quite a granular level of settings that you can monitor.

CHAPTER 7

Storage Solutions

Azure Storage is Microsoft's cloud storage solution for modern data storage scenarios. Azure Storage offers a massively scalable object store for data objects, a file system, a messaging store for reliable messaging, and a NoSQL store. Some of its salient features are listed here:

- Durable and highly available

- Secure

- Scalable

- Managed

- Accessible

In this chapter, you'll see how to implement and manage storage. Having said that, let's get started. Let's search for *storage* in "All services," as shown in Figure 7-1.

© Rahul Sahay 2020
R. Sahay, *Microsoft Azure Architect Technologies Study Companion*,
https://doi.org/10.1007/978-1-4842-6200-9_7

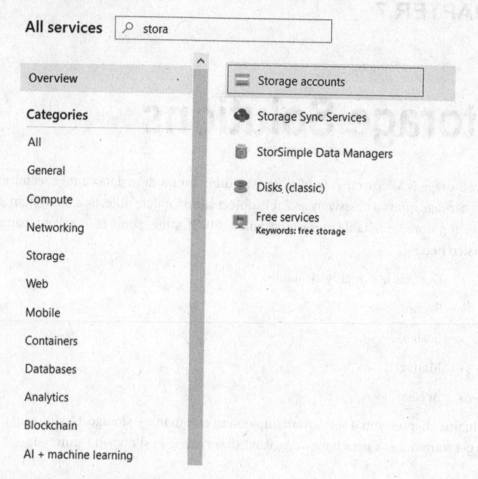

Figure 7-1. *Storage accounts search*

I already have a couple of storage accounts under my resource group, as shown in Figure 7-2.

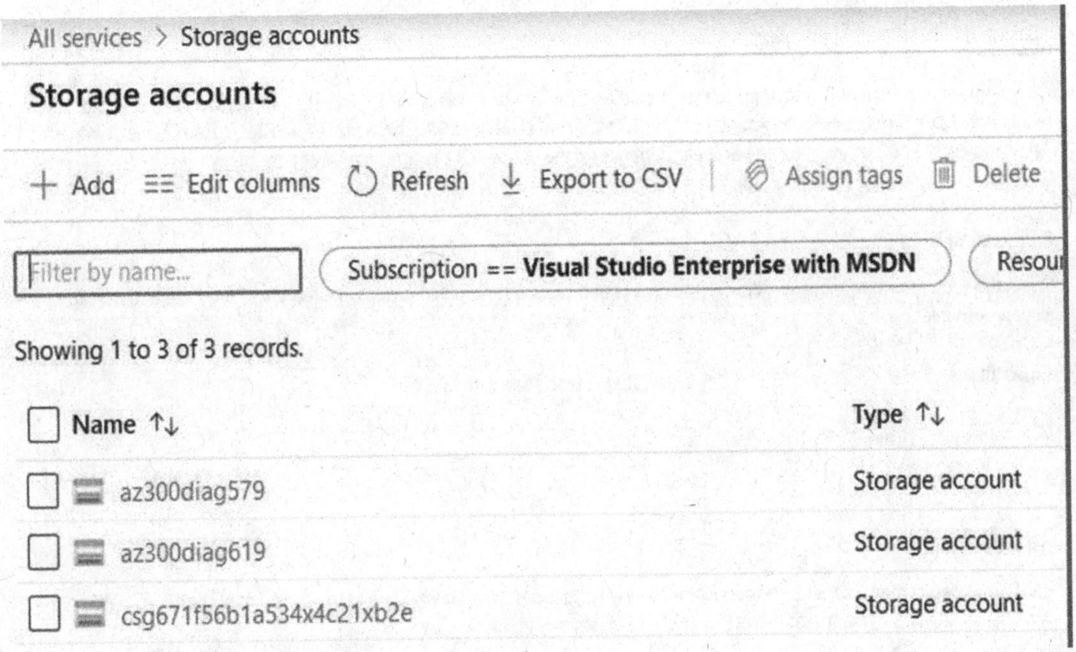

All services > Storage accounts

Storage accounts

+ Add   ≡≡ Edit columns   ○ Refresh   ↓ Export to CSV   ⊘ Assign tags   🗑 Delete

| Filter by name... | Subscription == **Visual Studio Enterprise with MSDN** | Resour |

Showing 1 to 3 of 3 records.

☐ Name ↑↓	Type ↑↓
☐ 📼 az300diag579	Storage account
☐ 📼 az300diag619	Storage account
☐ 📼 csg671f56b1a534x4c21xb2e	Storage account

Figure 7-2. *Storage accounts*

But, let's create one from scratch and see how it works. Click the Add button. This will give you the UI shown in Figure 7-3. The UI is pretty much similar to the virtual machine interface UI. In fact, more or less you will get the same UI when creating any new resource.

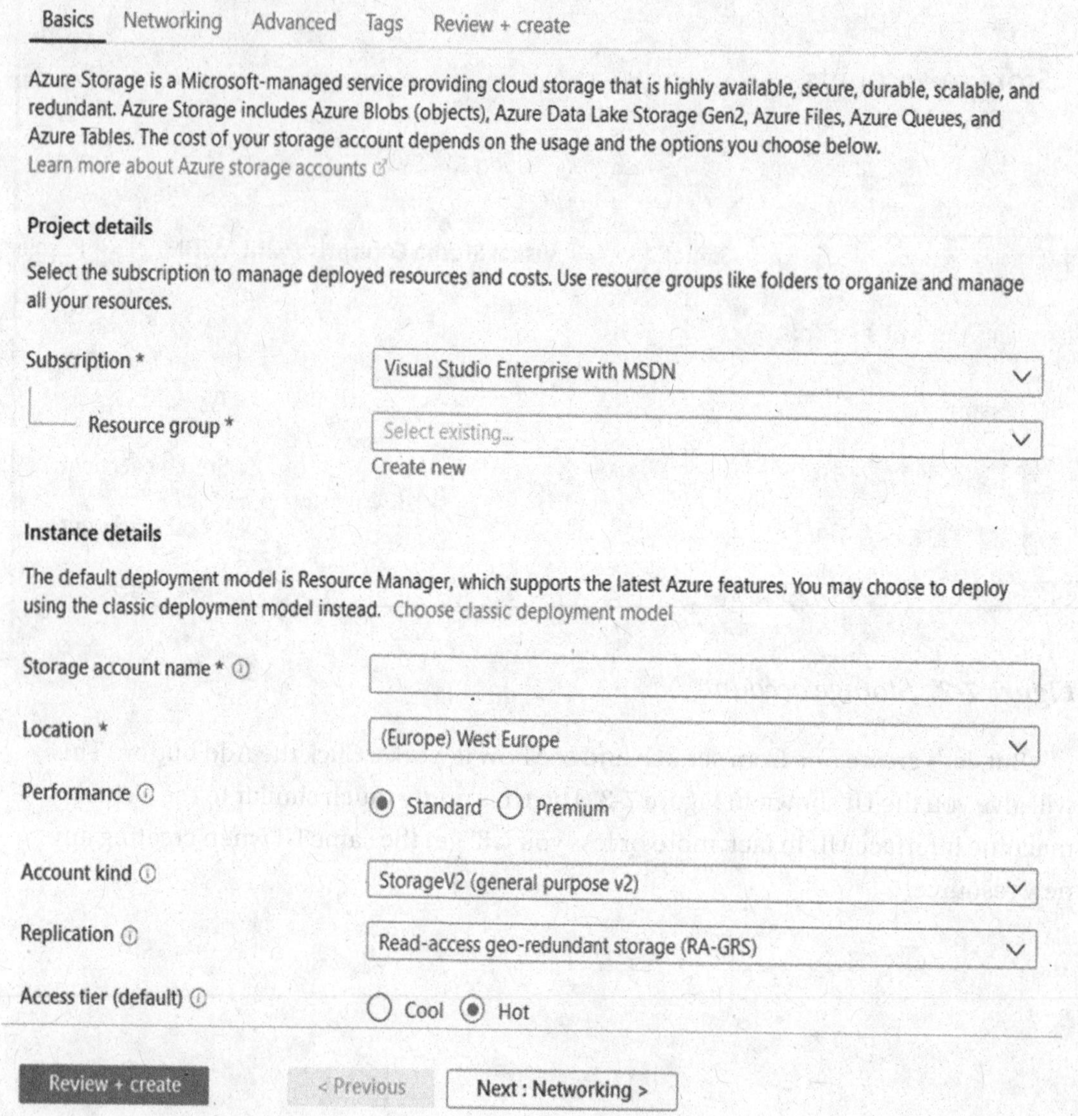

Basics   Networking   Advanced   Tags   Review + create

Azure Storage is a Microsoft-managed service providing cloud storage that is highly available, secure, durable, scalable, and redundant. Azure Storage includes Azure Blobs (objects), Azure Data Lake Storage Gen2, Azure Files, Azure Queues, and Azure Tables. The cost of your storage account depends on the usage and the options you choose below.
Learn more about Azure storage accounts ☐

Project details

Select the subscription to manage deployed resources and costs. Use resource groups like folders to organize and manage all your resources.

Subscription * | Visual Studio Enterprise with MSDN   ⌄ |

    Resource group * | Select existing...   ⌄ |
                     Create new

Instance details

The default deployment model is Resource Manager, which supports the latest Azure features. You may choose to deploy using the classic deployment model instead. Choose classic deployment model

Storage account name * ⓘ | _____ |

Location * | (Europe) West Europe   ⌄ |

Performance ⓘ   ◉ Standard ○ Premium

Account kind ⓘ | StorageV2 (general purpose v2)   ⌄ |

Replication ⓘ | Read-access geo-redundant storage (RA-GRS) ⌄ |

Access tier (default) ⓘ   ○ Cool ◉ Hot

[Review + create]   [< Previous]   [Next : Networking >]

Figure 7-3. *Storage account basics*

The difference between standard and premium accounts is that standard storage is a physical storage account, which is magnetic storage. Basically, it's a hard disk drive (HDD). A premium storage account, on the other hand, is a solid-state disk (SSD). When you choose premium storage, it significantly reduces the supported types, as shown in Figure 7-4.

Performance ⓘ	◯ Standard ⦿ Premium
Account kind ⓘ	StorageV2 (general purpose v2) ⌄
Replication ⓘ	Locally-redundant storage (LRS) ⌄

> ⓘ Accounts with the selected kind, replication and performance type only support page blobs. Block blobs, append blobs, file shares, tables, and queues will not be available.

Figure 7-4. *Supported storage types*

Figure 7-5 shows the account types available.

Storage account name * ⓘ	rahulstorage1 ✓
Location *	(US) East US ⌄
Performance ⓘ	⦿ Standard ◯ Premium
Account kind ⓘ	StorageV2 (general purpose v2) ⌃
Replication ⓘ	StorageV2 (general purpose v2)
Access tier (default) ⓘ	Storage (general purpose v1)
	BlobStorage

Figure 7-5. *Storage account types*

General-purpose storage will provide storage for blobs, tables, files, and queues in a unified account. You can find more details at `https://bit.ly/az-storage-account`.

Let's say you go with a blob storage account. In that case, the biggest advantage is that it can be made public. Therefore, you can turn this into a public account and start storing files in Azure that you can share in your web applications. Here, images, videos, etc., can be stored in a blob account.

Figure 7-6 shows the replication options.

Storage account name * ⓘ	Locally-redundant storage (LRS)
	Zone-redundant storage (ZRS)
Location *	Geo-redundant storage (GRS)
Performance ⓘ	Read-access geo-redundant storage (RA-GRS)
	Geo-zone-redundant storage (GZRS) (preview)
Account kind ⓘ	Read-access geo-zone-redundant storage (RA-GZRS) (preview)
Replication ⓘ	Locally-redundant storage (LRS) ︿
Access tier (default) ⓘ	◯ Cool ⦿ Hot

Figure 7-6. *Replication options*

Based on your location, the drop-down options vary.

- Locally redundant storage (LRS) means it stores your data plus two additional copies within the region. This takes advantage of availability zones. Availability zones allow you to create VMs in specific data centers.

- Zone-redundant storage (ZRS) replicates your data synchronously across three storage clusters in a single region. Each storage cluster is physically separated from the others and is located in its own availability zone (AZ).

- Georedundant storage (GRS) replicates your data to another data center in a secondary region, but that data is available to be read-only if Microsoft initiates a failover from the primary to secondary region.

- Read-access georedundant storage (RA-GRS) maximizes availability for your storage account. RA-GRS provides read-only access to the data in the secondary location, in addition to georeplication across two regions.

- Geozone-redundant storage (GZRS) (preview) marries the high availability of zone-redundant storage (ZRS) with protection from regional outages as provided by GRS. Data in a GZRS storage account is replicated across three Azure availability zones in the primary region and also replicated to a secondary geographic region for protection from regional disasters.

- You can optionally enable read access to data in the secondary region with RA-GZRS if your applications need to be able to read data in the event of a disaster in the primary region.

- Access tiers are divided into two, like hot and cold storage. Hot storage is immediately available. This means if you have stored something in an account, it should have the lowest latency time in terms of retrieval. If you choose cold storage, it's actually a cheaper option when you consider the price per gigabyte. But, here the latency time is high.

- Let's say you have data that you don't need to access frequently, like archival data or backup data; then you should go for cold storage.

My finished storage solution looks like Figure 7-7.

Create storage account

Basics   Networking   Advanced   Tags   Review + create

Azure Storage is a Microsoft-managed service providing cloud storage that is highly available, secure, durable, scalable, and redundant. Azure Storage includes Azure Blobs (objects), Azure Data Lake Storage Gen2, Azure Files, Azure Queues, and Azure Tables. The cost of your storage account depends on the usage and the options you choose below.
Learn more about Azure storage accounts

Project details

Select the subscription to manage deployed resources and costs. Use resource groups like folders to organize and manage all your resources.

Subscription *

| Visual Studio Enterprise with MSDN | ∨ |

Resource group *

| az300 | ∨ |

Create new

Instance details

The default deployment model is Resource Manager, which supports the latest Azure features. You may choose to deploy using the classic deployment model instead. Choose classic deployment model

Storage account name * ⓘ

| rahulstorage1 | ✓ |

Location *

| (US) East US | ∨ |

Performance ⓘ

⦿ Standard   ○ Premium

Account kind ⓘ

| StorageV2 (general purpose v2) | ∨ |

Replication ⓘ

| Locally-redundant storage (LRS) | ∨ |

Access tier (default) ⓘ

⦿ Cool   ○ Hot

[Review + create]   < Previous   [Next : Networking >]

Figure 7-7. *Storage account, basic setup*

Next comes networking. I will go with the default option, as shown in Figure 7-8.

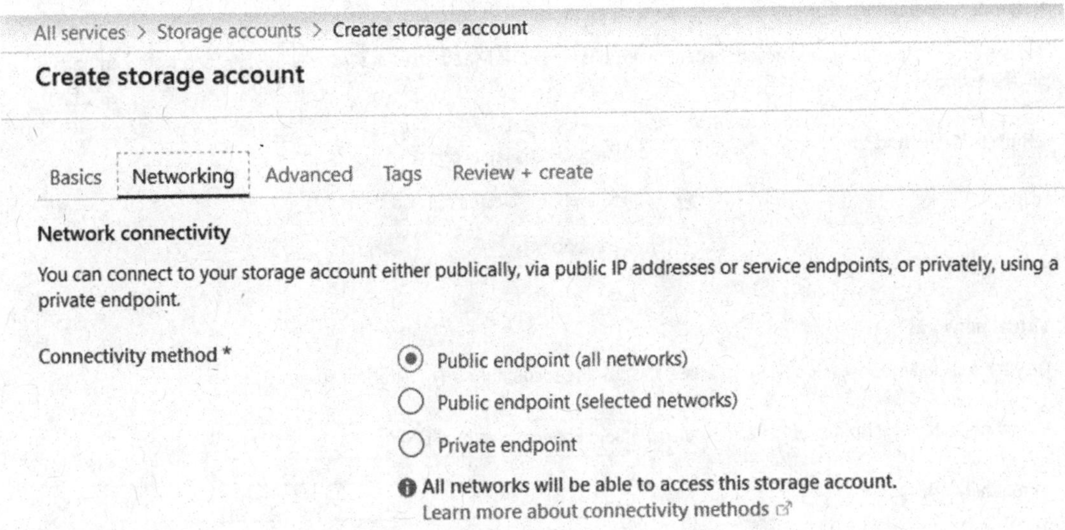

All services > Storage accounts > Create storage account

Create storage account

Basics   Networking   Advanced   Tags   Review + create

Network connectivity

You can connect to your storage account either publically, via public IP addresses or service endpoints, or privately, using a private endpoint.

Connectivity method *

⦿ Public endpoint (all networks)

◯ Public endpoint (selected networks)

◯ Private endpoint

ℹ️ All networks will be able to access this storage account.
Learn more about connectivity methods ↗

Figure 7-8. *Storage account, networking*

In this case, select the second option called "Public endpoint (selected networks)," as shown in Figure 7-9.

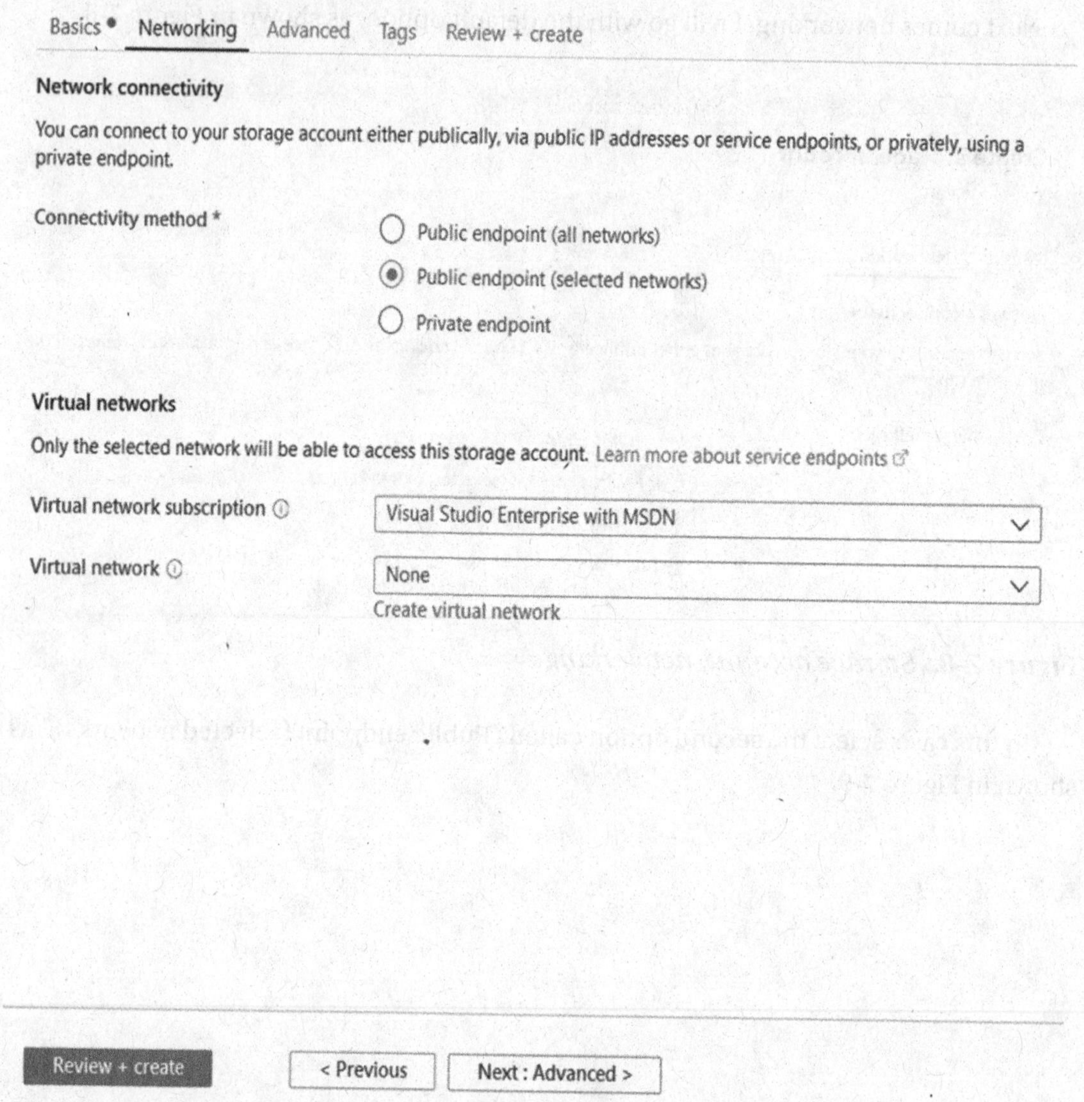

Basics • Networking Advanced Tags Review + create

Network connectivity

You can connect to your storage account either publically, via public IP addresses or service endpoints, or privately, using a private endpoint.

Connectivity method *

○ Public endpoint (all networks)

◉ Public endpoint (selected networks)

○ Private endpoint

Virtual networks

Only the selected network will be able to access this storage account. Learn more about service endpoints ☐

Virtual network subscription ⓘ

    Visual Studio Enterprise with MSDN   ⌄

Virtual network ⓘ

    None   ⌄
    Create virtual network

[Review + create]   [< Previous]   [Next : Advanced >]

Figure 7-9. *Storage account, selected network*

Then, you have to set up networking. This is also called the *virtual network service endpoints* in other places. This will turn off the public access. Even if you have access keys but you are outside of this virtual network, then you won't be able to access this network. You can use a network security group to secure the network such as when you need virtual network peering or global virtual network peering.

Hence, this adds an extra security layer to your storage account. I have kept the default settings.

Next comes the advanced section. I have kept the default settings for this as well, as shown in Figure 7-10.

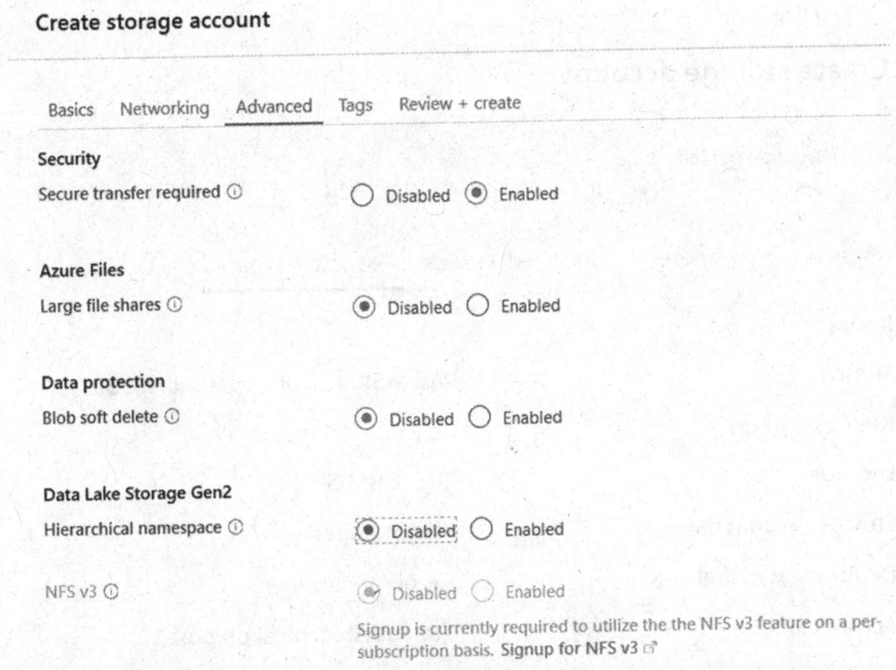

Create storage account

Basics   Networking   Advanced   Tags   Review + create

Security

Secure transfer required ⓘ   ○ Disabled   ⦿ Enabled

Azure Files

Large file shares ⓘ   ⦿ Disabled   ○ Enabled

Data protection

Blob soft delete ⓘ   ⦿ Disabled   ○ Enabled

Data Lake Storage Gen2

Hierarchical namespace ⓘ   ⦿ Disabled   ○ Enabled

NFS v3 ⓘ   ⦿ Disabled   ○ Enabled

Signup is currently required to utilize the the NFS v3 feature on a per-subscription basis. Signup for NFS v3 ↗

Figure 7-10. *Storage account, advanced section*

The next tab is Tags. I have provided a tag named env with a build value, as shown in Figure 7-11.

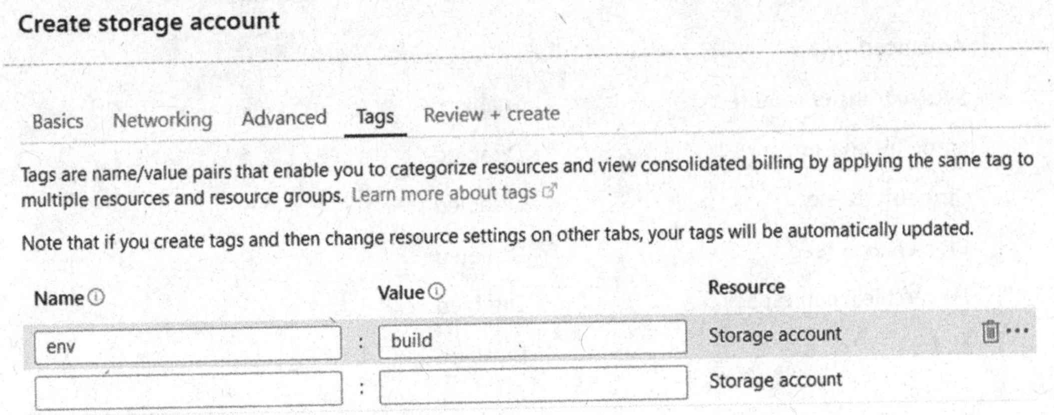

Create storage account

Basics   Networking   Advanced   Tags   Review + create

Tags are name/value pairs that enable you to categorize resources and view consolidated billing by applying the same tag to multiple resources and resource groups. Learn more about tags ↗

Note that if you create tags and then change resource settings on other tabs, your tags will be automatically updated.

Name ⓘ		Value ⓘ	Resource	
env	:	build	Storage account	🗑 •••
	:		Storage account	

Figure 7-11. *Storage account, tags*

Finally comes the summary page. This is an overview of all selections that you have made in the creation process. Let's go ahead and create the storage account, as shown in Figure 7-12.

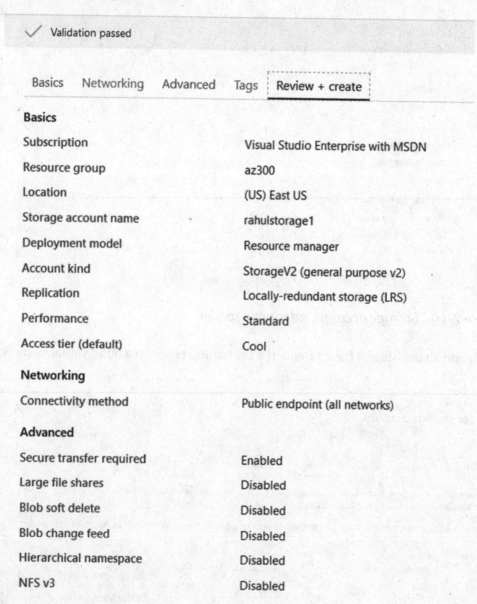

Create storage account

✓ Validation passed

Basics   Networking   Advanced   Tags   Review + create

Basics

Subscription	Visual Studio Enterprise with MSDN
Resource group	az300
Location	(US) East US
Storage account name	rahulstorage1
Deployment model	Resource manager
Account kind	StorageV2 (general purpose v2)
Replication	Locally-redundant storage (LRS)
Performance	Standard
Access tier (default)	Cool

Networking

Connectivity method	Public endpoint (all networks)

Advanced

Secure transfer required	Enabled
Large file shares	Disabled
Blob soft delete	Disabled
Blob change feed	Disabled
Hierarchical namespace	Disabled
NFS v3	Disabled

Figure 7-12. *Storage account, review page*

Azure has created the required storage, as shown in Figure 7-13.

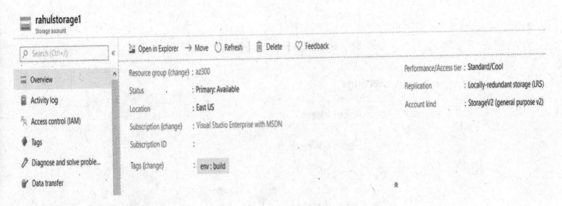

Figure 7-13. *Storage account, overview*

Configuring an Endpoint

In this section, you will see how to configure the virtual network endpoint. Click "Firewalls and virtual networks" in the Settings section, as shown in Figure 7-14.

Figure 7-14. *Firewall settings*

This will bring up the screen shown in Figure 7-15.

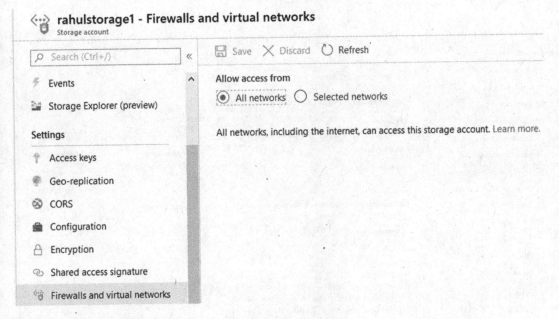

Figure 7-15. Firewall and virtual network settings

I created a storage account for all the networks. Now, I want to add a virtual network. Hence, I will select the second option and continue, as shown in Figure 7-16.

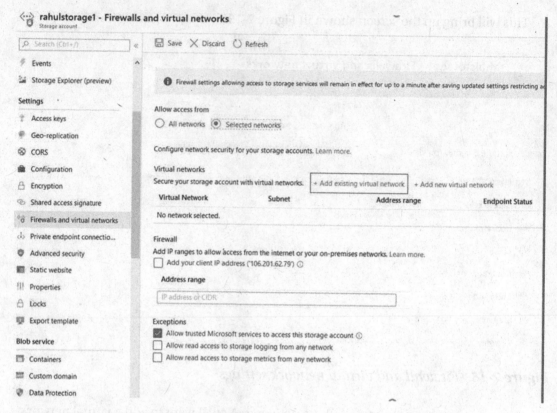

Figure 7-16. Firewall, selected networks

You can add an existing virtual network by clicking the link "Add existing virtual network." This will bring up the screen shown in Figure 7-17.

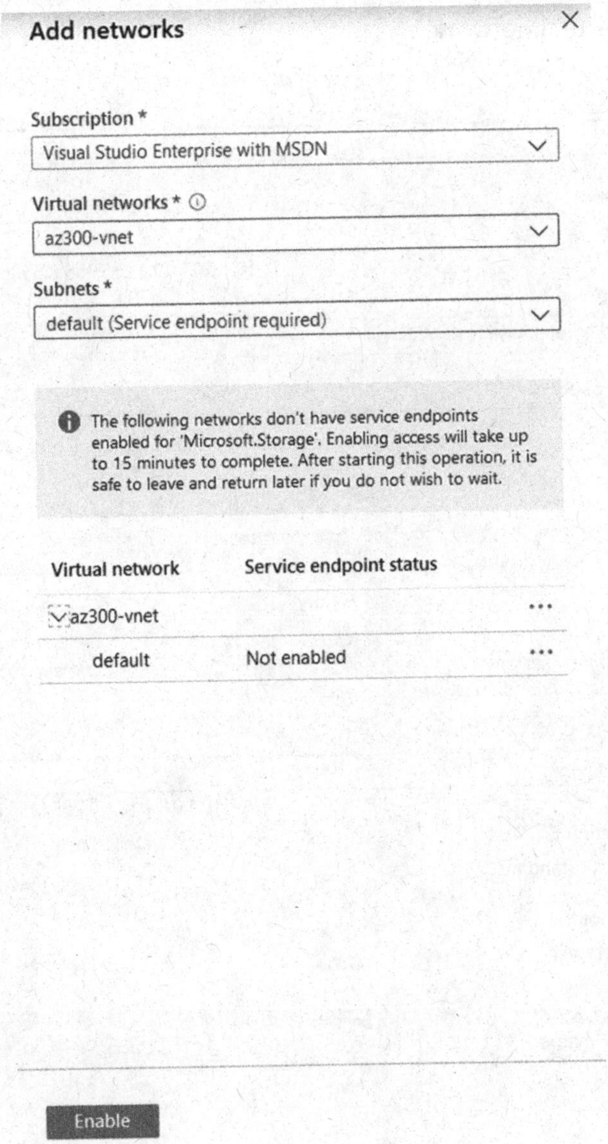

Add networks   ✕

Subscription *

| Visual Studio Enterprise with MSDN | ⌄ |

Virtual networks * ⓘ

| az300-vnet | ⌄ |

Subnets *

| default (Service endpoint required) | ⌄ |

> ⓘ The following networks don't have service endpoints
> enabled for 'Microsoft.Storage'. Enabling access will take up
> to 15 minutes to complete. After starting this operation, it is
> safe to leave and return later if you do not wish to wait.

Virtual network	Service endpoint status	
⌵ az300-vnet		•••
default	Not enabled	•••

Enable

Figure 7-17. *Adding networks*

From here, you can add an existing network, or you can create a new one by clicking "Add new virtual network," as shown in Figure 7-18.

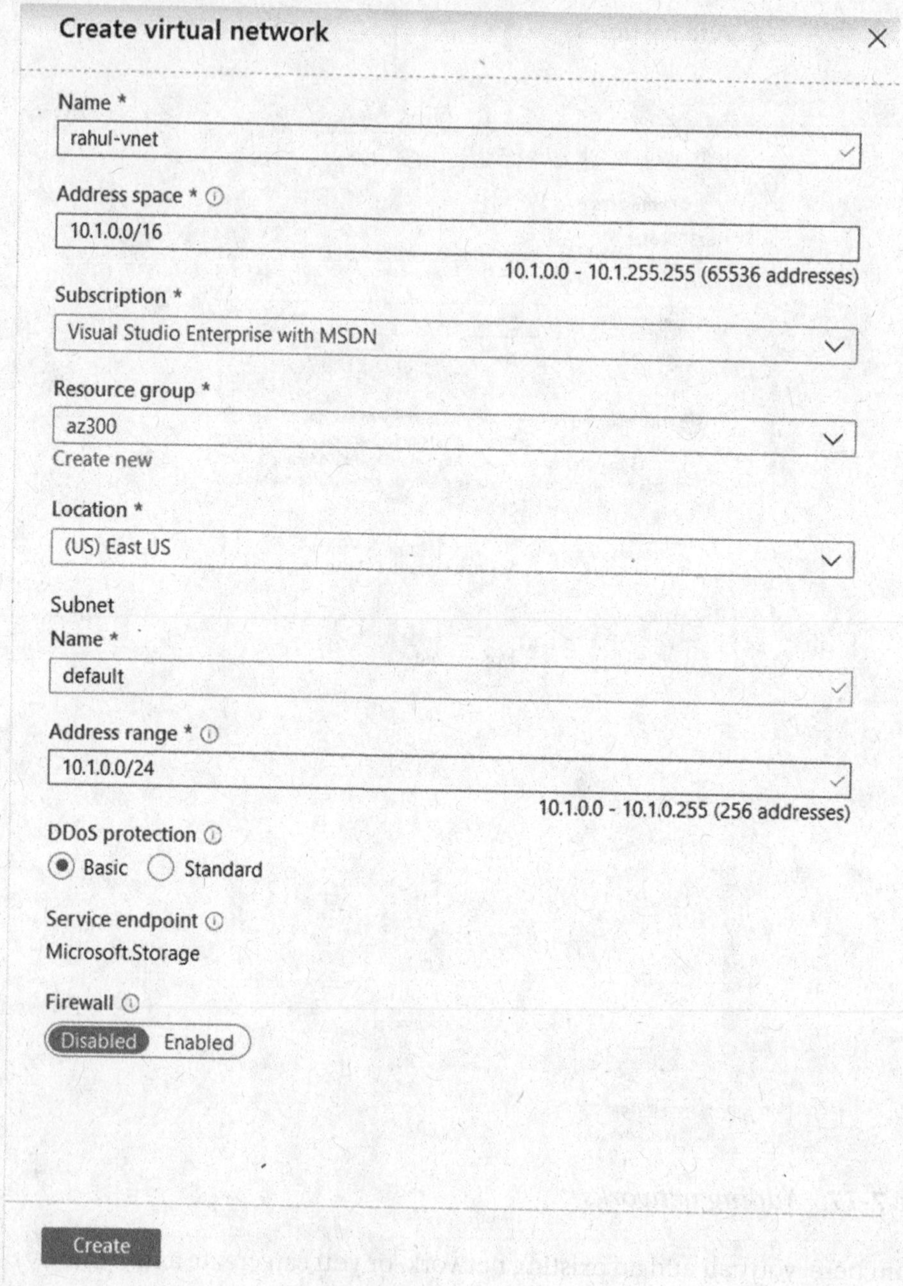

Figure 7-18. *Creating a virtual network*

Here, I have just kept the default settings. If you want to modify the address space, you can certainly do that. Upon creation, the screen looks like Figure 7-19.

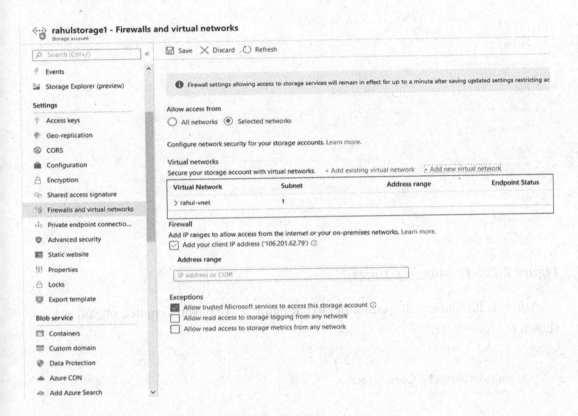

Figure 7-19. *Firewall and virtual networks*

You can also configure a firewall from this page. Basically, you can whitelist the required IPs. Save the settings and return to the overview page.

Configuring a Container

Let's go ahead and configure a container. Click Containers, as shown in Figure 7-20.

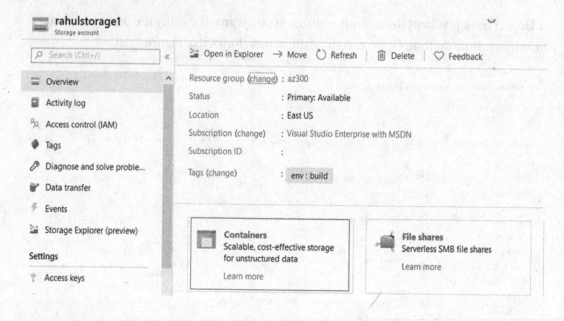

Figure 7-20. Container settings

You can click an existing container to configure it; we haven't created on yet, as shown in Figure 7-21.

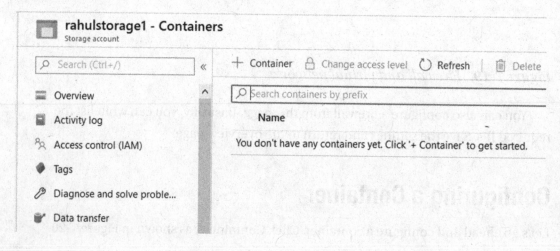

Figure 7-21. Container settings page

Let's go ahead and create a new container now by clicking Container at the top, as shown in Figure 7-22.

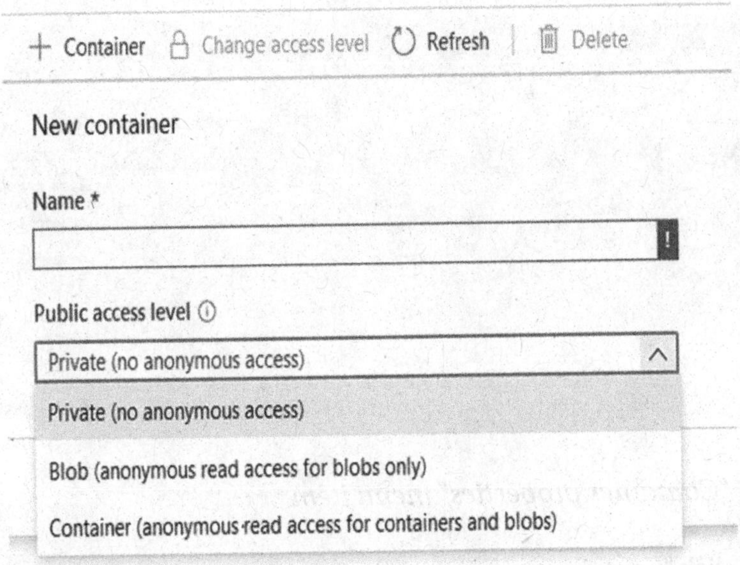

Figure 7-22. *"New container" settings*

I will select the first one listed and continue, as shown in Figure 7-23.

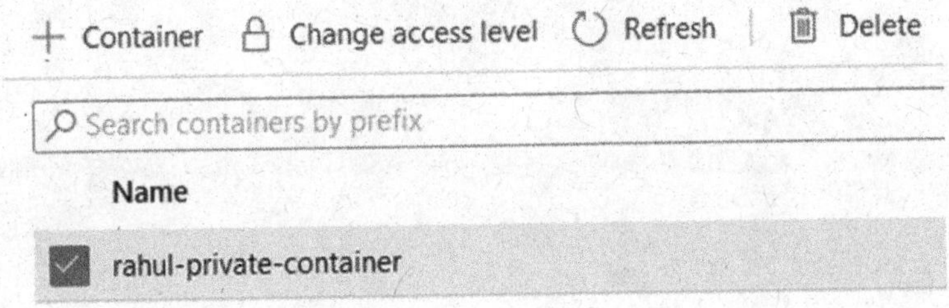

Figure 7-23. *Selected private container*

By clicking "Container properties," you will get the URL to access the storage. But it won't be accessible publicly, as shown in Figure 7-24.

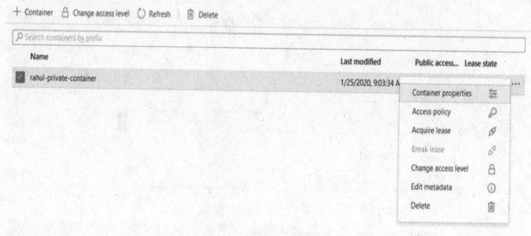

Figure 7-24. *"Container properties" menu item*

When you click "Container properties," the Properties page opens, as shown in Figure 7-25.

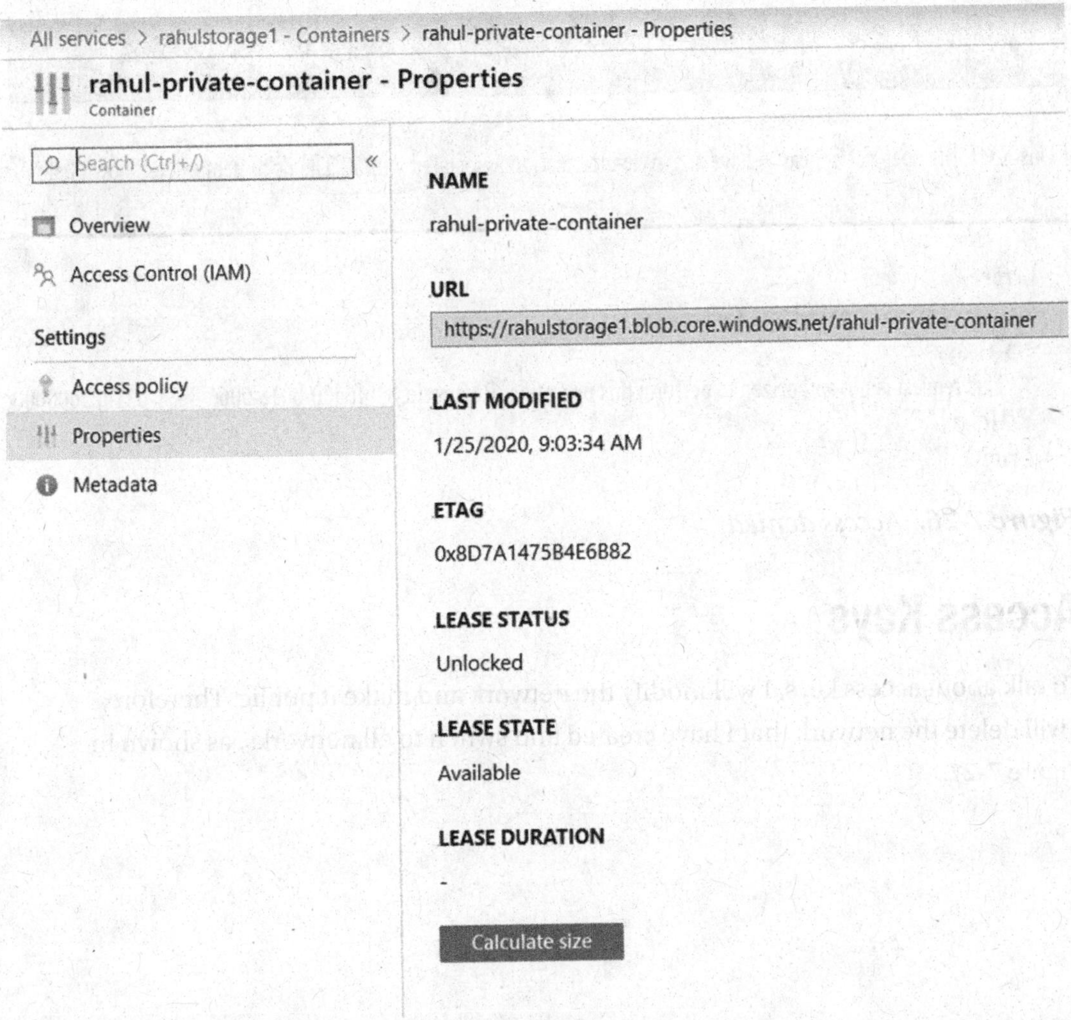

All services > rahulstorage1 - Containers > rahul-private-container - Properties

⫴ rahul-private-container - Properties
Container

🔍 Search (Ctrl+/) «
🖥 Overview
🧑 Access Control (IAM)
Settings
🔑 Access policy
⫴ Properties
ⓘ Metadata

NAME

rahul-private-container

URL

https://rahulstorage1.blob.core.windows.net/rahul-private-container

LAST MODIFIED

1/25/2020, 9:03:34 AM

ETAG

0x8D7A1475B4E6B82

LEASE STATUS

Unlocked

LEASE STATE

Available

LEASE DURATION

-

Calculate size

Figure 7-25. *Private container properties*

If you try to access the URL, it will return a 401 error, as shown in Figure 7-26.

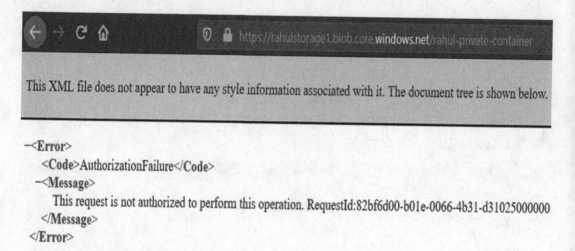

```
-<Error>
    <Code>AuthorizationFailure</Code>
  -<Message>
      This request is not authorized to perform this operation. RequestId:82bf6d00-b01e-0066-4b31-d31025000000
    </Message>
  </Error>
```

Figure 7-26. *Access denied*

Access Keys

To talk about access keys, I will modify the network and make it public. Therefore, I will delete the network that I have created and switch to all networks, as shown in Figure 7-27.

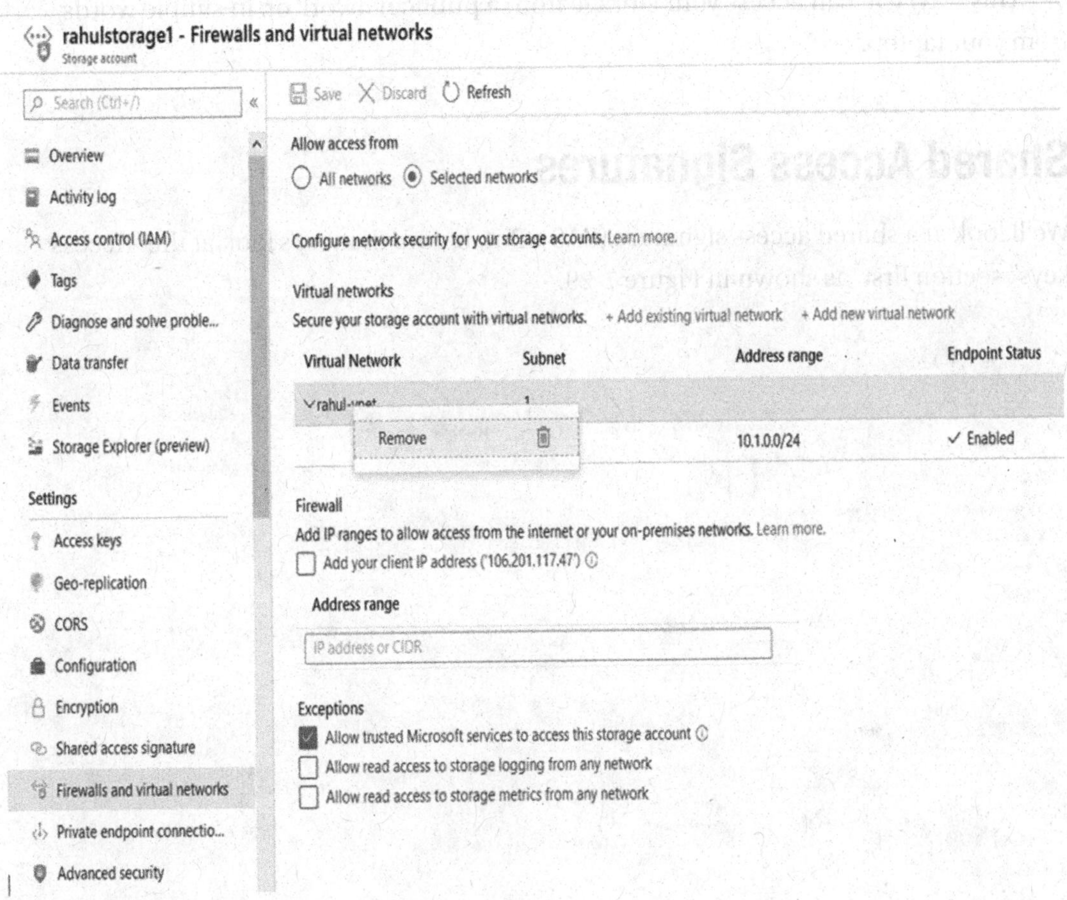

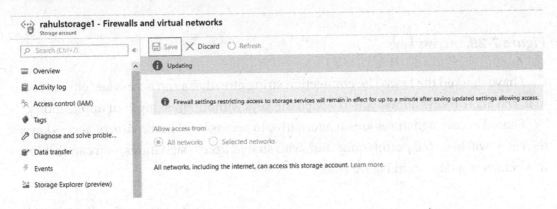

Figure 7-27. *Firewall and virtual network settings*

Figure 7-28 shows the settings updating.

Figure 7-28. *Settings updating*

This way, you can access your storage from a public network or, in simple words, from your laptop.

Shared Access Signatures

We'll look at a shared access signature (SAS). But, before that, let's look at the "Access keys" section first, as shown in Figure 7-29.

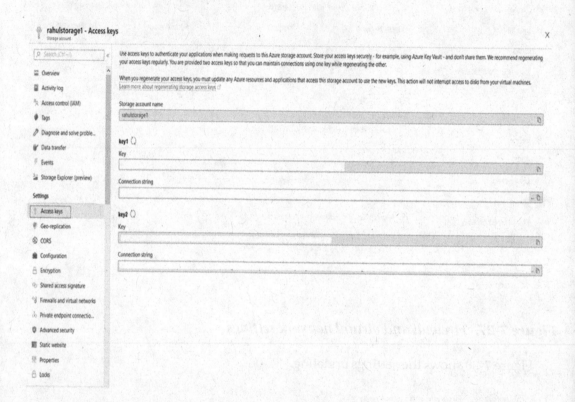

Figure 7-29. *Access keys*

I have masked the keys. The connection string already has an access key embedded in it. Having two keys allows you to switch the keys without breaking your applications.

Shared access signatures are an alternative to access keys. In the case of access keys, the client will have full permissions. But, with shared access signatures, you can restrict this behavior, as shown in Figure 7-30.

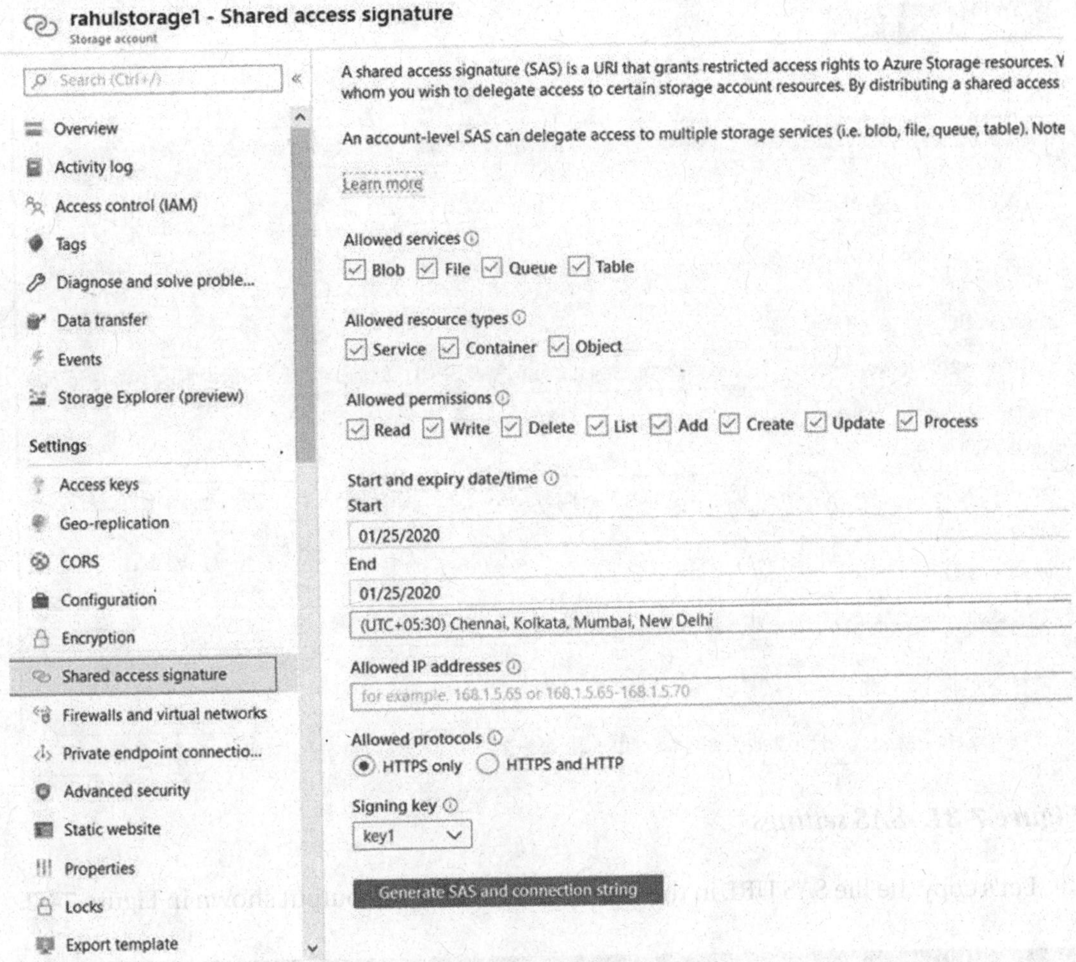

rahulstorage1 - Shared access signature
Storage account

Search (Ctrl+/)

- Overview
- Activity log
- Access control (IAM)
- Tags
- Diagnose and solve proble...
- Data transfer
- Events
- Storage Explorer (preview)

Settings

- Access keys
- Geo-replication
- CORS
- Configuration
- Encryption
- Shared access signature
- Firewalls and virtual networks
- Private endpoint connectio...
- Advanced security
- Static website
- Properties
- Locks
- Export template

A shared access signature (SAS) is a URI that grants restricted access rights to Azure Storage resources. Y whom you wish to delegate access to certain storage account resources. By distributing a shared access

An account-level SAS can delegate access to multiple storage services (i.e. blob, file, queue, table). Note

Learn more

Allowed services ⓘ
☑ Blob ☑ File ☑ Queue ☑ Table

Allowed resource types ⓘ
☑ Service ☑ Container ☑ Object

Allowed permissions ⓘ
☑ Read ☑ Write ☑ Delete ☑ List ☑ Add ☑ Create ☑ Update ☑ Process

Start and expiry date/time ⓘ
Start
01/25/2020
End
01/25/2020
(UTC+05:30) Chennai, Kolkata, Mumbai, New Delhi

Allowed IP addresses ⓘ
for example. 168.1.5.65 or 168.1.5.65-168.1.5.70

Allowed protocols ⓘ
◉ HTTPS only ○ HTTPS and HTTP

Signing key ⓘ
key1

Generate SAS and connection string

Figure 7-30. *"Shared access signature" screen*

Notice at the bottom that we are signing this with an access key. Now, click the button "Generate SAS and connecting string." This page shown in Figure 7-31 will open.

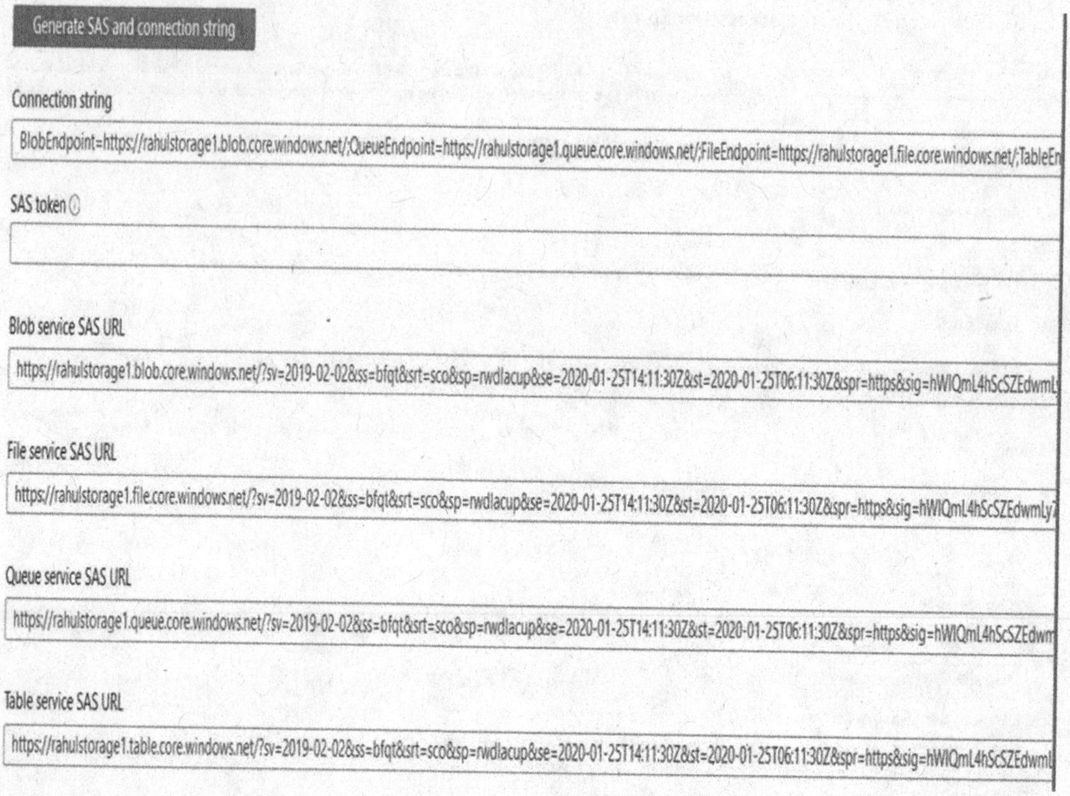

Generate SAS and connection string

Connection string

BlobEndpoint=https://rahulstorage1.blob.core.windows.net/;QueueEndpoint=https://rahulstorage1.queue.core.windows.net/;FileEndpoint=https://rahulstorage1.file.core.windows.net/;TableEn

SAS token ⓘ

Blob service SAS URL

https://rahulstorage1.blob.core.windows.net/?sv=2019-02-02&ss=bfqt&srt=sco&sp=rwdlacup&se=2020-01-25T14:11:30Z&st=2020-01-25T06:11:30Z&spr=https&sig=hWIQmL4hScSZEdwmL

File service SAS URL

https://rahulstorage1.file.core.windows.net/?sv=2019-02-02&ss=bfqt&srt=sco&sp=rwdlacup&se=2020-01-25T14:11:30Z&st=2020-01-25T06:11:30Z&spr=https&sig=hWIQmL4hScSZEdwmLy

Queue service SAS URL

https://rahulstorage1.queue.core.windows.net/?sv=2019-02-02&ss=bfqt&srt=sco&sp=rwdlacup&se=2020-01-25T14:11:30Z&st=2020-01-25T06:11:30Z&spr=https&sig=hWIQmL4hScSZEdwm

Table service SAS URL

https://rahulstorage1.table.core.windows.net/?sv=2019-02-02&ss=bfqt&srt=sco&sp=rwdlacup&se=2020-01-25T14:11:30Z&st=2020-01-25T06:11:30Z&spr=https&sig=hWIQmL4hScSZEdwmL

Figure 7-31. *SAS settings*

Let's copy the file SAS URL in the browser. It gave me the output shown in Figure 7-32.

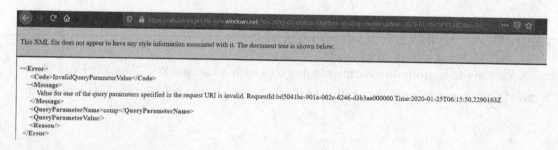

Figure 7-32. *Invalid URL*

This didn't work because we haven't supplied a key to it. However, when you supply it with a key, the URL will work. One point to note here is that if you revoke your access keys, then you have to regenerate the SAS with a new key; otherwise, it will become invalid.

Using Azure Storage Explorer

On the overview page, you can open Storage Explorer in two ways, as shown in Figure 7-33.

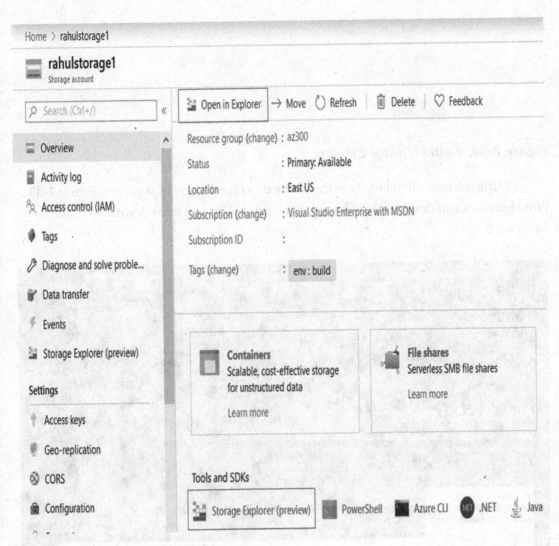

Figure 7-33. *Opening Storage Explorer*

This will bring up the screen shown in Figure 7-34.

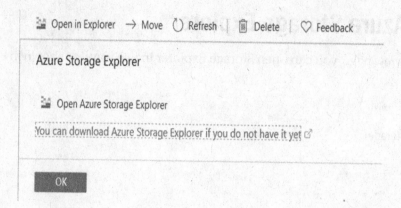

Figure 7-34. *Azure Storage Explorer*

Clicking the link will take you to the utility download page, as shown in Figure 7-35. From here you can download the kit and get started. You can even download different flavors of it.

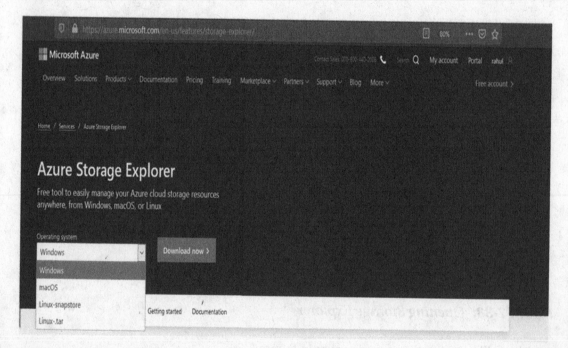

Figure 7-35. *Storage Explorer download*

Or, you can use the web version, as highlighted in Figure 7-36.

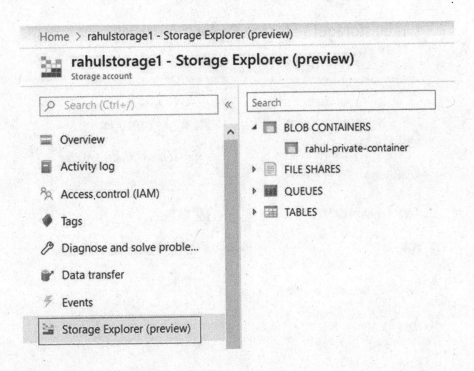

Figure 7-36. *Storage Explorer preview*

From the Storage Explorer, you can upload/download files, open files, create a new folder, and more, as shown in Figure 7-37.

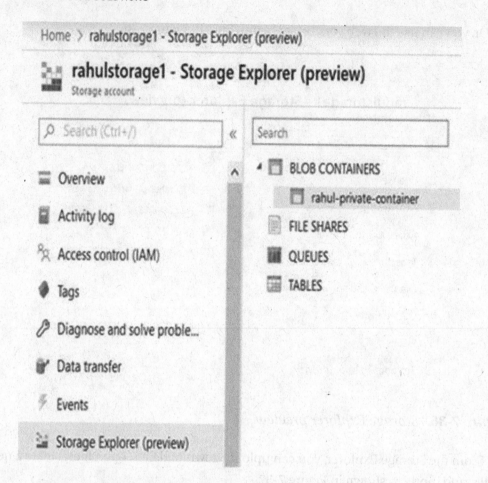

Figure 7-37. *Private container settings*

Clicking rahul-private-container will open a new window, as shown in Figure 7-38.

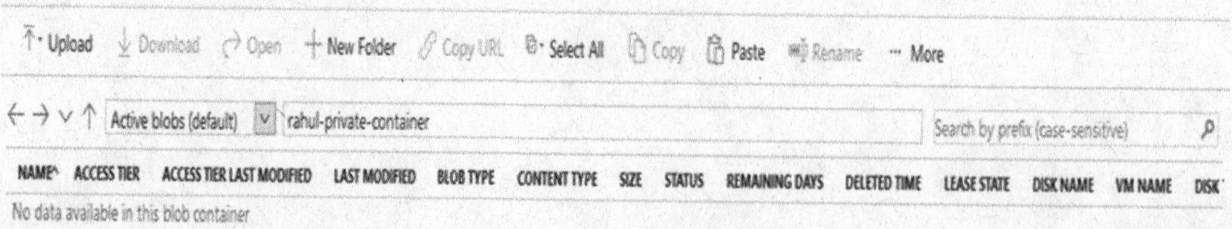

NAME^	ACCESS TIER	ACCESS TIER LAST MODIFIED	LAST MODIFIED	BLOB TYPE	CONTENT TYPE	SIZE	STATUS	REMAINING DAYS	DELETED TIME	LEASE STATE	DISK NAME	VM NAME	DISK

No data available in this blob container

Figure 7-38. *Private container*

Now, let's go ahead and create a new folder from here. This will open a new dialog box, as shown in Figure 7-39.

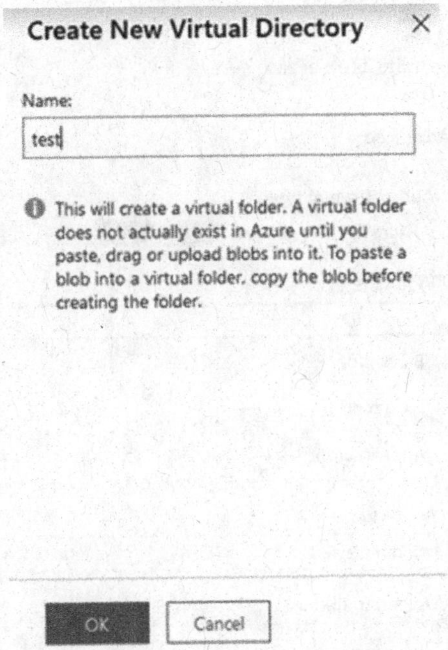

Create New Virtual Directory   ✕

Name:

```
test
```

ⓘ This will create a virtual folder. A virtual folder
  does not actually exist in Azure until you
  paste, drag or upload blobs into it. To paste a
  blob into a virtual folder, copy the blob before
  creating the folder.

[OK]   [Cancel]

Figure 7-39. *New virtual directory*

Now, you can click the Upload button on the test directory, as shown in Figure 7-40.

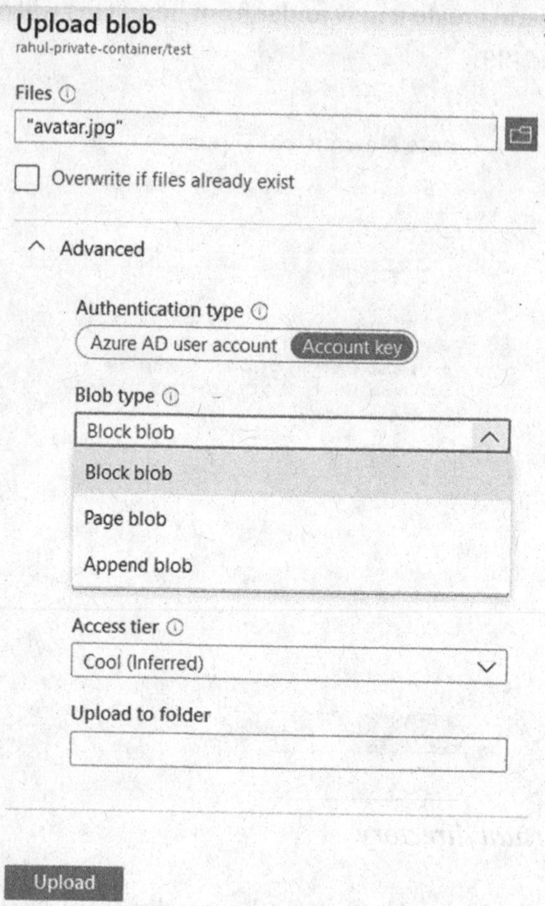

Figure 7-40. *Uploading a blob*

Three types are available, as shown in Figure 7-41.

- Block blobs are mainly meant for images and videos stored with full filenames. However, they can also store text.

- Page blobs mean you can access individual pages in that blob.

- Append blobs are just meant for log files or files that are meant to be appended. But, in this case, I am fine with block blobs.

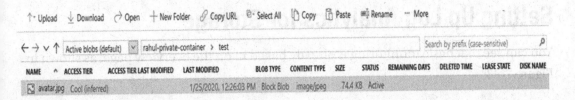

Figure 7-41. *Image uploaded*

You can also see an image's properties by right-clicking it, as shown in Figure 7-42.

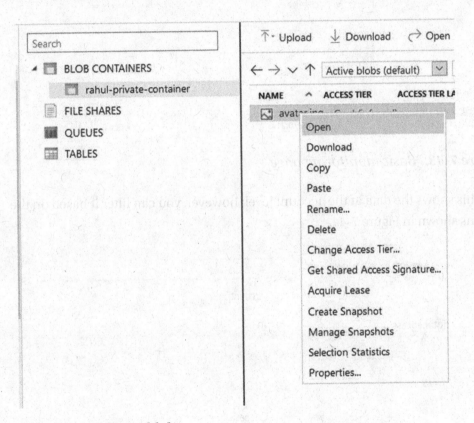

Figure 7-42. *Uploading a blob*

Setting Up Log Analytics for Storage

You can see that basic monitoring is already baked in on the overview page, as shown in Figure 7-43.

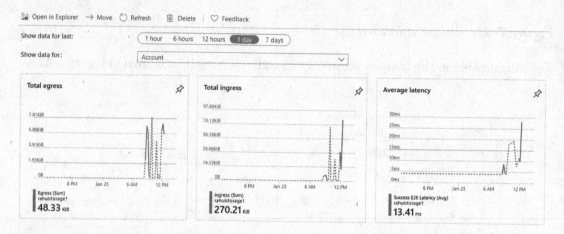

Figure 7-43. *Basic monitoring page*

This shows the data at the account level; however, you can filter it based on the options shown in Figure 7-44.

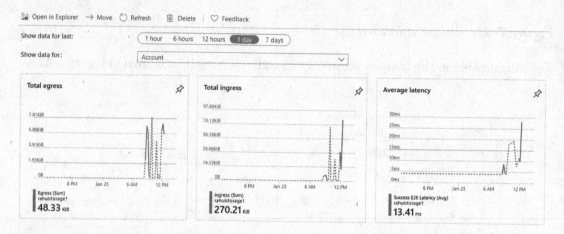

Figure 7-44. *Filter options*

When you search for *Log Analytics* under "All services" in the Azure portal, you will see the screen shown in Figure 7-45.

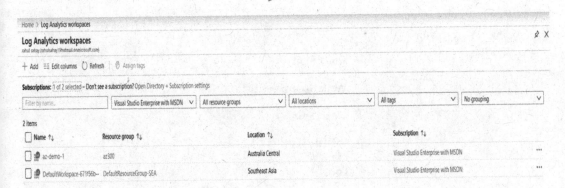

Figure 7-45. *Log Analytics workspace*

This is the same Log Analytics workspace that I created earlier. Let's look at the different resources that are here, as shown in Figure 7-46.

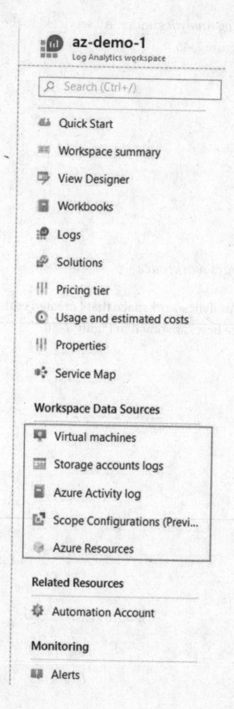

Figure 7-46. *Workspace data sources*

Let's add the storage account logs as the data source, as shown in Figure 7-47.

Figure 7-47. Storage account logs

This will bring up the screen shown in Figure 7-48.

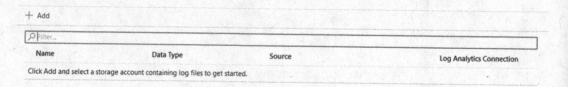

Figure 7-48. *Adding a storage account log*

Click Add and enter the details shown in Figure 7-49.

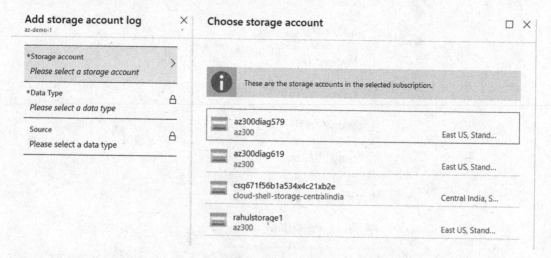

Figure 7-49. *Choosing a storage account*

Select the storage account, as shown in Figure 7-49. Then select the data type, as shown in Figure 7-50.

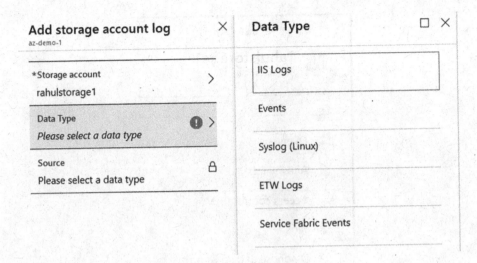

Figure 7-50. *Choosing a data type*

If you are using a storage account for logging purposes, then you can definitely add one of them. But, at the top level, the Azure activity is going to monitor ingress and egress traffic to the storage account.

Setting Up Azure AD Authentication for Storage

Azure gives you many different ways to access the content of the storage account. You have already learned about access keys and shared access signatures. Microsoft also offers role-based access control (RBAC), as shown in Figure 7-51.

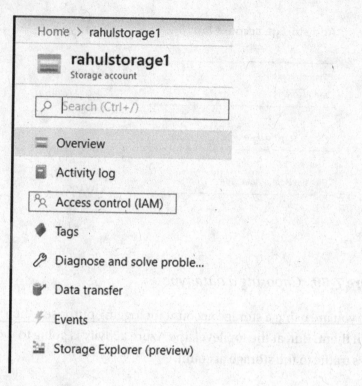

Figure 7-51. *Access control (IAM)*

Click the "Access control (IAM)" item, as highlighted in Figure 7-51. This will bring up the screen in Figure 7-52.

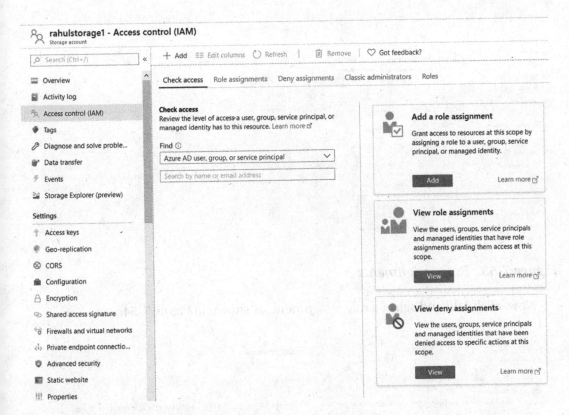

Figure 7-52. Checking the access page

This access control is pretty familiar and available to almost every resource. You can now click to view the role assignments. You will see the list of applications that are granted access, as shown in Figure 7-53.

Figure 7-53. *Role assignments*

Now, click Add and select a role assignment, as shown in Figure 7-54.

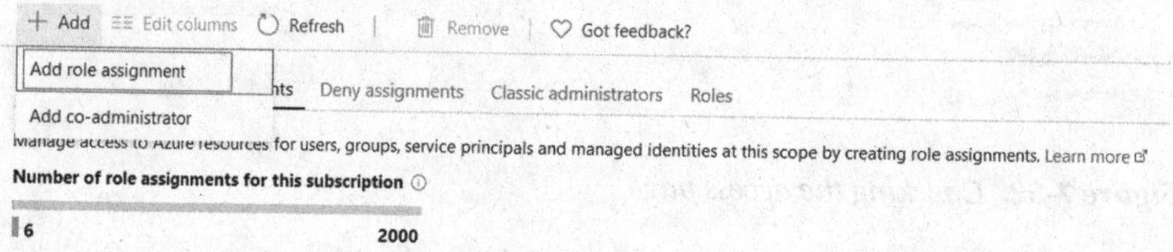

Figure 7-54. *Adding role assignments*

You can see variety of role assignments that can be assigned to the user. As you can see, by default I have six role assignments assigned for this subscription. In your case, it may differ, but here you can increase or decrease the role assignments as per your needs, as shown in Figure 7-55.

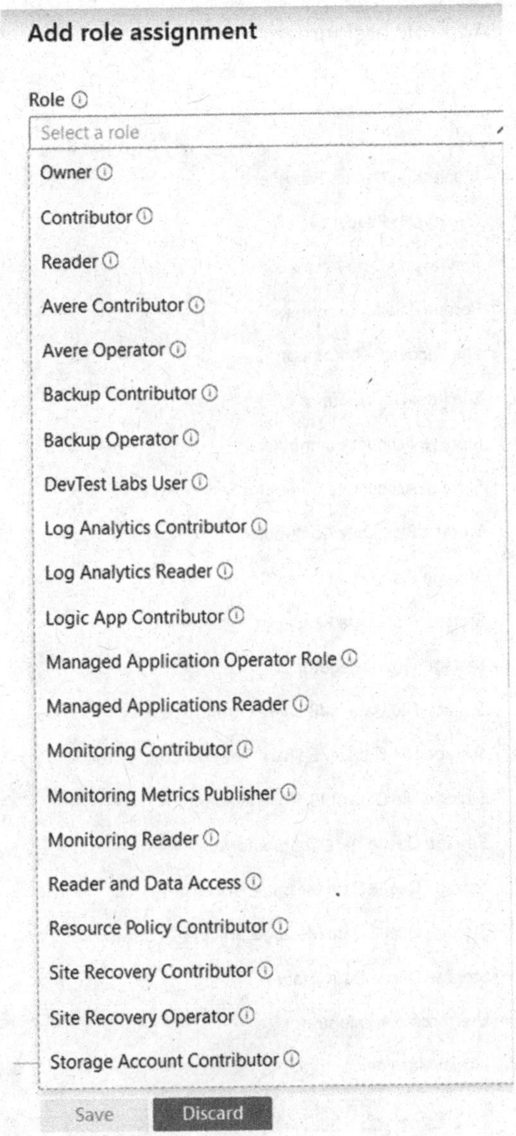

Add role assignment

Role ⓘ

Select a role

Owner ⓘ

Contributor ⓘ

Reader ⓘ

Avere Contributor ⓘ

Avere Operator ⓘ

Backup Contributor ⓘ

Backup Operator ⓘ

DevTest Labs User ⓘ

Log Analytics Contributor ⓘ

Log Analytics Reader ⓘ

Logic App Contributor ⓘ

Managed Application Operator Role ⓘ

Managed Applications Reader ⓘ

Monitoring Contributor ⓘ

Monitoring Metrics Publisher ⓘ

Monitoring Reader ⓘ

Reader and Data Access ⓘ

Resource Policy Contributor ⓘ

Site Recovery Contributor ⓘ

Site Recovery Operator ⓘ

Storage Account Contributor ⓘ

Save   Discard

Figure 7-55. *Adding a role assignment*

You can grant access to an owner, contributor, reader, etc. If you scroll further down, then you can see the storage-level access, as shown in Figure 7-56.

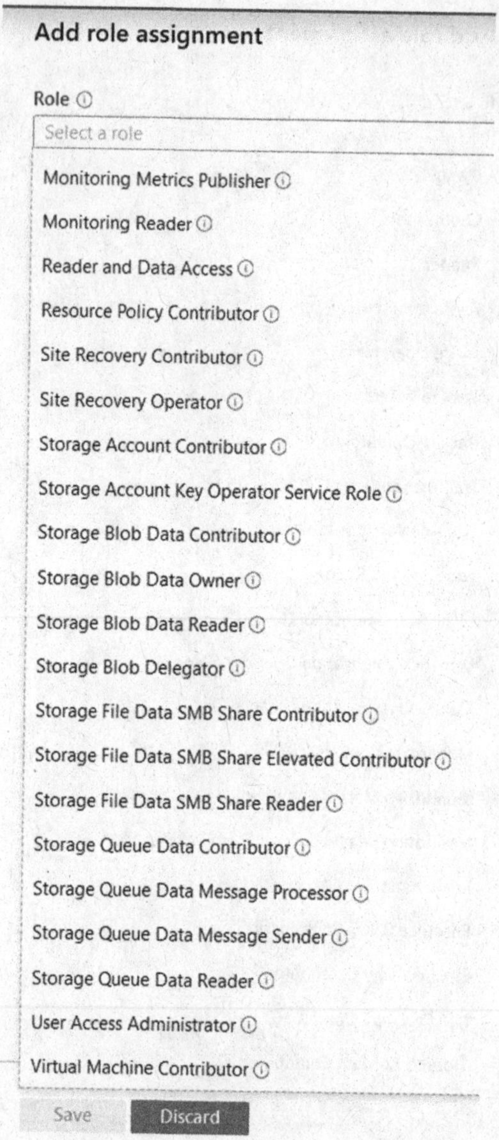

Add role assignment

Role ⓘ

Select a role

Monitoring Metrics Publisher ⓘ

Monitoring Reader ⓘ

Reader and Data Access ⓘ

Resource Policy Contributor ⓘ

Site Recovery Contributor ⓘ

Site Recovery Operator ⓘ

Storage Account Contributor ⓘ

Storage Account Key Operator Service Role ⓘ

Storage Blob Data Contributor ⓘ

Storage Blob Data Owner ⓘ

Storage Blob Data Reader ⓘ

Storage Blob Delegator ⓘ

Storage File Data SMB Share Contributor ⓘ

Storage File Data SMB Share Elevated Contributor ⓘ

Storage File Data SMB Share Reader ⓘ

Storage Queue Data Contributor ⓘ

Storage Queue Data Message Processor ⓘ

Storage Queue Data Message Sender ⓘ

Storage Queue Data Reader ⓘ

User Access Administrator ⓘ

Virtual Machine Contributor ⓘ

Save   Discard

Figure 7-56. *Role assignments list*

Let's add one, as shown in Figure 5-57.

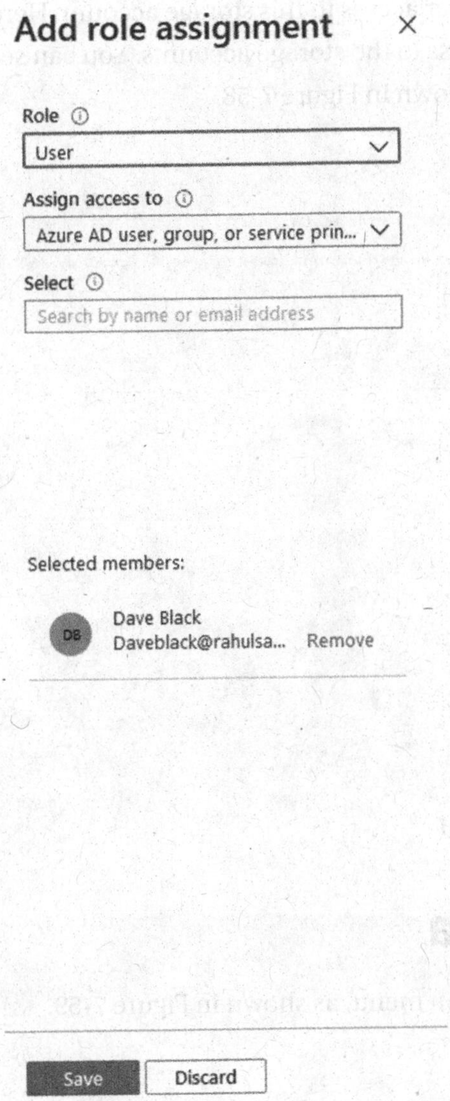

Add role assignment   ✕

Role ⓘ

| User | ∨ |

Assign access to ⓘ

| Azure AD user, group, or service prin... | ∨ |

Select ⓘ

| Search by name or email address |

Selected members:

DB   Dave Black
         Daveblack@rahulsa...   Remove

| Save | Discard |

Figure 7-57. *Adding a role assignment*

I have given Dave Black storage blob reader access. This will take a couple of minutes to propagate. Any application that authenticates with Azure AD with a user named Dave Black will have reader access to this storage account. Here we are using role-based access to control the access to the storage accounts. You can see that the user is added to the storage account, as shown in Figure 7-58.

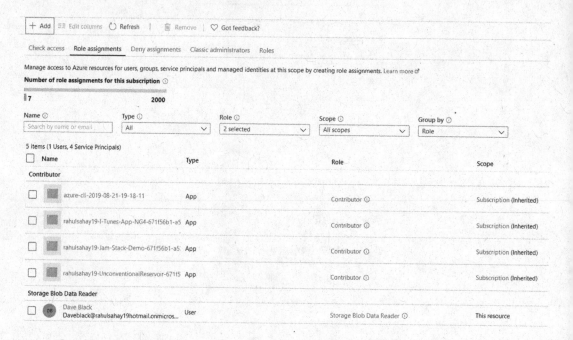

Figure 7-58. *User added*

Replicating Data

Let's click the Configuration menu, as shown in Figure 7-59.

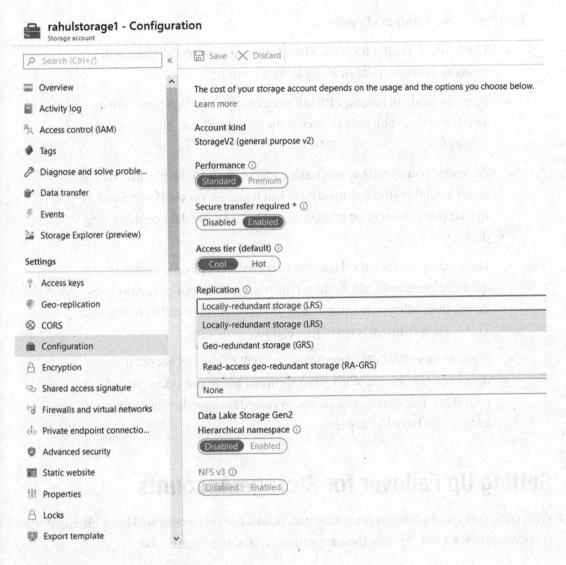

Figure 7-59. Storage configuration

Here, you have a couple of options.

- LRS is the default. LRS is the cheapest option, wherein Microsoft is going to keep the data in its local data center.

- The downside of having LRS is if the entire data center goes down. Then, you won't be able to access the data until the data center gets restored.

- To rescue you from that scenario, ZRS comes into the picture, which is not available in the drop-down, but it can be set via PowerShell. In that case, you will be protected against a single data center going down.

- The next option is GRS. This makes sure that your data center is in a different geography altogether. This means if the entire region goes down, then Microsoft can retrieve your data from a different region. This is an additional level of protection.

- If you choose RA-GRS, then Microsoft will have read access to your data from other area. With other options, Microsoft takes care of your data. You don't have access to your data specifically. With read access, you have the access.

Setting Up Failover for Storage Accounts

With GRS, you can do failover on storage accounts. For this example, I have changed the replication to RA-GRS. To view the properties of GRS, see Figure 7-60.

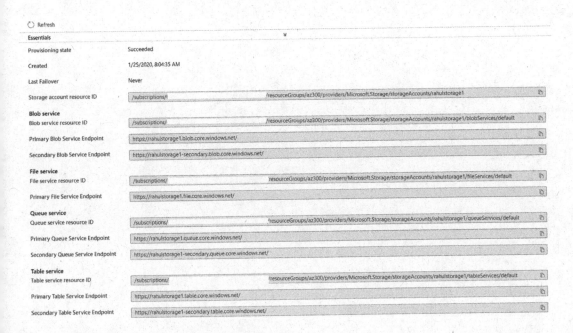

Figure 7-60. Replication properties

This basically means that when your primary data center goes out, you can use the secondary data center keys to replicate the same data. Currently, at the time of this writing, this is a preview feature only.

CHAPTER 8

Managing Virtual Networks

An Azure virtual network (aka a VNet) is a representation of your network in the cloud. It is a logical isolation of the cloud tied to your subscription. You can use VNets to provision and manage virtual private networks (VPNs) in Azure. You can also connect VNets with another VNets with a variety of techniques. Each VNet you create has its own Classless Internet Domain Routing (CIDR) block and can be linked with other VNets as long as the CIDR blocks do not overlap.

Virtual networking is the backbone that allows resources to talk to each other in different regions or in the same region. There are various techniques Microsoft offers to allow us to do that.

Creating a Virtual Network

Let's start by creating a virtual network. You can search in "All services" for *virtual network*. This will take you to the screen shown in Figure 8-1.

Figure 8-1. *Virtual networks search page*

237

© Rahul Sahay 2020
R. Sahay, *Microsoft Azure Architect Technologies Study Companion*,
https://doi.org/10.1007/978-1-4842-6200-9_8

Let's click Add, which will present the screen shown in Figure 8-2. Let's fill in the details first.

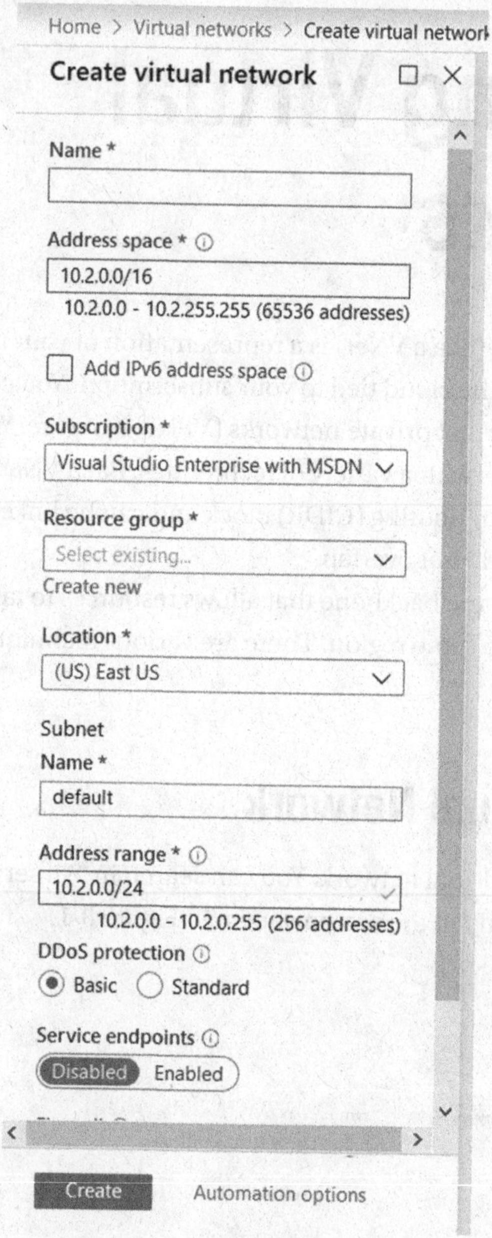

Figure 8-2. Virtual network creation screen

The first big decision you have to make is about the address space. Since this is private address space, you can use any range you want.

The Internet authorities have reserved IP addresses starting with 10 for private use. There are some other ranges such as 192.168, etc., but you can use any random network address such as 190.0.0.0, because it's mapped under a private virtual network. Hence, that's what I will use in this example.

Also, I will create a new resource group while sitting in India.

Each virtual network needs to have one subnet at a minimum. A *subnet*, as the name implies, is part of the virtual network. I have called my subnet *frontend*.

The reason why you will want to use subnets is because you might want to divide your tiers into the frontend, backend, middleware, or firewall, which can be mapped to specific subnets. Hence, you should keep some kind of buffer for each subnet.

If you are sure that you are not going to need any additional address space for subnets, then you can simply copy the same address space into the subnet itself.

This address naming scheme is called Classless Inter-domain Routing notation. This is an alternative to what was called the A block, B block, C block, etc.

For distributed denial-of-service (DDOS) protection, I have chosen basic. Basically, this will make it harder for people to send traffic to this network in a malicious manner.

If you upgrade to a standard subscription, then you can do more adaptive tuning. It sends notifications for any kind DDOS attacks.

Service endpoints are a pretty cool security feature. If you enable this option, your screen will look like Figure 8-3.

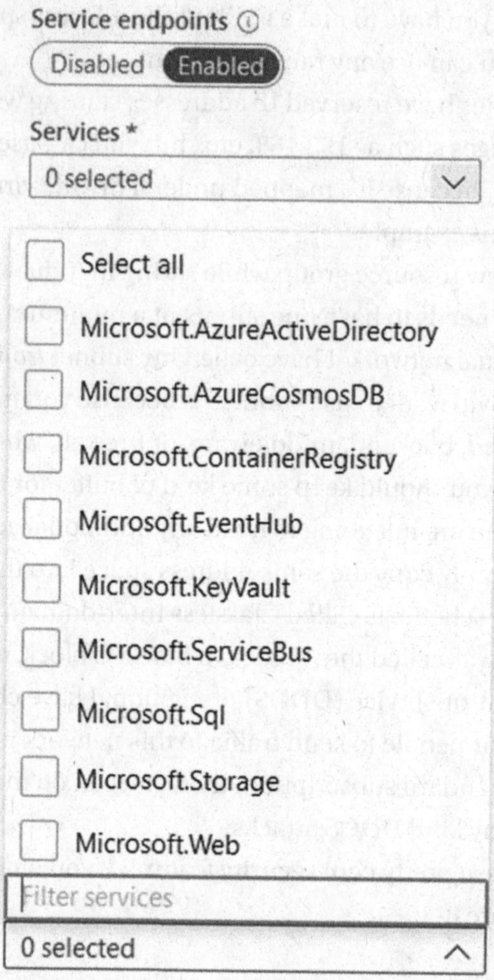

Service endpoints ⓘ

Disabled   **Enabled**

Services *

| 0 selected | ⌄ |

☐ Select all

☐ Microsoft.AzureActiveDirectory

☐ Microsoft.AzureCosmosDB

☐ Microsoft.ContainerRegistry

☐ Microsoft.EventHub

☐ Microsoft.KeyVault

☐ Microsoft.ServiceBus

☐ Microsoft.Sql

☐ Microsoft.Storage

☐ Microsoft.Web

Filter services

| 0 selected | ⌃ |

Figure 8-3. *Service endpoints options*

This means you can open this virtual network to exclusively connect with some of the built-in Azure services. You can set the virtual network to connect to any of these services on this secure channel, which means traffic won't be traveling on the open Internet.

Without it, the traffic that goes from these addresses into the resources in this network will travel on an open network.

Optionally, you can enable a firewall with a new subnet on a standard SKU, as shown in Figure 8-4.

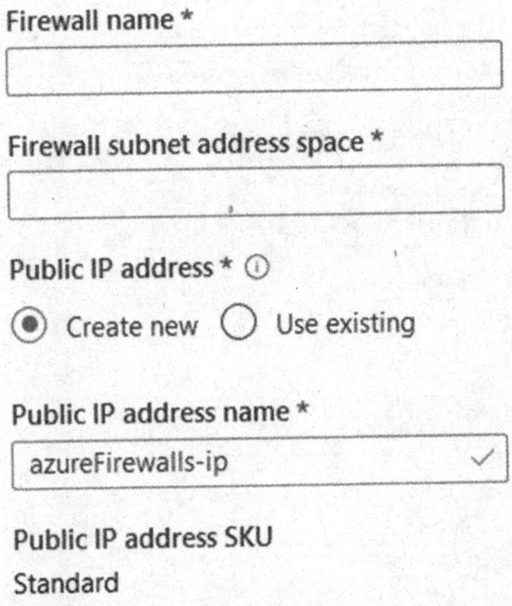

Firewall name *

Firewall subnet address space *

Public IP address * ⓘ

◉ Create new   ◯ Use existing

Public IP address name *

azureFirewalls-ip   ✓

Public IP address SKU
Standard

Figure 8-4. *Firewall settings*

Enabling this will cost you extra. Figure 8-5 shows the completed settings.

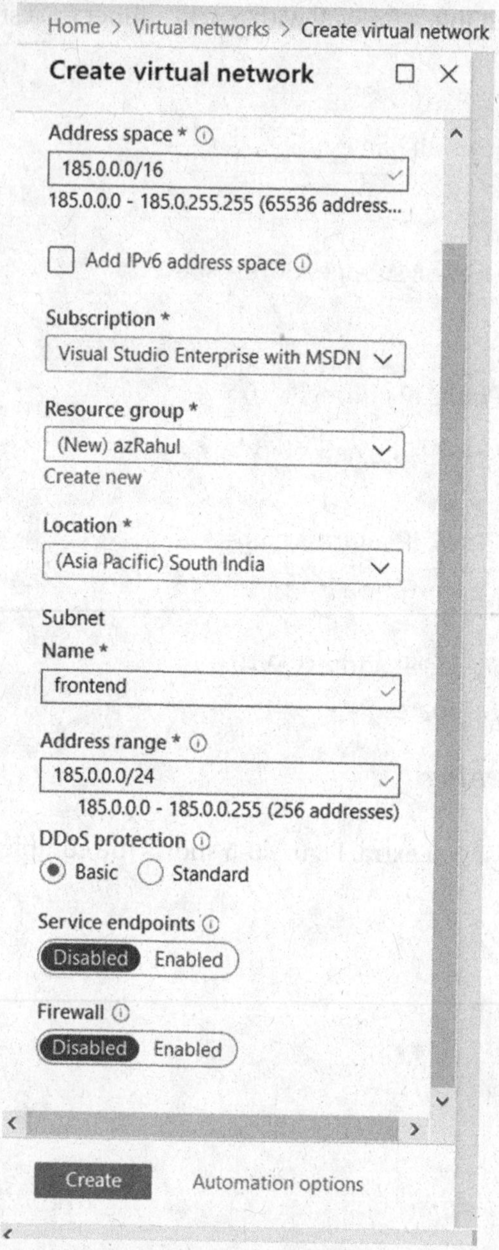

Figure 8-5. *Virtual network finished page*

Once the virtual network is created, you will see the Overview page for it, as shown in Figure 8-6.

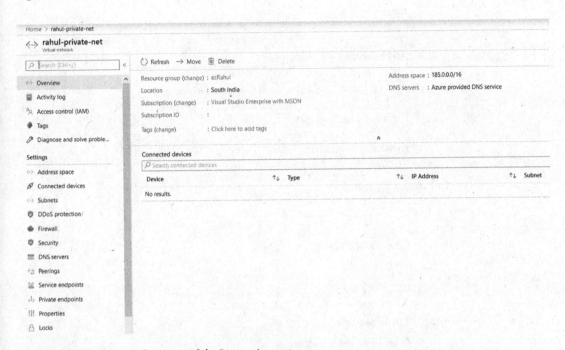

Figure 8-6. *Virtual network's Overview page*

As you can see, by default, there are no connected devices, of course. But, you do have a subnet associated with this VNet. Click Subnets, as shown in the left menu. This will list the newly created subnet, as shown in Figure 8-7.

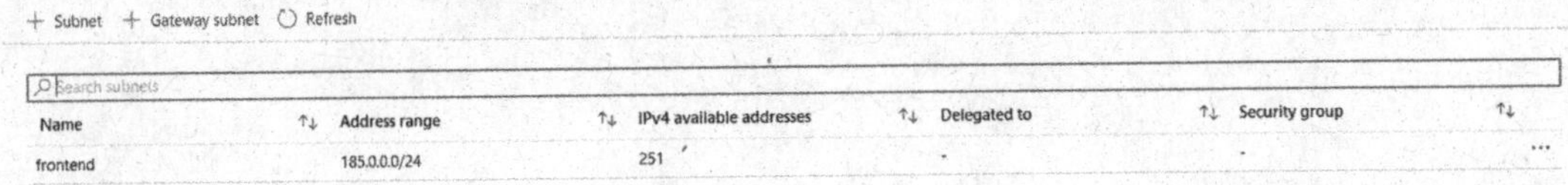

Name	Address range	IPv4 available addresses	Delegated to	Security group
frontend	185.0.0.0/24	251		

Figure 8-7. *Subnet screen*

Here, I have 251 available addresses. You can also create a subnet from here by clicking + Subnet. This will take you to the screen in Figure 8-8.

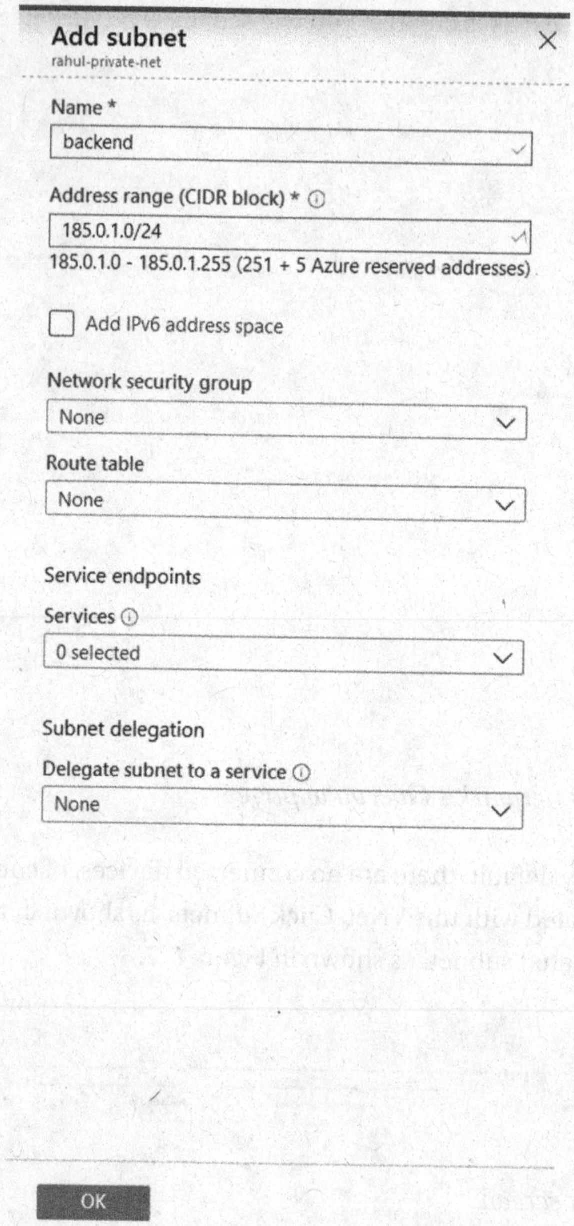

Add subnet   ✕
rahul-private-net

Name *

backend

Address range (CIDR block) * ⓘ

185.0.1.0/24

185.0.1.0 - 185.0.1.255 (251 + 5 Azure reserved addresses)

☐ Add IPv6 address space

Network security group

None   ⌄

Route table

None   ⌄

Service endpoints

Services ⓘ

0 selected   ⌄

Subnet delegation

Delegate subnet to a service ⓘ

None   ⌄

OK

Figure 8-8. *Adding a subnet*

Here, I won't make any changes. I will discuss network security groups and other options later in the chapter . As you can see, I have two subnets, as shown in Figure 8-9.

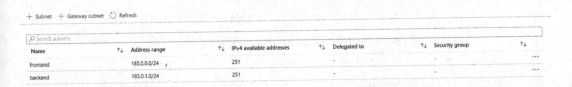

Name	Address range	IPv4 available addresses	Delegated to	Security group	
frontend	185.0.0.0/24	251	-	-	...
backend	185.0.1.0/24	251	-	-	...

Figure 8-9. *Subnet list*

Setting Up Public and Private IP Addresses

At the beginning of this chapter, you saw that these addresses are private. So, how do you create public IP addresses? To start, search for *public IP* in "All services," as shown in Figure 8-10.

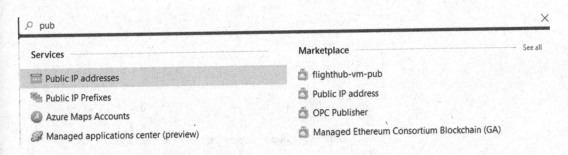

Figure 8-10. *IP address page*

Click "Public IP addresses," which will bring you to the screen shown in Figure 8-11.

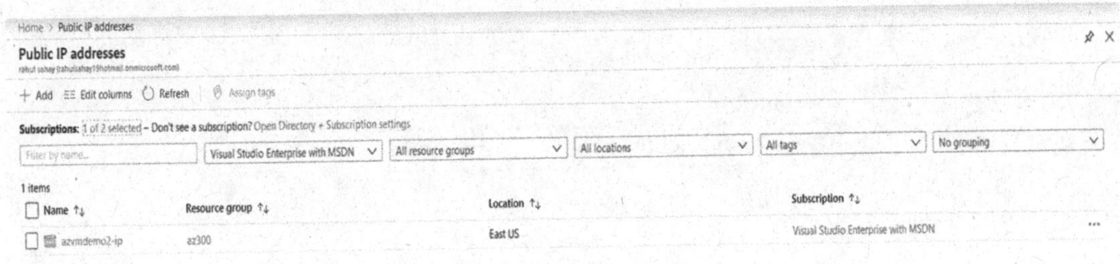

Figure 8-11. *Public IP addresses*

Here, I already have one public IP address that was created automatically when I was creating a VM. Let's go ahead and create one now by clicking the Add button. This will bring up the screen shown in Figure 8-12.

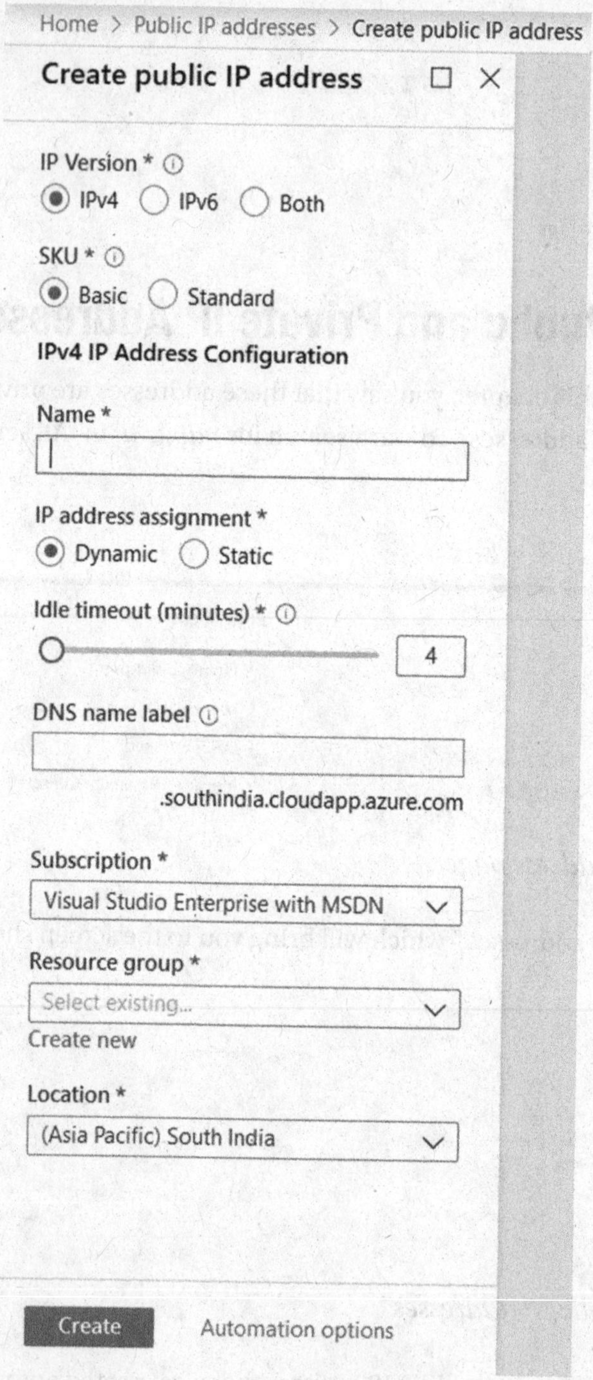

Home > Public IP addresses > Create public IP address

Create public IP address   □   ×

IP Version * ⓘ
◉ IPv4   ○ IPv6   ○ Both

SKU * ⓘ
◉ Basic   ○ Standard

IPv4 IP Address Configuration

Name *

IP address assignment *
◉ Dynamic   ○ Static

Idle timeout (minutes) * ⓘ

○───────────────────── | 4 |

DNS name label ⓘ

.southindia.cloudapp.azure.com

Subscription *
| Visual Studio Enterprise with MSDN   ⌄ |

Resource group *
| Select existing...   ⌄ |
Create new

Location *
| (Asia Pacific) South India   ⌄ |

Create   Automation options

Figure 8-12. *Public IP creation*

One thing to note here is that the public IP SKU plan must match the load balancer SKU.

You do have an option to configure IPv6 at the load balancer level. But, if you like to use it, then you need to put a load balancer in front of it so that IPv6 traffic will travel into the virtual machine and be converted from an IPv6 IP address to an IPv4 address.

You have a choice between dynamic IP addresses and static IP addresses. A static IP address is an address that never changes. This is good when you want the IP address in some kind of settings like firewall need to be opened up or DNS registration, etc.

In addition, you can choose a connection opening timeout. The default is four minutes. Then, you can enter fully qualified name.

Now, you can map DNS name label to a custom domain name; if you need to use your domain name registrar, you can use a cname record.

You get an IPv4 address for free, but you can create an IPv6 address for an extra cost. Having said that, Figure 8-13 shows my final choice.

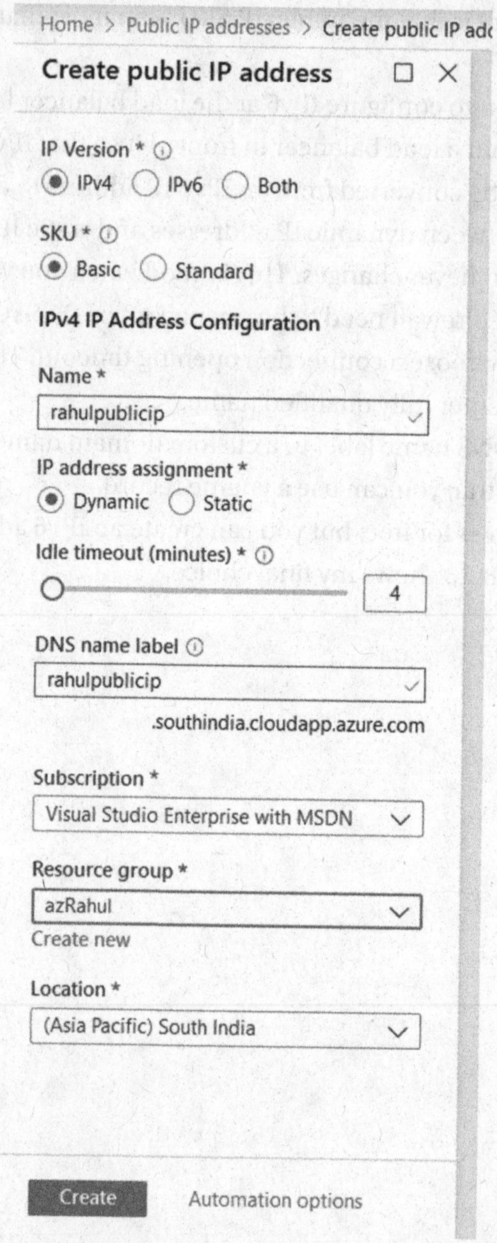

Home > Public IP addresses > Create public IP add

Create public IP address   □   ✕

IP Version * ⓘ
◉ IPv4   ○ IPv6   ○ Both

SKU * ⓘ
◉ Basic   ○ Standard

IPv4 IP Address Configuration

Name *

rahulpublicip

IP address assignment *
◉ Dynamic   ○ Static

Idle timeout (minutes) * ⓘ

4

DNS name label ⓘ

rahulpublicip

.southindia.cloudapp.azure.com

Subscription *

Visual Studio Enterprise with MSDN

Resource group *

azRahul

Create new

Location *

(Asia Pacific) South India

Create   Automation options

Figure 8-13. *Public IP address settings*

After it's created, the public IP address will be listed, as shown in Figure 8-14.

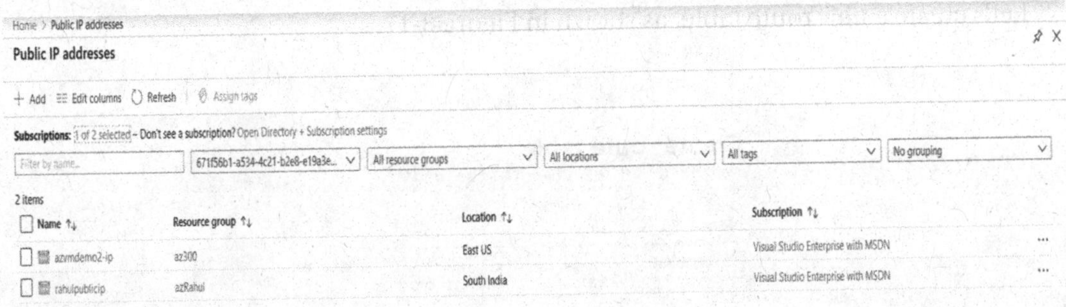

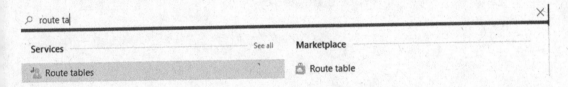

Figure 8-14. *IP address list*

Creating a Route Table

Next, you will see how to create a route table. A route table is basically a list of IP address ranges. This will tell Microsoft Azure how to send traffic that is traveling over your network. Hence, let's search for this in "All services," as shown in Figure 8-15.

Figure 8-15. *Route tables search*

Upon clicking "Route tables," you will see the screen in Figure 8-16.

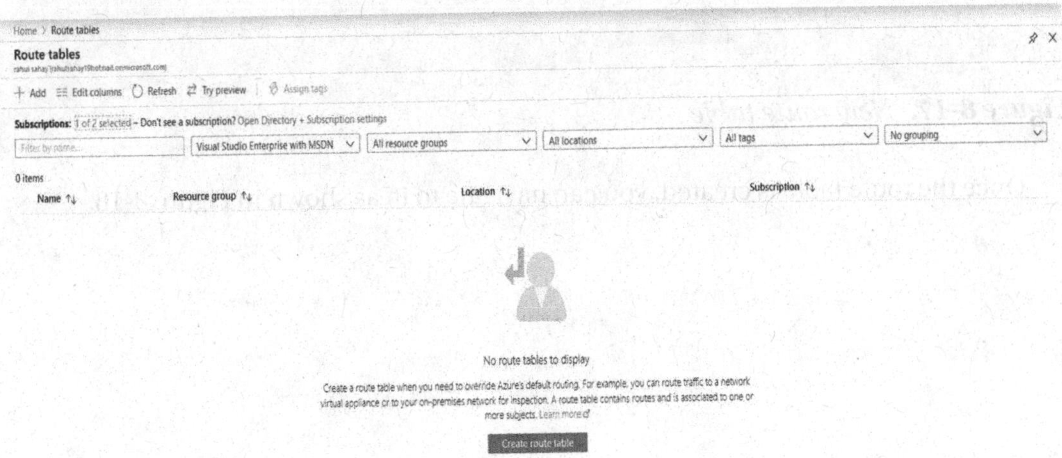

Figure 8-16. *"Route tables" screen*

Let's create a new route table, as shown in Figure 8-17.

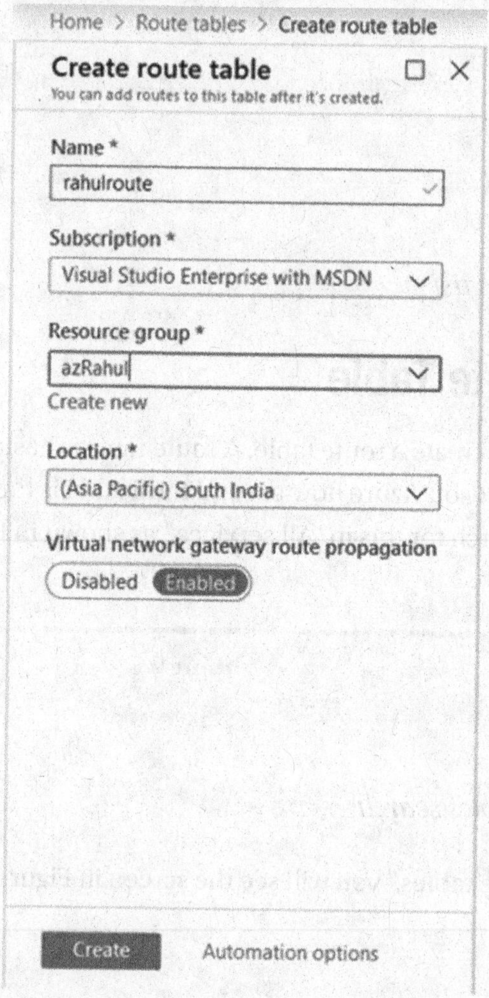

Figure 8-17. *New route table*

Once the route table is created, you can navigate to it, as shown in Figure 8-18.

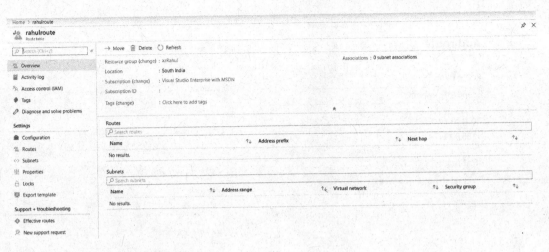

Figure 8-18. *Route table overview*

Now, click Routes, which will open the screen shown in Figure 8-19.

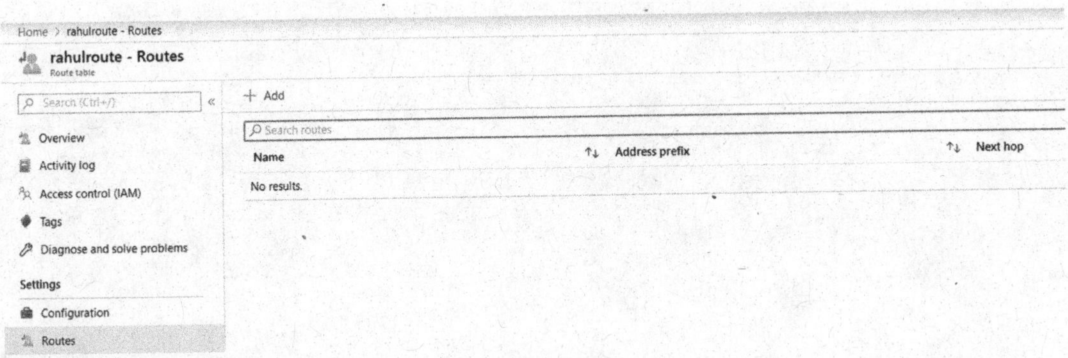

Figure 8-19. *Routes screen*

Let's add a route. Let's say you want to implement a rule that says that for any traffic that originates from a server running on the backend, you want it to go to a firewall before it leaves the network. In Figure 8-20, I have also copied the backend network address.

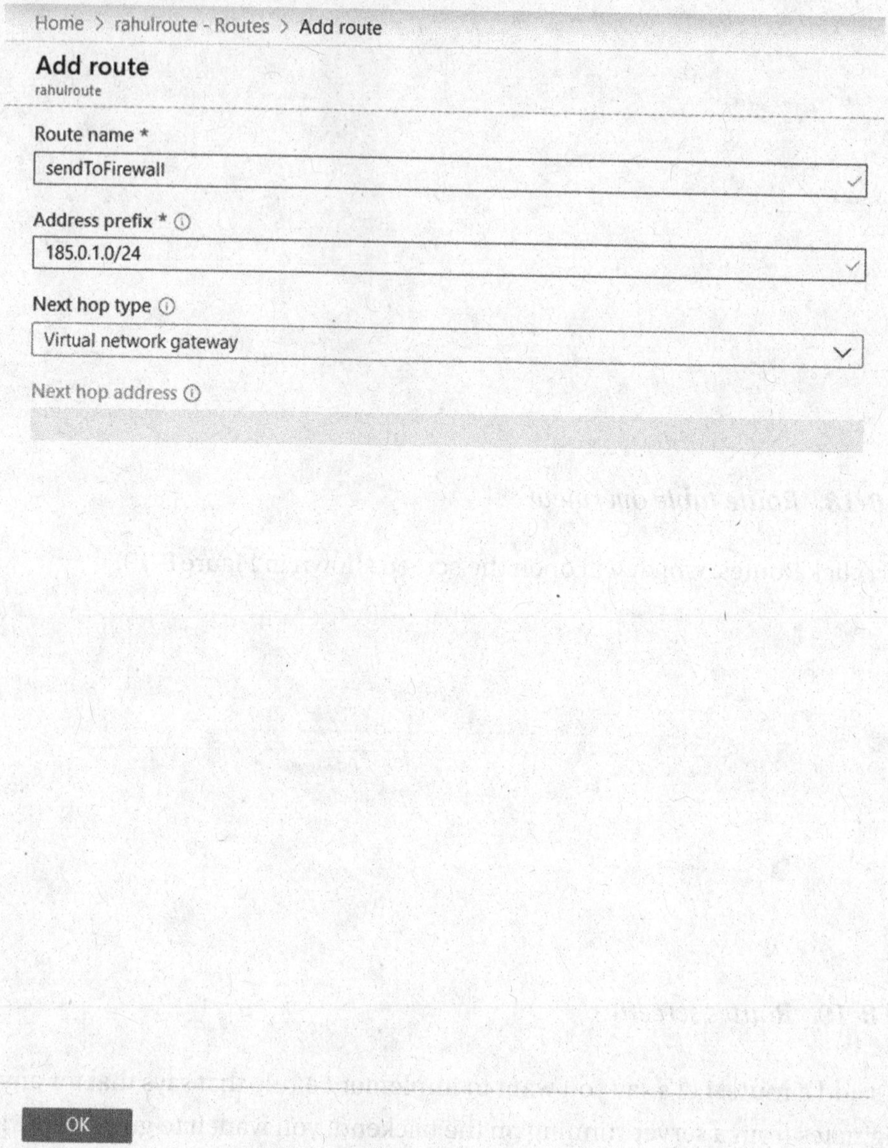

Home > rahulroute - Routes > Add route

Add route
rahulroute

Route name *

sendToFirewall

Address prefix * ⓘ

185.0.1.0/24

Next hop type ⓘ

Virtual network gateway

Next hop address ⓘ

OK

Figure 8-20. *Adding a route*

I want this traffic to be sent to a virtual appliance, which just means setting the hop type, as shown in Figure 8-21.

Next hop type ⓘ

Virtual network gateway	∧
Virtual network gateway	
Virtual network	
Internet	
Virtual appliance	
None	

Figure 8-21. Hop type

This virtual appliance ends up being a firewall, which we haven't created yet. But, let's say there is a firewall sitting at some IP address, say 185.0.4.1. Therefore, traffic originating from the backend source will be sent to the firewall, as shown in Figure 8-22 and Figure 8-23.

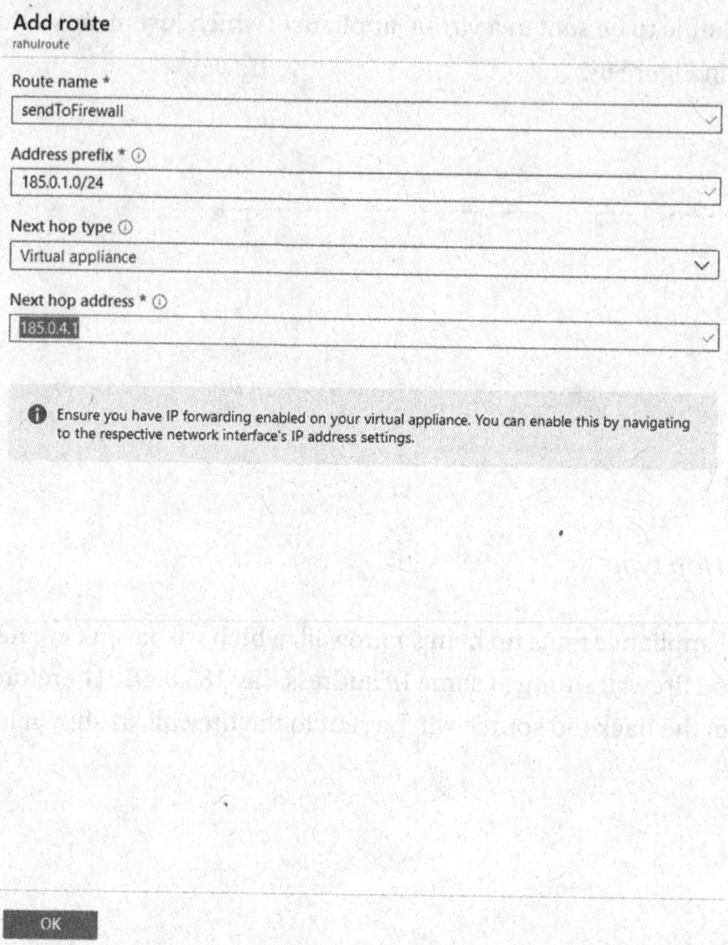

Add route
rahulroute

Route name *

sendToFirewall

Address prefix * ⓘ

185.0.1.0/24

Next hop type ⓘ

Virtual appliance

Next hop address * ⓘ

185.0.4.1

ⓘ Ensure you have IP forwarding enabled on your virtual appliance. You can enable this by navigating
to the respective network interface's IP address settings.

OK

Figure 8-22. *Route addition*

+ Add			
Search routes			
Name ↑↓	Address prefix ↑↓	Next hop ↑↓	
sendToFirewall	185.0.1.0/24	185.0.4.1	...

Figure 8-23. *Route added*

Associating a Subnet

We haven't associated this route table with our subnet yet. Therefore, let's go to the Subnets section and click Associate, as shown in Figure 8-24.

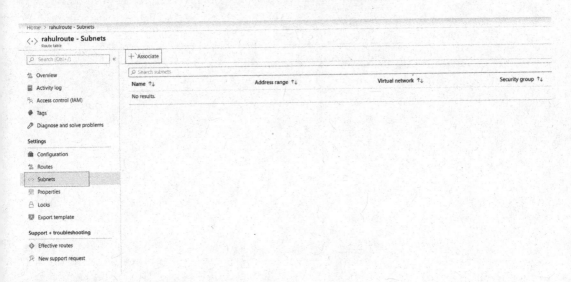

Figure 8-24. *Associating a subnet*

This will bring up the screen shown in Figure 8-25.

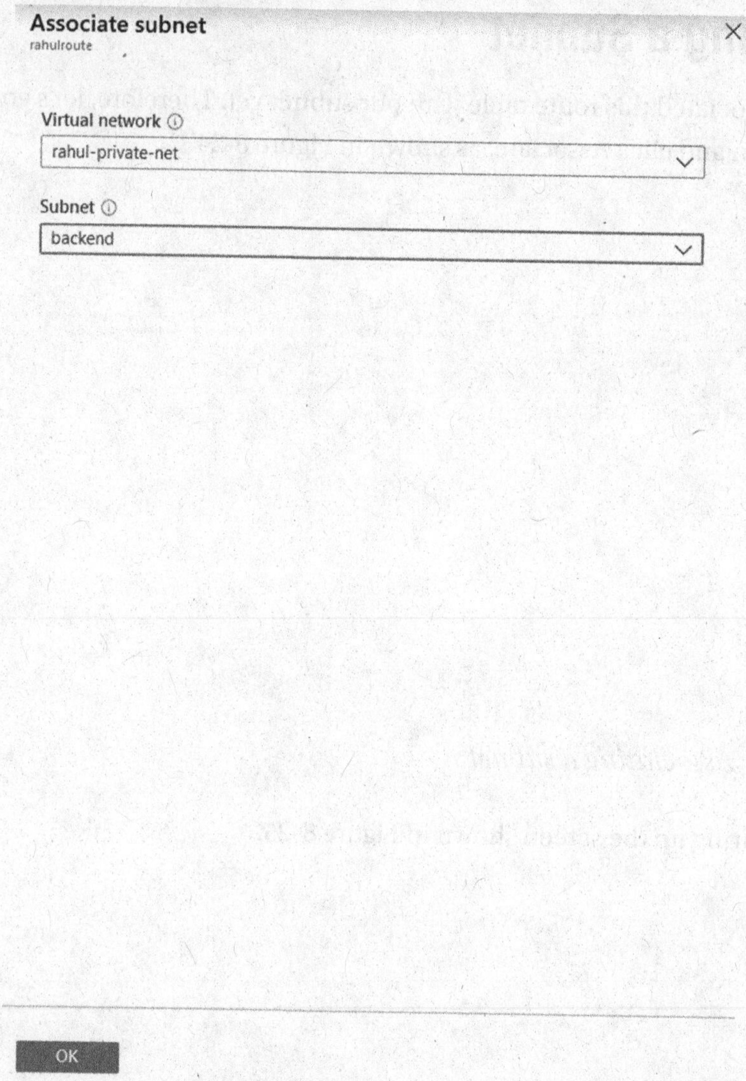

Associate subnet
rahulroute   ✕

Virtual network ⓘ

    rahul-private-net   ⌄

Subnet ⓘ

    backend   ⌄

OK

Figure 8-25. *Associating a subnet*

I have chosen the virtual network, which I have created and associated with the
backend subnet. The traffic that travels over the backend subnet has to follow this route
table.

Creating Application Security Groups

Application security groups (ASGs) are enhancements of network security groups. They allow you to reduce the number of network security groups (NSGs) you require or the number of security rules that you require.

The way Azure does that is by grouping resources based on the same rules. Instead of creating network security groups for every subnet that you have and then creating separate rules for each resource, you can put all of your SQL Server databases and all of your app servers and web servers into the same security group, for example.

Let's create an ASG. Search for *application security groups* in "All services," as shown in Figure 8-26.

Figure 8-26. *Application security groups screen*

I have put this ASG in the East US region, in a resource group called az300, as shown in Figure 8-27.

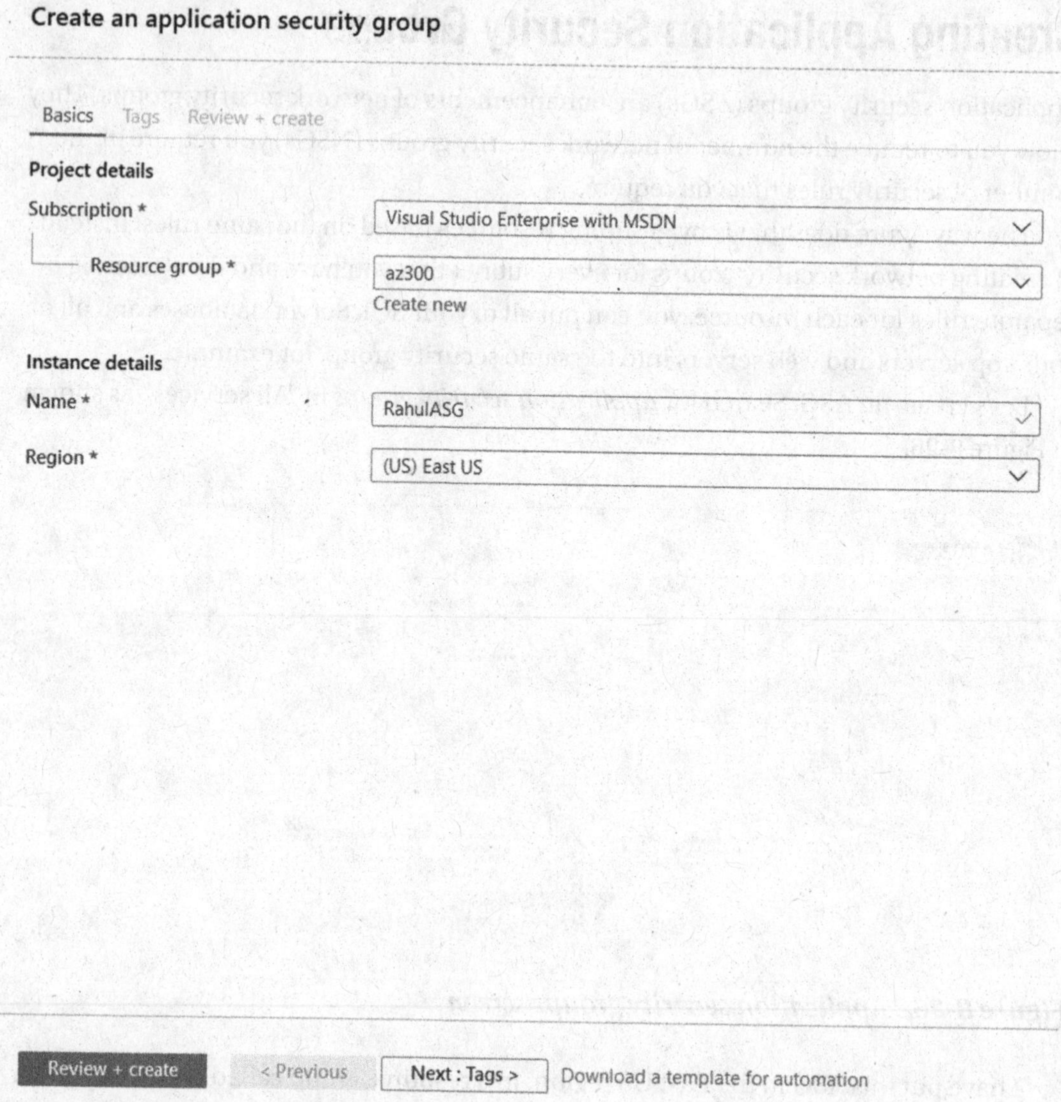

Create an application security group

Basics   Tags   Review + create

Project details

Subscription *

Visual Studio Enterprise with MSDN

Resource group *

az300

Create new

Instance details

Name *

RahulASG

Region *

(US) East US

Review + create   < Previous   Next : Tags >   Download a template for automation

Figure 8-27. *ASG basic page*

Next comes tags, as shown in Figure 8-28.

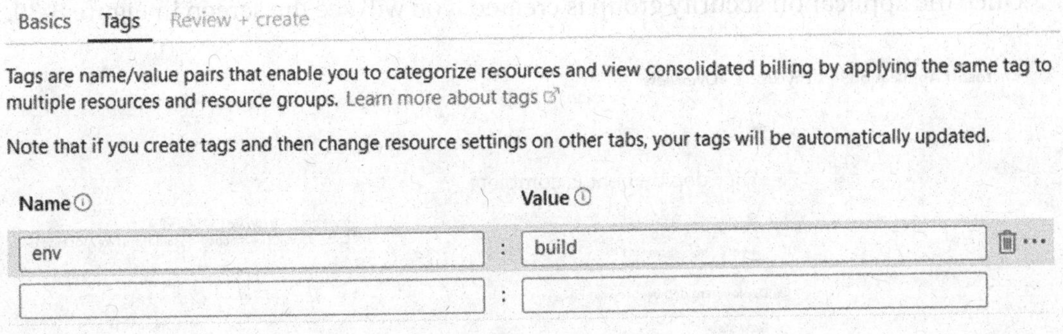

Basics   **Tags**   Review + create

Tags are name/value pairs that enable you to categorize resources and view consolidated billing by applying the same tag to multiple resources and resource groups. Learn more about tags ⍐

Note that if you create tags and then change resource settings on other tabs, your tags will be automatically updated.

Name ⓘ		Value ⓘ	
env	:	build	🗑 ···
	:		

Figure 8-28. *ASG tags*

Finally, you'll see the review screen, as shown in Figure 8-29.

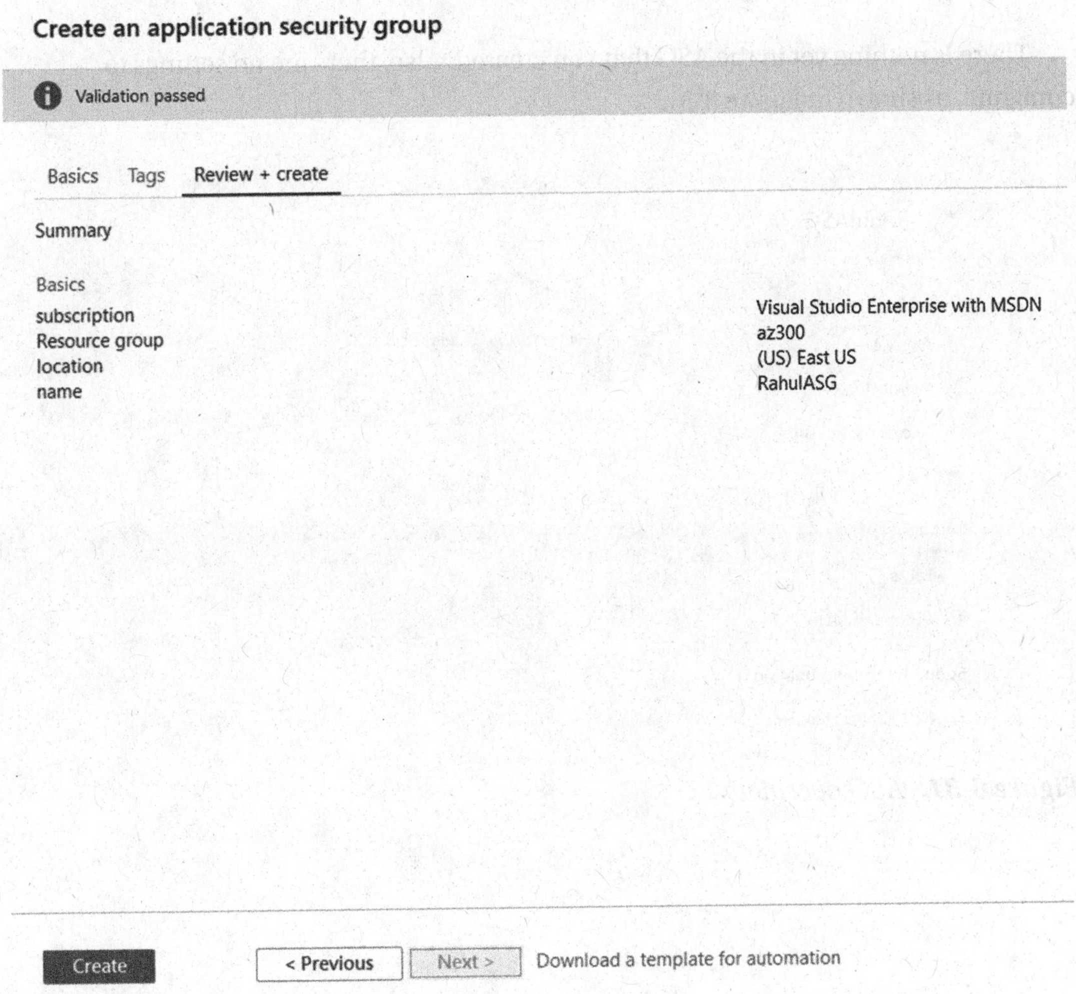

Create an application security group

ⓘ Validation passed

Basics   Tags   **Review + create**

Summary

Basics
subscription   Visual Studio Enterprise with MSDN
Resource group   az300
location   (US) East US
name   RahulASG

[Create]   [< Previous] [Next >]   Download a template for automation

Figure 8-29. *ASG review page*

Once the application security group is created, you will see the screen in Figure 8-30.

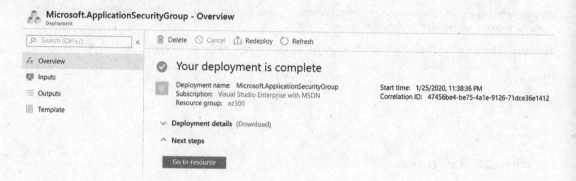

Figure 8-30. *ASG deployment details*

There is nothing yet in the ASG that you created. Also, there are no settings to configure, as shown in Figure 8-31.

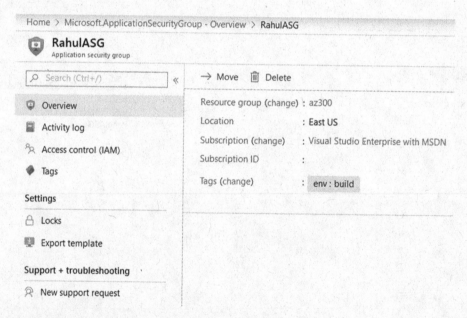

Figure 8-31. *ASG overview*

Assigning an Application Security Group to a Resource

Next, you need to assign this ASG to a resource. ASGs are limited to the region in which they were created. For that, go to the virtual machine that you created in your resource group. On the Networking tab, you can see the ASG option, as shown in Figure 8-32.

Priority	Name	Port	Protocol	Source	Destination	Action	
300	RDP	3389	TCP	Any	Any	Allow	...
65000	AllowVnetInBound	Any	Any	VirtualNetwork	VirtualNetwork	Allow	...
65001	AllowAzureLoadBalancerInBound	Any	Any	AzureLoadBalancer	Any	Allow	...
65500	DenyAllInBound	Any	Any	Any	Any	Deny	...

Figure 8-32. *Inbound port rules*

Currently, there is no ASG associated with the network interface, as shown in Figure 8-33.

Attach network interface   Detach network interface

Network Interface: rahulnic123   Effective security rules   Topology
Virtual network/subnet: az300-vnet/default   NIC Public IP: 40.121.66.136   NIC Private IP: **10.0.0.4**   Accelerated networking: **Disabled**

Inbound port rules   Outbound port rules   Application security groups   Load balancing

Configure the application security groups

Figure 8-33. *ASG list*

Next, click the save button, as shown in Figure 8-34.

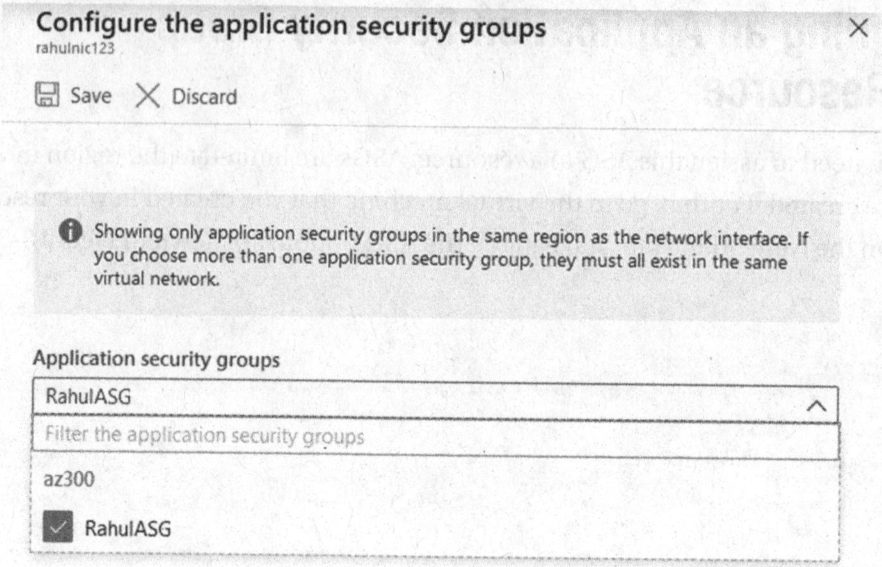

Configure the application security groups
rahulnic123   ✕

💾 Save   ✕ Discard

> ℹ️ Showing only application security groups in the same region as the network interface. If
> you choose more than one application security group, they must all exist in the same
> virtual network.

Application security groups

RahulASG	∧

Filter the application security groups

az300

✅ RahulASG

Figure 8-34. Configuring the ASG

Figure 8-35 shows how the ASG is updated.

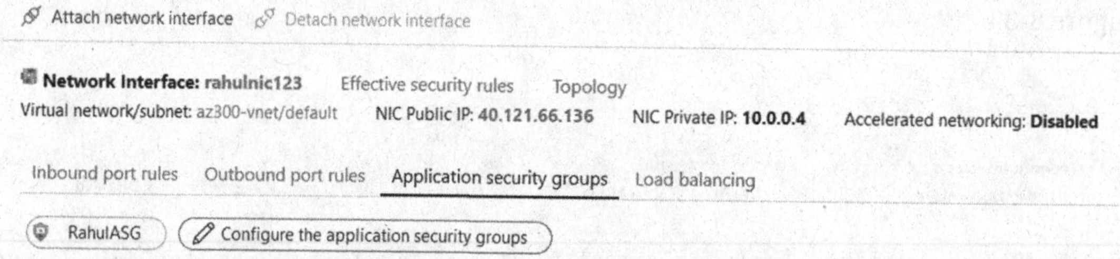

📎 Attach network interface   📎 Detach network interface

🖥️ **Network Interface: rahulnic123**   Effective security rules   Topology
Virtual network/subnet: az300-vnet/default   NIC Public IP: **40.121.66.136**   NIC Private IP: **10.0.0.4**   Accelerated networking: **Disabled**

Inbound port rules   Outbound port rules   Application security groups   Load balancing

🛡️ RahulASG   ✏️ Configure the application security groups

Figure 8-35. The updated ASG

Updating Inbound Rules

Next, you can go to the NSG and update the "Add inbound security rule" option with the
ASG, as shown in Figure 8-36.

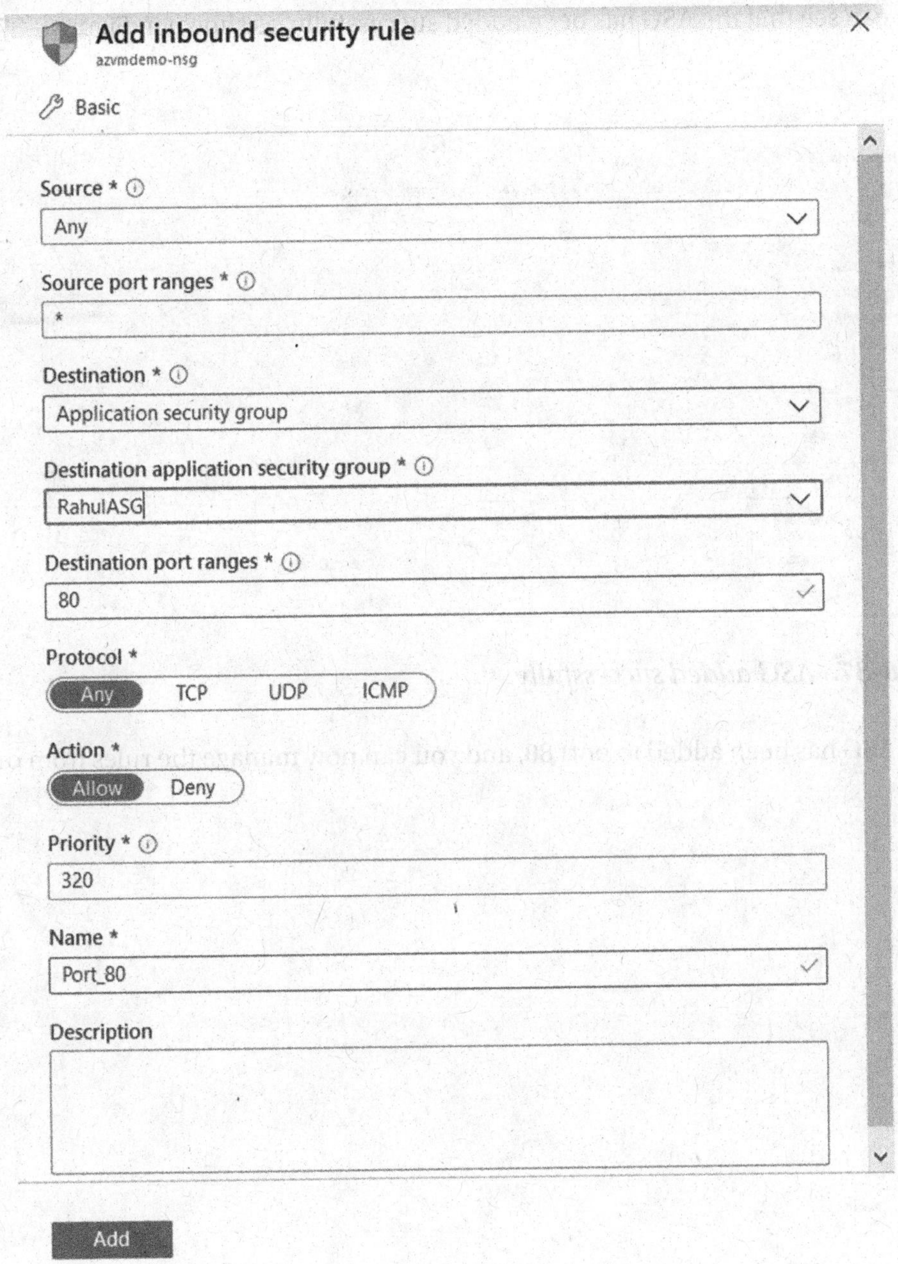

Add inbound security rule
azvmdemo-nsg   ×

🔧 Basic

Source * ⓘ

| Any | ∨ |

Source port ranges * ⓘ

| * |

Destination * ⓘ

| Application security group | ∨ |

Destination application security group * ⓘ

| RahulASG | ∨ |

Destination port ranges * ⓘ

| 80 | ✓ |

Protocol *

(Any)   TCP   UDP   ICMP

Action *

(Allow)   Deny

Priority * ⓘ

| 320 |

Name *

| Port_80 | ✓ |

Description

| |

Add

Figure 8-36. *Adding an inbound security rule*

You can see that the ASG has been added successfully, as shown in Figure 8-37.

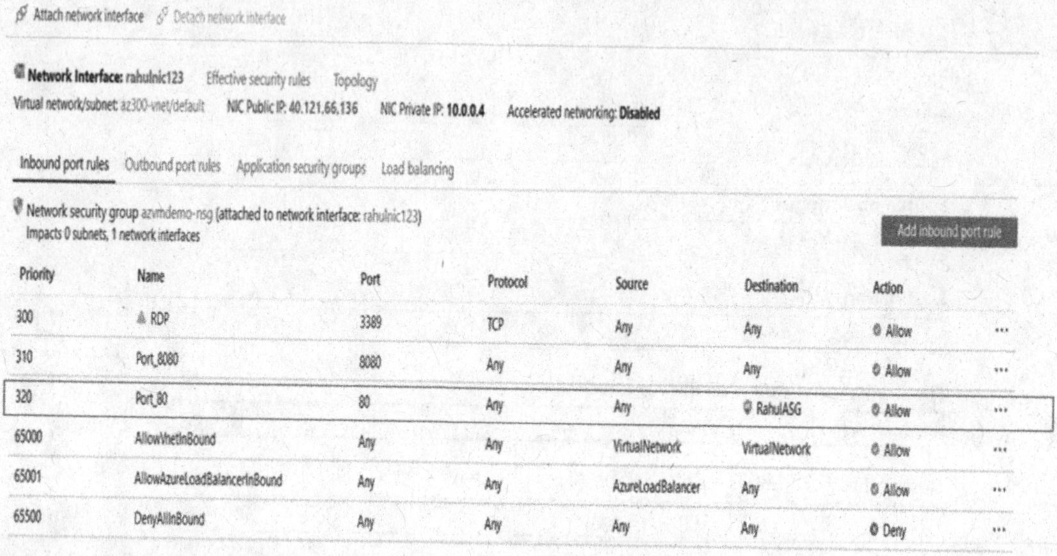

Figure 8-37. *ASG added successfully*

The ASG has been added to port 80, and you can now manage the rules from one place.

CHAPTER 9

Connecting Networks

It's important to understand how Azure implements security across virtual networks. By default, a machine that is on one virtual network cannot communicate with a machine or any other resource on another virtual network.

Any storage resource can communicate via public endpoints and associated keys. But, if you have associated your storage account with a private endpoint on a virtual network, then you will find that any virtual machine on another network cannot communicate with that storage account.

But, that doesn't stop networking. You can set up peering relationships between the two networks. See Figure 9-1.

Figure 9-1. *Virtual networks*

Setting Up Peering

Let's select the private network that we created in the previous chapter. Next, click Peerings, as shown in Figure 9-2.

265

© Rahul Sahay 2020
R. Sahay, *Microsoft Azure Architect Technologies Study Companion*,
https://doi.org/10.1007/978-1-4842-6200-9_9

Figure 9-2. *Peerings menu item*

On the Overview screen, as shown in Figure 9-3, you can see that there is a connected device listed.

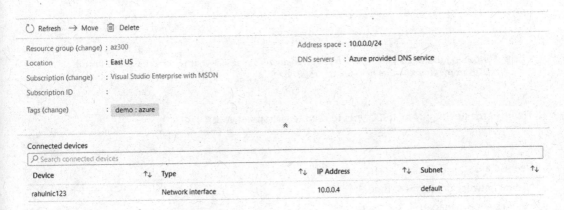

Figure 9-3. *Overview screen*

Now, click Peerings (shown earlier in Figure 9-2). This will bring up the screen shown in Figure 9-4.

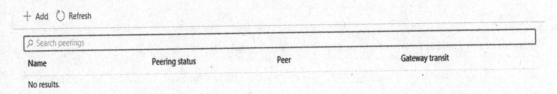

Figure 9-4. *Adding peering*

Then click Add. This will open the screen shown in Figure 9-5.

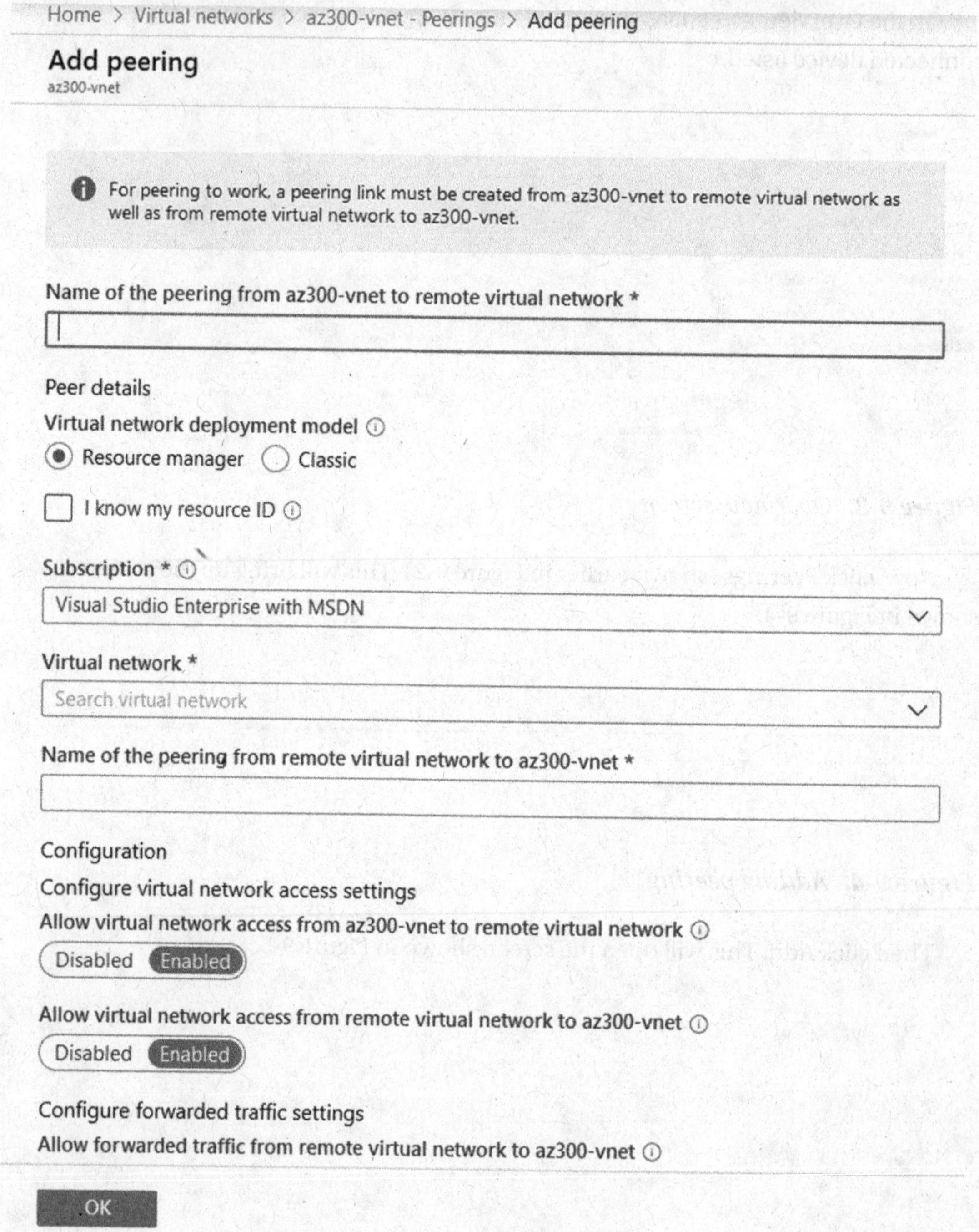

Home > Virtual networks > az300-vnet - Peerings > Add peering

Add peering
az300-vnet

ℹ️ For peering to work, a peering link must be created from az300-vnet to remote virtual network as well as from remote virtual network to az300-vnet.

Name of the peering from az300-vnet to remote virtual network *

Peer details

Virtual network deployment model ⓘ

◉ Resource manager   ○ Classic

☐ I know my resource ID ⓘ

Subscription * ⓘ

Visual Studio Enterprise with MSDN   ⌄

Virtual network *

Search virtual network   ⌄

Name of the peering from remote virtual network to az300-vnet *

Configuration

Configure virtual network access settings

Allow virtual network access from az300-vnet to remote virtual network ⓘ

(Disabled Enabled)

Allow virtual network access from remote virtual network to az300-vnet ⓘ

(Disabled Enabled)

Configure forwarded traffic settings

Allow forwarded traffic from remote virtual network to az300-vnet ⓘ

OK

Figure 9-5. *Peering details screen*

On this screen, you have to create a network connection from one network to another. Let's give name it a name first.

Here we are using the resource manager model. If you want to connect to a network that is across subscriptions, then you can select the checkbox "I know my resource ID."

I have selected another virtual network, called rahul-vnet.

Now, you need to again give a name for the reverse connection. I will call mine Rahul-VM-2-To-1. Next, you have the option of whether you want to allow traffic to go in both directions or in only one direction. I have enabled this connection to go in both directions.

Now, there is also a concept of forwarded traffic. Forwarded traffic means traffic that comes from another source to VM 1 or VM 2. In other words, there is another peering relationship wherein traffic from a third source wants to go to VM 1, and the other way as well.

You'll also see the gateway transit setting. If you want to set up a network gateway, then gateway transit will allow traffic to go across the VPN, such as if you want to connect to a corporate network or via ExpressRoute. See Figure 9-6.

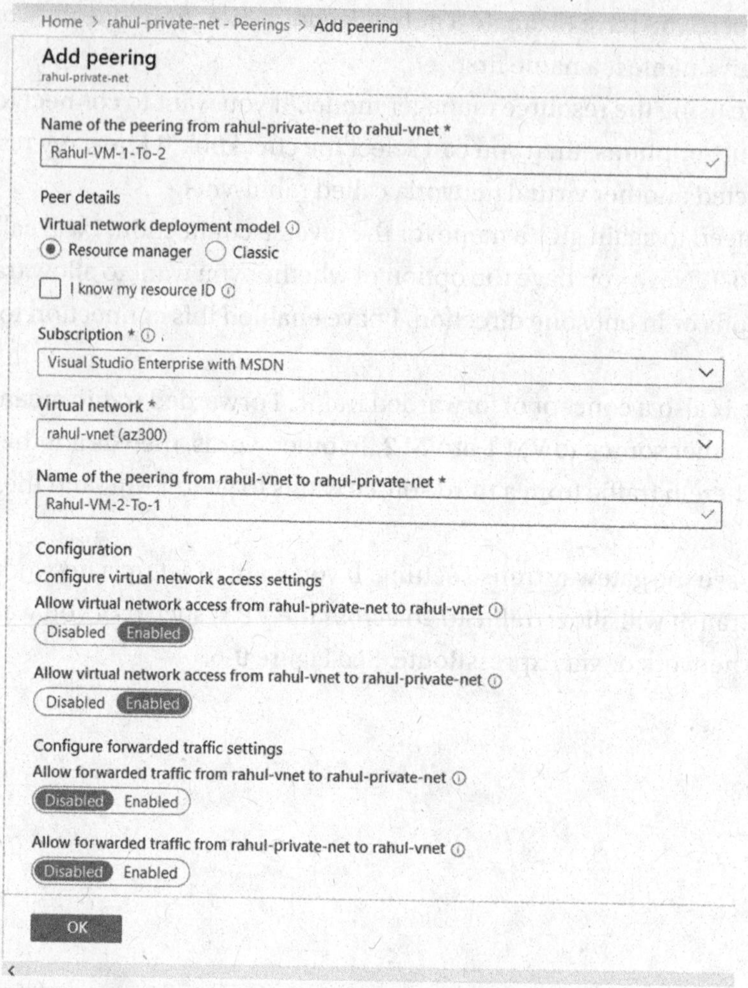

Figure 9-6. *Peering finished screen*

Once you click OK, then Azure will start doing a dual deployment. This means it's deploying a peering relationship on both sides. Figure 9-7 shows that peering has been set up successfully.

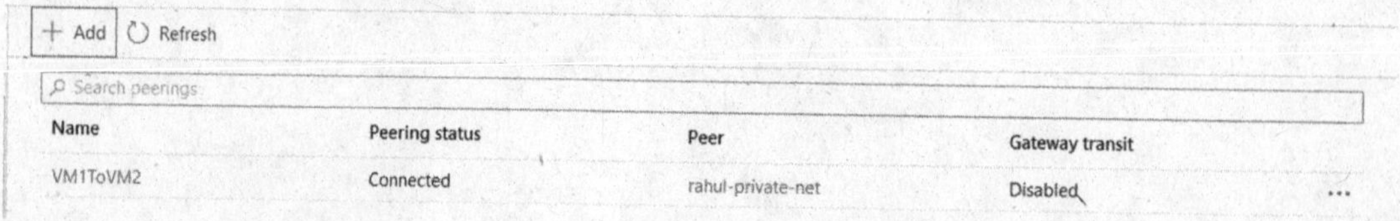

Figure 9-7. *Peerings list*

If you go to another network and check the settings in the Peerings list, as shown in Figure 9-8, you can see that the peering is set up there too.

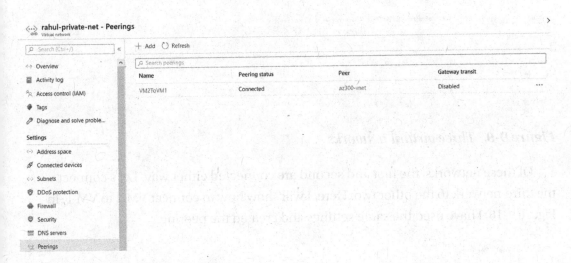

Figure 9-8. *Peering setup done*

Later in the chapter you will learn how to deal with a network security group, which is going to block a certain type of traffic traveling over the network. You will also learn about firewalls and other settings as well. Setting up these two networks in this way allows them to understand that the IP address range of the other network actually exists and configures how they get traffic there.

Configuring Global Peering

Right now, you have two virtual networks that are set up to talk to each other over a peering relationship. But what you didn't know was that you have actually set up global peering, which means a virtual network in one region is talking to one in another region. The same peering relationship can be set up within the same region.

Figure 9-9 shows three virtual networks.

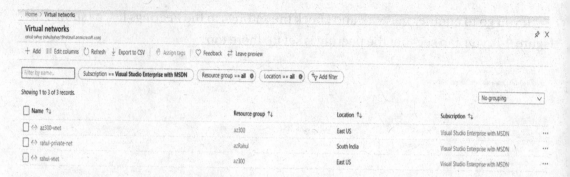

Figure 9-9. *Three virtual networks*

Of these networks, the first and second are connected either way. Let's connect the third network to the other two. Here, I will show how to connect VM 3 to VM 1. In Figure 9-10, I have used the same settings and created the peering.

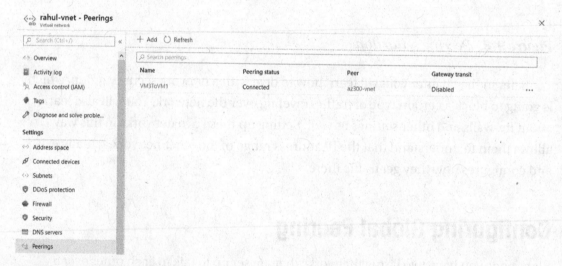

Figure 9-10. *Peerings list*

Now, in the current scenario, VM 3 can talk to VM 1. VM 2 can talk VM 1, but VM 2 can't talk to VM 3. To solve this, you can obviously set up a peering relationship between VM 2 and VM 3. But, the other option you have is to set up a chaining relationship via forwarded traffic.

Forwarded Traffic

This allows traffic forwarded by a network virtual appliance in a virtual network (that didn't originate from the virtual network) to flow this network through a peering. While enabling this capability allows the forwarded traffic through the peering, it doesn't require any user-defined routes or network virtual appliances. Figure 9-11 shows the Peerings list.

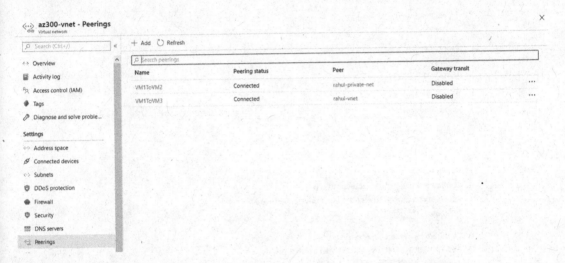

Figure 9-11. *Peerings list*

I can now go to VM 2 and into the VM2ToVM1 peerings, as shown in Figure 9-12.

Figure 9-12. *Adding peering*

Now, click VM2ToVM1 and enable the forwarded traffic, as shown in Figure 9-13.

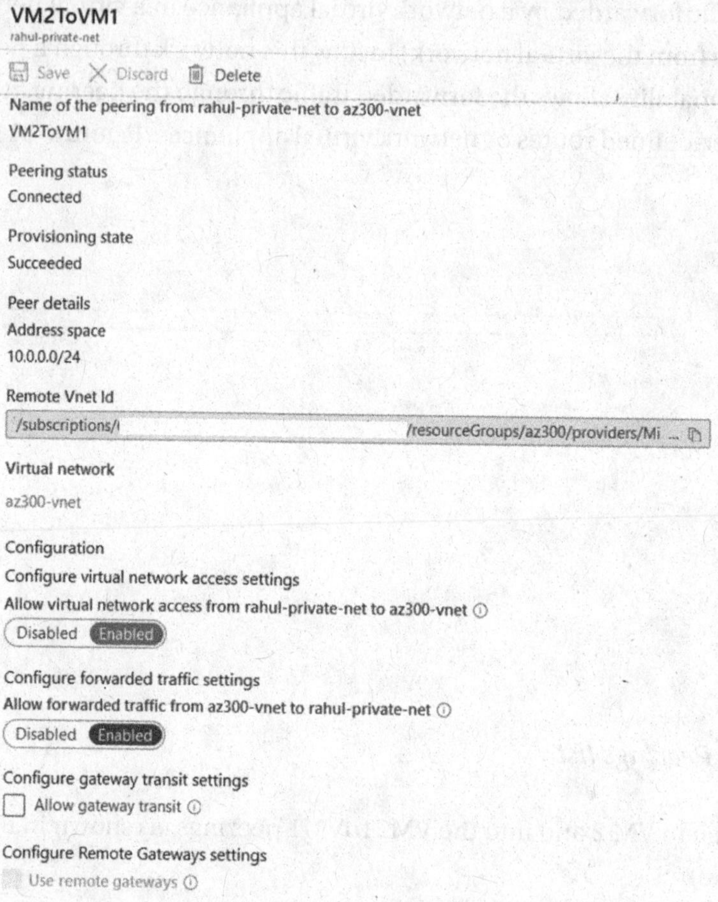

VM2ToVM1
rahul-private-net

🖫 Save   ✕ Discard   🗑 Delete

Name of the peering from rahul-private-net to az300-vnet
VM2ToVM1

Peering status
Connected

Provisioning state
Succeeded

Peer details
Address space
10.0.0.0/24

Remote Vnet Id

| /subscriptions/l   /resourceGroups/az300/providers/Mi ... 🗋 |

Virtual network

az300-vnet

Configuration
Configure virtual network access settings
Allow virtual network access from rahul-private-net to az300-vnet ⓘ
(Disabled **Enabled**)

Configure forwarded traffic settings
Allow forwarded traffic from az300-vnet to rahul-private-net ⓘ
(Disabled **Enabled**)

Configure gateway transit settings
☐ Allow gateway transit ⓘ

Configure Remote Gateways settings
▨ Use remote gateways ⓘ

Figure 9-13. *Enabling forwarded traffic*

This is where you enable any traffic from VM 3 to travel to VM 2. You also need to enable VM 1 to talk to VM 3. Specifically, go to the first VM and then into the Peerings list; then click VM1ToVM3 and enable it. See Figure 9-14 and see Figure 9-15.

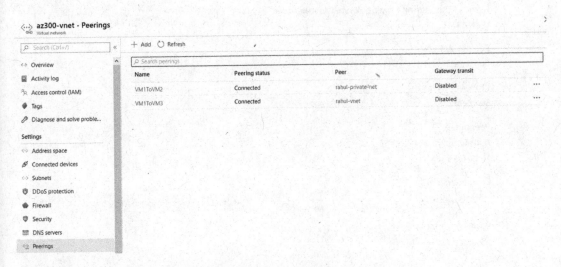

Figure 9-14. *Peerings list showing two peerings*

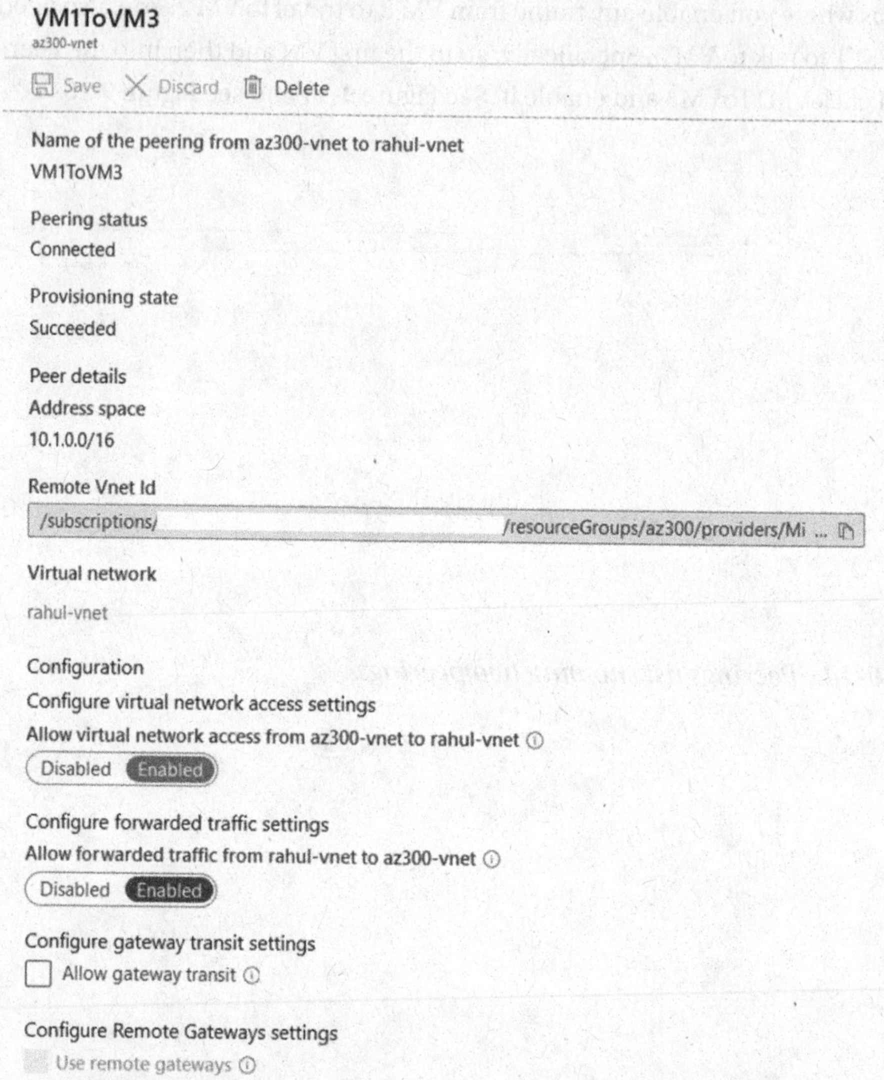

VM1ToVM3
az300-vnet

💾 Save   ✕ Discard   🗑 Delete

Name of the peering from az300-vnet to rahul-vnet
VM1ToVM3

Peering status
Connected

Provisioning state
Succeeded

Peer details
Address space
10.1.0.0/16

Remote Vnet Id
| /subscriptions/   /resourceGroups/az300/providers/Mi ... 🗋 |

Virtual network
rahul-vnet

Configuration
Configure virtual network access settings
Allow virtual network access from az300-vnet to rahul-vnet ⓘ
(Disabled **Enabled**)

Configure forwarded traffic settings
Allow forwarded traffic from rahul-vnet to az300-vnet ⓘ
(Disabled **Enabled**)

Configure gateway transit settings
☐ Allow gateway transit ⓘ

Configure Remote Gateways settings
☐ Use remote gateways ⓘ

Figure 9-15. *Enabling forwarded traffic*

With this, the chaining relationship has been set up.

VNet Pricing

Although having up to 50 virtual networks is free, peering comes with a cost. Figure 9-16 shows some high-level costs of virtual network peering.

Region:
Central US

Currency:
US Dollar ($)

Virtual network peering

Virtual network peering links virtual networks, enabling you to route traffic between them using private IP addresses. Ingress and egress traffic is charged at both ends of the peered networks.

VNET Peering within the same region

Inbound data transfer	$0.01 per GB
Outbound data transfer	$0.01 per GB

VNET Peering

	ZONE 1	ZONE 2	ZONE 3	US GOV
Inbound data transfer	$0.035 per GB	$0.09 per GB	$0.16 per GB	$0.044 per GB
Outbound data transfer	$0.035 per GB	$0.09 per GB	$0.16 per GB	$0.044 per GB

*Global VNET Peering pricing is based on a zonal structure. For instance, if data is being transferred from a VNET in zone 1 to a VNET in zone 2, customers will incur outbound data transfer rates for zone 1 and inbound data transfer rates for zone 2.

Virtual Network TAP preview

Virtual Network TAP is a feature that allows customers to enable mirroring of their virtual machine network traffic to a packet collector.

	GLOBAL	US GOV
VTAP	$0.0125 per hour	$0.0125 per hour

*Per hour charge is per IP endpoint in a Virtual Network enabled with Virtual Network TAP. During public preview, pricing reflects a 50% discount.

Figure 9-16. *Peering cost sheet*

The cost is applicable to both directions, meaning inbound and outbound traffic. You can find detailed pricing information per region at `https://bit.ly/az-vnet-pricing`.

Creating a Gateway Subnet

In the previous section, you learned how to set up a peering network, but there is another way to do it, and that is via network gateways. Let's go into one of the virtual networks and then into a subnet, as shown in Figure 9-17.

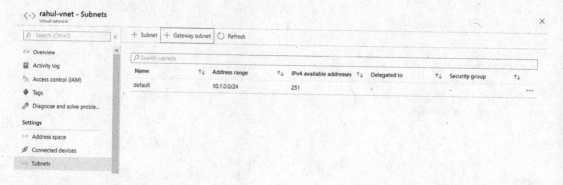

Figure 9-17. *Gateway subnet screen*

Currently, you have only one default subnet, but I will discuss in the coming chapter how to create more subnets. From here, you can create a gateway subnet in which you can install a network gateway.

- You can have a network gateway set up with a site-to-site VPN between two points. Normally, this will be used as a VPN between your office and Azure. Therefore, you can set up a VPN device and a physical device on your premises to connect to this network gateway and allow people on your network to talk to Azure and vice versa.

- You can use the same network gateway to set up a site-to-site connection between two VNets. This is why I have left the IPv4 addresses unused.

Let's go ahead create a gateway subnet, as shown in Figure 9-18.

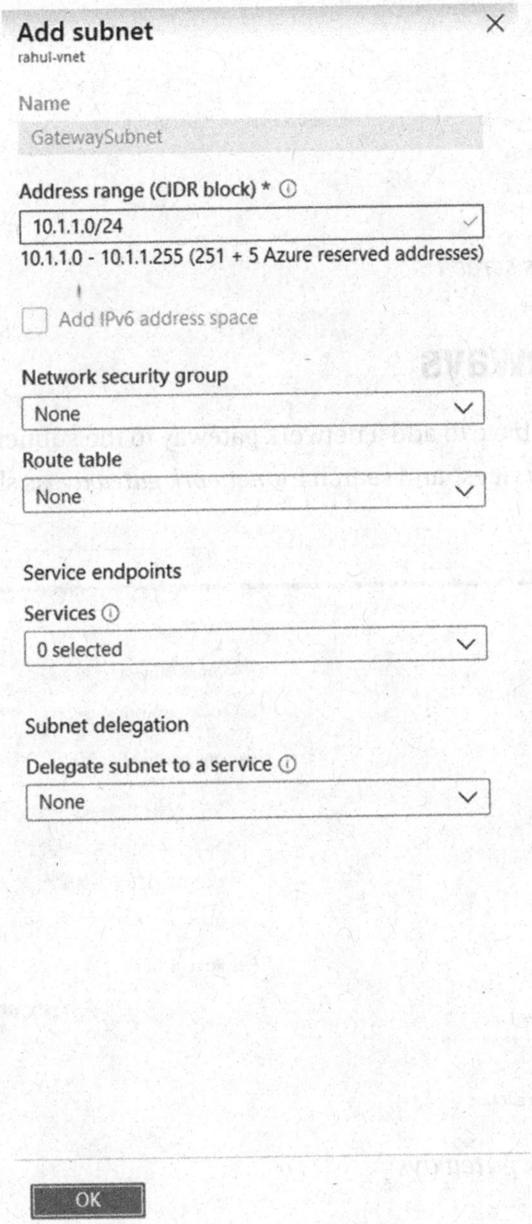

Add subnet   ✕
rahul-vnet

Name

GatewaySubnet

Address range (CIDR block) * ⓘ

10.1.1.0/24   ✓

10.1.1.0 - 10.1.1.255 (251 + 5 Azure reserved addresses)

☐ Add IPv6 address space

Network security group

None   ⌄

Route table

None   ⌄

Service endpoints

Services ⓘ

0 selected   ⌄

Subnet delegation

Delegate subnet to a service ⓘ

None   ⌄

OK

Figure 9-18. *Adding a subnet*

Once you click OK, Azure will create a new gateway subnet, as shown in Figure 9-19. I have left the other settings at their defaults.

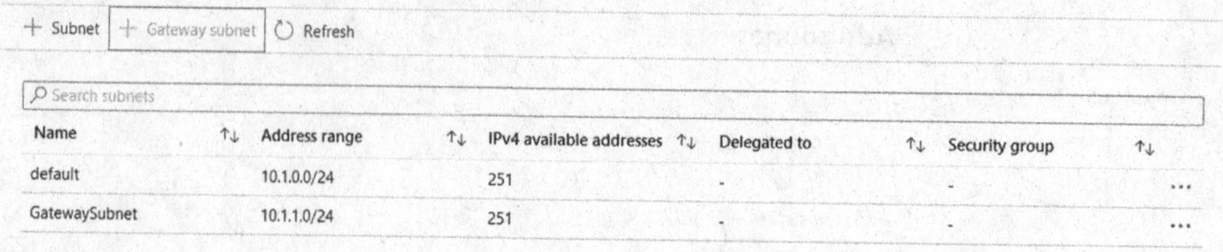

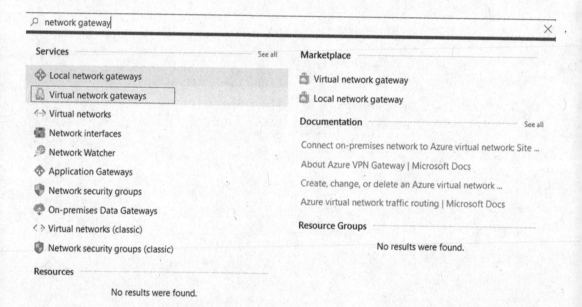

Name	↑↓	Address range	↑↓	IPv4 available addresses ↑↓	Delegated to	↑↓	Security group	↑↓
default		10.1.0.0/24		251	-		-	...
GatewaySubnet		10.1.1.0/24		251	-		-	...

Figure 9-19. Subnets screen

Network Gateways

To use the subnet, you have to add a network gateway to the subnet as a virtual device. To do that, go to "All services" and search for *network gateway*, as shown in Figure 9-20.

Figure 9-20. Network gateways

Clicking "Virtual network gateways" will take you to the screen shown in Figure 9-21.

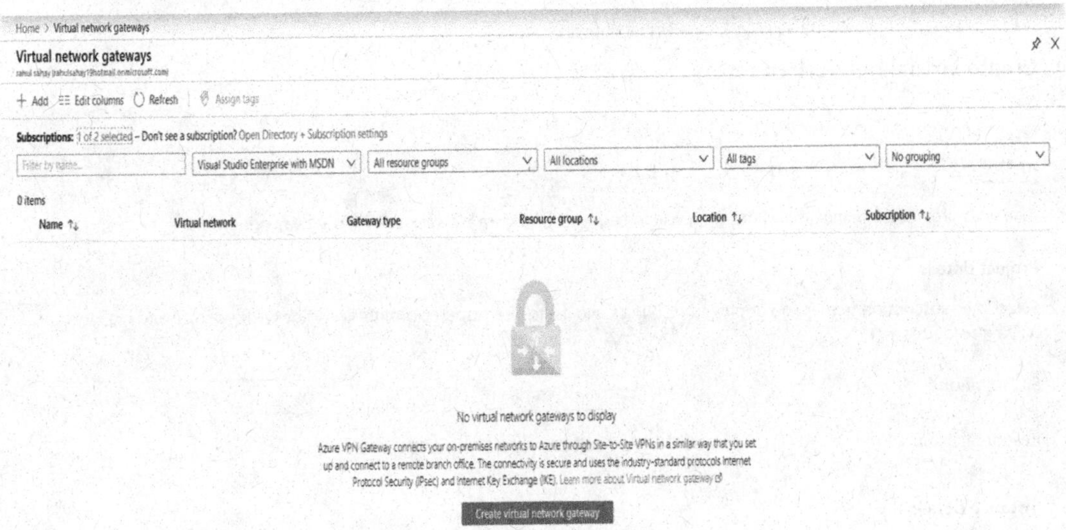

Figure 9-21. *Virtual network gateways screen*

You can give the virtual network gateway a name and a location, which should be the same as the virtual network, and then you will put one in a different location. Then you will set up these two. I have kept the other options at the defaults, as shown in Figure 9-22.

Home > Virtual network gateways > Create virtual network gateway

Create virtual network gateway

Basics   Tags   Review + create

Azure has provided a planning and design guide to help you configure the various VPN gateway options. Learn more.

Project details

Select the subscription to manage deployed resources and costs. Use resource groups like folders to organize and manage all your resources.

Subscription *

| Visual Studio Enterprise with MSDN | ⌄ |

Resource group ⓘ

az300 (derived from virtual network's resource group)

Instance details

Name *

| rahul-vnet-gateway | ✓ |

Region *

| (US) East US | ⌄ |

Gateway type * ⓘ

◉ VPN   ○ ExpressRoute

VPN type * ⓘ

◉ Route-based   ○ Policy-based

SKU * ⓘ

| VpnGw1 | ⌄ |

Generation ⓘ

| Generation1 | ⌄ |

VIRTUAL NETWORK

Virtual network * ⓘ

| rahul-vnet | ⌄ |

ⓘ Only virtual networks in the currently selected subscription and region are listed.

| Review + create | | < Previous | | Next : Tags > | Download a template for automation |

Figure 9-22.   *VNet gateway's Basics tab*

Next, select the virtual network where you have a gateway. Azure already picked up the gateway address range, as shown in Figure 9-23.

Home > Virtual network gateways > Create virtual network gateway

Create virtual network gateway

VPN type * ⓘ	◉ Route-based ○ Policy-based

SKU * ⓘ	VpnGw1 ⌄
Generation ⓘ	Generation1 ⌄

VIRTUAL NETWORK

Virtual network * ⓘ	rahul-vnet ⌄

> ⓘ Only virtual networks in the currently selected subscription and region are listed.

Gateway subnet address range	10.1.1.0/24

Public IP address

Public IP address * ⓘ	◉ Create new ○ Use existing

Public IP address name *	NewGateway1 ✓
Public IP address SKU	Basic
Assignment	◉ Dynamic ○ Static

Enable active-active mode * ⓘ	○ Enabled ◉ Disabled

Configure BGP ASN * ⓘ	○ Enabled ◉ Disabled

Azure recommends using a validated VPN device with your virtual network gateway. To view a list of validated devices and instructions for configuration, refer to Azure's documentation regarding validated VPN devices.

Review + create   < Previous   Next : Tags >   Download a template for automation

Figure 9-23. *VNet gateway address range*

The gateway does require a public IP address name; give it a name and leave the other settings as they are. Now, click the Create button. This deployment will take some time. Now, you can see in my virtual network that the device is connected, as shown in Figure 9-24.

Figure 9-24. *VNet device*

Let's go into the newly created gateway, as shown in Figure 9-25.

Figure 9-25. *VNet gateway Overview screen*

Similarly, let's create another gateway in another virtual network. Following the same approach, I have created another resource group, as shown in Figure 9-26.

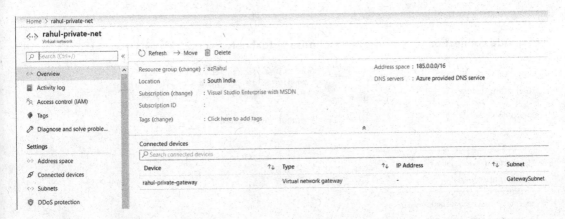

Figure 9-26. Another VNet gateway's Overview screen

VNet-to-VNet Connection

Let's go to the previous gateway that we created and click Connections in the left panel, as shown in Figure 9-27.

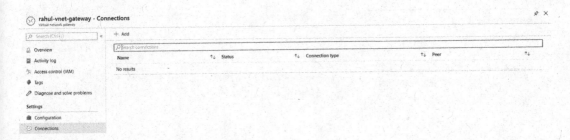

Figure 9-27. VNet gateway connections

As you can see, there are no connections available. Here, you will set up a VNet-to-VNet connection. You could also set up a point-to-site VPN or a site-to-site VPN.

Click Add, and enter the details shown in Figure 9-28.

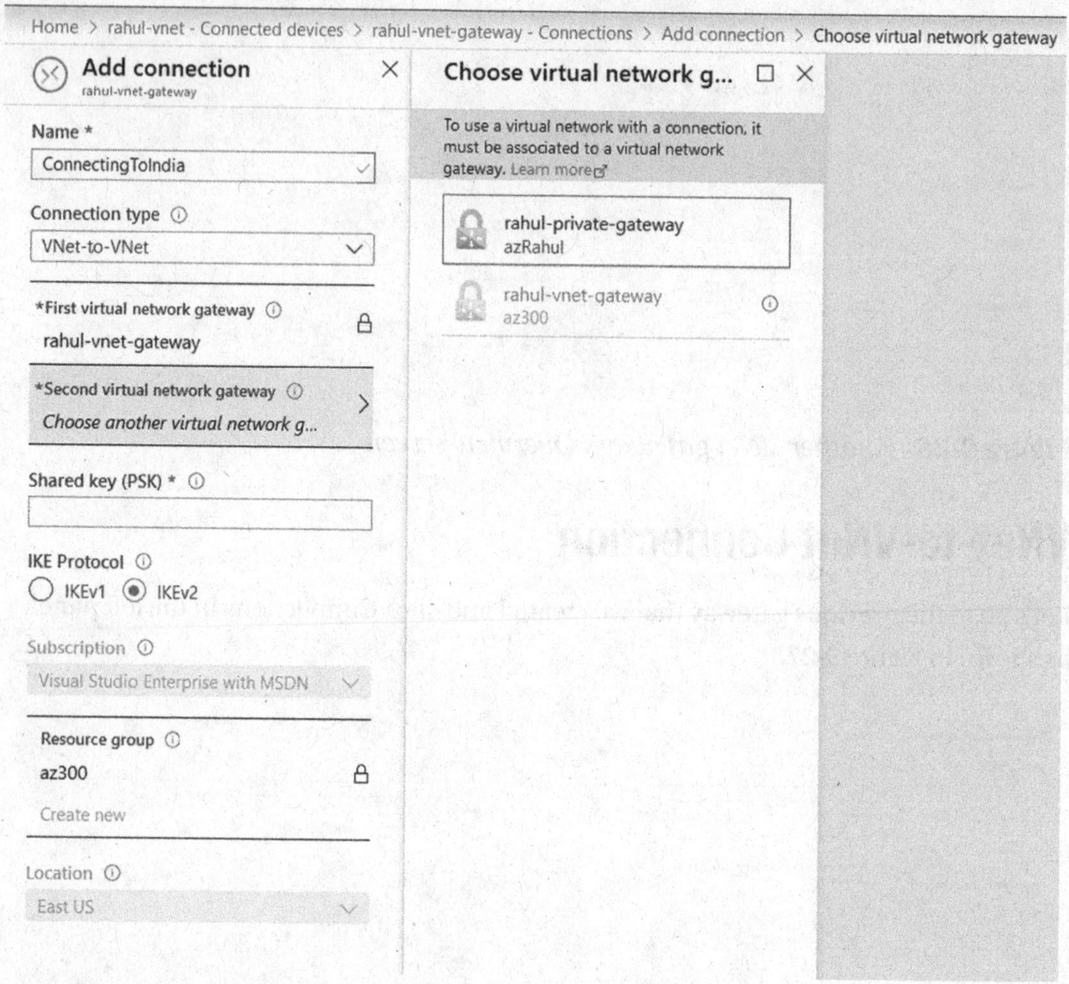

Figure 9-28. *VNet gateway's "Add connection" screen*

Next, select the other gateway that you want to connect to.

Then you need to create a shared key that both gateways need to have to communicate. In the case of a physical device, you could have used that physical device's ID. But, since this is a VNet-to-VNet connection, you need to have a key.

We will keep other settings as they are, as shown in Figure 9-29, and click OK.

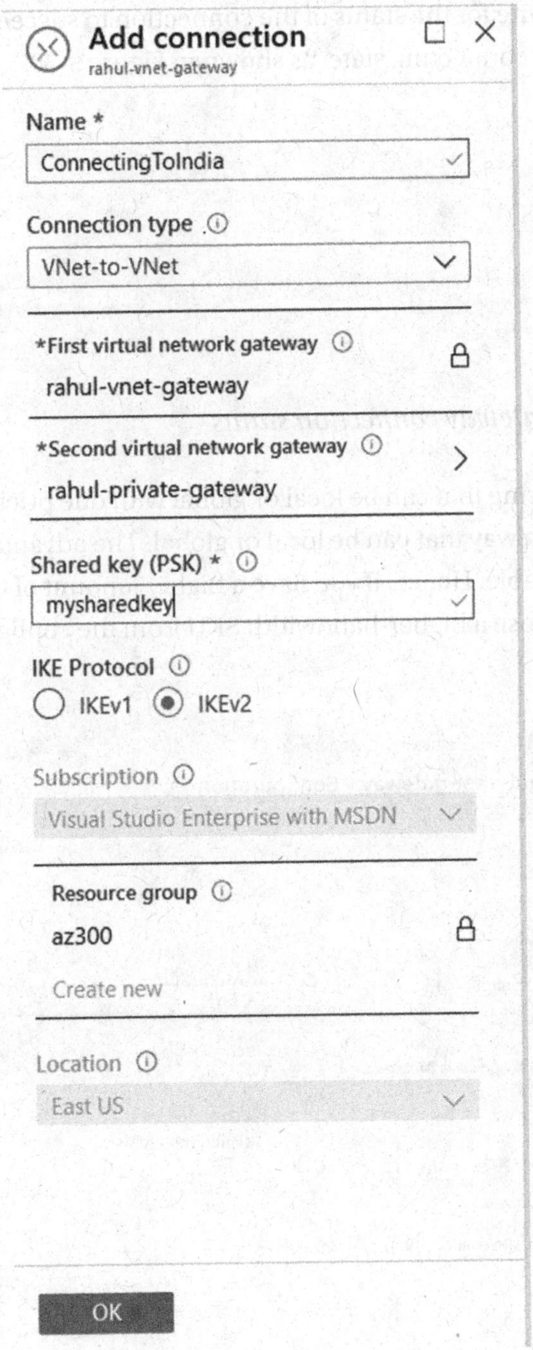

Figure 9-29. *VNet gateway details*

It will take some time for the status of the connection to succeed. Currently, it is in a connecting state, as shown in Figure 9-30.

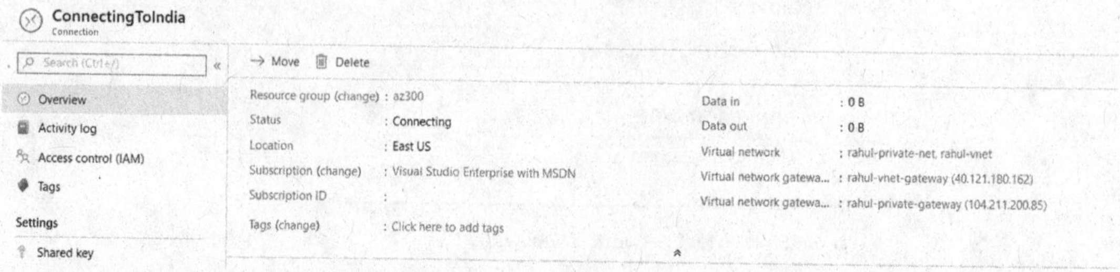

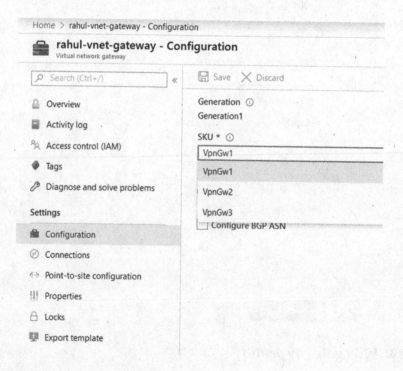

Figure 9-30. VNet gateway connection status

You have seen peering that can be local or global with one pricing structure, or you can have a network gateway that can be local or global. The advantage of a network gateway is that it's scalable. Hence, if you have a higher amount of traffic coming in or going out, you can choose a higher-bandwidth SKU from the configuration, as shown in Figure 9-31.

Figure 9-31. VNet gateway configuration

You can also configure a corporate network by using a site-to-site VPN option into Azure via a gateway and then connecting to other networks from there through a peering relationship.

You learned how to set up a gateway on both ends, which is not required in a peering relationship, as shown in Figure 9-32.

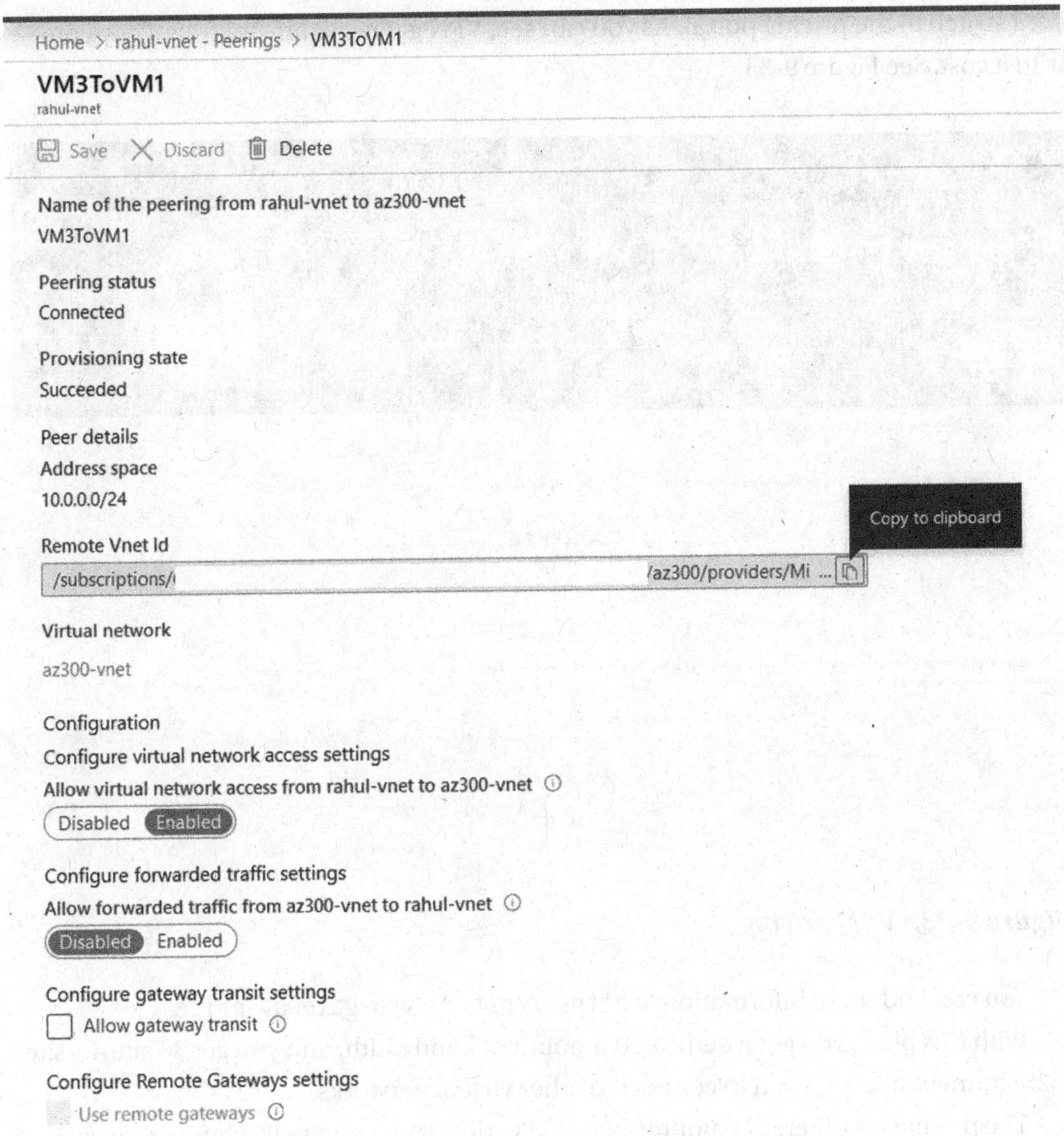

Home > rahul-vnet - Peerings > VM3ToVM1

VM3ToVM1
rahul-vnet

🖫 Save   ✕ Discard   🗑 Delete

Name of the peering from rahul-vnet to az300-vnet
VM3ToVM1

Peering status
Connected

Provisioning state
Succeeded

Peer details
Address space
10.0.0.0/24

Remote Vnet Id

Copy to clipboard

/subscriptions/   /az300/providers/Mi ... 🗋

Virtual network

az300-vnet

Configuration
Configure virtual network access settings
Allow virtual network access from rahul-vnet to az300-vnet ⓘ

(Disabled **Enabled**)

Configure forwarded traffic settings
Allow forwarded traffic from az300-vnet to rahul-vnet ⓘ

(**Disabled** Enabled)

Configure gateway transit settings
☐ Allow gateway transit ⓘ

Configure Remote Gateways settings
☐ Use remote gateways ⓘ

Figure 9-32. *VNet configuration*

Here, you could have enabled the remote gateway settings. This concept of a remote gateway means having one VPN device and then remote gateways that use the VPN device to communicate on the corporate network.

VPN Pricing

Let's switch to the pricing portal. As you can see, VPN gateways are not free. They come with a cost. See Figure 9-33.

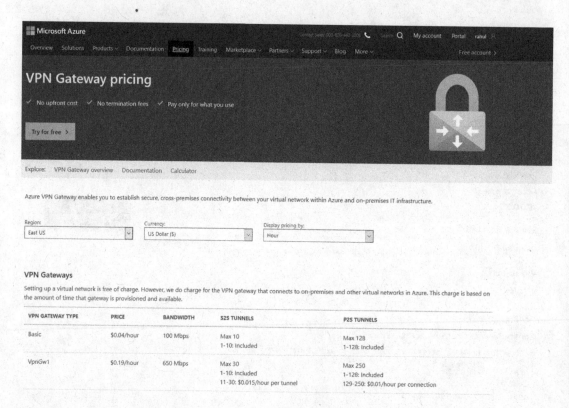

Figure 9-33. *VPN pricing*

You can find more information at https://bit.ly/vpn-gateway-price.

With this plan , you get a dedicated amount of bandwidth, and you get 30 site-to-site (S2S) tunnels, allowing you to connect to other virtual networks.

The pricing for different amounts of traffic varies, and it's actually cheaper to use a network gateway connection than peering. But, you are paying here for the device itself.

But, you do get free inbound traffic; hence, you are paying for only one side of a gateway connection.

However, you have different traffic rates for outbound cases. Hence, you need to do a little bit of math here before choosing an optimal one for our case.

Virtual Private Networks

A VPN is a connection between your computer and a virtual network within Azure or between a whole network of computers and virtual networks within Azure.

You may be using a VPN now to connect to your office network from your laptop. It's quite a common setup, and the technology has been available for quite some time now. The advantage of this is that you might have tons of data, services, and files in Azure that you don't want to transfer over an open network.

You could set up resources such as network security groups and firewalls within Azure to make it safe and secure to access and transfer files. Or, you could use a VPN, which is a pretty secure way to connect to the devices, and then you are exposed to those resources as they are local to you.

Using a VPN means the data between yourself and the remote network is encrypted. Therefore, it can travel over the public Internet. To achieve this, there must be a client installed on your machine (aka a VPN client) and a remote virtual gateway. Here are some examples:

- Point-to-site (P2S) VPN

- Site-to-site (S2S) VPN

- ExpressRoute

- ExpressRoute Direct

Point-to-Site Connection

In this case, traffic from your computer will be sent over a network into the Azure virtual network. You can have multiple P2S VPNs, which means you can have a VPN client, and your co-workers can have the same VPN client.

This is a temporary nest to the connection, but it's not efficient. For long-time usage, it's a bit of an inconvenience.

Site-to-Site Connection

An S2S VPN is probably the answer to the previous problem. If you can connect an entire office network into Azure, all of the computers on the office network can connect into the resources in Azure. This means it's persistent.

For this, you need a physical VPN device in your office network. So, either you already have a one and you need to set it up or you need to acquire one. Microsoft provides a list of devices that it supports.

S2S supports redundancy, multiple gateways, and active gateways. S2S is great for most cases, but it does run over the public Internet where there are some speed restrictions.

ExpressRoute

ExpressRoute is a private connection between your location and Azure using IXP (aka Exchange Provider). This means you are still encrypted, but you are running a private fiber network. You do need to work with a private communication provider to set it up. It's extremely fast and also expensive.

ExpressRoute Direct

ExpressRoute requires you to go to an Internet service provider to connect to the Azure network. But by using ExpressRoute Direct, you can directly connect to Microsoft in order to connect to the global Microsoft backbone.

Microsoft has currently around 200 edge locations around the world that are outside the regions where VMs are hosted. If you are close to any of these edge locations, you can direct your servers directly to the Microsoft networks through ExpressRoute Direct.

One of the advantages of this is that you are going to get faster speeds than the other options. The speeds available are in the range of 10 Gbps to 100 Gbps. In this case, you get multiple circuits on one connection to support the speed.

This kind of speed is required for massive data ingestion. Let's say you have some big data services sitting in Azure and you need the data to be flowing from your network to Azure at high speed. In those kinds of scenarios, this kind of high speed is required. This also means you are going to need some specialized hardware that supports these speeds.

CHAPTER 10

Azure Active Directory

In this chapter, we will discuss Azure Active Directory (AD). You will see how to

- Create an Active Directory

- Upgrade to premium level

- Use many other features of AD

Azure AD is the Microsoft-recommended solution for providing security solutions to your applications. You register your application with Azure AD, and then you can delegate user ID management tasks such as login, user IDs/passwords, multifactor authentication, etc., to Azure AD. Of course, this comes with a price, but the solution is pretty robust and follows all the latest security standards. AD is known as an *identity as a service*.

Here are some of its features:

- One of the most commonly used features of AD is its integration with on-premises AD directories. The concept of single sign-on comes in handy in this case. This is when users already have a user ID and password with their organization accounts that are managed by their on-premises directory in an Active Directory server. So, Azure AD synchronizes with your on-premises server so that users who already have an identity can use the identity in the cloud. In a nutshell, Azure AD offers a big advantage to existing users.

- The developer tools allow you to register your application. You can use the roles and various things that can be set up within AD, and you don't need to code much of it; you just need to delegate this work to Azure.

© Rahul Sahay 2020
R. Sahay, *Microsoft Azure Architect Technologies Study Companion*,
https://doi.org/10.1007/978-1-4842-6200-9_10

- Azure AD works with external users, so even if you have an on-premises AD, your employees are covered by that. You don't need to add those users who are nonemployees. There are many different ways of how you can work with external users. We will cover this in detail in the coming sections.

Pricing

Figure 10-1 shows the pricing portal where you can see the different Azure AD categories.

Currency:
US Dollar ($)

Pricing details

Azure Active Directory comes in four editions—Free, Office 365 apps, Premium P1, and Premium P2. The Free edition is included with a subscription of a commercial online service, e.g. Azure, Dynamics 365, Intune and Power Platform. Office 365 subscriptions include the Free edition, but Office 365 E1, E3, E5 and F1 subscriptions also include the features listed under the Office 365 apps column. The Premium editions are available through your Microsoft representative, the Open Volume License Program, and the Cloud Solution Providers program. Azure and Office 365 subscribers can also buy Azure Active Directory Premium P1 and P2 online. Sign in here to purchase.

	FREE	OFFICE 365 APPS	PREMIUM P1	PREMIUM P2
Core Identity and Access Management				
Directory Objects[1]	5,00,000 Object Limit	No Object Limit	No Object Limit	No Object Limit
Single Sign-On (SSO) [2]	up to 10 apps	up to 10 apps	Unlimited	Unlimited
Easy provisioning	✔	✔	✔	✔
Federated Authentication (ADFS or 3rd party IDP)	✔	✔	✔	✔
User and group management (add/update/delete)	✔	✔	✔	✔
Device registration	✔	✔	✔	✔
Cloud Authentication (Pass-Through Auth, Password Hash sync, Seamless SSO)	✔	✔	✔	✔

Figure 10-1. *Azure AD pricing portal*

You can find a more detailed list at https://bit.ly/Azure-AD-Price.

Creating an Azure Active Directory

Let's create an Azure Active Directory. Just search for *Azure Active Directory* in the marketplace, and you will land on the screen shown in Figure 10-2.

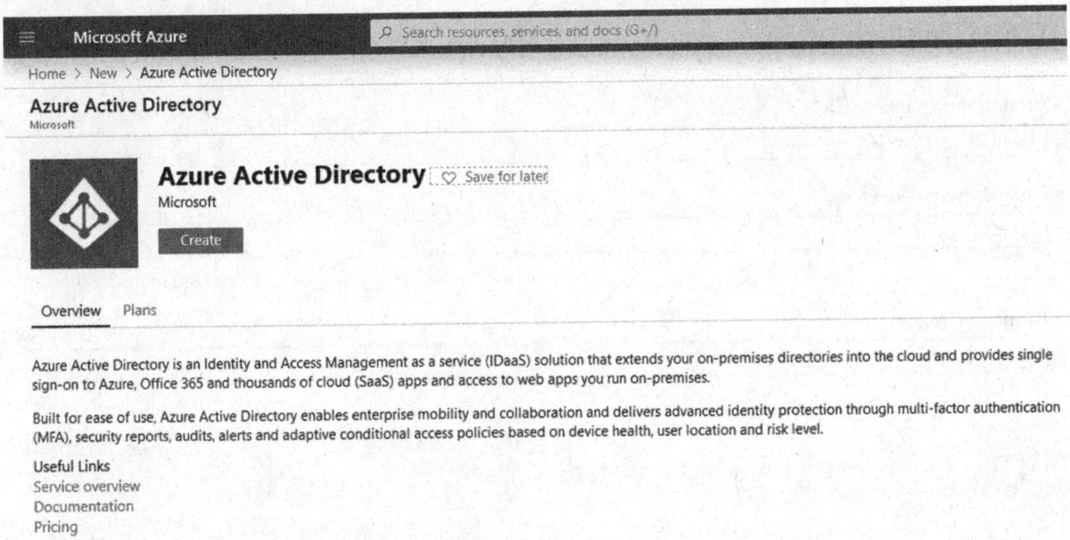

Figure 10-2. Azure AD creation screen

Click Create, which will open the screen in Figure 10-3.

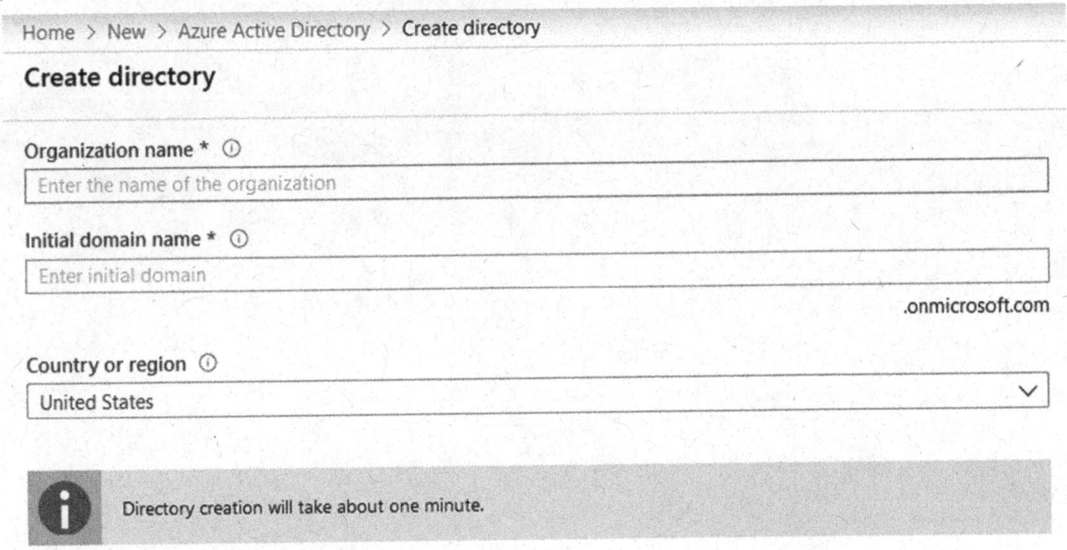

Figure 10-3. Starting to create an Azure AD

It's pretty simple to create an Azure AD. You just give it a name and give it an organization name that ends with `.onmicrosoft.com`. Then, Azure will create an empty, free Azure Active Directory for you, as shown in Figure 10-4.

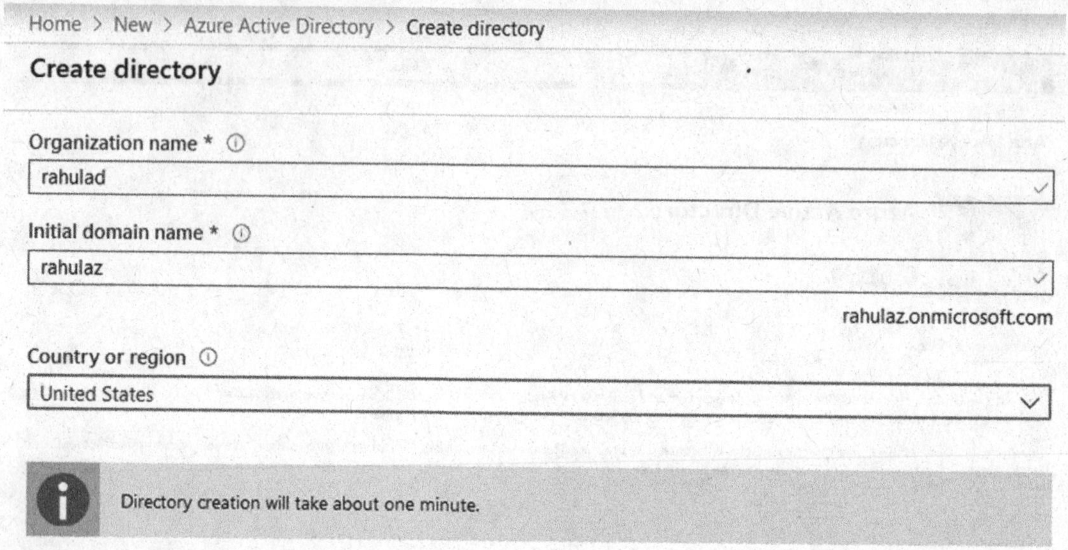

Home > New > Azure Active Directory > Create directory

Create directory

Organization name * ⓘ

rahulad

Initial domain name * ⓘ

rahulaz

rahulaz.onmicrosoft.com

Country or region ⓘ

United States

ⓘ   Directory creation will take about one minute.

Figure 10-4. *Naming the Azure AD*

Once the directory is created, your screen will look like Figure 10-5.

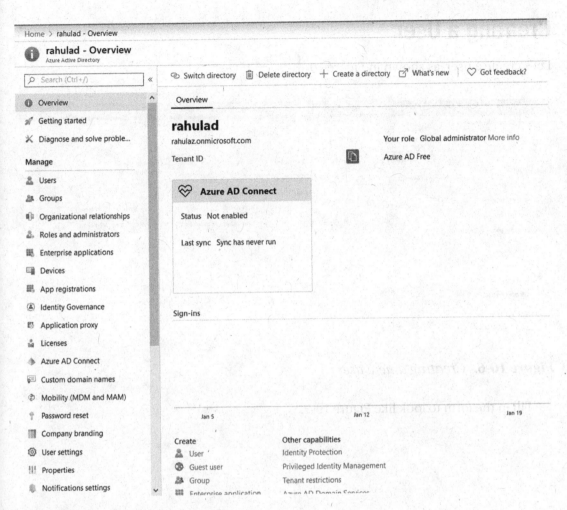

Figure 10-5. *Azure AD overview*

Here, I have masked the tenant ID. The basic concepts of Azure Active Directory are users, groups, and roles. Basically, you add applications into the Active Directory and then assign them roles.

Users or guest users can be added via a user's link, and then those users can be grouped into roles. For example, you can have a clients group and then add members into it.

Creating a User

Let's create a user, as shown in Figure 10-6.

Figure 10-6. *Creating a new user*

Fill in the form to look like Figure 10-7.

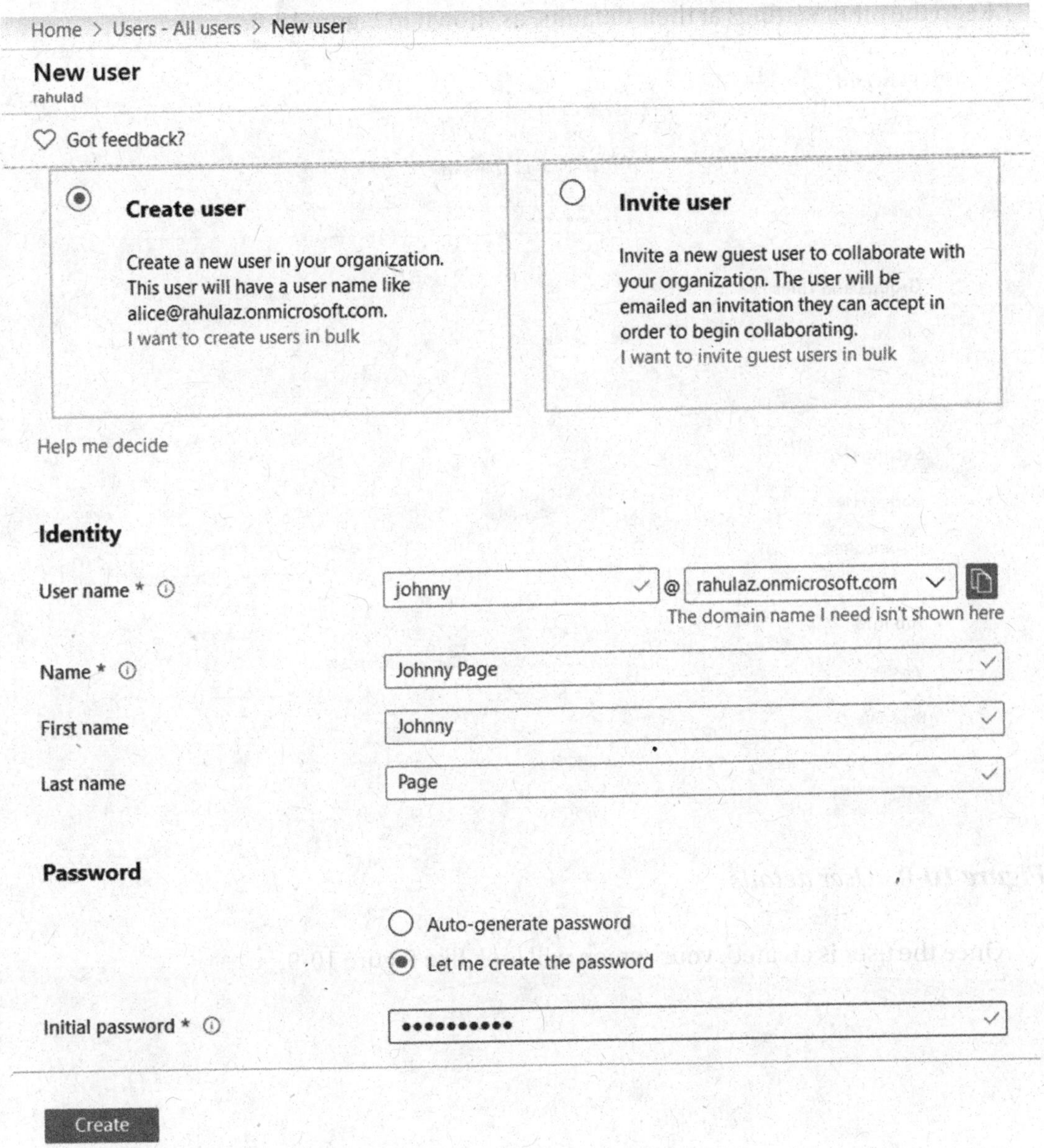

Home > Users - All users > New user

New user
rahulad

♡ Got feedback?

● **Create user**	○ **Invite user**
Create a new user in your organization. This user will have a user name like alice@rahulaz.onmicrosoft.com. I want to create users in bulk	Invite a new guest user to collaborate with your organization. The user will be emailed an invitation they can accept in order to begin collaborating. I want to invite guest users in bulk

Help me decide

Identity

User name * ⓘ   johnny ✓ @ rahulaz.onmicrosoft.com ∨ 🗋

The domain name I need isn't shown here

Name * ⓘ   Johnny Page ✓

First name   Johnny ✓

Last name   Page ✓

Password

○ Auto-generate password
● Let me create the password

Initial password * ⓘ   •••••••••• ✓

Create

Figure 10-7. *New user details*

Keep the other settings at their defaults, as shown in Figure 10-8.

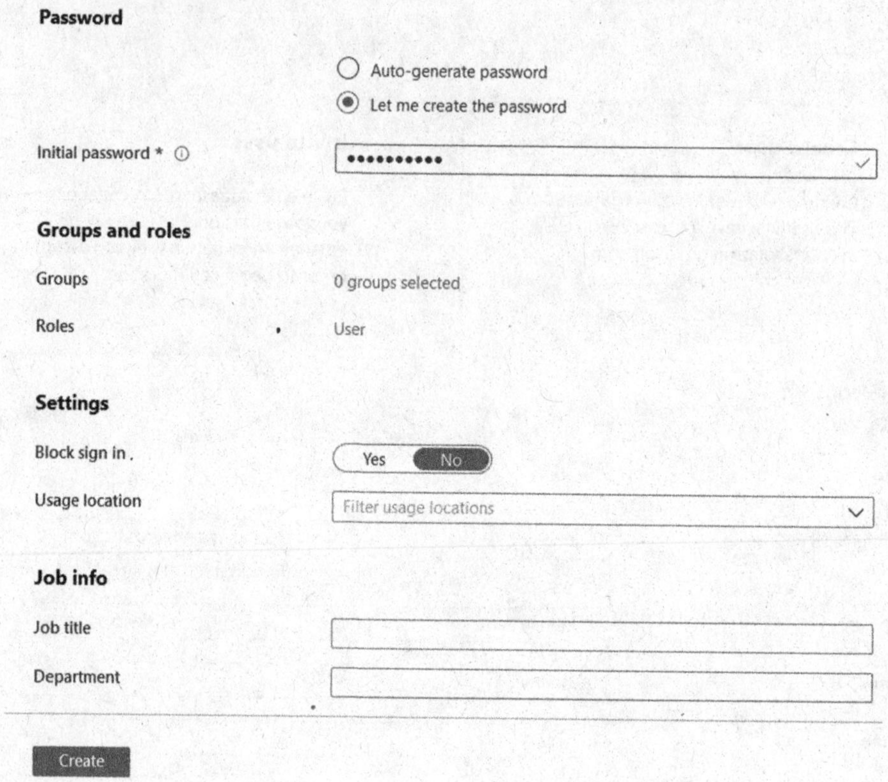

Password

○ Auto-generate password
◉ Let me create the password

Initial password * ⓘ   ●●●●●●●●●●   ✓

Groups and roles

Groups   0 groups selected

Roles   •   User

Settings

Block sign in .   (Yes   No)

Usage location   Filter usage locations   ⌄

Job info

Job title

Department

Create

Figure 10-8. *User details*

Once the user is created, your screen will look like Figure 10-9.

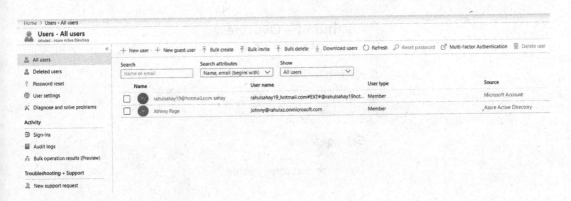

Figure 10-9. *Azure AD users*

Adding Custom Domain Names

In the previous section, you learned how to create one user with the name Johnny Page. In my example, it was created on the domain `rahulaz.onmicrosoft.com`, which many times isn't preferred in organizations.

Let's say you have a user on the company domain or on, let's say, a Gmail account and you want to use the single sign-on (SSO) feature. In that case, the previous example won't work. You need some way to add a custom domain here. You can certainly do this from Active Directory, as shown in Figure 10-10.

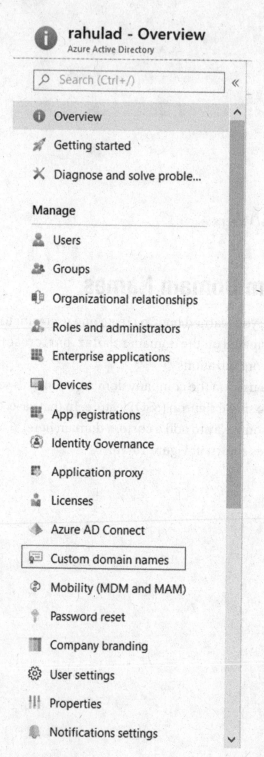

Figure 10-10. *Custom domain link*

Clicking "Custom domain names" will bring up the screen in Figure 10-11.

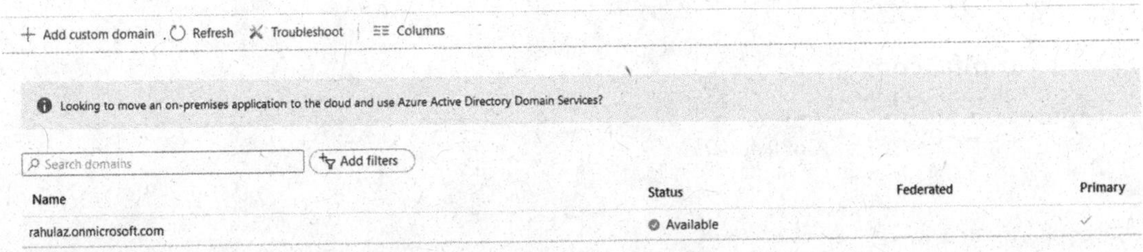

+ Add custom domain . ◯ Refresh ✕ Troubleshoot | ☷ Columns

ℹ Looking to move an on-premises application to the cloud and use Azure Active Directory Domain Services?

🔎 Search domains   ⊹ Add filters

Name	Status	Federated	Primary
rahulaz.onmicrosoft.com	⊘ Available		✓

Figure 10-11. *Custom domain screen*

You can see here that one default domain has already been added. Now, click "Add custom domain." See Figure 10-12.

Custom domain name   ✕
rahulad

Custom domain name * ⓘ

tripifai.com   ✓

Add domain

Figure 10-12. *Adding a custom domain*

I have added a custom domain that I own via my registrar Namecheap. Next, the screen shown in Figure 10-13 will give me some information about the custom domain.

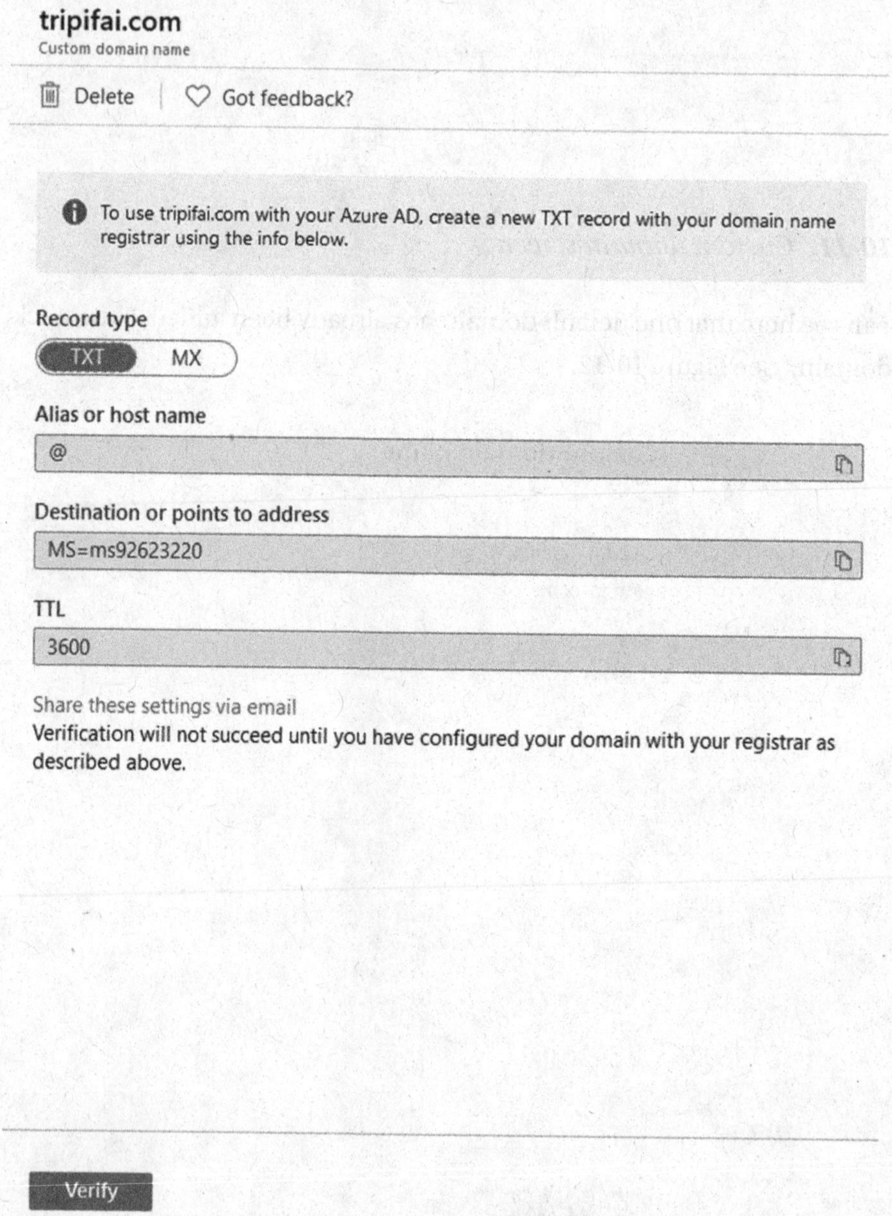
tripifai.com
Custom domain name
Delete
Got feedback?
To use tripifai.com with your Azure AD, create a new TXT record with your domain name registrar using the info below.
Record type
TXT
MX
Alias or host name
@
Destination or points to address
MS=ms92623220
TTL
3600
Share these settings via email
Verification will not succeed until you have configured your domain with your registrar as described above.
Verify

***Figure 10-13.** Custom domain settings*

To verify domain, I need to add this as a text record via my registrar under my site's DNS/host records settings, as shown in Figure 10-14.

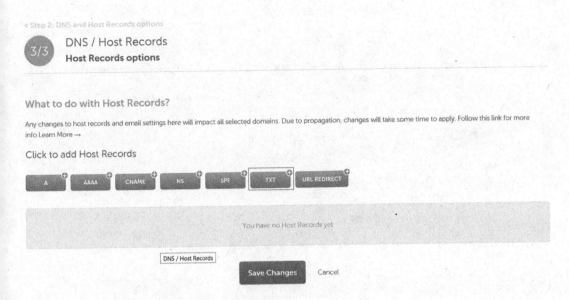

Figure 10-14. *DNS/Host Records screen*

To follow along, click TXT and fill in the details, as shown in Figure 10-15.

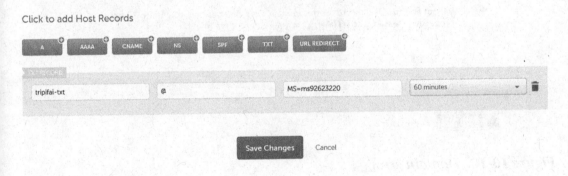

Figure 10-15. *Adding a text record*

Click Save Changes. This will take some to update. On the Azure side, if you click Verify now, it will show an error, as shown in Figure 10-16.

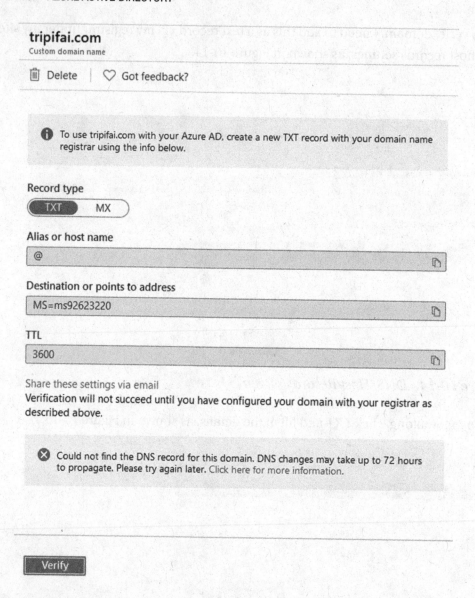

Figure 10-16. *Domain error*

Hence, let's give Azure a day or two to get this propagated. Ideally, you should be notified via email once it's done. Upon successful verification, the screen will look like Figure 10-17.

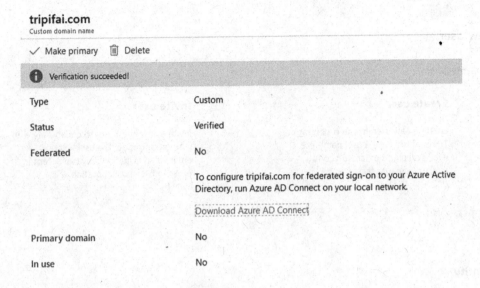

Figure 10-17. *Custom domain added*

Now the "Custom domain names" screen will look like Figure 10-18.

Figure 10-18. *Custom domain created*

You will now be allowed to create a user with this domain, since it's a valid domain now. See Figure 10-19.

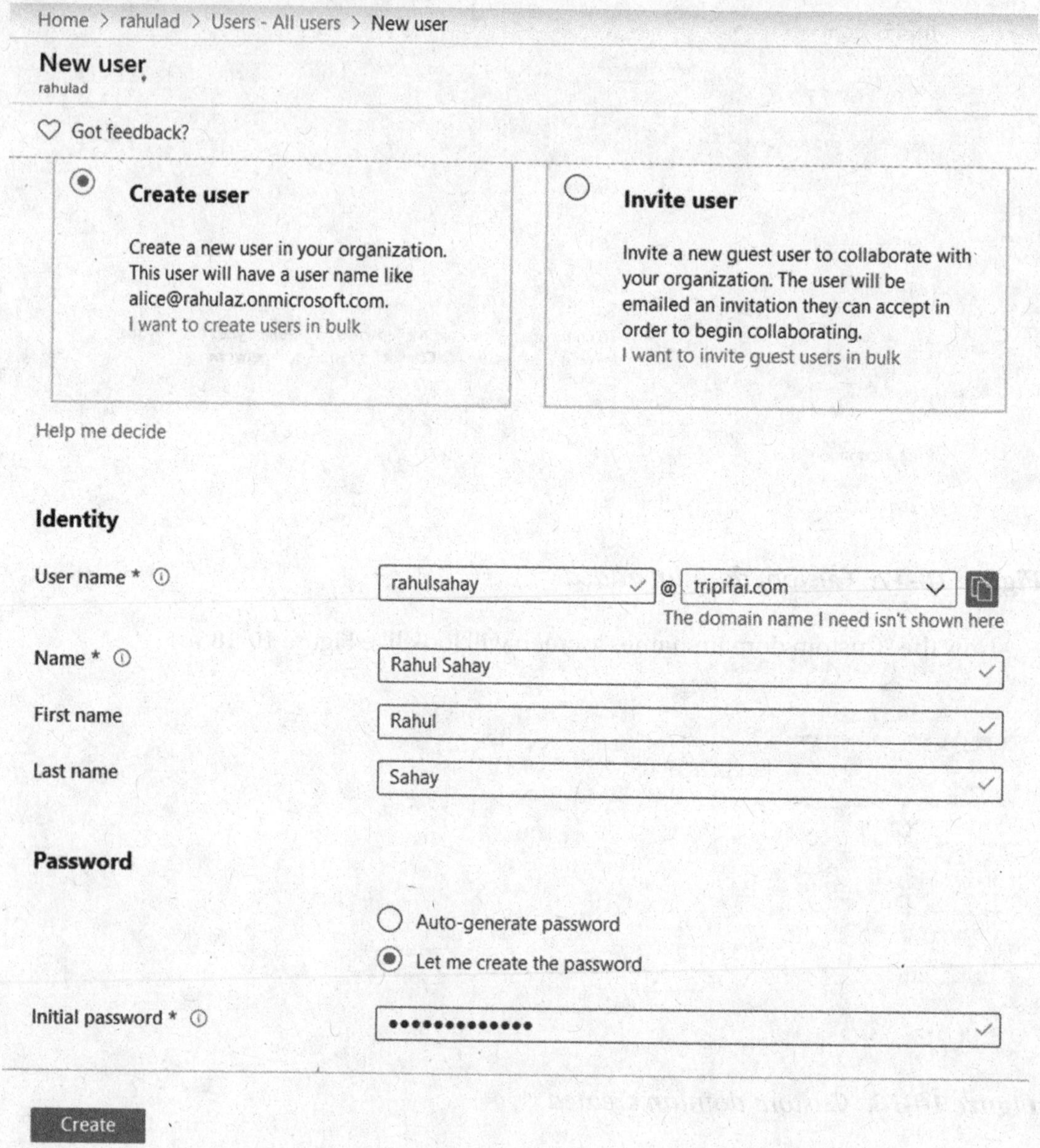

Home > rahulad > Users - All users > New user

New user
rahulad

♡ Got feedback?

⦿ **Create user**

Create a new user in your organization.
This user will have a user name like
alice@rahulaz.onmicrosoft.com.
I want to create users in bulk

○ **Invite user**

Invite a new guest user to collaborate with
your organization. The user will be
emailed an invitation they can accept in
order to begin collaborating.
I want to invite guest users in bulk

Help me decide

Identity

User name * ⓘ	rahulsahay ✓ @ tripifai.com ✓ 🗋
	The domain name I need isn't shown here
Name * ⓘ	Rahul Sahay ✓
First name	Rahul ✓
Last name	Sahay ✓

Password

○ Auto-generate password
⦿ Let me create the password

Initial password * ⓘ	•••••••••••••• ✓

Create

Figure 10-19. *Adding users to the new domain*

I have added several users, as shown in Figure 10-20. Feel free to do the same.

Figure 10-20. *Azure AD users*

Creating a Group

Let's now create a user group, which is a straightforward task. User groups are required to separate users based on different business units. See Figure 10-21.

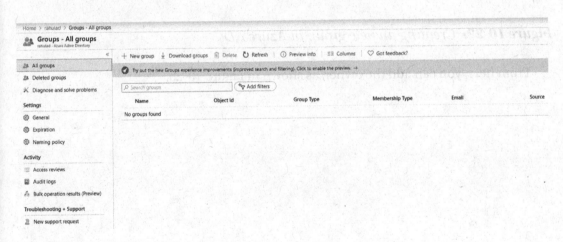

Figure 10-21. *Azure AD user groups*

Let's click "New group." The screen in Figure 10-22 opens.

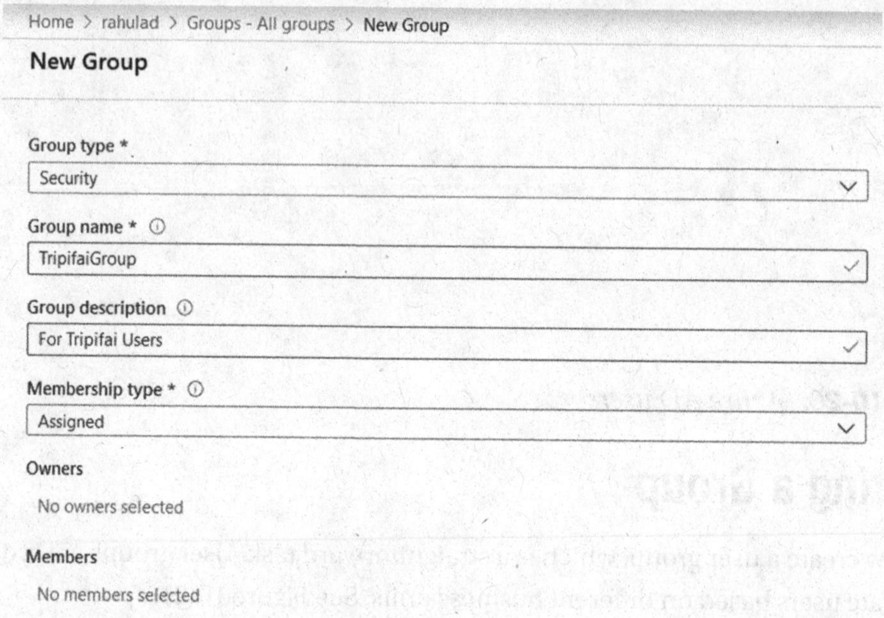

Home > rahulad > Groups - All groups > New Group

New Group

Group type *

| Security | ⌄ |

Group name * ⓘ

| TripifaiGroup | ✓ |

Group description ⓘ

| For Tripifai Users | ✓ |

Membership type * ⓘ

| Assigned | ⌄ |

Owners

No owners selected

Members

No members selected

Figure 10-22. *Creating an new group in Azure AD*

From here, you can add the owner, as shown in Figure 10-23.

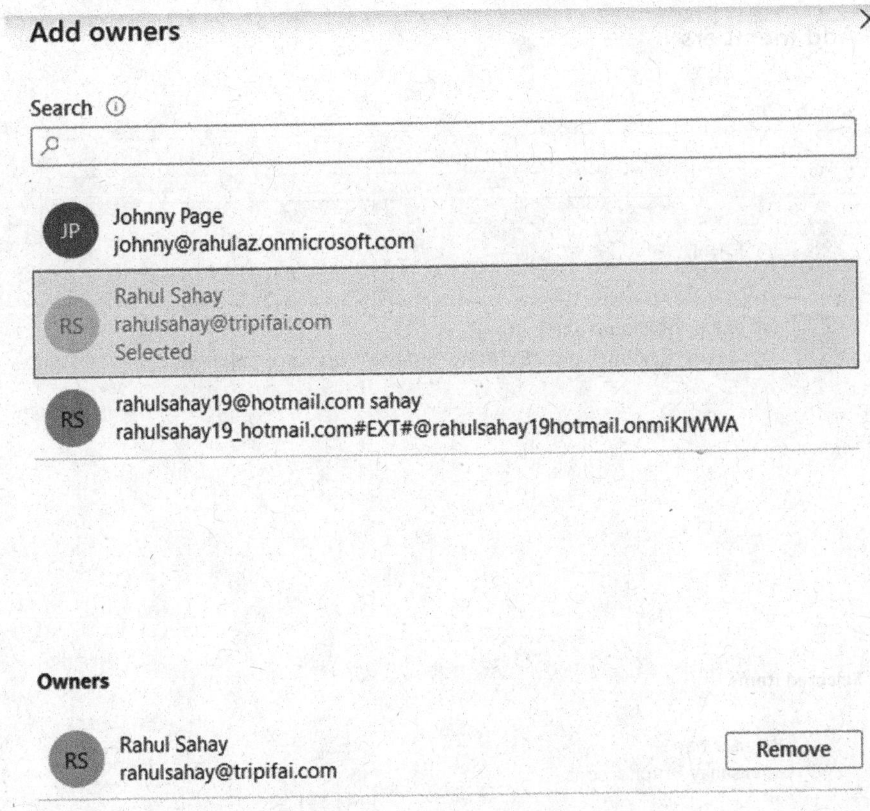

Add owners   ×

Search ⓘ

|🔍 |

JP Johnny Page
       johnny@rahulaz.onmicrosoft.com

RS Rahul Sahay
        rahulsahay@tripifai.com
        Selected

RS rahulsahay19@hotmail.com sahay
        rahulsahay19_hotmail.com#EXT#@rahulsahay19hotmail.onmiKIWWA

Owners

RS Rahul Sahay   [Remove]
        rahulsahay@tripifai.com

Figure 10-23. *Azure AD, adding an owner*

Similarly, you can add members to it, as shown in Figure 10-24.

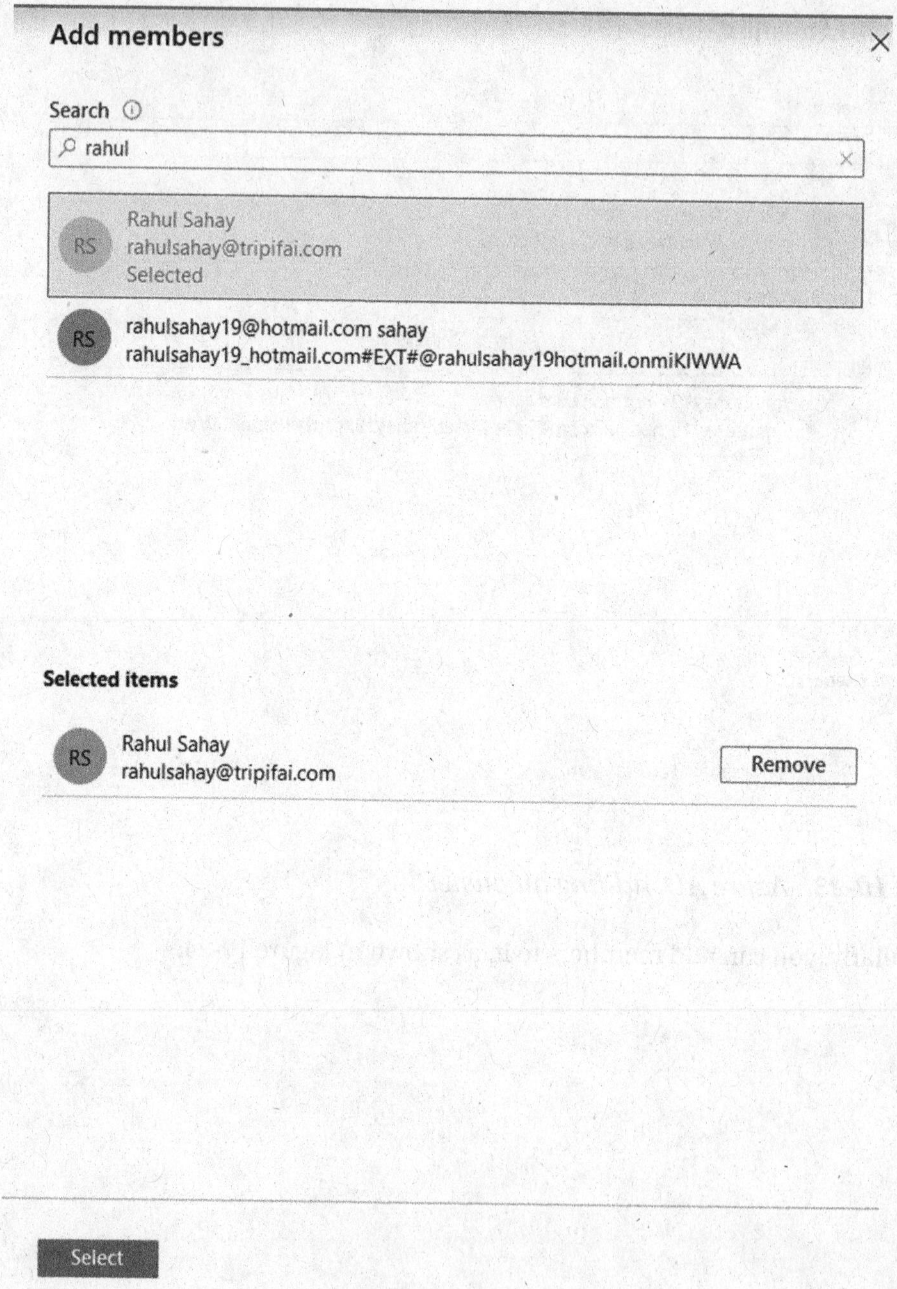

Add members   ✕

Search ⓘ

🔍 rahul   ✕

RS   Rahul Sahay
     rahulsahay@tripifai.com
     Selected

RS   rahulsahay19@hotmail.com sahay
     rahulsahay19_hotmail.com#EXT#@rahulsahay19hotmail.onmiKIWWA

Selected items

RS   Rahul Sahay
     rahulsahay@tripifai.com   Remove

Select

Figure 10-24. *Azure AD, adding members to a group*

My group settings look like Figure 10-25.

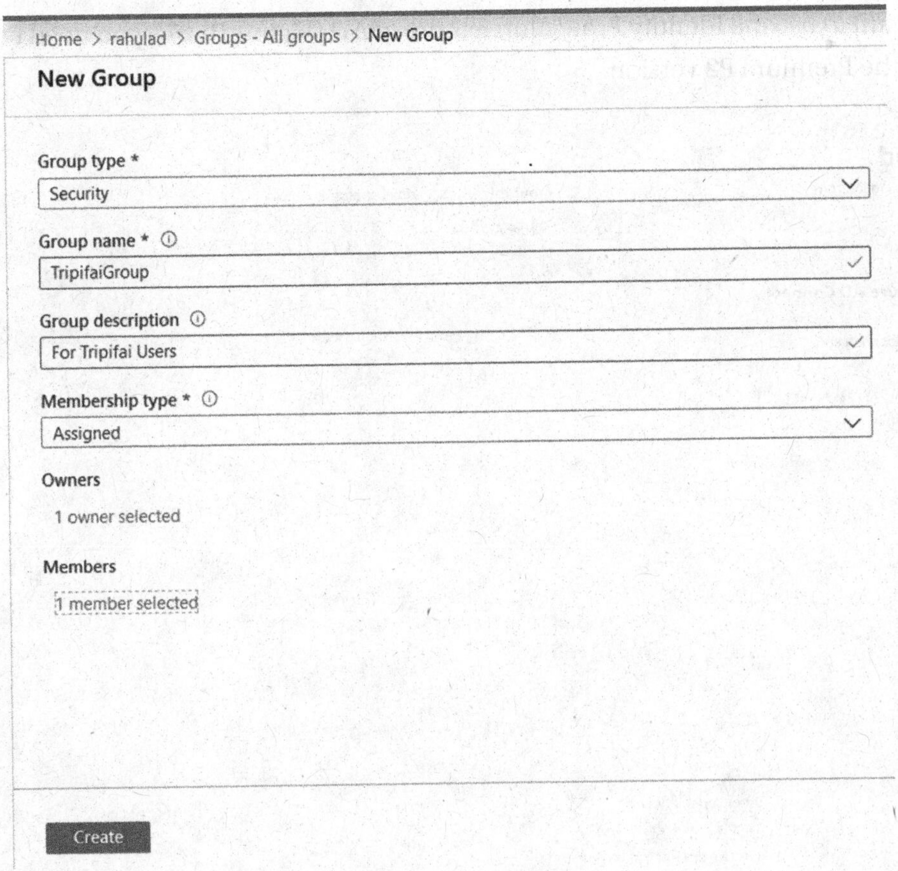

Figure 10-25. *Azure AD group settings*

You can see that the groups list has been populated now, as shown in Figure 10-26.

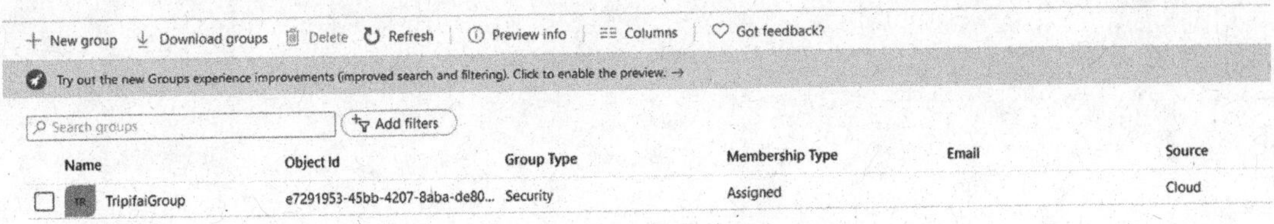

Figure 10-26. *Azure AD groups*

Using Identity Protection

If you want to use the Identity Protection feature of AD (Figure 10-27), you need to enable the Premium P2 version.

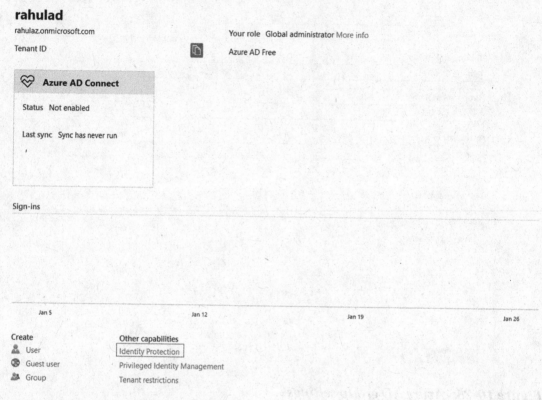

Figure 10-27. *Identity Protection*

Click Identity Protection and then click "Get a Premium trial to use this feature," as shown in Figure 10-28.

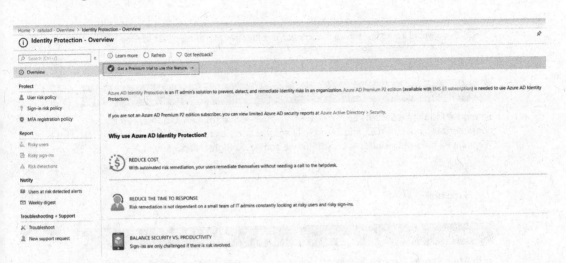

Figure 10-28. *Identity Protection overview*

This will take you to the required screen, as shown in Figure 10-29.

Activate   ✕

Browse available plans and features

 If you would like to purchase a subscription directly from Microsoft, please see the
Purchase services catalog.

ENTERPRISE MOBILITY + SECURITY E5

Enterprise Mobility + Security E5 is the comprehensive cloud solution to address your
consumerization of IT, BYOD, and SaaS challenges. In addition to Azure Active Directory
Premium P2 the suite includes Microsoft Intune and Azure Rights Management.

More information

∨ Free trial

AZURE AD PREMIUM P2

With Azure Active Directory Premium P2 you can gain access to advanced security features,
richer reports and rule based assignments to applications. Your end users will benefit from
self-service capabilities and customized branding.

More information

∧ Free trial

Azure Active Directory Premium P2 enhances your directory with additional
features that include multi-factor authentication, policy driven management and
end-user self-service. Learn more about features

The trial includes 100 licenses and will be active for 30 days beginning on the
activation date. If you wish to upgrade to a paid version, you will need to
purchase Azure Active Directory Premium P2. Learn more about pricing

Azure Active Directory Premium P2 is licensed separately from Azure Services. By
confirming this activation you agree to the Microsoft Online Subscription
Agreement and the Privacy Statement.

Activate

Figure 10-29. *Activation screen for Identity Protection*

From here, click the Azure AD Premium P2 option and activate Identity Protection, as shown in Figure 10-30. This will be available to you for 30 days.

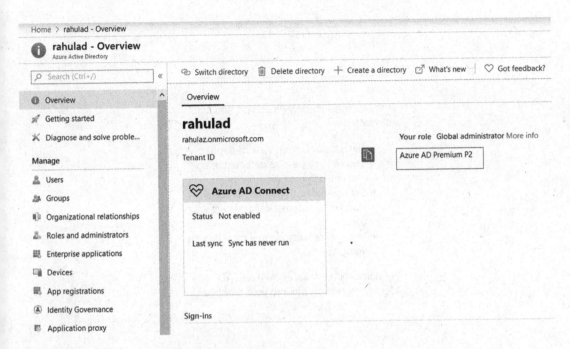

Figure 10-30. *Activating Premium P2*

The P2 level allows all of the premium features that we are about to discuss. Let's go to the marketplace and search for *Identity Protection*. This will take you to the screen shown in Figure 10-31.

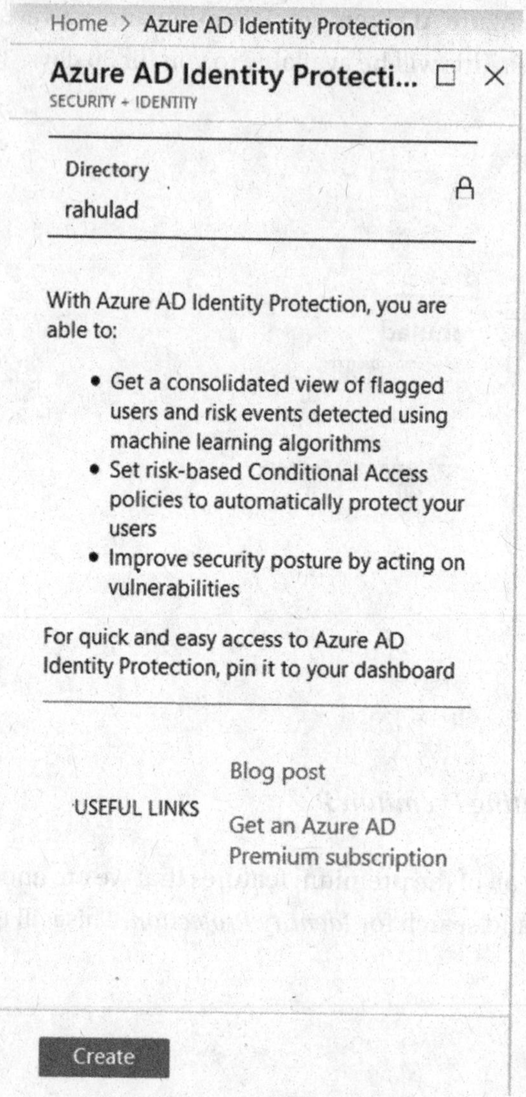

Home > Azure AD Identity Protection

Azure AD Identity Protecti... □ ✕
SECURITY + IDENTITY

Directory

rahulad

With Azure AD Identity Protection, you are able to:

- Get a consolidated view of flagged users and risk events detected using machine learning algorithms
- Set risk-based Conditional Access policies to automatically protect your users
- Improve security posture by acting on vulnerabilities

For quick and easy access to Azure AD Identity Protection, pin it to your dashboard

USEFUL LINKS

Blog post

Get an Azure AD Premium subscription

Create

Figure 10-31. *Security and Identity Protection*

My example shows rahulad as the account, which I created some time ago. If you would like to use another directory, then you can click "Switch directory," as shown in Figure 10-32.

Figure 10-32. *"Switch directory" option*

This will open the screen shown in Figure 10-33.

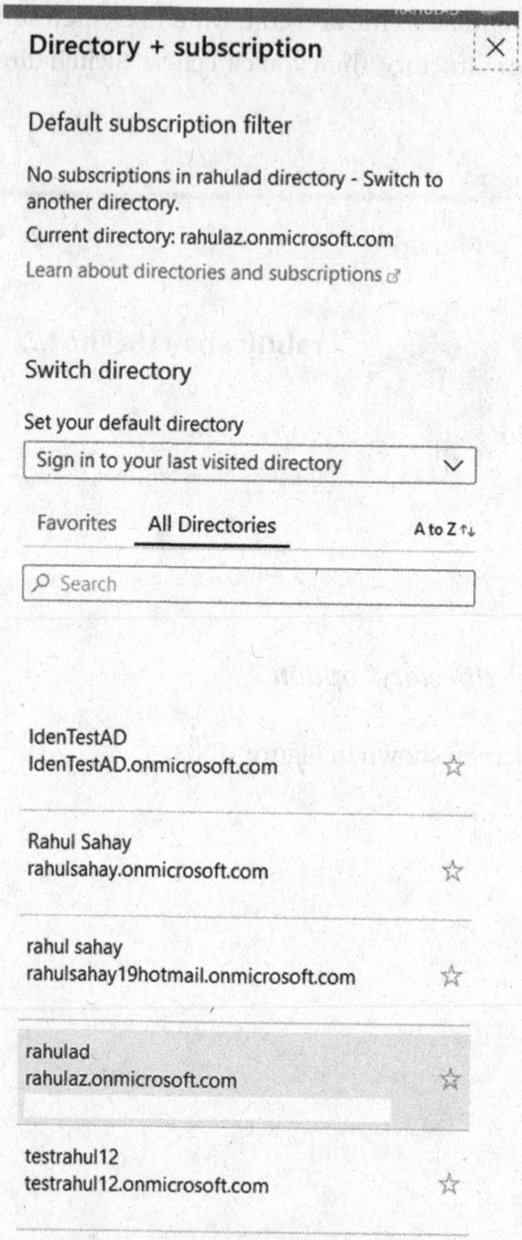

Directory + subscription   ×

Default subscription filter

No subscriptions in rahulad directory - Switch to
another directory.

Current directory: rahulaz.onmicrosoft.com

Learn about directories and subscriptions ⧉

Switch directory

Set your default directory

| Sign in to your last visited directory   ∨ |

Favorites   **All Directories**   A to Z ↑↓

| 🔎 Search |

IdenTestAD
IdenTestAD.onmicrosoft.com   ☆

Rahul Sahay
rahulsahay.onmicrosoft.com   ☆

rahul sahay
rahulsahay19hotmail.onmicrosoft.com   ☆

rahulad
rahulaz.onmicrosoft.com   ☆

testrahul12
testrahul12.onmicrosoft.com   ☆

Figure 10-33. *"Switch directory" options*

Identity Protection is a series of machine learning algorithms that will analyze the users, logins, and any sort of vulnerabilities in your Active Directory account. It can protect your account against any suspicious activity. Figure 10-34 shows the Overview screen.

Figure 10-34. *Identity Protection Overview screen*

Creating a User Risk Policy

You can click "User risk policy" in the left panel to see whether any risky user or any risky event is associated with this AD. Let's go ahead and set up a policy that alerts you to risky sign-ins, as shown in Figure 10-35.

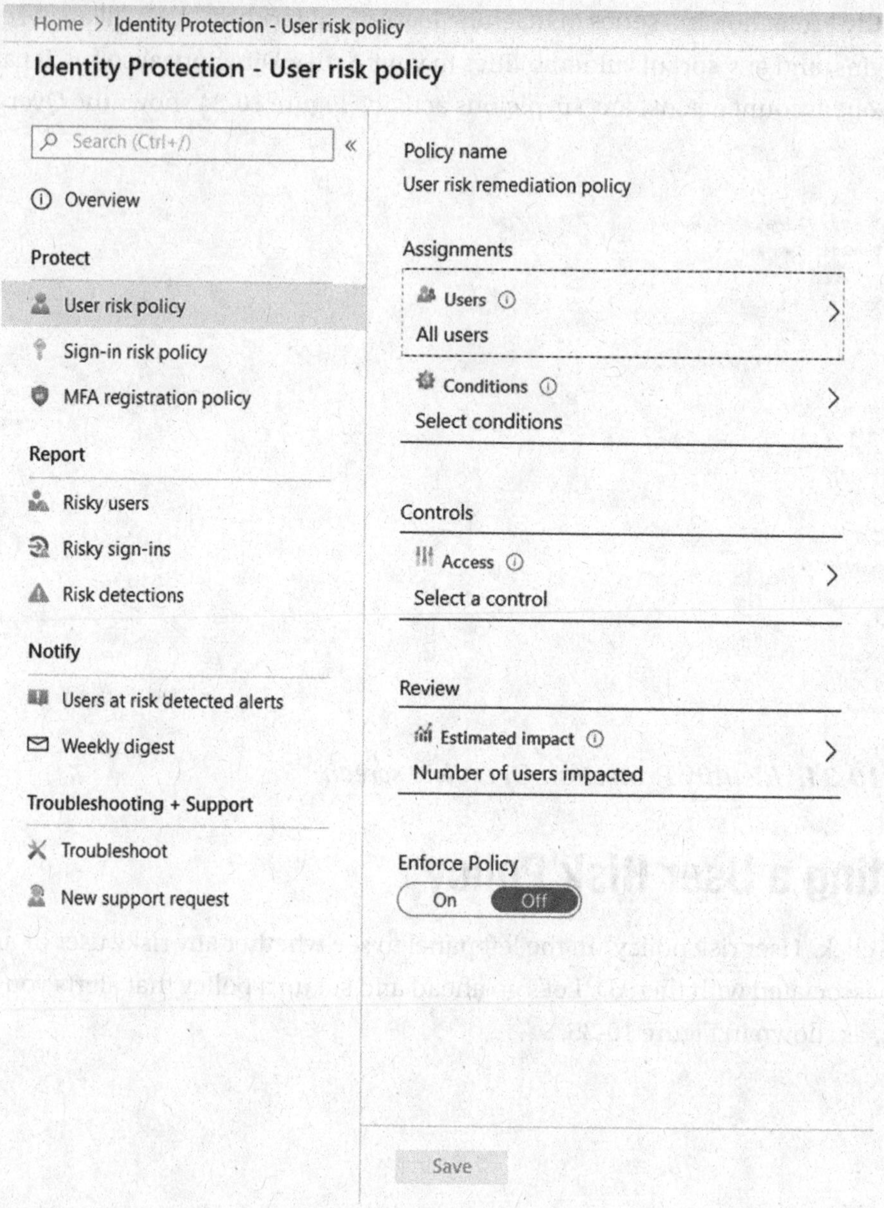

Home > Identity Protection - User risk policy

Identity Protection - User risk policy

Search (Ctrl+/) «

- ⓘ Overview

Protect

- 👤 User risk policy
- 🔑 Sign-in risk policy
- 🛡 MFA registration policy

Report

- 👥 Risky users
- 🔁 Risky sign-ins
- ⚠ Risk detections

Notify

- 📇 Users at risk detected alerts
- ✉ Weekly digest

Troubleshooting + Support

- 🔧 Troubleshoot
- 👤 New support request

Policy name
User risk remediation policy

Assignments

👥 Users ⓘ   >
All users

⚙ Conditions ⓘ   >
Select conditions

Controls

𝄃𝄃𝄃 Access ⓘ   >
Select a control

Review

📊 Estimated impact ⓘ   >
Number of users impacted

Enforce Policy
(On   Off)

Save

Figure 10-35. *Setting up a user risk policy*

Here, you can include all users or exclude a few. Basically, you want to exclude any users within the organization whom you know and include any that might attempt a risky sign-in, as shown in Figure 10-36.

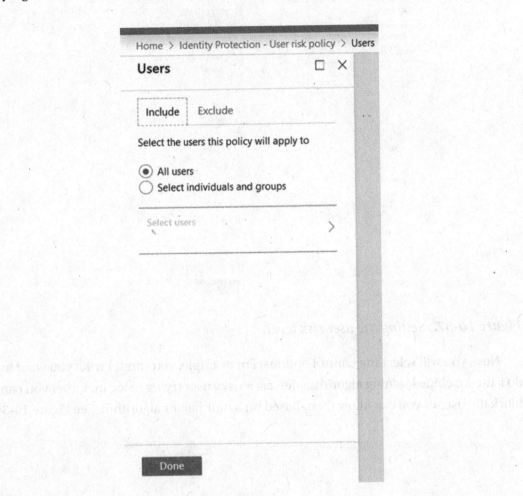

Figure 10-36. *Adding users to a risk policy*

Let's say you are not expecting someone from Brazil or Ukraine to log in to your application. In that case, you can select the risk level shown in Figure 10-37.

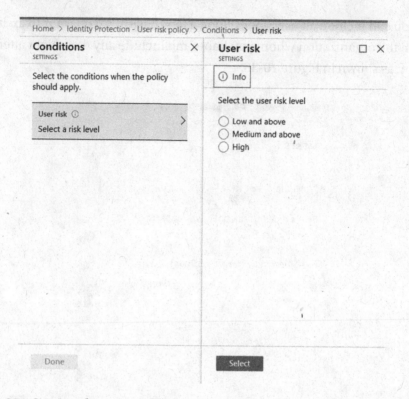

Figure 10-37. *Setting the user risk level*

Next, you will select the control options. For example, you can set what you want to do if the machine learning algorithm detects a risky user trying to log in. Either you can block the user or you can allow them based on a multifactor algorithm. See Figure 10-38.

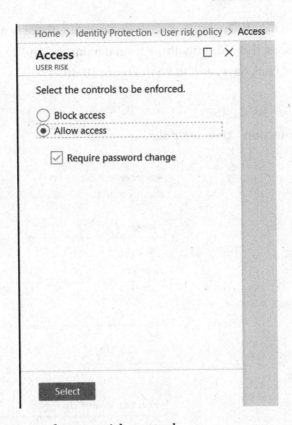

Figure 10-38. *Setting up the user risk controls*

Next, run the estimated impact report, as shown in Figure 10-39.

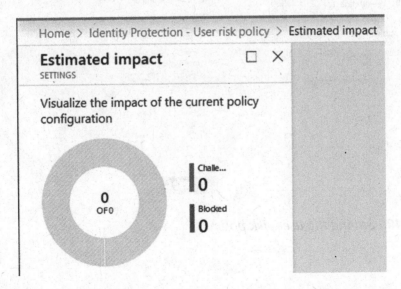

Figure 10-39. *Estimated impact*

Since I have only a handful users that were just created, there is no impact. But if you have 1,000 or more users, then Identity Protection becomes significant. Finally, you can enforce the policy and click Save, as shown in Figure 10-40.

Home > Identity Protection - User risk policy

Identity Protection - User risk policy

🔍 Search (Ctrl+/) «	Policy name
ⓘ Overview	User risk remediation policy
Protect	**Assignments**
🧑 User risk policy	👥 Users ⓘ >
🛡 Sign-in risk policy	All users
🛡 MFA registration policy	⚙ Conditions ⓘ >
Report	User risk
🧑‍🤝‍🧑 Risky users	
🔁 Risky sign-ins	**Controls**
⚠ Risk detections	▌▌▌ Access ⓘ >
Notify	Require password change
📧 Users at risk detected alerts	
✉ Weekly digest	**Review**
Troubleshooting + Support	📊 Estimated impact ⓘ >
🔧 Troubleshoot	Number of users impacted
🧑 New support request .	
	Enforce Policy
	(On) Off
	Save

Figure 10-40. *Saving the user risk policy*

Setting Up a Sign-in Risk Policy

Now you'll need to set up a sign-in risk policy. This is also pretty straightforward, as shown in Figure 10-41.

Home > Identity Protection - Sign-in risk policy

Identity Protection - Sign-in risk policy

🔍 Search (Ctrl+/) «	**Policy name** Sign-in risk remediation policy
ⓘ Overview	
Protect	**Assignments**
👤 User risk policy	👥 Users ⓘ ⟩ All users
⭐ Sign-in risk policy	
🛡 MFA registration policy	⚙ Conditions ⓘ ⟩ Select conditions
Report	
👥 Risky users	**Controls**
🔁 Risky sign-ins	⫼ Access ⓘ ⟩ Select a control
⚠ Risk detections	
Notify	**Review**
📣 Users at risk detected alerts	📊 Estimated impact ⓘ ⟩ Number of sign-ins impacted
✉ Weekly digest	
Troubleshooting + Support	
🔧 Troubleshoot	**Enforce Policy**
👤 New support request	On (Off)

Figure 10-41. Setting up a sign-in risk policy

MFA Registration Policy

Next, you can set up multifactor authentication, as shown in Figure 10-42.

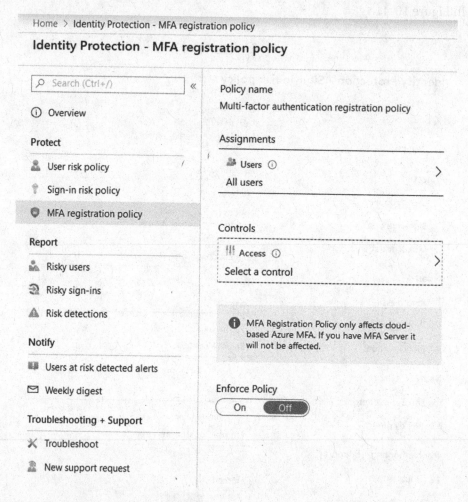

Figure 10-42. *MFA registration policy*

Once you have set up multifactor authentication, you can see relevant events on the Overview screen, or you can pin MFA to the dashboard as well.

Setting Up a Self-Service Password Reset

A self-service password reset means that Active Directory users will be able to reset their own passwords. Figure 10-43 shows the password reset properties.

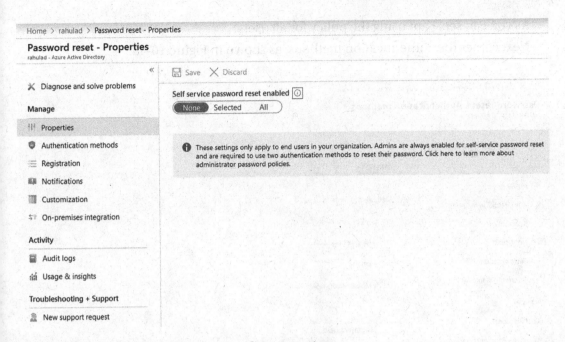

Figure 10-43. *Self-service password reset options*

If you want this to enable for a particular group, you can do so as shown in Figure 10-44. Currently, I don't have any groups, which is why the options are not populating.

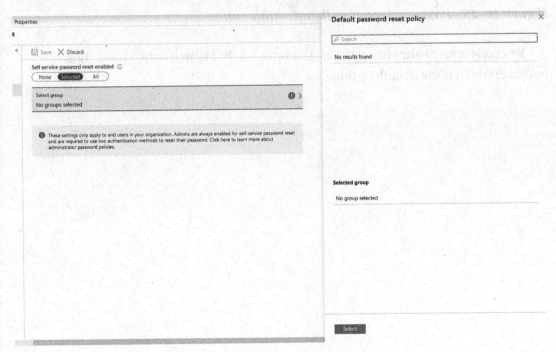

Figure 10-44. *Default password reset policy options*

As you can see, I am using the policy for all users.

Next comes the authentication methods, as shown in Figure 10-45.

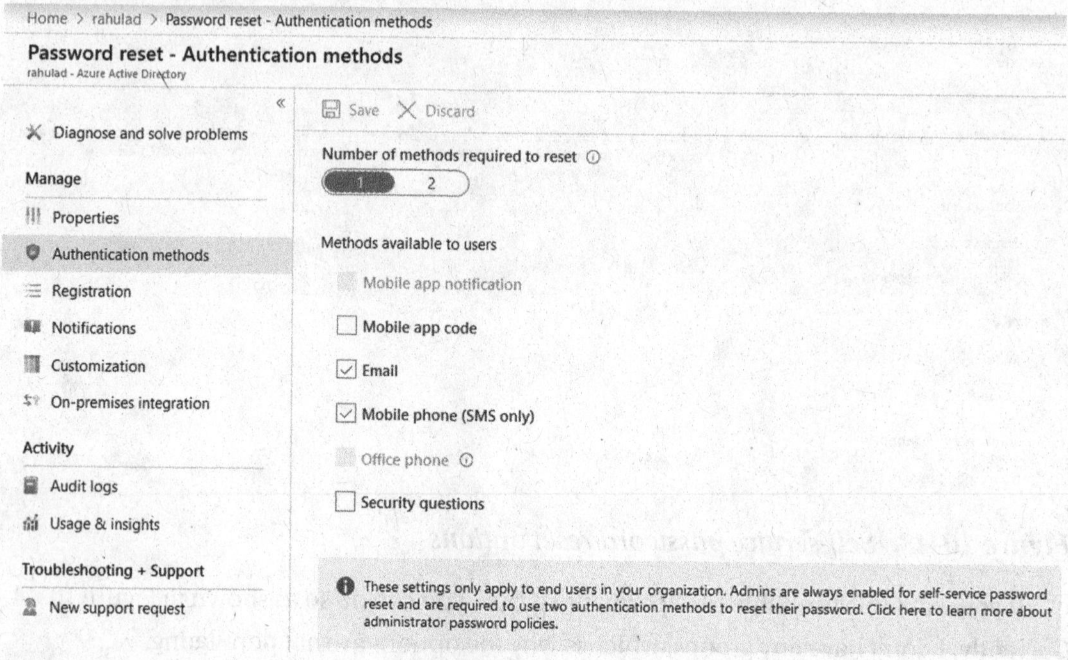

Figure 10-45. *Password reset, authentication options*

You can choose either from option 1 or option 2. In Figure 10-46, I have chosen option 2, which is the default option.

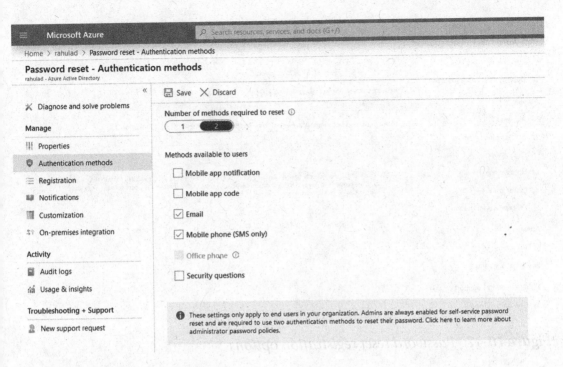

Figure 10-46. *Choosing option 2*

Normally, at an enterprise level, you usually use mobile app notifications, which is why option 2 is my choice here.

Next comes the registration settings, where you can set for how many days you want users to be prompted to verify their phone number or email address. See Figure 10-47.

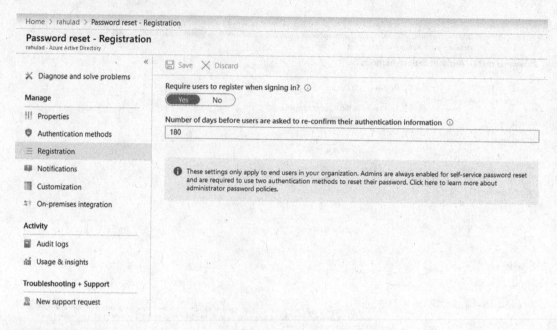

Figure 10-47. *Password reset registration options*

Testing the AD Flow

Now, let's go ahead and test the flow in this section. During an AD flow test, you can sign in with the temporary password that was generated during user creation, as shown in Figure 10-48 and Figure 10-49.

Figure 10-48. *Azure sign-in screen*

Figure 10-49. *Azure password screen*

Then, you need to change the password, as shown in Figure 10-50.

Figure 10-50. *Azure Sign-in password change screen*

Next, you need to complete the security clearance such as providing a phone number, etc., as shown in Figure 10-51.

Figure 10-51. *Azure sign-in, more information screen*

The next screen is where you will enter your phone details, as shown in Figure 10-52.

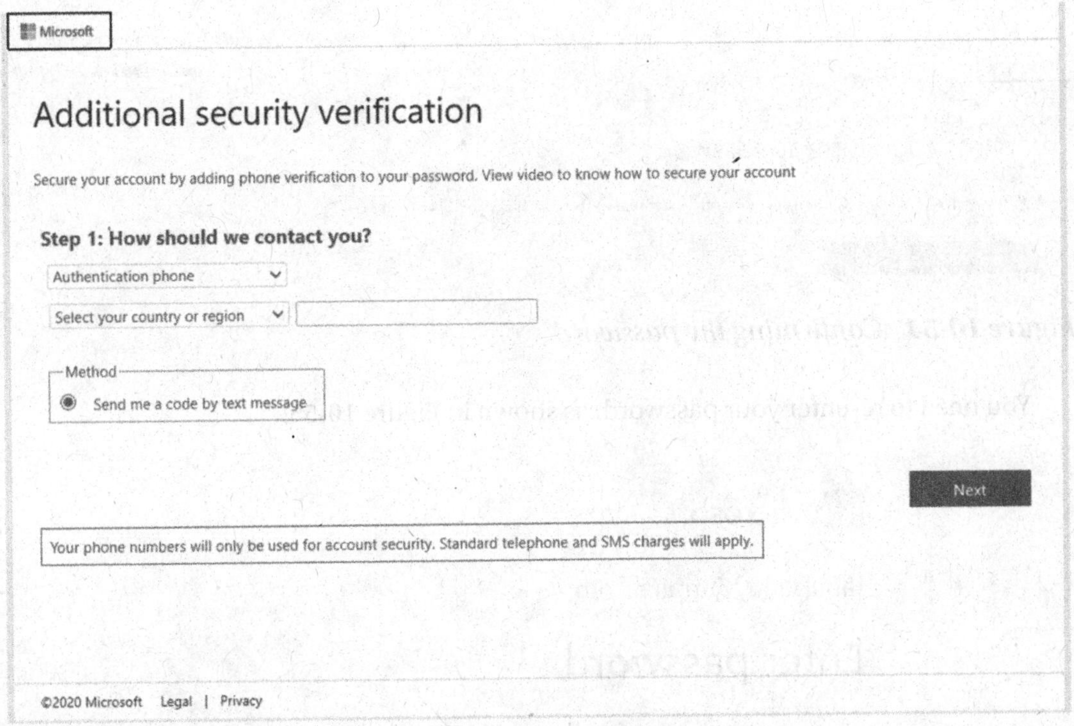

Figure 10-52. *Additional security information screen*

You will get a verification key on your number. After verification, your account will be enabled, as shown in Figure 10-53.

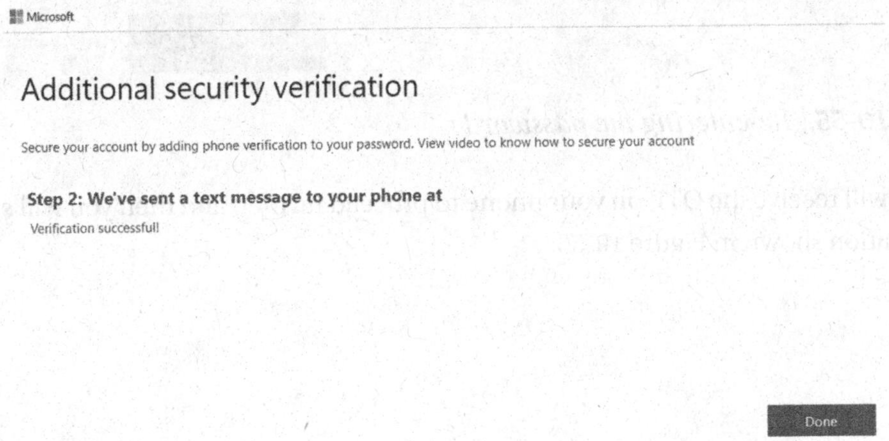

Figure 10-53. *Additional security confirmation screen*

After confirming, you will be taken to the "confirm your current password" screen, as shown in Figure 10-54.

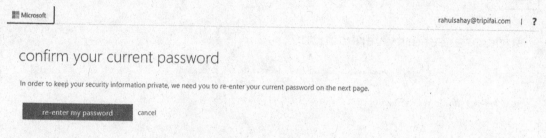

Figure 10-54. *Confirming the password*

You need to re-enter your password, as shown in Figure 10-55.

Figure 10-55. *Re-entering the password*

You will receive the OTP on your phone to proceed further, and then you will see the confirmation shown in Figure 10-56.

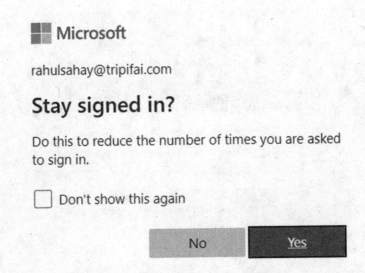

Figure 10-56. *Login process*

You have now come to the settings that you actually configured in the portal, as shown in Figure 10-57.

Figure 10-57. *Security settings*

After verification, you will be taken to the home screen, as shown in Figure 10-58.

Figure 10-58. *Azure AD home screen*

Conditional Access

In this section, you'll learn about conditional access, which is part of the security settings, as shown in Figure 10-59.

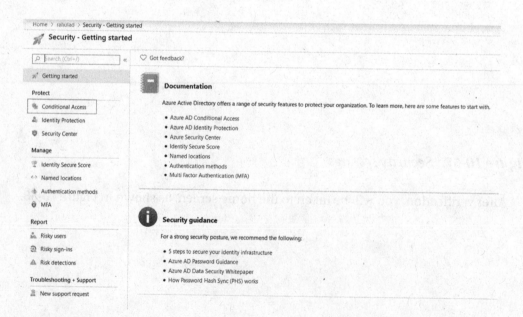

Figure 10-59. *Conditional access screen*

After clicking Azure AD Conditional Access, you will see the screen in Figure 10-60.

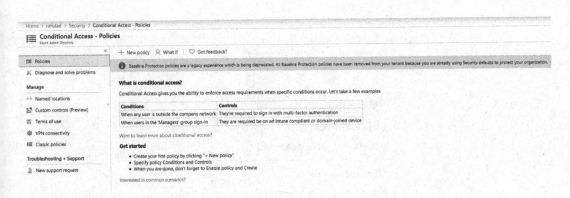

Figure 10-60. *Conditional access policies*

The concept of conditional access is pretty simple, as shown in Figure 10-61.

Conditions	Controls
When any user is outside the company network	They're required to sign in with multi-factor authentication
When users in the 'Managers' group sign-in	They are required be on an Intune compliant or domain-joined device

Figure 10-61. *Conditions and controls*

Click New Policy. This will bring up the screen in Figure 10-62.

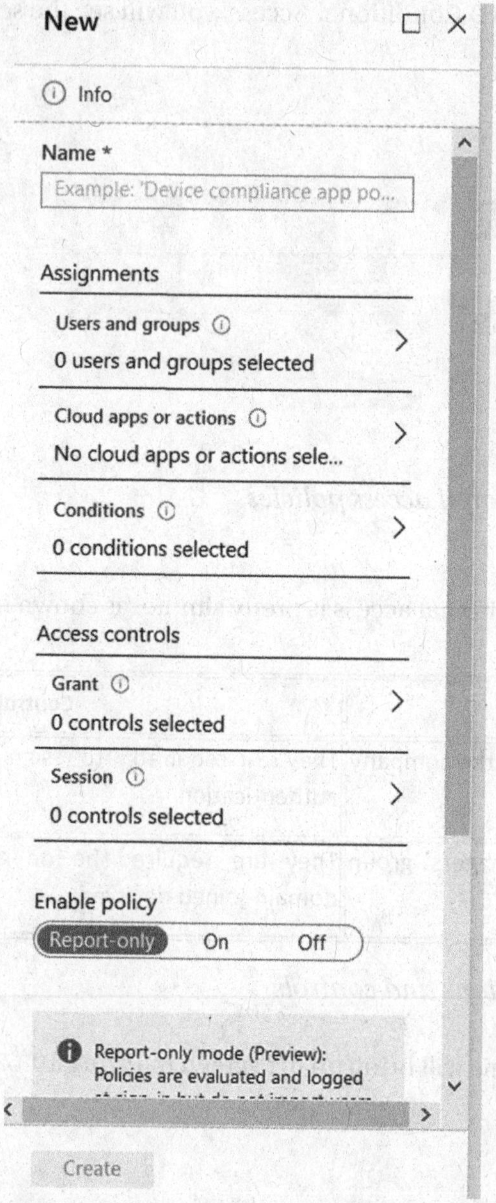

Figure 10-62. *New policy options*

Next, you can give the policy a name and go to the "Users and groups" section, as shown in Figure 10-63.

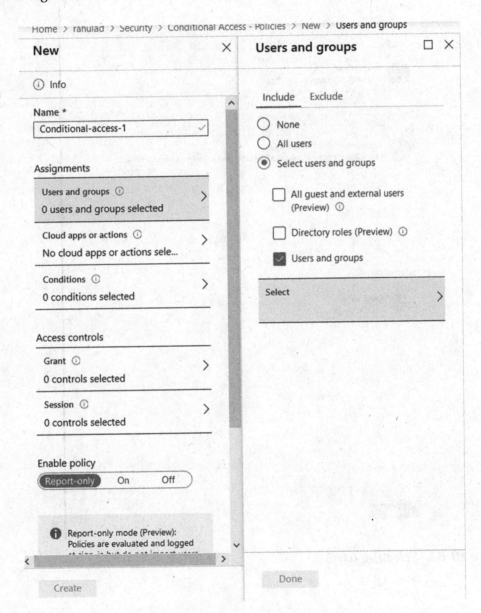

Figure 10-63. Adding users and groups to the policy

Then select the user, as shown in Figure 10-64.

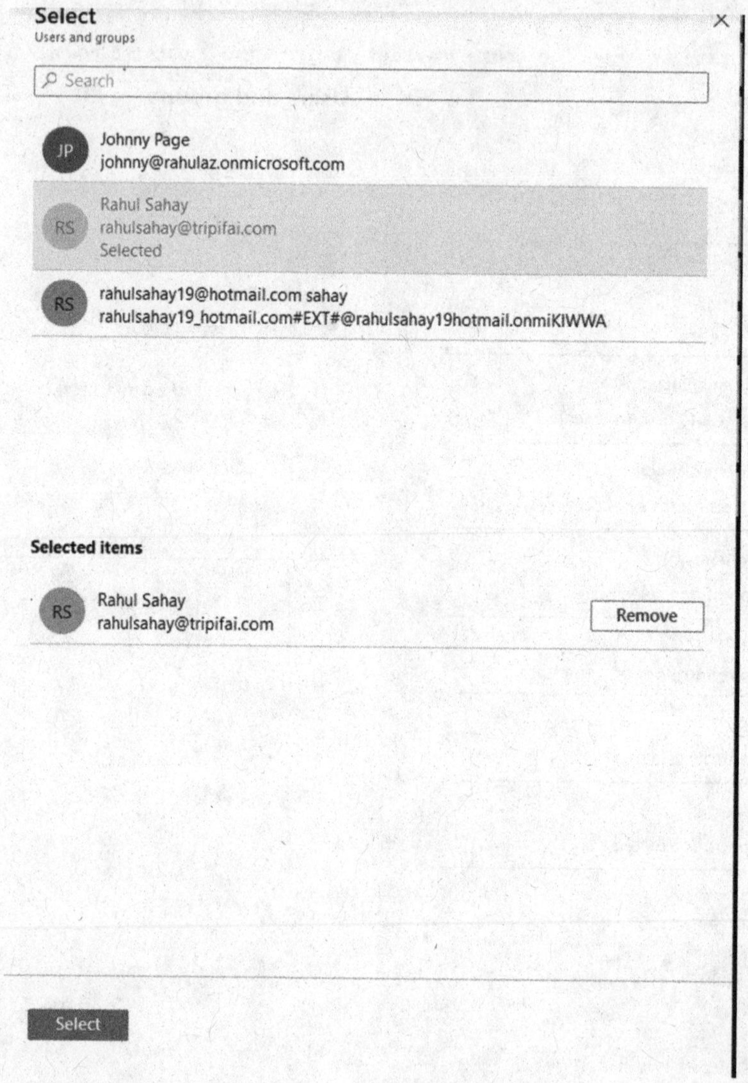

Figure 10-64. *Selecting users*

Next you need to select "Cloud apps" or "User actions," as shown in Figure 10-65.

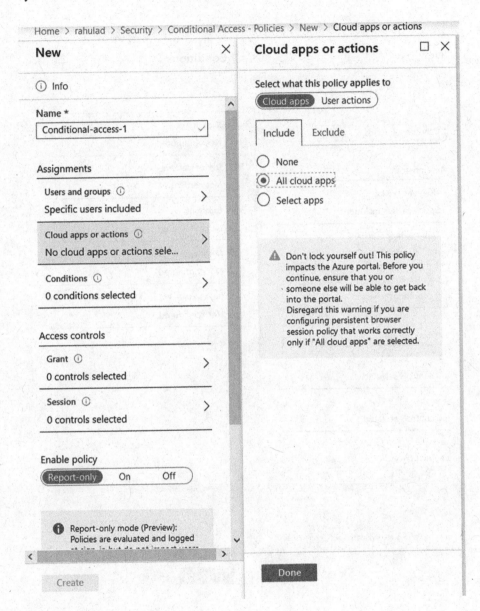

Figure 10-65. Adding apps or actions

Next comes the Conditions section, as shown in Figure 10-66.

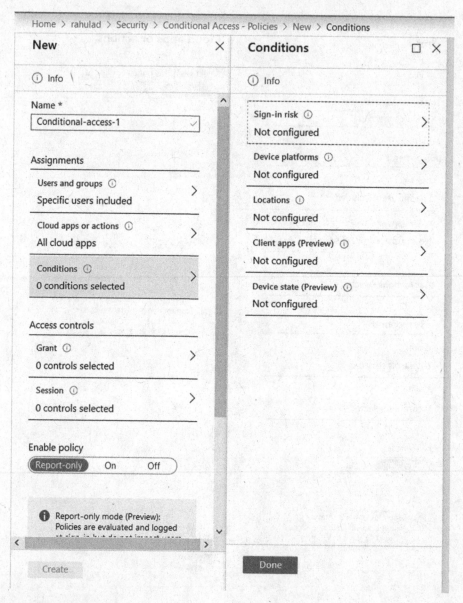

Figure 10-66. *Conditions section*

I have set the sign-in risk to Medium, as shown in Figure 10-67, which means the machine learning algorithm internally evaluates risk in medium way.

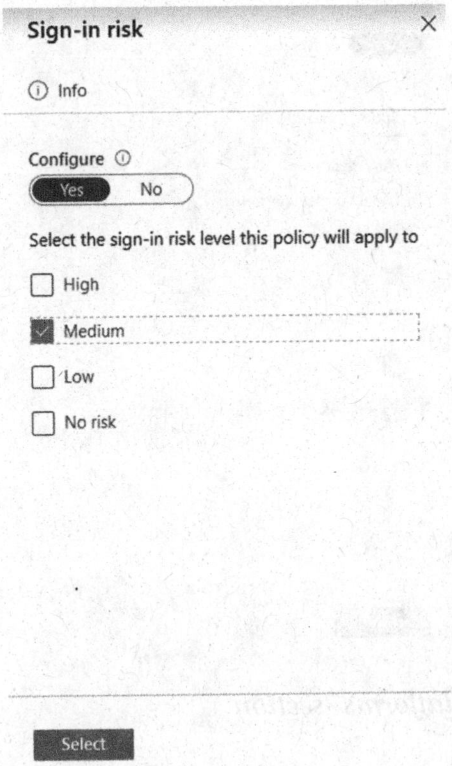

Sign-in risk   ✕

ⓘ Info

Configure ⓘ
Yes   No

Select the sign-in risk level this policy will apply to

☐ High

☑ Medium

☐ Low

☐ No risk

Select

Figure 10-67. *Sign-in risk levels*

Next comes the device platforms. Figure 10-68 shows the platforms that I have chosen.

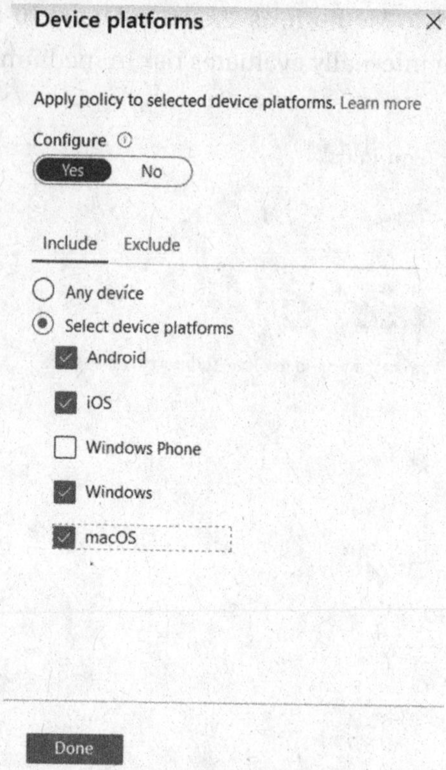

Figure 10-68. *"Device platforms" section*

Next comes the Locations section, as shown in Figure 10-69.

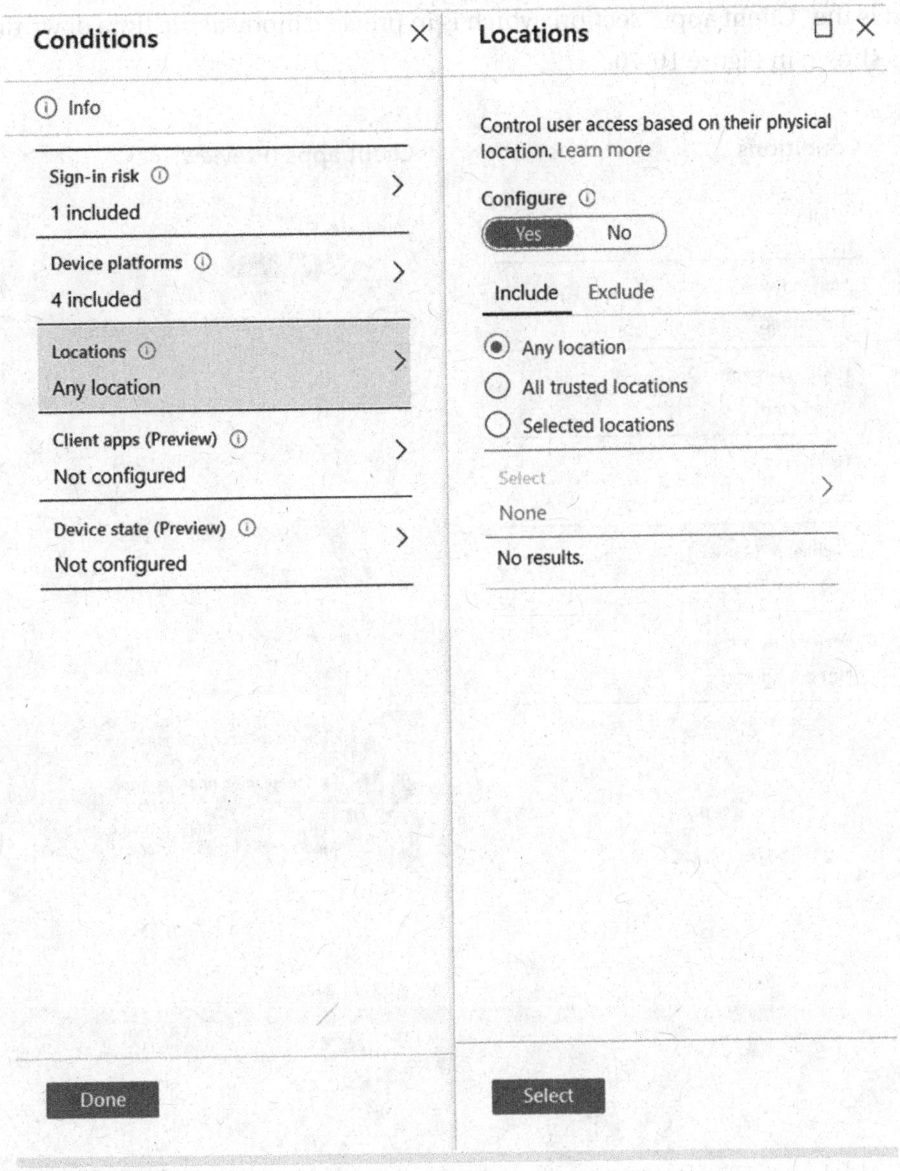

Conditions ✕   **Locations** ☐ ✕

ⓘ Info   Control user access based on their physical
                        location. Learn more

Sign-in risk ⓘ   〉   Configure ⓘ
1 included   (Yes) No

Device platforms ⓘ   〉   Include   Exclude
4 included
                        ⦿ Any location
Locations ⓘ   〉   ◯ All trusted locations
Any location   ◯ Selected locations

Client apps (Preview) ⓘ   〉   Select   〉
Not configured   None

Device state (Preview) ⓘ   〉   No results.
Not configured

Done   Select

Figure 10-69. Locations section

Next is the "Client apps" section, which is in preview mode at the time of writing this book, as shown in Figure 10-70.

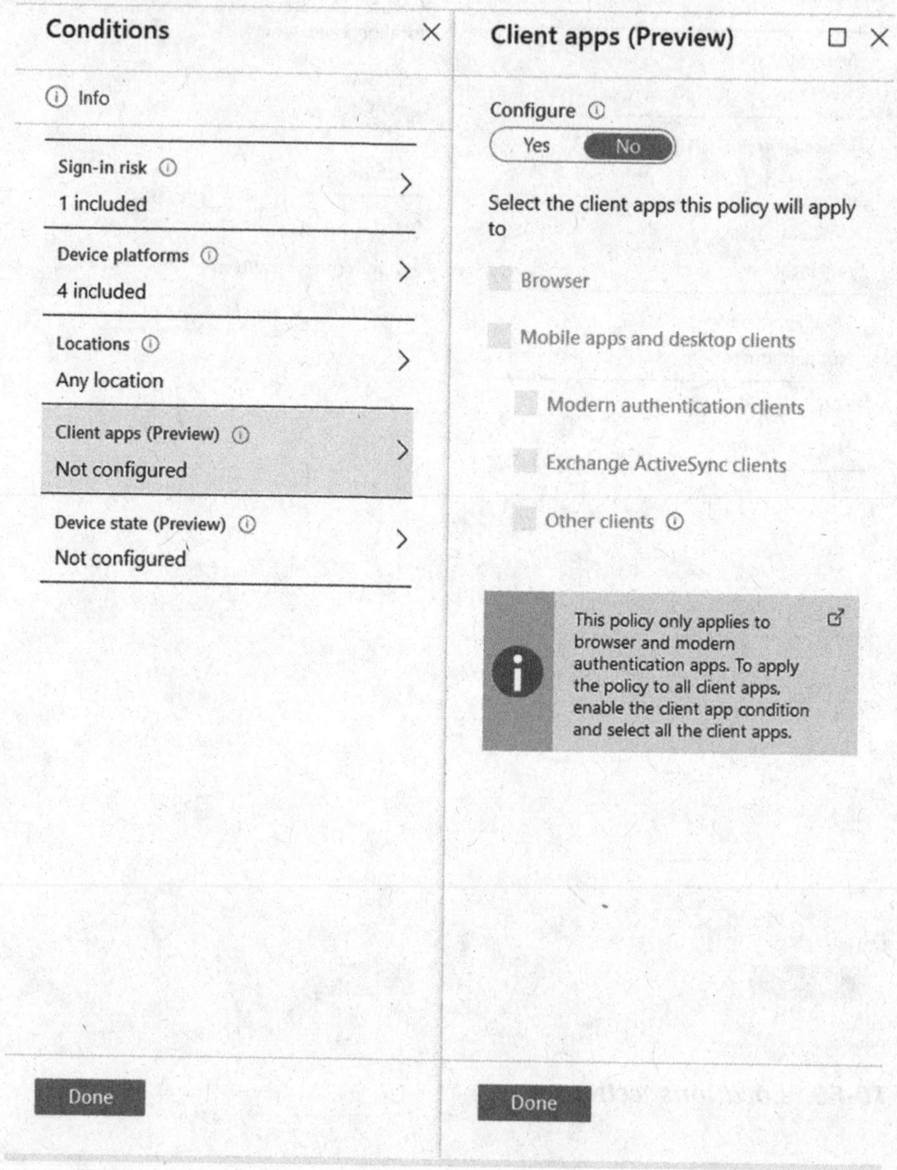

Conditions ✕	Client apps (Preview) ☐ ✕
ⓘ Info	Configure ⓘ
	(Yes (No))
Sign-in risk ⓘ >	
1 included	Select the client apps this policy will apply to
Device platforms ⓘ >	
4 included	▢ Browser
Locations ⓘ >	▢ Mobile apps and desktop clients
Any location	
Client apps (Preview) ⓘ >	▢ Modern authentication clients
Not configured	▢ Exchange ActiveSync clients
Device state (Preview) ⓘ >	▢ Other clients ⓘ
Not configured	
	ⓘ This policy only applies to browser and modern authentication apps. To apply the policy to all client apps, enable the client app condition and select all the client apps. ⬀
Done	Done

Figure 10-70. *"Client apps" section*

You can choose client apps to set conditions as a hybrid app, as shown in Figure 10-71.

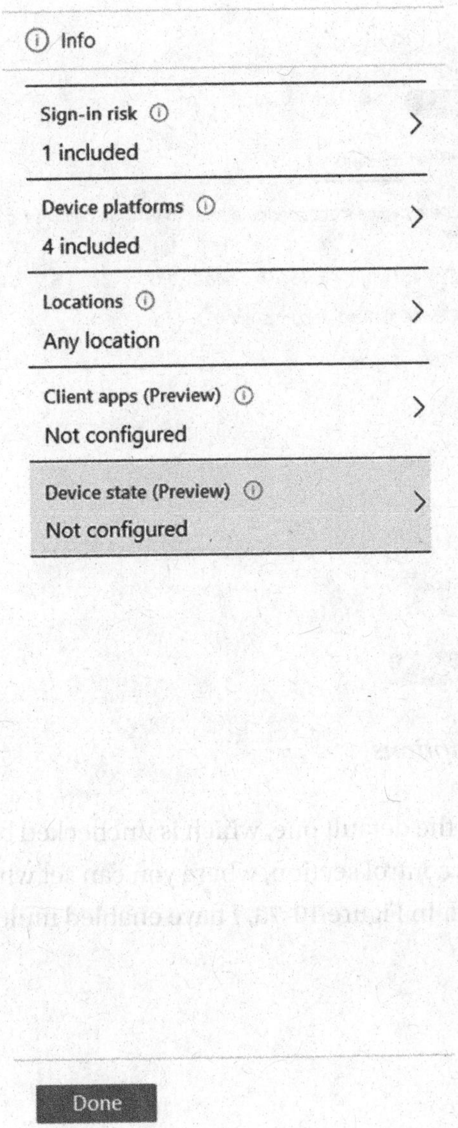

(i) Info

Sign-in risk (i)   >
1 included

Device platforms (i)   >
4 included

Locations (i)   >
Any location

Client apps (Preview) (i)   >
Not configured

Device state (Preview) (i)   >
Not configured

Done

Figure 10-71. *Device state link*

Figure 10-72 shows the Exclude options.

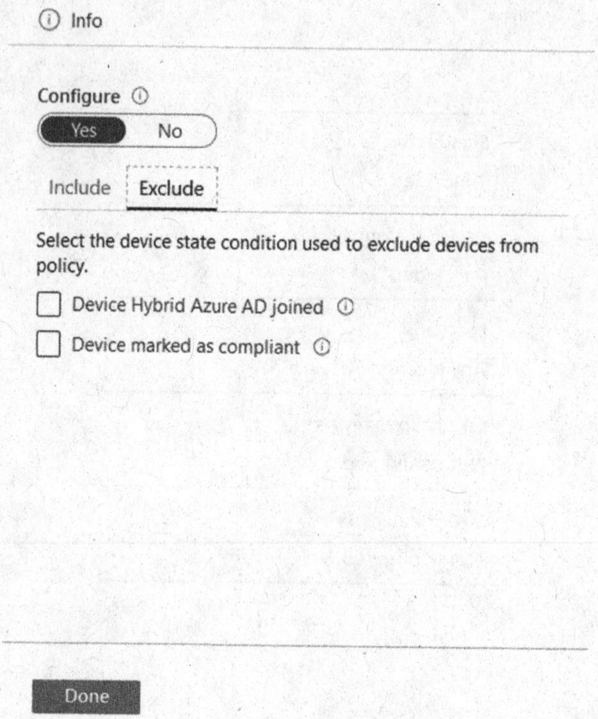

ⓘ Info

Configure ⓘ

Yes   No

Include │ **Exclude**

Select the device state condition used to exclude devices from policy.

☐ Device Hybrid Azure AD joined ⓘ

☐ Device marked as compliant ⓘ

Done

Figure 10-72. *Exclude options*

For now, I will go with the default one, which is unchecked by default.

Next comes the access control section, where you can set what action you would like to do when MFA requested. In Figure 10-73, I have enabled multifactor authentication.

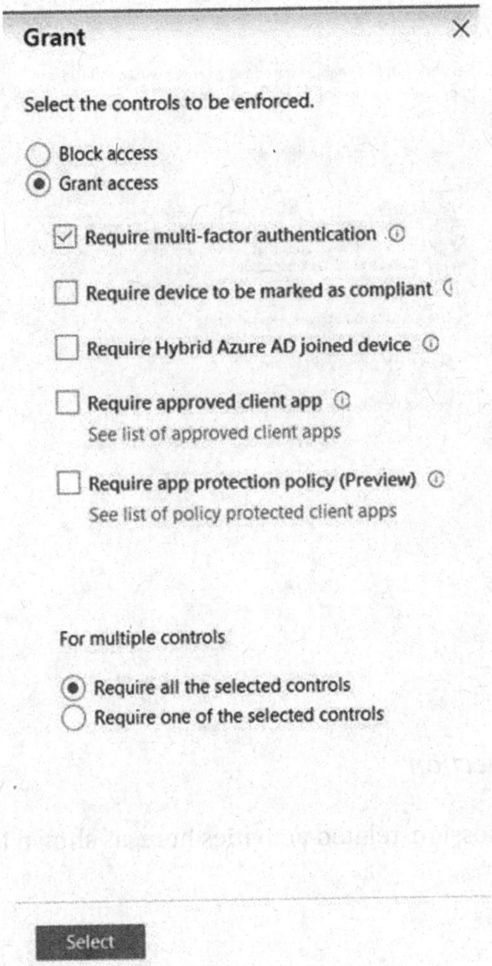

Figure 10-73. *Enabling multifactor authentication*

Next comes the session-level controls, as shown in Figure 10-74. In this case, you can allow them to log in to the application, but they can do limited activities for this single sign-on.

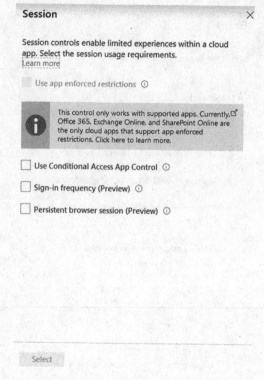

Figure 10-74. *Session section*

You can also control session-related activities here, as shown in Figure 10-75.

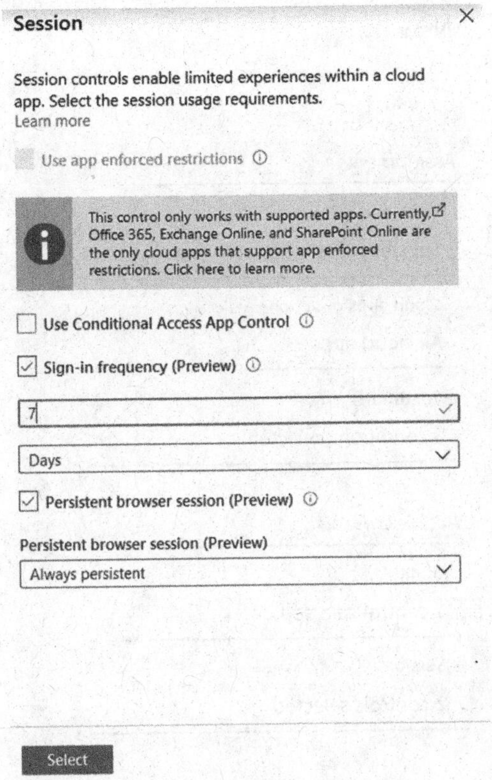

Figure 10-75. *Session details section*

Figure 10-76 shows the finished version of the conditional access configuration.

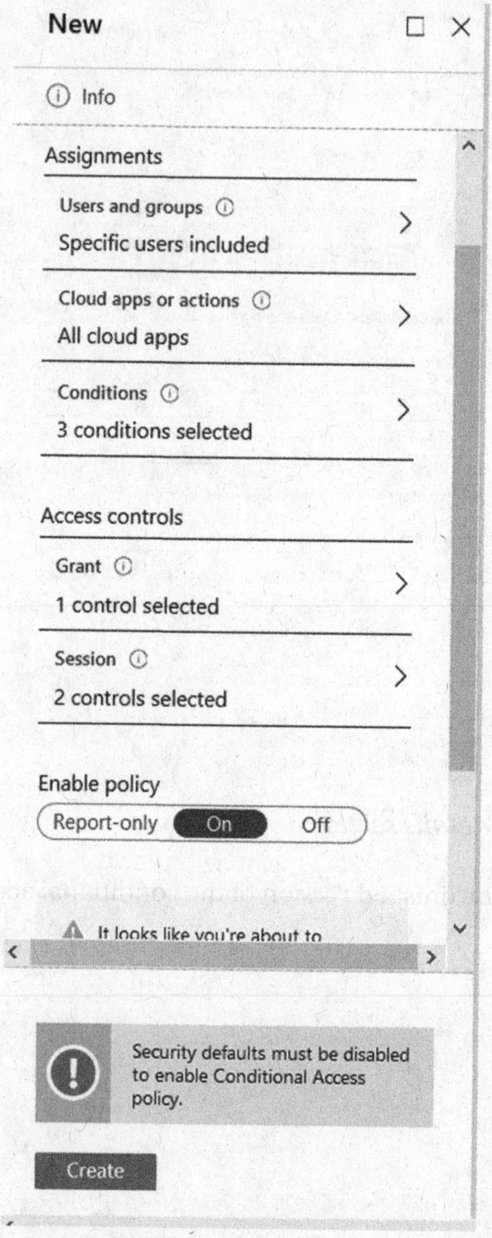

Figure 10-76. Conditional access finished settings

To disable this warning, you need disable the security defaults. For this, you need to go Azure Active Directory and then the Properties section and click the "Manage Security defaults" link. See Figure 10-77.

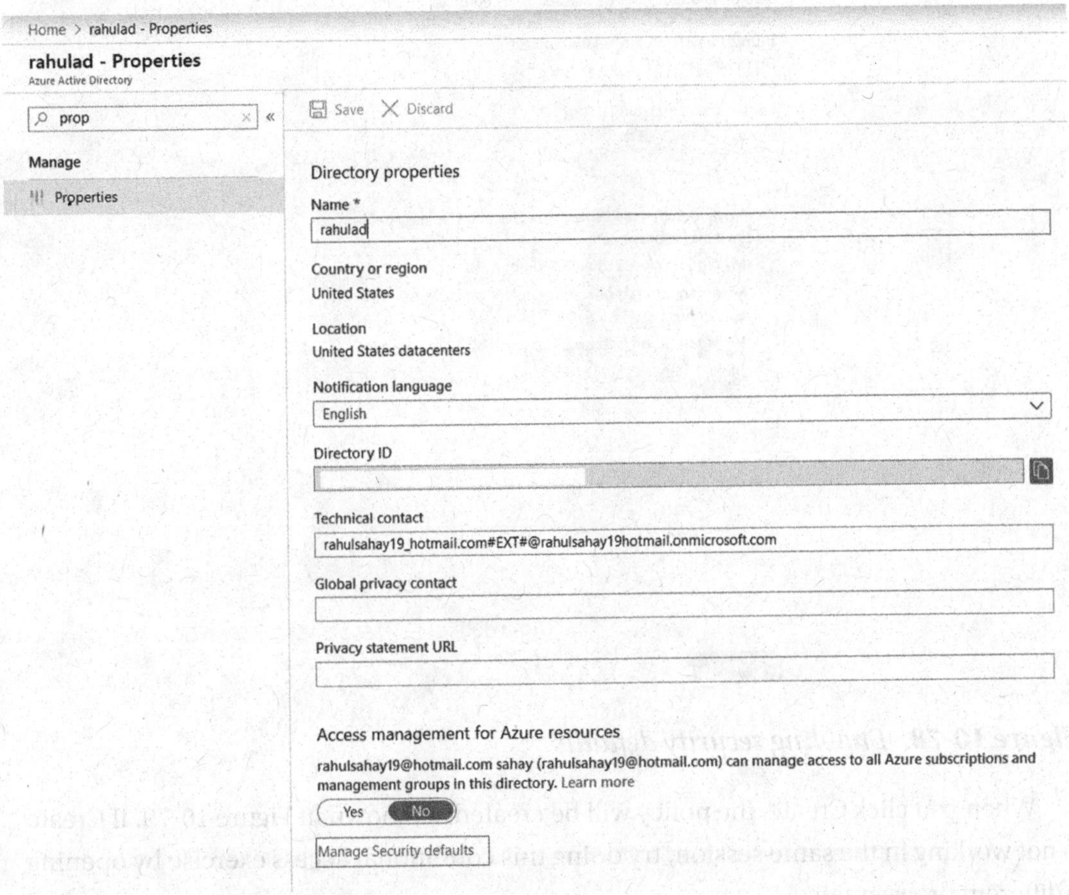

Home > rahulad - Properties

rahulad - Properties
Azure Active Directory

🔍 prop

Manage

Properties

💾 Save ✕ Discard

Directory properties

Name *

rahulad

Country or region
United States

Location
United States datacenters

Notification language

English

Directory ID

Technical contact

rahulsahay19_hotmail.com#EXT#@rahulsahay19hotmail.onmicrosoft.com

Global privacy contact

Privacy statement URL

Access management for Azure resources

rahulsahay19@hotmail.com sahay (rahulsahay19@hotmail.com) can manage access to all Azure subscriptions and management groups in this directory. Learn more

Yes   No

Manage Security defaults

Figure 10-77. *Azure AD Properties section*

Then save the settings, as shown in Figure 10-78.

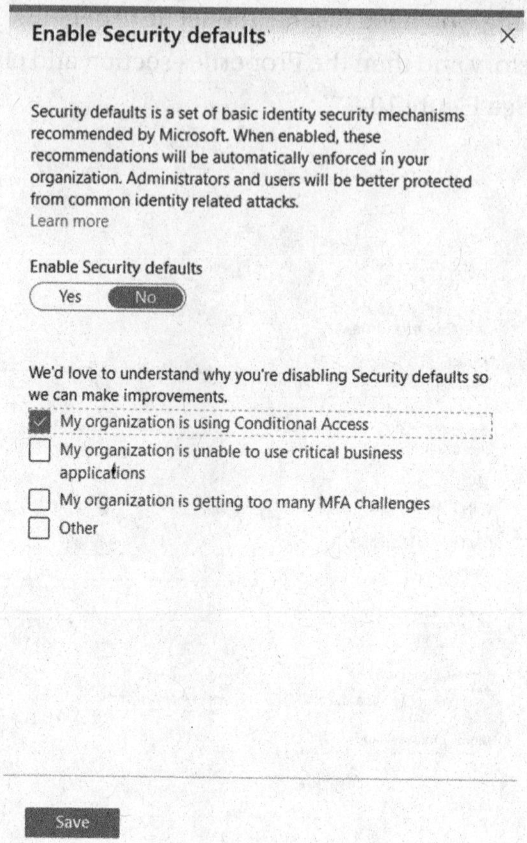

Figure 10-78. *Enabling security defaults*

When you click Create, the policy will be created, as shown in Figure 10-79. If Create is not working in the same session, try doing this conditional access exercise by opening a different browser tab.

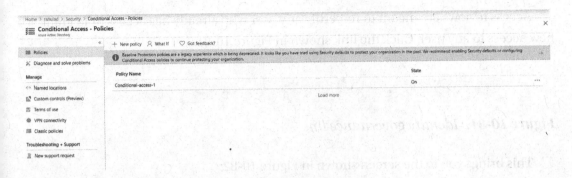

Figure 10-79. Conditional access policies list

Identity Governance

Identity governance is how you can do things like access reviews. You can search for this feature in the marketplace to get the service. One point to note here is that this feature is available only for EMS E5 or P2 level, as shown in Figure 10-80. Hence, to use it here, you first need to enable the trial version.

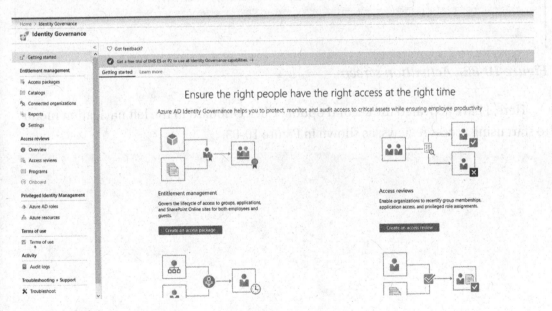

Figure 10-80. Conditional access finished version

Access reviews are meant to re-certify any user who already has access or to grant new access to any user. Click the link shown in Figure 10-81.

Figure 10-81. *Identity governance link*

This brings you to the screen shown in Figure 10-82.

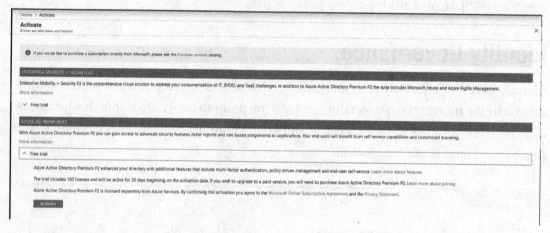

Figure 10-82. *Activation screen*

Here, I have activated the second option. Click Onboard in the left navigation menu to start using access reviews, as shown in Figure 10-83.

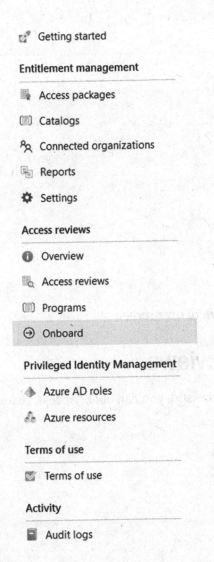

Figure 10-83. Onboard link

After clicking Onboard, the screen shown in Figure 10-84 will open.

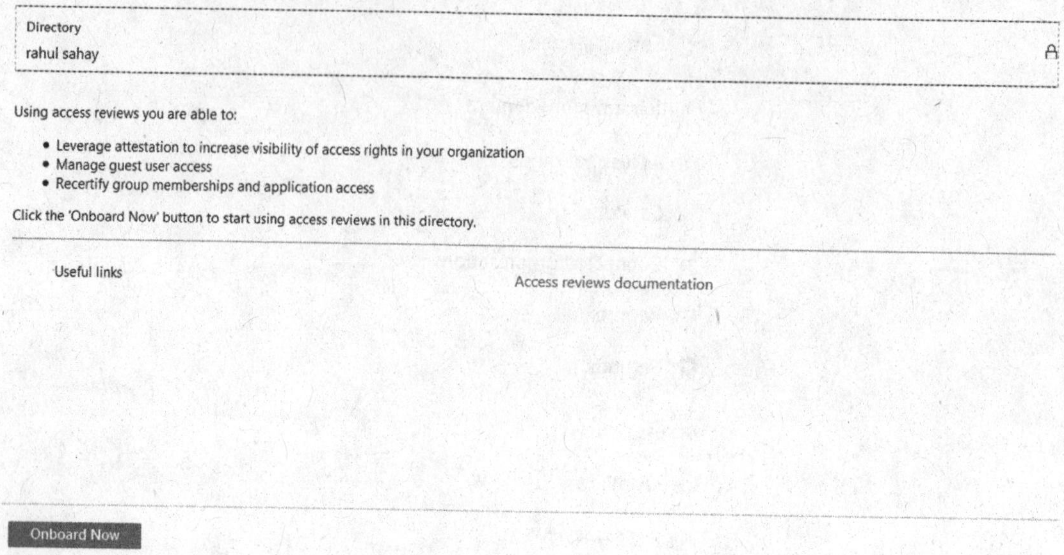

Directory
rahul sahay

Using access reviews you are able to:

- Leverage attestation to increase visibility of access rights in your organization
- Manage guest user access
- Recertify group memberships and application access

Click the 'Onboard Now' button to start using access reviews in this directory.

Useful links   Access reviews documentation

Onboard Now

Figure 10-84. *Onboard new user screen*

Using Access Reviews

Once the onboarding is successful, you can click "Access reviews," as shown in Figure 10-85.

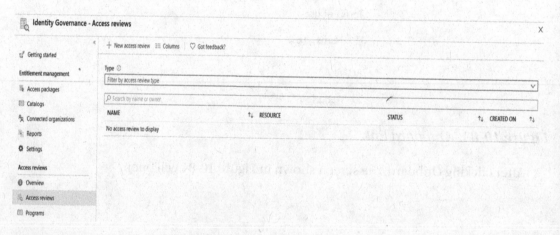

Figure 10-85. *Access review screen*

Click "New access review," and the screen in Figure 10-86 will open.

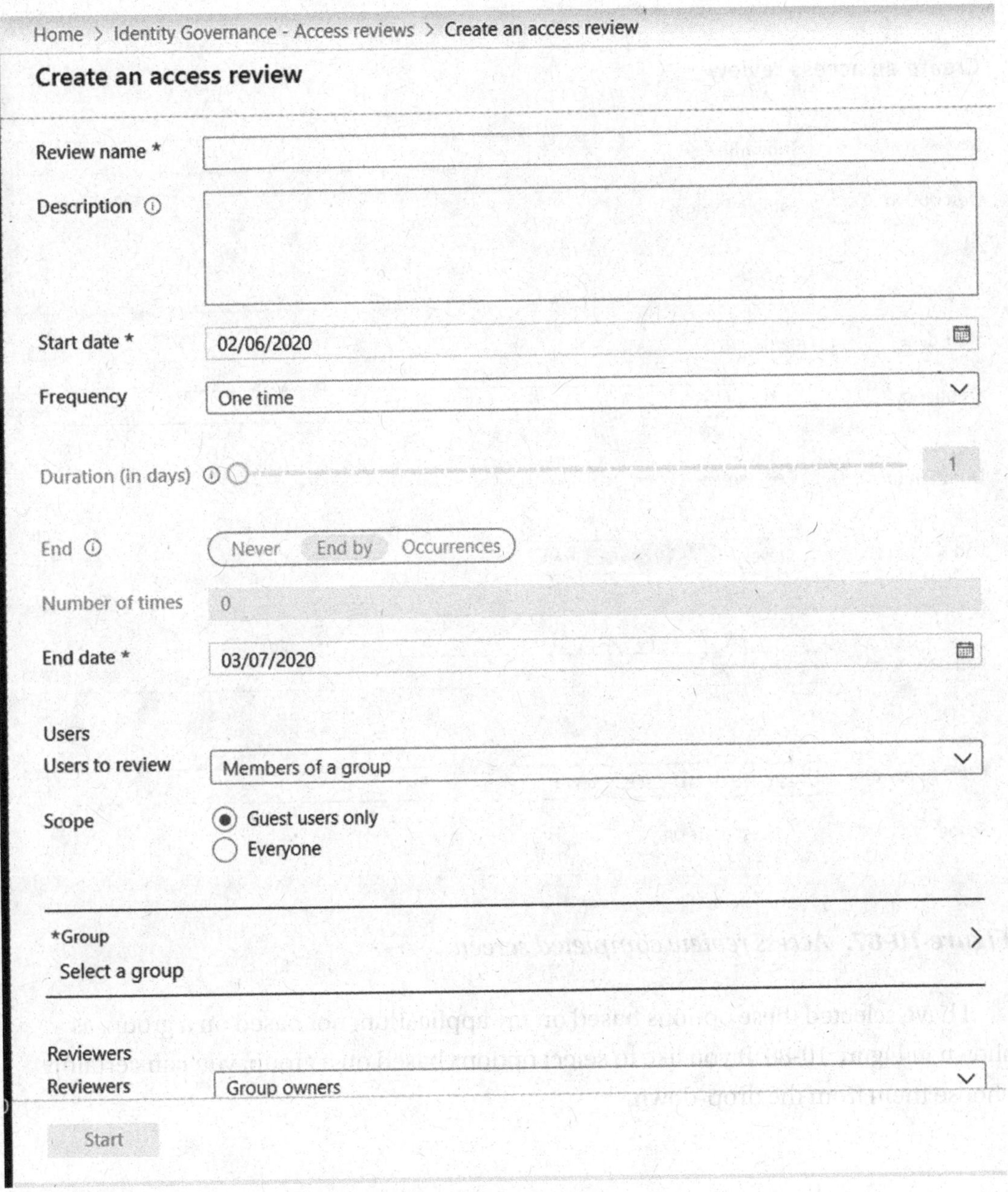

Home > Identity Governance - Access reviews > Create an access review

Create an access review

Review name *	
Description ⓘ	
Start date *	02/06/2020
Frequency	One time

Duration (in days) ⓘ ◯ ─────────────────────────── 1

End ⓘ	(Never End by Occurrences)
Number of times	0
End date *	03/07/2020

Users

Users to review	Members of a group
Scope	⦿ Guest users only
	◯ Everyone

*Group
 Select a group

Reviewers

Reviewers	Group owners

Start

Figure 10-86. *Access review creation screen*

This is pretty self-explanatory. Figure 10-87 shows the filled-in form.

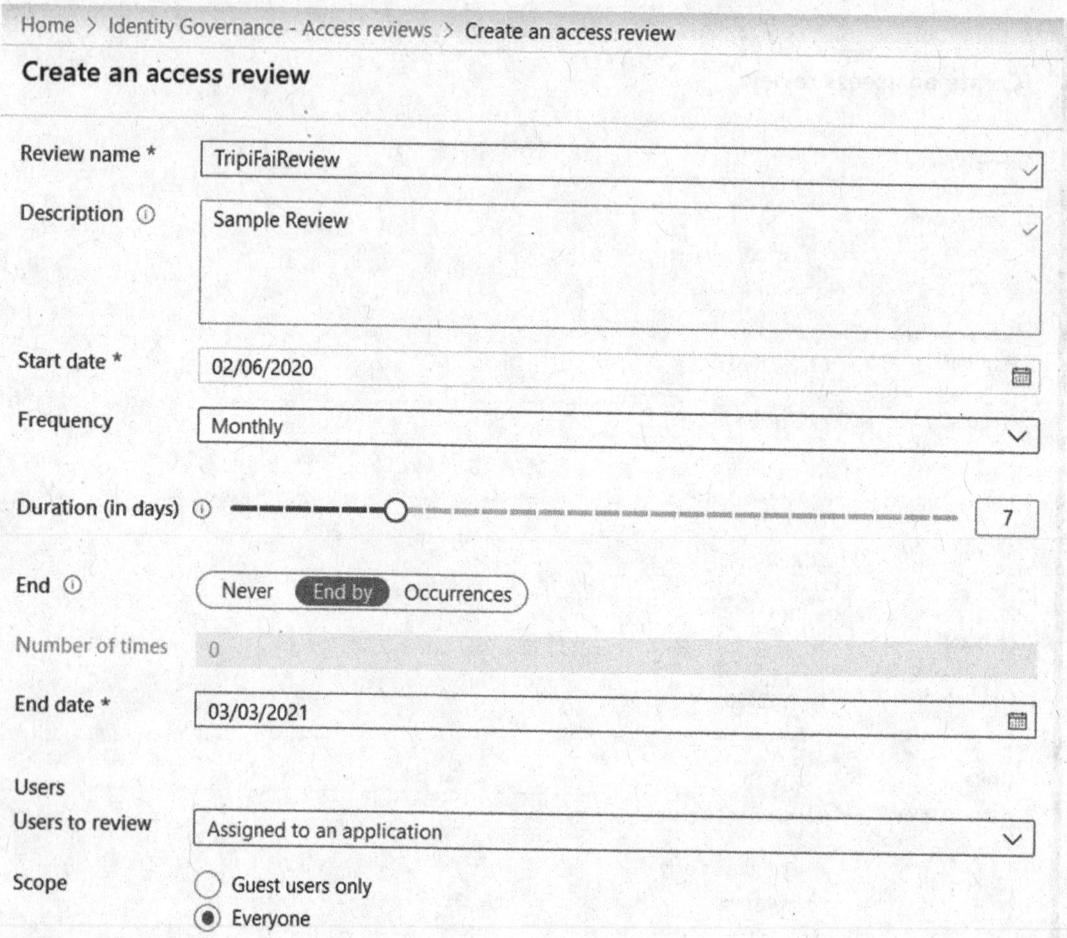

Figure 10-87. *Access review completed screen*

I have selected these options based on my application, not based on a group, as shown in Figure 10-88. If you like to select options based on a group, you can certainly choose them from the drop-down.

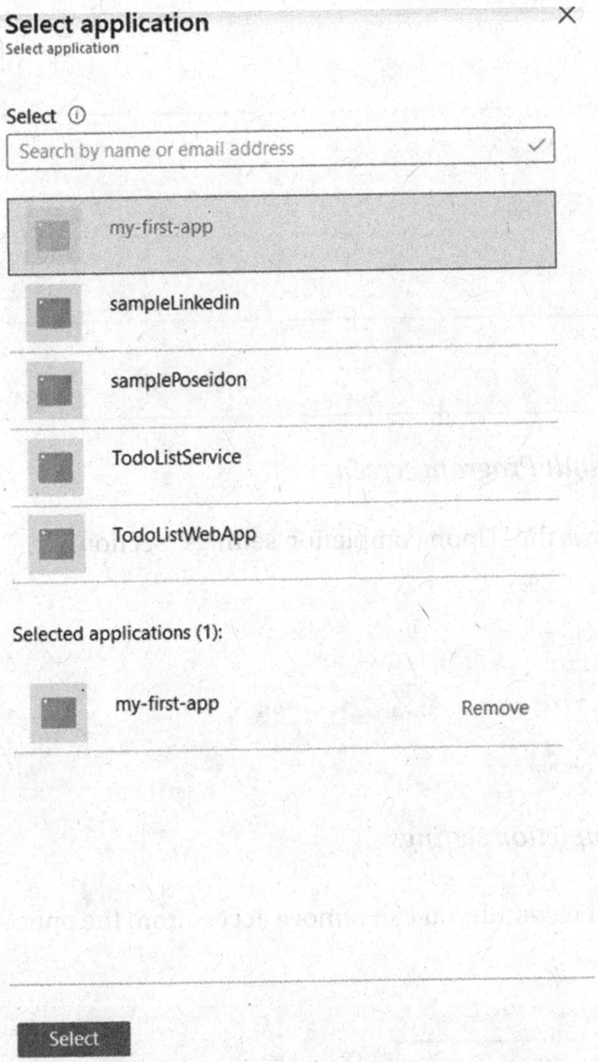

Select application

Select application   ✕

Select ⓘ

Search by name or email address   ✓

my-first-app

sampleLinkedin

samplePoseidon

TodoListService

TodoListWebApp

Selected applications (1):

my-first-app   Remove

Select

Figure 10-88. *Selecting application options*

You can also set yourself as a reviewer and select Default Program for the program, as shown in Figure 10-89.

---

*Application
my-first-app   >

Reviewers

Reviewers   [Assigned (self)   ∨]

Programs

Link to program
Default Program   >

Figure 10-89. *Default Program screen*

Figure 10-90 shows the "Upon completion settings" section.

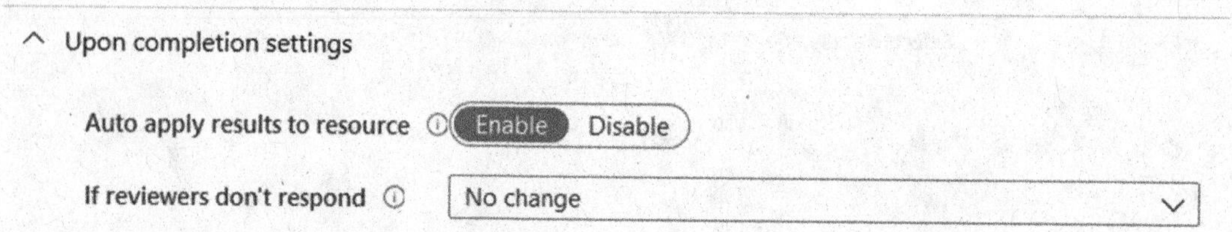

∧ Upon completion settings

Auto apply results to resource ⓘ (**Enable**   Disable)

If reviewers don't respond ⓘ   [No change   ∨]

Figure 10-90. *Completion settings*

If reviewers don't respond, you can remove access from the options, as shown in Figure 10-91.

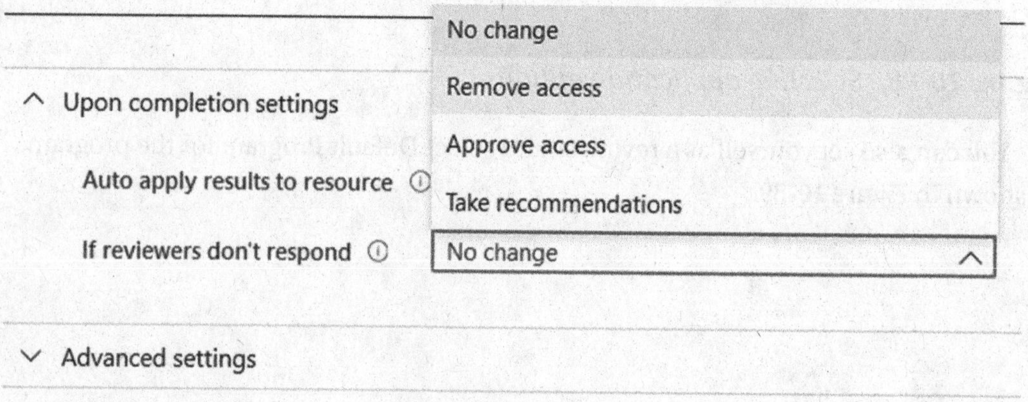

	No change
	Remove access
∧ Upon completion settings	Approve access
	Take recommendations
Auto apply results to resource ⓘ	
If reviewers don't respond ⓘ	[No change ∧]

∨ Advanced settings

Figure 10-91. *Reviewers not responding to settings*

364

You can also set up advanced settings, as shown in Figure 10-92.

∧ Advanced settings

Show recommendations ⓘ   (**Enable**   Disable)

Require reason on approval ⓘ(**Enable**   Disable)

Mail notifications ⓘ   (**Enable**   Disable)

Reminders ⓘ   (**Enable**   Disable)

Start

Figure 10-92. Advanced settings screen

Click the Start button. When you refresh the screen, you can see that the access review has been created, as shown in Figure 10-93.

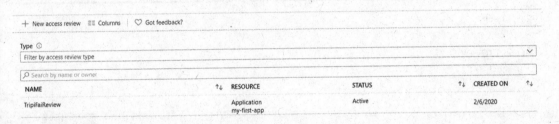

NAME		RESOURCE	STATUS		CREATED ON
TripiFaiReview		Application my-first-app	Active		2/6/2020

Figure 10-93. Access review created

At this stage, you will get an access review mail. When you click Review, you will see the screen shown in Figure 10-94.

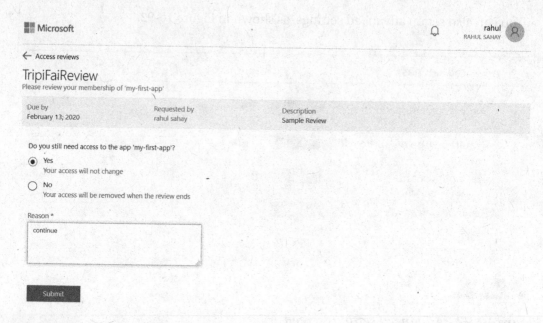

Figure 10-94. *Confirmation screen*

Next click Submit. After this, the screen shown in Figure 10-95 will open.

Figure 10-95. *Access review screen*

At this stage, the screen will look like Figure 10-96.

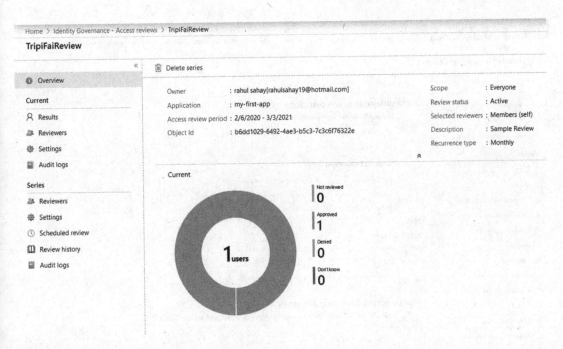

Home > Identity Governance - Access reviews > TripiFaiReview

TripiFaiReview

Overview

Current

Results

Reviewers

Settings

Audit logs

Series

Reviewers

Settings

Scheduled review

Review history

Audit logs

Delete series

Owner	: rahul sahay[rahulsahay19@hotmail.com]
Application	: my-first-app
Access review period	: 2/6/2020 - 3/3/2021
Object Id	: b6dd1029-6492-4ae3-b5c3-7c3c6f76322e

Scope	: Everyone
Review status	: Active
Selected reviewers	: Members (self)
Description	: Sample Review
Recurrence type	: Monthly

Current

1 users

Not reviewed
0

Approved
1

Denied
0

Don't know
0

Figure 10-96. *Access review detail screen*

Figure 10-96 shows that I have granted access to one user so far. But, this will give you an overall glimpse of the access review feature.

Creating an Azure AD Hybrid Identity

Hybrid basically means the AD directory is a combination of on-premises services and Microsoft services. In this case, the on-premises identity provider integrates with Azure Active Directory. If you go to the settings of Azure Active Directory, you can see in the left panel Azure AD Connect, as highlighted in Figure 10-97.

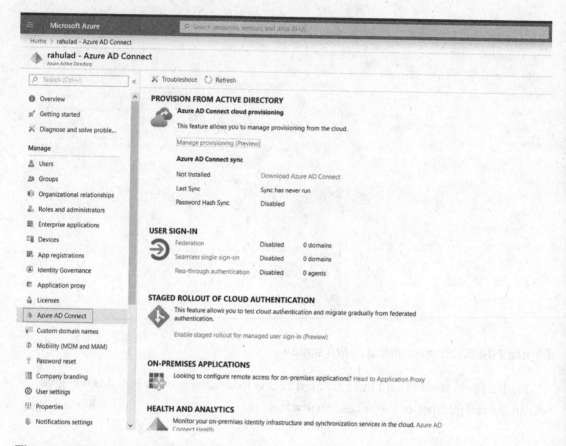

Figure 10-97. *Azure AD Connect option*

This screen contains a number of options you can set up to enable a hybrid identity. Once you set up a hybrid identity, you can synchronize your already existing on-premises user IDs and passwords with Azure Active Directory. You can learn more about this at `https://bit.ly/AZ-AD-Connect`. In that case, Azure Active Directory becomes an extension of the on-premises Active Directory. To do this, you first need to download the Azure AD Connect software and install it on your network.

The next step is part of the user sign-in process known as *federation*. Federation allows system to handle the user ID and password. This means you trust that other system, and if the person is able to log in to the other system, that means the person is a legitimate user. Federation is an alternative to the synchronization process.

Single sign-on is straightforward. It is seamless; because you already logged in, you don't have to log in again to access the cloud-based apps.

Pass-through also delegates the authentication process to on-premises server or to another authentication agent.

Azure AD B2C

In this section, we will discuss the newly minted workflow on top of Azure AD aka Azure AD Business to Customers (B2C). Figure 10-98 explains the high-level design behind Azure AD B2C.

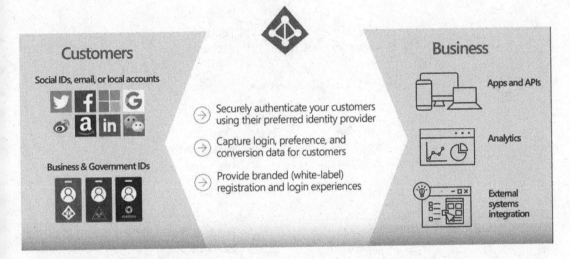

Figure 10-98.   *Azure AD B2C*

Azure AD B2C is a white-label authentication solution that enables businesses to provide their customers with access to public-facing web or mobile apps using the identities they already have.

Customers can use their social identity, enterprise identity, or local identity to get single sign-on access to any application. The entire experience can be completely branded and customized so that it blends seamlessly with each application.

B2C can also centralize the collection of user profile and preference information, as well as capture detailed analytics about behavior and sign-up conversions.

Figure 10-99 shows some of the features.

Figure 10-99. Azure AD B2C features

B2C also offers support from many identity providers. Some of them are listed in Figure 10-100.

Figure 10-100. *Azure AD B2C identity providers*

One point to note here is that at the time of writing this book, there is a bug in the Azure portal. Specifically, if you just search for *b2c*, it won't take you on the creation flow path. Rather, it will take you to the Overview screen, where all the options are disabled.

Let's go ahead and click "Create new resource" and search for *b2c*, as shown in Figure 10-101.

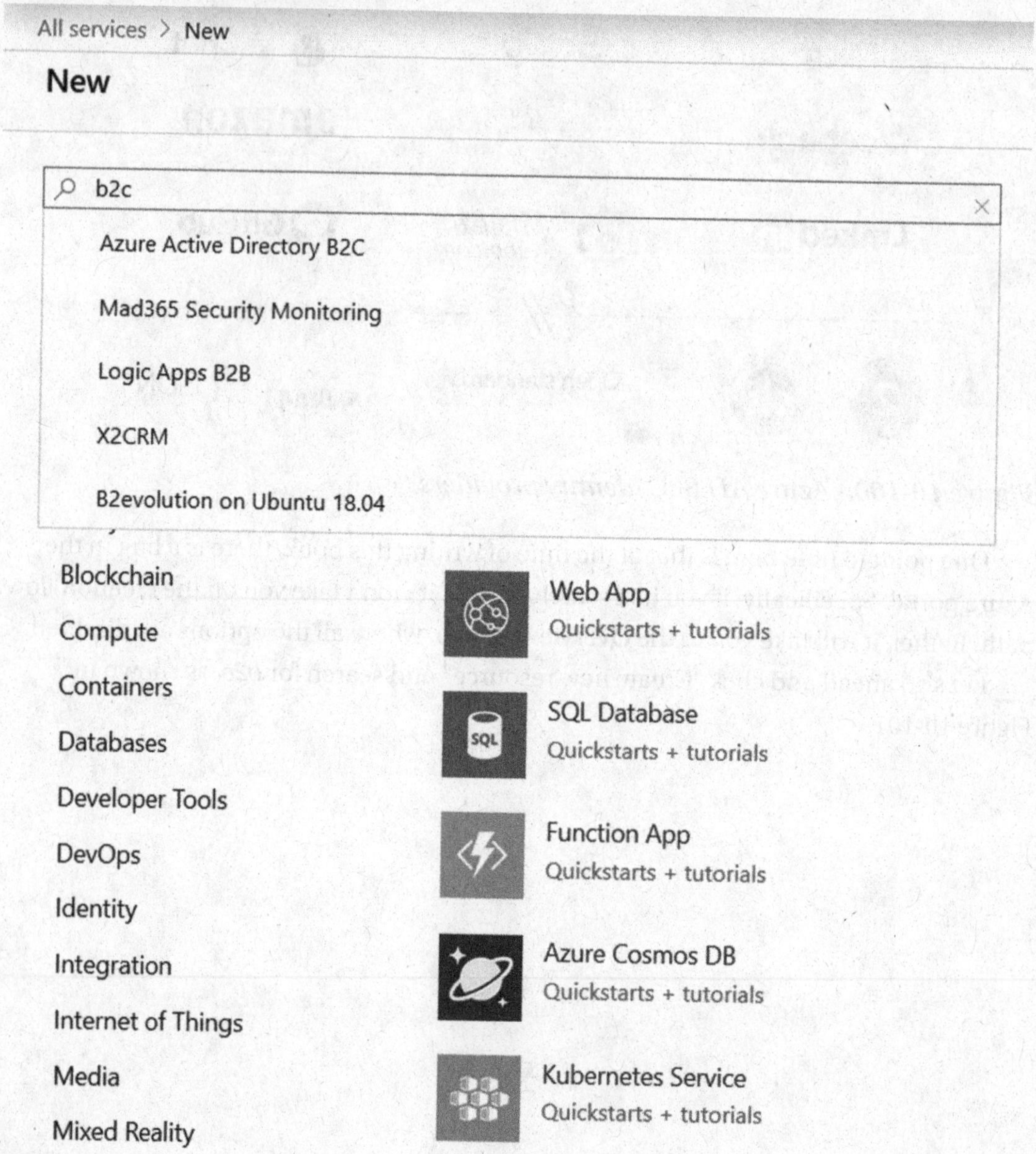

All services > New

New

🔍 b2c   ×

Azure Active Directory B2C

Mad365 Security Monitoring

Logic Apps B2B

X2CRM

B2evolution on Ubuntu 18.04

Blockchain

Compute

Containers

Databases

Developer Tools

DevOps

Identity

Integration

Internet of Things

Media

Mixed Reality

Web App
Quickstarts + tutorials

SQL Database
Quickstarts + tutorials

Function App
Quickstarts + tutorials

Azure Cosmos DB
Quickstarts + tutorials

Kubernetes Service
Quickstarts + tutorials

Figure 10-101. Azure AD B2C search screen

Click the first option, which will take you to the screen shown in Figure 10-102.

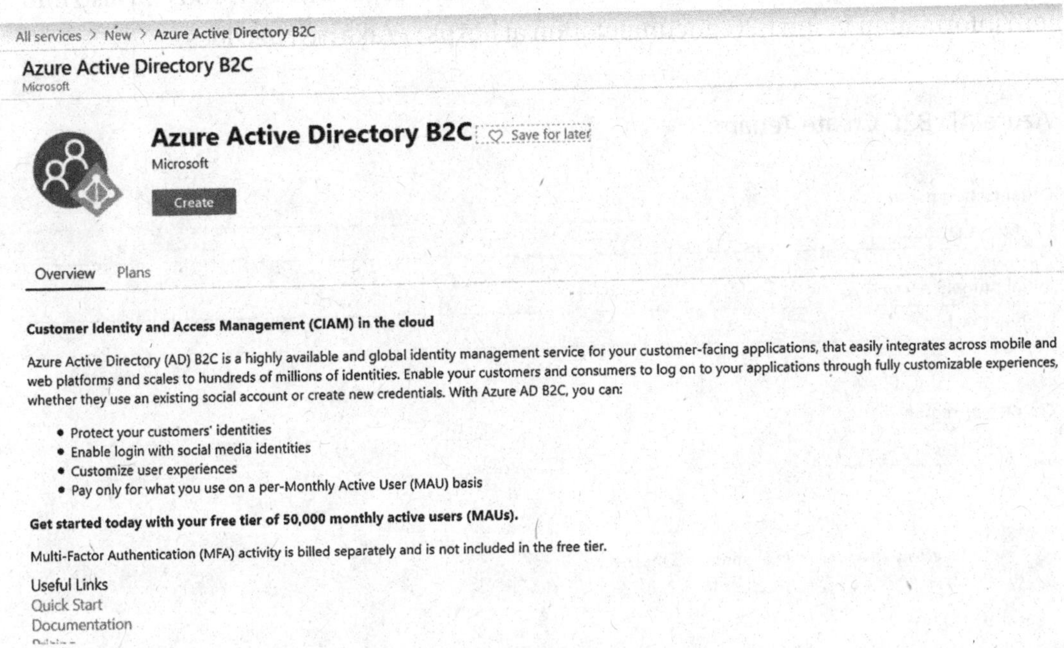

All services > New > Azure Active Directory B2C

Azure Active Directory B2C
Microsoft

Azure Active Directory B2C   ♡ Save for later
Microsoft

Create

Overview   Plans

Customer Identity and Access Management (CIAM) in the cloud

Azure Active Directory (AD) B2C is a highly available and global identity management service for your customer-facing applications, that easily integrates across mobile and web platforms and scales to hundreds of millions of identities. Enable your customers and consumers to log on to your applications through fully customizable experiences, whether they use an existing social account or create new credentials. With Azure AD B2C, you can:

- Protect your customers' identities
- Enable login with social media identities
- Customize user experiences
- Pay only for what you use on a per-Monthly Active User (MAU) basis

Get started today with your free tier of 50,000 monthly active users (MAUs).

Multi-Factor Authentication (MFA) activity is billed separately and is not included in the free tier.

Useful Links
Quick Start
Documentation

Figure 10-102. Azure AD Directory B2C screen

Next, click Create to open the screen in Figure 10-103.

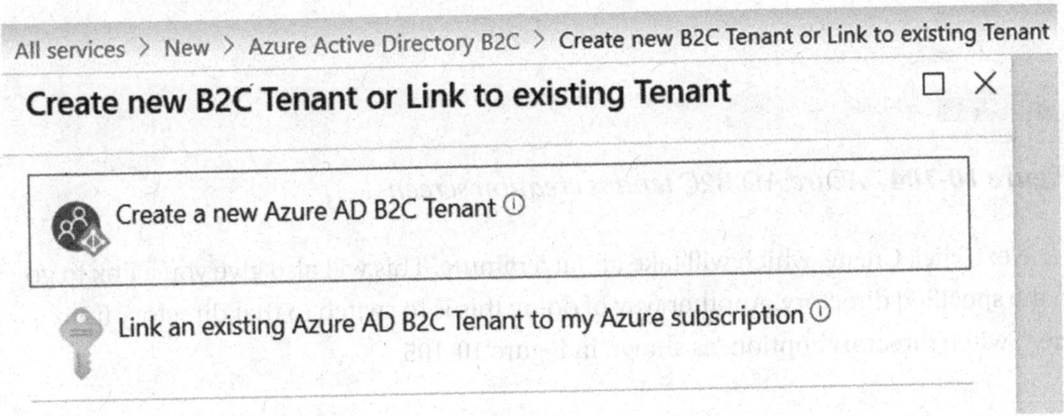

All services > New > Azure Active Directory B2C > Create new B2C Tenant or Link to existing Tenant

Create new B2C Tenant or Link to existing Tenant   □ ✕

Create a new Azure AD B2C Tenant ⓘ

Link an existing Azure AD B2C Tenant to my Azure subscription ⓘ

Figure 10-103. Tenant link screen

Here, you can either link to an existing Azure AD B2C tenant or create a new one, as shown earlier. This will take you to the screen shown in Figure 10-104. You can also find more information in the B2C documentation at `https://aka.ms/b2cdocs`.

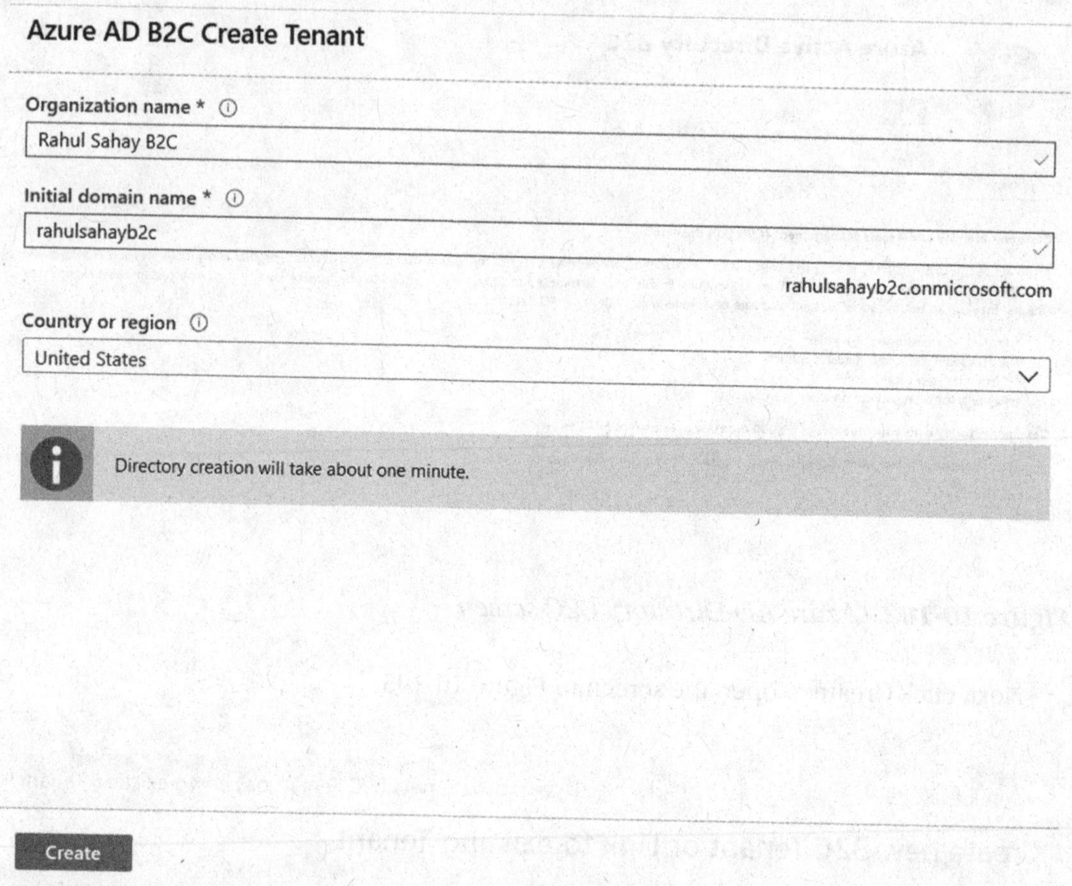

Azure AD B2C Create Tenant

Organization name * ⓘ

Rahul Sahay B2C ✓

Initial domain name * ⓘ

rahulsahayb2c ✓

rahulsahayb2c.onmicrosoft.com

Country or region ⓘ

United States ⌄

ⓘ Directory creation will take about one minute.

Create

Figure 10-104. *Azure AD B2C tenant creation screen*

Next, click Create, which will take about a minute. This will also give you a link to go to the specified directory. Another way of doing this is to switch to that directory from the "Switch directory" option, as shown in Figure 10-105.

Figure 10-105. Azure AD B2C, switching directories

The B2C screen looks like Figure 10-106.

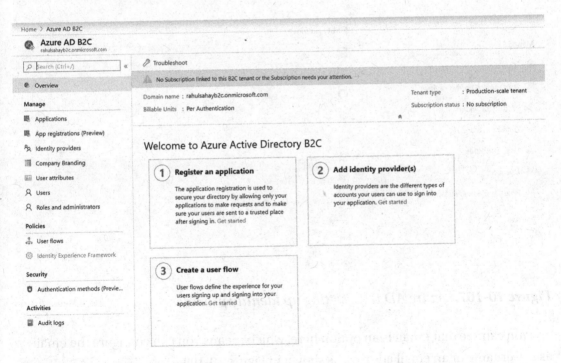

Figure 10-106. Azure AD B2C's Overview screen

On the left side, you can see that there are a couple of options that you can manage, including the following:

- Which applications are authenticating against your directory

- Which identity providers you offer for signing in

- Custom user attributes you can configure

- List of users

- User flows

- Custom policies that you can configure using the Identity Experience Framework

Let's go ahead and set up some identity providers. See Figure 10-107.

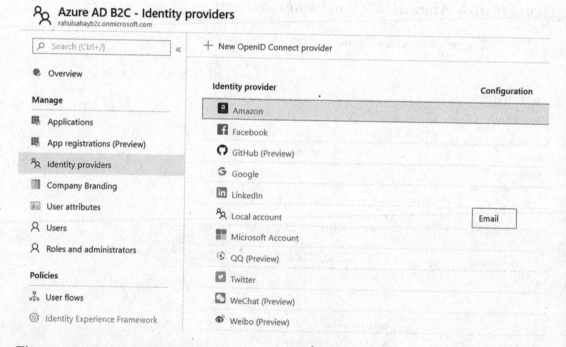

Figure 10-107. *Azure AD B2C, setting up identity providers*

You can see that Email is an option here, which means you can configure the email as a username or an email address, as shown in Figure 10-108.

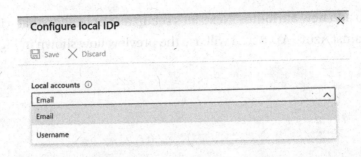

Figure 10-108. *Configuring a local IDP*

For different identity providers, the values will change. You can find the exact configuration values you can use here: `https://aka.ms/b2cdocs`. Let's look at the user attributes now. You can see that there are many user attributes already built in, as shown in Figure 10-109.

Name	Data Type	Description	Attribute type
City	String	The city in which the user is located.	Built-in
Country/Region	String	The country/region in which the user is located.	Built-in
Display Name	String	Display Name of the User.	Built-in
Email Addresses	StringCollection	Email addresses of the user.	Built-in
Given Name	String	The user's given name (also known as first name).	Built-in
Identity Provider	String	The social identity provider used by the user to access to your application.	Built-in
Job Title	String	The user's job title.	Built-in
Legal Age Group Classifi...	String	The legal age group that a user falls into based on their country and date of birth	Built-in
Postal Code	String	The postal code of the user's address.	Built-in
State/Province	String	The state or province in user's address.	Built-in
Street Address	String	The street address where the user is located.	Built-in
Surname	String	The user's surname (also known as family name or last name).	Built-in
User is new	Boolean	True, if the user has just signed-up for your application.	Built-in
User's Object ID	String	Object identifier (ID) of the user object in Azure AD.	Built-in

Home > Azure AD B2C - User attributes

Azure AD B2C - User attributes
rahulrahayb2c.onmicrosoft.com

- Overview
- **Manage**
- Applications
- App registrations (Preview)
- Identity providers
- Company Branding
- User attributes
- Users
- Roles and administrators
- **Policies**
- User flows
- Identity Experience Framework
- **Security**
- Authentication methods (Previe...
- **Activities**
- Audit logs

Figure 10-109. *Azure AD B2C "User attributes" screen*

You can also add new attributes. Next, let's set up an application that will authenticate against Azure AD B2C. I will use the preview flow shown in Figure 10-110.

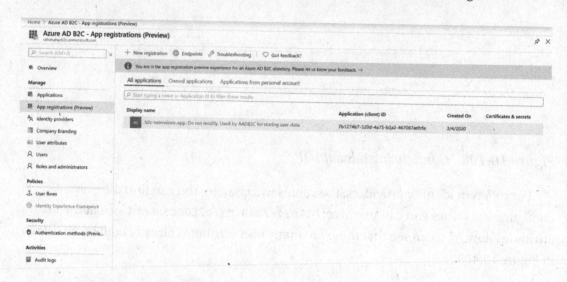

Figure 10-110. *Azure AD B2C app registrations list*

Click "New registration," and enter the details shown in Figure 10-111.

Home > Azure AD B2C - App registrations (Preview) > Register an application

Register an application

* Name

The display name for this application (this can be changed later).

| JWT.ms | ✓ |

Supported account types

Who can use this application or access this API?

○ Accounts in this organizational directory only (Rahul Sahay B2C only).

○ Accounts in any organizational directory (Any Azure AD directory – Multitenant).

⦿ Accounts in any organizational directory or any identity provider. For authenticating users with Azure AD B2C.

Help me choose...

Redirect URI (recommended)

We'll return the authentication response to this URI after successfully authenticating the user. Providing this now is optional and it can be changed later, but a value is required for most authentication scenarios.

| Web ⌄ | https://jwt.ms | ✓ |

Permissions

By proceeding, you agree to the Microsoft Platform Policies ☐

[Register]

Figure 10-111. *Azure AD B2C app registration screen*

This will bring up the screen shown in Figure 10-112.

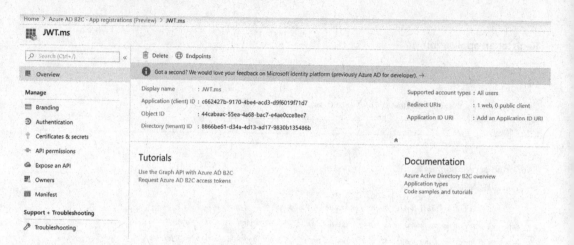

Figure 10-112. *Azure AD B2C app*

You can see that the application is a registered application now, as shown in Figure 10-113.

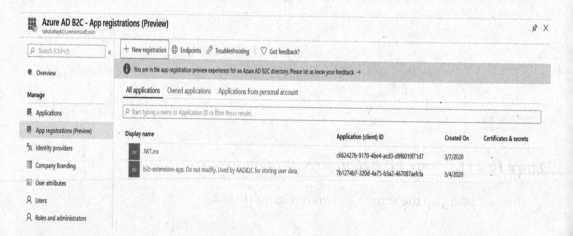

Figure 10-113. *Azure AD B2C app registrations list*

Let's go ahead and choose a basic user flow. For that, click "User flows" in the left panel, as shown in Figure 10-114.

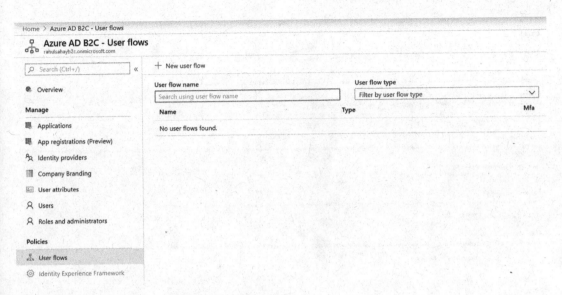

Figure 10-114. *Azure AD B2C user flows*

Click "New user flow" to open the screen shown in Figure 10-115.

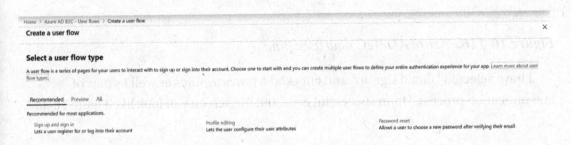

Figure 10-115. *Azure AD B2C user flow selection*

Click "Sign up and sign in" and you will see the screen in Figure 10-116.

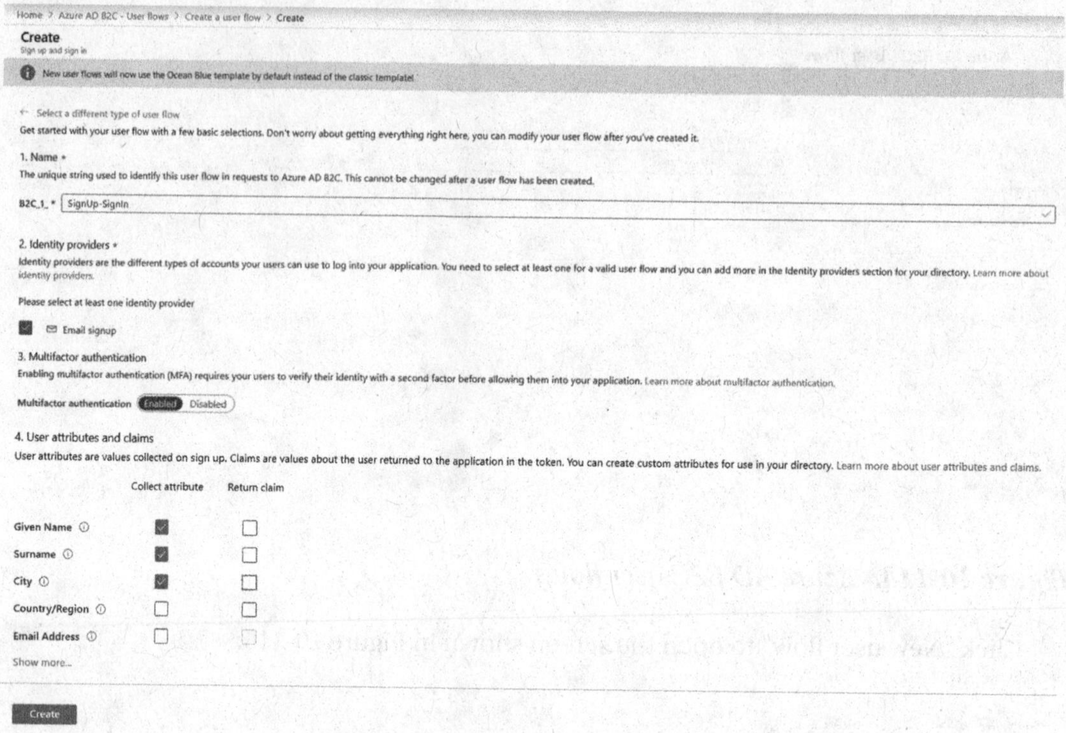

Figure 10-116. *Azure AD B2C new user flow*

I have selected "Email signup" and checked a few attributes as well as part of authentication process. Upon successful creation, the screen will look like Figure 10-117.

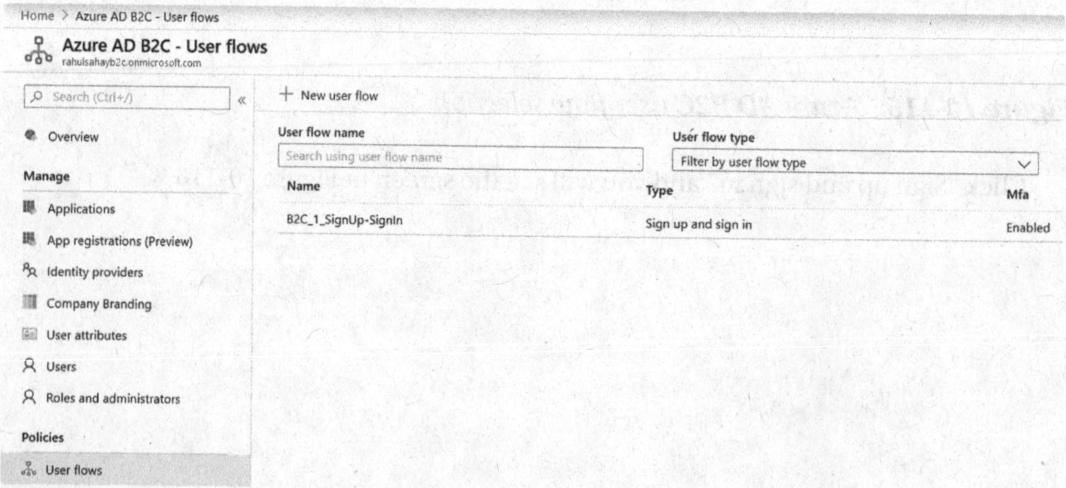

Figure 10-117. *Azure AD B2C user flows created*

After creating this user flow, you can configure more settings inside it. Once you click the user flow, you will see the screen in Figure 10-118.

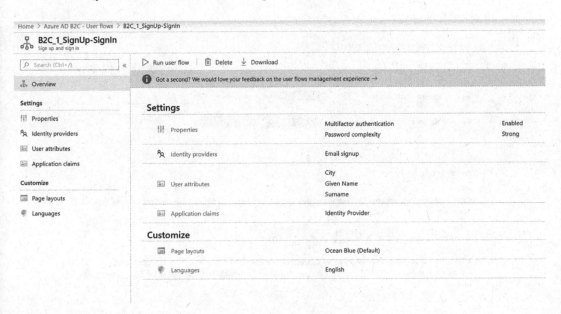

Figure 10-118. *Azure AD B2C sign-up settings*

Click Properties, which will open the complete list of settings, as shown in Figure 10-119.

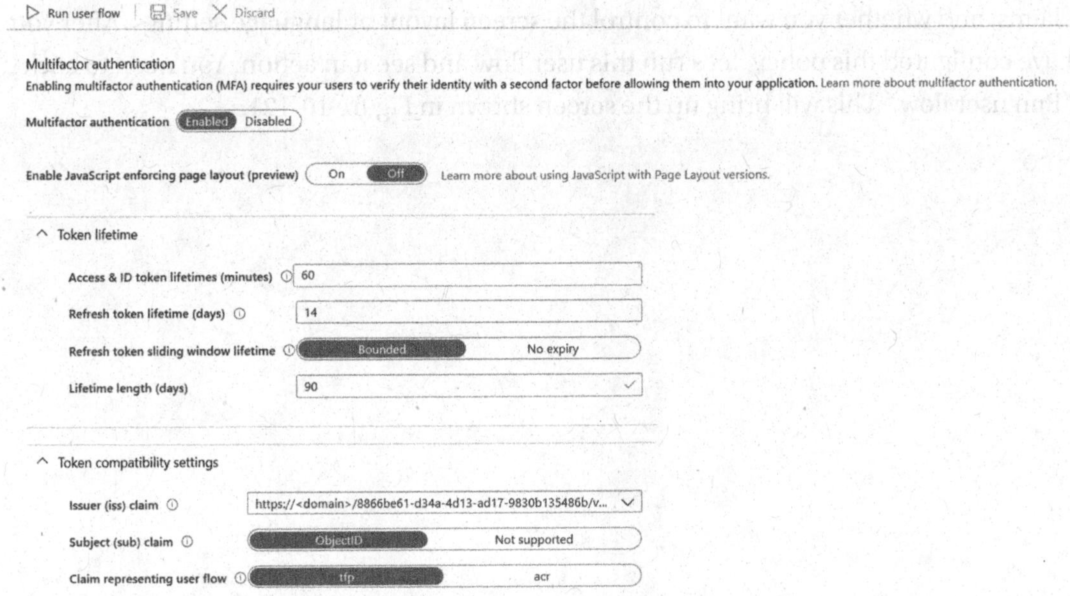

Figure 10-119. *Azure AD B2C properties*

Figure 10-120 shows the Azure AD B2C session and password settings.

∧ Session behavior

Web app session lifetime (minutes) ⓘ 1440

Web app session timeout ⓘ   Absolute   Rolling

Single sign-on configuration ⓘ   Tenant   Application   Policy   Disabled

Require ID Token in logout requests ⓘ   No   Yes

∧ Password complexity

Configure the requirements for your users' password. Use custom to define your own set of requirements.
Learn more about password complexity.

Complexity ⓘ Simple   Strong   Custom   Legacy

Minimum 8 characters and maximum 64 characters in length 3 of 4 character classes - uppercase,
lowercase, number, symbol. The error message for password validation is updated when a requirement is
met.

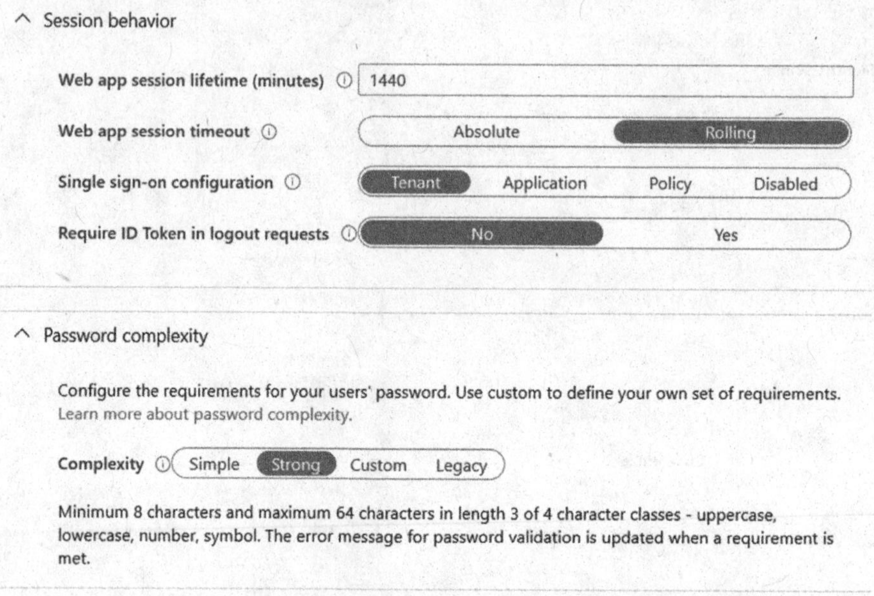

Figure 10-120. *Azure AD B2C session and password settings*

You can configure any of the settings on this screen. In addition, you can configure
which identity providers are selected, which user attributes can be collected, application
claims, and whether you want to control the screen layout or language settings. After you
have configured this policy, let's run this user flow and see it in action. You need to click
"Run user flow." This will bring up the screen shown in Figure 10-121.

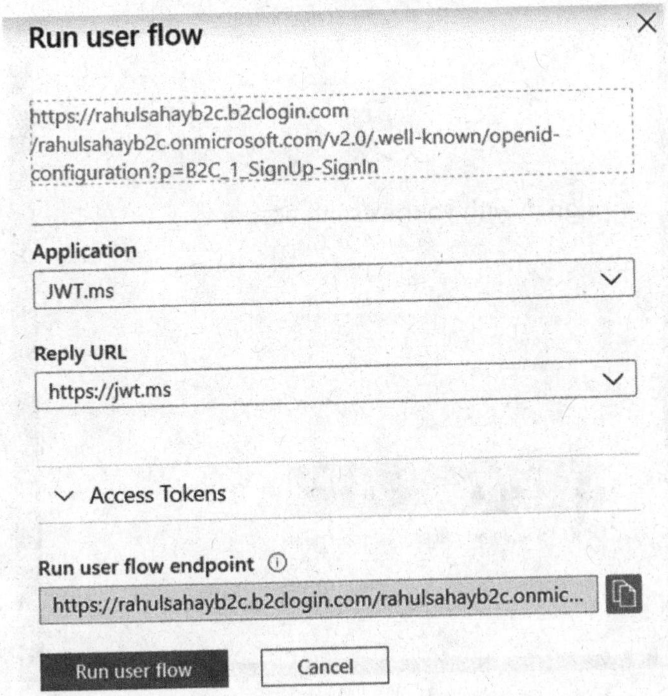

Run user flow   ×

https://rahulsahayb2c.b2clogin.com
/rahulsahayb2c.onmicrosoft.com/v2.0/.well-known/openid-
configuration?p=B2C_1_SignUp-SignIn

Application

JWT.ms   ∨

Reply URL

https://jwt.ms   ∨

∨ Access Tokens

Run user flow endpoint ⓘ

https://rahulsahayb2c.b2clogin.com/rahulsahayb2c.onmic...

Run user flow   Cancel

Figure 10-121. *Azure AD B2C's "Run user flow" screen*

The login screen shown in Figure 10-122 appears.

Figure 10-122. *Azure AD B2C login screen*

Go ahead and sign up now, as shown in Figure 10-123.

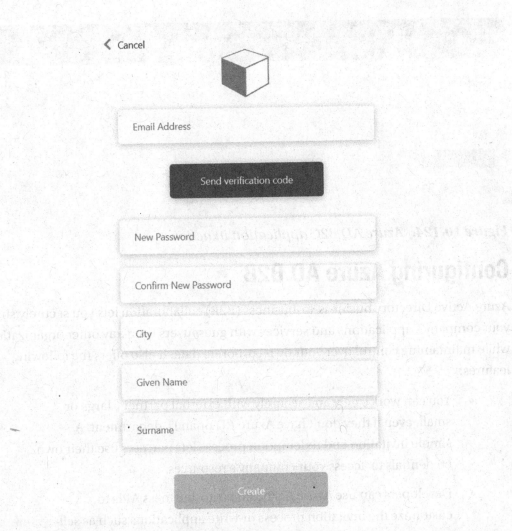

Figure 10-123. *Azure AD B2C sign-up screen*

Upon successful sign-up, you will be taken to the screen shown in Figure 10-124.

Figure 10-124. *Azure AD B2C application in action*

Configuring Azure AD B2B

Azure Active Directory business-to-business (B2B) collaboration lets you securely share your company's applications and services with guest users from any other organization, while maintaining control over your own corporate data. It also offers the following features:

- You can work safely and securely with external partners, large or small, even if they don't have Azure AD or an IT department. A simple invitation and redemption process lets partners use their own credentials to access your company's resources.

- Developers can use Azure AD business-to-business APIs to customize the invitation process or write applications such as self-service sign-up portals.

You can find complete details about this flow at http://aka.ms/b2bdocs.

Deleting an Active Directory

To delete any Active Directory, make sure to get rid of any user policies that you created in Active Directory.

Then, delete the registered applications. Delete the user that you created. Before deleting the Active Directory, you need to enable access management for Azure resources and save the properties. See Figure 100-125.

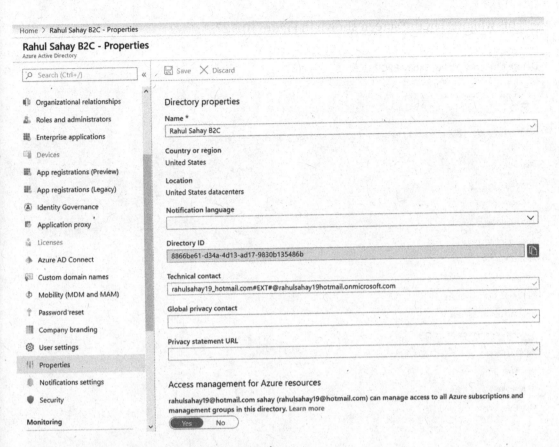

Figure 10-125. *Azure AD B2C properties*

To delete the Active Directory, go to the Active Directory's Overview screen and click "Delete directory," as shown in Figure 10-126.

Figure 10-126. *Azure AD "Delete directory" option*

This will present the screen shown in Figure 10-127.

Delete directory 'Rahul Sahay B2C'?
Azure Active Directory

⟳ Refresh   ✕ Troubleshoot

ⓘ To delete 'Rahul Sahay B2C', complete the required action(s) shown below. Then return here to try again. Learn more

Resource	Status	Required action
Users	✓	--
LinkedIn application ⓘ	✓	--
App registrations ⓘ	⚠	Delete all app registrations
Enterprise applications ⓘ	✓	--
Subscriptions ⓘ	✓	--
Microsoft Azure	✓	--
Self-service sign up products	✓	--
Azure AD Domain Services	✓	--
Multi-Factor Authentication	✓	--
Identity providers	✓	--
User flows	✓	--
IEF policy keys	✓	--
Identity Experience Framework (IEF) policies	✓	--

Figure 10-127. *Deleteing an Azure AD*

I am not saying that all applications should be deleted. Hence, before deleting the Active Directory, you need to delete that pending application as well. Once you have deleted it successfully, then click "Delete directory" again. See Figure 10-128.

Delete directory 'Rahul Sahay B2C'?
Azure Active Directory

○ Refresh   ✕ Troubleshoot

ⓘ All initial checks passed. Click 'Delete' to Delete directory 'Rahul Sahay B2C'. After deletion, you will need to sign out.

Resource	Status	Required action
Users	✓	--
LinkedIn application ⓘ	✓	--
App registrations ⓘ	✓	--
Enterprise applications ⓘ	✓	--
Subscriptions ⓘ	✓	--
Microsoft Azure	✓	--
Self-service sign up products	✓	--
Azure AD Domain Services	✓	--
Multi-Factor Authentication	✓	--
Identity providers	✓	--
User flows	✓	--
IEF policy keys	✓	--
Identity Experience Framework (IEF) policies	✓	--

Delete

Figure 10-128. *Deleting an Azure AD directory*

Click the Delete button now. This will present the screen shown in Figure 10-129.

Home > You do not have access > Delete directory 'Rahul Sahay B2C'?

Delete directory 'Rahul Sahay B2C'?
Azure Active Directory

○ Refresh   ✕ Troubleshoot

○ Directory 'Rahul Sahay B2C' was successfully scheduled for deletion. Please click here to sign out. After signing back in you can choose other directories to work with.

Figure 10-129. *Azure AD deleted directory confirmation*

Next sign out and sign in again. The Active Directory will have been deleted and won't be listed anymore. You can verify this using the "Switch directory" option as well.

CHAPTER 11

Implement and Manage Hybrid Identities

Today most businesses use a mixture of on-premises and cloud applications. Users need to access applications in both environments, and managing users both on-premises and in the cloud is a challenging task. That's way Microsoft has introduced the concept of hybrid identities.

Azure AD Connect

Azure AD Connect is the Microsoft tool that helps you accomplish your hybrid identity goals. It provides the following features:

- **Password hash synchronization:** Azure AD Connect offers a sign-in method that synchronizes a hash of a user's on-premises AD password with Azure AD.

- **Pass-through authentication:** Azure AD Connect offers a sign-in method that allows users to use the same password on-premises and in the cloud but doesn't require the additional infrastructure of a federated environment.

- **Federation integration:** Federation is an optional part of Azure AD Connect and can be used to configure a hybrid environment using an on-premises AD Federation Services infrastructure. It also provides AD Federation Services management capabilities such as certificate renewal and additional AD Federation Services server deployments.

© Rahul Sahay 2020
R. Sahay, *Microsoft Azure Architect Technologies Study Companion*,
https://doi.org/10.1007/978-1-4842-6200-9_11

- **Synchronization:** Azure AD Connect is responsible for creating users, groups, and other objects as well as making sure that the identity information for your on-premises users and groups matches the information in the cloud. This synchronization also includes password hashes.

- **Health monitoring:** Azure AD Connect Health can provide robust monitoring and provide a central location in the Azure portal to view this activity.

Password Hash Synchronization

Password hash synchronization is one of the sign-in methods that is used to achieve a hybrid identity. Azure AD Connect synchronizes the hash of a user's password from an on-premises Active Directory instance to a cloud-based instance. Figure 11-1 explains the process.

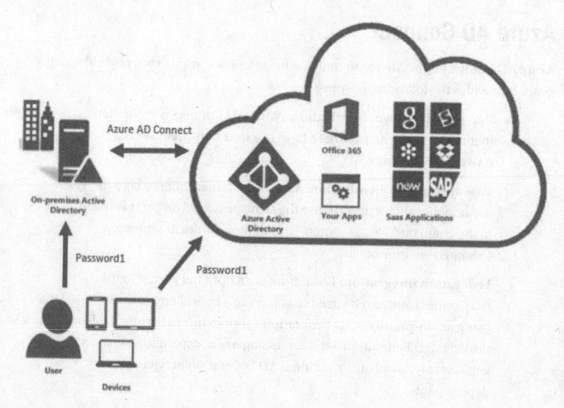

Figure 11-1. *Azure AD Connect*

Azure AD Connect reduces the number of passwords users need to maintain to just one password. To use this feature, users need to do the following steps:

1. Install Azure AD Connect.

2. Configure directory synchronization between your on-premises Active Directory and your cloud instance of Azure AD.

3. Enable password hash synchronization.

Pass-Through Synchronization

Pass-through synchronization allows users to sign in to both on-premises and cloud-based applications using the same passwords. This feature provides users with a better experience because there is one less password to remember. When users sign in using Azure AD, pass-through synchronization validates users' passwords directly against your on-premises Active Directory. This policy is used by organizations that want to enforce their on-premises Active Directory security and password policy. Figure 11-2 explains the concept.

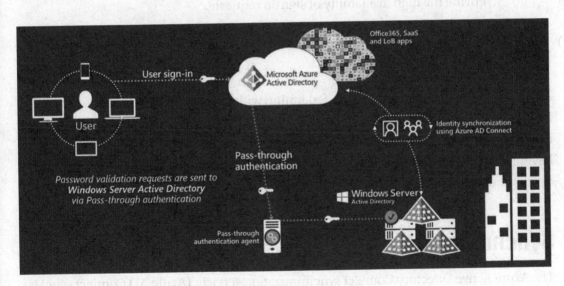

Figure 11-2. Pass-through synchronization

Benefits of Using Pass-Through Authentication

The following are the benefits of using pass-through authentication:

- Users use the same passwords to sign into both on-premises and cloud-based applications.

- There is no need for complex on-premises deployments or network configuration.

- You just need a lightweight agent installed on-premises.

- On-premises passwords are never stored in the cloud in any form.

- Pass-through authentication protects a user's account seamlessly by using Azure AD conditional policies, using MFA, blocking legacy authentication, and restricting brute-force attacks.

- The communication between an agent and Azure AD is secured using certificates.

- Additional agents can be installed on multiple on-premises servers to provide the high availability of sign-in requests.

Federation Integration

Azure AD Connect lets you configure federation with on-premises Active Directory Federation Services (AD FS) and Azure AD. With federation sign-in, you can enable a user to sign in to Azure AD–based services with an on-premises password without having to enter the password again while on the corporate network. You can find more details about this at https://bit.ly/Azure-AD-Connect-Fed.

Synchronization

The Azure Active Directory Connect synchronization services (Azure AD Connect sync) is a main component of Azure AD Connect. It takes care of all the operations that are related to synchronizing identity data between your on-premises environment and Azure AD. This is also known as the *sync engine*. The sync service consists of two components: the on-premises Azure AD Connect sync component and the Azure AD Connect sync service.

Azure AD Connect Health

Azure AD Connect Health provides robust monitoring of your on-premises identity infrastructure. It enables you to maintain a reliable connection to Office 365 and Microsoft Online Services. This reliability is achieved by providing monitoring capabilities for your key identity components. Also, it makes the key data points about these components easily accessible.

You can use the Azure AD Connect Health portal to view alerts, performance, monitoring, usage analytics, and other information. Figure 11-3 explains the concepts.

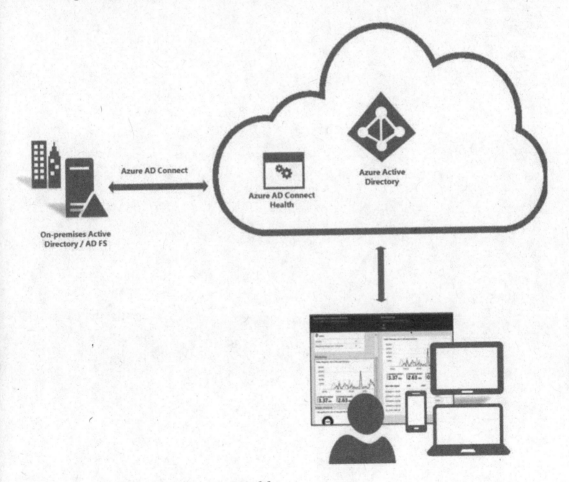

Figure 11-3. Azure AD Connect Health

CHAPTER 12

Migrate Servers to Azure

A *recovery service vault* is an entity that stores the backups and recovery points created over time. It also contains the backup policies. In this chapter, you'll learn how to get started with Azure site recovery.

Creating a Recovery Service

To create a recovery service, you can search in the marketplace for *site*. "Recovery Services vaults" will come up, as shown in Figure 12-1.

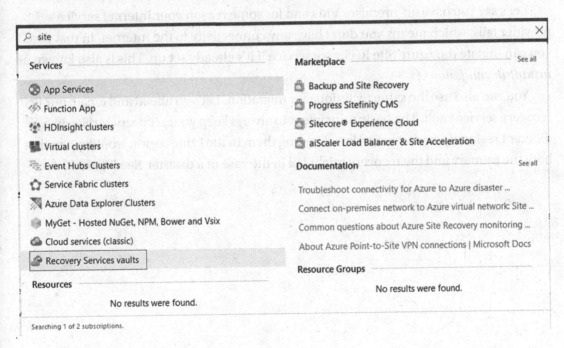

Figure 12-1. *Site recovery search*

© Rahul Sahay 2020
R. Sahay, *Microsoft Azure Architect Technologies Study Companion*,
https://doi.org/10.1007/978-1-4842-6200-9_12

Clicking "Recovery Services vaults" will take you to the screen shown in Figure 12-2.

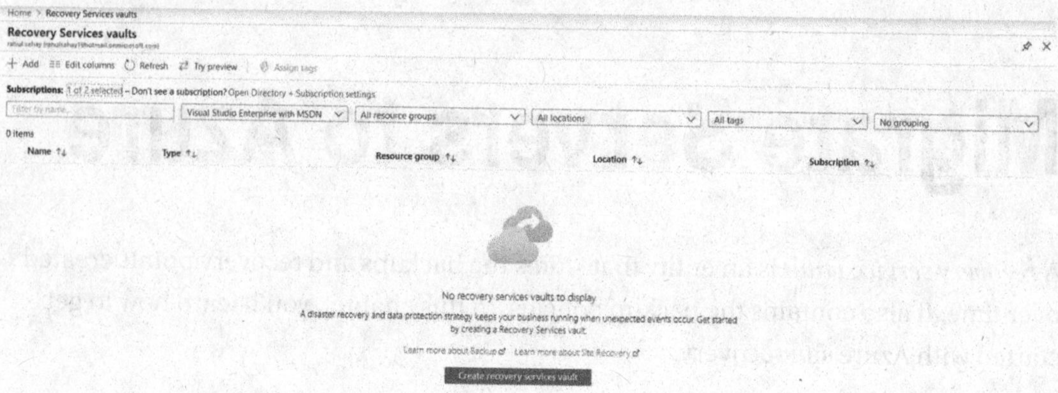

Figure 12-2. "Recovery Services vaults" screen

The Azure Site Recovery service is nothing but a disaster recovery system. For example, if you have a set of virtual machines running on Azure or on-premises, then you can have replicated versions of them ready to go in case a disaster happens.

Let's say you have on-premises VMs and for some reason your Internet service provider fails, which means you don't have any connectivity to the Internet. In that case, you can initiate the Azure Site Recovery service if it's already set up. This is also known as *instantaneous failover*.

You can also use the same technique for migration. Let's go ahead and create our first recovery service vault. The basic principle is to always keep your recovery service in a different region from your main data. Keeping them in the same region would mean that both the primary and the recovery might fail in the case of a disaster. See Figure 12-3.

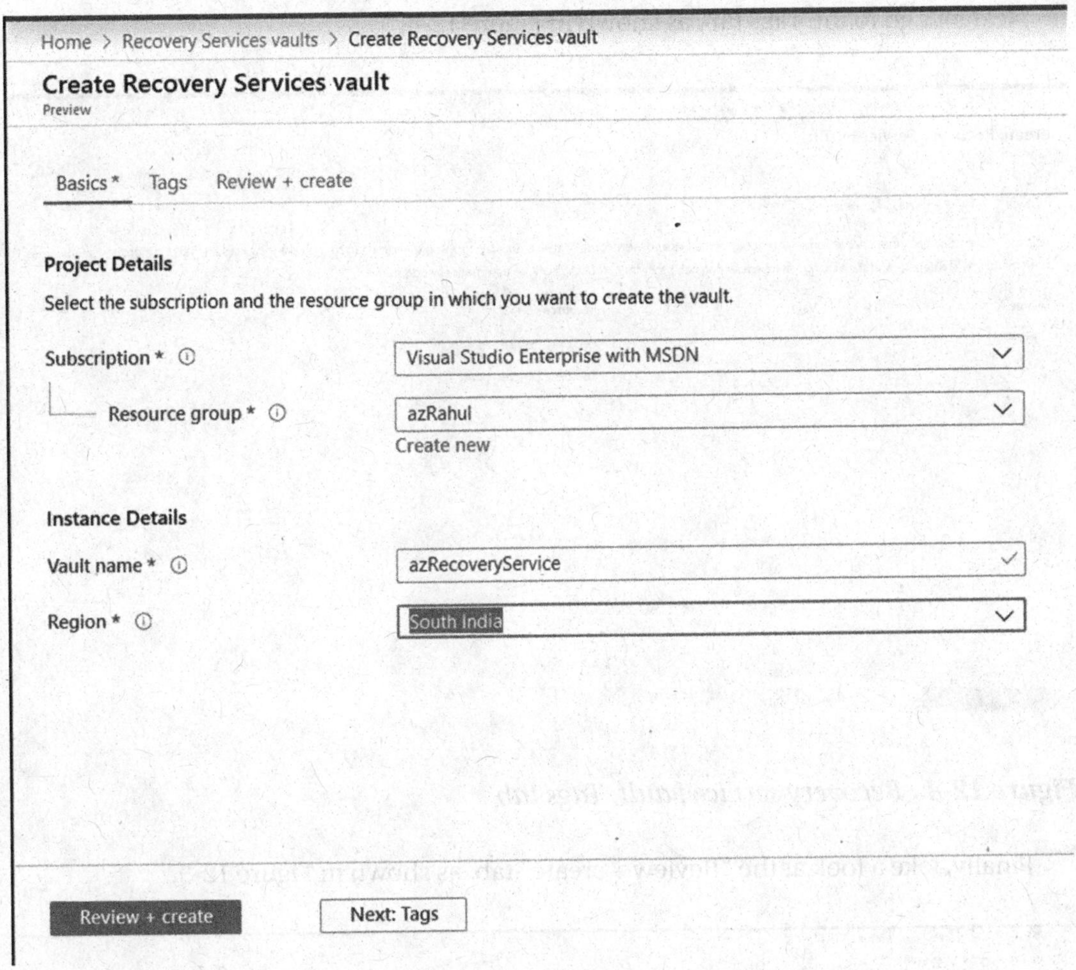

Home > Recovery Services vaults > Create Recovery Services vault

Create Recovery Services vault
Preview

Basics *   Tags   Review + create

Project Details

Select the subscription and the resource group in which you want to create the vault.

Subscription * ⓘ   Visual Studio Enterprise with MSDN   ⌄

     Resource group * ⓘ   azRahul   ⌄
                                         Create new

Instance Details

Vault name * ⓘ   azRecoveryService   ✓

Region * ⓘ   South India   ⌄

Review + create   Next: Tags

Figure 12-3. Recovery service vault, Basics tab

Next let's go to the Tags tab, as shown in Figure 12-4.

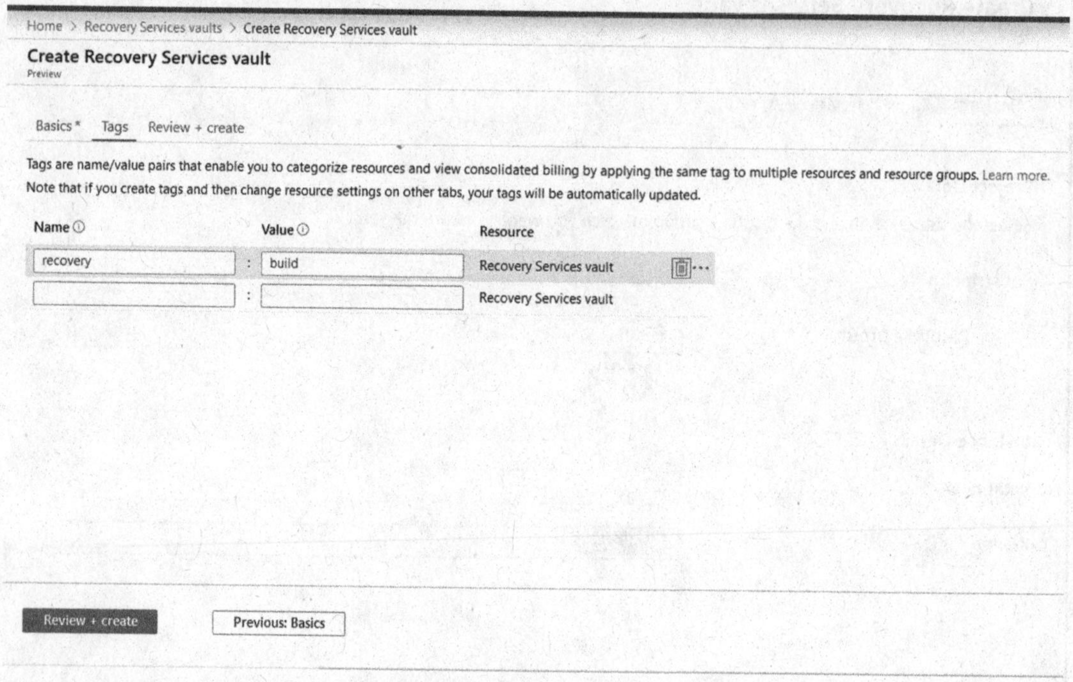

Figure 12-4. Recovery service vault, Tags tab

Finally, take a look at the "Review + create" tab, as shown in Figure 12-5.

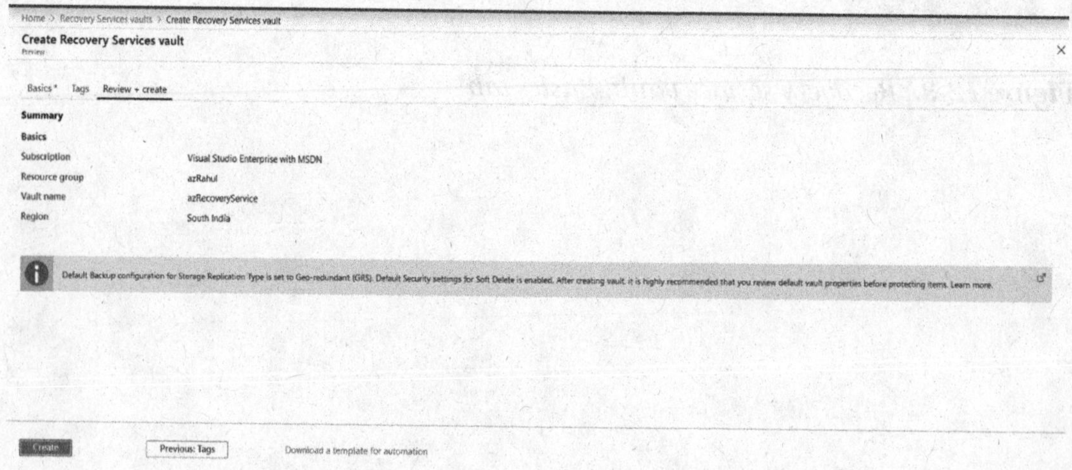

Figure 12-5. Recovery service, "Review + create" tab

If your deployment fails, you'll see the screen shown in Figure 12-6.

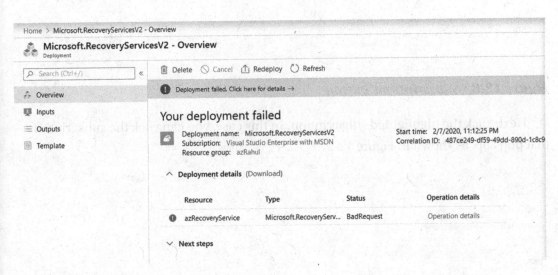

Figure 12-6. *Recovery service vault error*

You can check the Summary tab for more details, as shown in Figure 12-7.

Figure 12-7. *Recovery service vault error detail page*

Enabling Resource Providers

To fix this error, you need to enable this service from a subscription level. Click Subscriptions, as shown in Figure 12-8.

Figure 12-8. *Subscriptions button*

Next, click the highlighted subscription. In this case, you can click the subscription that pops up, as shown in Figure 12-9.

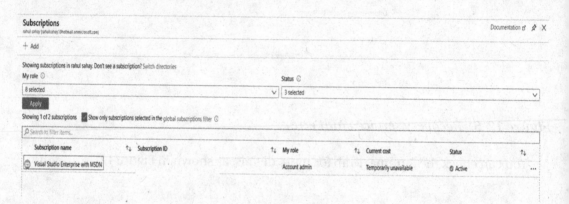

Figure 12-9. *Subscriptions list*

Click "Resource providers" in the left panel as highlighted in Figure 12-10 and look for the RecoveryServices resource on the right.

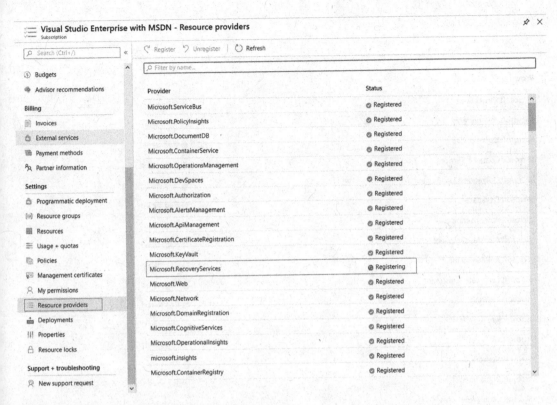

Figure 12-10. *Resource providers list*

If it appears like the resource provider is trying to register, then you need to re-register this service and then try to enable the recovery service vault again.

Hence, go ahead and select the same, and click the Re-register button, as shown in Figure 12-11. Or, if that doesn't help, then try unregistering it first and then re-registering it. This will take some time to take effect. You may want to close the browser and then come back and check later.

Re-register   Unregister   Refresh

Filter by name...

Provider	Status
Microsoft.ServiceBus	Registered
Microsoft.PolicyInsights	Registered
Microsoft.DocumentDB	Registered
Microsoft.ContainerService	Registered
Microsoft.OperationsManagement	Registered
Microsoft.DevSpaces	Registered
Microsoft.Authorization	Registered
Microsoft.AlertsManagement	Registered
Microsoft.ApiManagement	Registered
Microsoft.CertificateRegistration	Registered
Microsoft.KeyVault	Registered
Microsoft.RecoveryServices	Registered
Microsoft.Web	Registered
Microsoft.Network	Registered
Microsoft.DomainRegistration	Registered
Microsoft.CognitiveServices	Registered
Microsoft.OperationalInsights	Registered
microsoft.insights	Registered

Figure 12-11. *Resource providers list after re-registering*

Once the provider is registered, then you can go ahead and complete the recovery process. Once the process is complete, you will see the screen shown in Figure 12-12.

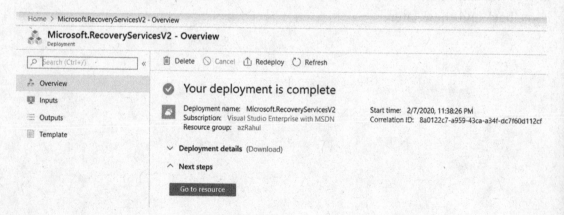

Figure 12-12. *Recovery service vault created*

Now, when you go to the resource, you will see the screen in Figure 12-13.

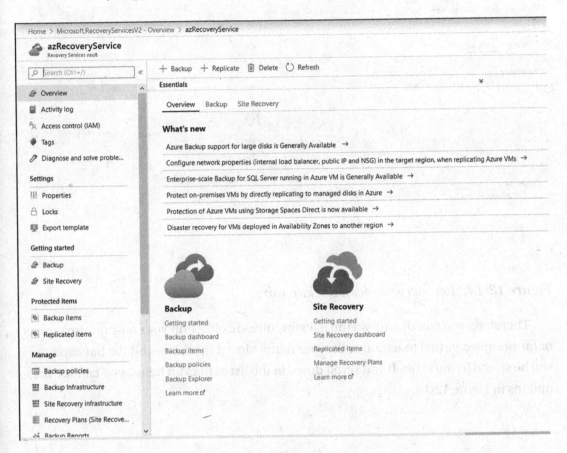

Figure 12-13. *Recovery service vault's Overview page*

The recovery service vault has a couple of purposes. One of them is that it's a destination for backups. When you click the Backup tab, you'll see the screen in Figure 12-14.

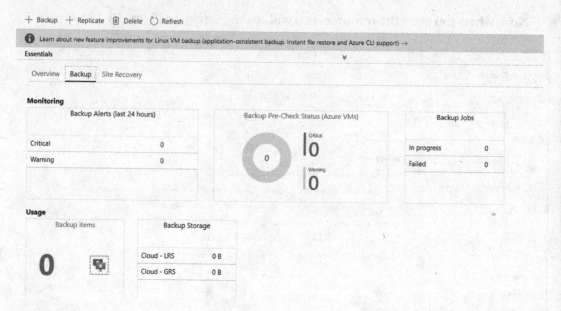

Figure 12-14. *Recovery service's Backup tab*

Therefore, you can download the backup software either on your on-premises server or on-premises virtual machine or on your Azure virtual machine, and the backups will be stored in the vault. If you scroll down in the list of backup items, you can see the options in Figure 12-15.

BACKUP MANAGEMENT TYPE	BACKUP ITEM COUNT
Azure Virtual Machine	0
Azure Backup Agent	0
Azure Backup Server	0
DPM	0
Azure Storage (Azure Files)	0
SQL in Azure VM	0

○ Refresh

Primary Region   Secondary Region

Figure 12-15. *Recovery service backup management screen*

You can see that the backup management types support the items listed in the figure.

Now, let's look at replication, which is just another destination for a migration. Therefore, click "Replicated items," as shown in Figure 12-16.

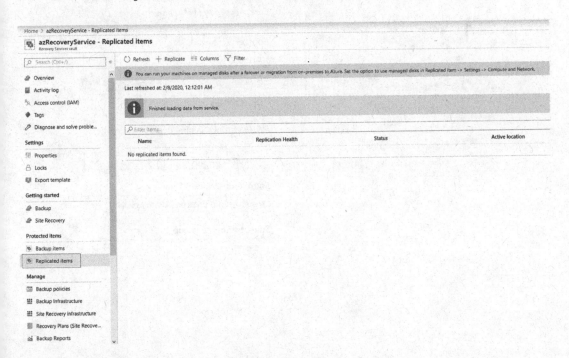

Figure 12-16. *Recovery service replicated items*

Creating a New Replication Item

Let's go ahead and create a new replication item, as shown in Figure 12-17.

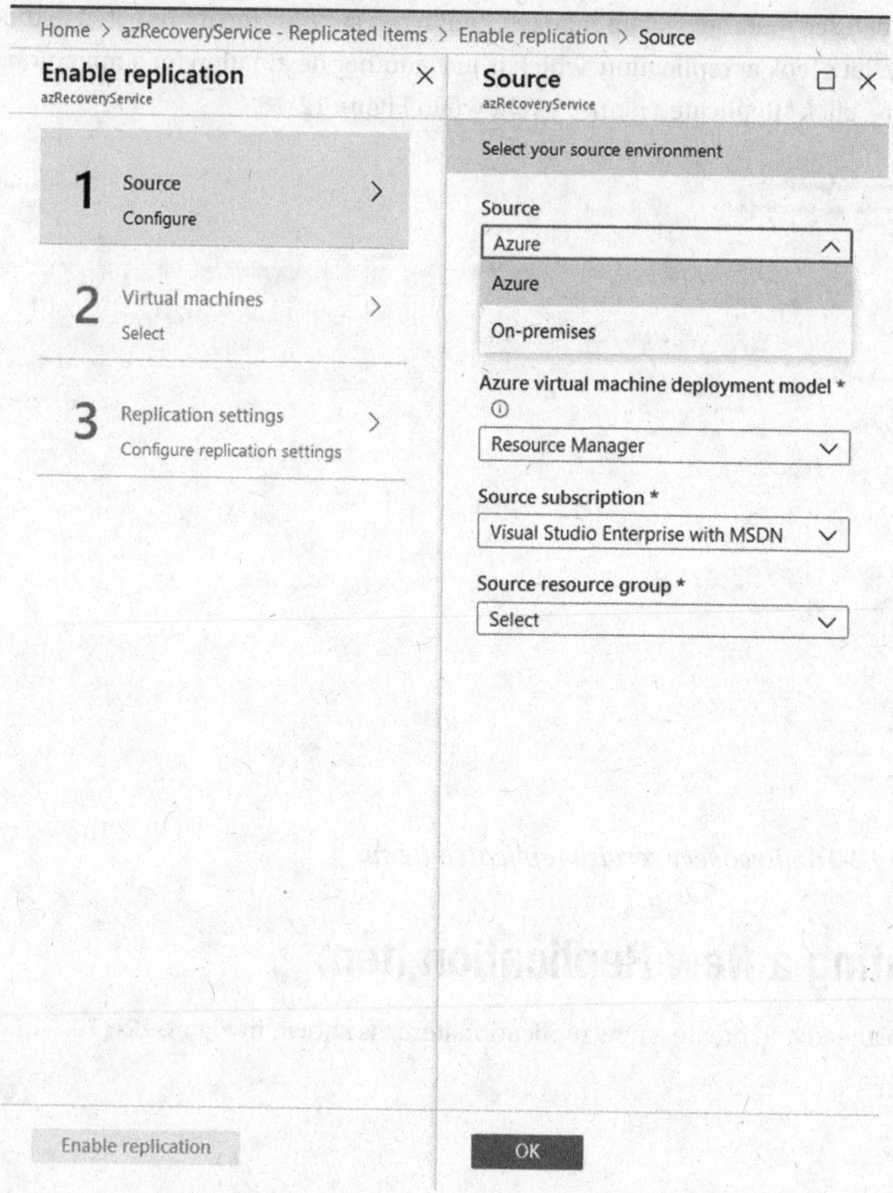

Figure 12-17. *Recovery service, enabling replication*

For this example, I will select the On-premise option from the drop-down, as shown in Figure 12-18.

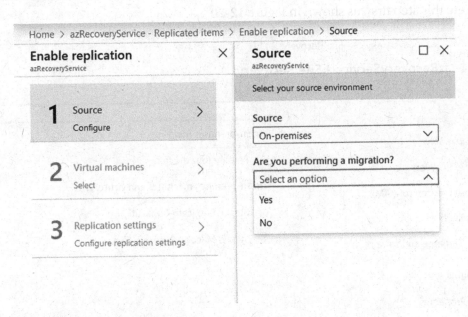

Figure 12-18. *Enabling replication*

Then I will select No to the next question, as shown in Figure 12-19.

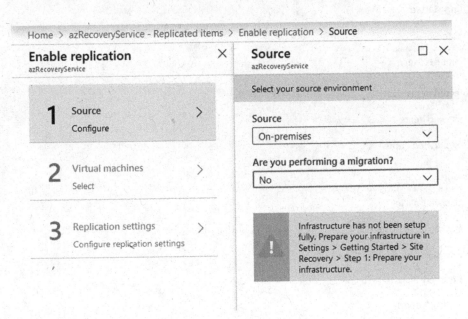

Figure 12-19. *Enabling replication on-premise*

The infrastructure has not been set up fully yet. Prepare your infrastructure in Settings ➤ Getting Started ➤ Site Recovery ➤ Step 1: Prepare your infrastructure. Let's complete this step first, as shown in Figure 12-20.

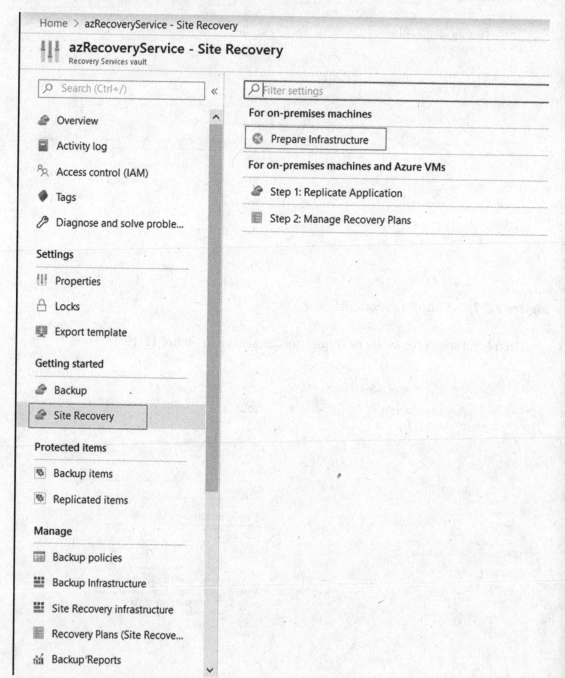

Figure 12-20. *Site recovery, preparing the infrastructure*

Next, select the options shown in Figure 12-21.

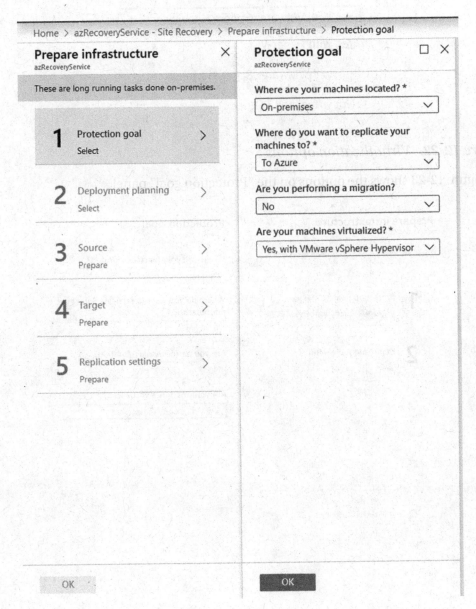

Figure 12-21. *Protection goal*

Figure 12-22 shows the option I have selected.

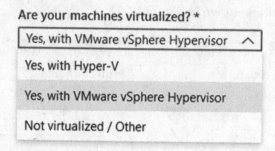

Figure 12-22. *Virtualization options*

Figure 12-23 shows the options on the "Protection goal" panel.

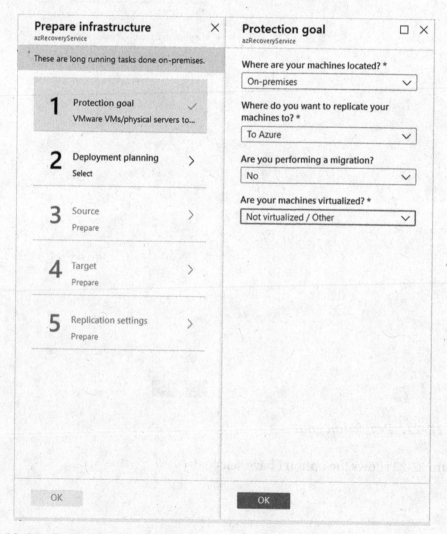

Figure 12-23. *Protection goal settings*

414

Next comes the "Deployment planning" panel, where it will ask you to estimate the network bandwidth, storage requirements, and other stuff. You can state that you will do this later, as shown in Figure 12-24. Basically, you can download a tool from here that can help you with this.

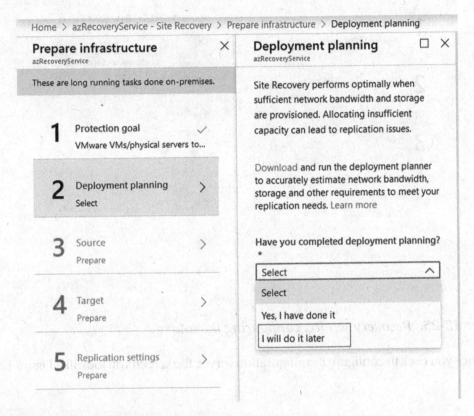

Figure 12-24. *Deployment planning*

Next comes Source, where you need to configure a source for the site recovery, as shown in Figure 12-25. Hence, you need to create a configuration server for this.

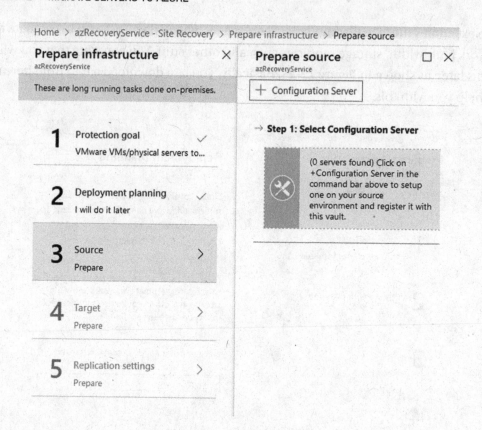

Figure 12-25. *Recovery service, configuring the source*

Once you click to configure a configuration server, the screen will look like Figure 12-26.

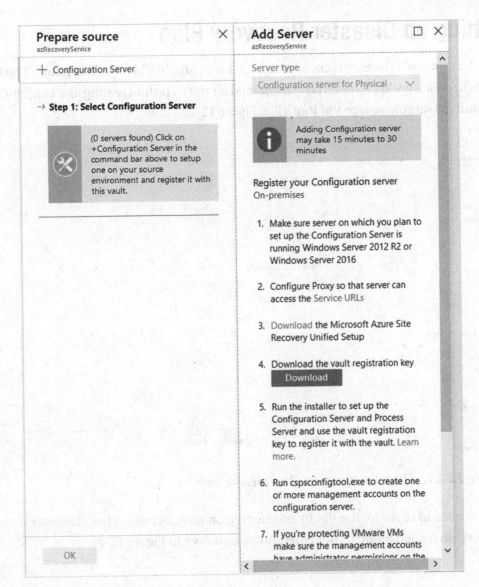

Prepare source   ✕
azRecoveryService

+ Configuration Server

→ **Step 1: Select Configuration Server**

⚒   (0 servers found) Click on
+Configuration Server in the
command bar above to setup
one on your source
environment and register it with
this vault.

OK

Add Server   ☐ ✕
azRecoveryService

Server type

Configuration server for Physical   ∨

ⓘ   Adding Configuration server
may take 15 minutes to 30
minutes

Register your Configuration server
On-premises

1. Make sure server on which you plan to
   set up the Configuration Server is
   running Windows Server 2012 R2 or
   Windows Server 2016

2. Configure Proxy so that server can
   access the Service URLs

3. Download the Microsoft Azure Site
   Recovery Unified Setup

4. Download the vault registration key
   Download

5. Run the installer to set up the
   Configuration Server and Process
   Server and use the vault registration
   key to register it with the vault. Learn
   more.

6. Run cspsconfigtool.exe to create one
   or more management accounts on the
   configuration server.

7. If you're protecting VMware VMs
   make sure the management accounts
   have administrator permissions on the

Figure 12-26. Recovery service, adding a server

Configuring this will take some time, perhaps around 15 to 30 minutes. First, you
need to download Microsoft Azure Site Recovery Unified Setup. It's a piece of software
that will be installed in your local environment, and then you can connect to your vault.
You need the vault registration key, and the software will pick up that key.

Once you run the installer, you need to create a service account for this tool on the
configuration server, which gives the administrator permission on the physical server.
Administrator permissions are obviously required for proper backup and replication.

Setting up Disaster Recovery Plan

Now, let's look at a disaster recovery example for a sample VM hosted in Azure. The first step is to create a VM I have already explained all the steps for creating and configuring a VM, and my sample source VM looks like Figure 12-27.

Figure 12-27. *Disaster recovery Overview screen*

You need to replicate the VM in another region now. For that, click "Disaster recovery" in the left menu under Operations, as shown in Figure 12-28.

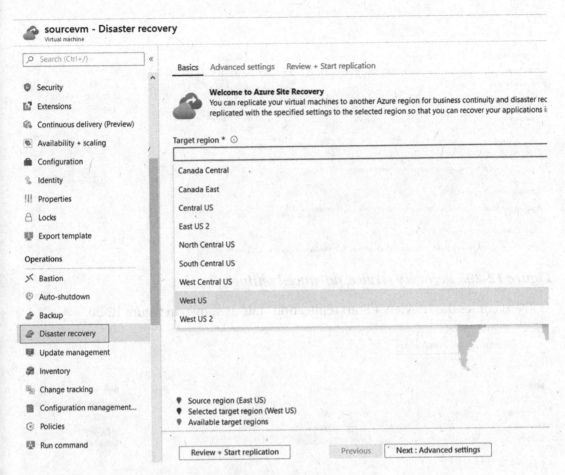

Figure 12-28. *Disaster recovery target options*

You can select any region from the options available. I selected West US. Then, click the next tab for the advanced settings. Figure 12-29 shows the default settings.

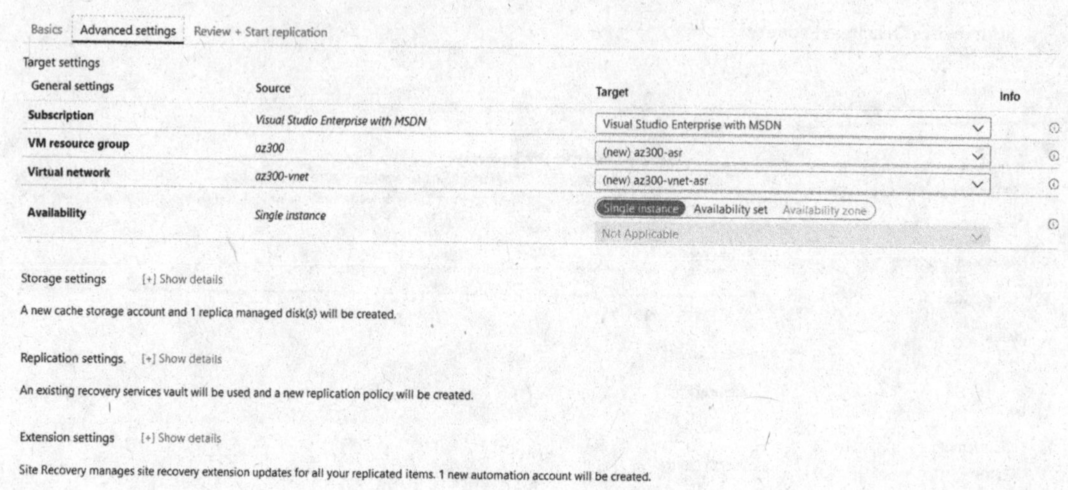

Figure 12-29. *Recovery service, advanced settings*

Next comes the "Review + Start replication" tab, as shown in Figure 12-30.

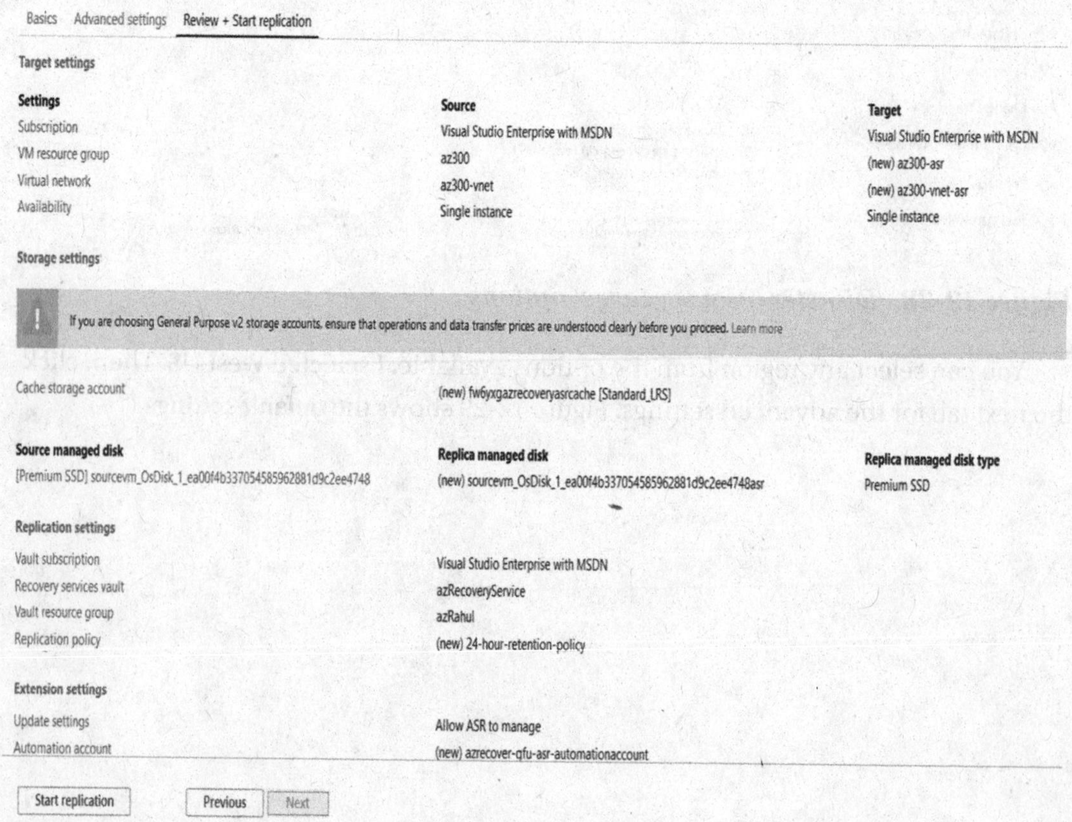

Figure 12-30. *Recovery service, review screen*

This replication process will take some time to complete. Under the hood, it will create a new destination resource group, service principal, NSG, VNet, and many other things associated with the VM. In total, it will take about an hour to complete.

Let's go ahead and check the recovery service that we created earlier and click "Replicated items" under "Protected items." See Figure 12-31.

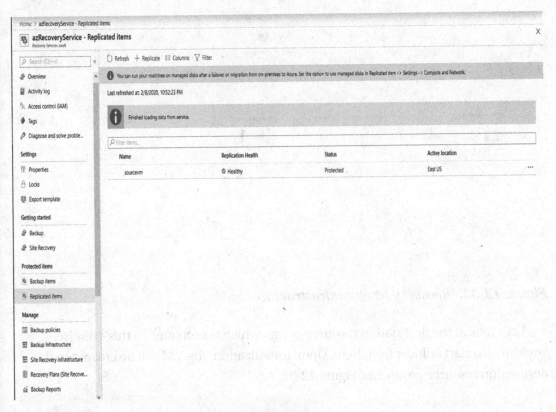

Figure 12-31. *Recovery service, replicated items*

The screen looks like Figure 12-32.

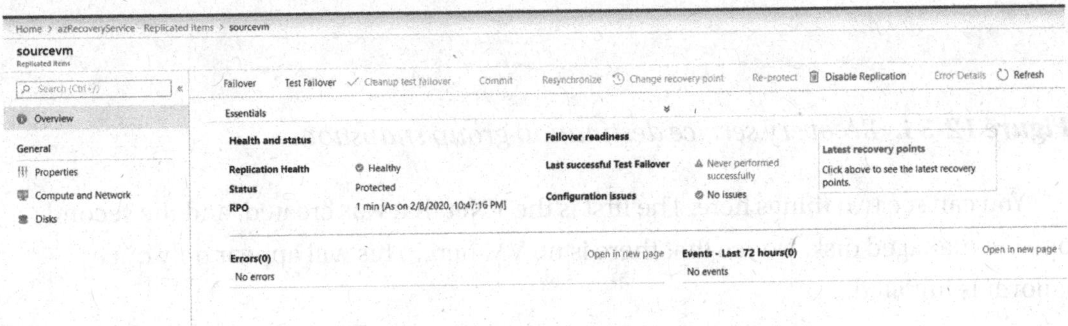

Figure 12-32. *Recovery service source VM's Overview screen*

The infrastructure view looks like Figure 12-33.

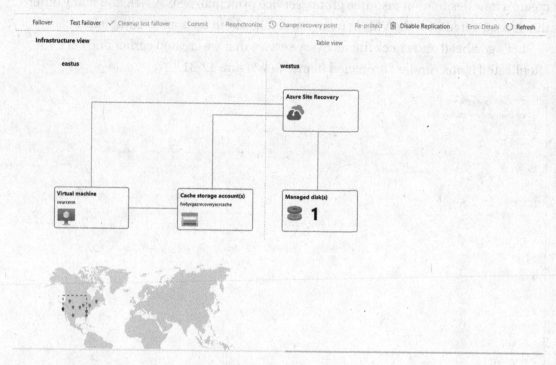

Figure 12-33. *Recovery service infrastructure view*

Let's look at the destination resource group, which was created in this exercise. You can also start failover from here. Upon initialization, the VM will be created in the destination resource group. See Figure 12-34.

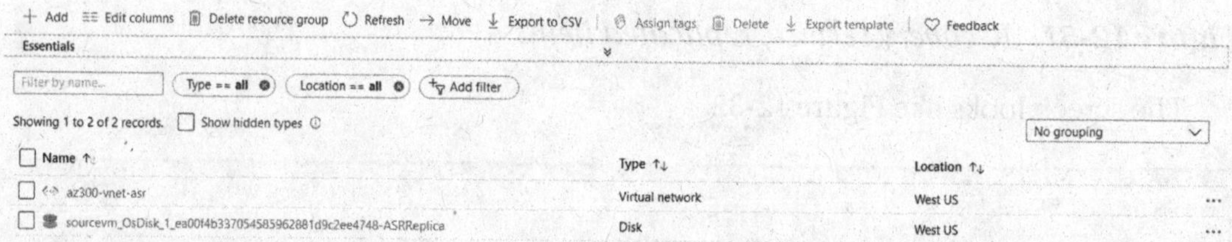

Name ↑	Type ↑↓	Location ↑↓
az300-vnet-asr	Virtual network	West US
sourcevm_OsDisk_1_ea00f4b337054585962881d9c2ee4748-ASRReplica	Disk	West US

Figure 12-34. *Recovery service destination group snapshot*

You can see two things here. The first is the VNet that was created, and the second one is a managed disk. Notice that there is no VM here. This will appear only once failover is initiated.

Creating a Virtual Network

Now, let's create a virtual network for testing, as shown in Figure 12-35.

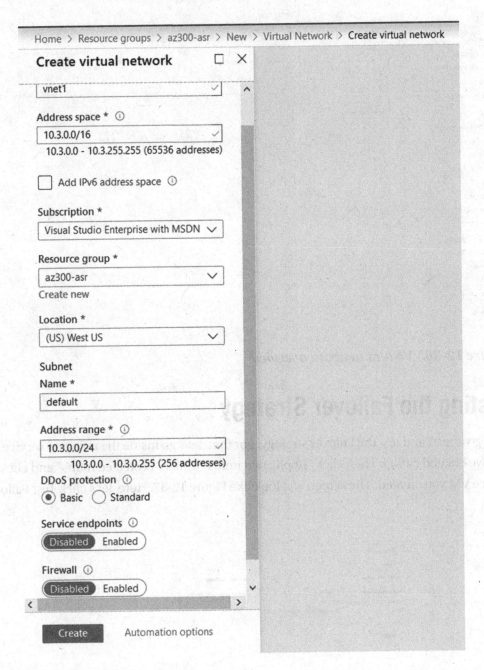

Figure 12-35. *Creating a virtual network*

Once the VM is created, the screen will look like Figure 12-36.

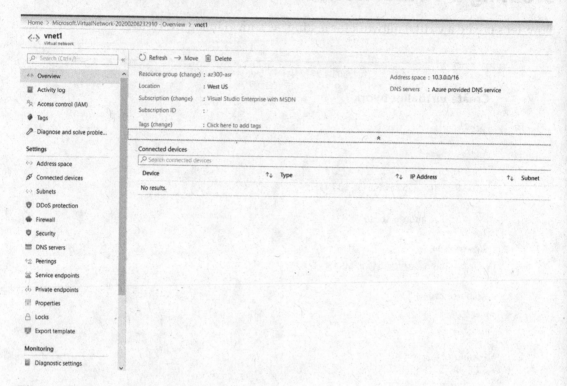

Figure 12-36. *Virtual network overview*

Testing the Failover Strategy

Let's go ahead and test the failover strategy. For that, let's go inside the recovery service that we created earlier. Then click "Replicated items" under "Protected items" and click the source VM you created. The screen will look like Figure 12-37. Here, let's click Test Failover.

Figure 12-37. *Recovery service failover option*

Choose vnet1, which we have created, from the list and click OK, as shown in Figure 12-38.

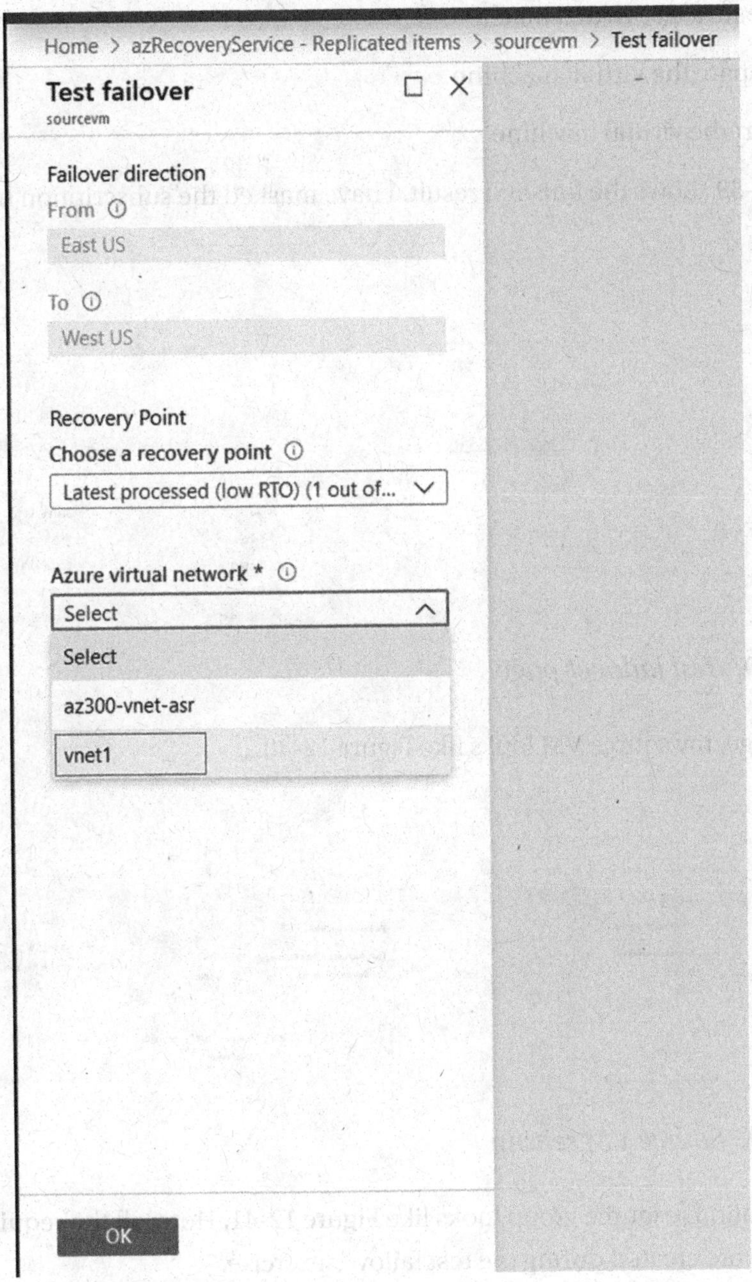

Figure 12-38. *Test failover setting*

This will do a couple of things under the hood.

- Check the prerequisites to test the failover

- Create a test virtual machine

- Prepare the virtual machine

- Start the virtual machine

Figure 12-39 shows the finished result. I have masked the subscription here.

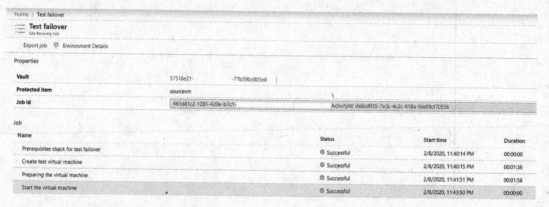

Figure 12-39. *Test failover page*

At this stage, my source VM looks like Figure 12-40.

Figure 12-40. *Source VM setting*

My destination resource group looks like Figure 12-41. Here, all the required components were created during the test failover exercise.

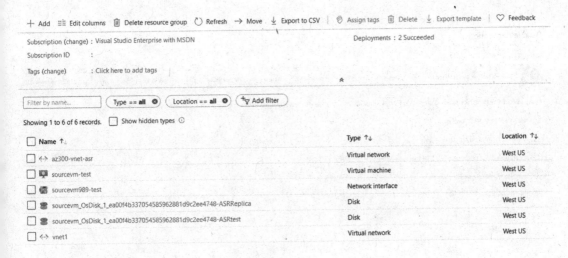

Figure 12-41. Destination resource group

Deleting a Recovery Service

Cleanup is one of the most important things you can do to keep the billing low. As you can see in Figure 12-42, first you need to disable the replication feature for the source VM.

Figure 12-42. Disabling the replication

Figure 12-43 shows how to disable the replication.

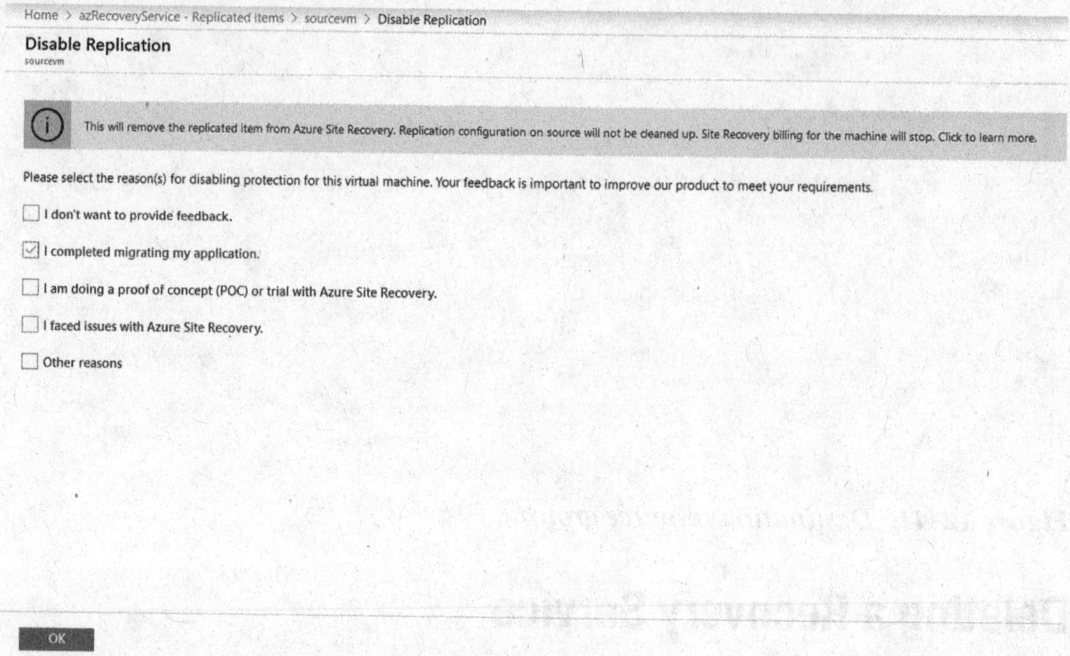

Home > azRecoveryService - Replicated items > sourcevm > Disable Replication

Disable Replication
sourcevm

(i)   This will remove the replicated item from Azure Site Recovery. Replication configuration on source will not be cleaned up. Site Recovery billing for the machine will stop. Click to learn more.

Please select the reason(s) for disabling protection for this virtual machine. Your feedback is important to improve our product to meet your requirements.

☐ I don't want to provide feedback.

☑ I completed migrating my application.

☐ I am doing a proof of concept (POC) or trial with Azure Site Recovery.

☐ I faced issues with Azure Site Recovery.

☐ Other reasons

OK

Figure 12-43. *Disabling the replication*

Click OK. At this stage, when you see the replicated items, they will be empty. Next, you can delete the recovery service that you created, as shown in Figure 12-44.

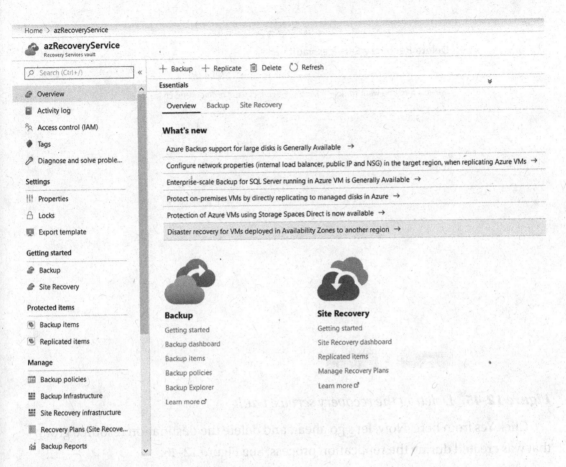

Figure 12-44. *Recovery service overview*

Click Delete, and your screen will look like Figure 12-45.

Figure 12-45. *Deleting the recovery service vault*

Click Yes from here. Now, let's go ahead and delete the destination resource group that was created during the replication process. See Figure 12-46.

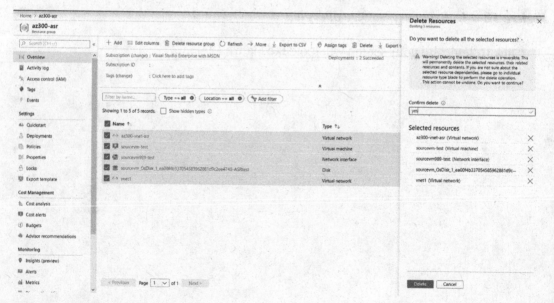

Figure 12-46. *Deleting resources*

I am deleting resources first (Figure 12-47) and then the resource group for graceful deletion (Figure 12-48).

Figure 12-47. *Deleting the resource group*

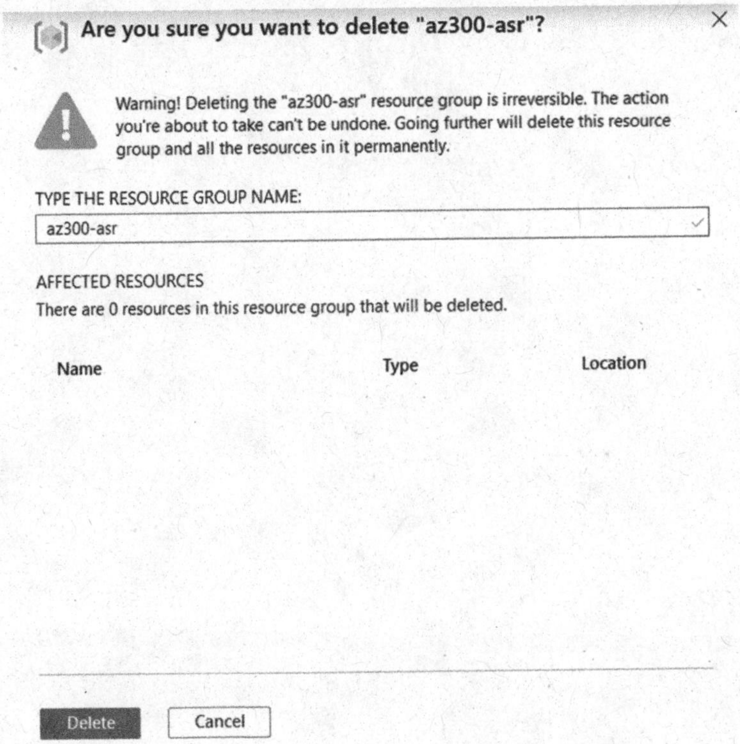

Figure 12-48. *Deleting a resource group confirmation*

This will take a couple of minutes. You can check the status in the notification bar. That wraps up this chapter.

CHAPTER 13

Serverless Computing

Serverless computing enables developers to build applications faster by eliminating the need for them to manage infrastructure. With serverless applications, the cloud service provider automatically provisions, scales, and manages the infrastructure required to run the code. It is important to understand here that servers are still running the code. The *serverless* name comes from the fact that the tasks associated with infrastructure provisioning are not visible to users. This approach enables developers to increase their focus on the business logic.

The following are the top benefits of serverless computing:

- Dynamic scalability
- No infrastructure management
- More efficient use of resources
- Faster time to market

Function App

The Function app is how you implement serverless functions. Let's search in the marketplace for *function*. Then, click the Create button, as shown in Figure 13-1.

433

© Rahul Sahay 2020
R. Sahay, *Microsoft Azure Architect Technologies Study Companion*,
https://doi.org/10.1007/978-1-4842-6200-9_13

Figure 13-1. *Function app*

You can choose the language of your choice from the list of languages, as shown in Figure 13-2.

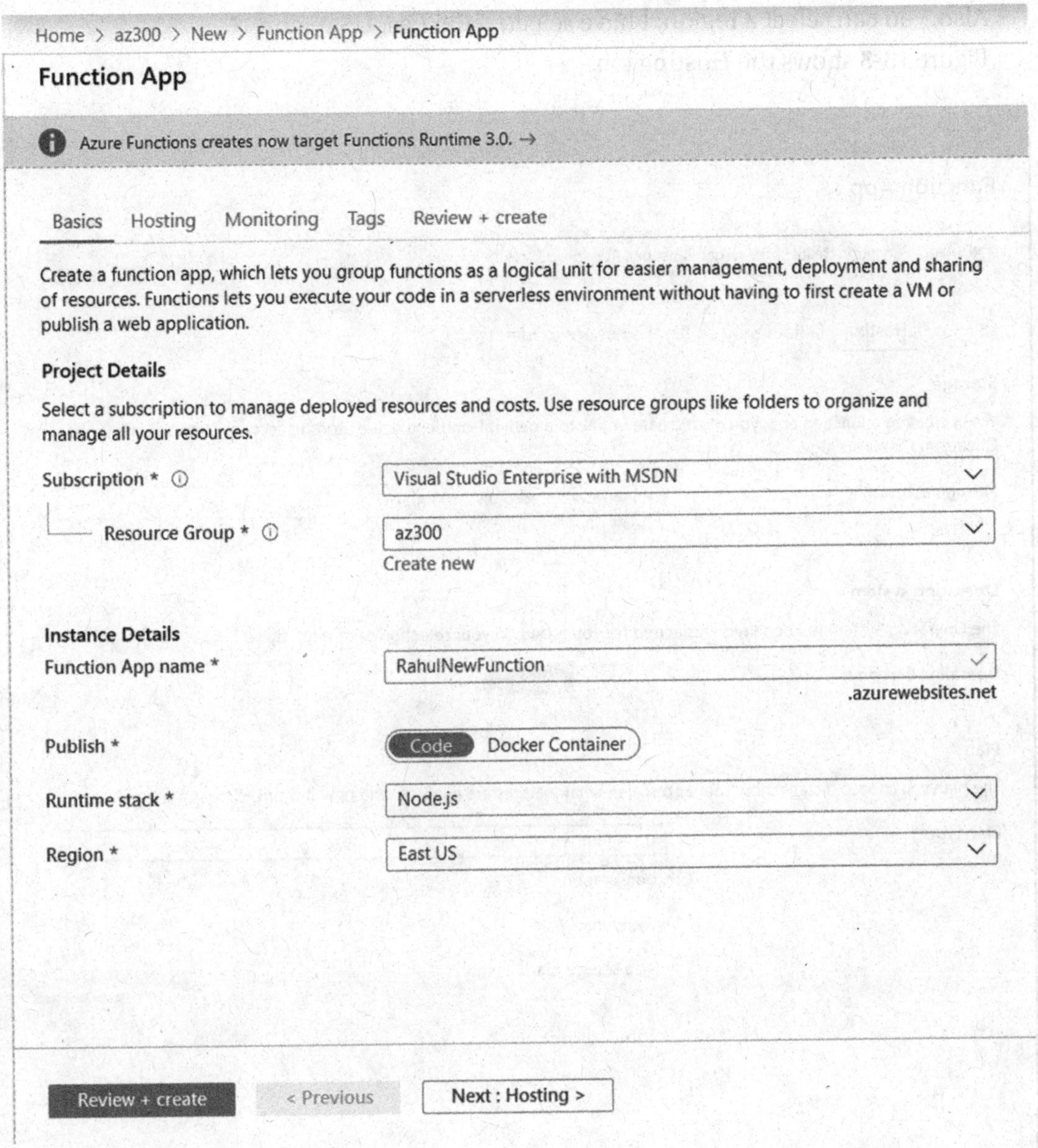

Home > az300 > New > Function App > **Function App**

Function App

> ⓘ Azure Functions creates now target Functions Runtime 3.0. →

Basics   Hosting   Monitoring   Tags   Review + create

Create a function app, which lets you group functions as a logical unit for easier management, deployment and sharing of resources. Functions lets you execute your code in a serverless environment without having to first create a VM or publish a web application.

Project Details

Select a subscription to manage deployed resources and costs. Use resource groups like folders to organize and manage all your resources.

Subscription * ⓘ	Visual Studio Enterprise with MSDN ⌄
└── Resource Group * ⓘ	az300 ⌄
	Create new

Instance Details

Function App name *	RahulNewFunction ✓
	.azurewebsites.net
Publish *	(Code) Docker Container
Runtime stack *	Node.js ⌄
Region *	East US ⌄

Review + create   < Previous   Next : Hosting >

Figure 13-2. *Function app, Basics tab*

435

Also, you can select a region; I have selected the East US region.

Figure 13-3 shows the Hosting tab.

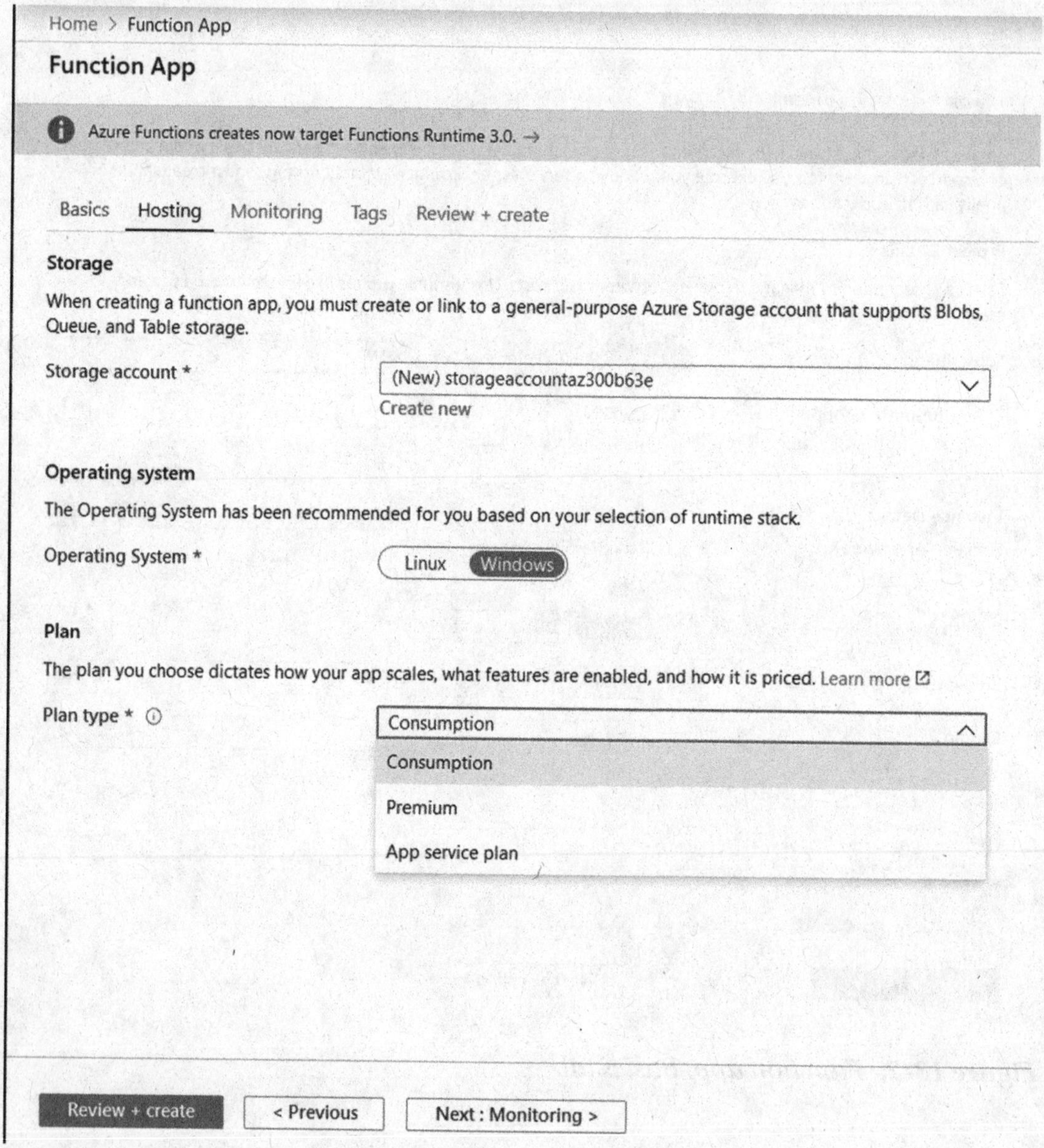

Home > Function App

Function App

ℹ️ Azure Functions creates now target Functions Runtime 3.0. →

Basics   **Hosting**   Monitoring   Tags   Review + create

Storage

When creating a function app, you must create or link to a general-purpose Azure Storage account that supports Blobs, Queue, and Table storage.

Storage account *   (New) storageaccountaz300b63e ⌄
Create new

Operating system

The Operating System has been recommended for you based on your selection of runtime stack.

Operating System *   (Linux **Windows**)

Plan

The plan you choose dictates how your app scales, what features are enabled, and how it is priced. Learn more ☒

Plan type * ⓘ   Consumption ⌃
Consumption
Premium
App service plan

Review + create   < Previous   Next : Monitoring >

Figure 13-3. *Function app, Hosting tab*

For a complete serverless feature, select the Consumption plan. The "App service plan" option is the traditional web app plan where you choose a server, as shown in Figure 13-4.

Plan

The plan you choose dictates how your app scales, what features are enabled, and how it is priced. Learn more ☒

Plan type * ⓘ	App service plan ⌄
	❶ Not finding your plan? Try a different location in Basics tab.
Windows Plan (East US) * ⓘ	(New) ASP-az300-8d2a ⌄
	Create new
Sku and size *	**Standard S1**
	100 total ACU, 1.75 GB memory
	Change size

Figure 13-4. *App service plan setting*

The Premium plan is similar, but with it the premium SKU becomes available, as shown in Figure 13-5.

Plan

The plan you choose dictates how your app scales, what features are enabled, and how it is priced. Learn more ☒

Plan type * ⓘ	Premium ⌄
	❶ Not finding your plan? Try a different location in Basics tab.
Windows Plan (East US) * ⓘ	(New) ASP-az300-a1cd ⌄
	Create new
Sku and size *	**Elastic Premium EP1**
	210 total ACU, 3.5 GB memory
	Change size

Figure 13-5. *"Sku and size" option*

Hence, in this example, we will stick to the Consumption plan. Let's look at the pricing model for it, as shown in Figure 13-6.

Azure Functions pricing

Azure Functions consumption plan is billed based on per-second resource consumption and executions. Consumption plan pricing includes a monthly free grant of 1 million requests and 4,00,000 GB-s of resource consumption per month per subscription in pay-as-you-go pricing across all function apps in that subscription. Azure Functions Premium plan provides enhanced performance and is billed on a per second basis based on the number of vCPU-s and GB-s your Premium Functions consume. Customers can also run Functions within their App Service plan at regular App Service plan rates.

METER	PRICE	FREE GRANT (PER MONTH)
Execution Time*	$0.000016/GB-s	4,00,000 GB-s
Total Executions*	$0.20 per million executions	1 million executions

*Free grants apply to paid consumption subscriptions only.

Note—A storage account is created by default with each Functions app. The storage account is not included in the free grant. Standard storage rates and networking rates charged separately as applicable.

View details on regional availability

Figure 13-6.   *Azure Functions pricing*

The price makes Azure Functions a good choice for code that doesn't frequently run. If you fall below the limit, then it's not going to cost you anything. You can calculate your price in the pricing portal based on your needs: `https://bit.ly/Azure-functions-pricing`.

Figure 13-7 shows the Monitoring tab.

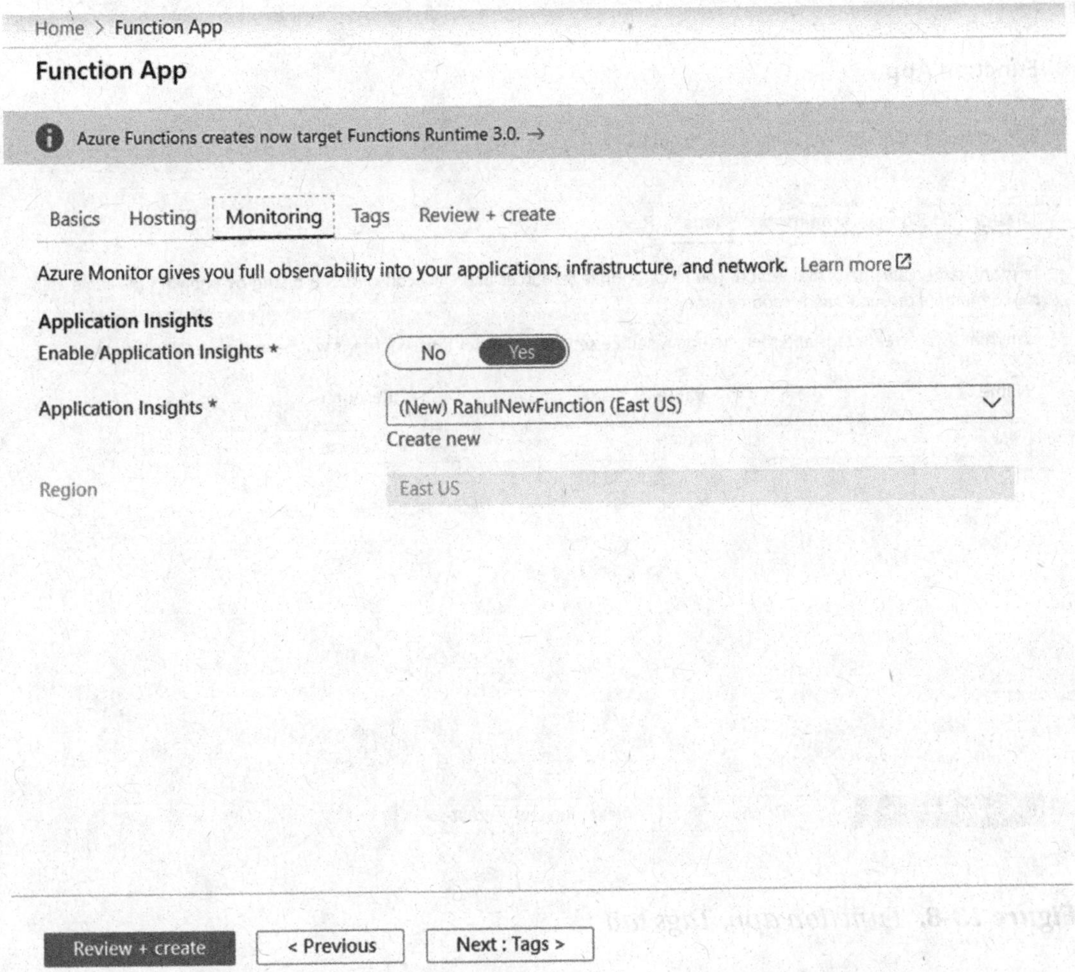

Home > Function App

Function App

ⓘ Azure Functions creates now target Functions Runtime 3.0. →

Basics   Hosting   **Monitoring**   Tags   Review + create

Azure Monitor gives you full observability into your applications, infrastructure, and network. Learn more ☒

Application Insights

Enable Application Insights *   (No   Yes)

Application Insights *   (New) RahulNewFunction (East US)   ˅
                               Create new

Region   East US

Review + create   < Previous   Next : Tags >

Figure 13-7. Function app, Monitoring tab

Next comes the Tags tab. You can supply the usual values here, as shown in Figure 13-8.

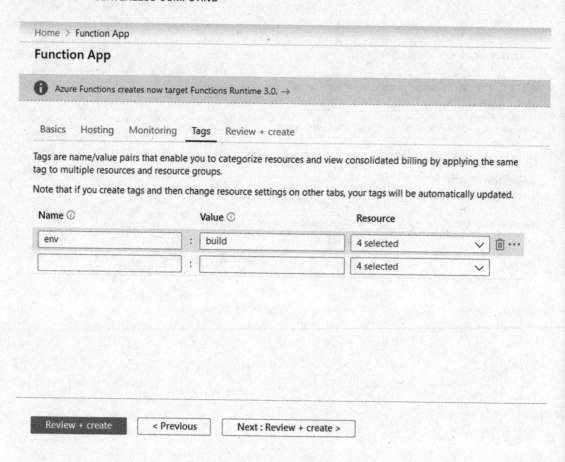

Figure 13-8. *Function app, Tags tab*

Finally comes the "Review + create" tab, as shown in Figure 13-9.

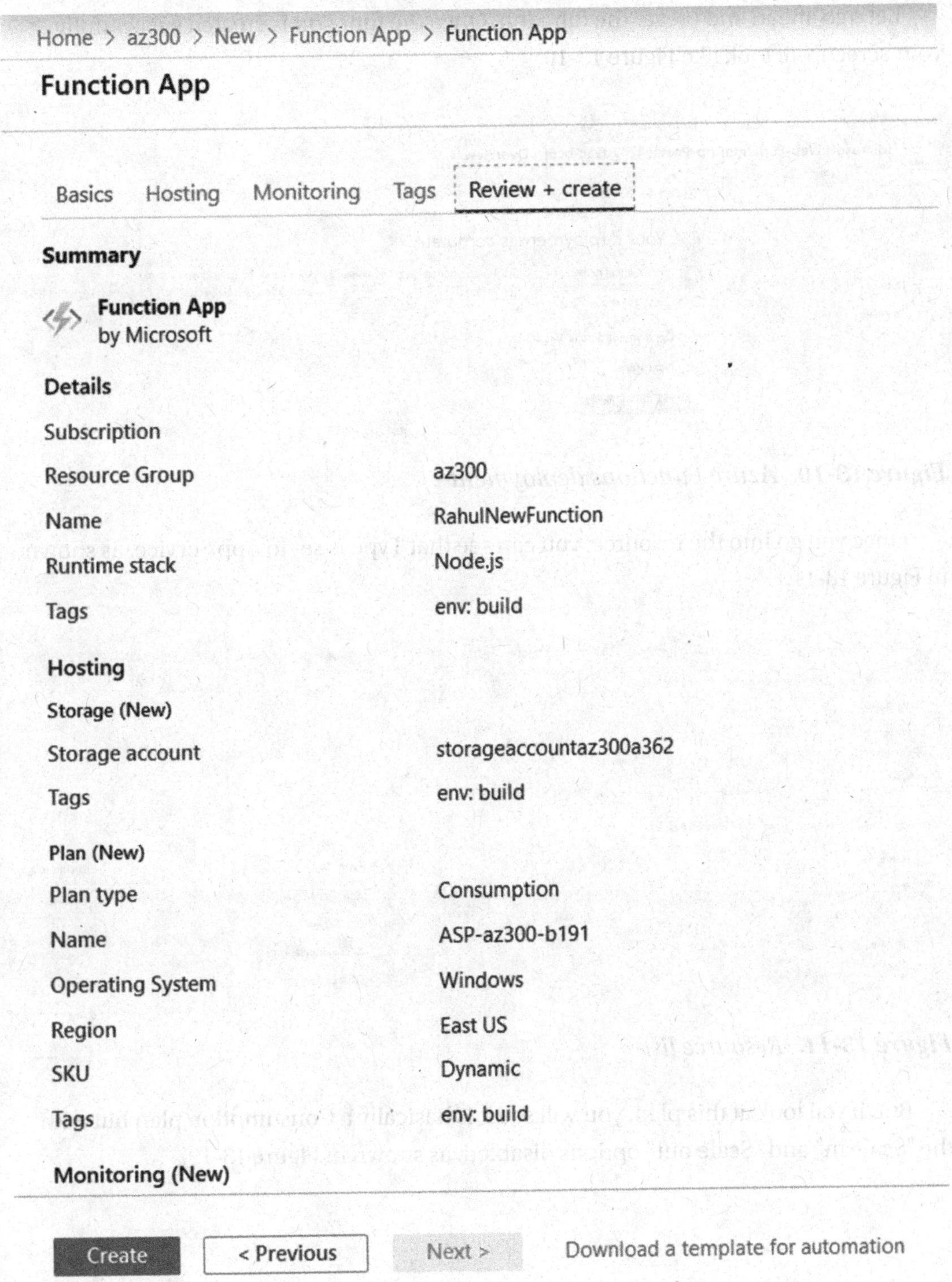

Home > az300 > New > Function App > Function App

Function App

Basics   Hosting   Monitoring   Tags   **Review + create**

Summary

⚡ **Function App**
by Microsoft

Details

Subscription	
Resource Group	az300
Name	RahulNewFunction
Runtime stack	Node.js
Tags	env: build

Hosting

Storage (New)

Storage account	storageaccountaz300a362
Tags	env: build

Plan (New)

Plan type	Consumption
Name	ASP-az300-b191
Operating System	Windows
Region	East US
SKU	Dynamic
Tags	env: build

Monitoring (New)

Create   < Previous   Next >   Download a template for automation

Figure 13-9. Function app, "Review + create" tab

Let's go ahead and create the function. Once the function is created successfully, your screen will look like Figure 13-10.

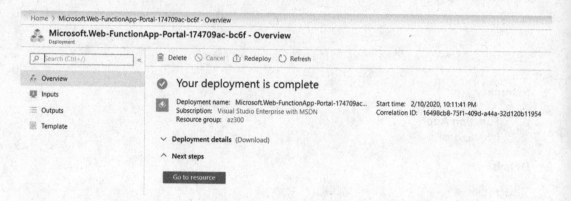

Figure 13-10. *Azure Functions deployment*

Once you go into the resource, you can see that Type is set to App Service, as shown in Figure 13-11.

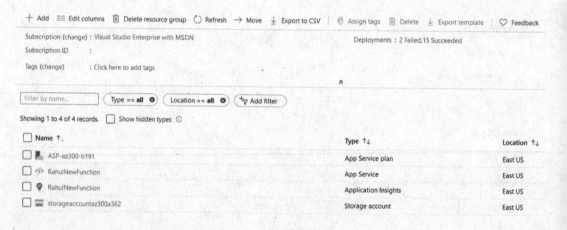

Figure 13-11. *Resource list*

But, if you look at this plan, you will see it is basically a Consumption plan but with the "Scale in" and "Scale out" options disabled, as shown in Figure 13-12.

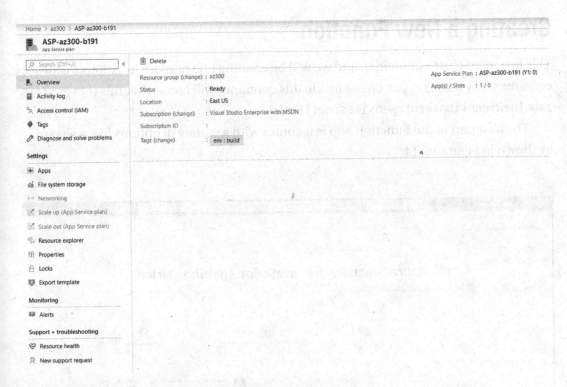

Figure 13-12. *App Service plan's Overview screen*

If you go to the Function Apps list, you will see the screen shown in Figure 13-13.

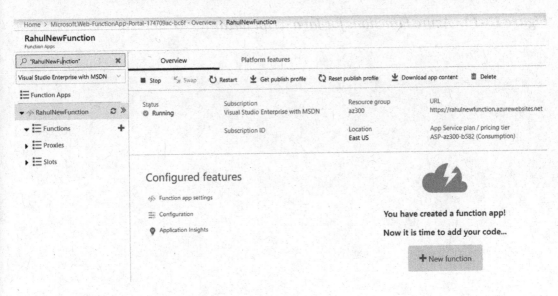

Figure 13-13. *Function Apps screen*

Creating a New Function

This instance is just a container, and we will be creating one or more functions inside this container. Any function you create inside this container will come after this (https://rahulnewfunction.azurewebsites.net) URL.

The best part of the Function app is it comes with a variety of options like a wizard, as shown in Figure 13-14.

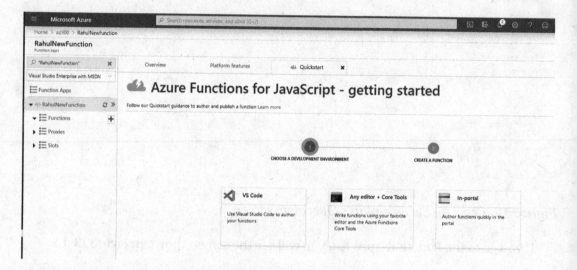

Figure 13-14. *Azure Functions for JavaScript wizard*

Click In-portal and then Continue, as shown in Figure 13-15.

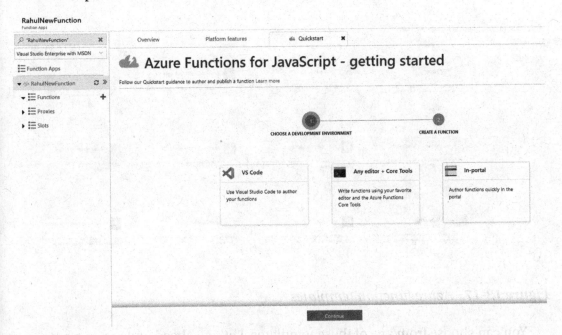

Figure 13-15. *Azure Functions for JavasScript wizard, getting started screen*

Then, it will present some templates, as shown in Figure 13-16.

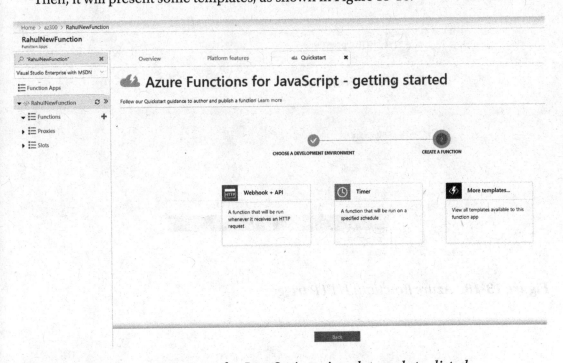

Figure 13-16. *Azure Functions for JavaScript wizard, templates listed*

Clicking "More templates" will give you even more options, as shown in Figure 13-17.

Figure 13-17. Azure function templates

You can choose from any of these templates. Let's go ahead and create a new HTTP trigger function. Click "HTTP trigger," which will open the screen shown in Figure 13-18.

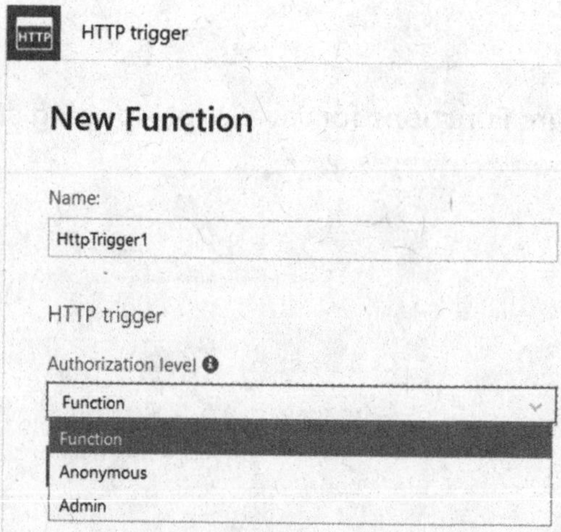

Figure 13-18. Azure function: HTTP trigger

Here, you can create a function with anonymous-level access or a function with admin-level access. For this example, you will see how to create an anonymous function, as shown in Figure 13-19.

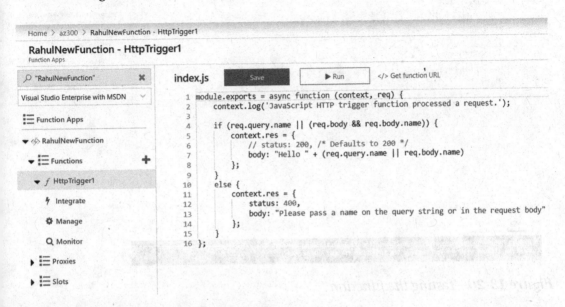

Figure 13-19.   *Azure function HttpTrigger1*

Testing the Function App

The Azure function HttpTrigger1 was created in Node JS because I chose Node JS as my framework while installing the Function app. Here, it's basically going to look at either the query string parameter or the body parameter, and then it will say "Hello {name}." Let's test the function, as shown in Figure 13-20.

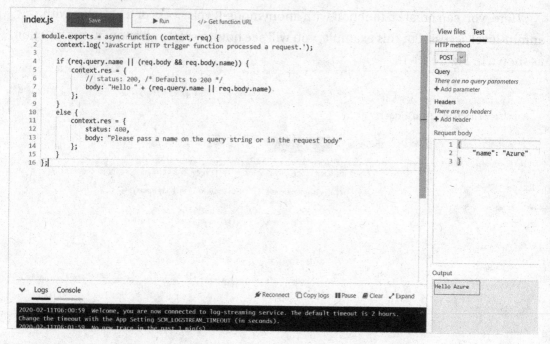

Figure 13-20. *Testing the function*

Click the Run button; the function runs with the POST method and the name set to Azure. Therefore, it prints "Hello, Azure" to the screen. Now, let's test this as a query string in the browser. For that, you need to copy the function URL from the link shown in Figure 13-21.

Figure 13-21. *Function app link*

For this example, the link is `https://rahulnewfunction.azurewebsites.net/api/HttpTrigger1`.

To test this in a browser, go to `https://rahulnewfunction.azurewebsites.net/api/HttpTrigger1?name=Rahul`.

This will print "Hello, Rahul" in the browser, as shown in Figure 13-22.

Figure 13-22. *Testing the function in a browser*

If you don't pass the name parameter, then you will get the error shown in Figure 13-23.

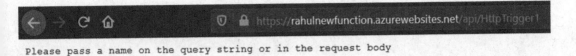

Please pass a name on the query string or in the request body

Figure 13-23. Function app error

Function Integration with Azure Blob

This is one part of using it like by just creating the function. However, functions really shine at various levels of integration. Let's look at the Integrate screen, as shown in Figure 13-24.

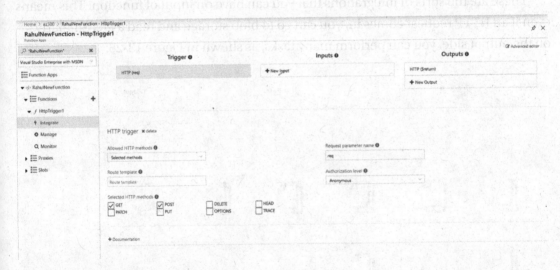

Figure 13-24. Function integration

When you click New Input, you will see the options shown in Figure 13-25.

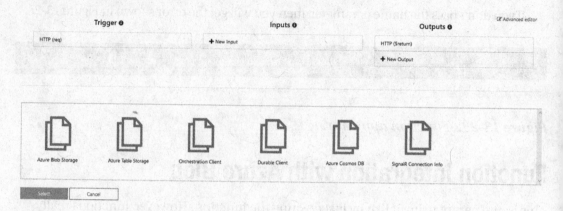

Figure 13-25. *Integration options*

These are the sorts of integrations that you can have on input of function. This means even if an HTTP request comes in, you can go to blob storage and read a file. Similarly, on the output side, you can perform many tasks, as shown in Figure 13-26.

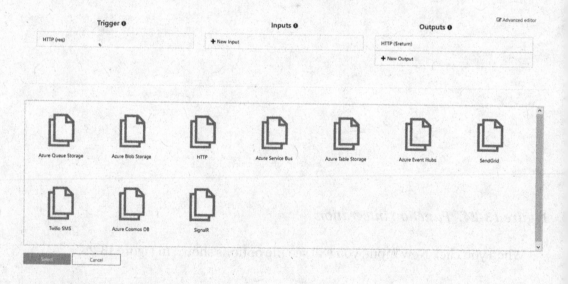

Figure 13-26. *More integration options*

In the output options, let's select Azure Blob Storage, as shown in Figure 13-27.

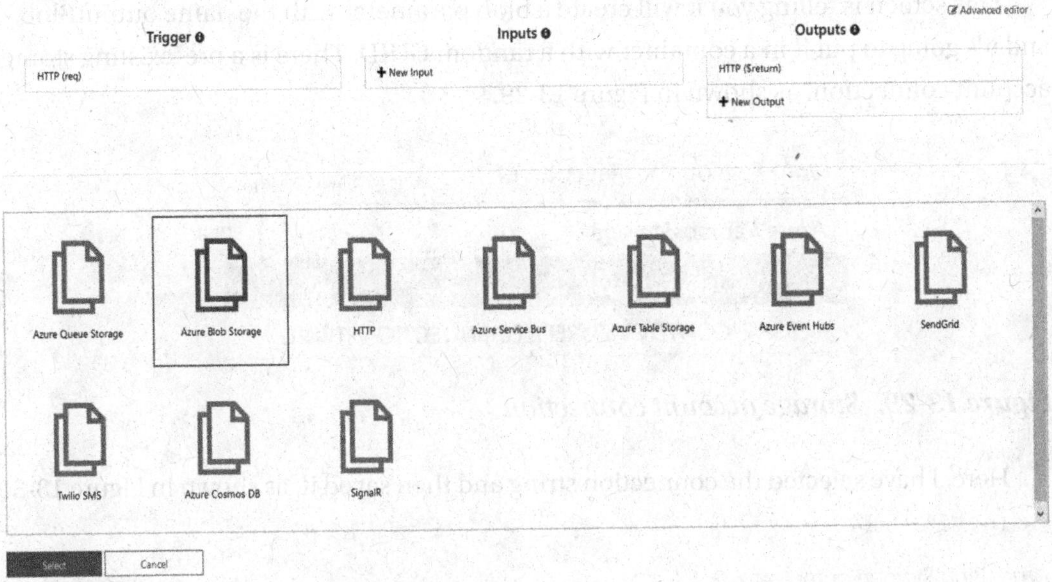

Figure 13-27. *Azure Blob Storage option*

The screen shown in Figure 13-28 will appear.

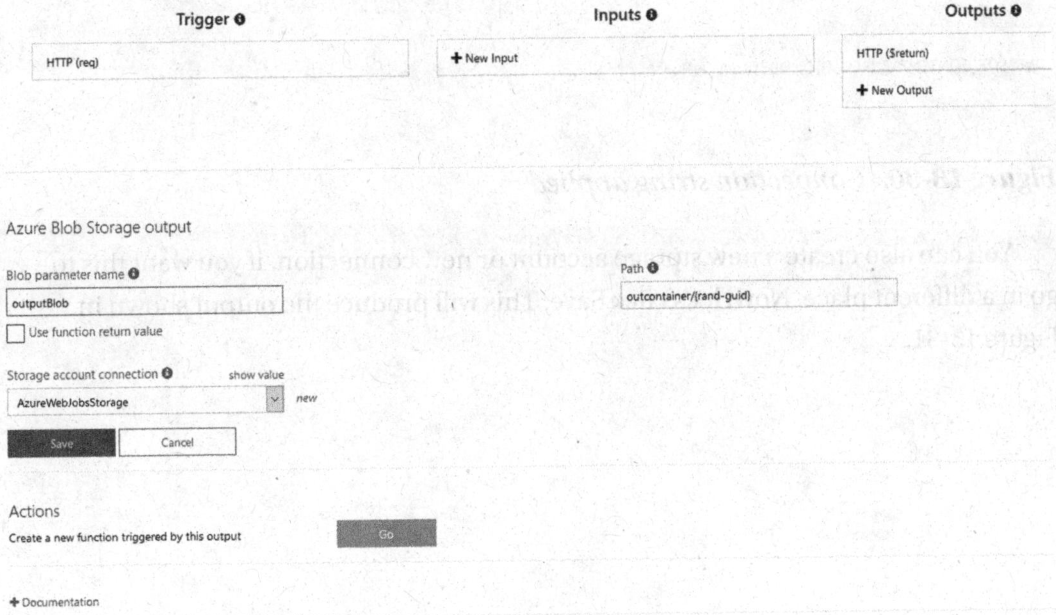

Figure 13-28. *Output blob*

This screen is telling you it will create a blob parameter with the name outputBlob, and it's going to put it in a container with a random GUID. There is a pre-existing storage account connection, as shown in Figure 13-29.

Storage account connection
show value
AzureWebJobsStorage
new
AzureWebJobsStorage
WEBSITE_CONTENTAZUREFILECONNECTIONSTRING

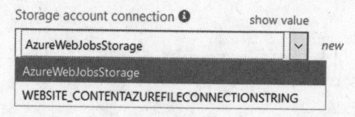

***Figure 13-29.** Storage account connection*

Here, I have selected the connection string and then saved it, as shown in Figure 13-30.

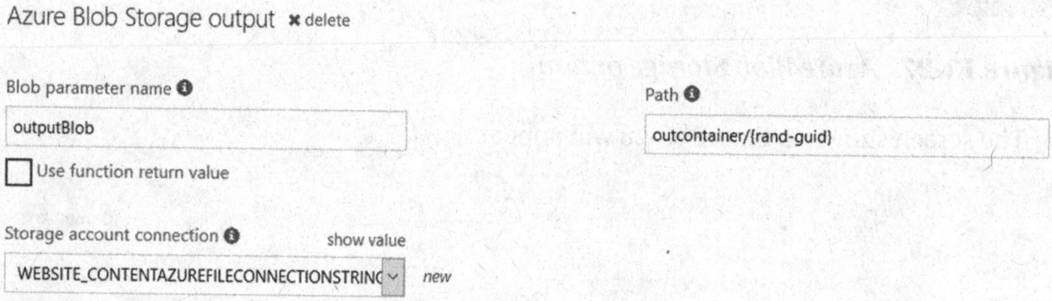

Azure Blob Storage output
delete
Blob parameter name
outputBlob
Use function return value
Path
outcontainer/{rand-guid}
Storage account connection
show value
WEBSITE_CONTENTAZUREFILECONNECTIONSTRING
new

***Figure 13-30.** Connection string applied*

You can also create a new storage account or new connection, if you want this to go in a different place. Now, let's click Save. This will produce the output shown in Figure 13-31.

Trigger ❶	Inputs ❶	Outputs ❶
HTTP (req)	+ New Input	HTTP ($return)
		Azure Blob Storage (outputBlob)
		+ New Output

Azure Blob Storage output ✖ delete

Blob parameter name ❶   Path ❶

outputBlob   outcontainer/{rand-guid}

☐ Use function return value

Storage account connection ❶   show value

AzureWebJobsStorage   ⌄   new

Figure 13-31. *Connection string information*

This means you can go back to your function and start acting on your output blob, as shown in Figure 13-32.

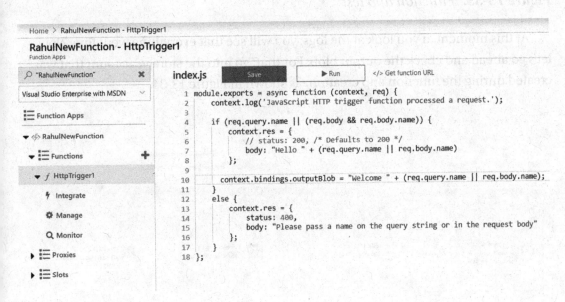

Home > RahulNewFunction - HttpTrigger1

RahulNewFunction - HttpTrigger1
Function Apps

```
index.js
1  module.exports = async function (context, req) {
2      context.log('JavaScript HTTP trigger function processed a request.');
3
4      if (req.query.name || (req.body && req.body.name)) {
5          context.res = {
6              // status: 200, /* Defaults to 200 */
7              body: "Hello " + (req.query.name || req.body.name)
8          };
9
10         context.bindings.outputBlob = "Welcome " + (req.query.name || req.body.name);
11     }
12     else {
13         context.res = {
14             status: 400,
15             body: "Please pass a name on the query string or in the request body"
16         };
17     }
18 };
```

Figure 13-32. *Function code changes*

Testing the Integrated Function

In this section, you will put a welcome message into the output blob. Now, let's go ahead and run it, as shown in Figure 13-33.

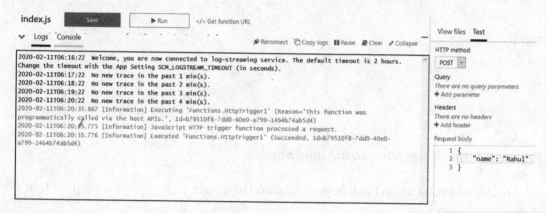

Figure 13-33. *Function app test*

At this moment, if you look at the logs, you will see that everything went fine. Now, let's go ahead and check the output blob. For that, go into the storage account that was created during the function app creation, as shown in Figure 13-34.

Figure 13-34. *Container creation*

Click Containers and select the container named outcontainer that was created after executing the function, as shown in Figure 13-35. The screen shown in Figure 13-36 will open.

Figure 13-35. Container setting

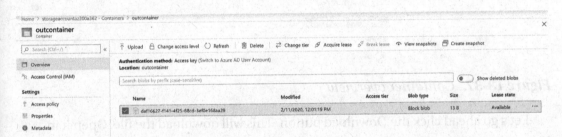

Figure 13-36. Container overview

When you click the selected file, the screen shown in Figure 13-37 will open.

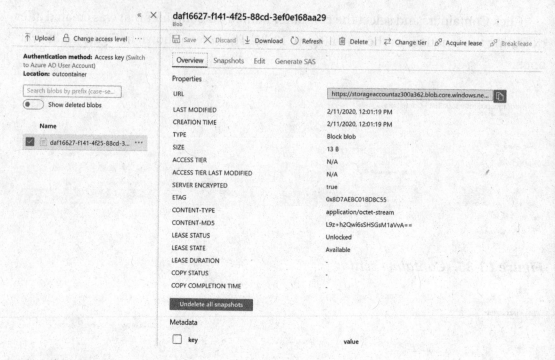

Figure 13-37. *Container overview*

Let's go ahead click the Download button. This will download the file. Open it in Notepad, as shown in Figure 13-38.

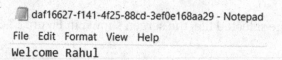

Figure 13-38. *Container output*

Notice that the same message as output in the blob container via the function app has been printed in the file.

Logic Apps

In this section, we will discuss the Logic Apps service. Logic apps are different from functions. Functions are basically small pieces of functionality that run in the cloud, whereas logic apps are more like workflows that can tie those pieces of functionality together. This means you can take a number of functions and chain them together using logic apps. Logic apps also integrate with many other Azure services and external services as well, so that you can have one step leading to another in the workflow.

Creating a New Logic App

Let's create a logic app. Search for *logic* in the marketplace, as shown in Figure 13-39.

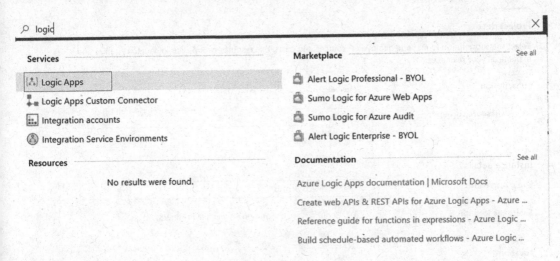

Figure 13-39. *Logic Apps service search*

When you click Logic Apps, you will be taken to the screen shown in Figure 13-40.

Figure 13-40. *Logic Apps screen*

Click Add or "Create logic app," which will take you to the screen shown in Figure 13-41. If you want to expose the logs of your logic apps in Log Analytics, then you can turn the Log Analytics setting on. Let's turn this on now and select the default workspace.

Home > Logic Apps > Logic App

Logic App

Basics *   Review + create

Project details

Select the subscription to manage deployed resources and costs. Use resource groups like folders to organize and manage all your resources.

Subscription *	Visual Studio Enterprise with MSDN
Resource group *	az300
	Create new

Instance details

Logic App name *	RahulNewLogicApp
Select the location	⦿ Region ◯ Integration Service Environment
Location *	East US
Log Analytics ⓘ	On Off
Log Analytics workspace *	DefaultWorkspace-671f56b1-a534-4c21-b2e8-e19a3ea94b89-SEA

Review + create   Download a template for automation ⓘ

***Figure 13-41.** Logic App screen, Basics tab*

Next, click "Review + create," as shown in Figure 13-42.

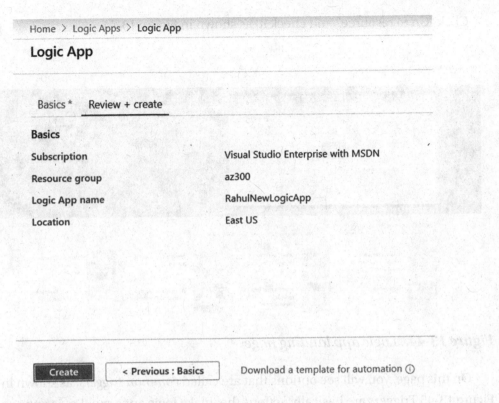

Figure 13-42. Logic App screen, "Review + create" tab

After the logic app is successfully deployed, you will see the screen in Figure 13-43.

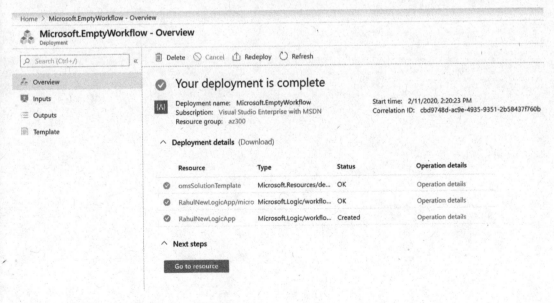

Figure 13-43. Deployment completed

Click "Go to resource" and check it, as shown in Figure 13-44.

Figure 13-44. *Logic app landing page*

On this page, you will see options that are called *common triggers*, as shown in
Figure 13-45 Triggers are basically actions that make logic apps run. Logic apps need one
trigger to get started.

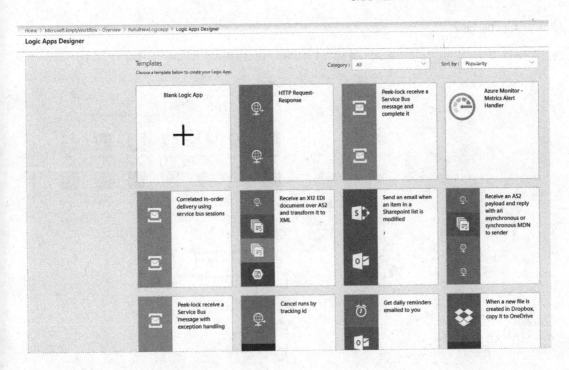

Figure 13-45. *Commong triggers*

Let's create a blank logic app from these options by clicking Blank Logic App. The screen shown in Figure 13-46 will appear.

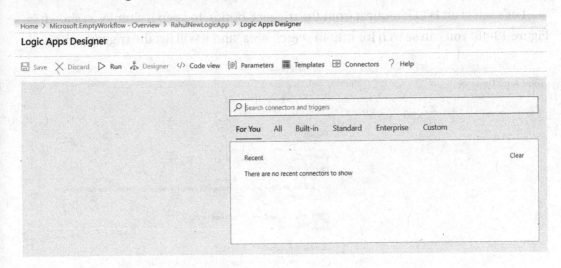

Figure 13-46. *Logic Apps Designer, blank*

Next, check for the available triggers. You can see here that we have a plethora of triggers available, as shown in Figure 13-47.

461

Logic Apps Designer

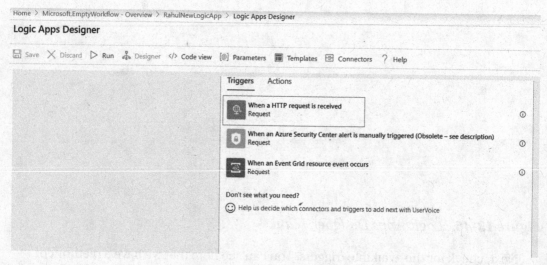

Figure 13-47. *Logic Apps Designer, trigger options*

Let's select an HTTP request from the triggers' option to keep it simple, as shown in Figure 13-48. You can search for http in search area, and it will list the trigger.

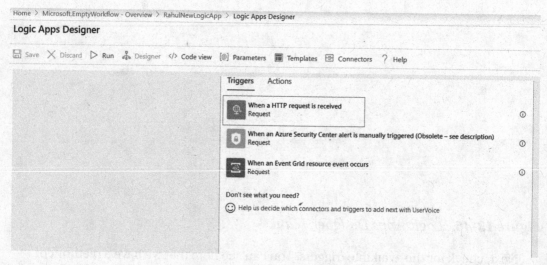

Figure 13-48. *Logic Apps Designer, HTTP request*

I have selected Get as the method, and then in the URL, I have provided a REST kind of URL pattern to accept the employee ID, as shown in Figure 13-49.

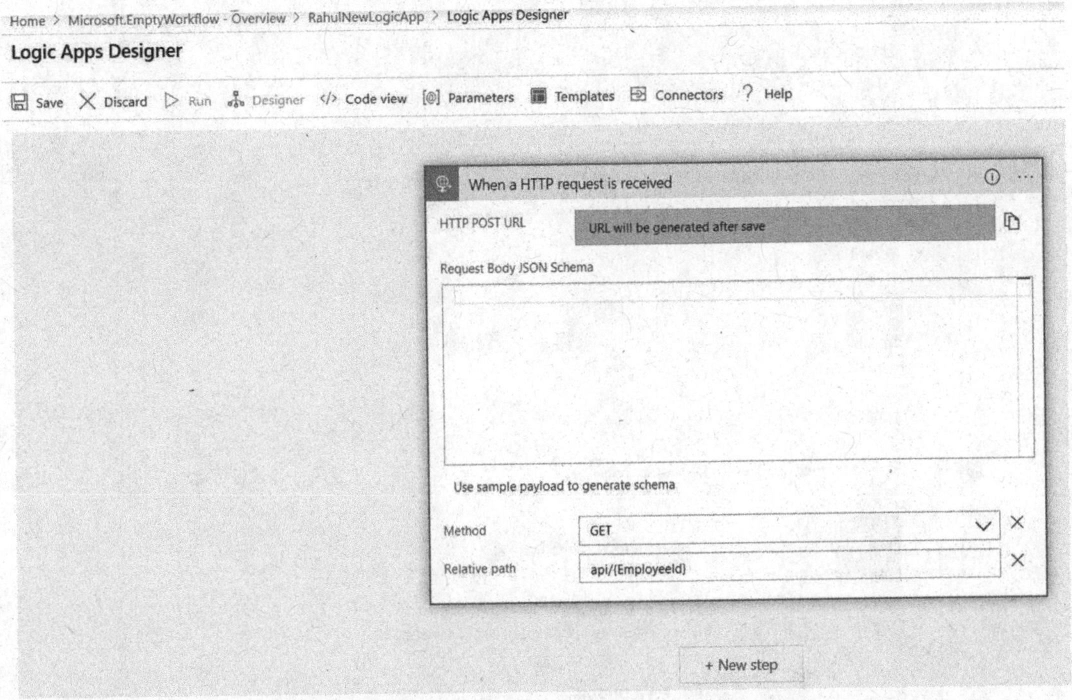

Figure 13-49. *Logic Apps Designer, HTTP request trigger*

Once you save the trigger, the URL will be generated. For now, just click the title bar to minimize it and choose the next step for the workflow, as shown in Figure 13-50.

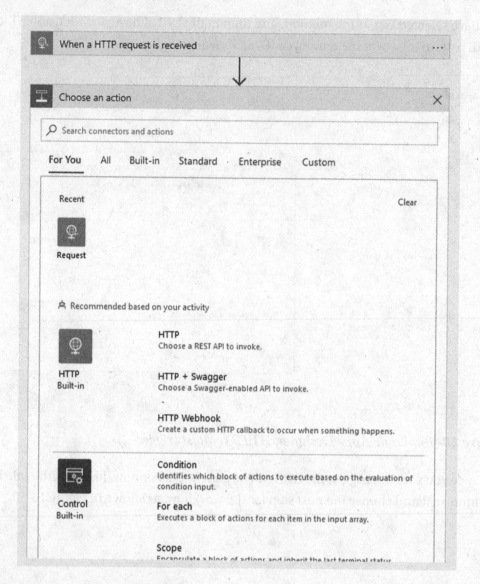

Figure 13-50. *Choosing an action*

From here, you can choose a condition, as shown in Figure 13-51.

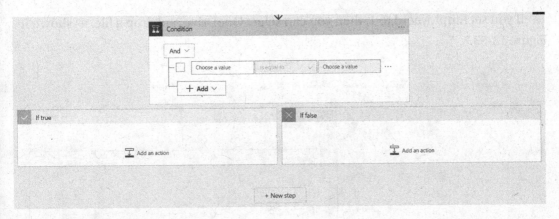

Figure 13-51. *If-else ladder*

Select EmployeeId, as shown in Figure 13-52.

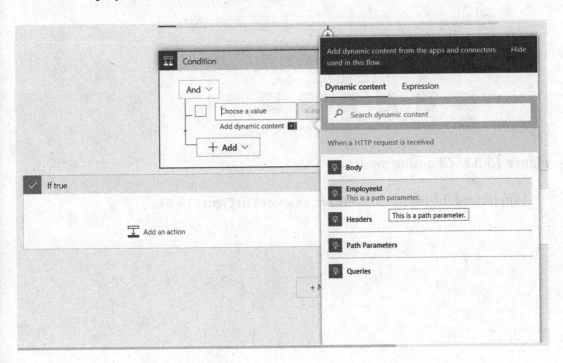

Figure 13-52. *Applying a condition*

If you set EmployeeId to 1, then you can select OneDrive and drop a file, as shown in Figure 13-53.

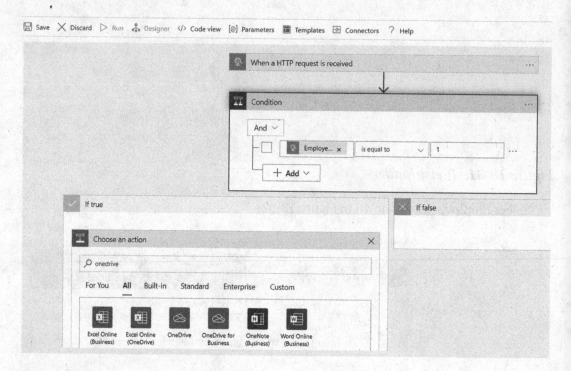

Figure 13-53. *Choosing an action*

I am picking the file from OneDrive, as shown in Figure 13-54.

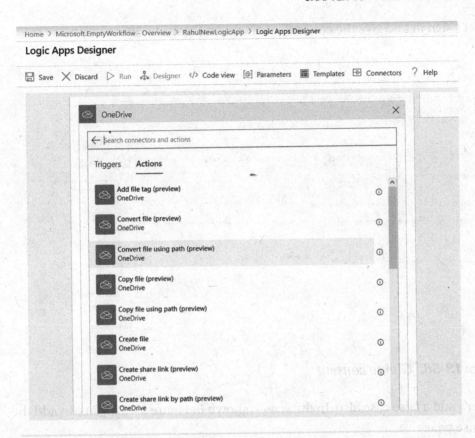

Figure 13-54. *Selecting from options*

A true condition looks like Figure 13-55.

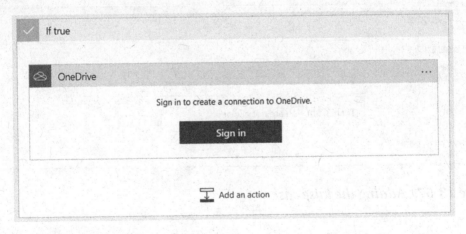

Figure 13-55. *Sign-in option selected*

Let's sign in and give the consent, as shown in Figure 13-56.

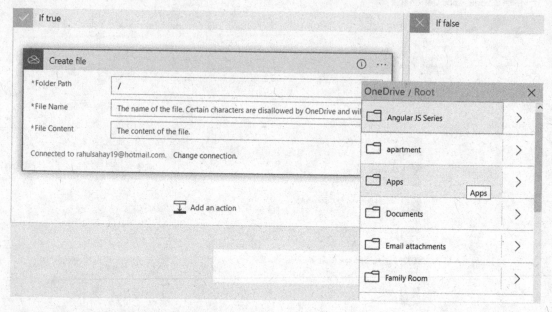

Figure 13-56. *Giving consent*

Let's add a false case also. In the screen shown in Figure 13-57, you can add the response type.

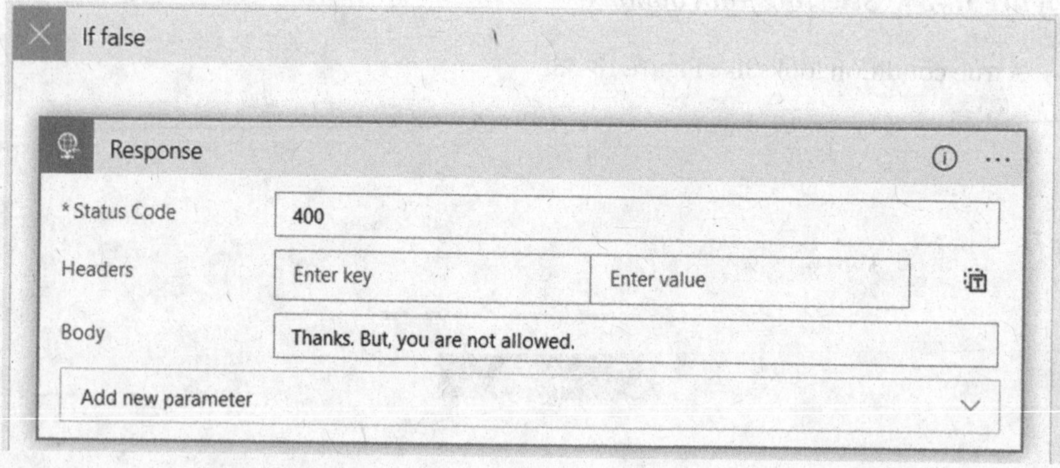

Figure 13-57. *Adding the false case*

You can append the incoming EmployeeId value with the `.txt` extension, as shown in Figure 13-58.

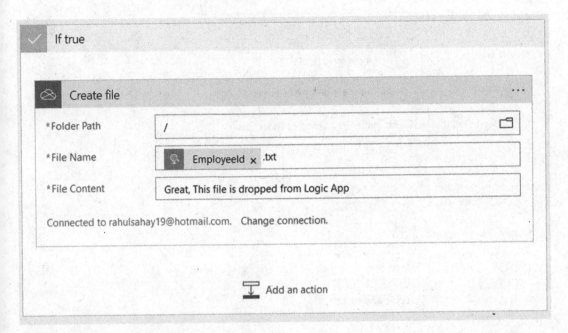

Figure 13-58. *Applying a true condition*

Figure 13-59 shows that it's a true case.

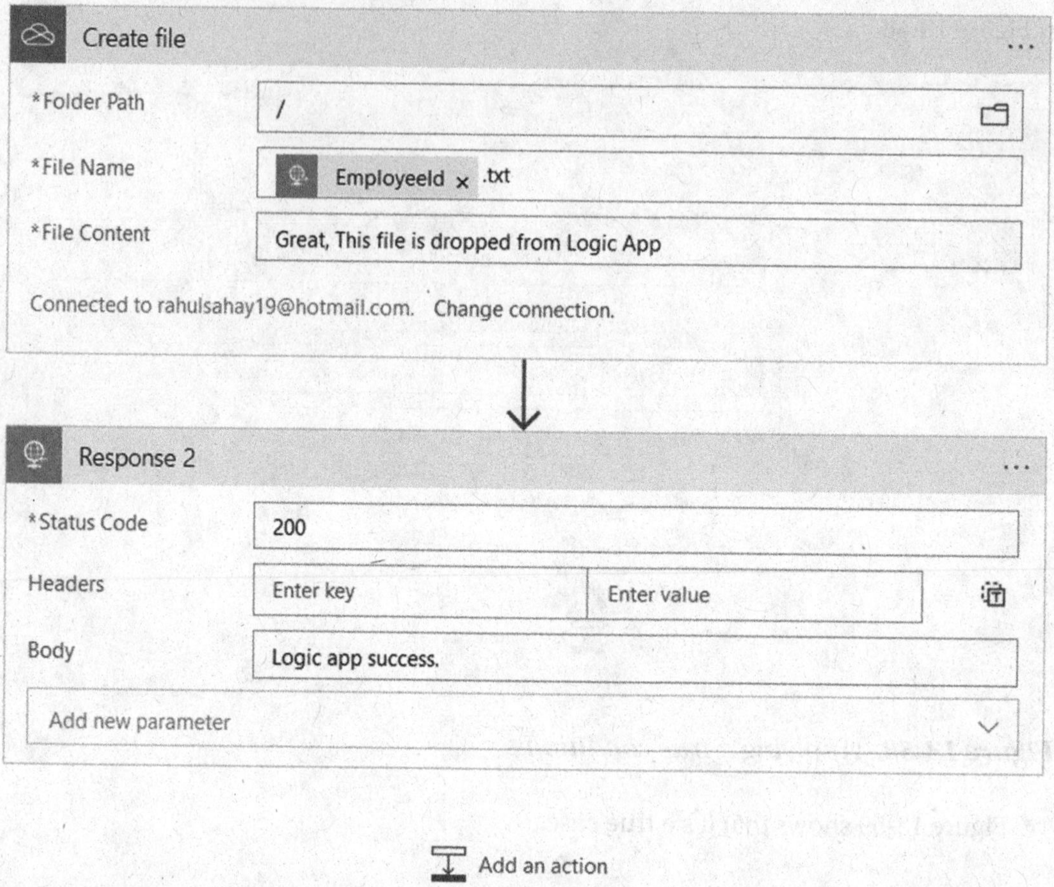

Figure 13-59. *Added another response*

Let's go ahead and add the function app that was created earlier, as shown in Figure 13-60.

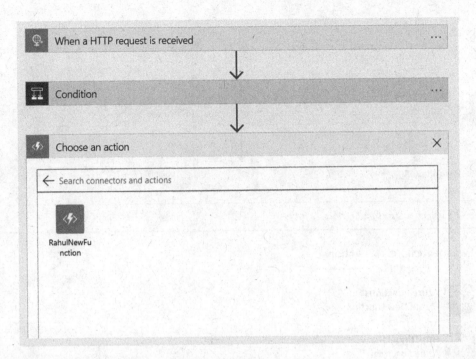

Figure 13-60. *Option to connect function app*

The screen will look like Figure 13-61.

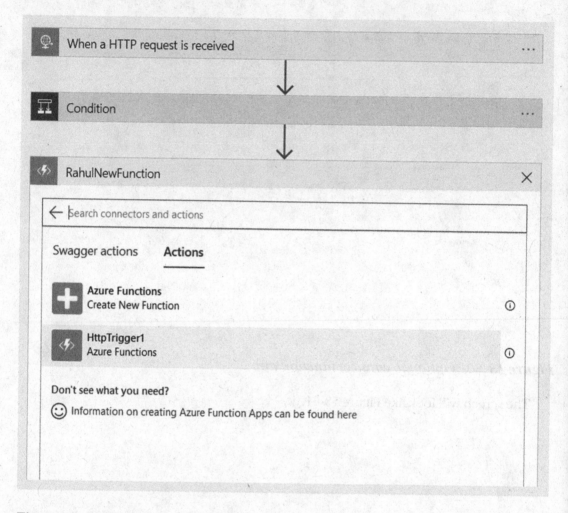

Figure 13-61. *Function app connected*

This shows the finished version of the function. You can go deeper into this with complex feature chaining, but this is more than enough for demonstration purposes, as shown in Figure 13-62.

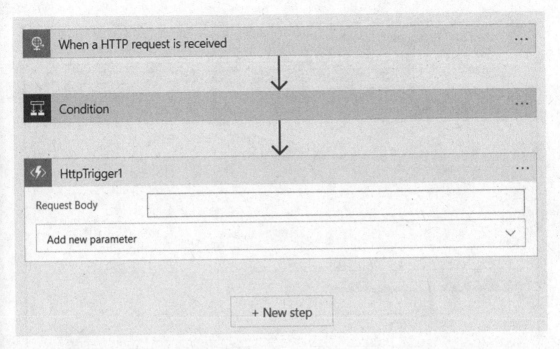

Figure 13-62. *Logic app in finished state*

To fetch the URL, you can get it from the root level, as shown in Figure 13-63. After saving the designer, it will be available.

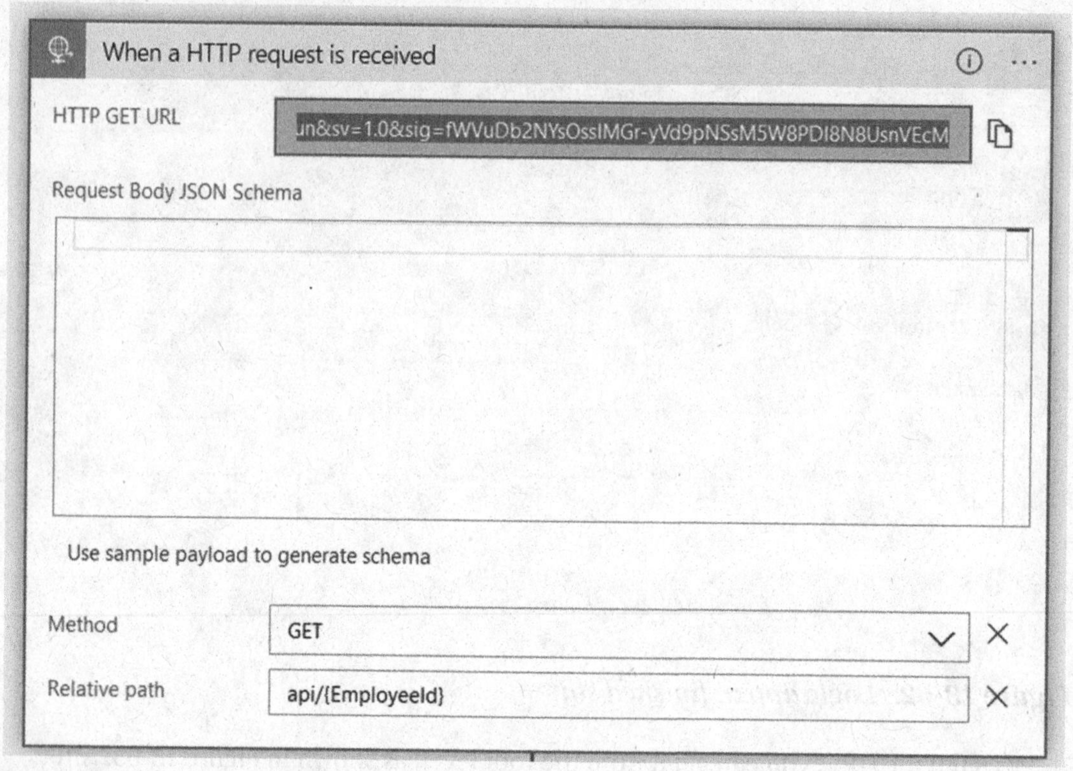

When a HTTP request is received

HTTP GET URL

un&sv=1.0&sig=fWVuDb2NYsOssIMGr-yVd9pNSsM5W8PDI8N8UsnVEcM

Request Body JSON Schema

Use sample payload to generate schema

Method

GET

Relative path

api/{EmployeeId}

Figure 13-63. *Retrieving the logic app URL*

Copy the URL and paste in the browser. It should look like this:

https://prod-88.eastus.logic.azure.com/workflows/
cfae30f204e245f4a115da2ec09db1a4/triggers/manual/paths/invoke/api/2?api-
version=2016-10-01&sp=%2Ftriggers%2Fmanual%2Frun&sv=1.0&sig=fWVuDb2NYsOssIM
Gr-yVd9pNSsM5W8PDI8N8UsnVEcM, as shown in Figure 13-64.

Thanks. But, you are not allowed.

Figure 13-64. *Getting the URL*

Notice in Figure 13-65 that you're seeing the same message that we configured. You
are seeing this message because app resulted in the false case. For a true scenario, it will
drop a file in my OneDrive folder. If you want to see the code view of this, you can refer to
Figure 13-65.

Home > Microsoft.EmptyWorkflow - Overview > RahulNewLogicApp > Logic Apps Designer

Logic Apps Designer

🖫 Save   ✕ Discard   ▷ Run   ⚙ Designer   </> Code view   ⚙ Parameters   ▦ Templates   ⊞ Connectors   ? Help

```
1    {
2        "definition": {
3            "$schema": "https://schema.management.azure.com/providers/Microsoft.Logic/schemas/2016-06-01/workflowdefinition.json#",
4            "actions": {
5                "Condition": {
6                    "actions": {
7                        "Create_file": {
8                            "inputs": {
9                                "body": "Great, This file is dropped from Logic App",
10                               "host": {
11                                   "connection": {
12                                       "name": "@parameters('$connections')['onedrive']['connectionId']"
13                                   }
14                               },
15                               "method": "post",
16                               "path": "/datasets/default/files",
17                               "queries": {
18                                   "folderPath": "/Angular JS Series",
19                                   "name": "@{triggerOutputs()['relativePathParameters']['EmployeeId']}.txt"
20                               }
21                           },
22                           "runAfter": {},
23                           "runtimeConfiguration": {
24                               "contentTransfer": {
25                                   "transferMode": "Chunked"
26                               }
27                           },
28                           "type": "ApiConnection"
29                       },
```

Figure 13-65. *Logic app, code view*

Event Grid

Event Grid is a fully managed event service that enables you to easily manage events across many different Azure services and applications. Made for performance and scale, it simplifies the process of building event-driven applications and serverless architectures.

- Therefore, it the glue between events that happen and the types of programs that can handle these events. You can learn more about Event Grid at `https://bit.ly/azure-event-grid`. Figure 13-66 shows the simple architecture for this.

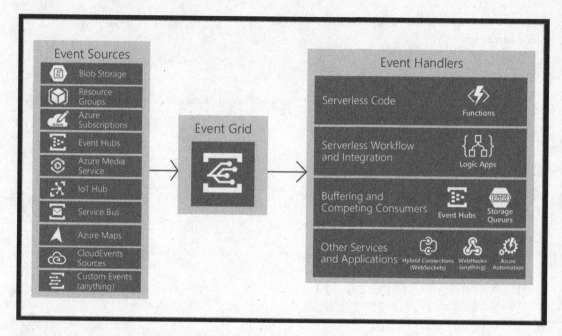

Figure 13-66. *Event Grid architecture*

Creating a New Event Grid

Before creating an event grid in the Azure portal, let's check whether our subscription can handle this. Hence, navigate to your subscription, click "Resource providers," and search for *event*. In Figure 13-67, you can see that Event Grid is not registered.

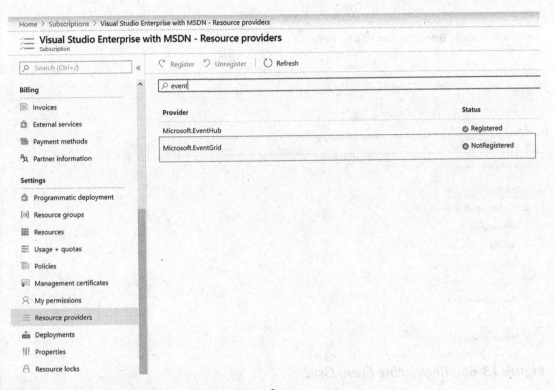

Figure 13-67. *Creating a new event grid*

You need to register Event Grid first, as shown in Figure 13-68.

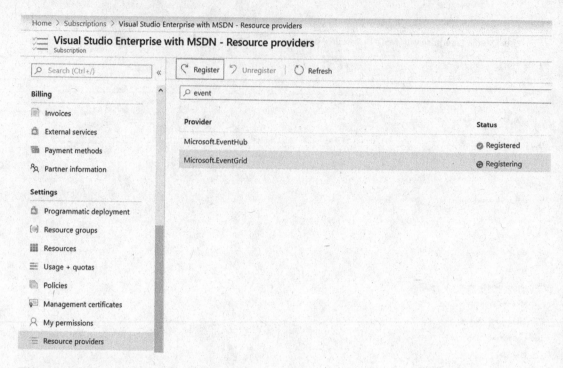

Figure 13-68. *Registering Event Grid*

You can see that Azure has started registering it. After a couple of minutes, try refreshing the page. Your screen should look like Figure 13-69.

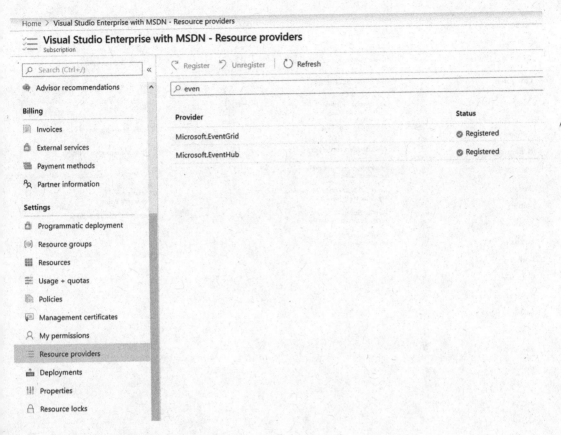

Figure 13-69. *Resource providers*

Let's search for *event* in "All services." You'll see Event Grid Subscriptions in the list, as shown in Figure 13-70.

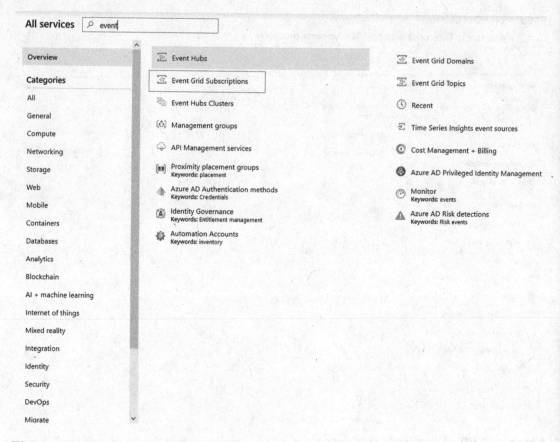

Figure 13-70. *Event Grid Subscriptions*

When you click the Event Grid Subscriptions link, you will be taken to the screen shown in Figure 13-71.

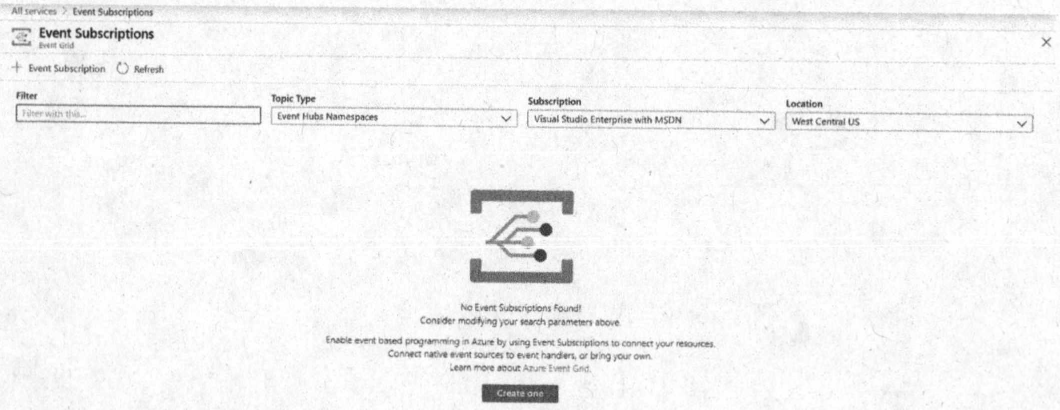

Figure 13-71. *Event Subscriptions screen*

You have two choices here. There is a basic editor that is UI based, and there is an advanced editor that is basically code based. I will start from the basic editor, as shown in Figure 13-72.

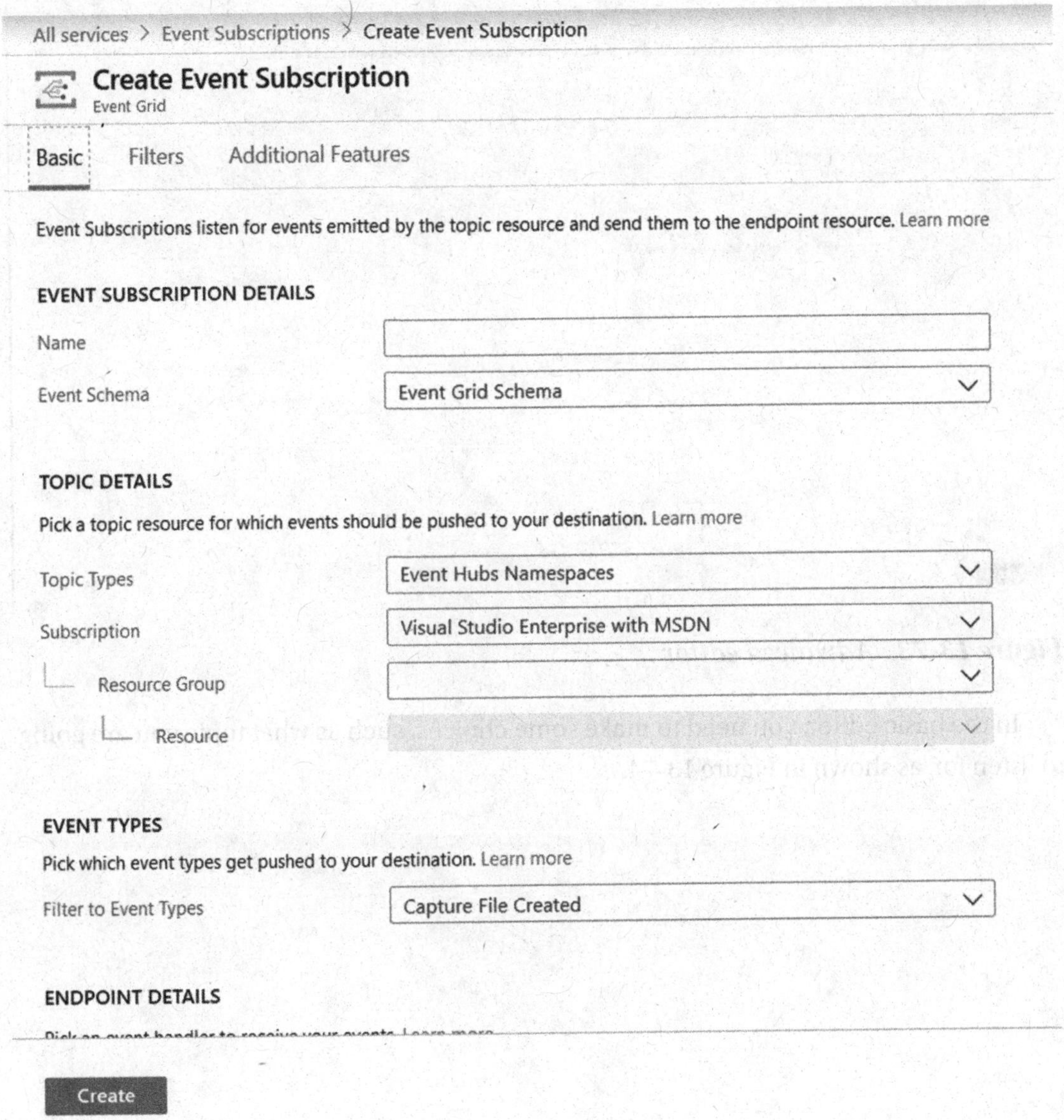

All services > Event Subscriptions > Create Event Subscription

Create Event Subscription
Event Grid

Basic   Filters   Additional Features

Event Subscriptions listen for events emitted by the topic resource and send them to the endpoint resource. Learn more

EVENT SUBSCRIPTION DETAILS

Name

Event Schema   Event Grid Schema   ∨

TOPIC DETAILS

Pick a topic resource for which events should be pushed to your destination. Learn more

Topic Types   Event Hubs Namespaces   ∨

Subscription   Visual Studio Enterprise with MSDN   ∨

└─ Resource Group   ∨

   └─ Resource   ∨

EVENT TYPES

Pick which event types get pushed to your destination. Learn more

Filter to Event Types   Capture File Created   ∨

ENDPOINT DETAILS

Pick an event handler to receive your events. Learn more

Create

Figure 13-72. *Basic editor*

Figure 13-73 shows the advanced editor.

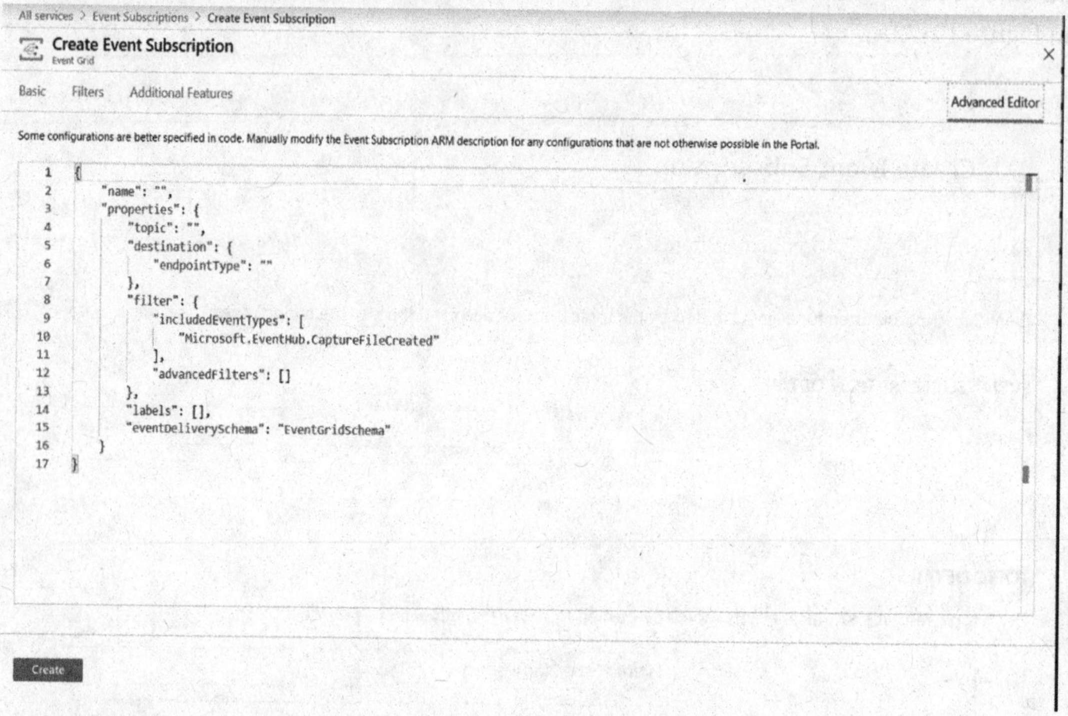

All services > Event Subscriptions > Create Event Subscription

Create Event Subscription
Event Grid

Basic   Filters   Additional Features

Advanced Editor

Some configurations are better specified in code. Manually modify the Event Subscription ARM description for any configurations that are not otherwise possible in the Portal.

```
1   {
2       "name": "",
3       "properties": {
4           "topic": "",
5           "destination": {
6               "endpointType": ""
7           },
8           "filter": {
9               "includedEventTypes": [
10                  "Microsoft.EventHub.CaptureFileCreated"
11              ],
12              "advancedFilters": []
13          },
14          "labels": [],
15          "eventDeliverySchema": "EventGridSchema"
16      }
17  }
```

Create

Figure 13-73. *Advanced editor*

In the basic editor, you need to make some choices, such as what topic you are going to listen for, as shown in Figure 13-74.

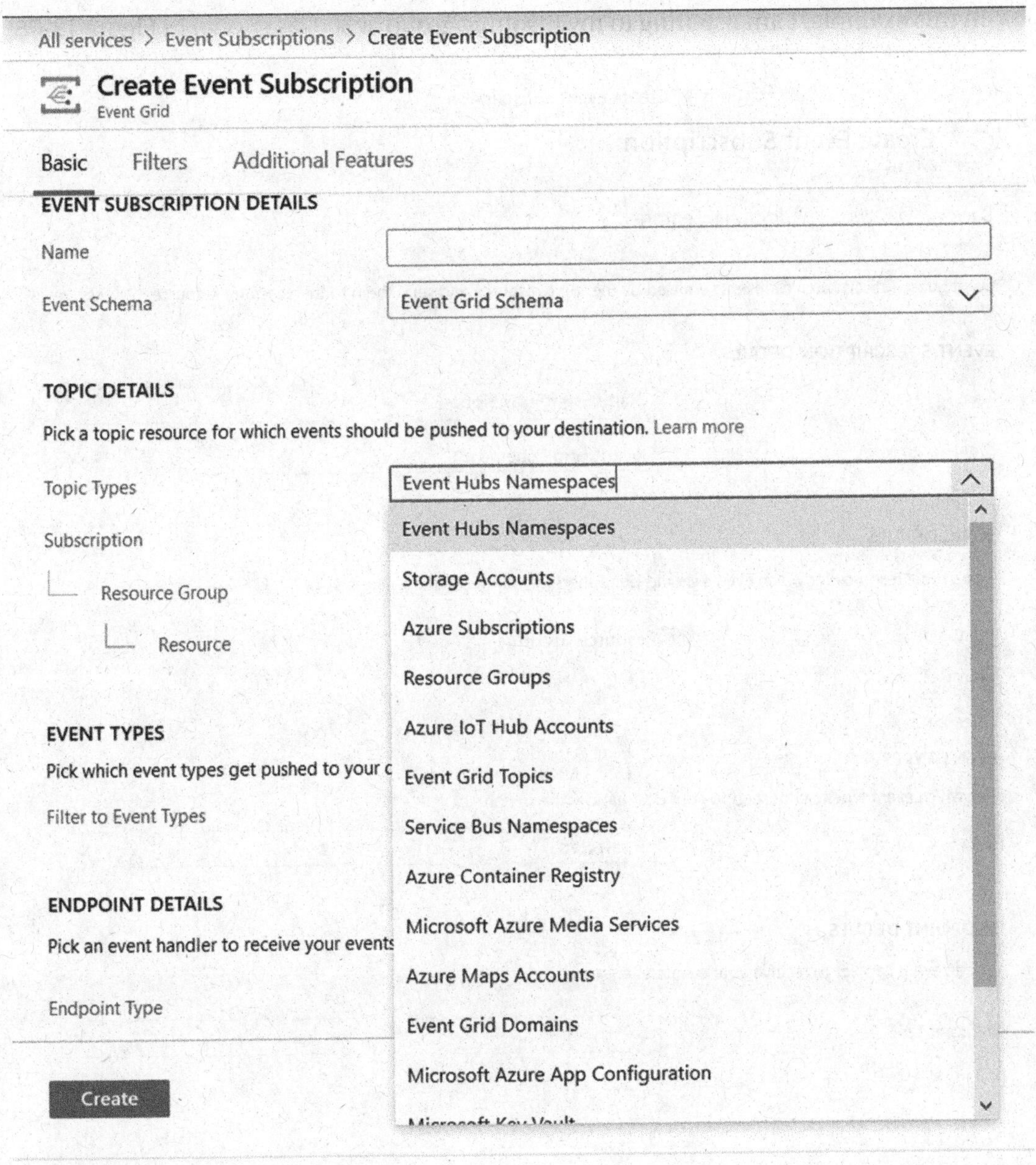

All services > Event Subscriptions > Create Event Subscription

Create Event Subscription
Event Grid

Basic   Filters   Additional Features

EVENT SUBSCRIPTION DETAILS

Name

Event Schema | Event Grid Schema ∨ |

TOPIC DETAILS

Pick a topic resource for which events should be pushed to your destination. Learn more

Topic Types | Event Hubs Namespaces ∧ |

Subscription   Event Hubs Namespaces

└── Resource Group   Storage Accounts

    └── Resource   Azure Subscriptions

                               Resource Groups

EVENT TYPES   Azure IoT Hub Accounts

Pick which event types get pushed to your c   Event Grid Topics

Filter to Event Types   Service Bus Namespaces

                               Azure Container Registry

                               Microsoft Azure Media Services

ENDPOINT DETAILS   Azure Maps Accounts

Pick an event handler to receive your events   Event Grid Domains

Endpoint Type   Microsoft Azure App Configuration

                               Microsoft Key Vault

    Create

Figure 13-74. Topic options

In this example, I am listening to my resource group az300, as shown in Figure 13-75.

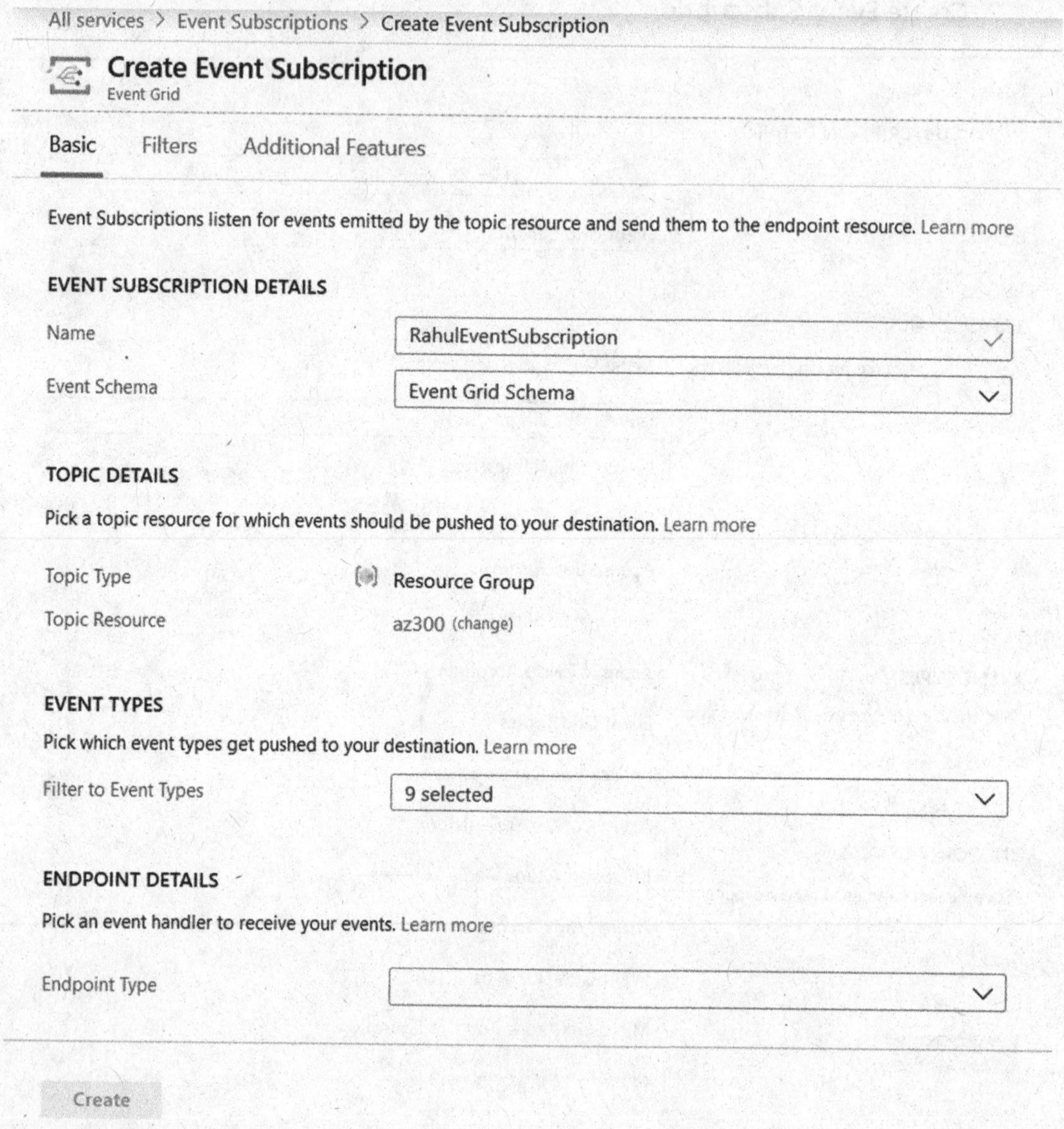

Figure 13-75. *Basic editor finished version*

Once you select event types dropdown, you can see that all the event types are by default selected. You can also filter the list, as shown in Figure 13-76.

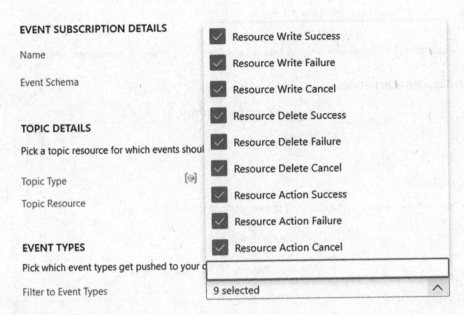

Figure 13-76. *Event types*

For this example, I am fine with all the events select. You also need to specify where you want these events to go. You will see options like those shown in Figure 13-77.

Figure 13-77. *Endpoint details*

I will choose a web hook for the sake of the demo, and I will pass the logic app URL into the endpoint, as shown in Figure 13-78 and Figure 13-79.

All services > Event Subscriptions > Create Event Subscription

Create Event Subscription
Event Grid

Basic   Filters   Additional Features

Event Subscriptions listen for events emitted by the topic resource and send them to the endpoint resource. Learn more

EVENT SUBSCRIPTION DETAILS

Name	RahulEventSubscription
Event Schema	Event Grid Schema

TOPIC DETAILS

Pick a topic resource for which events should be pushed to your destination. Learn more

Topic Type	(•) Resource Group
Topic Resource	az300 (change)

EVENT TYPES

Pick which event types get pushed to your destination. Learn more

Filter to Event Types	9 selected

ENDPOINT DETAILS

Pick an event handler to receive your events. Learn more

Endpoint Type	Web Hook (change)
Endpoint	Select an endpoint

Figure 13-78. *Endpoint type selected*

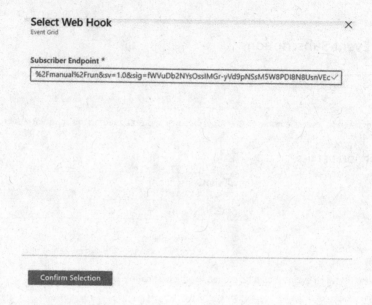

Figure 13-79. Web hook selected

After this, you can create the subscription by clicking Confirm Selection. Then you can verify it's created on the Event Subscriptions screen under the Resource Groups topic, as shown in Figure 13-80.

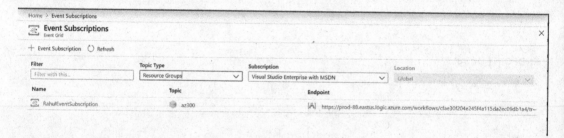

Figure 13-80. Event Subscriptions screen

Service Bus

Microsoft Azure Service Bus is a fully managed enterprise integration message broker. Service Bus can decouple applications and services. It offers a reliable and secure platform for the asynchronous transfer of data and state.

Data is transferred between different applications and services using messages. A message can be in binary format and can contain JSON, XML, or just text. Service Bus is also known as *messaging as a service* (MAAS). It gives applications the ability to send messages to each other. Let's go ahead and create one.

Creating a New Service Bus

To create a new service bus, search for *service bus* in "All services," as shown in Figure 13-81.

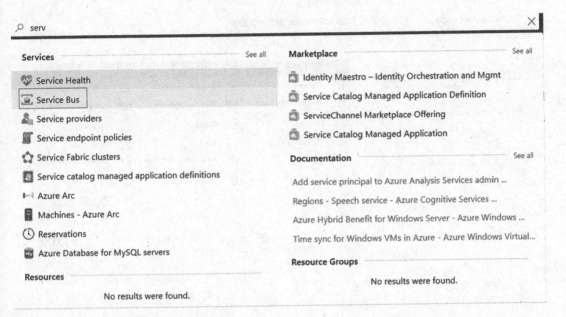

Figure 13-81. *Service Bus option*

Clicking Service Bus will take you to the screen shown in Figure 13-82.

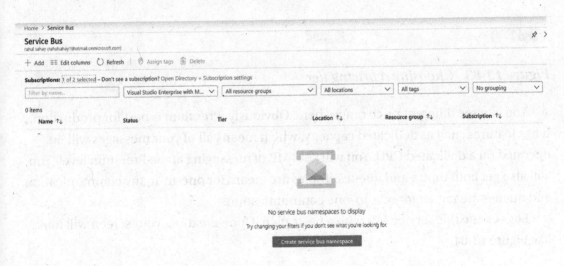

Figure 13-82. *Service Bus screen*

Figure 13-83 shows the pricing snapshot for a service bus. You need to pick a tier to proceed.

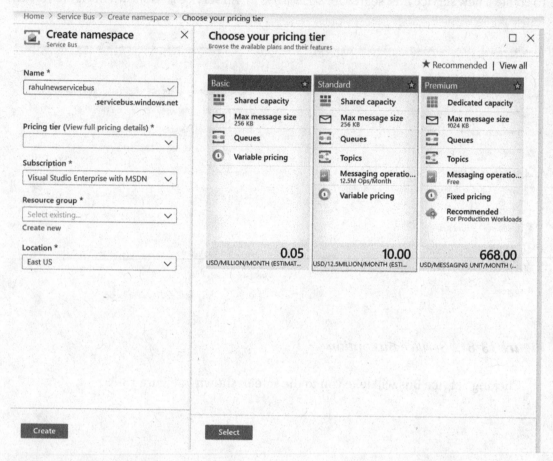

Figure 13-83. *Choosing a pricing tier*

You can see different price ranges here. Obviously, Premium is best for production. It has features such as dedicated capacity, which means all of your messages will be operated on a dedicated CPU. You will get 1MB of messaging at the Premium level. You will also get both topics and queues. Topics are meant for one-to-many communication, and queues are meant for one-to-one communication.

Let's create this service bus with a basic plan. Upon creation, your screen will look like Figure 13-84.

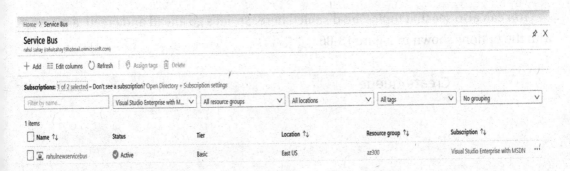

Figure 13-84. *Service Bus screen*

The service bus dashboard looks like Figure 13-85. You will have sections for requests and messages, as shown in Figure 13-85.

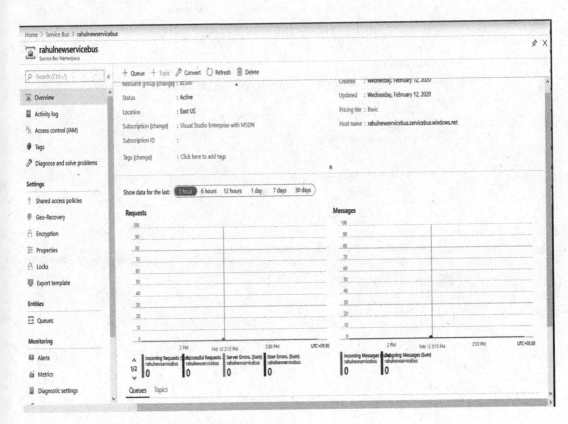

Figure 13-85. *Service bus Overview page*

You can also see that topics are disabled here. So, let's go ahead and create a queue with the options shown in Figure 13-86.

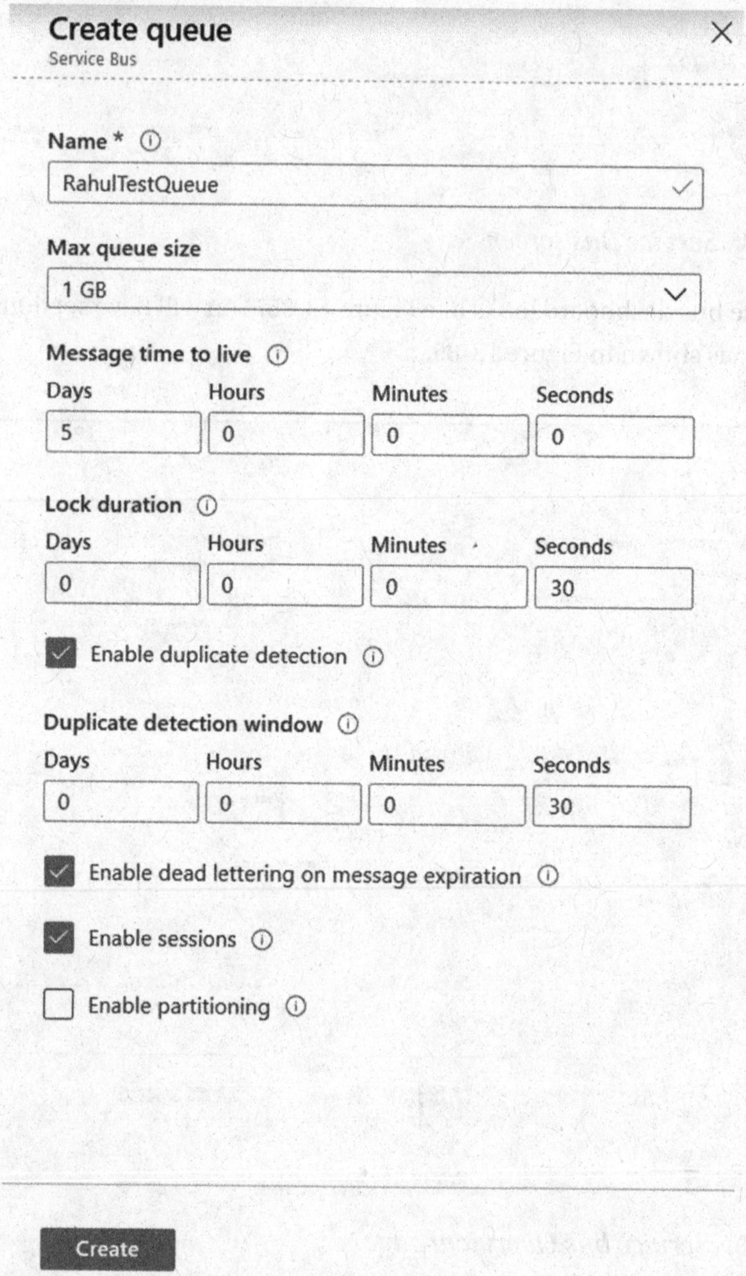

Create queue
Service Bus   ✕

Name * ⓘ

| RahulTestQueue | ✓ |

Max queue size

| 1 GB | ⌄ |

Message time to live ⓘ

Days	Hours	Minutes	Seconds
5	0	0	0

Lock duration ⓘ

Days	Hours	Minutes	Seconds
0	0	0	30

☑ Enable duplicate detection ⓘ

Duplicate detection window ⓘ

Days	Hours	Minutes	Seconds
0	0	0	30

☑ Enable dead lettering on message expiration ⓘ

☑ Enable sessions ⓘ

☐ Enable partitioning ⓘ

Create

Figure 13-86. Service bus "Create queue" panel

I have provided a queue name, the max queue size, and the message time to live. The lock duration means that for that period of time, messages won't be available for other receivers.

- *Duplicate detection* means during that interval, your queue will not accept any duplicate messages. Enabling this property guarantees exactly-once delivery over a user-defined span of time.

- *Dead-lettering messages* involves holding messages that cannot be successfully delivered to any receiver in a separate queue after they have expired. Messages do not expire in the dead-letter queue, and it supports peek-lock delivery and all transactional operations.

- Service bus *sessions* allow the ordered handling of unbounded sequences of related messages. With sessions enabled, a queue can guarantee first-in, first-out delivery of messages.

- *Partitions* separate a queue across multiple message brokers and message stores. This disconnects the overall throughput of a partitioned entity from any single message broker or messaging store. This property is not modifiable after a queue has been created.

The queue creation failed for me because duplication can't be enabled with a basic plan. However, I would expect this option to be disabled if the selected plan doesn't support this. Nevertheless, let's create it again with the options shown in Figure 13-87.

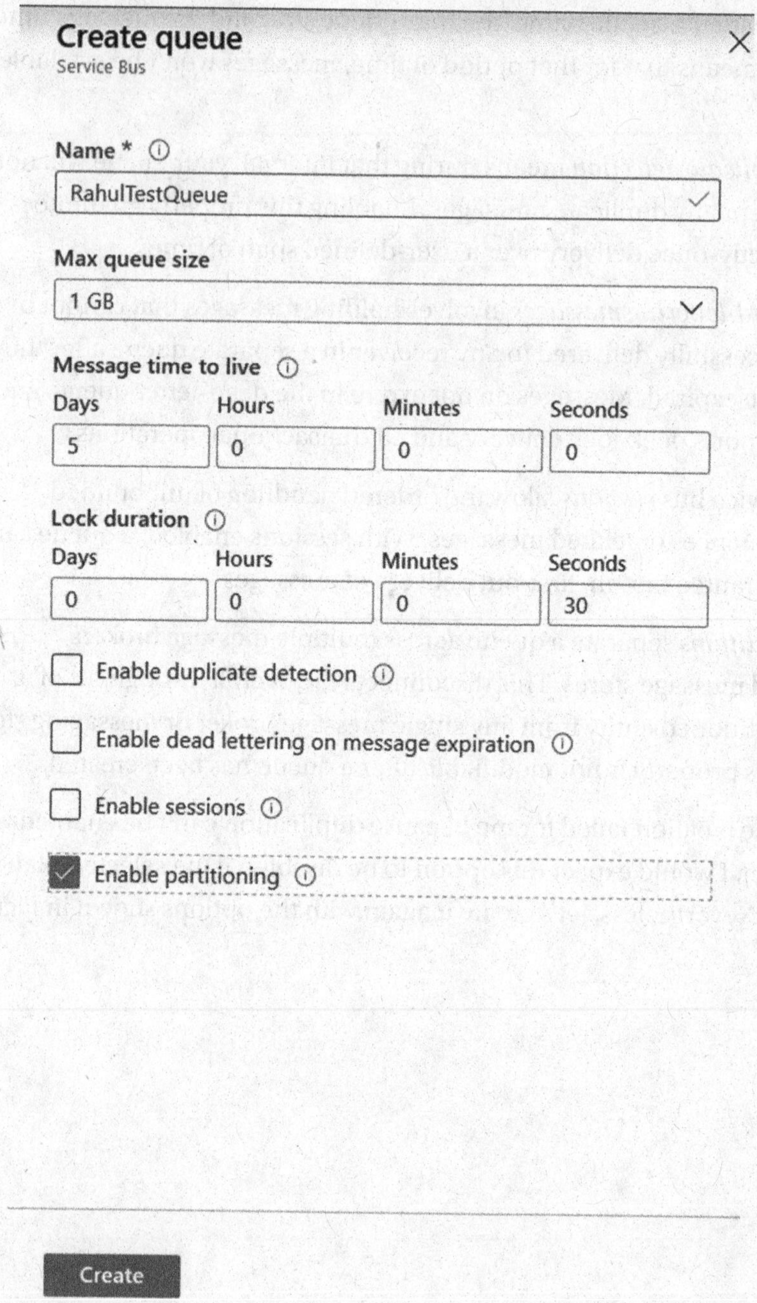

Figure 13-87. *"Create queue" options*

Having changed the settings, the queue is now created successfully, as shown in Figure 13-88.

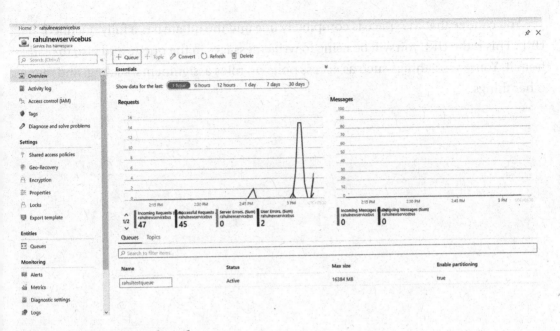

Figure 13-88. *Queue listed*

Let's click the queue. The screen shown in Figure 13-89 appears.

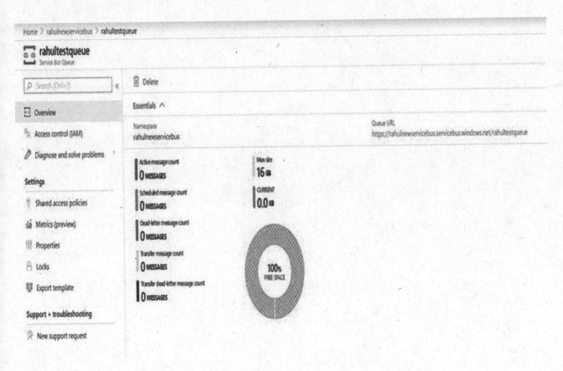

Figure 13-89. *Queue's Overview screen*

You can see that the space is completely free and the queue has a fully qualified URL. This is the URL you will be using to write messages in the queue and also to read from it. You can set things such as access policies, roles assignments, scaling, and many other things.

CHAPTER 14

Load Balancing

Load balancing evenly distributes the incoming load across a group of dedicated backend resources or servers. Azure Load Balancer operates at layer 4 of the Open Systems Interconnection (OSI) model. Basically, it distributes inbound flows arriving at the load balancer's front end to the backend pool of servers.

There are two types of load balancing that Microsoft provides. The first one is through Azure Load Balancer, and the second one is through Application Gateway. Let's first discuss Azure Load Balancer.

Load balancing is a concept where you have traffic coming from multiple sources trying to reach one server. But instead of one server doing the job, the traffic is distributed among multiple servers. The load balancer does the distribution to ensure that one server doesn't get overwhelmed with traffic. See Figure 14-1.

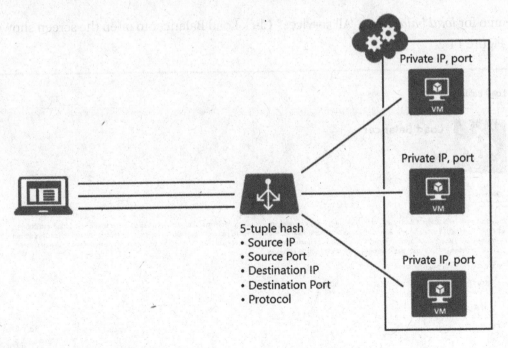

Figure 14-1. *Load balancer*

As mentioned, Azure Load Balancer operates at layer 4 of the OSI model, which makes termination based on five factors.

- Source IP

- Source port

- Destination IP

- Destination port

- Protocol

Based on these factors, Azure Load Balancer will decide which call will go to which server. Internally it uses a round-robin algorithm to distribute the load accordingly. This means not much intelligence is baked into the decision; that's why load balancers are often called *dumb devices*.

A benefit of using a load balancer is if any of these servers behind the load balancer go down, the load balancer can automatically take that server out of the pool.

Let's go ahead and set up Azure Load Balancer.

Creating a Load Balancer

Search for *load balancer* in "All services." Click Load Balancer to open the screen shown in Figure 14-2.

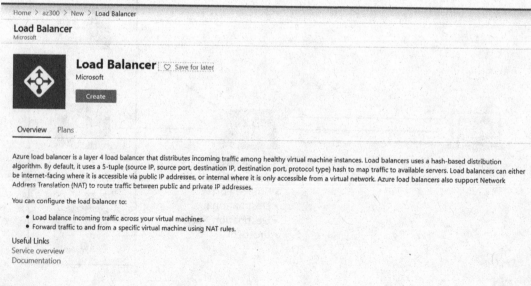

Figure 14-2. Load Balancer app screen

Click the Create button and fill in all the required details, as shown in Figure 14-3.

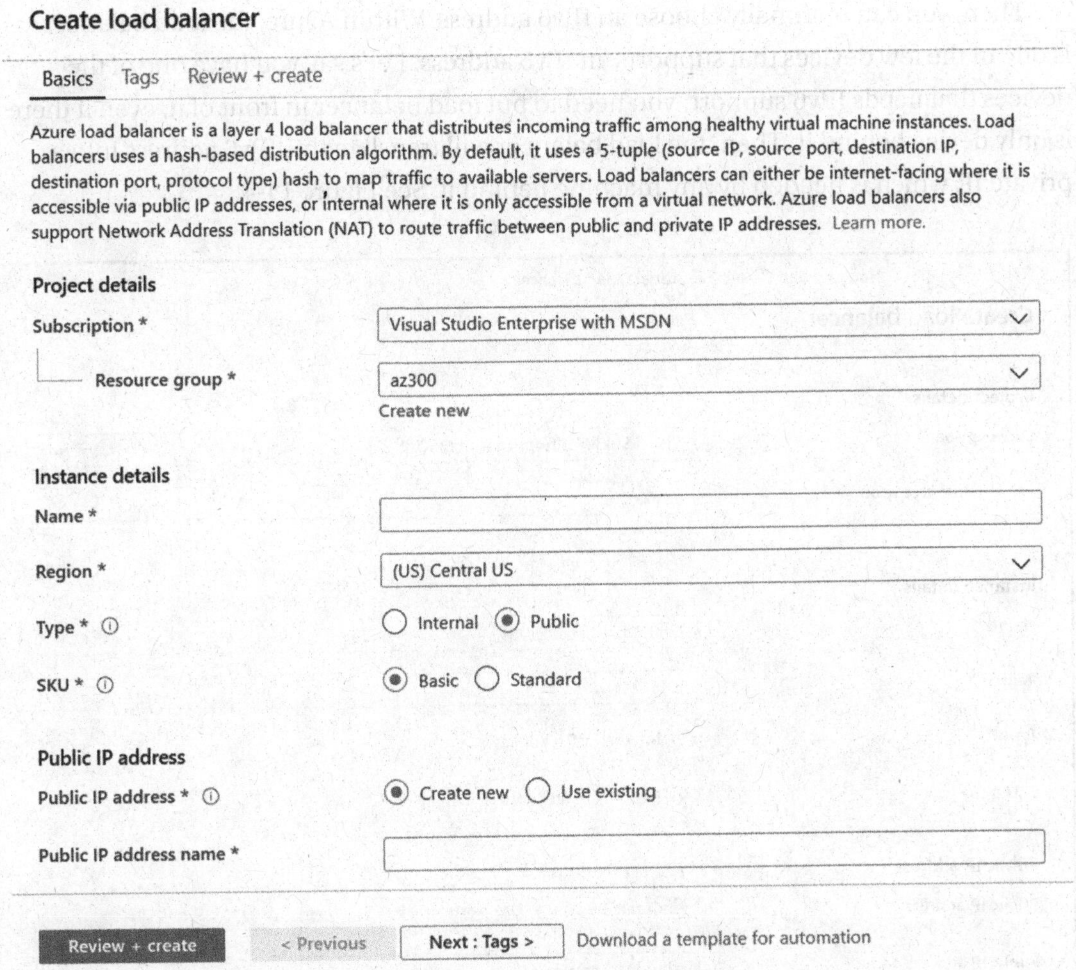

Create load balancer

Basics   Tags   Review + create

Azure load balancer is a layer 4 load balancer that distributes incoming traffic among healthy virtual machine instances. Load balancers uses a hash-based distribution algorithm. By default, it uses a 5-tuple (source IP, source port, destination IP, destination port, protocol type) hash to map traffic to available servers. Load balancers can either be internet-facing where it is accessible via public IP addresses, or internal where it is only accessible from a virtual network. Azure load balancers also support Network Address Translation (NAT) to route traffic between public and private IP addresses. Learn more.

Project details

Subscription *   Visual Studio Enterprise with MSDN   ∨

   ┗━ Resource group *   az300   ∨
                          Create new

Instance details

Name *   _____

Region *   (US) Central US   ∨

Type * ⓘ   ◯ Internal ⦿ Public

SKU * ⓘ   ⦿ Basic ◯ Standard

Public IP address

Public IP address * ⓘ   ⦿ Create new ◯ Use existing

Public IP address name *   _____

[Review + create]   [< Previous]   [Next : Tags >]   Download a template for automation

Figure 14-3. Load balancer creation screen, Basics tab

If you choose Internal as the type, then the load balancer will have a private IP address that won't be exposed to the outside world. For this example, we will use a public load balancer.

For now, I am fine with the Basic setting for SKU. But, it has tons of differences from a standard one. You can check out the details at https://docs.microsoft.com/en-us/azure/load-balancer/skus.

Mostly, for production use, I prefer to use standard SKUs because of their offerings. Next, you should give the public IP address a name.

For now, I will keep the IP settings as dynamic for this example because I am going to use a public IP address name to address it, not the IP address itself.

Then, you can optionally choose an IPv6 address. Within Azure, the load balancer is one of the few devices that supports an IPv6 address. Let's say you have one of the devices that needs IPv6 support; you need to put load balancer in front of it, even if there is only device behind it. Then, the load balancer will translate this IPv6 address into a private IP, which is needed by any machine behind it. See Figure 14-4.

Home > az300 > New > Load Balancer > Create load balancer

Create load balancer

Project details

Subscription *	Visual Studio Enterprise with MSDN
Resource group *	az300
	Create new

Instance details

Name *	rahul-load-balancer
Region *	(US) East US
Type * ⓘ	○ Internal ⦿ Public
SKU * ⓘ	⦿ Basic ○ Standard

Public IP address

Public IP address * ⓘ	⦿ Create new ○ Use existing
Public IP address name *	rahul-load-new-ip
Public IP address SKU	Basic
Assignment *	⦿ Dynamic ○ Static
Add a public IPv6 address ⓘ	No Yes

Review + create   < Previous   Next : Tags >   Download a template for automation

Figure 14-4. Load balancer details

Next comes the Tags tab, as shown in Figure 14-5.

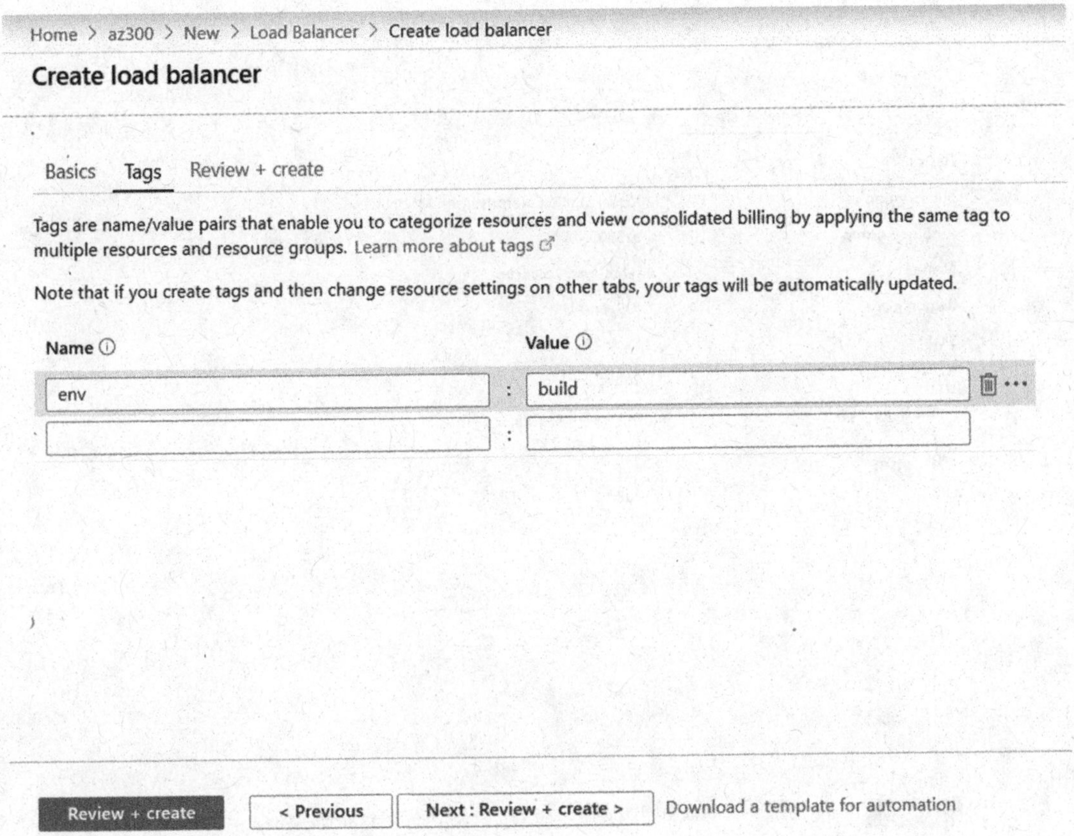

Home > az300 > New > Load Balancer > Create load balancer

Create load balancer

Basics   **Tags**   Review + create

Tags are name/value pairs that enable you to categorize resources and view consolidated billing by applying the same tag to multiple resources and resource groups. Learn more about tags ☐

Note that if you create tags and then change resource settings on other tabs, your tags will be automatically updated.

Name ⓘ		Value ⓘ	
env	:	build	🗑 •••
	:		

| Review + create | | < Previous | | Next : Review + create > | | Download a template for automation |

Figure 14-5. Load balancer tags

Finally comes the "Review + create" screen, as shown in Figure 14-6.

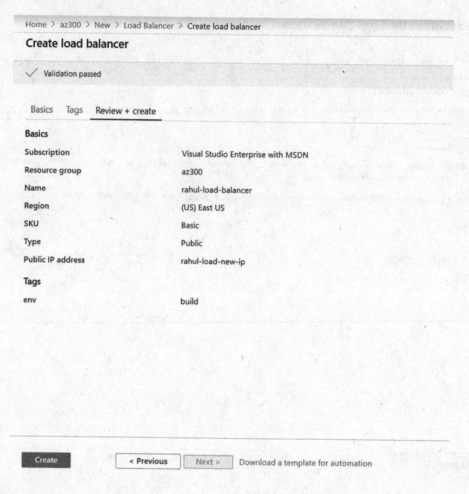

Figure 14-6. *Load balancer's "Review + create" screen*

The load balancer will take some time to create. Once it has been created, your screen will look like Figure 14-7.

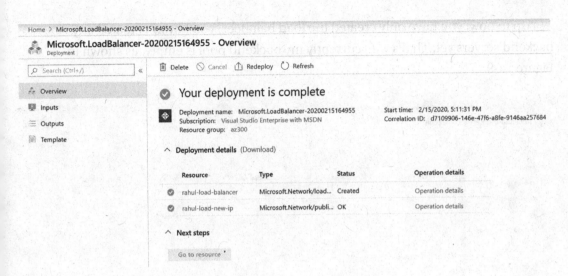

Figure 14-7. *Load balancer deployed*

You have now created a load balancer and the public IP address. Now, go ahead and click the load balancer, which will take you to the screen shown in Figure 14-8.

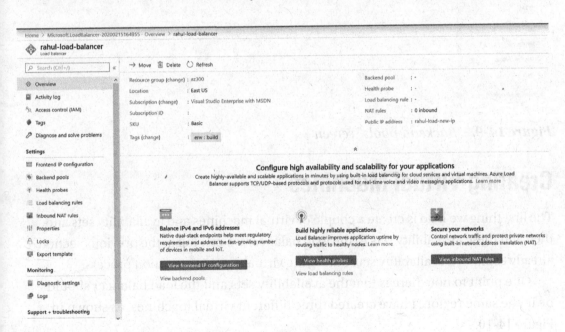

Figure 14-8. *Load balancer's Overview screen*

Up to now, you have only created the load balancer; you haven't created any backend servers yet. That's why currently my backend pool is empty, as shown in Figure 14-9.

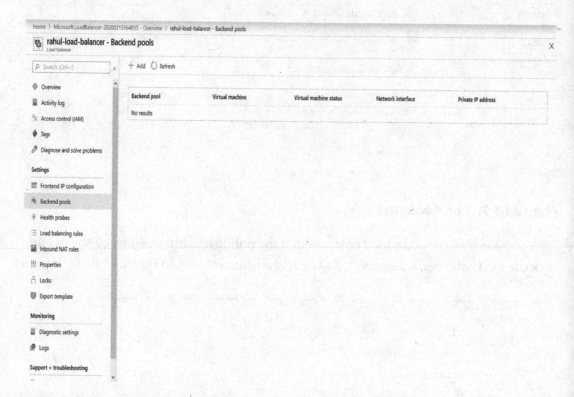

Figure 14-9. "Backend pools" screen

Creating Virtual Machines

The first thing we'll do is create a couple of virtual machines and availability sets and then add these availability sets to the load balancer we created in the previous section. I already explained availability sets during the virtual machine creation process.

One point to note here is that the availability sets and the load balancer should be in the same region. I have created three different virtual machines, as shown in Figure 14-10.

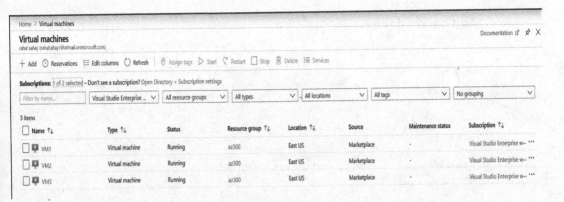

Figure 14-10. *Virtual machines*

Configuring a Backend Pool

Next, you can configure the backend pool under the load balancer's backend pool, as shown in Figure 14-11.

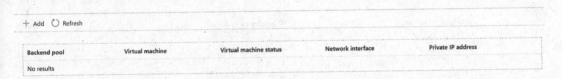

Figure 14-11. *Backend pool configuration*

Click the Add button, as shown in Figure 14-12.

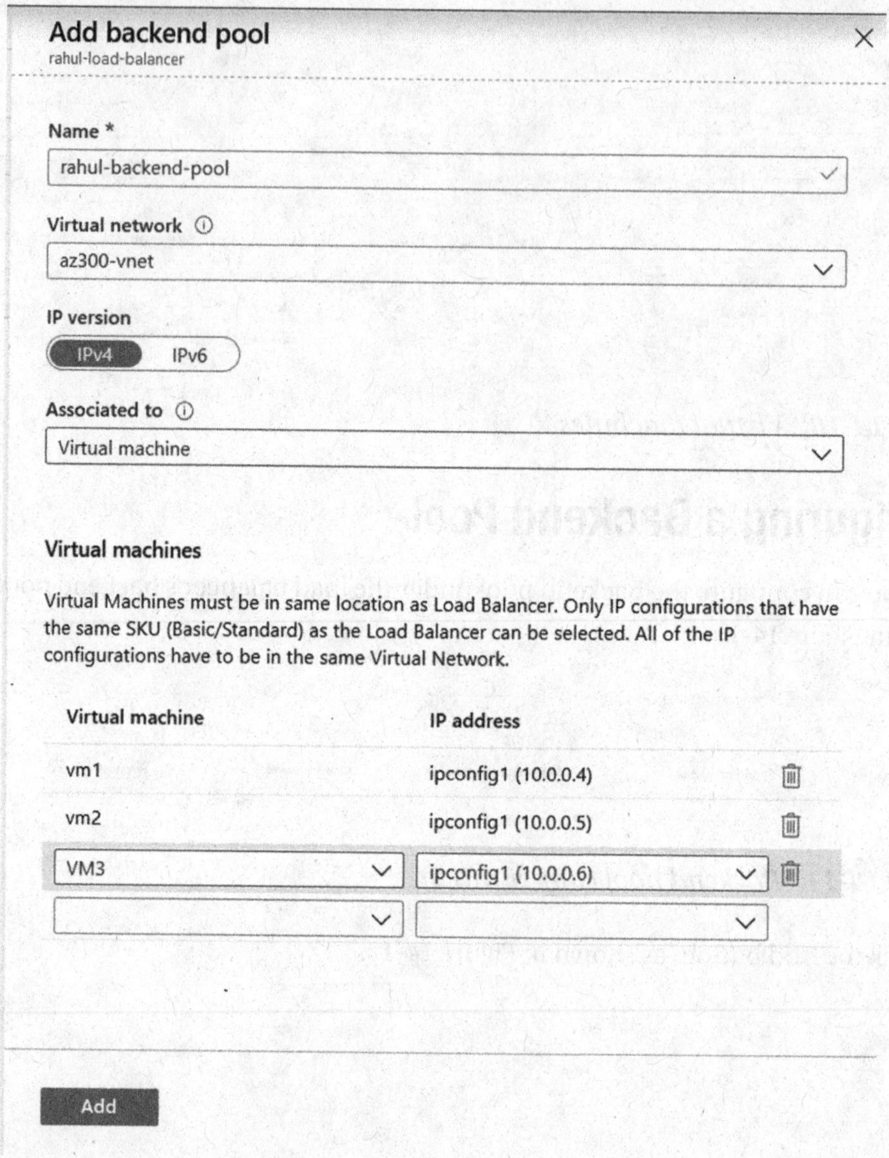

Figure 14-12. *Adding a backend pool*

Unfortunately, I didn't see the availability set in the drop-down option, so I had to add all the VMs individually. The associated IP addresses got populated in the adjacent drop-downs, as shown in Figure 14-13.

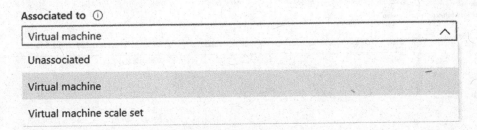

Figure 14-13. *"Associated to" option*

It will take a couple of minutes for the backend pool to get set up. Upon completion, your screen will look like Figure 14-14.

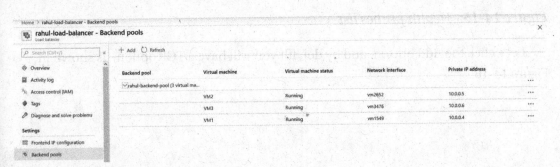

Figure 14-14. *Backend pools list*

You can see that the backend pool was created and is running fine.

Configuring a Health Probe

Next, let's set up a health probe. A health probe is the place where Azure will check whether a particular server is up and running and pinging correctly. If not, the server will be taken offline. Figure 14-15 shows the "Health probes" screen.

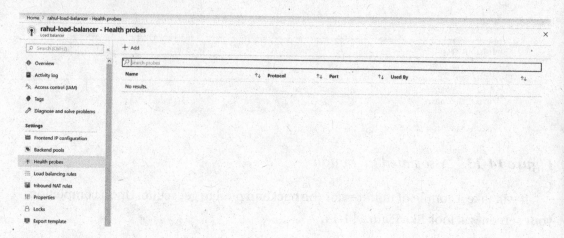

Figure 14-15. *Health probes list*

Let's click the Add button, and by default you will have a TCP option, as shown in Figure 14-16.

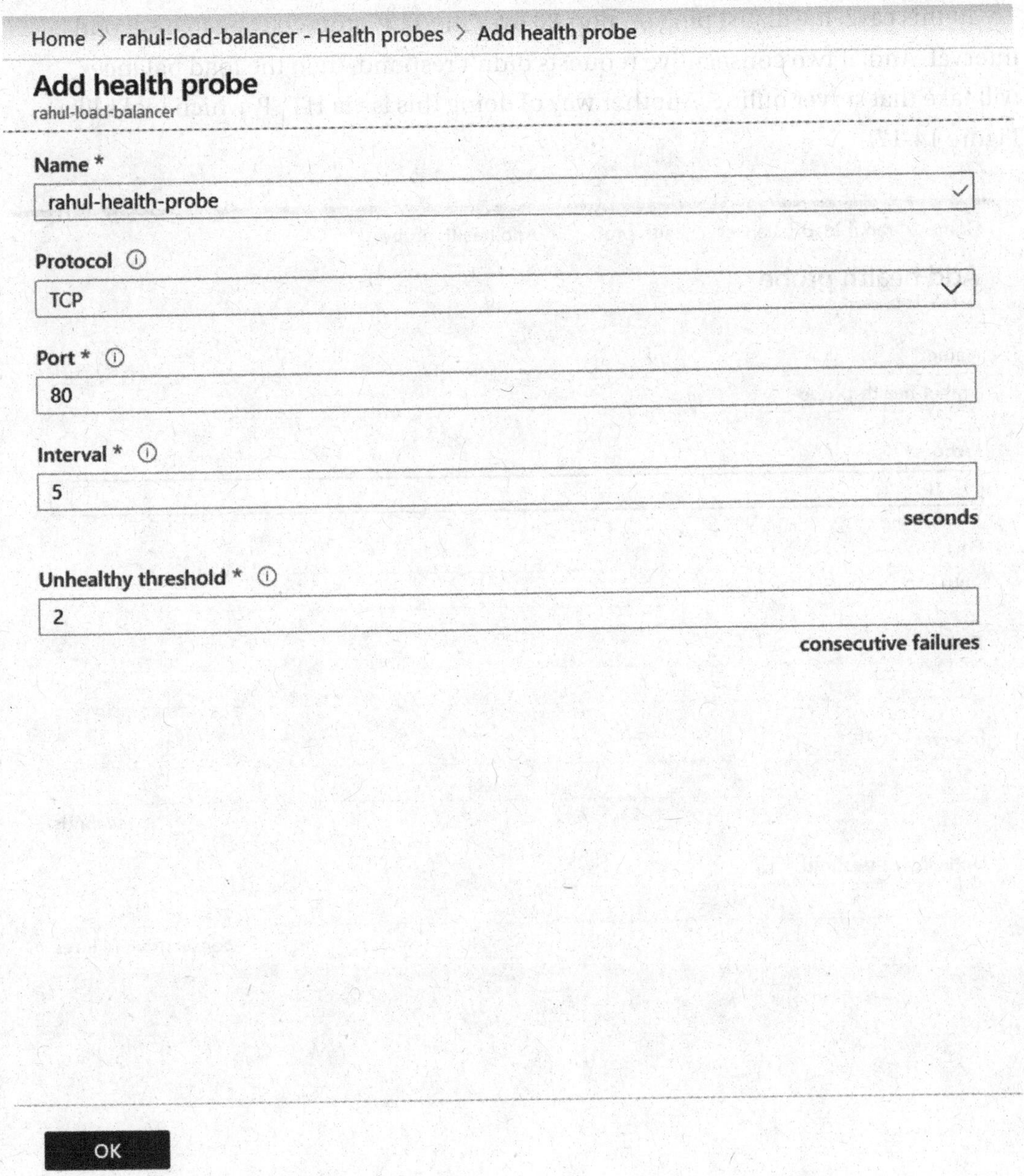

Home > rahul-load-balancer - Health probes > Add health probe

Add health probe
rahul-load-balancer

Name *

rahul-health-probe ✓

Protocol ⓘ

TCP ∨

Port * ⓘ

80

Interval * ⓘ

5

seconds

Unhealthy threshold * ⓘ

2

consecutive failures

OK

Figure 14-16. *Adding a health probe*

In this case, it will just ping on port 80 over the TCP protocol, at a five-second interval. And, if two consecutive requests didn't respond, then the load balancer will take that server offline. Another way of doing this is via HTTP, which looks like Figure 14-17.

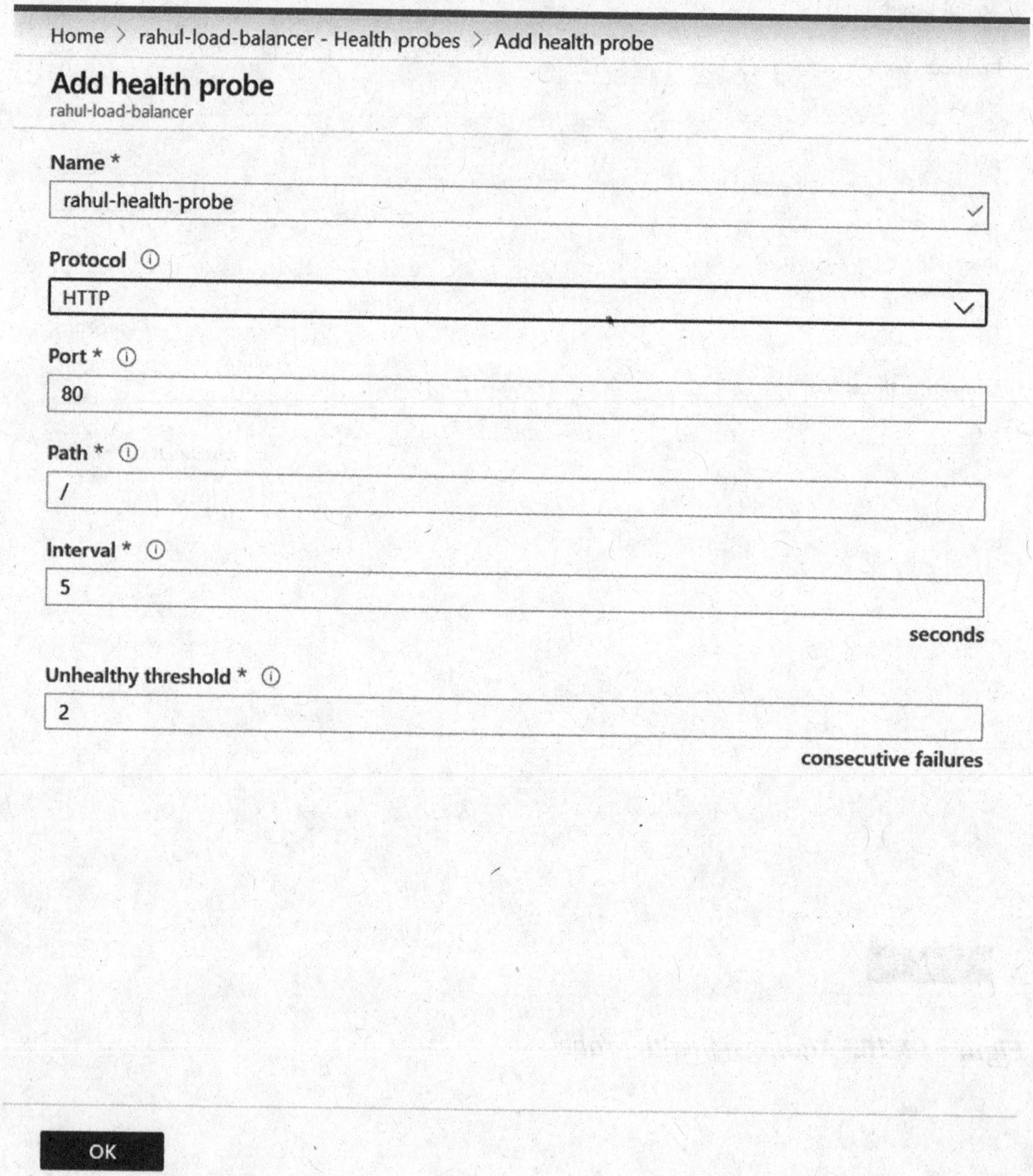

Home > rahul-load-balancer - Health probes > Add health probe

Add health probe
rahul-load-balancer

Name *

rahul-health-probe

Protocol ⓘ

HTTP

Port * ⓘ

80

Path * ⓘ

/

Interval * ⓘ

5

seconds

Unhealthy threshold * ⓘ

2

consecutive failures

OK

Figure 14-17. *Health probe configuration*

It will try to retrieve the landing screen of the app to judge whether the server is up and running. Many times the home page may end up being too resource-intensive or not efficient. In that case, generally developers' keep one page, say, `health.htm`, just to return a text. For this demonstration, I am fine with the TCP setting; hence, let's go ahead and create health probe. See Figure 14-18.

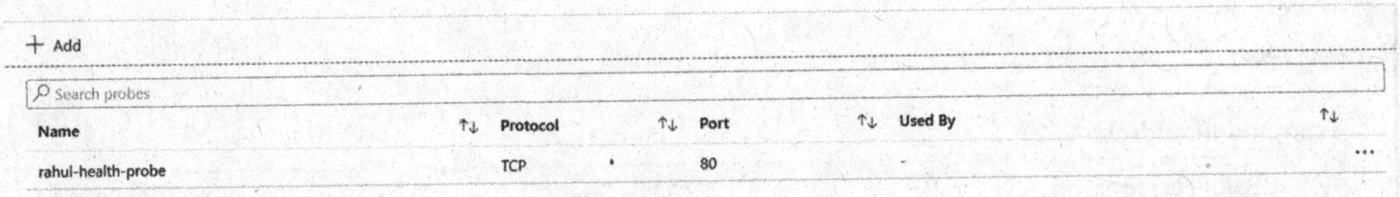

+ Add					
🔎 Search probes					
Name ↑↓	**Protocol** ↑↓	**Port** ↑↓	**Used By** ↑↓		↑↓
rahul-health-probe	TCP	80	-		...

Figure 14-18. *Health probe screen*

Creating a Load Balancing Rule

Next, let's create some load balancing rules, as shown in Figure 14-19.

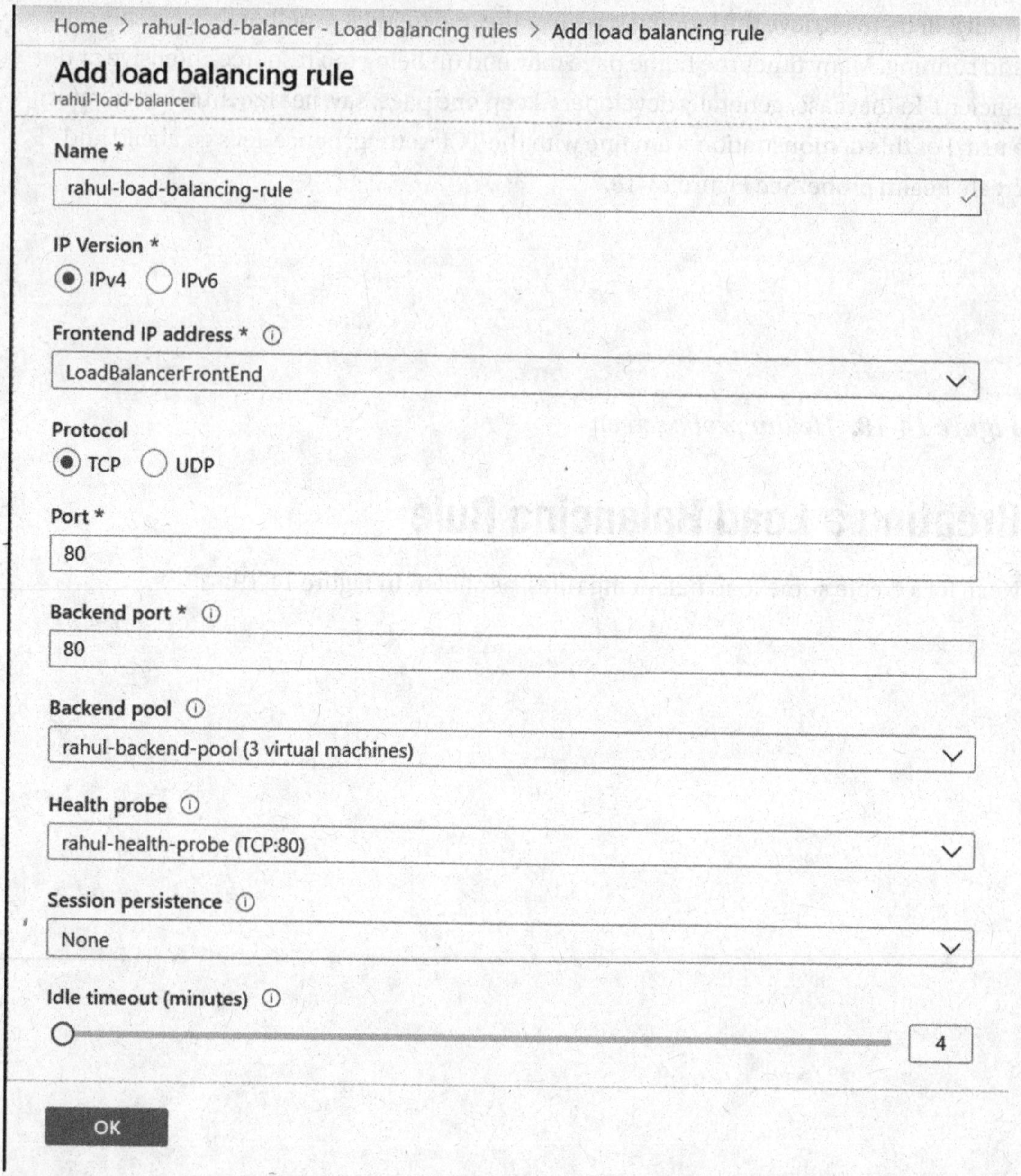

Home > rahul-load-balancer - Load balancing rules > Add load balancing rule

Add load balancing rule
rahul-load-balancer

Name *

rahul-load-balancing-rule

IP Version *
◉ IPv4   ◯ IPv6

Frontend IP address * ⓘ

LoadBalancerFrontEnd

Protocol
◉ TCP   ◯ UDP

Port *

80

Backend port * ⓘ

80

Backend pool ⓘ

rahul-backend-pool (3 virtual machines)

Health probe ⓘ

rahul-health-probe (TCP:80)

Session persistence ⓘ

None

Idle timeout (minutes) ⓘ

4

OK

Figure 14-19. *Azure load balancing rule*

Here, I have given a name to this rule that the front-end IP address automatically picked up.

For the protocol, I am fine with TCP. The front-end port is configured to accept traffic from port 80, and internally it will send traffic over port 80. You can modify this to use Network Address Translation (NAT) rules, for instance if you want to send traffic across port 8080 or some other port.

There are some other settings the rule has automatically picked up. Currently, I am not using sessions, which is why I selected None for session persistence. If you like to preserve sessions, then you can select Client IP from the drop-down, which means it will save the session on the same virtual machine, as shown in Figure 14-20.

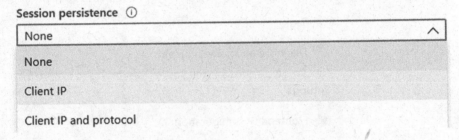

Figure 14-20. *"Session persistence" drop-down*

Let's create the rule. After the rule has been created, your screen will look like Figure 14-21.

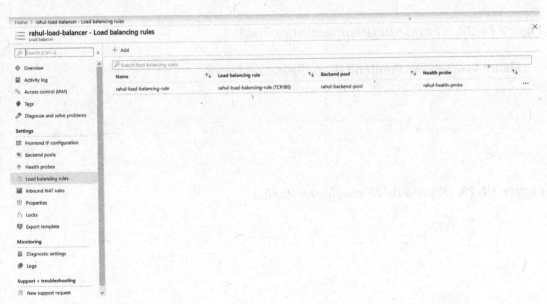

Figure 14-21. *Load balancing rules*

Configuring a Front-End IP Address

To configure the front-end IP address, select "Frontend IP configuration," as shown in Figure 14-22.

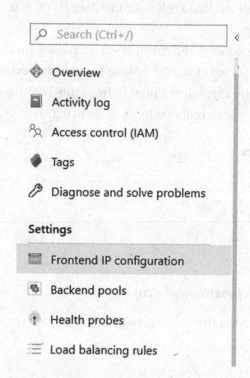

Figure 14-22. "Frontend IP configuration" link

Figure 14-23 shows Frontend IP configuration menu.

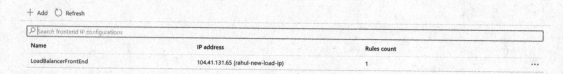

Figure 14-23. Front-end IP configuration list

On this screen, you can add more front-end IP addresses and then create a different load balancing rule for accepting traffic from different IP addresses. Let's see that flow as well. Search for *public IP addresses* to load the screen shown in Figure 14-24.

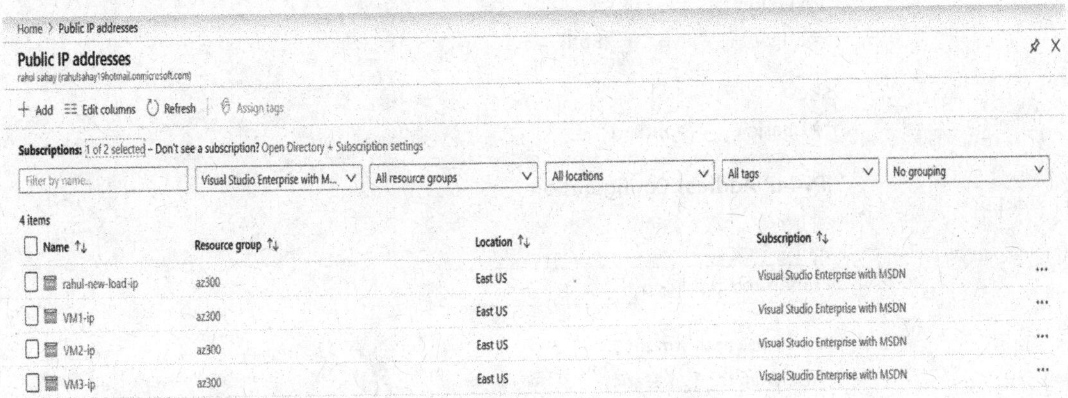

Figure 14-24. *Public IP addresses*

Now, add the configuration shown in Figure 14-25. It's pretty straightforward.

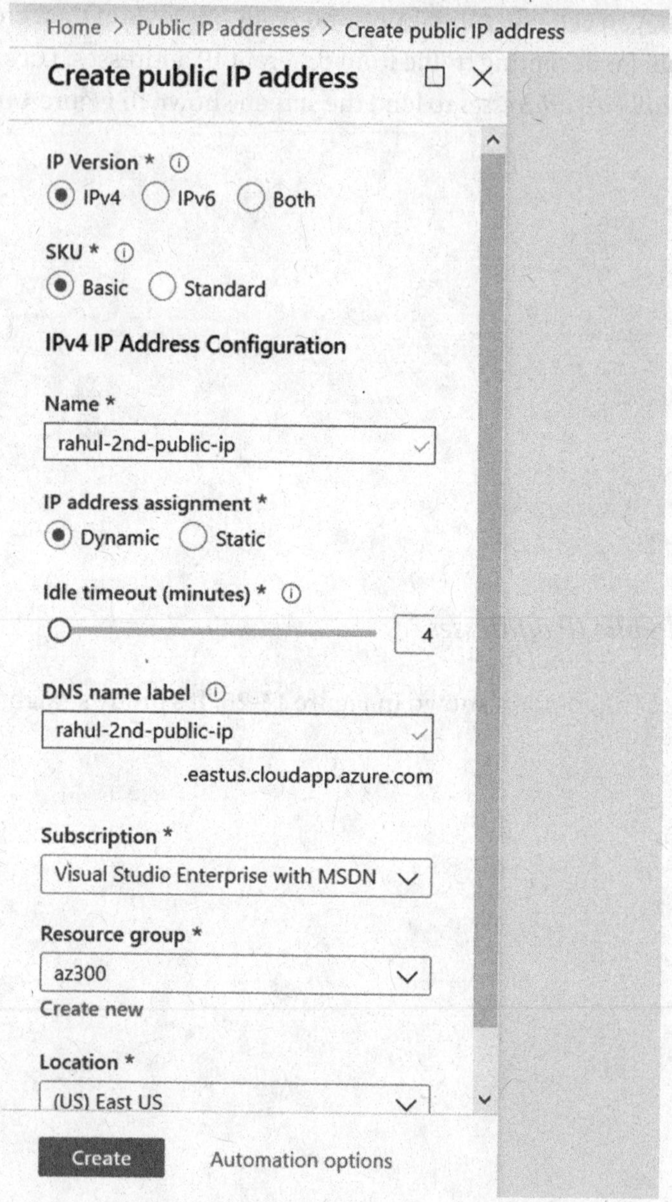

Home > Public IP addresses > Create public IP address

Create public IP address   ☐ ✕

IP Version * ⓘ
◉ IPv4   ◯ IPv6   ◯ Both

SKU * ⓘ
◉ Basic   ◯ Standard

IPv4 IP Address Configuration

Name *

rahul-2nd-public-ip   ✓

IP address assignment *
◉ Dynamic   ◯ Static

Idle timeout (minutes) * ⓘ

◯────────────────────────   4

DNS name label ⓘ

rahul-2nd-public-ip   ✓

.eastus.cloudapp.azure.com

Subscription *

Visual Studio Enterprise with MSDN ∨

Resource group *

az300   ∨
Create new

Location *

(US) East US   ∨

Create   Automation options

Figure 14-25. *Public IP address creation*

Upon successful creation, the screen will look like Figure 14-26.

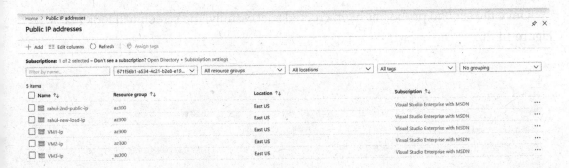

Figure 14-26. *Public IP address list with additions*

Creating a Secondary Health Probe

Next, let's create another health probe, which will check the health on port 8080, as
shown in Figure 14-27.

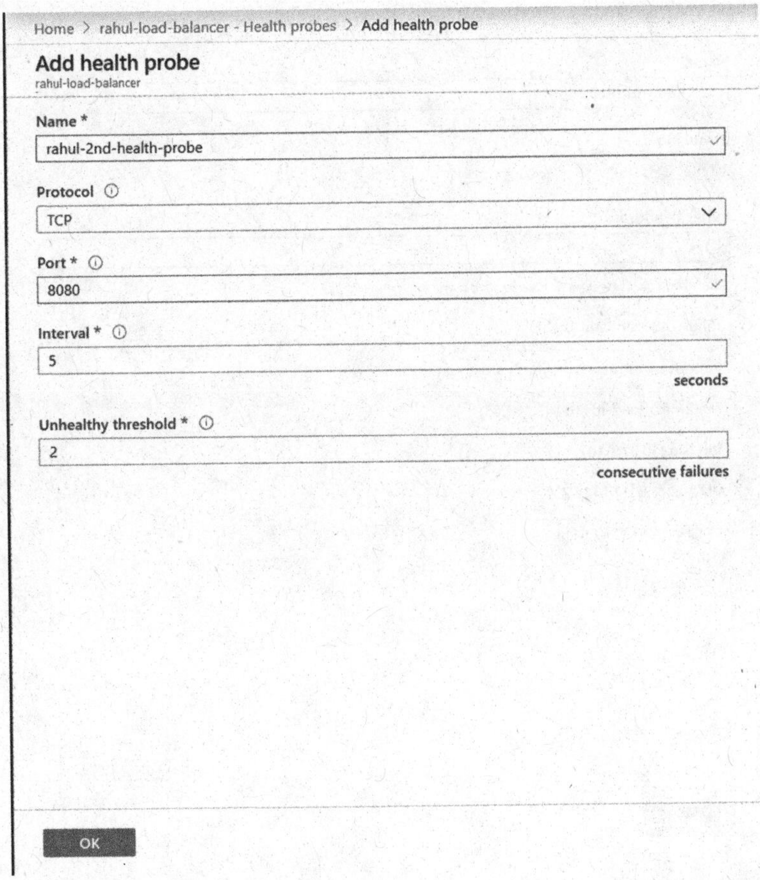

Figure 14-27. *Secondary health probe*

Once the second probe has been created successfully, the screen will look like Figure 14-28.

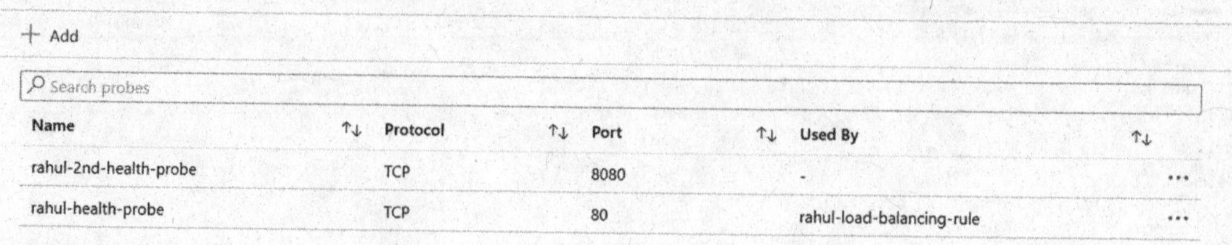

Name		Protocol		Port		Used By	
rahul-2nd-health-probe		TCP		8080		-	...
rahul-health-probe		TCP		80		rahul-load-balancing-rule	...

Figure 14-28. Health probes

Next, add the newly created IP address under "Frontend IP configuration," as shown in Figure 14-29.

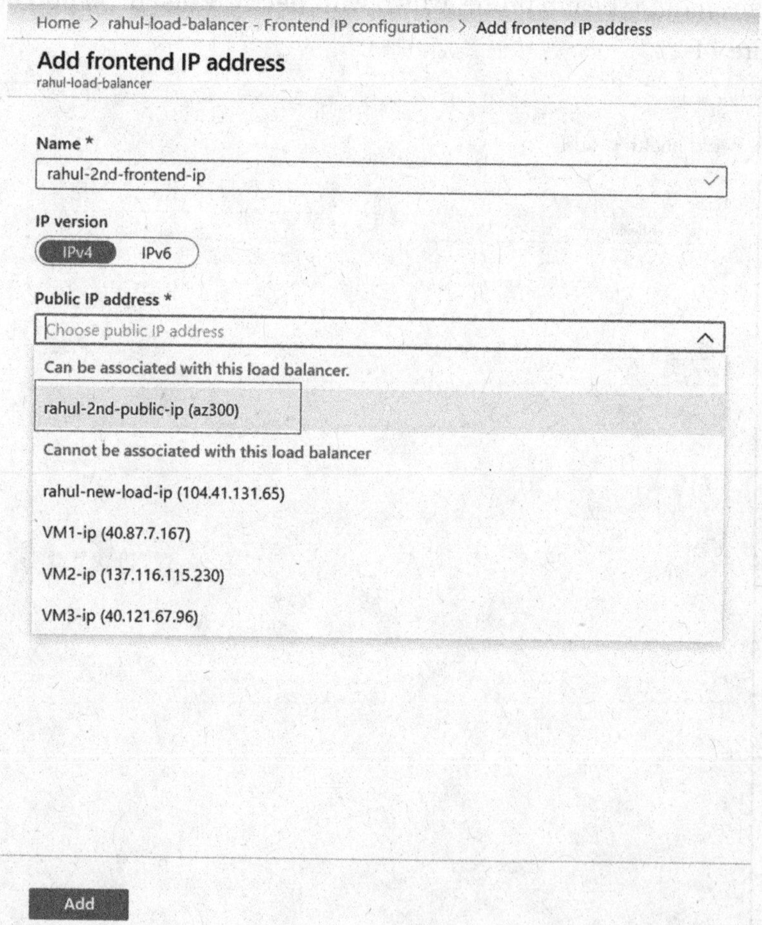

Figure 14-29. Adding a front-end IP address

After the IP address is successfully created, the screen will look like Figure 14-30.

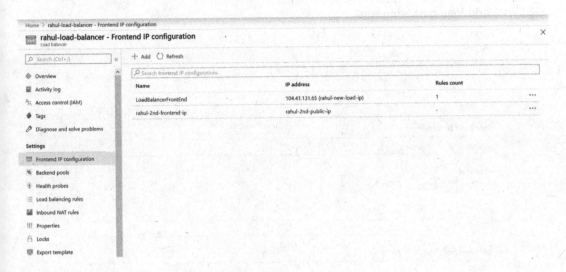

Figure 14-30. *Front-end IP configurations*

Click the newly added front-end IP configuration and then save it. The configuration will then become available in the load balancing rule; otherwise, you won't see this IP configuration there.

Next, let's create a new load balancing rule, which will take traffic from port 80 via the newly created public IP address and send it to port 8080. This kind of configuration becomes important when you are running multiple apps within the same virtual machine.

Creating a Second Load Balancing Rule

We will create another load balancer in this section, as shown in Figure 14-31.

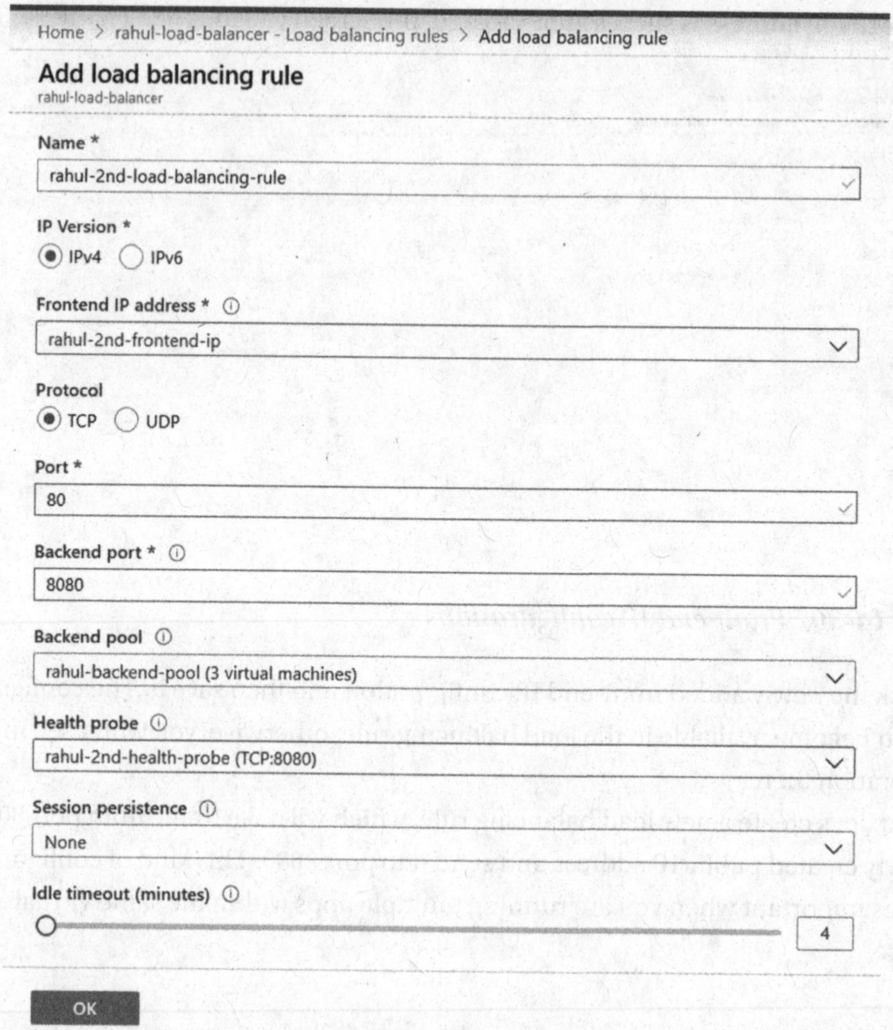

Home > rahul-load-balancer - Load balancing rules > Add load balancing rule

Add load balancing rule
rahul-load-balancer

Name *

rahul-2nd-load-balancing-rule

IP Version *
◉ IPv4   ○ IPv6

Frontend IP address * ⓘ

rahul-2nd-frontend-ip

Protocol
◉ TCP   ○ UDP

Port *

80

Backend port * ⓘ

8080

Backend pool ⓘ

rahul-backend-pool (3 virtual machines)

Health probe ⓘ

rahul-2nd-health-probe (TCP:8080)

Session persistence ⓘ

None

Idle timeout (minutes) ⓘ

4

OK

Figure 14-31. *Second load balancing rule*

After the second rule has been created successfully, the screen will look like
Figure 14-32.

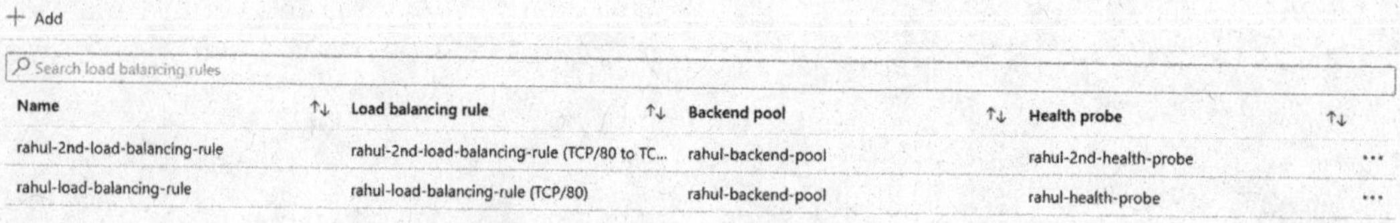

+ Add

🔍 Search load balancing rules

Name	↑↓	Load balancing rule	↑↓	Backend pool	↑↓	Health probe	↑↓
rahul-2nd-load-balancing-rule		rahul-2nd-load-balancing-rule (TCP/80 to TC...		rahul-backend-pool		rahul-2nd-health-probe	•••
rahul-load-balancing-rule		rahul-load-balancing-rule (TCP/80)		rahul-backend-pool		rahul-health-probe	•••

Figure 14-32. *Load balancers list*

Using Application Gateway

Azure Application Gateway is a web traffic load balancer that enables you to manage traffic to your web applications. Application Gateway can make routing decisions based on additional attributes of an HTTP request, say, a URI path or host headers. This type of routing is known as *application layer load balancing* (and happens on OSI layer 7). Figure 14-33 explains the high-level workings of Application Gateway based on the path.

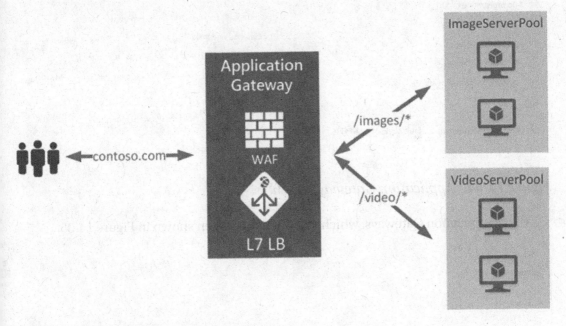

Figure 14-33. *Application Gateway flow*

Creating a Gateway

Unlike a load balancer, Application Gateway is smart device. Let's create a gateway, as shown in Figure 14-34.

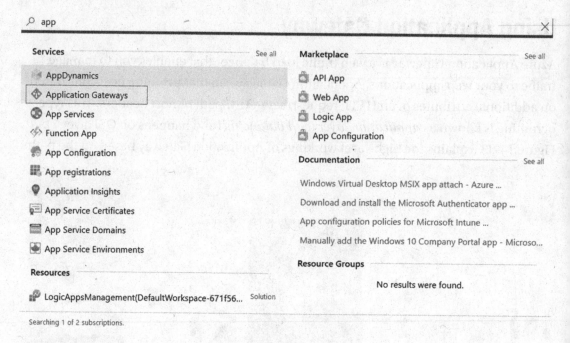

Figure 14-34. *Application Gateway search*

Click Application Gateways, which will open the screen shown in Figure 14-35.

Figure 14-35. *Application Gateways screen*

Let's provide the information shown in Figure 14-36.

Create an application gateway

① Basics   ② Frontends   ③ Backends   ④ Configuration   ⑤ Tags   ⑥ Review + create

An application gateway is a web traffic load balancer that enables you to manage traffic to your web application.
Learn more about application gateway

Project details

Select the subscription to manage deployed resources and costs. Use resource groups like folders to organize and manage all
your resources.

Subscription * ⓘ	Visual Studio Enterprise with MSDN ⌄
└── Resource group * ⓘ	az300 ⌄
	Create new

Instance details

Application gateway name *	rahul-app-gateway ✓
Region *	(US) East US ⌄
Tier ⓘ	Standard V2 ⌄
Enable autoscaling	⦿ Yes ◯ No
Minimum autoscale instances * ⓘ	0
Maximum autoscale instances	10
Availability zone ⓘ	None ⌄

< Previous   Next : Frontends >

Figure 14-36. *Application Gateway basics*

If you want higher availability, then you can choose the availability zones as well.
This specifies which data center your gateway is going to reside in. Availability zones also
depend on the region that you have selected. For a few regions, availability zones won't
be available.

Also notice the autoscale option, which means if the network traffic is high,
additional reserved capacity will get attached to it.

Next, let's create a virtual network, as shown in Figure 14-37.

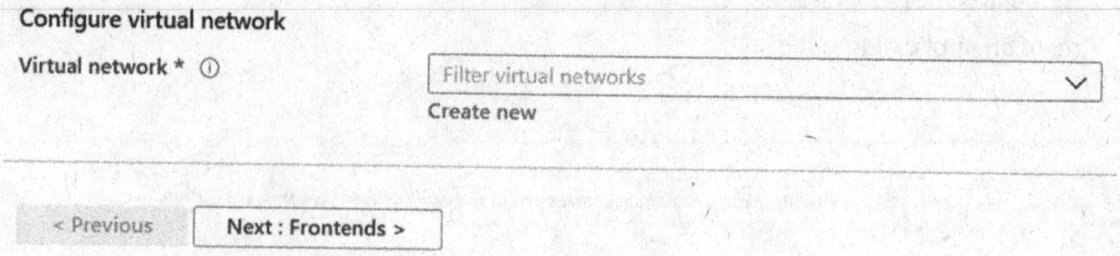

Configure virtual network

Virtual network * ⓘ

Filter virtual networks ⌄

Create new

< Previous   Next : Frontends >

Figure 14-37. *Virtual network setup*

Here are the settings to use:

- **Name:** Use *app-gateway-vnet* for the name of the virtual network, as shown in Figure 14-38.

- **Subnet name (Application Gateway subnet):** The subnets grid will show a subnet named Default. Change the name of this subnet to *app-gateway-subnet*. The application gateway subnet can contain only application gateways. No other resources are allowed.

- **Subnet name (backend server subnet):** In the second row of the Subnets section, use *app-gateway-backend-subnet* in the "Subnet name" column.

- **Address range (backend server subnet):** In the second row of the Subnets section, enter an address range that doesn't overlap with the address range of app-gateway-subnet. For example, if the address range of app-gateway-subnet is 10.0.0.0/24, use 10.0.1.0/24 for the address range of app-gateway-backend-subnet.

Create virtual network   ✕

The Microsoft Azure Virtual Network service enables Azure resources to securely communicate with each other in a virtual network which is
a logical isolation of the Azure cloud dedicated to your subscription. You can connect virtual networks to other virtual networks, or your on-
premises network. Learn more

Name * | app-gateway-vnet   ✓ |

Address space

The virtual network's address space, specified as one or more address prefixes in CIDR notation (e.g. 192.168.1.0/24).

	Address range	Addresses	Overlap	
☐	10.21.0.0/16 ✓	10.21.0.0 - 10.21.255.255 (65536 addresses)	None	🗑 ···
☐		(0 Addresses)	None	

Subnets

The subnet's address range in CIDR notation. It must be contained by the address space of the virtual network.

	Subnet name	Address range	Addresses	
☐	app-gateway-subnet	10.21.0.0/24	10.21.0.0 - 10.21.0.255 (256 addresses)	🗑 ···
☐	app-gateway-backend-subnet ✓	10.21.1.0/24 ✓	10.21.1.0 - 10.21.1.255 (256 addresses)	🗑 ···
			(0 Addresses)	

| OK | Discard |

Figure 14-38. *Virtual network creation screen*

Let's create a public IP address, as shown in Figure 14-39.

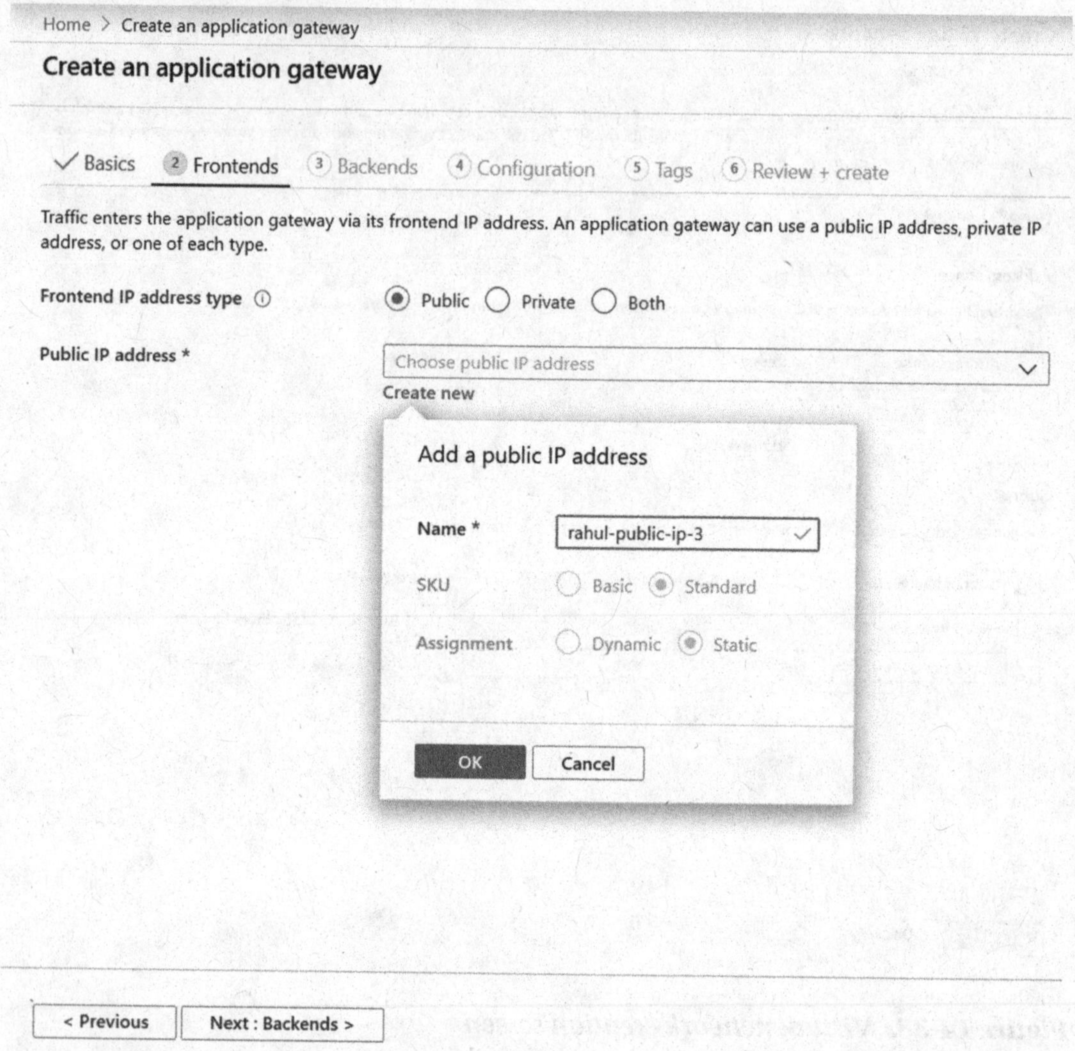

Home > Create an application gateway

Create an application gateway

✓ Basics   ② Frontends   ③ Backends   ④ Configuration   ⑤ Tags   ⑥ Review + create

Traffic enters the application gateway via its frontend IP address. An application gateway can use a public IP address, private IP address, or one of each type.

Frontend IP address type ⓘ   ● Public ○ Private ○ Both

Public IP address *   [Choose public IP address   ⌄]
                                       Create new

> ### Add a public IP address
>
> Name *   [rahul-public-ip-3   ✓]
>
> SKU   ○ Basic ● Standard
>
> Assignment   ○ Dynamic ● Static
>
> [OK]   [Cancel]

[< Previous]   [Next : Backends >]

Figure 14-39. *Front-end configuration*

On the Backends tab, the backend pool is used to route requests to the backend servers that serve the request. Backend pools can be composed of network interface cards (NICs), virtual machine scale sets, public IP addresses, internal IP addresses, fully qualified domain names (FQDNs), and multitenant backends like Azure App Service. In this example, you'll create an empty backend pool with an application gateway and then add backend targets to the backend pool, as shown in Figure 14-40.

Home > Resource groups > az300 > New > Application Gateway > Create an application gateway

Create an application gateway

✓ Basics ✓ Frontends ③ Backends ④ Configuration ⑤ Tags ⑥ Review + create

A backend pool is a collection of resources to which your application gateway can send traffic. A backend pool can contain virtual machines, virtual machine scale sets, IP addresses, or fully qualified domain names (FQDN).

+Add a backend pool

Backend pool	Targets
No results	

Add a backend pool   ✕

A backend pool is a collection of resources to which your application gateway can send traffic. A backend pool can contain virtual machines, virtual machine scale sets, IP addresses, or a valid Internet hostname.

Name *   [rahul-backend-pool   ✓]

Add backend pool without   (Yes   No)
targets

[Add] [Cancel]

< Previous   [Next : Configuration >]

Figure 14-40. *Adding a backend pool*

Next comes the Configuration tab, as shown in Figure 14-41. Here, you will connect the front-end and back-end pools using a routing rule.

Home > Resource groups > az300 > New > Application Gateway > Create an application gateway

Create an application gateway   ✕

✓ Basics ✓ Frontends ✓ Backends ④ Configuration ⑤ Tags ⑥ Review + create

Create routing rules that link your frontends and backends. You can also add more backend pools, add a second frontend IP configuration if you haven't already, or edit previous configurations.

Frontends   **Routing rules**   **Backend pools**

+ Add a frontend IP   ╋   + Add a backend pool

Public: (new) rahul-public-ip-3 🗑 ⋯   Add a rule   rahul-backend-pool 🗑 ⋯

< Previous   [Next : Tags >]

Figure 14-41. *Routing rule*

Click Add a Rule, and enter the details shown in Figure 14-42.

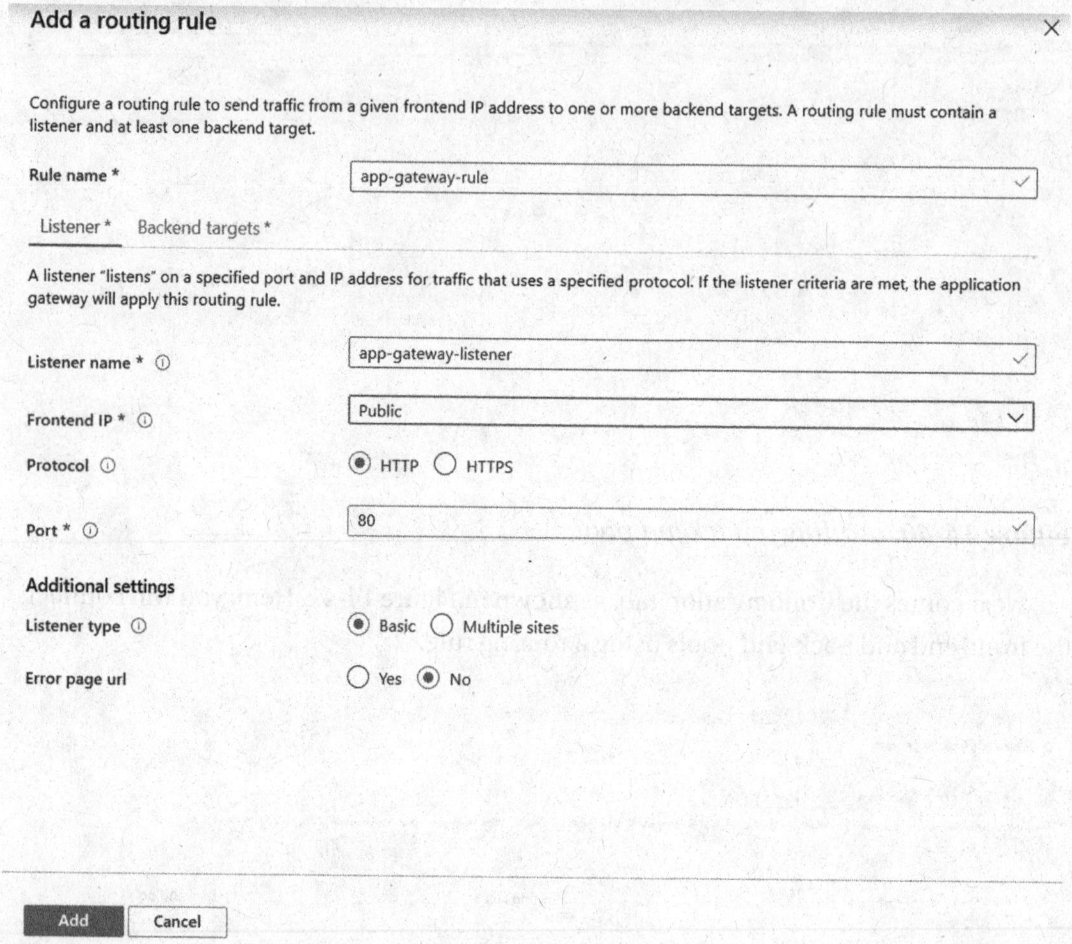

Figure 14-42. *Adding a routing rule*

Then, click Add and enter the details shown in Figure 14-43 on the "Backend targets" tab. Here, you need to select the backend pool from the drop-down menu, as shown in Figure 14-43.

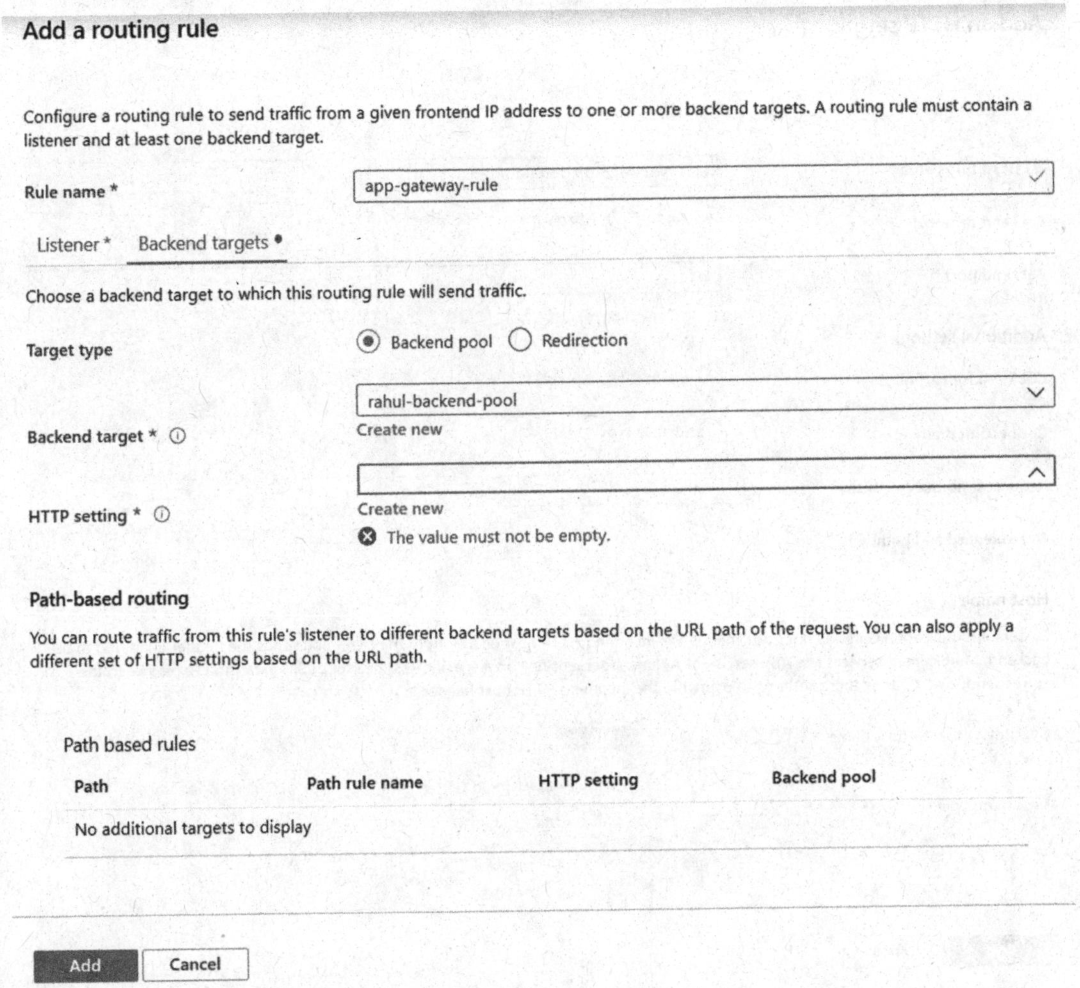

Add a routing rule

Configure a routing rule to send traffic from a given frontend IP address to one or more backend targets. A routing rule must contain a listener and at least one backend target.

Rule name *

> app-gateway-rule ✓

Listener *   Backend targets •

Choose a backend target to which this routing rule will send traffic.

Target type
● Backend pool ○ Redirection

Backend target * ⓘ
> rahul-backend-pool ∨

Create new

> ∧

HTTP setting * ⓘ
Create new
❌ The value must not be empty.

Path-based routing

You can route traffic from this rule's listener to different backend targets based on the URL path of the request. You can also apply a different set of HTTP settings based on the URL path.

Path based rules

Path	Path rule name	HTTP setting	Backend pool
No additional targets to display			

Add   Cancel

Figure 14-43. Adding backend targets

Under "HTTP setting," click "Create new" and enter the details shown in Figure 14-44.

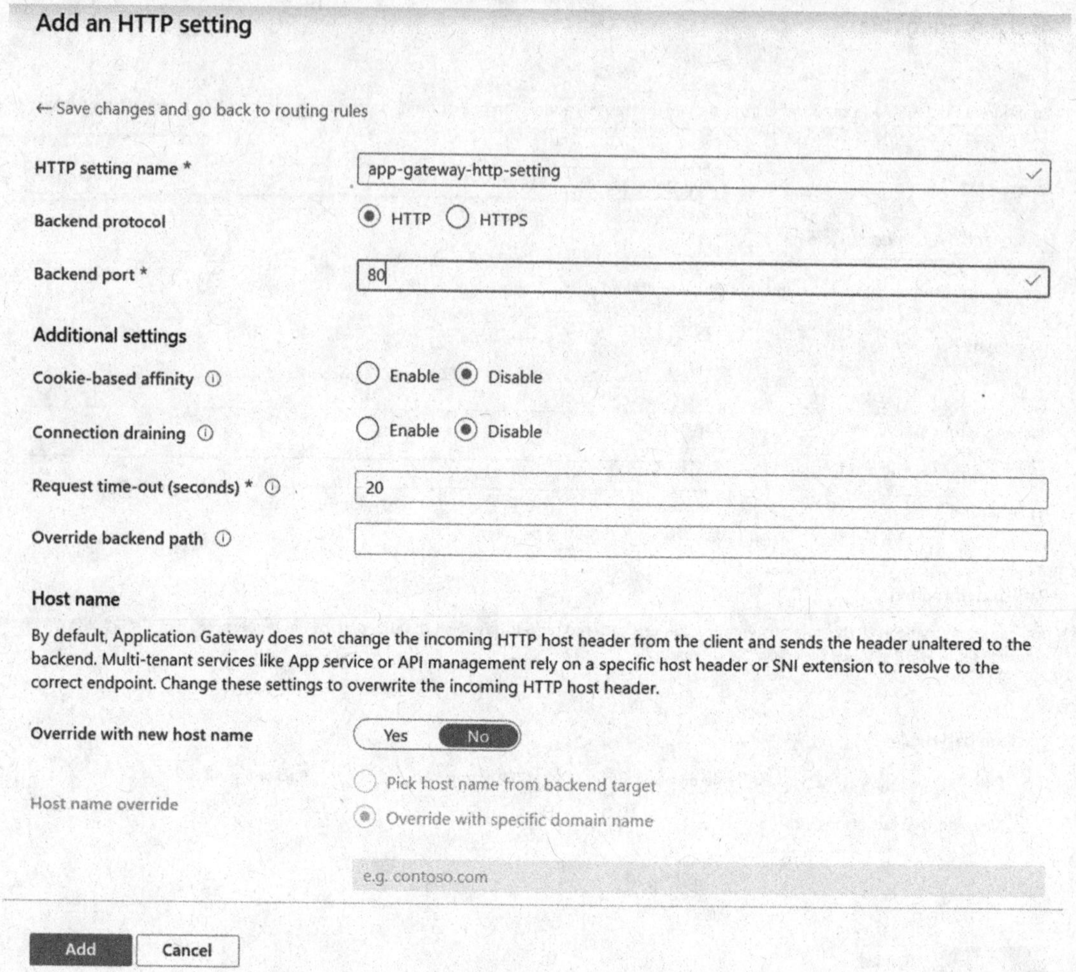

Add an HTTP setting

← Save changes and go back to routing rules

HTTP setting name *	app-gateway-http-setting ✓
Backend protocol	⦿ HTTP ◯ HTTPS
Backend port *	80 ✓

Additional settings

Cookie-based affinity ⓘ	◯ Enable ⦿ Disable
Connection draining ⓘ	◯ Enable ⦿ Disable
Request time-out (seconds) * ⓘ	20
Override backend path ⓘ	

Host name

By default, Application Gateway does not change the incoming HTTP host header from the client and sends the header unaltered to the backend. Multi-tenant services like App service or API management rely on a specific host header or SNI extension to resolve to the correct endpoint. Change these settings to overwrite the incoming HTTP host header.

Override with new host name	Yes **No**
Host name override	◯ Pick host name from backend target
	⦿ Override with specific domain name
	e.g. contoso.com

[Add] [Cancel]

Figure 14-44. *Adding an HTTP setting*

Finally, your screen will look like Figure 14-45. Click Add.

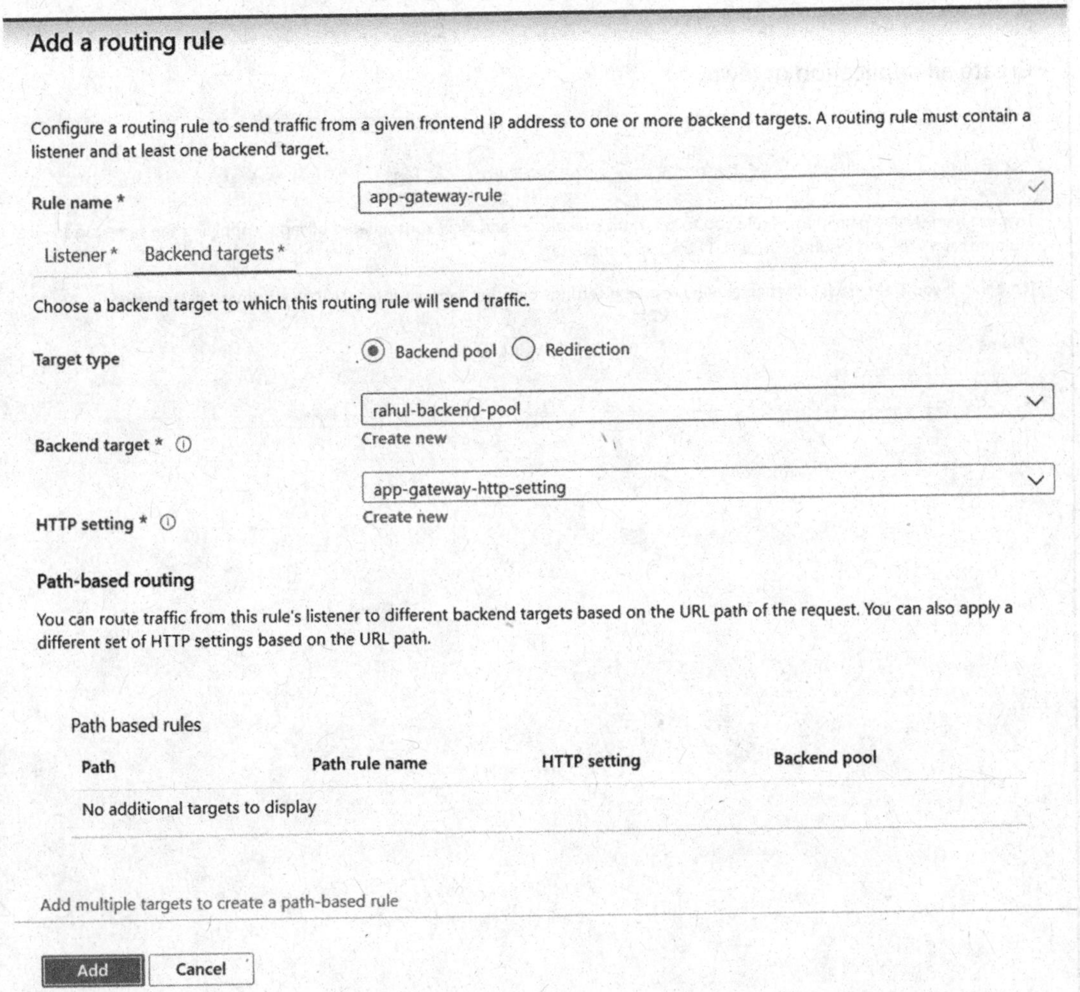

Add a routing rule

Configure a routing rule to send traffic from a given frontend IP address to one or more backend targets. A routing rule must contain a listener and at least one backend target.

Rule name *   app-gateway-rule   ✓

Listener *   Backend targets *

Choose a backend target to which this routing rule will send traffic.

Target type   ◉ Backend pool   ○ Redirection

Backend target * ⓘ   rahul-backend-pool   ⌄
                               Create new

HTTP setting * ⓘ   app-gateway-http-setting   ⌄
                               Create new

Path-based routing

You can route traffic from this rule's listener to different backend targets based on the URL path of the request. You can also apply a different set of HTTP settings based on the URL path.

Path based rules

Path	Path rule name	HTTP setting	Backend pool
No additional targets to display			

Add multiple targets to create a path-based rule

Add   Cancel

Figure 14-45. *Completed setup*

Next comes the Tags tab, as shown in Figure 14-46.

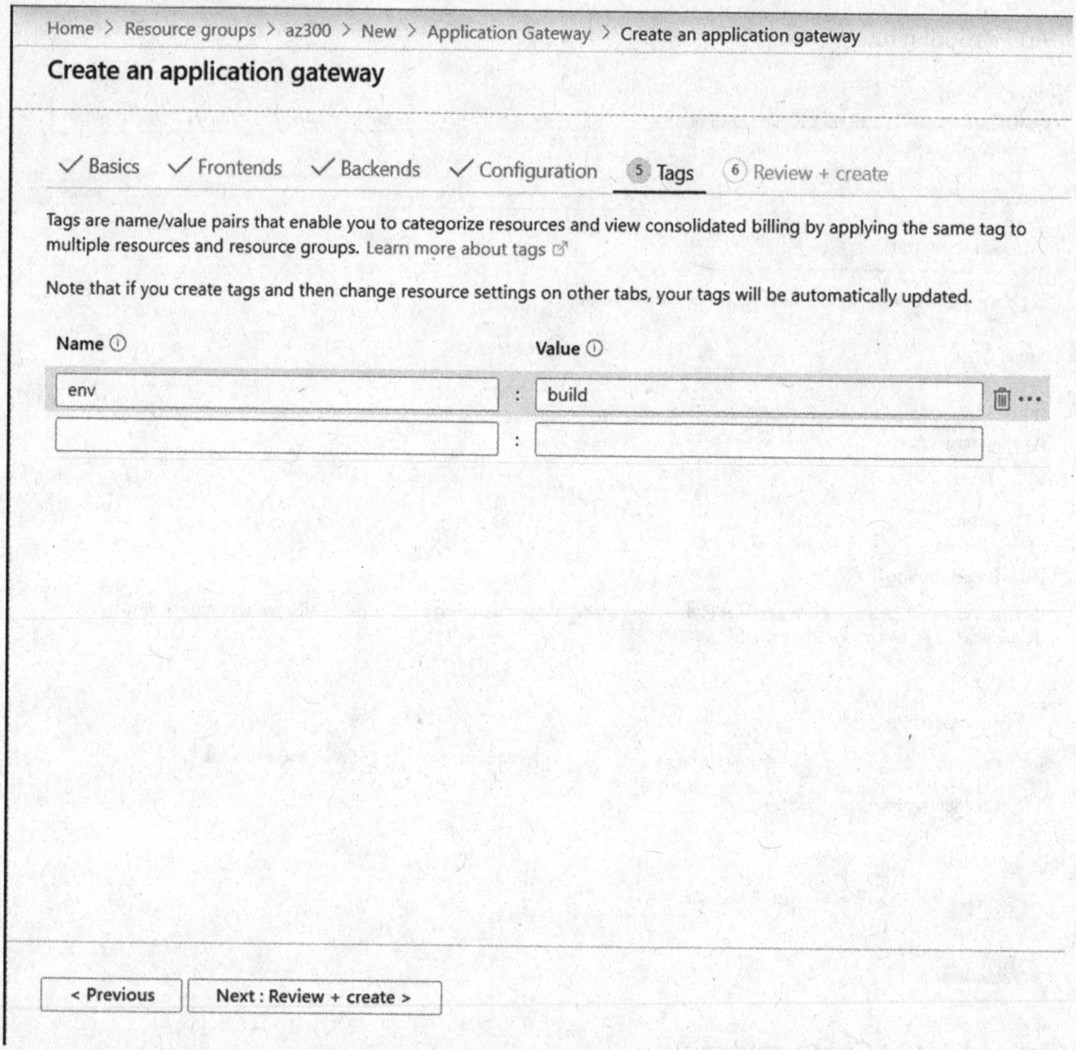

Home > Resource groups > az300 > New > Application Gateway > Create an application gateway

Create an application gateway

✓ Basics   ✓ Frontends   ✓ Backends   ✓ Configuration   ⑤ Tags   ⑥ Review + create

Tags are name/value pairs that enable you to categorize resources and view consolidated billing by applying the same tag to multiple resources and resource groups. Learn more about tags ⬀

Note that if you create tags and then change resource settings on other tabs, your tags will be automatically updated.

Name ⓘ   Value ⓘ

| env | : | build | 🗑 ••• |
| | : | | |

< Previous   Next : Review + create >

Figure 14-46. *Tags tab*

Finally, click the "Review + create" screen, as shown in Figure 14-47.

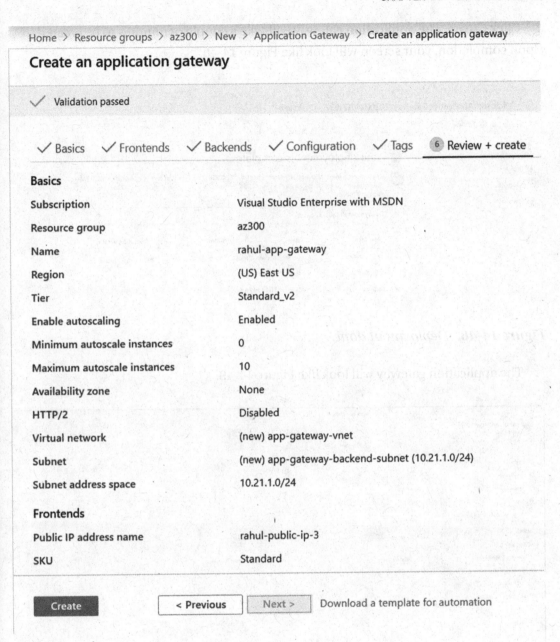

Create an application gateway

✓ Validation passed

✓ Basics   ✓ Frontends   ✓ Backends   ✓ Configuration   ✓ Tags   ⑥ Review + create

Basics

Subscription	Visual Studio Enterprise with MSDN
Resource group	az300
Name	rahul-app-gateway
Region	(US) East US
Tier	Standard_v2
Enable autoscaling	Enabled
Minimum autoscale instances	0
Maximum autoscale instances	10
Availability zone	None
HTTP/2	Disabled
Virtual network	(new) app-gateway-vnet
Subnet	(new) app-gateway-backend-subnet (10.21.1.0/24)
Subnet address space	10.21.1.0/24

Frontends

Public IP address name	rahul-public-ip-3
SKU	Standard

Create   < Previous   Next >   Download a template for automation

Figure 14-47. *"Review + create" screen*

Click Create. The application gateway will take a couple of minutes to be created. Upon completion, your screen will look like Figure 14-48.

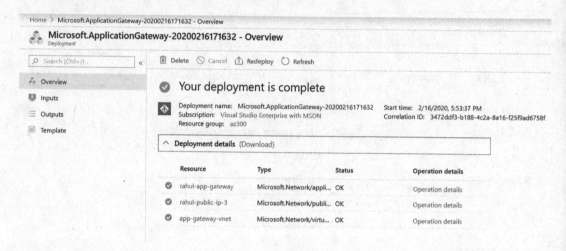

Figure 14-48. Deployment done

The application gateway will look like Figure 14-49.

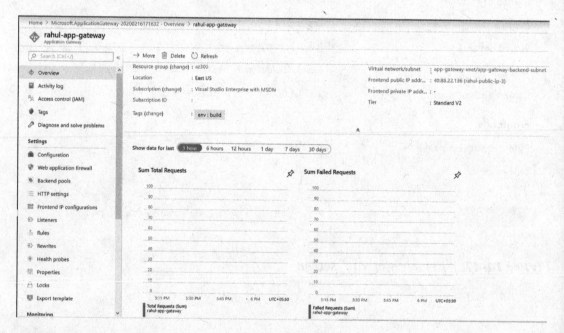

Figure 14-49. Application gateway's Overview screen

Next, you need to create backend servers for this gateway. You can utilize the same virtual machines, if they haven't been deleted, or create a new one. While creating a virtual machine, you can configure the load balancing options on the Networking tab as well. You can see this in Figure 14-50.

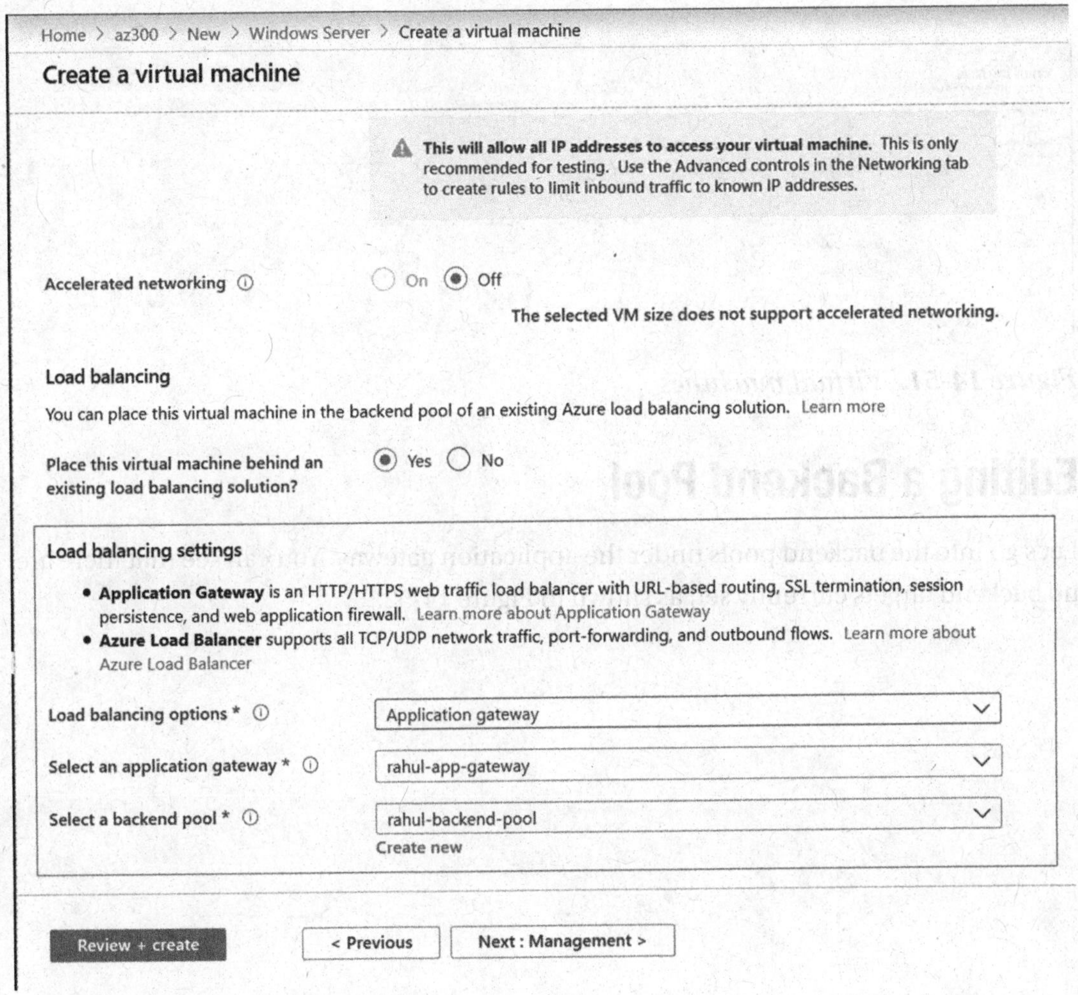

Home > az300 > New > Windows Server > Create a virtual machine

Create a virtual machine

⚠ **This will allow all IP addresses to access your virtual machine.** This is only recommended for testing. Use the Advanced controls in the Networking tab to create rules to limit inbound traffic to known IP addresses.

Accelerated networking ⓘ   ○ On ⦿ Off
                                              The selected VM size does not support accelerated networking.

Load balancing

You can place this virtual machine in the backend pool of an existing Azure load balancing solution. Learn more

Place this virtual machine behind an   ⦿ Yes ○ No
existing load balancing solution?

Load balancing settings

- **Application Gateway** is an HTTP/HTTPS web traffic load balancer with URL-based routing, SSL termination, session persistence, and web application firewall. Learn more about Application Gateway
- **Azure Load Balancer** supports all TCP/UDP network traffic, port-forwarding, and outbound flows. Learn more about Azure Load Balancer

Load balancing options * ⓘ | Application gateway   ∨ |

Select an application gateway * ⓘ | rahul-app-gateway   ∨ |

Select a backend pool * ⓘ | rahul-backend-pool   ∨ |
                                      Create new

[Review + create]   [< Previous]   [Next : Management >]

Figure 14-50. *Load balancing setup*

But, let's backtrack from here so I can show how to add backend targets from the application gateway section. Here, I have a set of three virtual machines, which will be my backend target. Make sure that you use the same virtual network that you used while creating the app gateway during VM creation on the Networking tab, as shown in Figure 14-51.

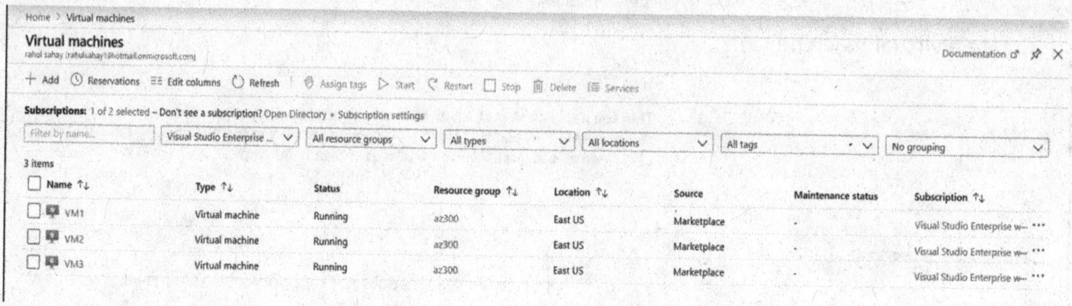

Figure 14-51. Virtual machines

Editing a Backend Pool

Let's go into the backend pools under the application gateway. You can see that there are no backend targets currently set, as shown in Figure 14-52.

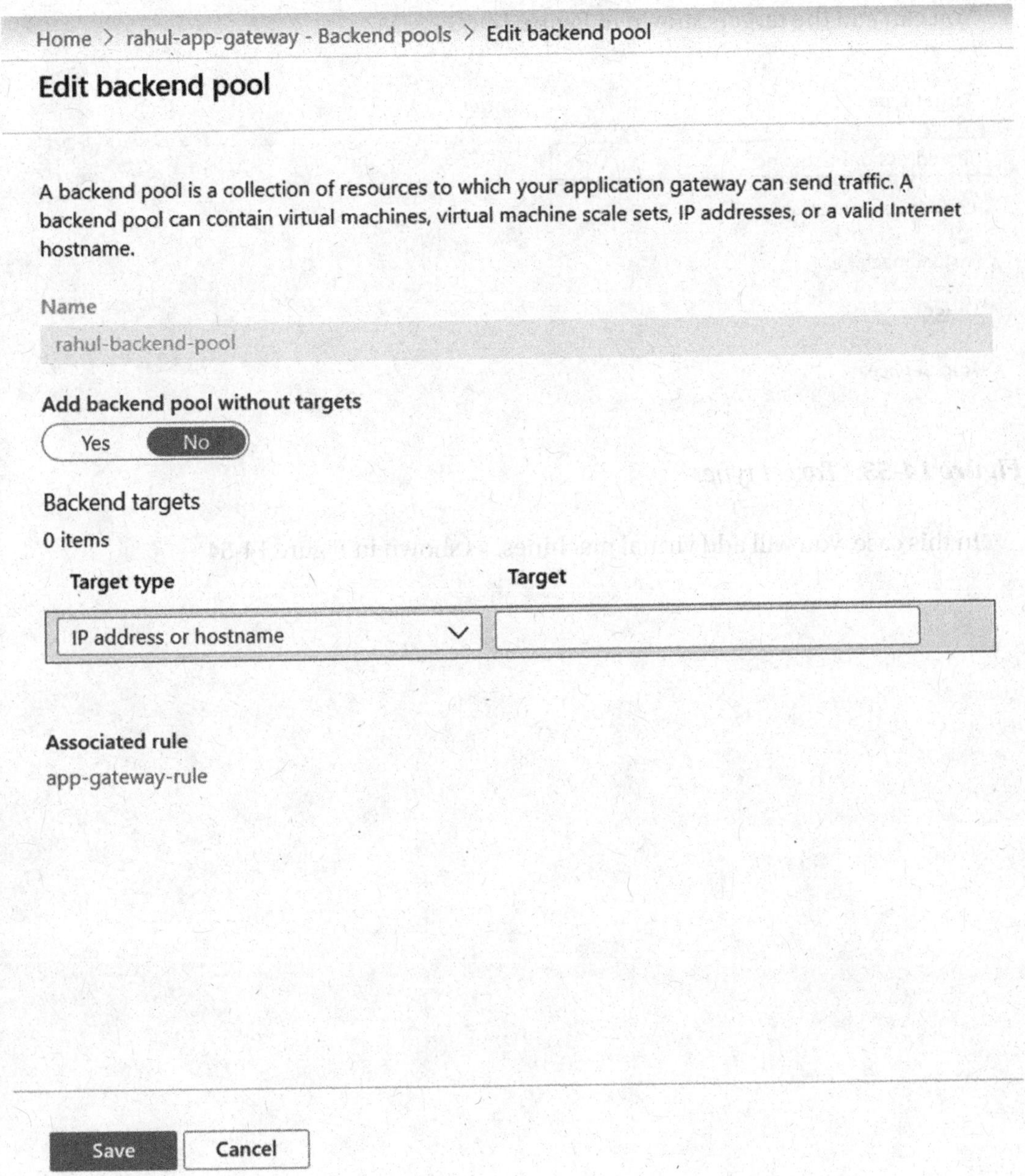

Home > rahul-app-gateway - Backend pools > Edit backend pool

Edit backend pool

A backend pool is a collection of resources to which your application gateway can send traffic. A backend pool can contain virtual machines, virtual machine scale sets, IP addresses, or a valid Internet hostname.

Name

rahul-backend-pool

Add backend pool without targets

Yes   No

Backend targets

0 items

Target type	Target
IP address or hostname ⌄	

Associated rule

app-gateway-rule

Save   Cancel

Figure 14-52. *Editing a backend pool*

You can add the targets shown in Figure 14-53.

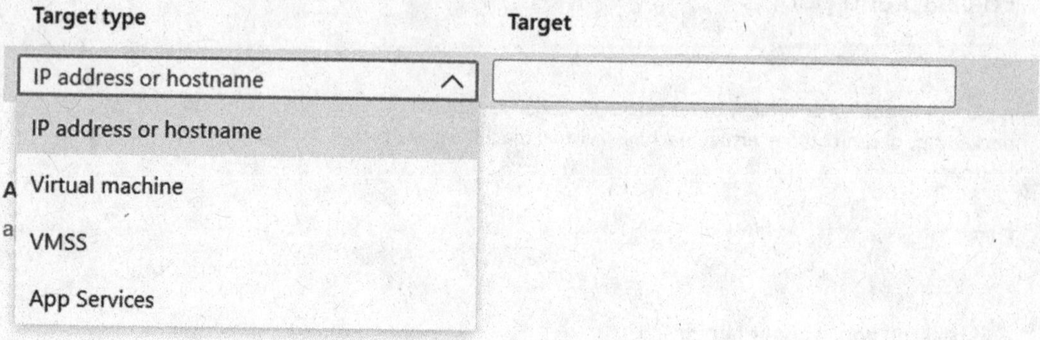

Target type   **Target**

| IP address or hostname   ∧ |

IP address or hostname

A Virtual machine

a VMSS

App Services

Figure 14-53. *Target types*

In this case, you will add virtual machines, as shown in Figure 14-54.

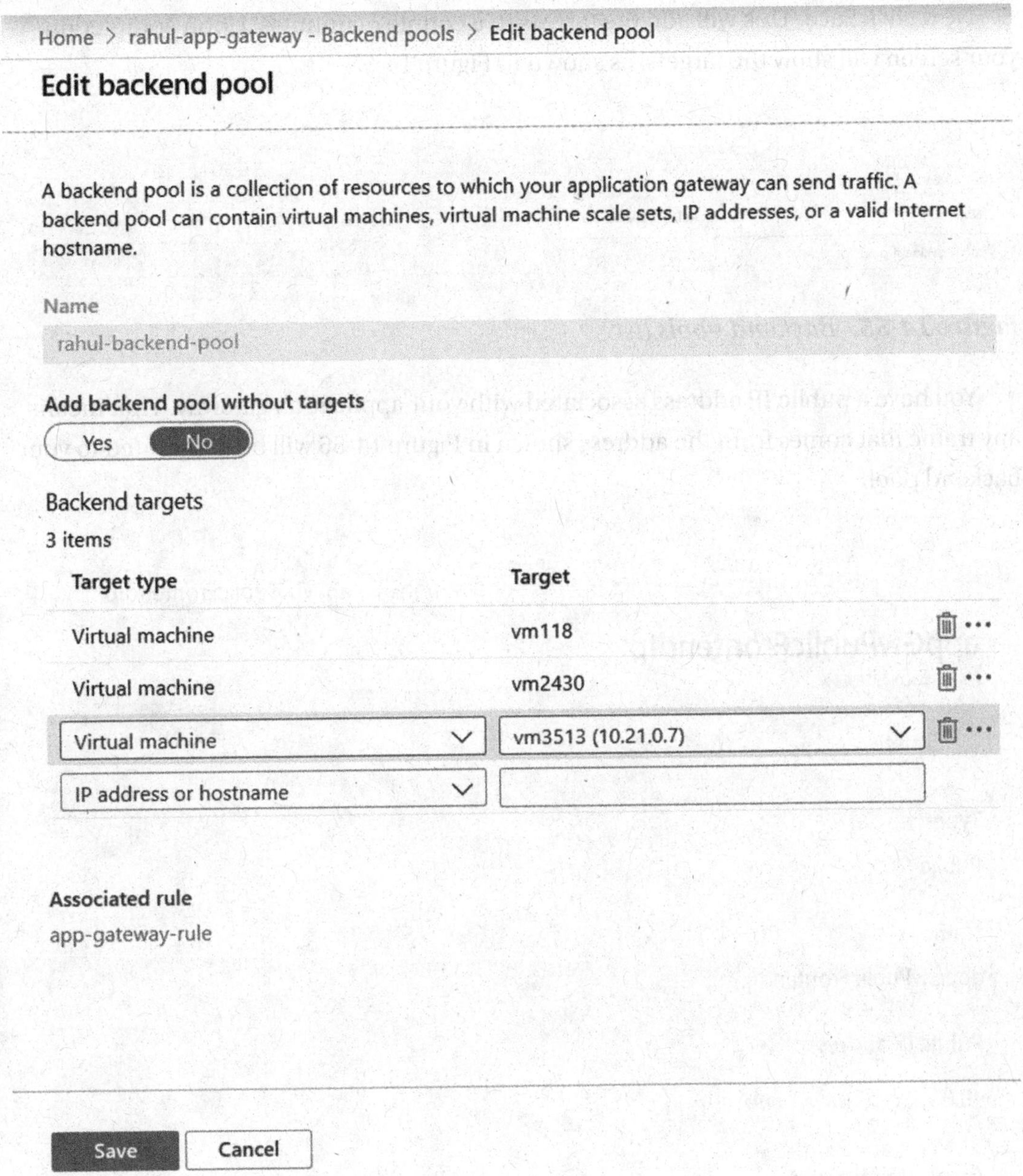

Home > rahul-app-gateway - Backend pools > Edit backend pool

Edit backend pool

A backend pool is a collection of resources to which your application gateway can send traffic. A backend pool can contain virtual machines, virtual machine scale sets, IP addresses, or a valid Internet hostname.

Name

rahul-backend-pool

Add backend pool without targets

Yes   No

Backend targets

3 items

Target type	Target	
Virtual machine	vm118	🗑 ...
Virtual machine	vm2430	🗑 ...
Virtual machine ∨	vm3513 (10.21.0.7) ∨	🗑 ...
IP address or hostname ∨		

Associated rule

app-gateway-rule

Save   Cancel

Figure 14-54. *Added virtual machine*

Next click Save. This will add the targets in a couple of minutes. Upon completion, your screen will show the targets, as shown in Figure 14-55.

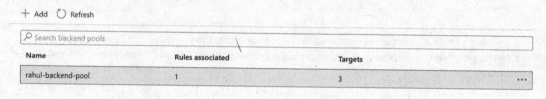

Figure 14-55. *Backend pools list*

You have a public IP address associated with your application gateway. That means any traffic that comes from the address shown in Figure 14-56 will be distributed to your backend pool.

Home > rahul-app-gateway - Frontend IP configurations > appGwPublicFrontendIp

appGwPublicFrontendIp
rahul-app-gateway

🗑 Delete

Type
Public

Name
appGwPublicFrontendIp

Public IP address
40.88.22.136 (rahul-public-ip-3)

Associated listeners
app-gateway-listener

Figure 14-56. *Front-end IP configuration*

It also has a listener setup that is listening for traffic over port 80, as shown in Figure 14-57.

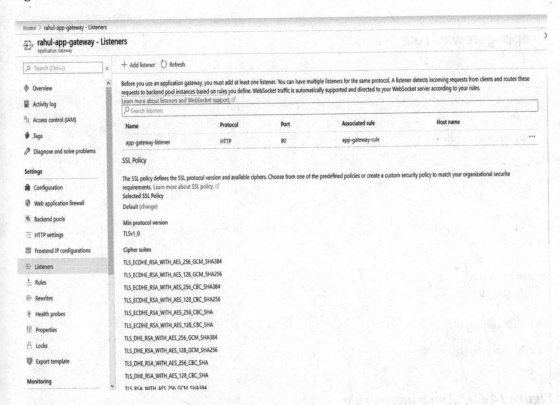

Figure 14-57. *App gateway listener*

This is using the rule shown in Figure 14-58.

Home > rahul-app-gateway - Listeners > app-gateway-listener > Rules

Rules
rahul-app-gateway

+ Basic   + Path-based

Search rules

Name	Type	Listener	
app-gateway-rule	Basic	app-gateway-listener	•••

Figure 14-58. *App gateway rule*

Next, you need to set up the app gateway rule, as shown in Figure 14-59.

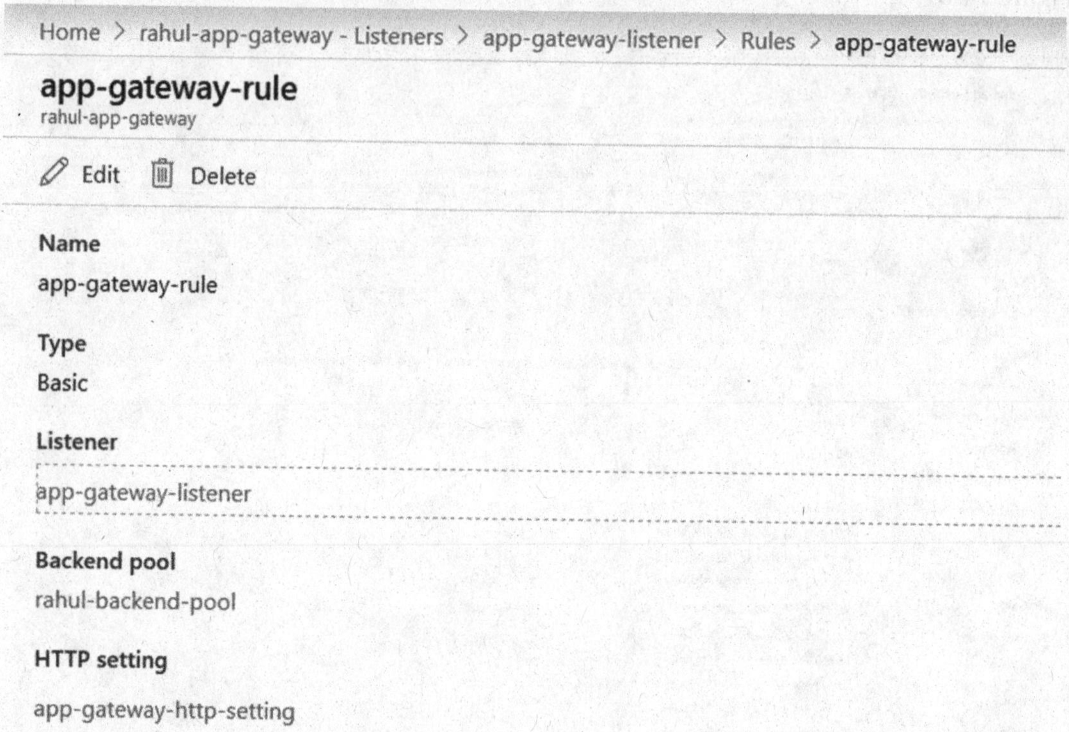

Home > rahul-app-gateway - Listeners > app-gateway-listener > Rules > **app-gateway-rule**

app-gateway-rule
rahul-app-gateway

✏ Edit   🗑 Delete

Name
app-gateway-rule

Type
Basic

Listener
app-gateway-listener

Backend pool
rahul-backend-pool

HTTP setting
app-gateway-http-setting

Figure 14-59. *App gateway rule*

Adding a Listener

Here, you can add another set of rules that are path based. But, before that, we will be needing another listener, which will be listening to some port, say, 8080, as shown in Figure 14-60.

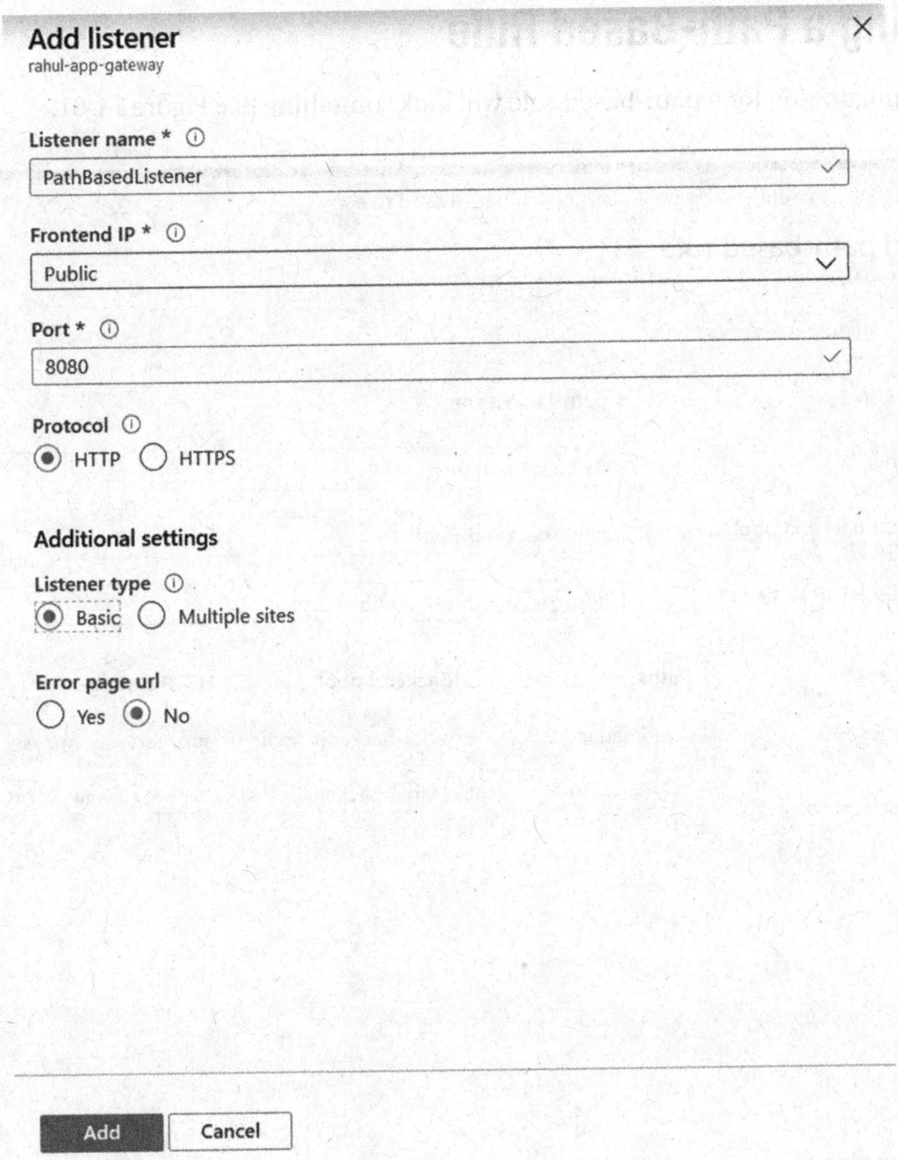

Add listener   ✕

rahul-app-gateway

Listener name * ⓘ

| PathBasedListener   ✓ |

Frontend IP * ⓘ

| Public   ⌄ |

Port * ⓘ

| 8080   ✓ |

Protocol ⓘ

⦿ HTTP   ◯ HTTPS

Additional settings

Listener type ⓘ

⦿ Basic   ◯ Multiple sites

Error page url

◯ Yes   ⦿ No

[Add]   [Cancel]

Figure 14-60. Adding another listener

Adding a Path-Based Rule

The configuration for a path-based rule will look something like Figure 14-61.

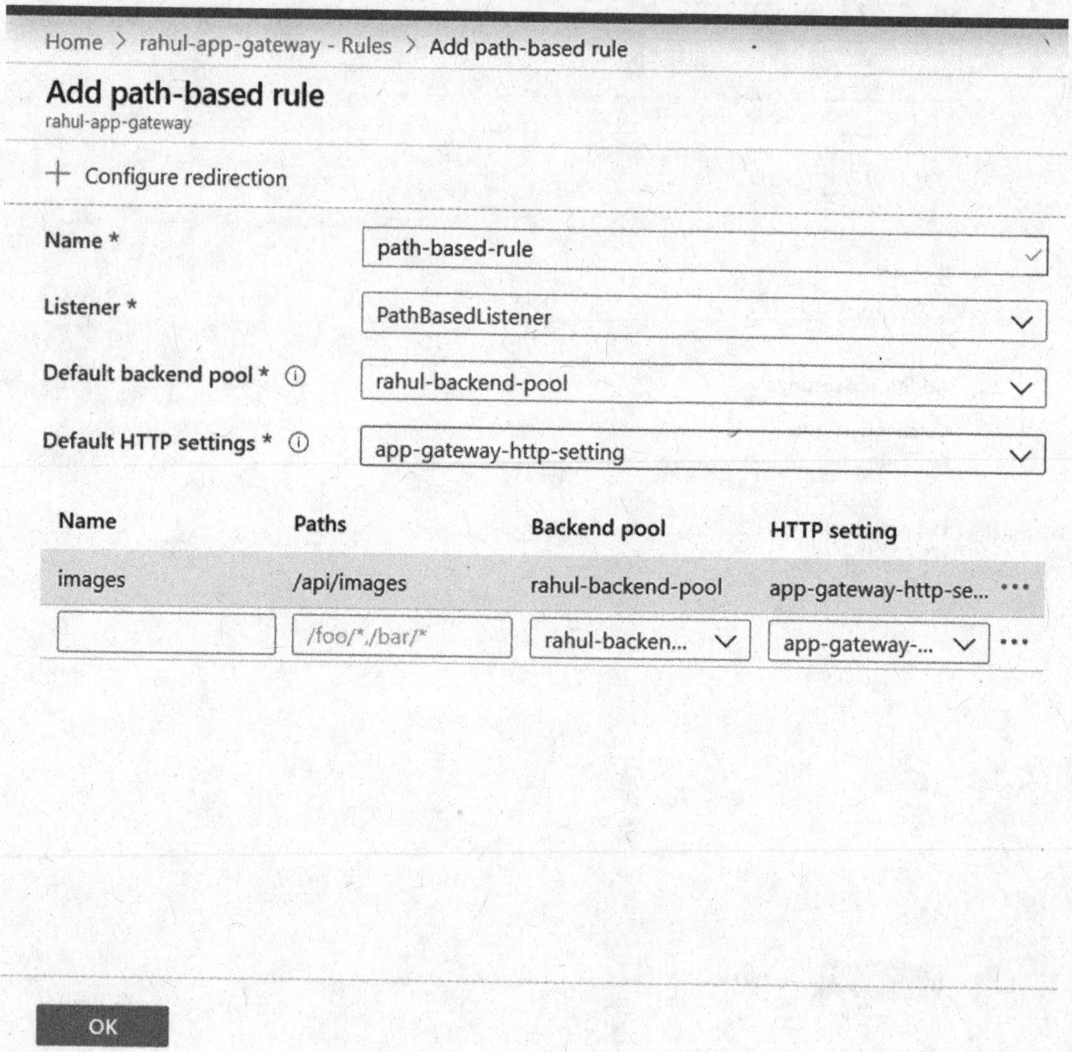

Figure 14-61. *Adding a path-based rule*

You can have different sets of servers for different sets of paths. Therefore, you can set up more sophisticated route rules here. This gives more granular control to users. This makes application gateways completely different from load balancers.

Using Front Door

Microsoft recently added a new service to its suite of services called Front Door. This runs like a load balancer but at a global scale. Therefore, instead of having a regional load balancer or application gateway, you can have a global load balancer.

Front Door is a real load balancer. It also has an acceleration platform built in. It has high availability. You can put things like app services, virtual machines, etc., behind the Front Door service.

Using Front Door

Hence, let's get started. Search for *Front door* in "All services," as shown in Figure 14-62.

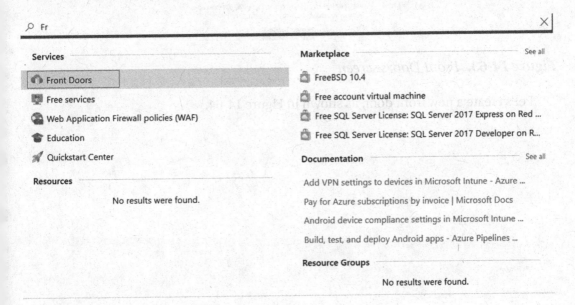

Figure 14-62. *Front Door search screen*

After clicking Front Doors, your screen will look like Figure 14-63.

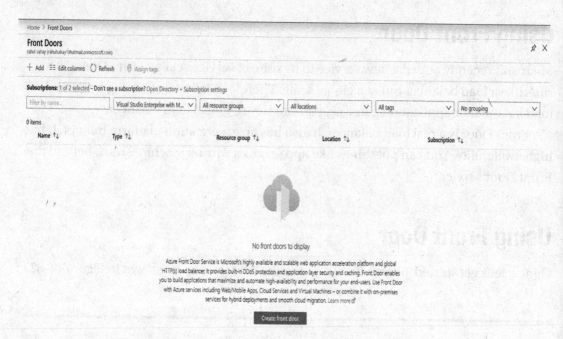

Figure 14-63. *Front Doors screen*

Let's create a new front door, as shown in Figure 14-64.

Home > Front Doors > Create a Front Door

Create a Front Door

Basics   Configuration   Tags   Review + create

Azure Front Door Service is Microsoft's highly available and scalable web application acceleration platform and global HTTP(s) load balancer. It provides built-in DDoS protection and application layer security and caching. Front Door enables you to build applications that maximize and automate high-availability and performance for your end-users. Use Front Door with Azure services including Web/Mobile Apps, Cloud Services and Virtual Machines – or combine it with on-premises services for hybrid deployments and smooth cloud migration. Learn more about Front Door

PROJECT DETAILS

Select a subscription to manage deployed resources and costs. Use resource groups like folders to organize and manage all your resources.

Subscription * ⓘ

| Visual Studio Enterprise with MSDN | ∨ |

Resource group * ⓘ

| az300 | ∨ |

Create new

Resource group location ⓘ

| (US) East US | ∨ |

| Review + create | | < Previous | | Next : Configuration > | | Download a template for automation |

Figure 14-64. *Front Door screen, Basics tab*

Next, click the Configuration tab, as shown in Figure 14-65.

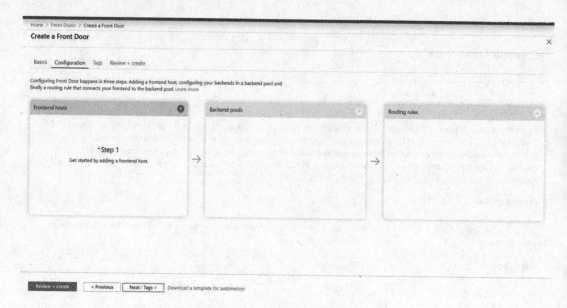

Figure 14-65. *Front Door screen, Configuration tab*

A front door looks similar to an application gateway. Let's create the front-end host first, as shown in Figure 14-66.

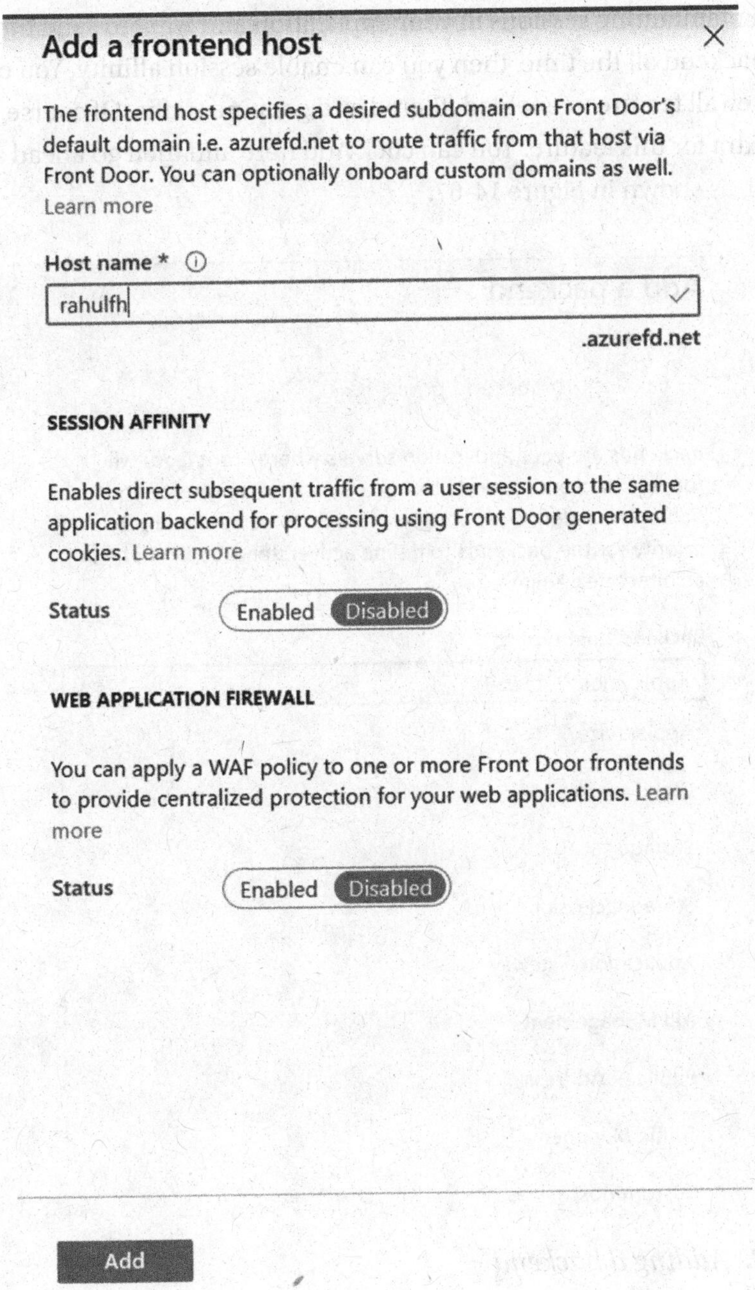

Add a frontend host

The frontend host specifies a desired subdomain on Front Door's default domain i.e. azurefd.net to route traffic from that host via Front Door. You can optionally onboard custom domains as well. Learn more

Host name * ⓘ

```
rahulfh
```
                                                      .azurefd.net

SESSION AFFINITY

Enables direct subsequent traffic from a user session to the same application backend for processing using Front Door generated cookies. Learn more

Status   Enabled   Disabled

WEB APPLICATION FIREWALL

You can apply a WAF policy to one or more Front Door frontends to provide centralized protection for your web applications. Learn more

Status   Enabled   Disabled

Add

Figure 14-66. *Adding the front-end host*

If you are maintaining sessions in your application and want to send them to the application backend all the time, then you can enable session affinity. You can also enable the firewall feature to enabled filtered and genuine traffic. Of course, you will be charged extra for this feature. You can click Add here and then go ahead and add a backend pool, as shown in Figure 14-67.

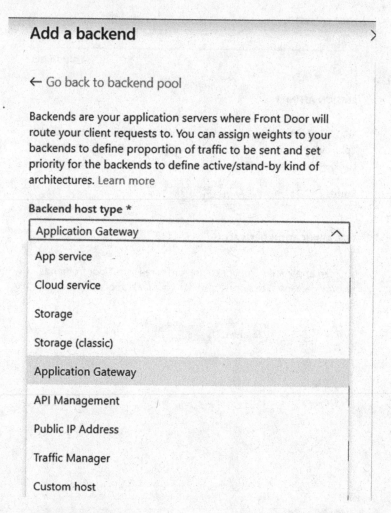

Figure 14-67. Adding a backend

Let's select Application Gateway in the list. This opens the screen shown in Figure 14-68.

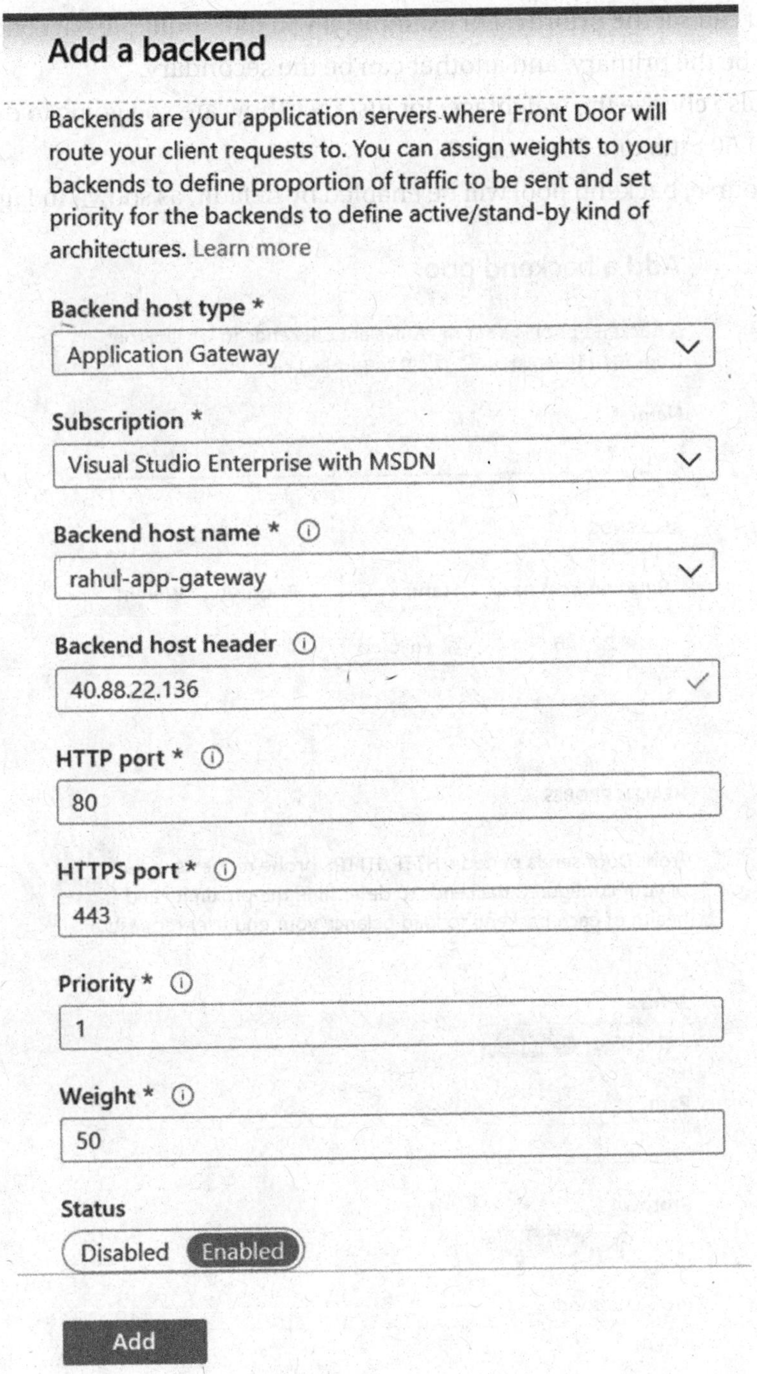

Add a backend

Backends are your application servers where Front Door will route your client requests to. You can assign weights to your backends to define proportion of traffic to be sent and set priority for the backends to define active/stand-by kind of architectures. Learn more

Backend host type *

| Application Gateway | ⌄ |

Subscription *

| Visual Studio Enterprise with MSDN | ⌄ |

Backend host name * ⓘ

| rahul-app-gateway | ⌄ |

Backend host header ⓘ

| 40.88.22.136 | ✓ |

HTTP port * ⓘ

| 80 |

HTTPS port * ⓘ

| 443 |

Priority * ⓘ

| 1 |

Weight * ⓘ

| 50 |

Status

Disabled **Enabled**

Add

Figure 14-68. *Adding a backend continuation*

Here, you can set the priority. For example, if you have multiple backends, then one backend can be the primary, and another can be the secondary.

You can also choose the weightage; for instance, how are you going to distribute traffic, in a 50-50 ratio or a 90-10 ratio?

And, of course, backend pool will be enabled by default, as shown in Figure 14-69.

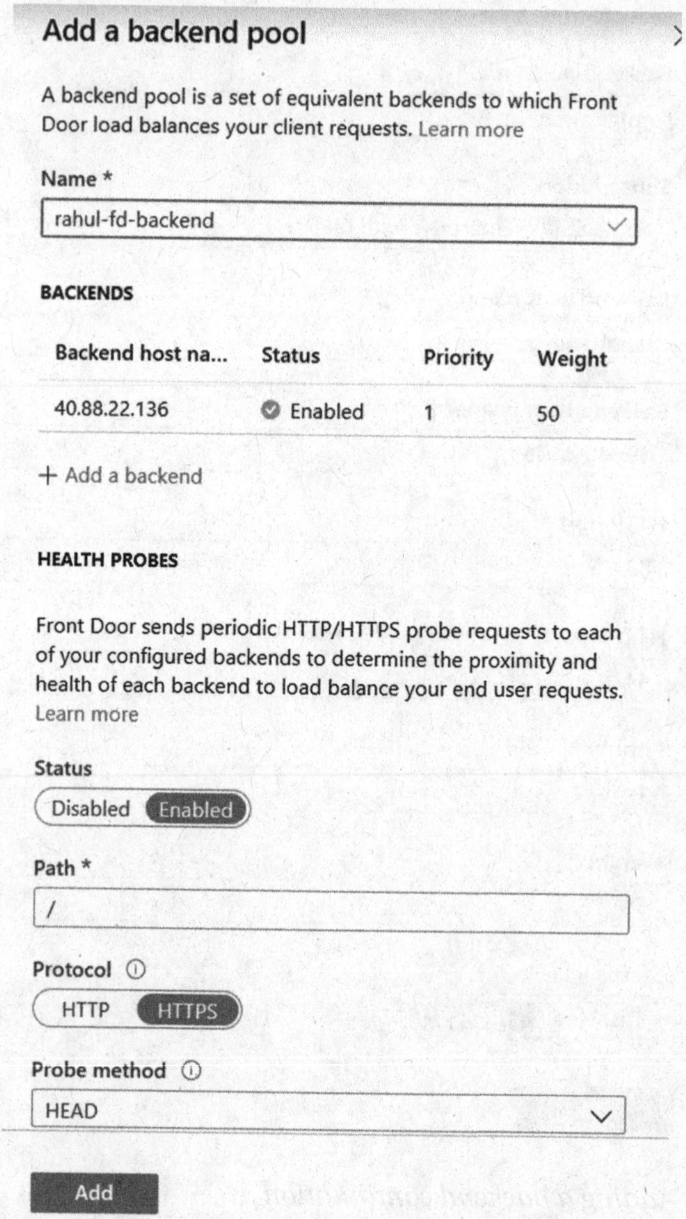

Add a backend pool

A backend pool is a set of equivalent backends to which Front Door load balances your client requests. Learn more

Name *

rahul-fd-backend

BACKENDS

Backend host na...	Status	Priority	Weight
40.88.22.136	✅ Enabled	1	50

+ Add a backend

HEALTH PROBES

Front Door sends periodic HTTP/HTTPS probe requests to each of your configured backends to determine the proximity and health of each backend to load balance your end user requests. Learn more

Status

Disabled | Enabled

Path *

/

Protocol ⓘ

HTTP | HTTPS

Probe method ⓘ

HEAD

Add

Figure 14-69. *Adding a backend pool*

Similarly, you can add another app gateway and mark it to receive the remaining 50 percent of traffic, as shown in Figure 14-70.

Protocol ⓘ

(HTTP   **HTTPS**)

Probe method ⓘ

| HEAD   ⌄ |

Interval (seconds) * ⓘ

| 30 |

LOAD BALANCING

Configure the load balancing settings to define what sample set we need to use to call the backend as healthy or unhealthy. The latency sensitivity with value zero (0) means always send it to the fastest available backend, else Front Door will round robin traffic between the fastest and the next fastest backends within the configured latency sensitivity. Learn more

Sample size * ⓘ

| 4 |

Successful samples required * ⓘ

| 2 |

Latency sensitivity (in milliseconds) * ⓘ

| 0 |

[Add]

Figure 14-70. Adding another gateway

Like with the load balancer, you can set up a health probe here that will be checked every 30 seconds.

Next comes the load balancing settings, where it checks the sample set. In this case, if two successful samples come in, then it's a healthy backend. Now, click Add.

Next come the routing rules. Since you have only one backend, 100 percent of the traffic should go to that backend, as shown in Figure 14-71 and Figure 14-72.

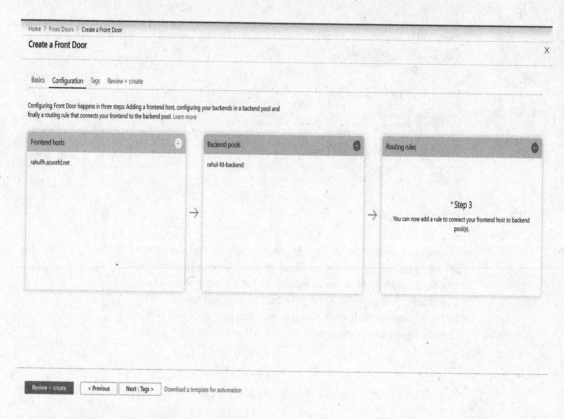

Figure 14-71. *Create a Front Door screen*

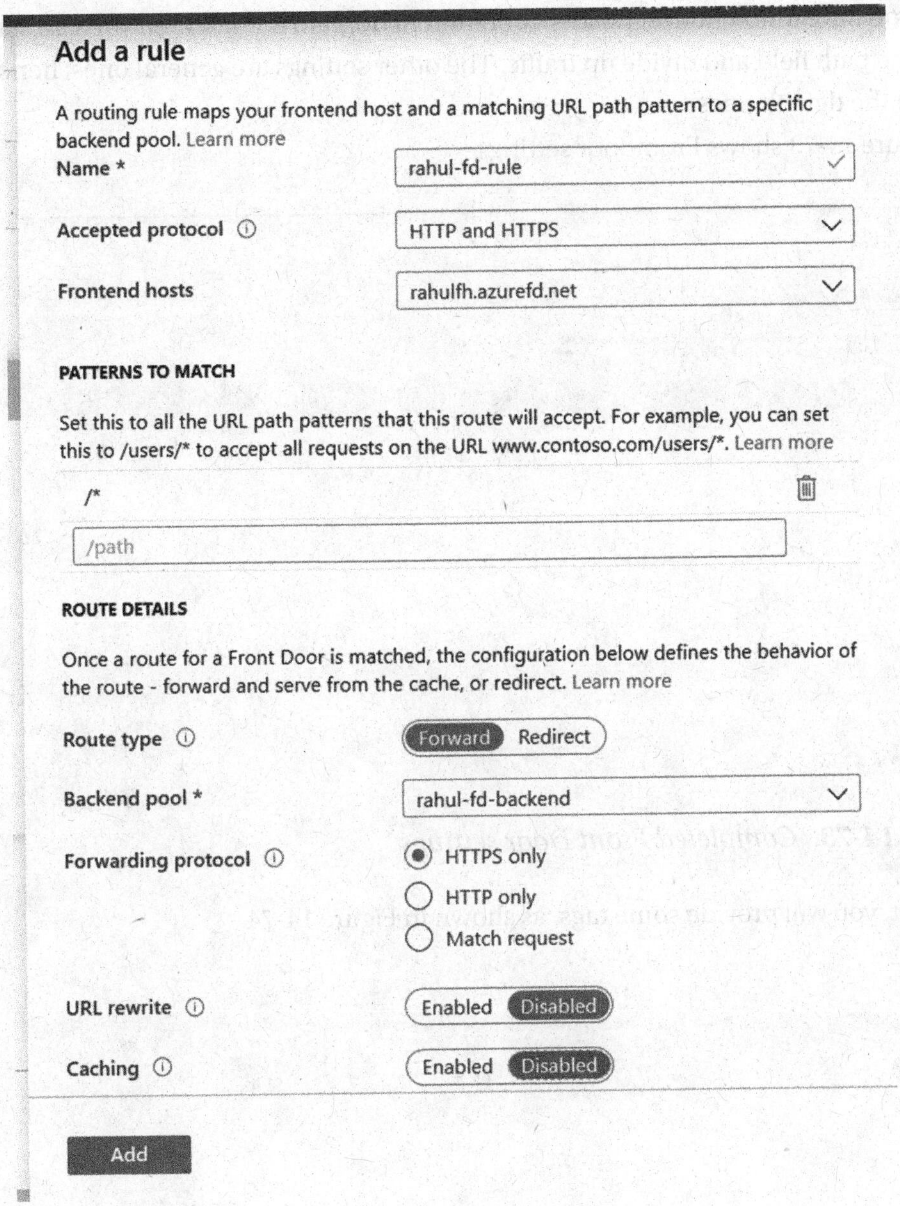

Add a rule

A routing rule maps your frontend host and a matching URL path pattern to a specific backend pool. Learn more

Name *   rahul-fd-rule   ✓

Accepted protocol ⓘ   HTTP and HTTPS   ⌄

Frontend hosts   rahulfh.azurefd.net   ⌄

PATTERNS TO MATCH

Set this to all the URL path patterns that this route will accept. For example, you can set this to /users/* to accept all requests on the URL www.contoso.com/users/*. Learn more

/*   🗑

/path

ROUTE DETAILS

Once a route for a Front Door is matched, the configuration below defines the behavior of the route - forward and serve from the cache, or redirect. Learn more

Route type ⓘ   (Forward   Redirect)

Backend pool *   rahul-fd-backend   ⌄

Forwarding protocol ⓘ   ◉ HTTPS only
                                ○ HTTP only
                                ○ Match request

URL rewrite ⓘ   (Enabled   Disabled)

Caching ⓘ   (Enabled   Disabled)

    Add

Figure 14-72. Adding a rule

If you have different host headers or different domain names, then you can set them up in the path field and divide up traffic. The other settings are general ones; hence, let's go with the default ones.

Figure 14-73 shows Frontdoor settings.

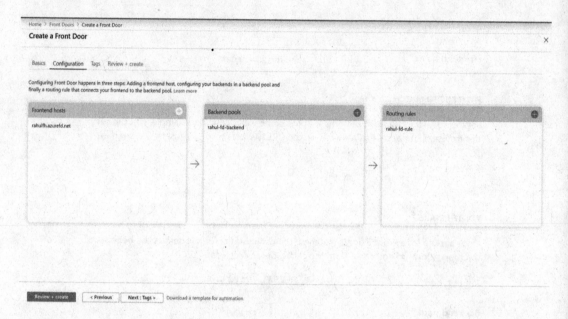

Figure 14-73. *Completed Front Door settings*

Next, you will provide some tags, as shown in Figure 14-74.

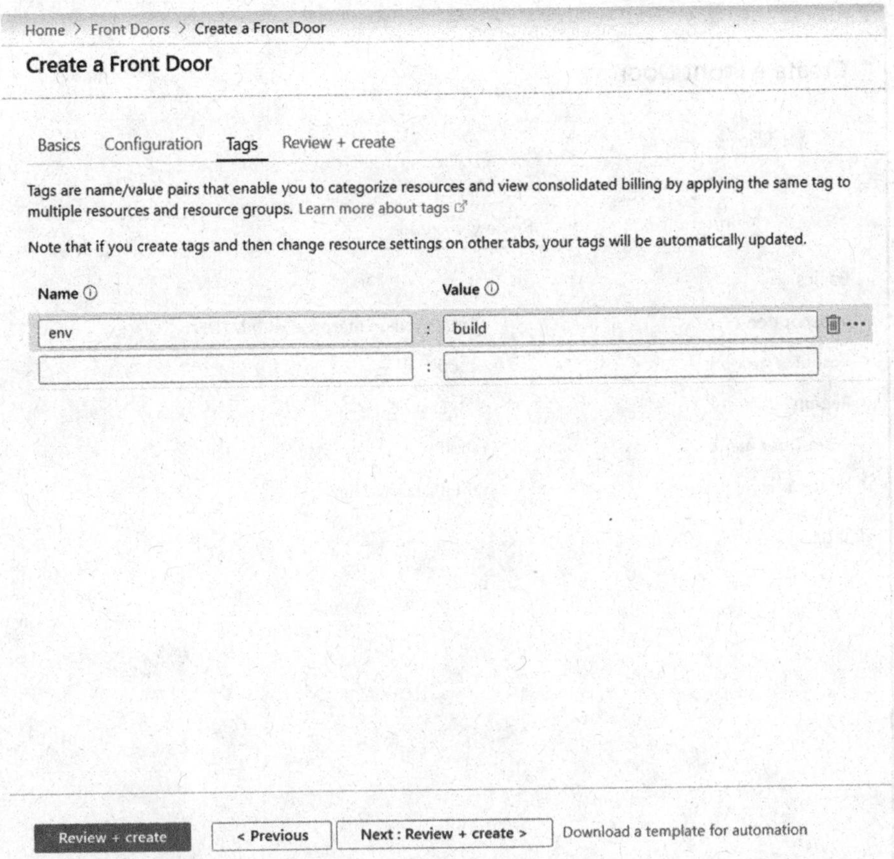

Home > Front Doors > Create a Front Door

Create a Front Door

Basics   Configuration   **Tags**   Review + create

Tags are name/value pairs that enable you to categorize resources and view consolidated billing by applying the same tag to multiple resources and resource groups. Learn more about tags ☐

Note that if you create tags and then change resource settings on other tabs, your tags will be automatically updated.

Name ⓘ		Value ⓘ	
env	:	build	🗑 ⋯
	:		

[Review + create]   [< Previous]   [Next : Review + create >]   Download a template for automation

Figure 14-74. *Front Door tags*

Finally, you will see the "Review + create" screen, as shown in Figure 14-75

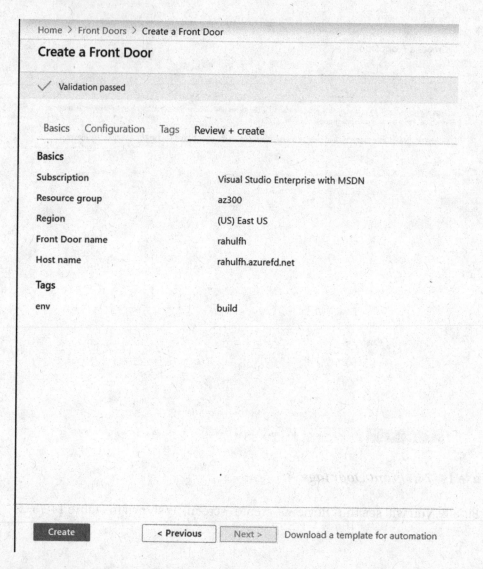

Figure 14-75. *Front Door, "Review + create" screen*

Let's click Create. After the probe is successfully created, your screen will look like Figure 14-76.

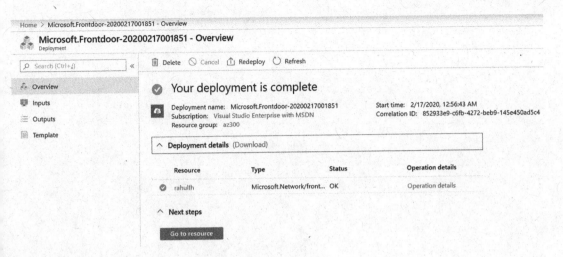

Figure 14-76. *Front Door deployment complete*

The resource will look like Figure 14-77.

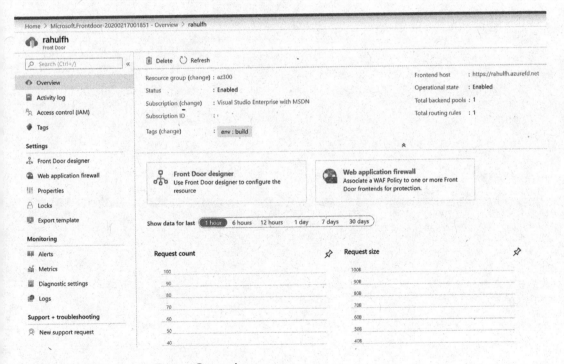

Figure 14-77. *Front Door, Overview screen*

And that finishes our load balancing chapter.

CHAPTER 15

Multifactor Authentication

In this chapter, we will discuss multifactor authentication. *Multifactor authentication* is when you add another way, besides a username and password, to authenticate users. This creates another layer to help secure your apps, services, and more.

Microsoft Azure Active Directory supports multifactor authentication. It does have an extra cost unless you are a Premium Active Directory user.

In this chapter, before discussing multifactor authentication, I will explain how you add a guest user, say, a user with a Yahoo account.

Adding a Guest User

In this section, you will see how to add a guest user. Go to Active Directory, and in the Users section, click "New guest user," as shown in Figure 15-1.

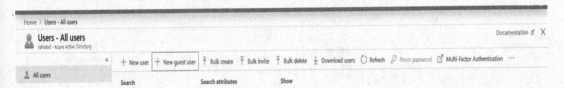

Figure 15-1. *Clicking "New guest user"*

561

© Rahul Sahay 2020
R. Sahay, *Microsoft Azure Architect Technologies Study Companion*,
https://doi.org/10.1007/978-1-4842-6200-9_15

I have created a user with a Yahoo mail, as shown in Figure 15-2. You can give your user an email ID. Then click Invite.

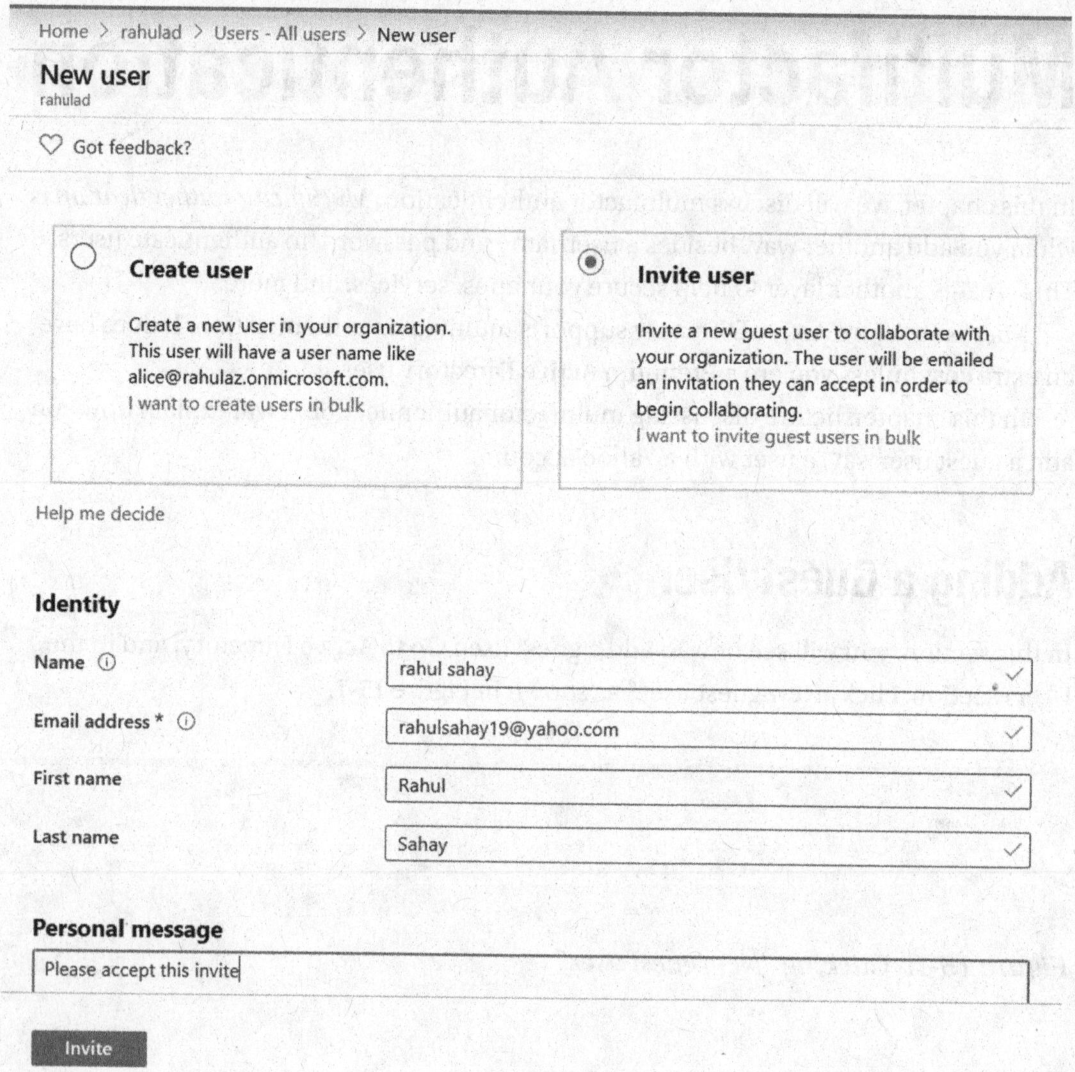

Home > rahulad > Users - All users > New user

New user
rahulad

♡ Got feedback?

○ **Create user**

Create a new user in your organization. This user will have a user name like alice@rahulaz.onmicrosoft.com.
I want to create users in bulk

◉ **Invite user**

Invite a new guest user to collaborate with your organization. The user will be emailed an invitation they can accept in order to begin collaborating.
I want to invite guest users in bulk

Help me decide

Identity

Name ⓘ	rahul sahay ✓
Email address * ⓘ	rahulsahay19@yahoo.com ✓
First name	Rahul ✓
Last name	Sahay ✓

Personal message

Please accept this invite

Invite

***Figure 15-2.** Inviting a user*

Then, check your email for an invitation from Microsoft, as shown in Figure 15-3.

Please only act on this email if you trust the organization represented below. In rare cases, individuals may receive fraudulent invitations from bad actors posing as legitimate companies. **If you were not expecting this invitation, proceed with caution.**

Organization: rahulad
Domain: rahulaz.onmicrosoft.com

This message was provided by the sender and is not from Microsoft Corporation.

RS   **Message from rahulad:**

Please accept this invite

If you accept this invitation, you'll be sent to https://myapps.microsoft.com/?tenantid=0226f998-5340-44f9-a238-3e7e5b9da535&login_hint=rahulsahay19@yahoo.com.

Accept invitation

Figure 15-3. *Email from Microsoft*

Click the "Accept invitation" button in the email. This will take you to the screen shown in Figure 15-4.

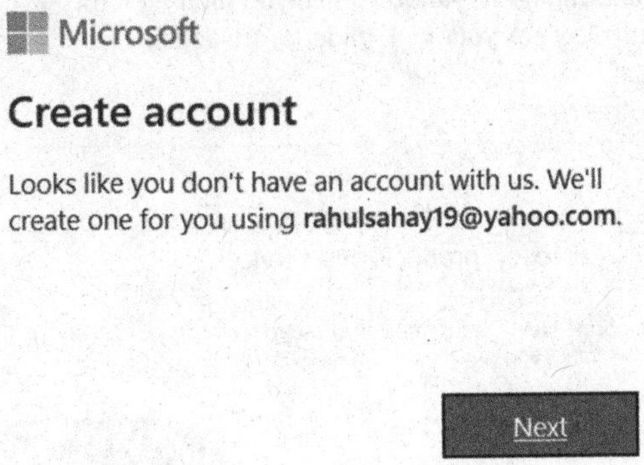

■■ Microsoft

Create account

Looks like you don't have an account with us. We'll create one for you using **rahulsahay19@yahoo.com**.

Next

Figure 15-4. *Microsoft confirmation*

Click the Next button and provide the password that you want to use, as shown in Figure 15-5.

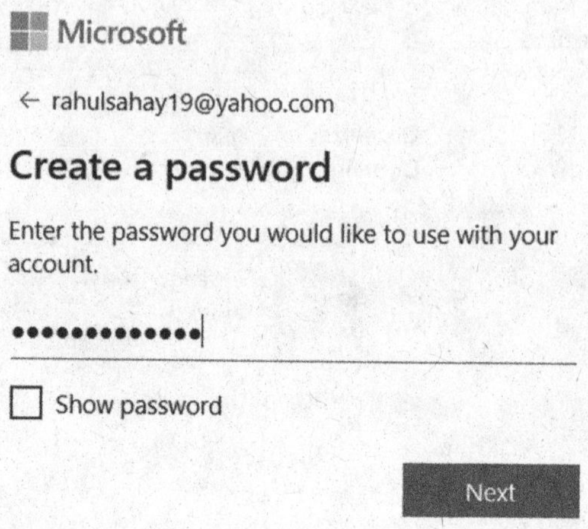

Figure 15-5. Password screen

Next, verify your address with the code that you receive in email, as shown in Figure 15-6.

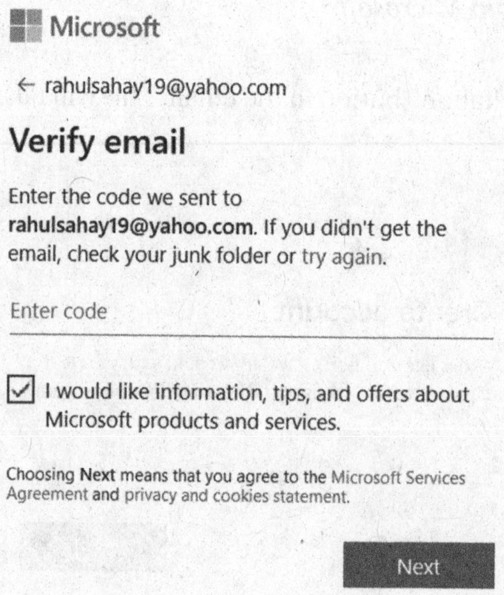

Figure 15-6. Verifying email address

Next, you need to enter the captcha code and click Next, as shown in Figure 15-7.

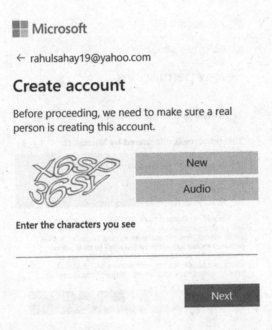

Figure 15-7. *Captcha confirmation*

Next, click the "Looks good!" button to continue, as shown in Figure 15-8.

Figure 15-8. *Security information*

Next comes the consent screen, as shown in Figure 15-9.

Figure 15-9. *Consent screen*

Next, you need to verify your phone number for additional security, as shown in Figure 15-10.

Figure 15-10. *More information required*

Click Next to continue. You'll see the screen in Figure 15-11.

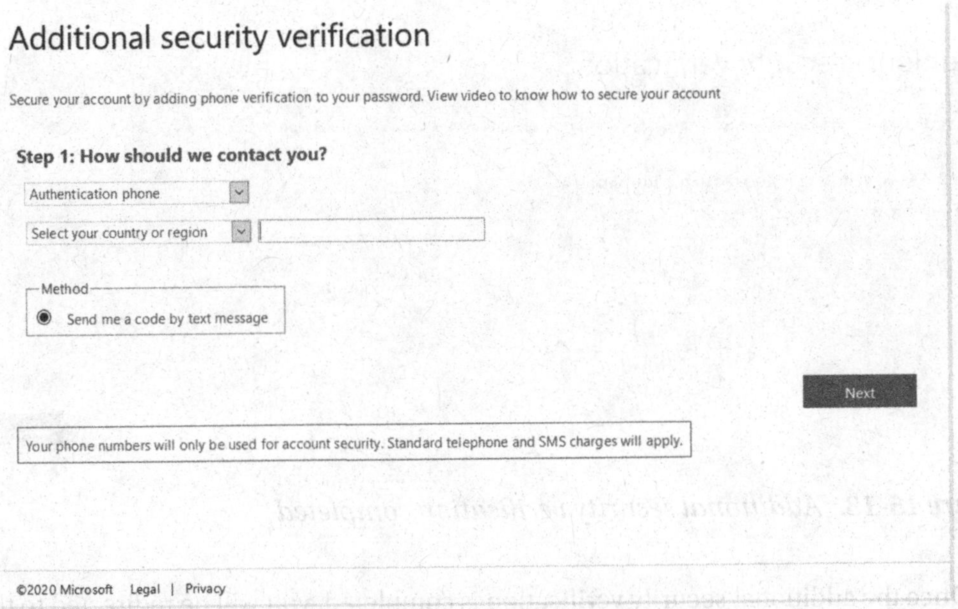

Additional security verification

Secure your account by adding phone verification to your password. View video to know how to secure your account

Step 1: How should we contact you?

Authentication phone ⌄

Select your country or region ⌄

— Method —
◉   Send me a code by text message

Next

Your phone numbers will only be used for account security. Standard telephone and SMS charges will apply.

©2020 Microsoft   Legal | Privacy

Figure 15-11. *Additional security verification*

You can enter your cell phone number and click Next, as shown in Figure 15-12.

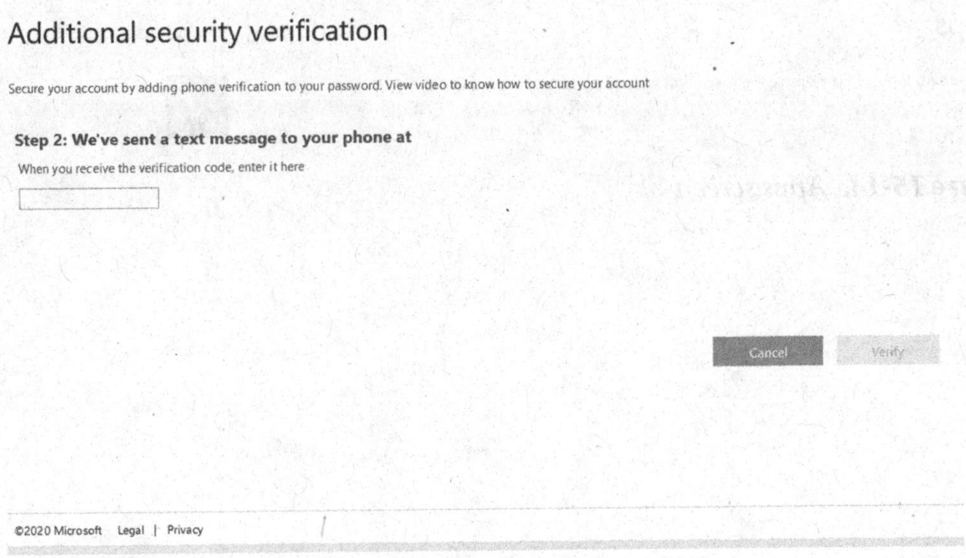

Additional security verification

Secure your account by adding phone verification to your password. View video to know how to secure your account

Step 2: We've sent a text message to your phone at
When you receive the verification code, enter it here

Cancel   Verify

©2020 Microsoft   Legal | Privacy

Figure 15-12. *Additional security verification, step 2*

Enter the code sent to your call phone and click Verify, as shown in Figure 15-13.

Additional security verification

Secure your account by adding phone verification to your password. View video to know how to secure your account

Step 2: We've sent a text message to your phone at

Verification successful!

Figure 15-13. *Additional security verification completed*

Once the additional security verification is completed, you will be redirected to the Apps screen, as shown in Figure 15-14.

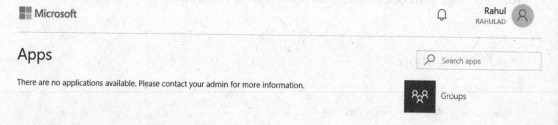

Figure 15-14. *Apps screen*

With the newly created credentials, you can log in to the Azure portal. Upon login, you will land on the screen shown in Figure 15-15.

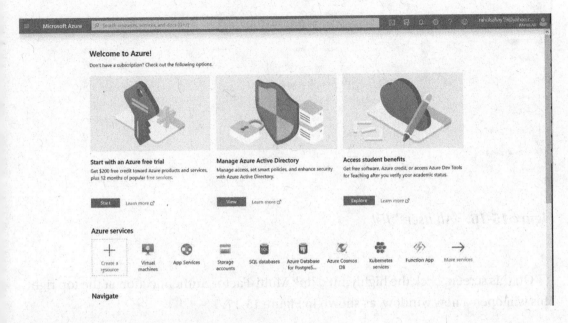

Figure 15-15. *Azure AD home page*

Enabling Multifactor Authentication

In this section, you will learn how to enable multifactor authentication. As an example, when I go to Azure Active Directory, I can see the users shown in Figure 15-16.

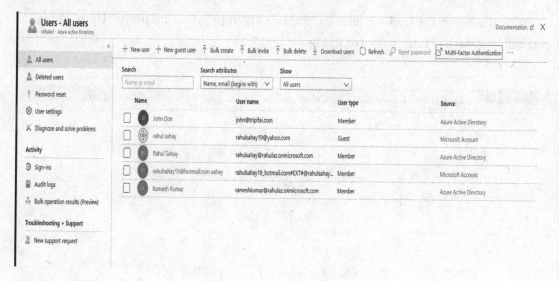

Figure 15-16. *"All users" list*

On this screen, click the highlighted link Multi-Factor Authentication at the top right. This will open a new window, as shown in Figure 15-17.

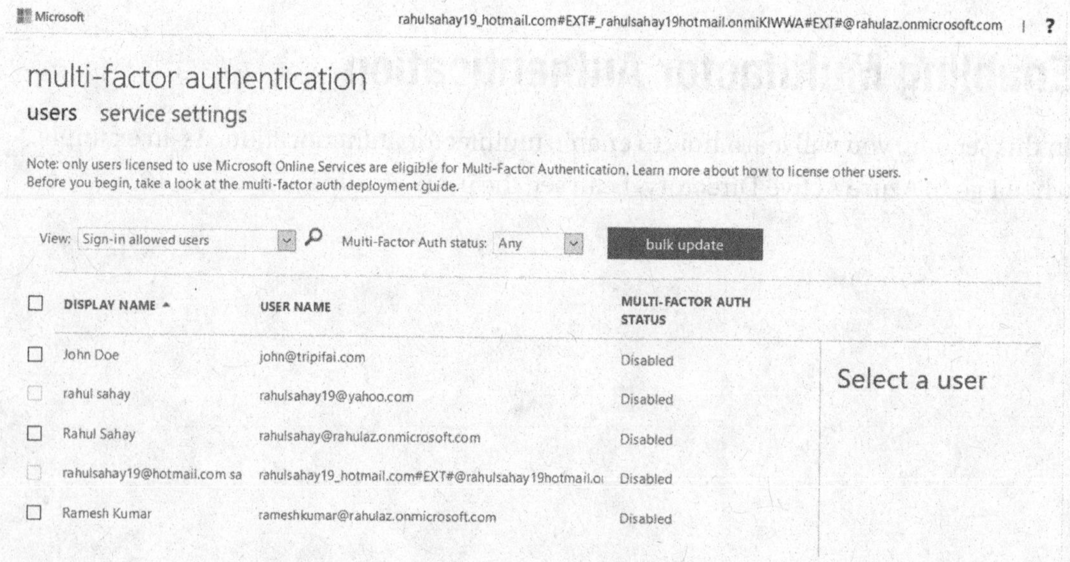

Figure 15-17. *MFA page*

Here, you can see that the accounts with Yahoo and Hotmail addresses are disabled because they are not part of this Active Directory; hence, you can't enable multifactor for these two accounts, as shown in Figure 15-18.

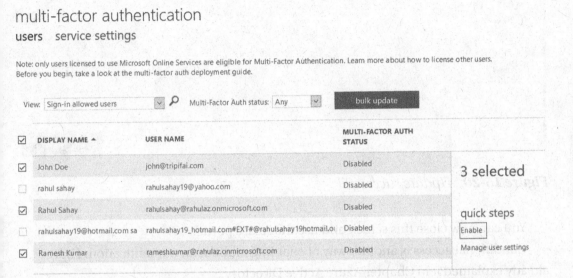

Figure 15-18. *Enabling MFA for Yahoo and Hotmail accounts*

After you click Enable, the screen shown in Figure 15-19 will open.

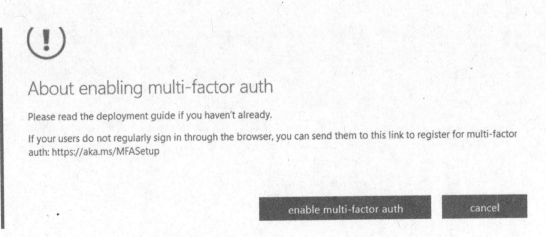

Figure 15-19. *About enabling MFA screen*

Click the button to enable multifactor authentication one account at a time. Or, you can select all the accounts and enable them in one shot. Your screen will look like Figure 15-20.

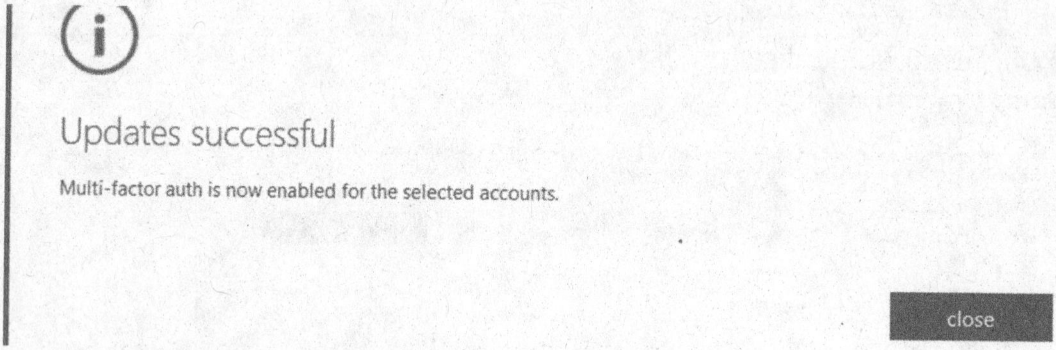

Updates successful

Multi-factor auth is now enabled for the selected accounts.

close

Figure 15-20. Update successful

You can now close this screen and use the Azure portal.

Conditional access is another way of enabling multifactor authentication. I have already explained it in Chapter Azure Active Directory..

Setting Up Fraud Alerts

To set up a fraud alert, you need to click MFA in the left panel, as shown in Figure 15-21.

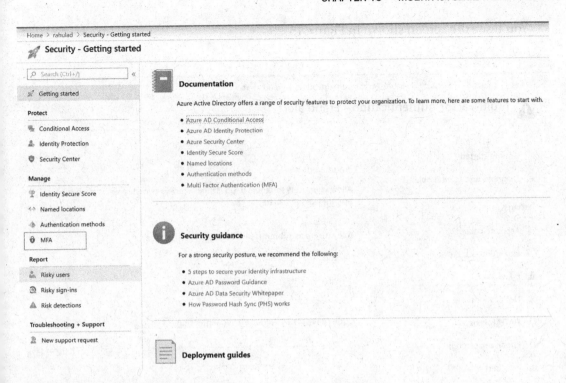

Figure 15-21. *Fraud alert setup*

Next click "Fraud alert," as shown in Figure 15-22.

Figure 15-22. *"Fraud alert" link*

You'll see the screen shown in Figure 15-23.

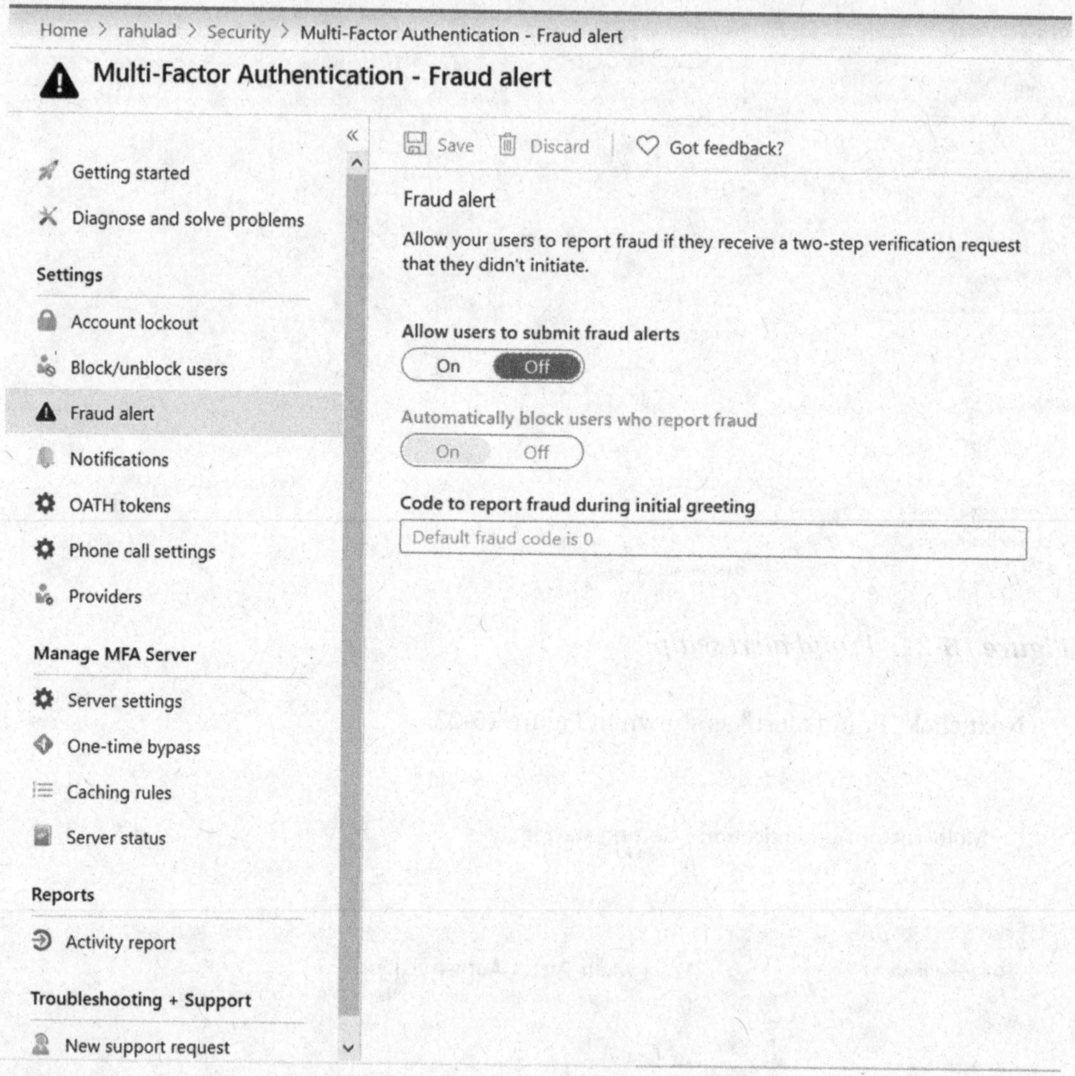

Home > rahulad > Security > Multi-Factor Authentication - Fraud alert

⚠ **Multi-Factor Authentication - Fraud alert**

«

💾 Save   🗑 Discard | ♡ Got feedback?

🚀 Getting started
✂ Diagnose and solve problems

Settings

🔒 Account lockout
👥 Block/unblock users
⚠ Fraud alert
🔔 Notifications
⚙ OATH tokens
⚙ Phone call settings
👥 Providers

Manage MFA Server

⚙ Server settings
⬦ One-time bypass
☰ Caching rules
▦ Server status

Reports

⟳ Activity report

Troubleshooting + Support

👤 New support request

Fraud alert

Allow your users to report fraud if they receive a two-step verification request that they didn't initiate.

Allow users to submit fraud alerts

[On | **Off**]

Automatically block users who report fraud

[On | Off]

Code to report fraud during initial greeting

[Default fraud code is 0]

Figure 15-23. *"Fraud alert" screen*

By default, fraud alerts will be off, but you can turn them on with the options shown in Figure 15-24. If you have enabled fraud alerts on an account, you will be notified if your user ID and password are compromised. Also, if you get a one-time password sent to your mobile phone, then you can go ahead and block the account.

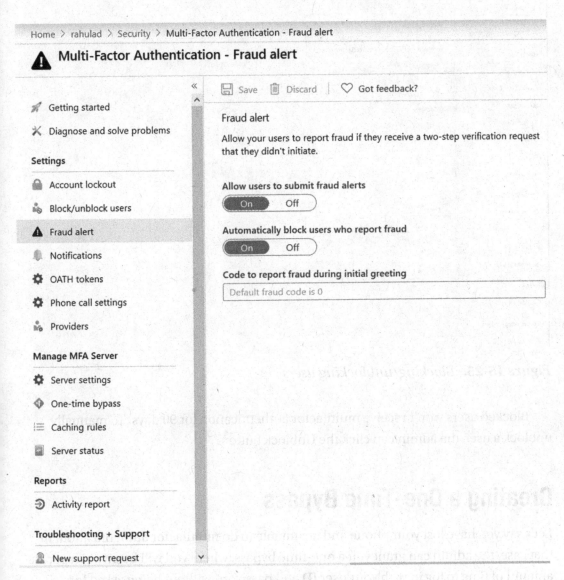

Figure 15-24. Enabled automatic blocking of users

Now, you can block or unblock users on the screen shown in Figure 15-25.

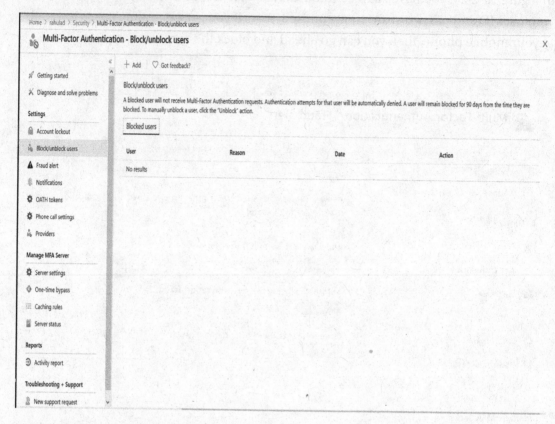

Figure 15-25. Blocking/unblocking users

Blocked users won't receive multifactor authentication for 90 days. To manually unblock a user, the admin can click the Unblock button.

Creating a One-Time Bypass

Let's say you have lost your phone and are unable to do multifactor authentication. In that case, the admin can grant you a one-time bypass, where you will be given a specific amount of time to log in with your user ID and password without being asked for multifactor authentication. Figure 15-26 shows the flow for a one-time bypass.

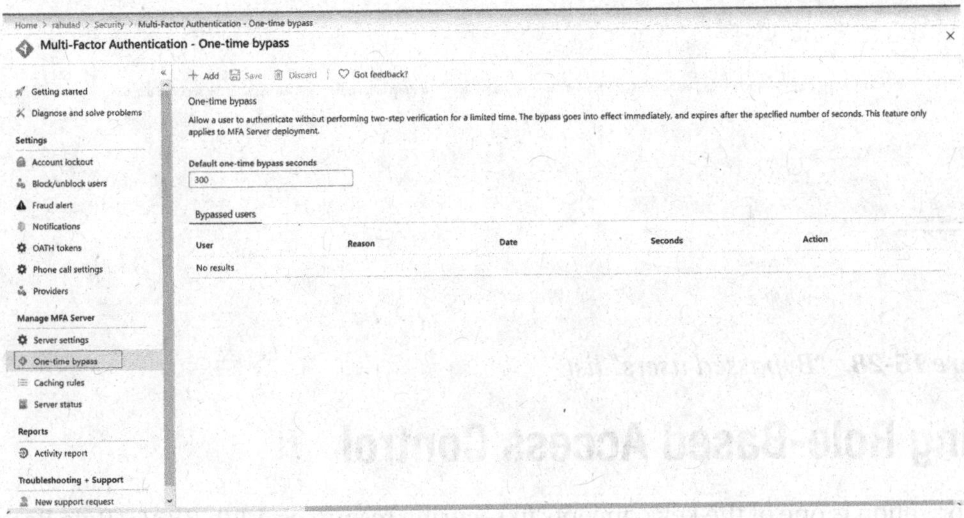

Figure 15-26. *"One-time bypass" screen*

Click Add, as shown in Figure 15-27.

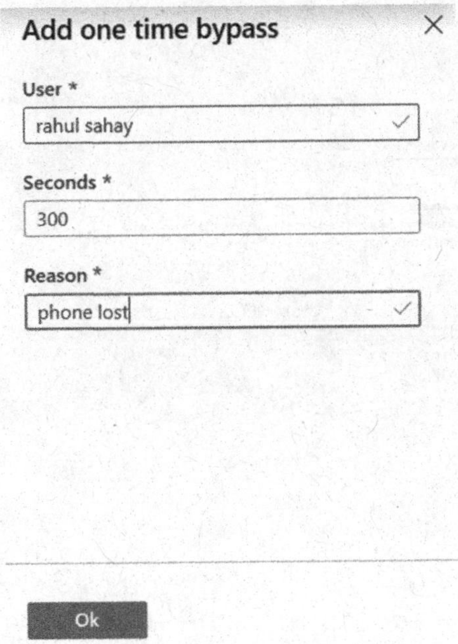

Figure 15-27. *One-time bypass setting*

Once you've added a user, you will see the user reflected in the "Bypassed users" list, as shown in Figure 15-28. The countdown for the time limit starts immediately.

+ Add   💾 Save   🗑 Discard | ♡ Got feedback?

One-time bypass

Allow a user to authenticate without performing two-step verification for a limited time. The bypass goes into effect immediately, and expires after the specified number of seconds. This feature only applies to MFA Server deployment.

Default one-time bypass seconds

| 300 |

Bypassed users

User	Reason	Date	Seconds	Action
rahul sahay	phone lost	02/17/2020, 11:49:00 PM	300	Cancel

Figure 15-28. *"Bypassed users" list*

Using Role-Based Access Control

Authorization is one of the key concepts in securing resources. With RBAC (Role Based Access Control) you can grant access to users to specify the exact resources that they can access. This can be applied at the resource group level or the resource level, as shown in Figure 15-29.

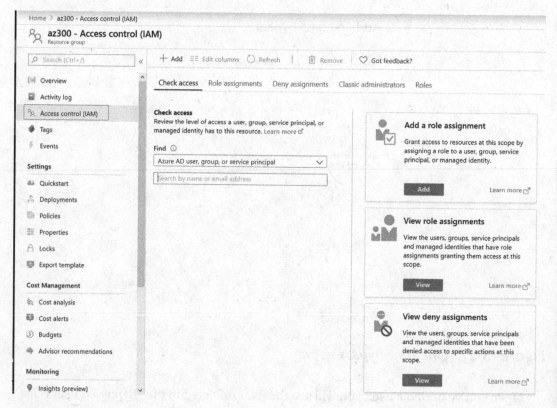

Figure 15-29. *Access control*

Let's first check the access I have here. You can see that I have a user with the address rahulsahay19@yahoo.com. Hence, I can search for that user, as shown in Figure 15-30.

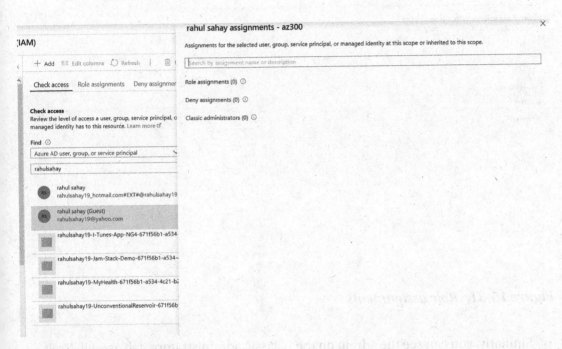

Figure 15-30. Adding a role

You can see that this user doesn't have any access. Now, let's check the default access. By default, you usually have some role assignments already set up. Some of them are inherited from the subscription level, as shown in Figure 15-31.

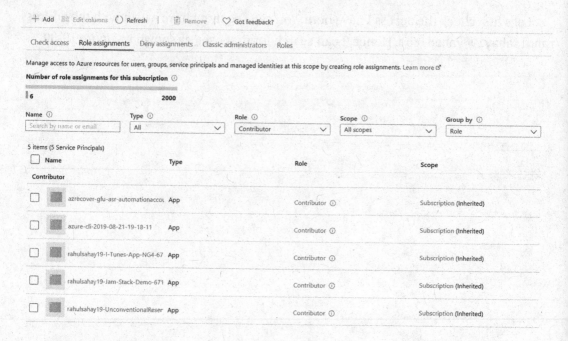

Figure 15-31. Role assignments

Similarly, you can see the admin on the "Classic administrators" tab as well. Now, let's say you want to grant access to the newly created user. For that case, you can go to the "Role assignments" tab and click the "Add role assignment" button, as shown in Figure 15-32.

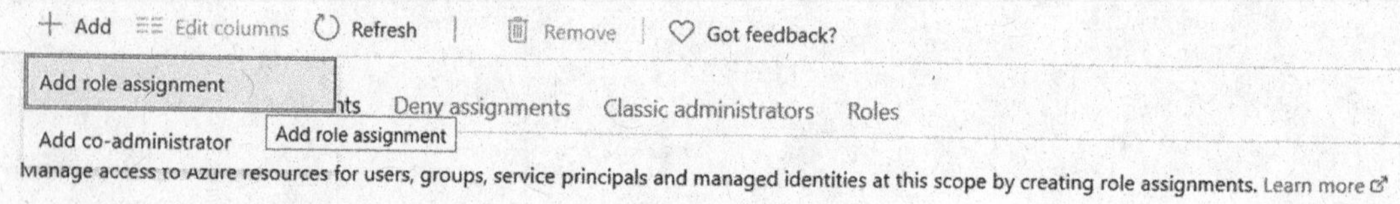

Figure 15-32. Adding the role assignment option

Click "Role assignment." This will bring you to the next screen, where you will see a bunch of roles. The most important are the owner, contributor, and reader roles.

- The Reader role means users will have read-only access. They can log in to the portal and view the resources, but that's it. They can't perform any actions on them.

- The Contributor role is like a full set of permissions. Contributors can create, delete, and edit resources. They can't give those permissions to other users.

- The Owner role is the most powerful. Owners can do all the things that a contributor can do plus grant access to other users.

You will also see service-associated roles like the API management reader role, Azure service bus data owner, etc. This means you can even grant very fine-grained permissions to one user.

Let's grant Contributor access to a new user, as shown in Figure 15-33.

Figure 15-33. *Adding a role assignment*

Once the role gets applied successfully, the list will look like Figure 15-34.

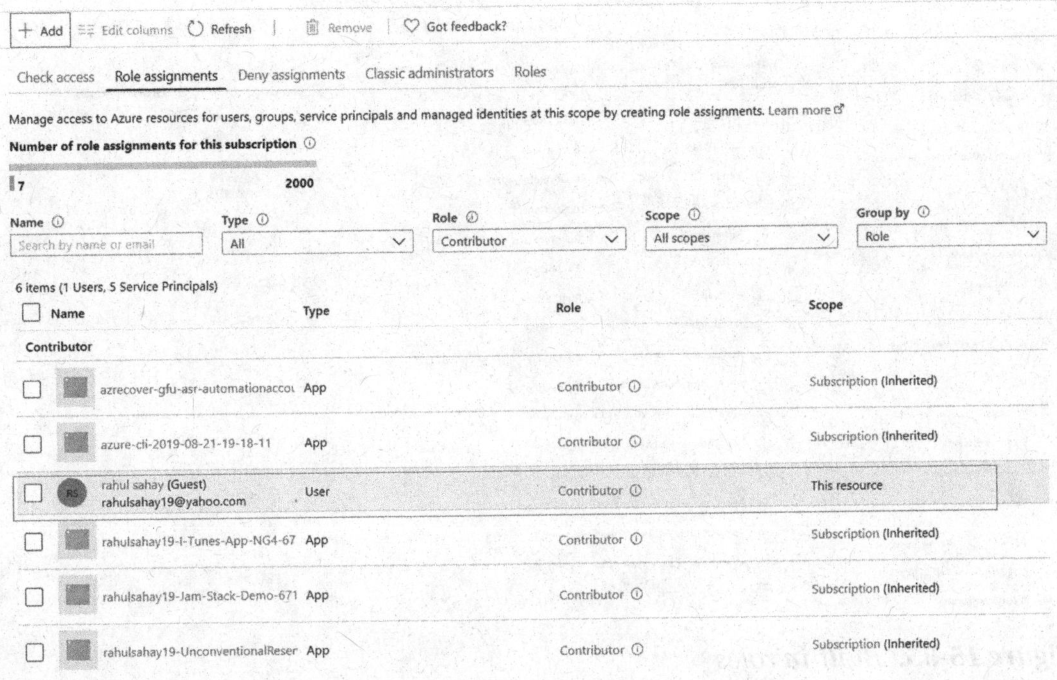

Figure 15-34. Added role assignment

Also, you can do the opposite by granting access such as Deny access from the "Deny assignments" tab. Here, you can select the user and block them from doing specific operations. Let's see what built-in roles there are. You can go to the subscription level and look at the Roles tab. In Figure 15-35, you can see tons of roles are there, even at the granular level.

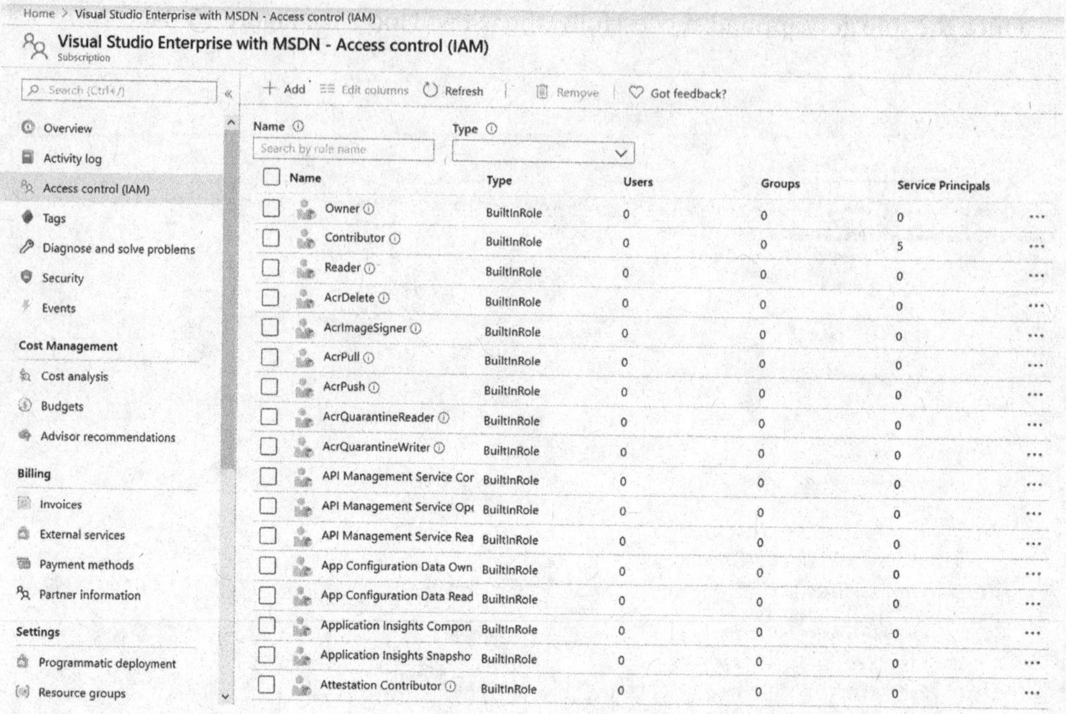

Figure 15-35. *Built-in roles*

Many times a built-in role is not sufficient; hence, you will need some kind of custom role. For that, you can create your own role with a PowerShell script or with the CLI.

Refer to `http://bit.ly/rbac-azure` to see how to create custom roles. Basically, you take an existing role like the Reader role, save it in JSON format, and then modify it. Finally, you execute the script.

CHAPTER 16

App Services

The Azure App Service platform gives you the flexibility to quickly build, deploy, and scale web apps created with popular frameworks such as .NET, .NET Core, Node.js, Java, PHP, etc., in containers or running on any operating system. An app service is a platform as a service. App services help to streamline the deployment process.

Creating an App Service

Let's create an app service. In this section, you will see how to create a web app. Let's search for *web or App Services* in "All services," as shown in Figure 16-1.

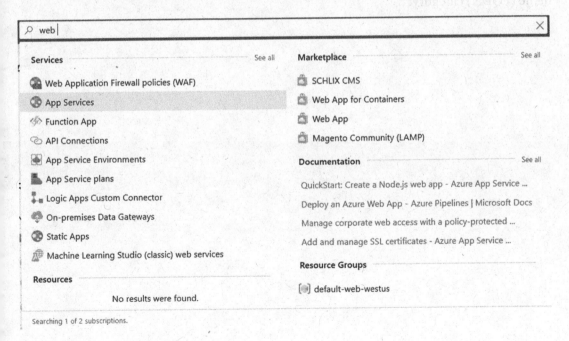

Figure 16-1. *App Services search*

585

© Rahul Sahay 2020
R. Sahay, *Microsoft Azure Architect Technologies Study Companion*,
https://doi.org/10.1007/978-1-4842-6200-9_16

Click App Services. The screen shown in Figure 16-2 will open.

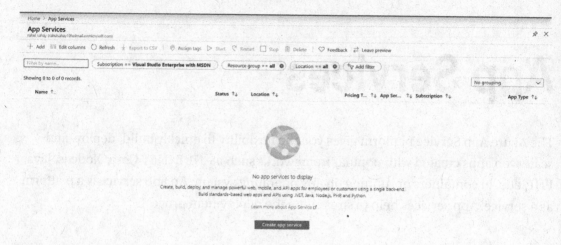

Figure 16-2. *App Services screen*

Click the Add button and enter the details on the Basics tab shown in Figure 16-3. Make sure to give the URL a unique name as it falls under the fully qualified domain name (FQDN) category.

Home > App Services > Web App

Web App

Basics   Monitoring   Tags   Review + create

App Service Web Apps lets you quickly build, deploy, and scale enterprise-grade web, mobile, and API apps running on any platform. Meet rigorous performance, scalability, security and compliance requirements while using a fully managed platform to perform infrastructure maintenance. Learn more 🗗

Project Details

Select a subscription to manage deployed resources and costs. Use resource groups like folders to organize and manage all your resources.

Subscription * ⓘ	Visual Studio Enterprise with MSDN ⌄
└─ Resource Group * ⓘ	az300 ⌄
	Create new

Instance Details

Name *	rahulsahaytes ✓
	.azurewebsites.net
Publish *	(Code) Docker Container
Runtime stack *	.NET Core 3.0 (Current) ⌄
Operating System *	(Linux) **Windows**
Region *	East US ⌄
	ⓘ Not finding your App Service Plan? Try a different region.

Figure 16-3. *Web App screen, Basics tab*

You can select several different frameworks as the runtime stack, as shown in Figure 16-4.

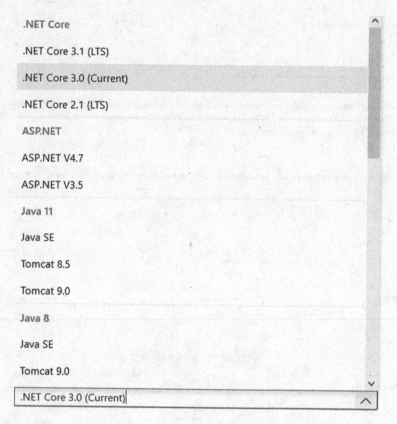

Figure 16-4. Framework options

Similarly, you can choose to publish the web app as a container, as shown in Figure 16-5.

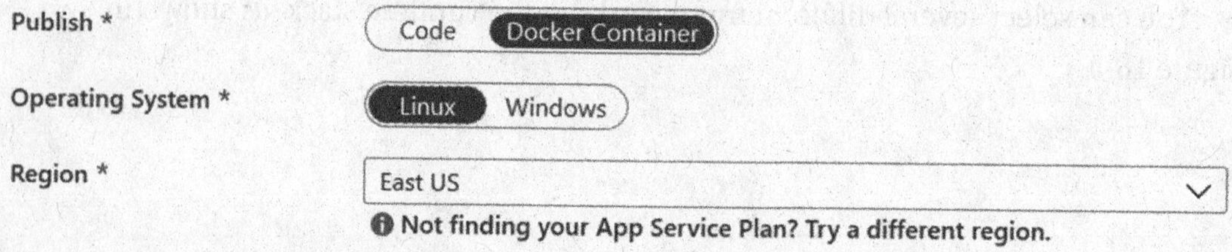

Publish *	Code · Docker Container
Operating System *	Linux · Windows
Region *	East US

ⓘ Not finding your App Service Plan? Try a different region.

Figure 16-5. Publish settings

I will discuss containers in more detail in Chapter 18. For now, let's switch to code mode with Windows Server. Click on Code and then Windows as shown in Figure 16-5.

Next you'll see the App Service Plan section. Figure 16-6 shows the default settings.

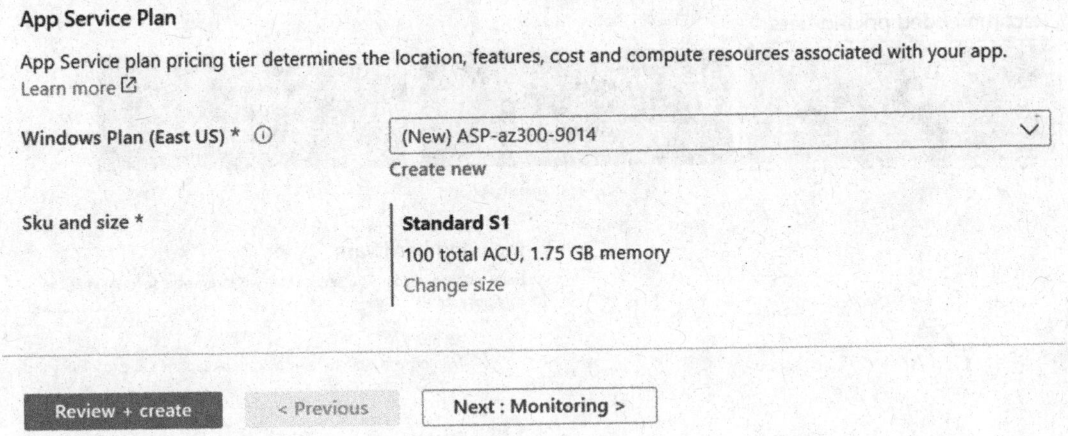

App Service Plan

App Service plan pricing tier determines the location, features, cost and compute resources associated with your app.
Learn more 🗗

Windows Plan (East US) * ⓘ   (New) ASP-az300-9014   ∨
                                  Create new

Sku and size *   **Standard S1**
                                  100 total ACU, 1.75 GB memory
                                  Change size

Review + create   < Previous   Next : Monitoring >

Figure 16-6. *App Service Plan section*

You can choose to change the size from the Spec Picker, as shown in Figure 16-7.

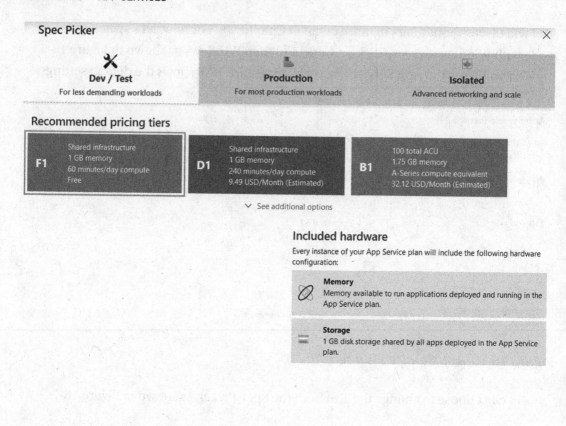

Figure 16-7. Spec Picker screen

As you can see, I have chosen the free one. The other options are going to cost you. For staging or production, you should a plan that best suits you. You can make a more educated decision by visiting the app service plan comparison available at https://bit.ly/app-service-plans.

Next, click Monitoring and keep the default settings, as shown in Figure 16-8.

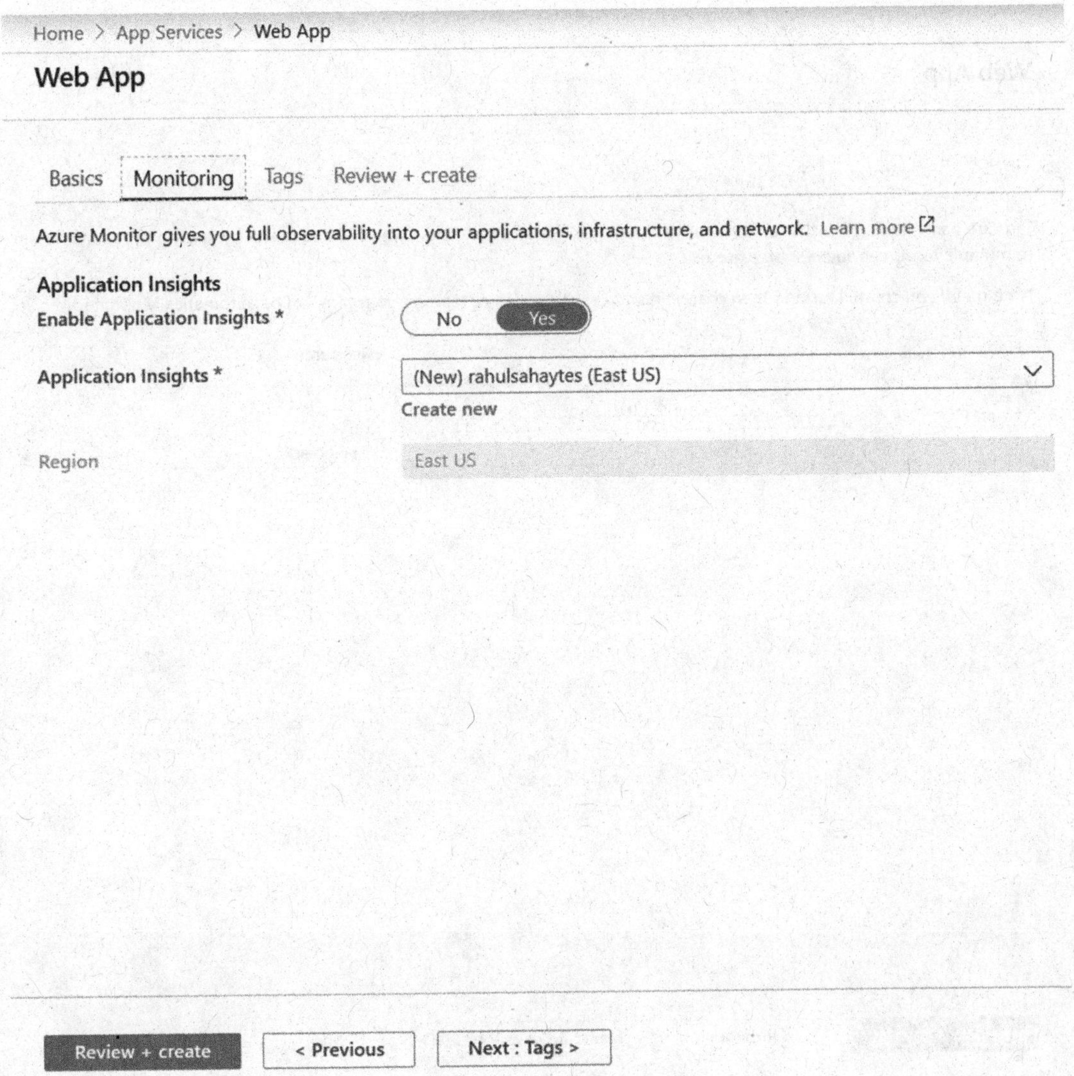

Home > App Services > Web App

Web App

Basics | Monitoring | Tags   Review + create

Azure Monitor gives you full observability into your applications, infrastructure, and network. Learn more ☒

Application Insights

Enable Application Insights *   (No   Yes)

Application Insights *   (New) rahulsahaytes (East US)   ⌄
                          Create new

Region   East US

Review + create   < Previous   Next : Tags >

Figure 16-8. *Web App screen, Monitoring tab*

Next comes the Tags tab, as shown in Figure 16-9.

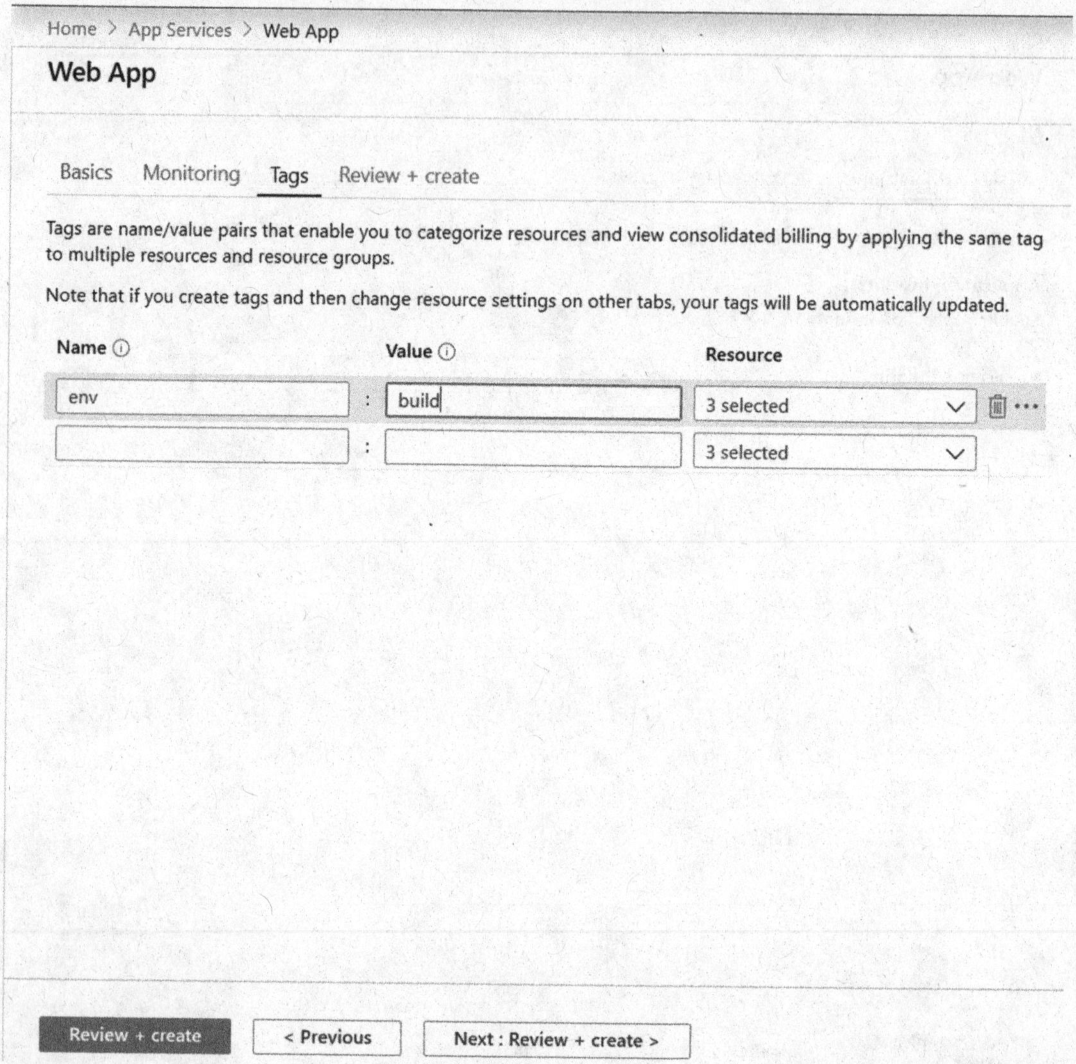

Home > App Services > Web App

Web App

Basics   Monitoring   **Tags**   Review + create

Tags are name/value pairs that enable you to categorize resources and view consolidated billing by applying the same tag to multiple resources and resource groups.

Note that if you create tags and then change resource settings on other tabs, your tags will be automatically updated.

Name ⓘ		Value ⓘ	Resource	
env	:	build	3 selected ⌄	🗑 •••
	:		3 selected ⌄	

Review + create   < Previous   Next : Review + create >

Figure 16-9. *Web App screen, Tags tab*

Finally comes the "Review + create" tab, as shown in Figure 16-10.

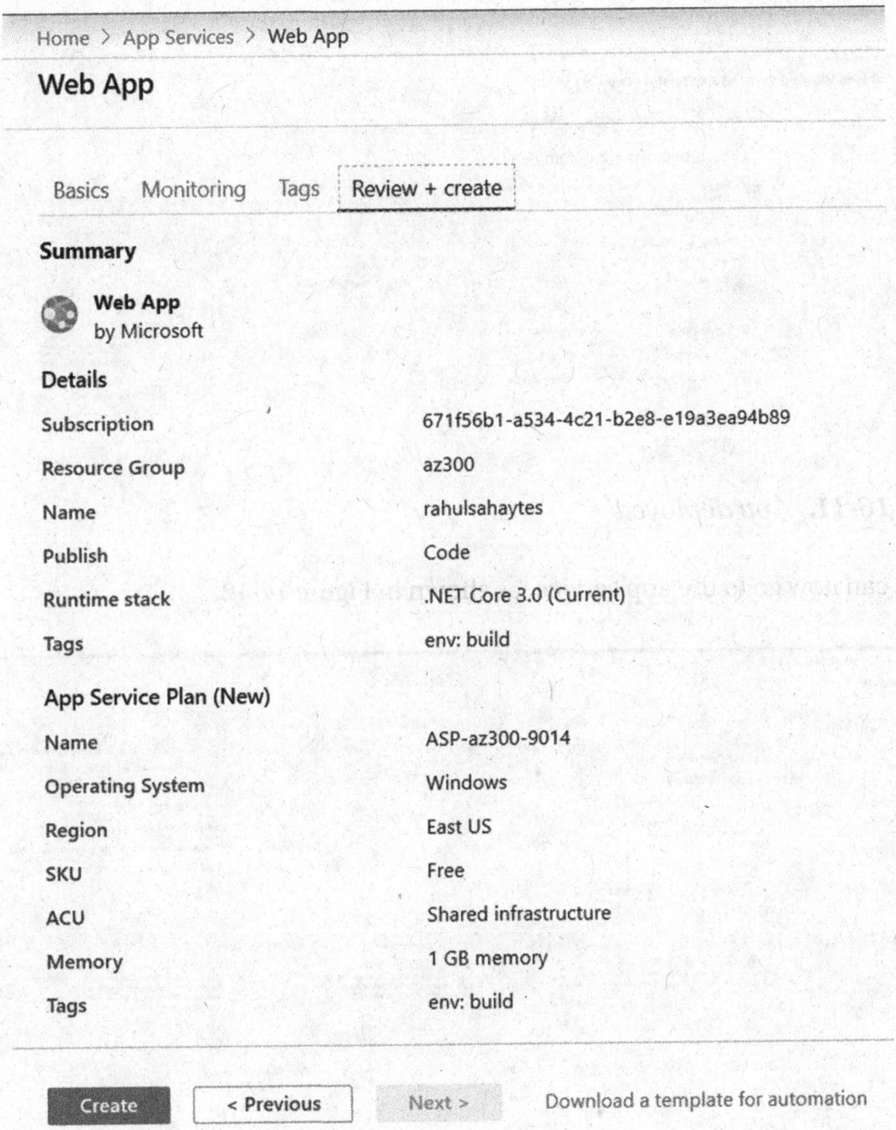

Home > App Services > Web App

Web App

Basics   Monitoring   Tags   **Review + create**

Summary

Web App
by Microsoft

Details

Subscription	671f56b1-a534-4c21-b2e8-e19a3ea94b89
Resource Group	az300
Name	rahulsahaytes
Publish	Code
Runtime stack	.NET Core 3.0 (Current)
Tags	env: build

App Service Plan (New)

Name	ASP-az300-9014
Operating System	Windows
Region	East US
SKU	Free
ACU	Shared infrastructure
Memory	1 GB memory
Tags	env: build

Create   < Previous   Next >   Download a template for automation

Figure 16-10. Web App screen, "Review + create" tab

Click the Create button. After the web app has been successfully create, your screen will look like Figure 16-11.

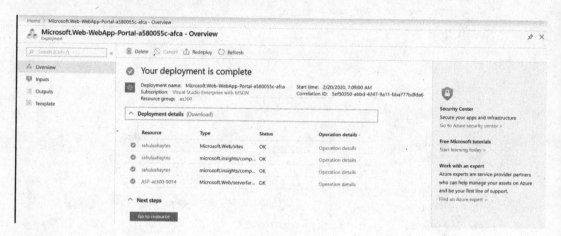

Figure 16-11. *App deployed*

You can now go to the app service, as shown in Figure 16-12.

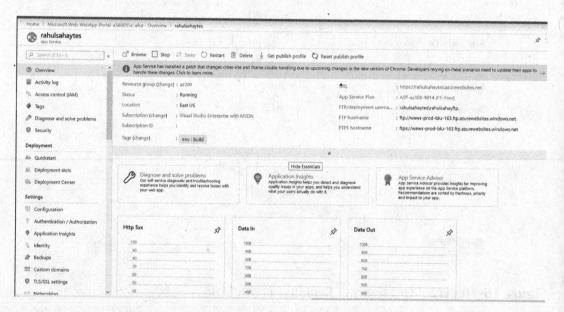

Figure 16-12. *App Service, Overview screen*

You can see the URL that is associated with the app. When you click the URL, you will be taken to the newly created app; for me, this is at `https://rahulsahaytes.azurewebsites.net/`.

You can learn more about deployment options from the Quickstart reference, as shown in Figure 16-13.

Figure 16-13. *Your app service's landing page*

Scale Up/Out Options

In the Settings section, you will see the "Scale up" and "Scale out" options. You can choose the required plan and scale up accordingly, as shown in Figure 16-14.

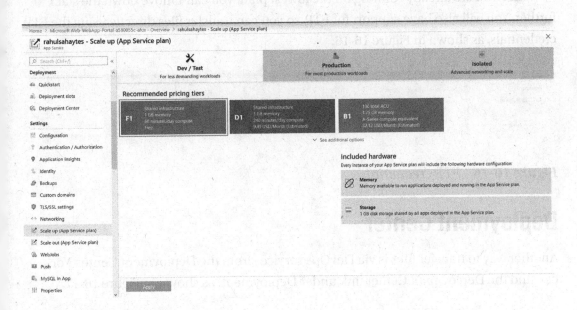

Figure 16-14. *"Scale up" options*

Similarly, you can choose to scale out, as shown in Figure 16-15.

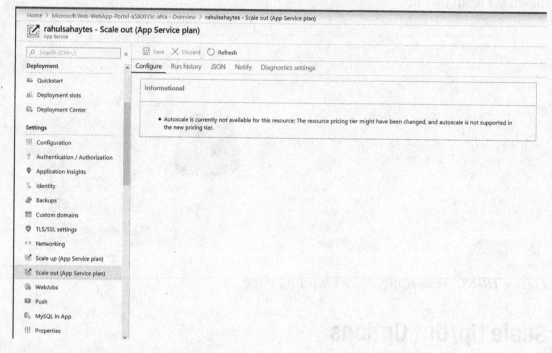

Figure 16-15. "Scale out" options

Since you are already running on the lowest plan, you can't move down the stack further. You will also have support for FTP, so you can transfer files directly using the FTP credentials, as shown in Figure 16-16.

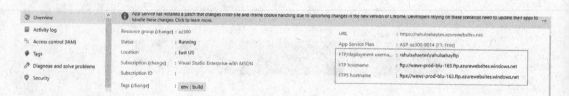

Figure 16-16. FTP credentials

Deployment Center

Another way to transfer files is via DevOps services from the Deployment Center. You can find the Deployment Center link under Deployment, as shown in Figure 16-17.

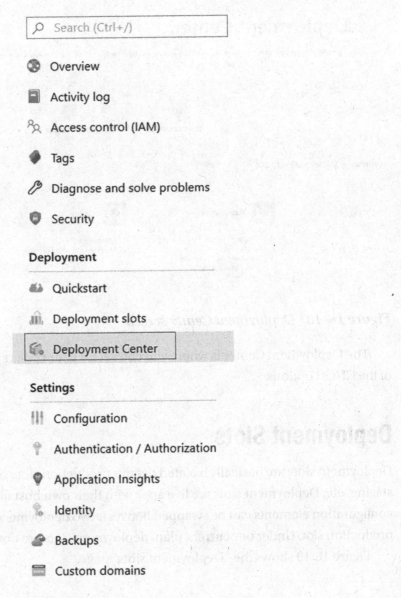

Figure 16-17. *Deployment Center link*

After clicking the Deployment Center link, you will see the screen shown in Figure 16-18.

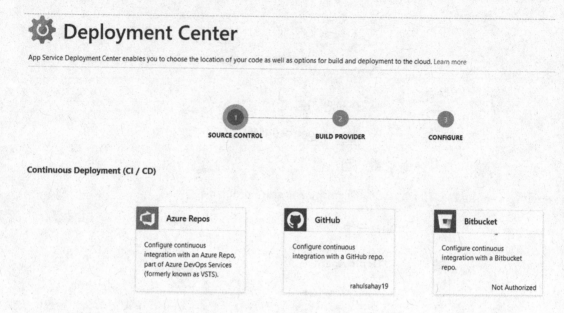

Figure 16-18. *Deployment Center screen*

The Deployment Center is where you can set up your code repo. You can select any of the CI/CD options.

Deployment Slots

Deployment slots are basically isolated default production slots such as development, staging, etc. Deployment slots are live apps with their own host names. App content and configuration elements can be swapped between two deployment slots, including the production slot. Under our current plan, deployment slots are not available.

Figure 16-19 shows the "Deployment slots" page.

Figure 16-19. *"Deployment slots" page*

Therefore, for this example, we need to scale up first to be able to use deployment slots. Let's go ahead and do this using the "Scale-up" option and then select one from production slot. In Figure 16-20, I have chosen the production slot.

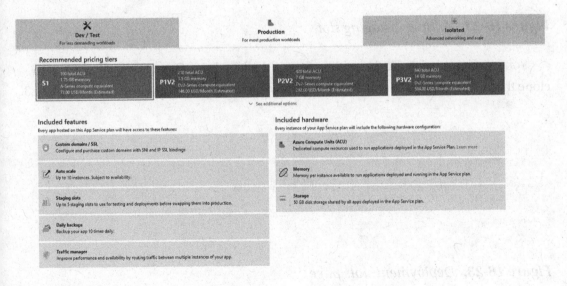

Figure 16-20. *Production slot*

After applying this change, you can see a deployment slot, as shown in Figure 16-21.

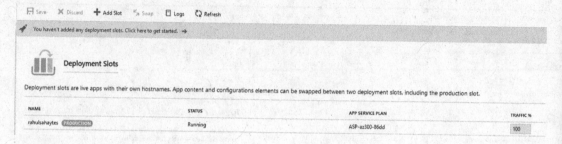

Figure 16-21. *Deployment slots*

By default, you can see there is a production slot here. You can go ahead and add another deployment slot like staging, as shown in Figure 16-22.

Figure 16-22. *Adding a staging slot*

You can choose to clone the settings from a deployed site. Or you may choose not to clone them. After adding the slot, your screen will look like the one shown in Figure 16-23.

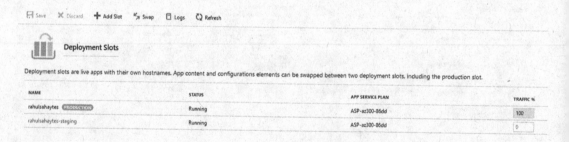

Figure 16-23. *Deployment slots page*

To learn more about deployment slots and this feature, you can refer to https://bit.ly/staging-environments.

App Services for Containers

Let's follow the same process that we followed before to create a web app for containers. Figure 16-24 shows the Basics tab of the Web App screen.

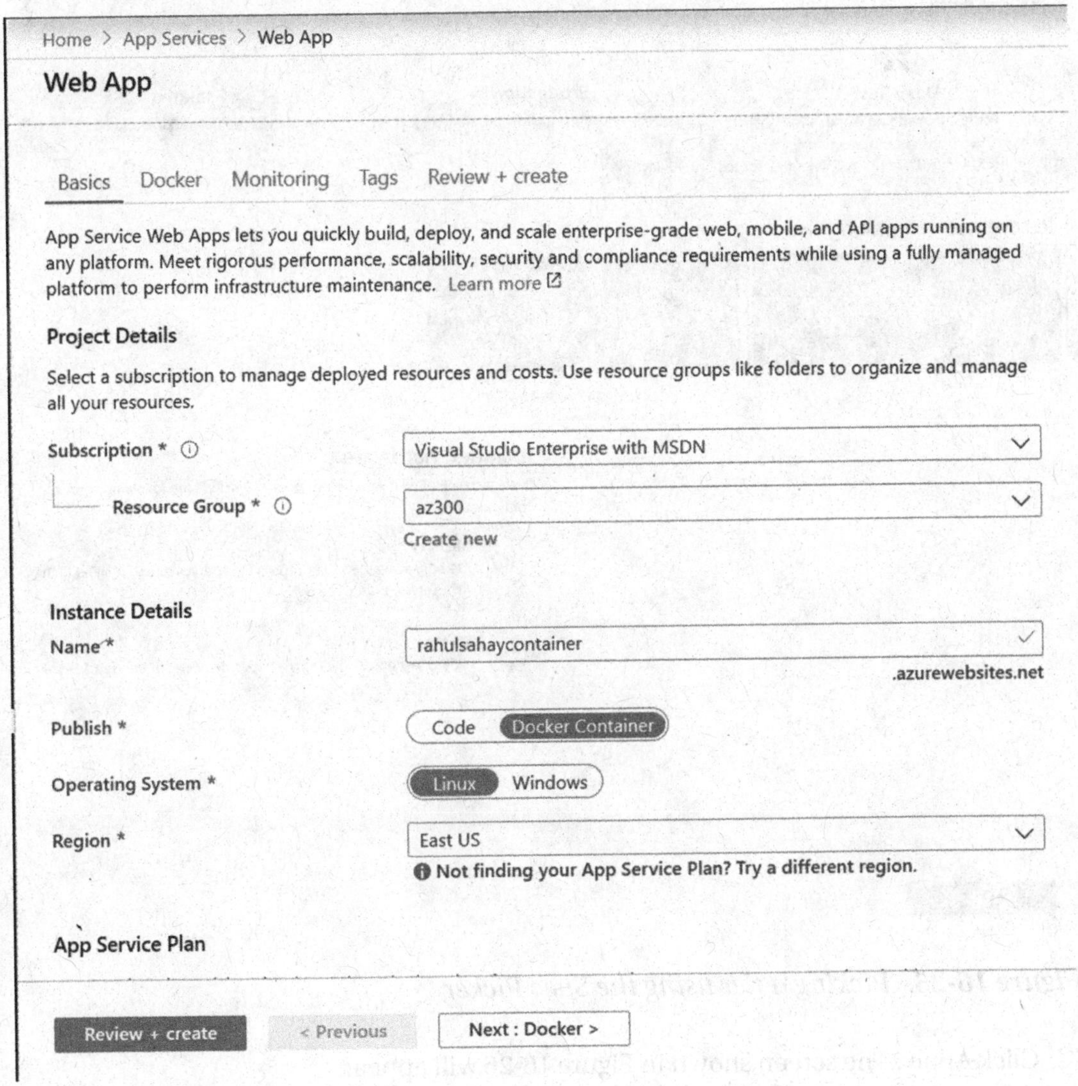

Home > App Services > Web App

Web App

Basics   Docker   Monitoring   Tags   Review + create

App Service Web Apps lets you quickly build, deploy, and scale enterprise-grade web, mobile, and API apps running on any platform. Meet rigorous performance, scalability, security and compliance requirements while using a fully managed platform to perform infrastructure maintenance. Learn more ☒

Project Details

Select a subscription to manage deployed resources and costs. Use resource groups like folders to organize and manage all your resources.

Subscription * ⓘ
Visual Studio Enterprise with MSDN ⌄

Resource Group * ⓘ
az300 ⌄
Create new

Instance Details

Name *
rahulsahaycontainer ✓
.azurewebsites.net

Publish *
Code   Docker Container

Operating System *
Linux   Windows

Region *
East US ⌄
ⓘ Not finding your App Service Plan? Try a different region.

App Service Plan

Review + create   < Previous   Next : Docker >

Figure 16-24. *Web App screen, Basics tab*

Note that I am now changing the SKU and using the free plan under the Linux tier, as shown in Figure 16-25. You can't put both Linux and Windows installations under the same app service plan.

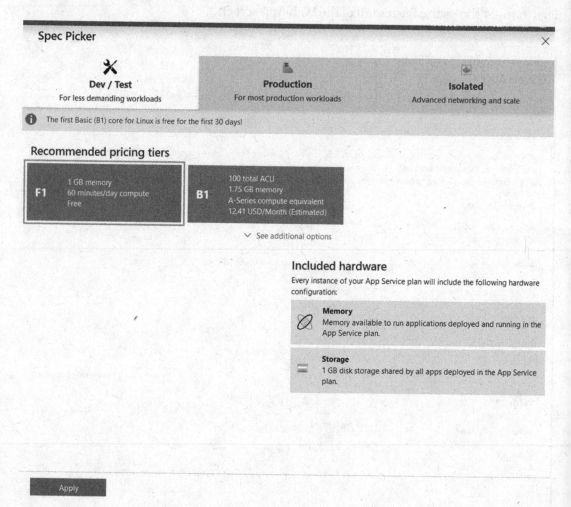

Figure 16-25. *Picking a tier using the Spec Picker*

Click Apply. The screen shown in Figure 16-26 will appear.

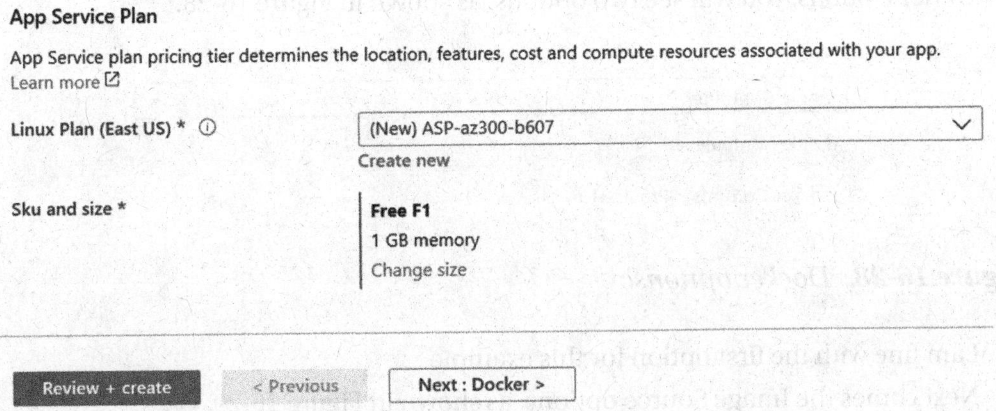

App Service Plan

App Service plan pricing tier determines the location, features, cost and compute resources associated with your app.
Learn more ☑

Linux Plan (East US) * ⓘ   (New) ASP-az300-b607   ∨
                                  Create new

Sku and size *   **Free F1**
                                  1 GB memory
                                  Change size

[Review + create]   [< Previous]   [Next : Docker >]

Figure 16-26. *App Service Plan section*

Next, go to the Docker section, as shown in Figure 16-27.

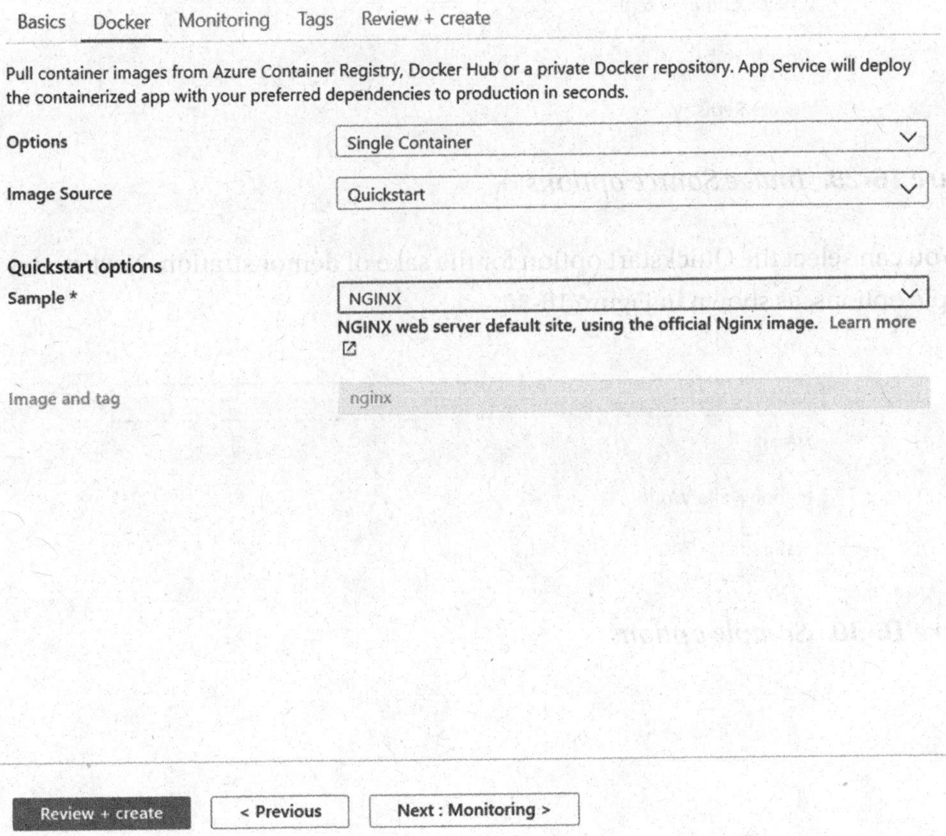

Basics   Docker   Monitoring   Tags   Review + create

Pull container images from Azure Container Registry, Docker Hub or a private Docker repository. App Service will deploy
the containerized app with your preferred dependencies to production in seconds.

Options   Single Container   ∨

Image Source   Quickstart   ∨

Quickstart options

Sample *   NGINX   ∨

                       NGINX web server default site, using the official Nginx image. Learn more
                       ☑

Image and tag   nginx

[Review + create]   [< Previous]   [Next : Monitoring >]

Figure 16-27. *Docker settings*

603

Under Options, you will see two options, as shown in Figure 16-28.

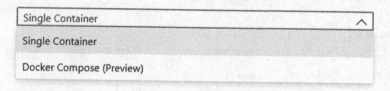

Figure 16-28. *Docker optionsc*

I am fine with the first option for this example.

Next comes the Image Source options, as shown in Figure 16-29.

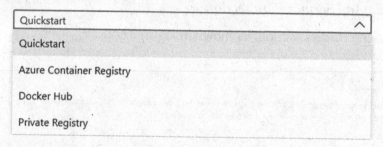

Figure 16-29. *Image Source options*

You can select the Quickstart option for the sake of demonstration. Next comes the Sample options, as shown in Figure 16-30.

NGINX

NGINX

Python Hello World

Static site

Figure 16-30. *Sample options*

Here, I will select the "Static site" option. Hence, the final version of the Docker tab will look like Figure 16-31.

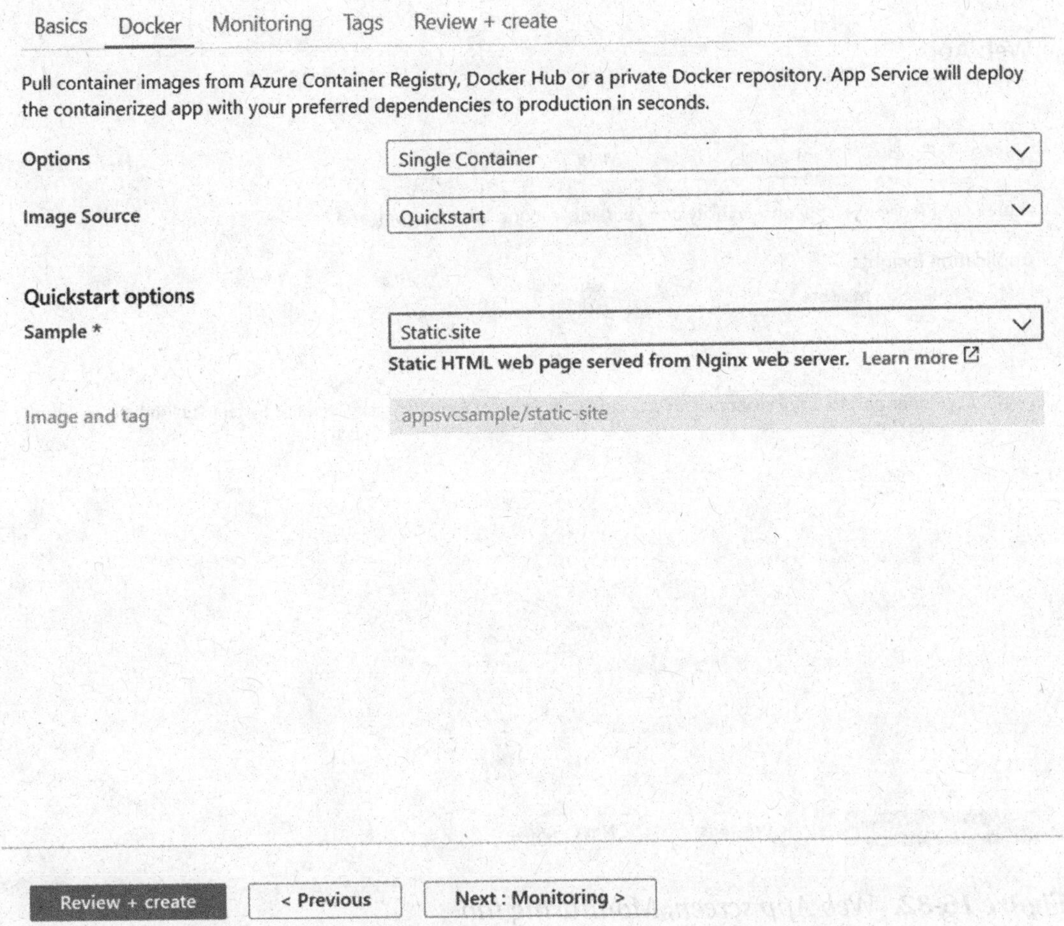

Basics   Docker   Monitoring   Tags   Review + create

Pull container images from Azure Container Registry, Docker Hub or a private Docker repository. App Service will deploy the containerized app with your preferred dependencies to production in seconds.

Options   Single Container   ⌄

Image Source   Quickstart   ⌄

Quickstart options
Sample *   Static.site   ⌄
                                Static HTML web page served from Nginx web server. Learn more ☐

Image and tag   appsvcsample/static-site

[Review + create]   [< Previous]   [Next : Monitoring >]

Figure 16-31. *Docker options*

Next comes the Monitoring tab. You can leave the settings at the defaults, as shown in Figure 16-32.

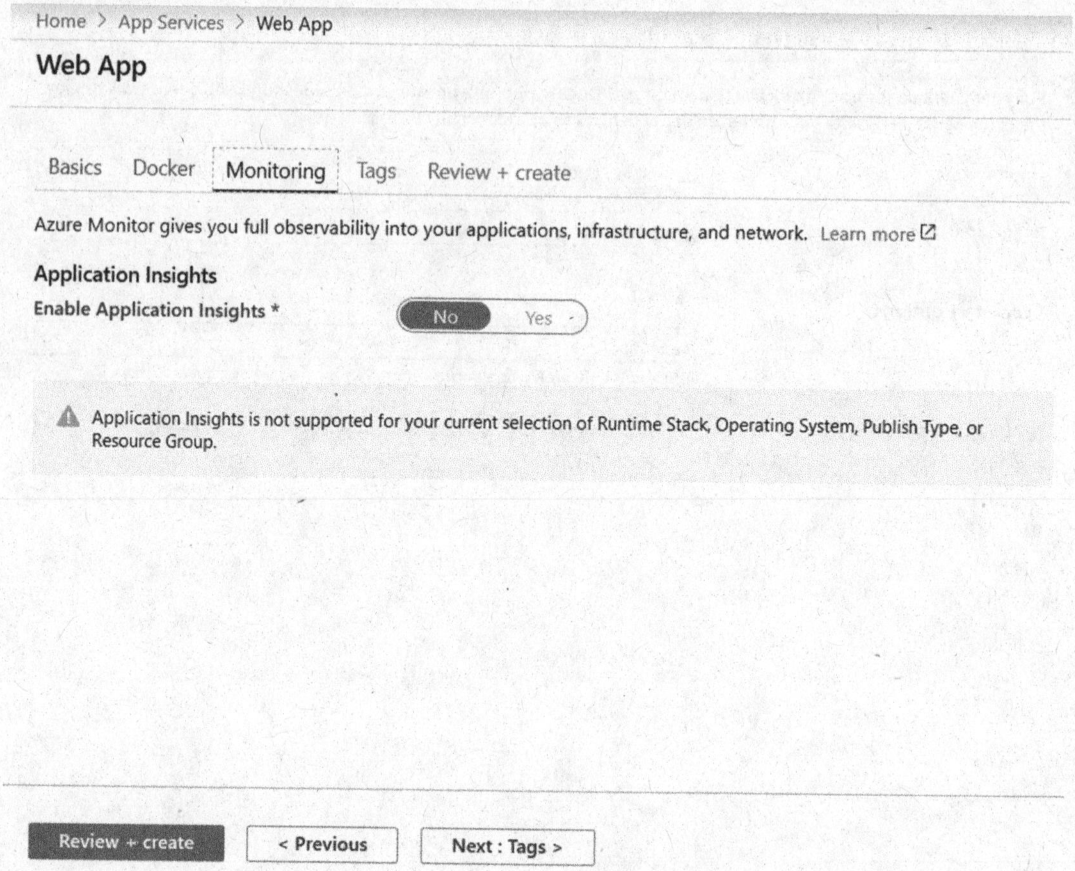

Figure 16-32.   Web App screen, Monitoring tab

Next comes Tags, as shown in Figure 16-33.

Home > App Services > Web App

Web App

Basics   Docker   Monitoring   **Tags**   Review + create

Tags are name/value pairs that enable you to categorize resources and view consolidated billing by applying the same tag to multiple resources and resource groups.

Note that if you create tags and then change resource settings on other tabs, your tags will be automatically updated.

Name ⓘ		Value ⓘ	Resource	
env	:	build	2 selected ⌄	🗑 ⋯
	:		2 selected ⌄	

Review + create		< Previous		Next : Review + create >

Figure 16-33. *Web App screen, Tags tab*

During the template validation, I got the error shown in Figure 16-34.

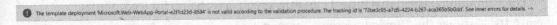

ℹ The template deployment 'Microsoft.Web-WebApp-Portal-e2f1d23d-8584' is not valid according to the validation procedure. The tracking id is '72be3c95-a7d5-4224-b267-aca365b5b0dd'. See inner errors for details. →

Figure 16-34. *Error occurred*

Once you click the error link, you will see more details about it. Basically, this error says you can't mix Windows items with Linux items under the same resource group. Hence, let's return to the first screen and create a new resource group for this Linux container, as shown in Figure 16-35.

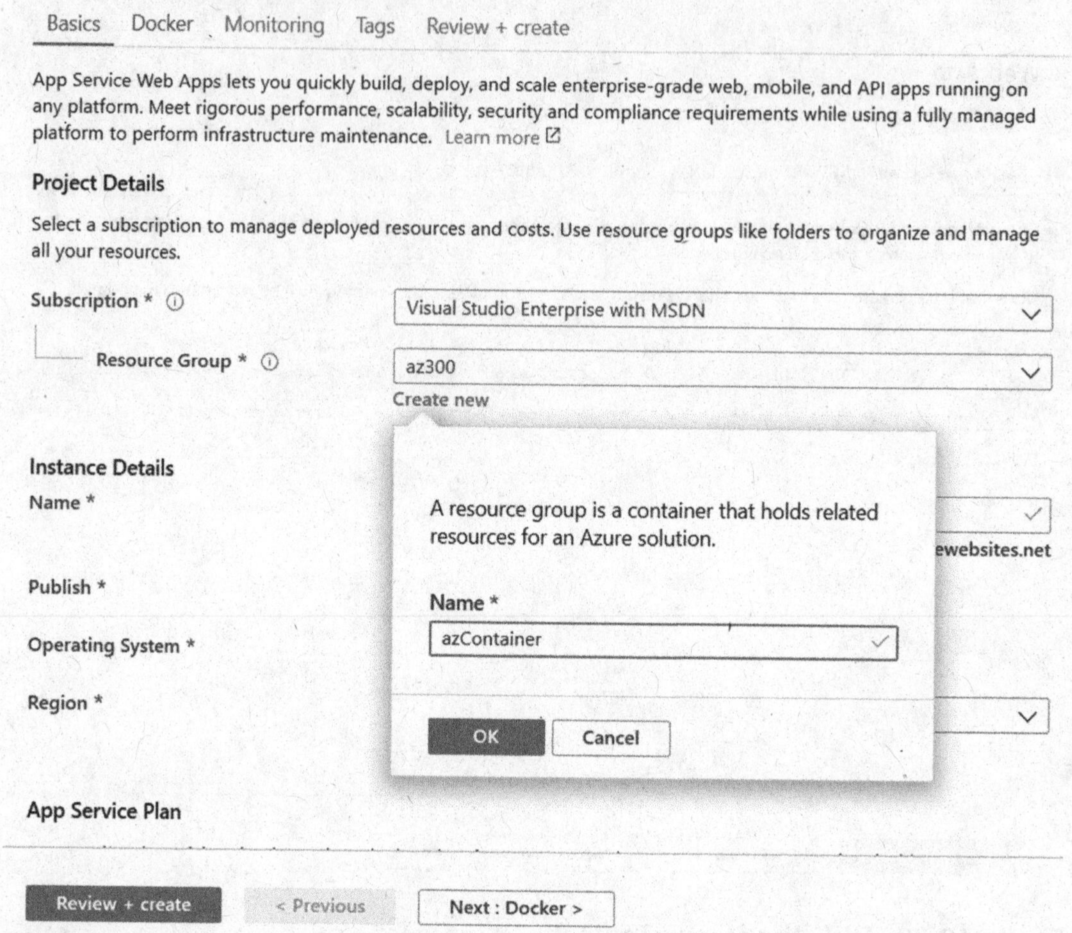

Basics   Docker   Monitoring   Tags   Review + create

App Service Web Apps lets you quickly build, deploy, and scale enterprise-grade web, mobile, and API apps running on any platform. Meet rigorous performance, scalability, security and compliance requirements while using a fully managed platform to perform infrastructure maintenance. Learn more ☒

Project Details

Select a subscription to manage deployed resources and costs. Use resource groups like folders to organize and manage all your resources.

Subscription * ⓘ   Visual Studio Enterprise with MSDN   ⌄

└──── Resource Group * ⓘ   az300   ⌄
                                    Create new

Instance Details

Name *   ✓

                                                                          ewebsites.net

Publish *

Operating System *

Region *   ⌄

A resource group is a container that holds related resources for an Azure solution.

Name *

azContainer   ✓

[OK]   [Cancel]

App Service Plan

───

[Review + create]   [< Previous]   [Next : Docker >]

Figure 16-35. *Creating a new resource group*

The validation passed this time. I can now create a web app for a container. Figure 16-36 shows the "Review + create" screen.

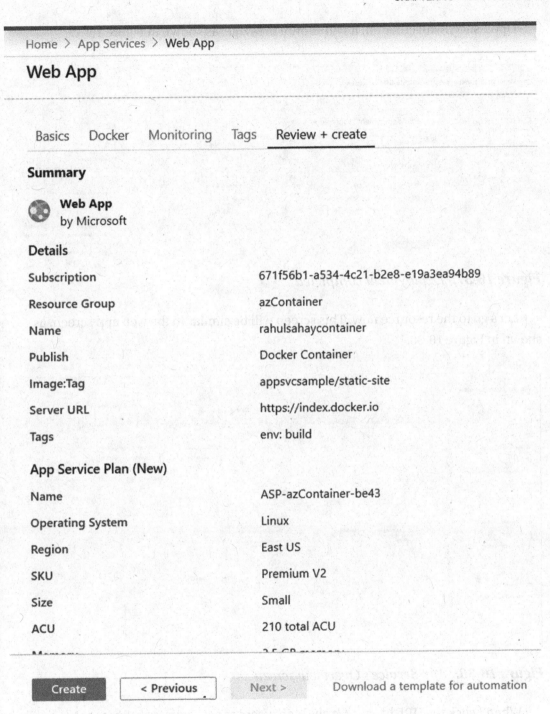

Home > App Services > Web App

Web App

Basics   Docker   Monitoring   Tags   **Review + create**

Summary

Web App
by Microsoft

Details

Subscription	671f56b1-a534-4c21-b2e8-e19a3ea94b89
Resource Group	azContainer
Name	rahulsahaycontainer
Publish	Docker Container
Image:Tag	appsvcsample/static-site
Server URL	https://index.docker.io
Tags	env: build

App Service Plan (New)

Name	ASP-azContainer-be43
Operating System	Linux
Region	East US
SKU	Premium V2
Size	Small
ACU	210 total ACU

| Create | < Previous | Next > | Download a template for automation |

Figure 16-36. Web app review screen

Upon successful creation, it will show a message, as shown in Figure 16-37.

Figure 16-37. *Deployment completed*

Let's go to the resource now. This screen will be similar to the web app screen, as shown in Figure 16-38.

Figure 16-38. *App Service's Overview screen*

When I click the URL https://rahulsahaycontainer.azurewebsites.net/, it will print the message shown in Figure 16-39.

Hello App Service!

This is being served from a **docker**
container running Nginx.

Figure 16-39. *Sample page*

This is being served from within the container. The other settings are more or less similar. The only difference we have here is in the Deployment Center, as shown in Figure 16-40.

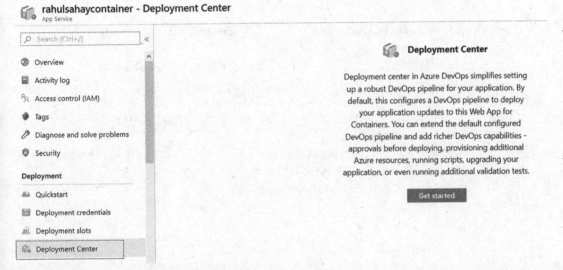

Figure 16-40. *Deployment Center link*

Click "Get started" and you will see the DevOps options shown in Figure 16-41.

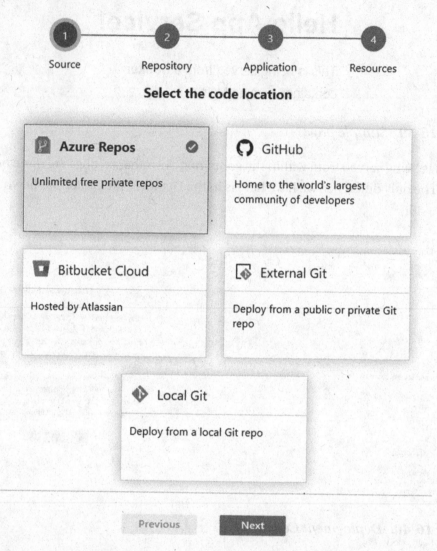

Figure 16-41. *Deployment options*

Background Jobs

In this section, we will discuss WebJobs. WebJobs are generally used when you need a task to run continuously irrespective of the website. Traditionally, you might have created a Windows service and installed it on the web server.

Web Jobs

Figure 16-42 shows the WebJobs link in the left panel.

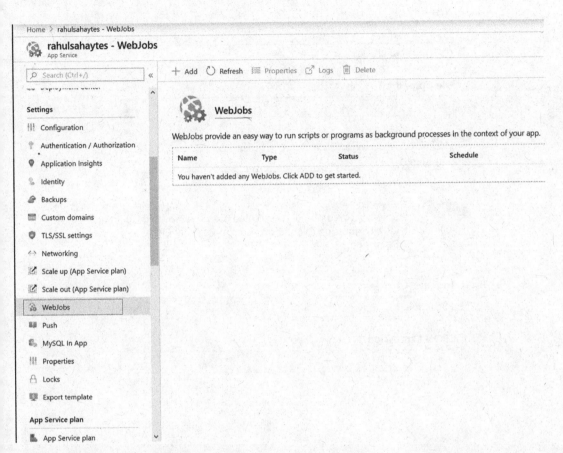

Figure 16-42. *WebJobs link*

Let's click the Add button. In the screen that opens, you can upload a manual job or a cron job. Of course, you need to upload the code in an acceptable format. In the case of a cron job, it will look like Figure 16-43, since it's a triggered job.

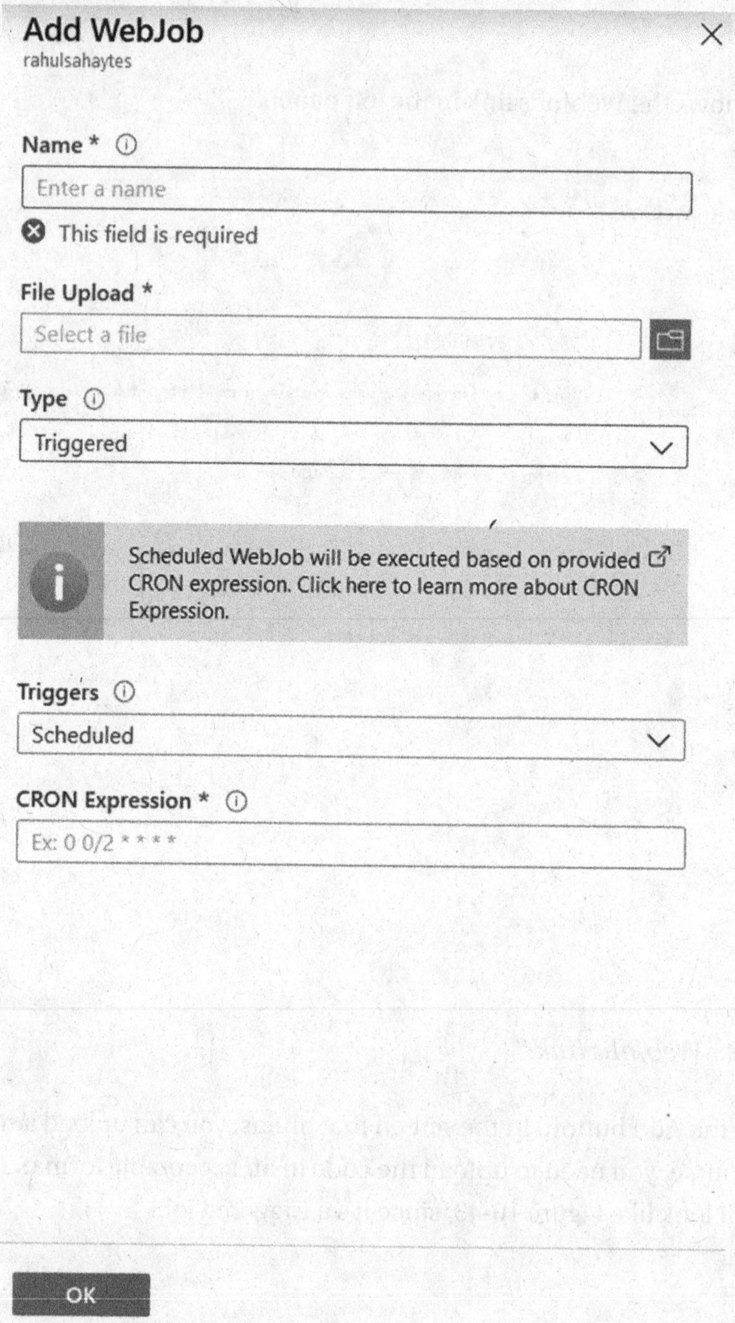

Add WebJob

rahulsahaytes

×

Name * ⓘ

Enter a name

❌ This field is required

File Upload *

Select a file

Type ⓘ

Triggered ⌄

ⓘ   Scheduled WebJob will be executed based on provided ⌐↗
CRON expression. Click here to learn more about CRON
Expression.

Triggers ⓘ

Scheduled ⌄

CRON Expression * ⓘ

Ex: 0 0/2 * * * *

OK

Figure 16-43. *Adding a WebJob*

If you select Continuous, your screen will look like Figure 16-44.

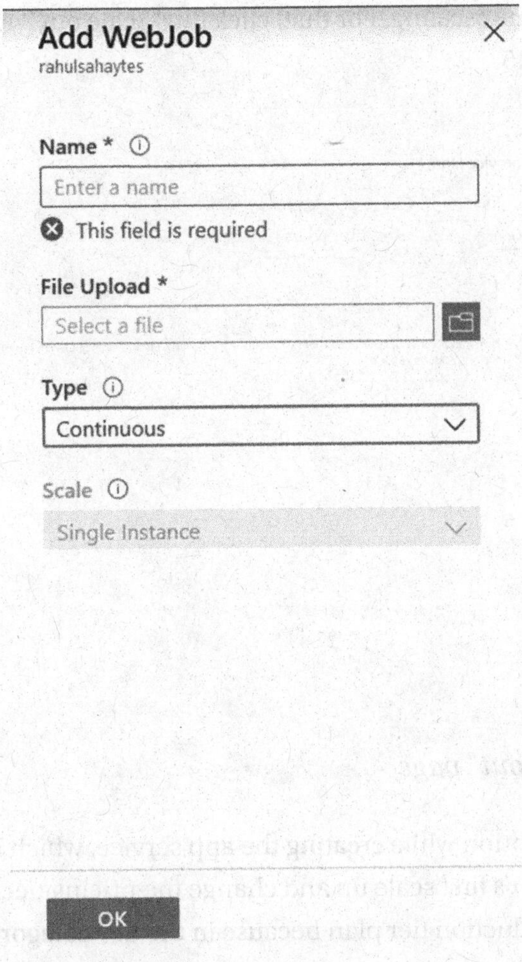

Figure 16-44. *Selecting Continuous*

The following file types are supported:

.cmd, .bat, .exe (using Windows commands), .ps1
(using PowerShell), .sh (using Bash), .php (using PHP), .py
(using Python), .js (using Node.js), and .jar (using Java)

You can find more details about WebJobs at http://bit.ly/2PAMzY7.

Autoscaling

Let's set up an app for autoscaling. For that, click the "Scale out" option in the left panel, as shown in Figure 16-45.

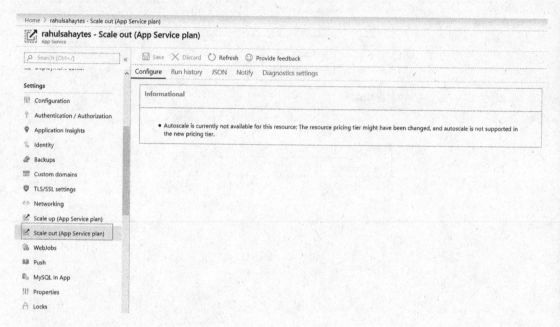

Figure 16-45. *"Scale out" page*

We chose the free option while creating the app service, which is why autoscaling is currently disabled. Let's first scale up and change the pricing tier. For this example, I have to choose one production tier plan because in the dev category, manually scaling is an option but autoscale is not, as shown in Figure 16-46 and Figure 16-47.

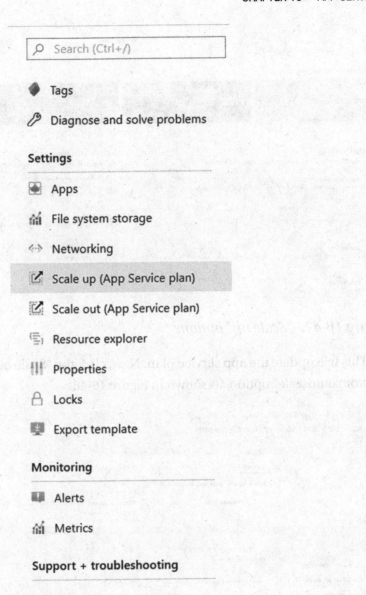

Figure 16-46. *"Scale up" link*

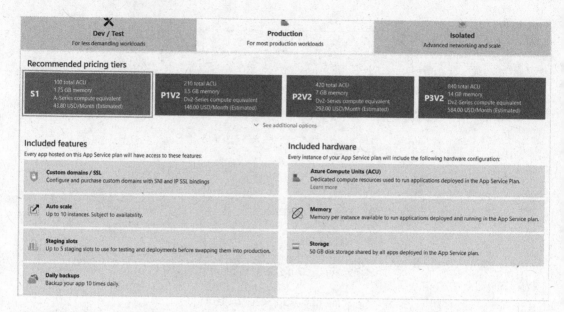

Figure 16-47. *"Scale up" options*

This will update the app service plan. Now, click the "Scale out" option and select the "Custom autoscale" option, as shown in Figure 16-48.

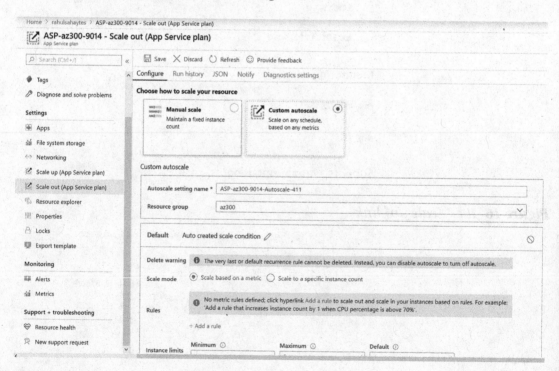

Figure 16-48. *Custom scale options*

After clicking, you will see a new form open, as shown in Figure 16-49. Either you can add a new scale condition or you can choose to modify the default one. I will create one from scratch. Let's delete the default one and click "Add a default scale condition."

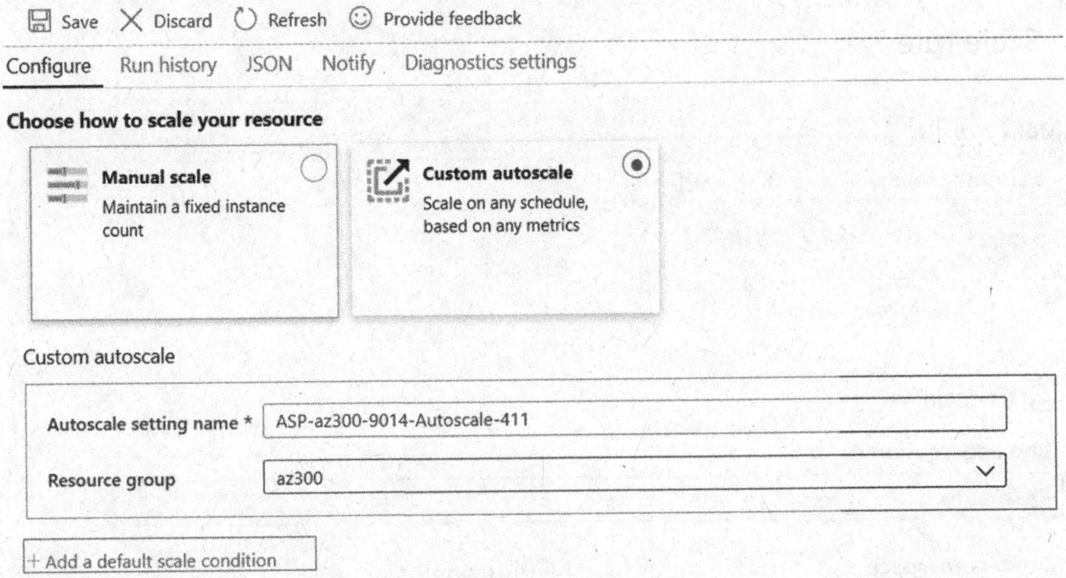

Figure 16-49. *Adding a default option*

Set the maximum instance limit to 5, as shown in Figure 16-50.

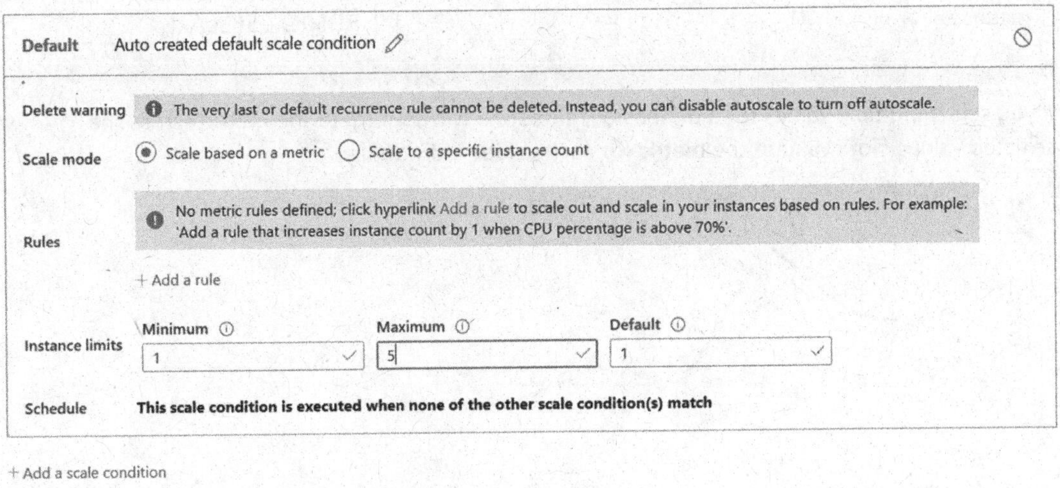

Figure 16-50. *Setting the maximum to 5*

Scale Rule

Next, click the "Add a rule" button. This will open the "Scale rule" window, as shown in Figure 16-51.

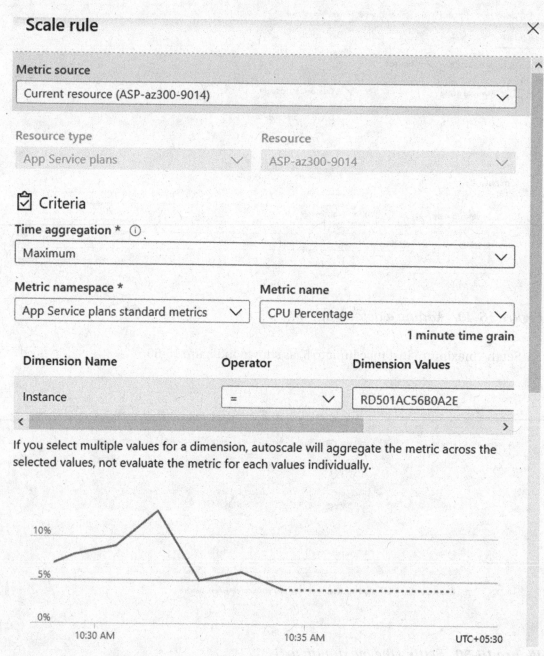

Figure 16-51. "Scale rule" window

I have set the CPU rule. When the CPU usage exceeds 70 percent, the instance count will be automatically increased by one. The highest instance limit is 5.

Similarly, you can set multiple scale factors for different rules or you can have multiple rules in the same scale condition as well.

Upon saving the scale rule, your screen will look like Figure 16-52.

💾 Save   ✕ Discard   ⟳ Refresh   ☺ Provide feedback.

Autoscale setting name ASP-az300-9014-Autoscale-411

Resource group   az300

Instance count   1

Default   Auto created default scale condition ✏️   ⊘

Delete warning   ℹ️ The very last or default recurrence rule cannot be deleted. Instead, you can disable autoscale to turn off autoscale.

Scale mode   ◉ Scale based on a metric   ○ Scale to a specific instance count

          ℹ️ It is recommended to have at least one scale in rule. New rules can be created by click hyperlink Add a rule .

Rules   Scale out

               When   ASP-az300-9014   (Maximum) CpuPercentage > 70 with filters   Increase count by 1

               + Add a rule

Instance limits | Minimum ⓘ | Maximum ⓘ | Default ⓘ |
               | --- | --- | --- |
               | 1 | 5 | 1 |

Schedule   **This scale condition is executed when none of the other scale condition(s) match**

+ Add a scale condition

Figure 16-52. *Final scale rule*

CHAPTER 17

Service Fabric

Azure Service Fabric is Microsoft's implementation of a microservice architecture. Azure Service Fabric is a distributed systems platform that makes it easy to package, deploy, and manage scalable and reliable microservices and containers. Service Fabric also addresses the significant challenges in developing and managing cloud-native applications. Developers and administrators can avoid complex infrastructure problems and focus on implementing mission-critical, demanding workloads that are scalable, reliable, and manageable. Service Fabric is a next-generation platform for building and managing these enterprise-class, tier-one, cloud-scale applications running in containers.

Azure Service Fabric runs as a pool of servers known as *clusters*, and multiple services can be deployed to each of these servers. This means you can start small and grow big as and when required.

Service Fabric Containers

Azure Service Fabric also supports containers. You learned about containers when you created a web app. In this chapter, you will see stand-alone container services such as Azure Kubernetes Service (AKS) and Azure Container Instances (ACI).

If you want to use an Azure Service Fabric style of architecture in conjunction with containers, you can use that as well. Figure 17-1 shows the high-level diagram for Azure Service Fabric.

623

© Rahul Sahay 2020
R. Sahay, *Microsoft Azure Architect Technologies Study Companion*,
https://doi.org/10.1007/978-1-4842-6200-9_17

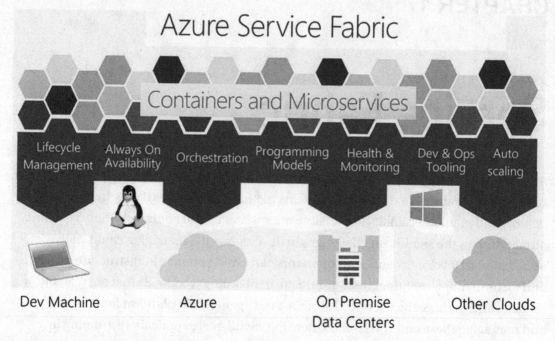

Figure 17-1. *Azure Service Fabric*

You can learn more about this at https://bit.ly/az-service-fabric. Another feature that Azure Service Fabric has is that it runs everywhere. This means it can run Windows or Linux. It can be set up on Azure, on AWS, or on premises. And you can use any type of runtime, say .NET, Java, Ruby, etc. Azure Service Fabric can be installed and developed on your local machine, which is not emulated. As far as deployment strategies are concerned, you can use pipelines such as Azure DevOps, Jenkins, etc.

Creating a Service Fabric

In this section, you will see how to create a service fabric. Search for *service fabric* under "All services," as shown in Figure 17-2.

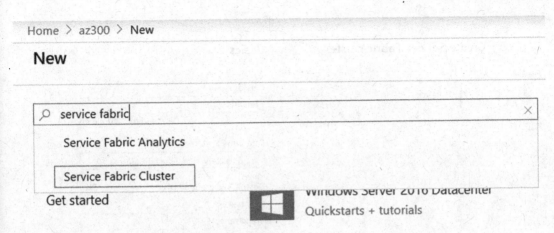

Figure 17-2. Service Fabric Cluster option

Click Service Fabric Cluster, and you will be taken to the screen shown in Figure 17-3.

Figure 17-3. Service Fabric Cluster screen

Click the Create button. Let's provide the information shown in Figure 17-4.

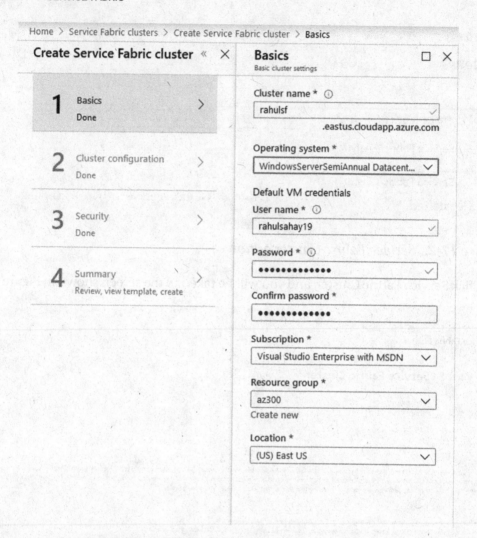

Figure 17-4. *Service fabric cluster basic settings*

After the basic settings, you'll work on the cluster configuration, as shown in Figure 17-5.

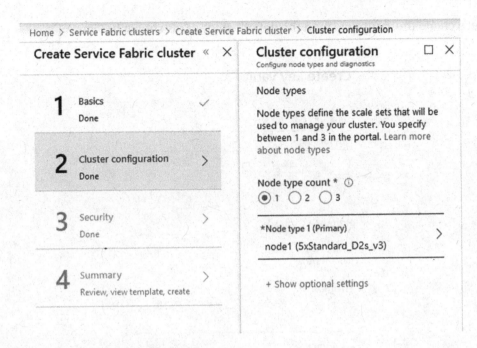

Figure 17-5. *Cluster configuration step*

Next, you will configure the security settings where you can configure a vault for storing a self-signed certificate, as shown in Figure 17-6.

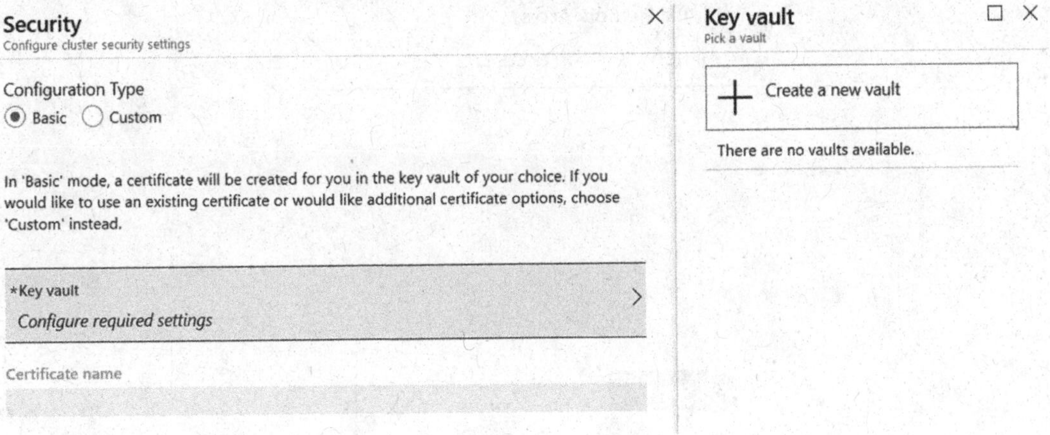

Security   ×   **Key vault**   □ ×
Configure cluster security settings   Pick a vault

Configuration Type   ┌──────────────────────────────┐
⦿ Basic ○ Custom   │ ╋ Create a new vault   │
                                                                                                    └──────────────────────────────┘
In 'Basic' mode, a certificate will be created for you in the key vault of your choice. If you   There are no vaults available.
would like to use an existing certificate or would like additional certificate options, choose
'Custom' instead.

┌───┐
│ *Key vault   > │
│ Configure required settings   │
└───┘

Certificate name

Figure 17-6. *Security settings*

Let's create the vault now with the default settings, as shown in Figure 17-7.

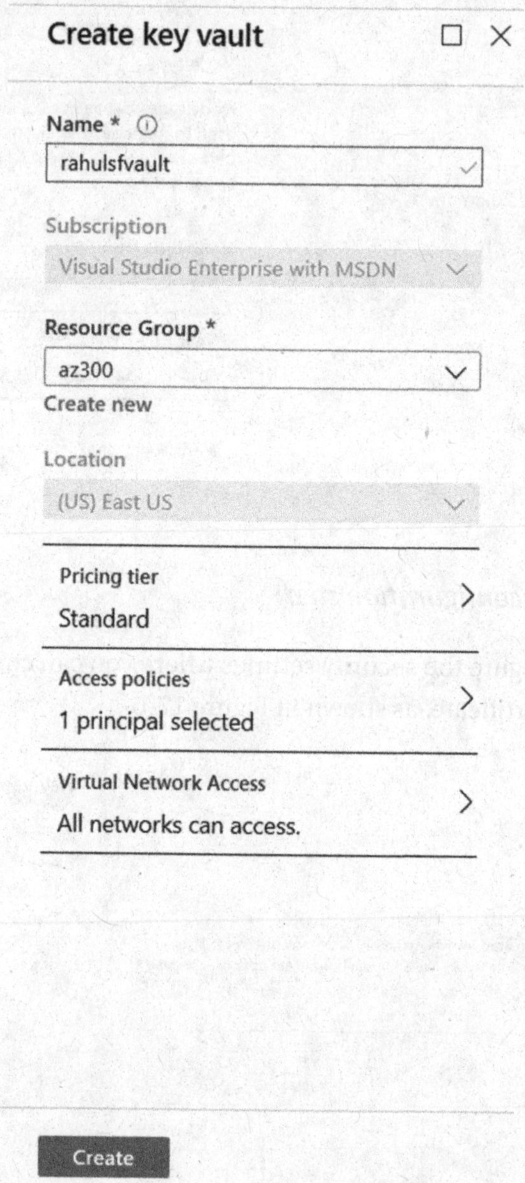

Create key vault   □ ✕

Name * ⓘ

rahulsfvault

Subscription

Visual Studio Enterprise with MSDN   ⌄

Resource Group *

az300   ⌄

Create new

Location

(US) East US   ⌄

Pricing tier
Standard   >

Access policies
1 principal selected   >

Virtual Network Access
All networks can access.   >

Create

Figure 17-7. *Azure key vault*

Make sure to edit the access policy and grant the required access, as shown in Figure 17-8.

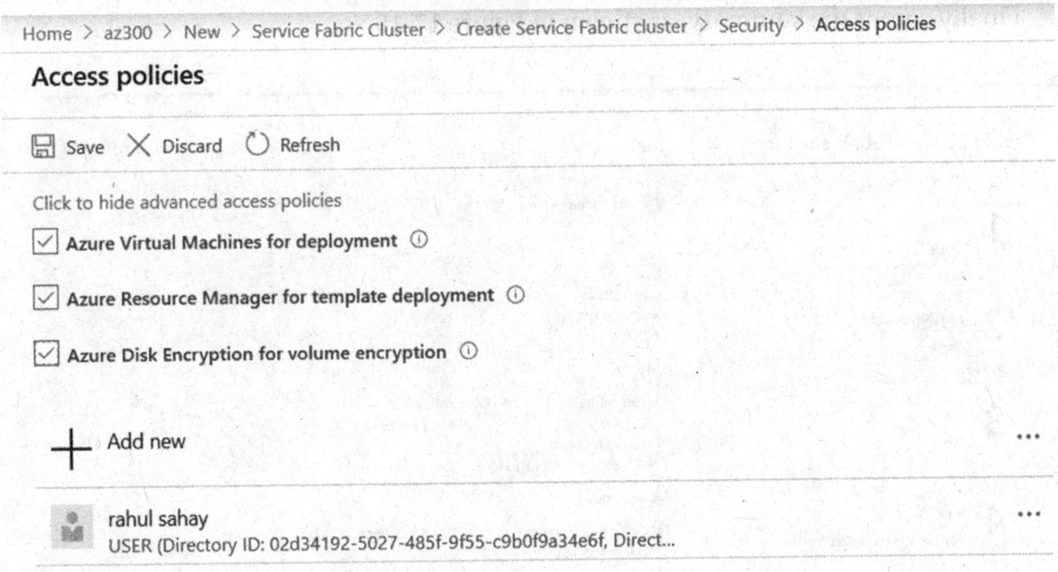

Home > az300 > New > Service Fabric Cluster > Create Service Fabric cluster > Security > Access policies

Access policies

💾 Save   ✕ Discard   ↻ Refresh

Click to hide advanced access policies

☑ **Azure Virtual Machines for deployment** ⓘ

☑ **Azure Resource Manager for template deployment** ⓘ

☑ **Azure Disk Encryption for volume encryption** ⓘ

╋   Add new   ...

👤   rahul sahay   ...
     USER (Directory ID: 02d34192-5027-485f-9f55-c9b0f9a34e6f, Direct...

***Figure 17-8.** Access policies*

Then provide the certificate name, as shown in Figure 17-9.

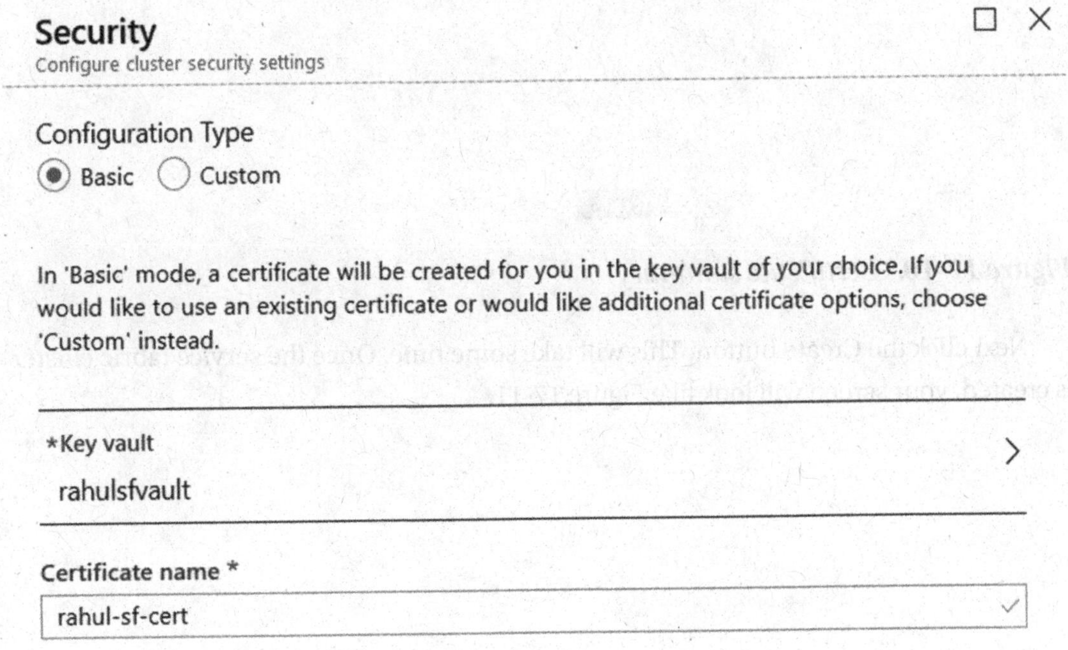

Security   ☐ ✕
Configure cluster security settings

Configuration Type
⦿ Basic   ◯ Custom

In 'Basic' mode, a certificate will be created for you in the key vault of your choice. If you would like to use an existing certificate or would like additional certificate options, choose 'Custom' instead.

*Key vault   ﹥
rahulsfvault

Certificate name *
┌───┐
│ rahul-sf-cert   ✓ │
└───┘

***Figure 17-9.** Certificate setting*

Finally comes the summary, as shown in Figure 17-10.

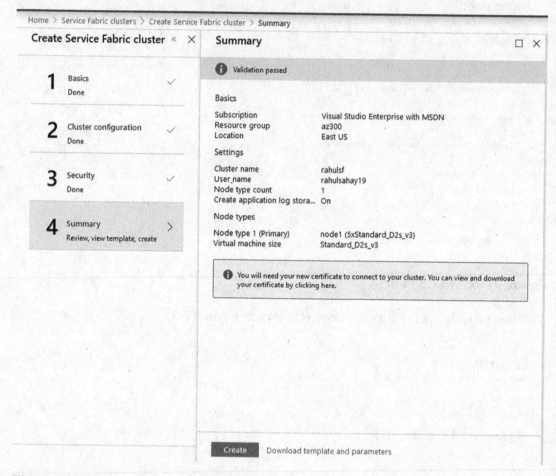

Figure 17-10. Certificate summary

Next click the Create button. This will take some time. Once the service fabric cluster is created, your screen will look like Figure 17-11.

✓ Your deployment is complete

Deployment name: Microsoft.ServiceFabricCluster-202022210929
Subscription: Visual Studio Enterprise with MSDN
Resource group: az300

Start time: 3/22/2020, 10:09:34 AM
Correlation ID: 59cc46a8-552c-4ef0-a0e9-f9c0ed28d4cc

∧ Deployment details (Download)

Resource	Type	Status	Operation details
✓ node1	Microsoft.Compute/virtualMachineScaleSets	OK	Operation details
✓ LB-rahulsf-node1	Microsoft.Network/loadBalancers	Created	Operation details
✓ rahulsf	Microsoft.ServiceFabric/clusters	OK	Operation details
✓ sflogsrahulsf6064	Microsoft.Storage/storageAccounts	OK	Operation details
✓ sfdgrahulsf9925	Microsoft.Storage/storageAccounts	OK	Operation details
✓ sflogsrahulsf6064	Microsoft.Storage/storageAccounts	OK	Operation details
✓ sfdgrahulsf9925	Microsoft.Storage/storageAccounts	OK	Operation details
✓ VNet-rahulsf	Microsoft.Network/virtualNetworks	OK	Operation details
✓ sflogsrahulsf6064	Microsoft.Storage/storageAccounts	OK	Operation details
✓ LBIP-rahulsf-node1	Microsoft.Network/publicIPAddresses	OK	Operation details

∧ Next steps

Go to resource

Figure 17-11. *Deployment complete*

If you go to the service fabric cluster, your screen will look like Figure 17-12.

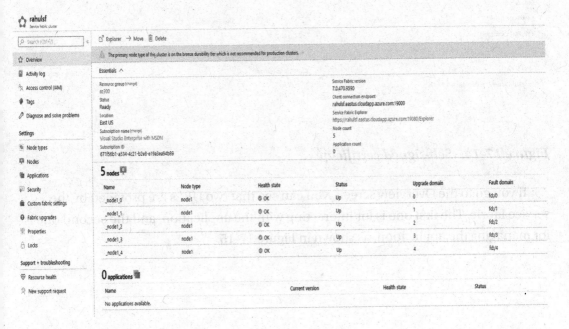

Figure 17-12. *Service fabric cluster, Overview screen*

When you click "Node types" in the menu, you will see that the endpoint information is listed, as shown in Figure 17-13.

Figure 17-13. *Endpoint information*

Other settings to look at right now are the security-related settings, as we created the self-signed certification as part of the process, as shown in Figure 17-14.

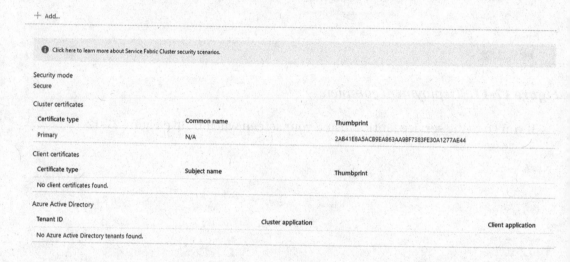

Figure 17-14. *Self-signed certificate*

If you go to the Overview screen, you can see that two URLs are provided by the service fabric. The first one is for interacting with the application, and the second one is for managing the application, as shown in Figure 17-15.

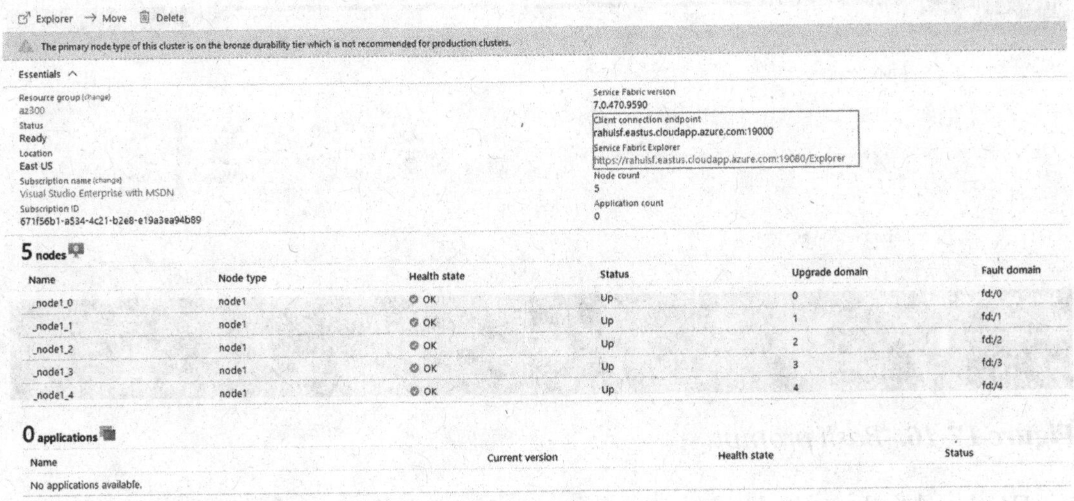

Figure 17-15. *Two URLs*

Regarding managing the service fabric on a local machine, I explain how to do this later in the chapter after I show how to create the cluster using PowerShell. I have given the same name for the cluster as when creating it using PowerShell. You may choose to use a different name so that they don't conflict. Other management processes will remain the same.

One more point to note here is that I created a Windows server using a portal; however, using PowerShell, I chose a Ubuntu machine. This way, you can get both the flavors.

Creating a Service Fabric Using the CLI

Let's get started with a service fabric using the cloud CLI terminal and Bash, as shown in Figure 17-16.

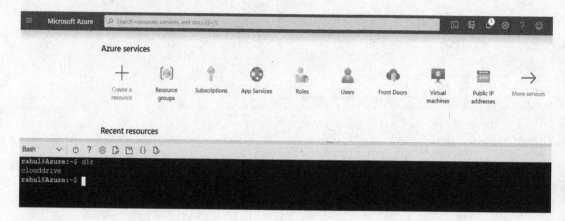

Figure 17-16. *Bash prompt*

Go ahead and create one directory, say `service-fabric`, and do all the service fabric–related operations there, as shown in Figure 17-17.

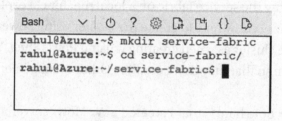

Figure 17-17. *In the service-fabric folder*

Next, create a service fabric using the `az cli` command, as shown in Figure 17-18. I first created a resource group with the command `az group create --name az300 --location eastus`.

```
Bash    ∨    ⏻  ?  ⚙  ⊡  ⊡  {}  ⊡
rahul@Azure:~/service-fabric$ az group create --name az300 --location eastus
{
  "id": "/subscriptions/671f56b1-a534-4c21-b2e8-e19a3ea94b89/resourceGroups/az300",
  "location": "eastus",
  "managedBy": null,
  "name": "az300",
  "properties": {
    "provisioningState": "Succeeded"
  },
  "tags": null,
  "type": "Microsoft.Resources/resourceGroups"
}
rahul@Azure:~/service-fabric$
```

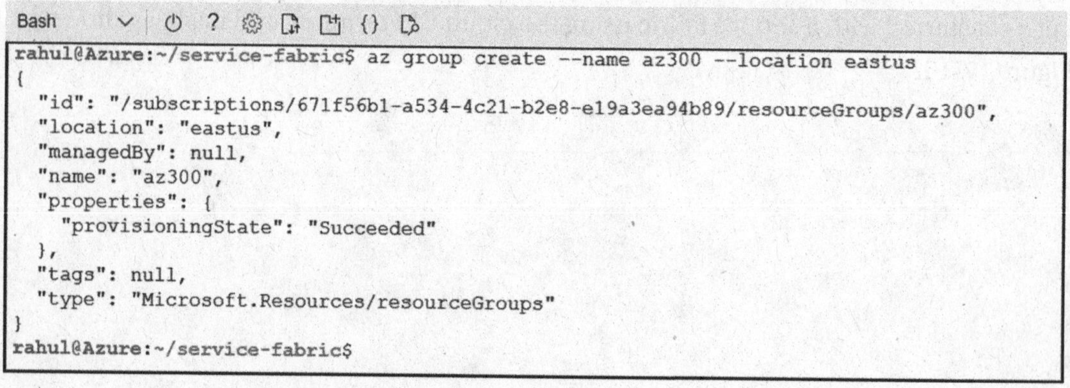

Figure 17-18. *Created resource group*

One thing to note with the CLI is that you should press Tab after entering a command.

Next, let's create a key vault and place self-signed certificates in it. Please follow the steps shown in Figure 17-19 to create it. Most of the steps are self-explanatory as I have just used the default settings.

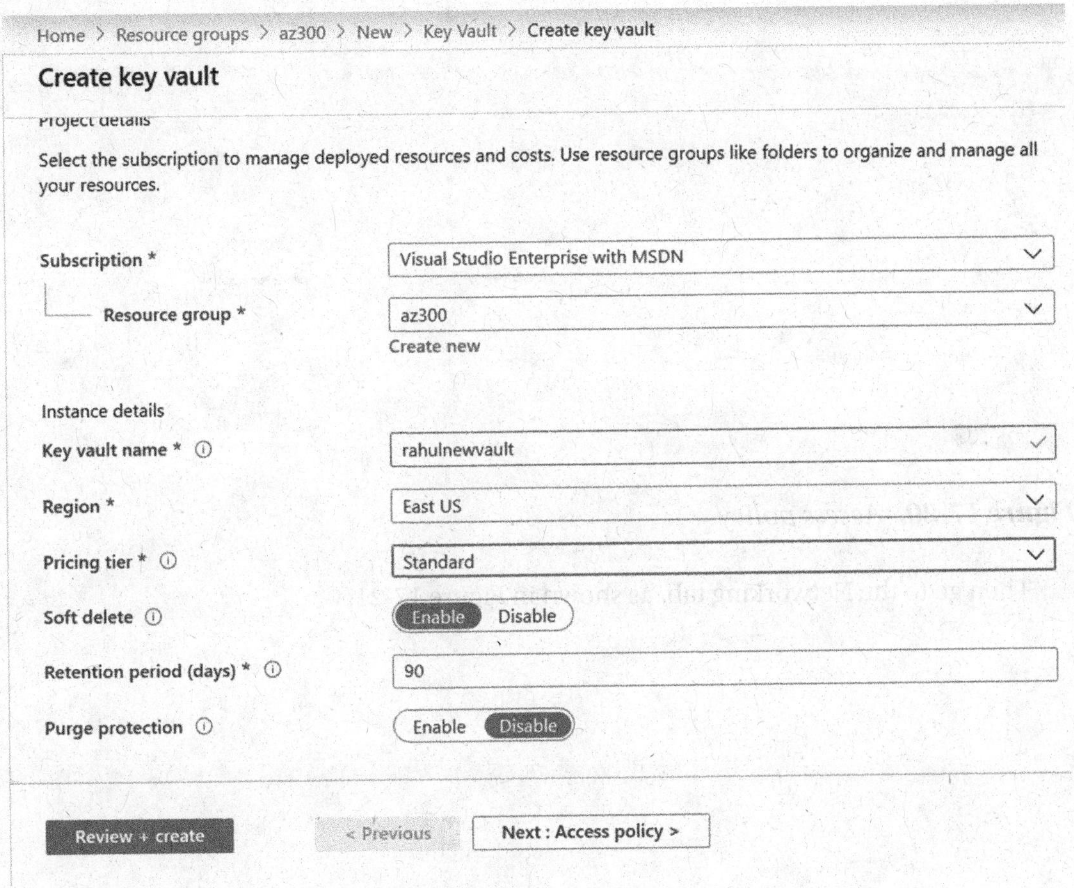

Home > Resource groups > az300 > New > Key Vault > Create key vault

Create key vault

Project details

Select the subscription to manage deployed resources and costs. Use resource groups like folders to organize and manage all your resources.

Subscription *	Visual Studio Enterprise with MSDN
Resource group *	az300
	Create new

Instance details

Key vault name * ⓘ	rahulnewvault
Region *	East US
Pricing tier * ⓘ	Standard
Soft delete ⓘ	(Enable) Disable
Retention period (days) * ⓘ	90
Purge protection ⓘ	Enable (Disable)

Review + create < Previous Next : Access policy >

Figure 17-19. *Creating an Azure vault*

Next comes the access policy, as shown in Figure 17-20.

Figure 17-20. *Access policy*

Then go to the Networking tab, as shown in Figure 17-21.

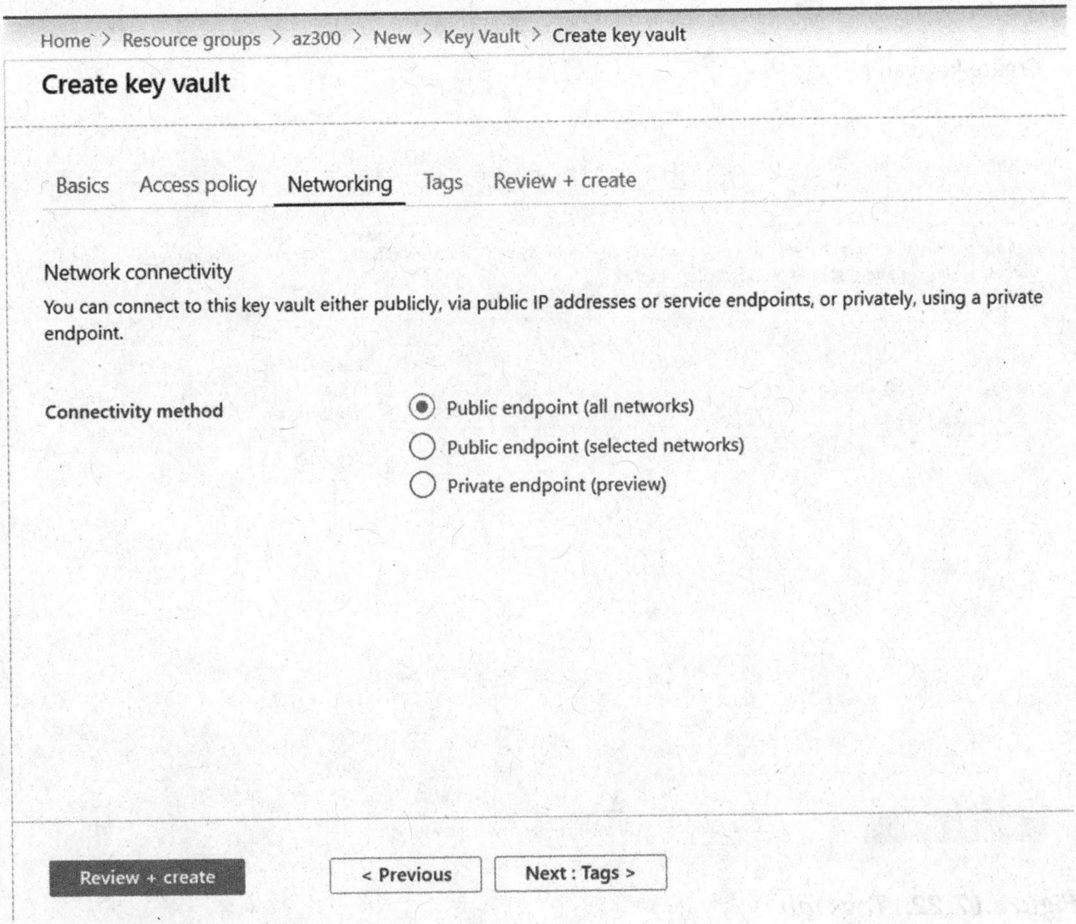

Home > Resource groups > az300 > New > Key Vault > **Create key vault**

Create key vault

Basics   Access policy   **Networking**   Tags   Review + create

Network connectivity
You can connect to this key vault either publicly, via public IP addresses or service endpoints, or privately, using a private endpoint.

Connectivity method   ⦿ Public endpoint (all networks)
                                        ○ Public endpoint (selected networks)
                                        ○ Private endpoint (preview)

| Review + create | | < Previous | Next : Tags > |

Figure 17-21. *Networking*

Next comes the Tags tab, as shown in Figure 17-22.

Home > Resource groups > az300 > New > Key Vault > Create key vault

Create key vault

Basics   Access policy   Networking   **Tags**   Review + create

Tags are name/value pairs that enable you to categorize resources and view consolidated billing by applying the same tag to multiple resources and resource groups. Learn more

Name ⓘ		Value ⓘ	Resource	
env	:	build	Key vault	🗑 ⋯
	:		Key vault	

Review + create		< Previous	Next : Review + create >

Figure 17-22. *Tags tab*

Finally, go to the "Review + create" screen, as shown in Figure 17-23.

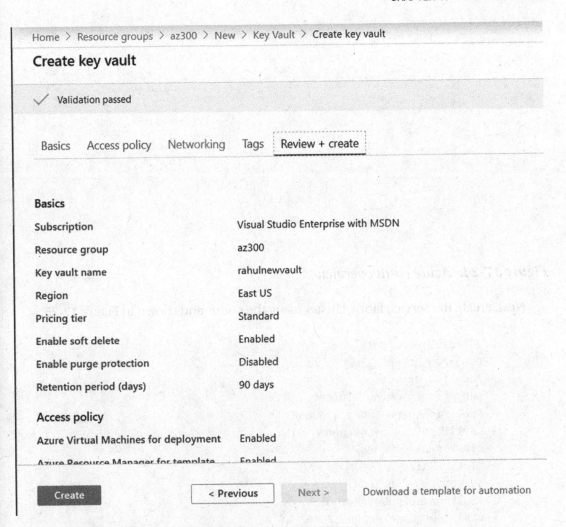

Home > Resource groups > az300 > New > Key Vault > Create key vault

Create key vault

✓ Validation passed

Basics   Access policy   Networking   Tags   Review + create

Basics

Subscription	Visual Studio Enterprise with MSDN
Resource group	az300
Key vault name	rahulnewvault
Region	East US
Pricing tier	Standard
Enable soft delete	Enabled
Enable purge protection	Disabled
Retention period (days)	90 days

Access policy

Azure Virtual Machines for deployment	Enabled
Azure Resource Manager for template	Enabled

Create   < Previous   Next >   Download a template for automation

Figure 17-23. *"Review + create" screen*

Once the vault is created, your screen will look like Figure 17-24.

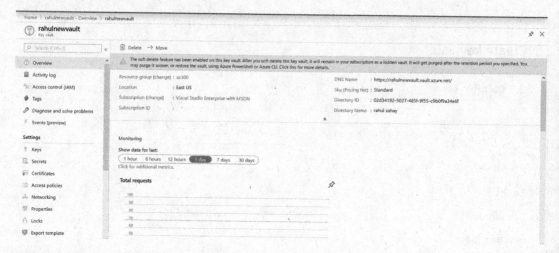

Figure 17-24. *Azure vault overview*

Next, create the service fabric cluster using the command shown in Figure 17-25.

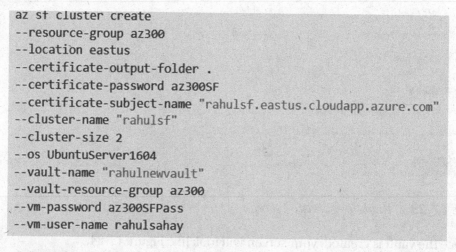

```
az sf cluster create
--resource-group az300
--location eastus
--certificate-output-folder .
--certificate-password az300SF
--certificate-subject-name "rahulsf.eastus.cloudapp.azure.com"
--cluster-name "rahulsf"
--cluster-size 2
--os UbuntuServer1604
--vault-name "rahulnewvault"
--vault-resource-group az300
--vm-password az300SFPass
--vm-user-name rahulsahay
```

Figure 17-25. *Service fabric cluster creation*

Let me explain the command step by step. Basically, the command is saying the following:

1. Create the service fabric cluster in the resource group az300.

2. Put the cluster in the location eastus.

3. It needs to have self-signed certificates; hence, it should go in the certificate's output folder. Since we are already in the service-fabric folder, a dot (.) indicates the current folder.

4. Specify the service fabric password.

5. The certificate subject name has to be globally unique, and the domain name should match the cluster name; hence, I have specified rahulsf.

6. For the cluster size, I have kept 2 for the time being.

7. For the operating system, I have selected Ubuntu.

8. Certificates going to live in the Azure key vault. Hence, provide a vault name and its resource group.

9. Finally, give the virtual machine a username and password.

10. If you don't create a vault ahead of the service fabric creation, you will end up with an error like the NoneType object has no attribute get.

If everything goes well, then the service fabric should be running, as shown in Figure 17-26.

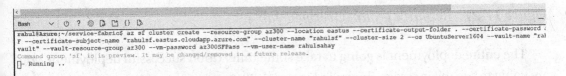

Figure 17-26. *Service fabric deploying*

However, before running cmd as shown in Figure 17-26, you may experience a cloud shell error, such as "request failed: Error occurred in request. HTTPError: 400 Client Error: Bad Request for url: http://localhost:50342/oauth2/token while creating service fabric in azure." In that case, just try running it again.

The Bash shell is not that self-explanatory. This you can verify in the portal itself inside a resource group, as shown in Figure 17-27.

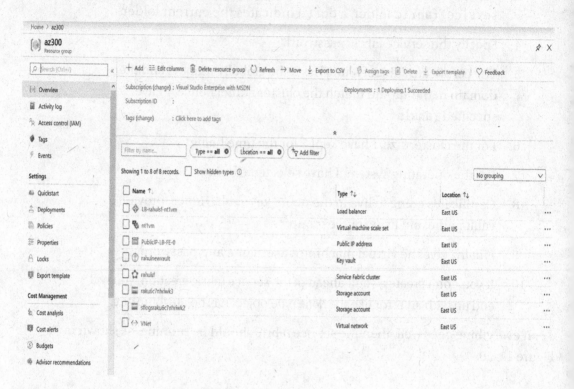

Figure 17-27.   *Resource group, Overview tab*

The entire deployment is going to take some time. Upon successful deployment, you are going to see the message shown in Figure 17-28.

```
Bash        ∨    ⏻  ?  ⚙  ⬀  ⬔  { }  ⬓

            "endPort": 30000,
            "startPort": 20000
        },
        "capacities": null,
        "clientConnectionEndpointPort": 19000,
        "durabilityLevel": "Bronze",
        "ephemeralPorts": {
          "endPort": 65534,
          "startPort": 49152
        },
        "httpGatewayEndpointPort": 19080,
        "isPrimary": true,
        "name": "nt1vm",
        "placementProperties": null,
        "reverseProxyEndpointPort": null,
        "vmInstanceCount": 2
      }
    ],
    "provisioningState": "Succeeded",
    "reliabilityLevel": "None",
    "resourceGroup": "az300",
    "reverseProxyCertificate": null,
    "reverseProxyCertificateCommonNames": null,
    "tags": {
      "clusterName": "rahulsf",
      "resourceType": "Service Fabric"
    },
    "type": "Microsoft.ServiceFabric/clusters",
    "upgradeDescription": null,
    "upgradeMode": "Automatic",
    "vmImage": "Linux"
  },
  "vm_user_name": "rahulsahay"
}
rahul@Azure:~/service-fabric$ ▌
```

Figure 17-28. *Service fabric deployed*

At this moment, when you go to the service fabric, you can see that it's still updating. It will take some time to enter a running state, as shown in Figure 17-29.

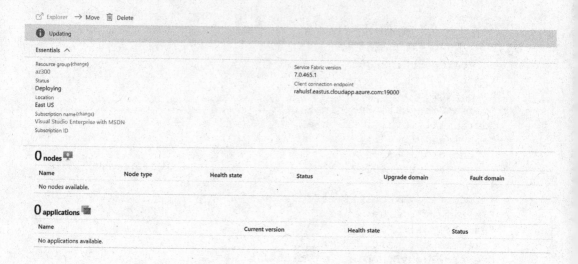

Figure 17-29. *Service fabric state*

In the meantime, take a look at the virtual machine scale set (VMSS), which was also created as part of this exercise, as shown in Figure 17-30.

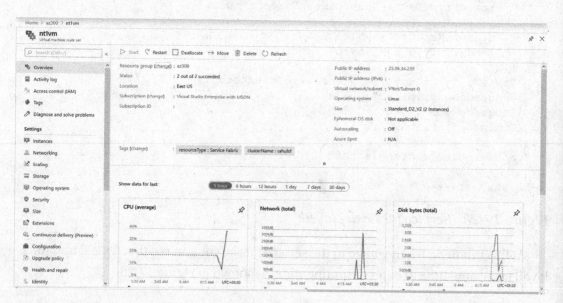

Figure 17-30. *Virtual machine scale set*

You can access this using a public IP address. You can also see running instances. There are two instances running currently, as shown in Figure 17-31.

Figure 17-31. *VMSS instances*

You can use manual scaling or autoscaling, as shown in Figure 17-32.

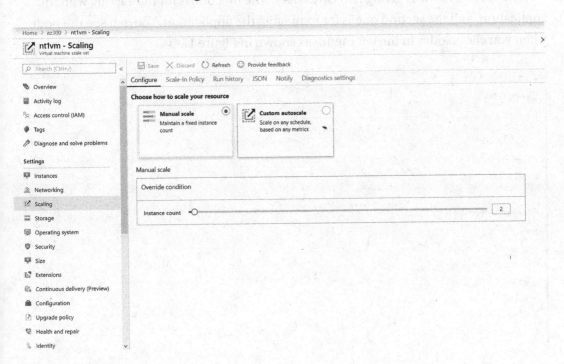

Figure 17-32. *Scaling options*

The service fabric is up now. You can now go to the Overview tab of the service fabric and copy the URL, as shown in Figure 17-33.

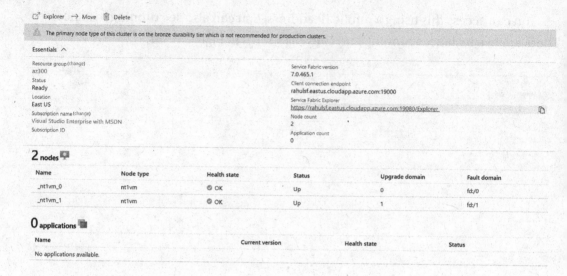

Figure 17-33. Copying the URL

The service fabric is giving two URLs here. The first one is for interacting with the application, and the second one is for managing the application. You can see the node when you click Nodes in the left menu, as shown in Figure 17-34.

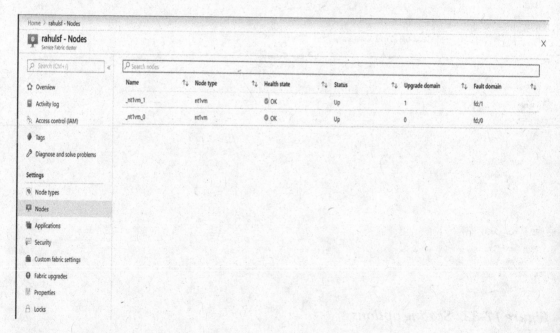

Figure 17-34. Service fabric nodes

You can also see the node types, as shown in Figure 17-35.

Name	Client endpoint	HTTP endpoint	App port range
nt1vm	19000	19080	20000-30000

Figure 17-35. *Service fabric node types*

This has an endpoint for the client and an endpoint for the management tool.

Managing the Service Fabric on a Local Machine

Let's grab the management URL, which in this case is `https://rahulsf.eastus.cloudapp.azure.com:19080/Explorer`.

Go to the URL in Firefox. You will see the warning shown in Figure 17-36.

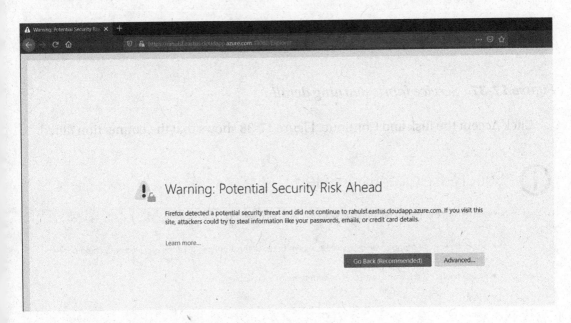

Figure 17-36. *Service fabric warning*

This is expected because we created the service fabric as a secure app with self-signed certificates. Figure 17-37 shows the warning details.

Warning: Potential Security Risk Ahead
Firefox detected a potential security threat and did not continue to rahulsf.eastus.cloudapp.azure.com. If you visit this site, attackers could try to steal information like your passwords, emails, or credit card details.
Learn more...
Go Back (Recommended)
Advanced...
rahulsf.eastus.cloudapp.azure.com:19080 uses an invalid security certificate.
The certificate is not trusted because it is self-signed.
Error code: MOZILLA_PKIX_ERROR_SELF_SIGNED_CERT
View Certificate
Go Back (Recommended)
Accept the Risk and Continue

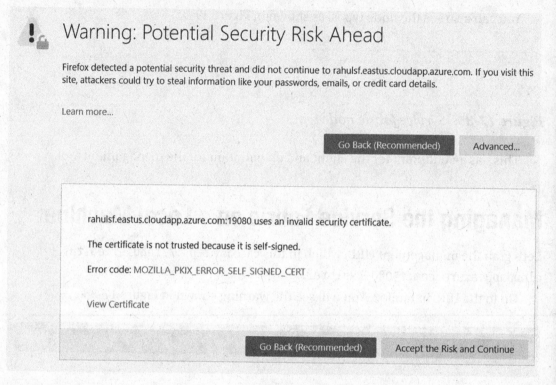

***Figure 17-37.** Service fabric warning detail*

Click Accept the Risk and Continue. Figure 17-38 shows that the connection failed.

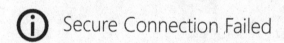

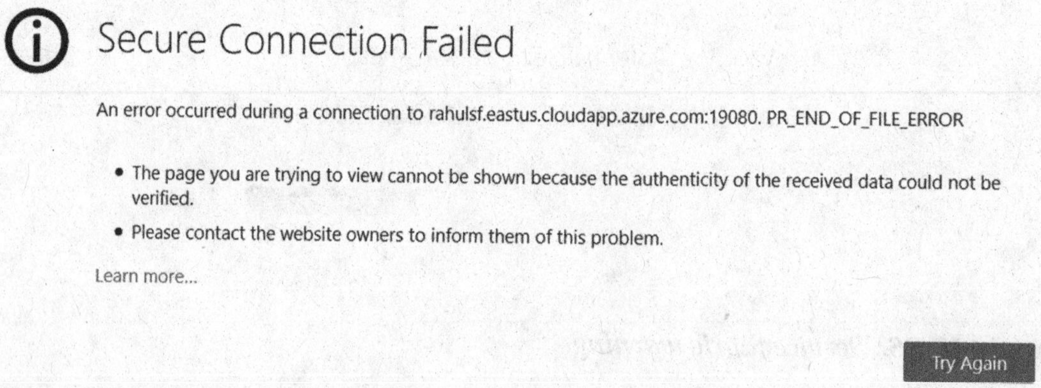

Secure Connection Failed
An error occurred during a connection to rahulsf.eastus.cloudapp.azure.com:19080. PR_END_OF_FILE_ERROR
The page you are trying to view cannot be shown because the authenticity of the received data could not be verified.
Please contact the website owners to inform them of this problem.
Learn more...
Try Again

***Figure 17-38.** Service fabric failed*

Now, it failed because it didn't find the required certificate locally. Either you can download and install the certificate locally on a machine or you can upload the certificate in Firefox itself.

Let's download the certificate from the shell, as shown in Figure 17-39.

Figure 17-39. *Azure cloud shell*

I can see the certificate in the directory. Let's click the "Upload/Download files" button, as shown in Figure 17-40.

```
Bash        ∨ |  ⏻  ?  ⚙  ⬆  ⬆  {}  ⬆
rahul@Azure:~$ cd service-fabric/
rahul@Azure:~/service-fa Upload/Download files
az300202002220044.pem   az300202002220044.pfx
rahul@Azure:~/service-fabric$ ▮
```

Figure 17-40. *Download icon*

Click Download, as shown in Figure 17-41.

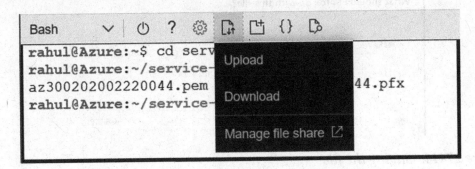

Figure 17-41. *Download link*

Provide the directory name and the filename, as shown in Figure 17-42.

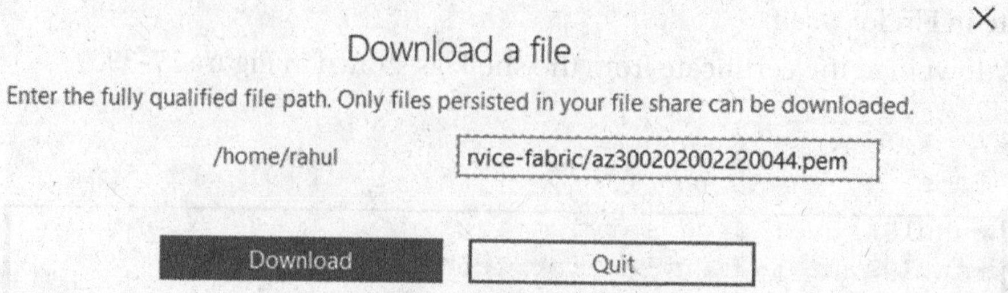

$\times$

Download a file

Enter the fully qualified file path. Only files persisted in your file share can be downloaded.

/home/rahul   rvice-fabric/az300202002220044.pem

| Download | Quit |

Figure 17-42. *Directory name with filename*

You will see a message at the bottom of the screen, as shown in Figure 17-43. Save the file, as shown in Figure 17-44.

Click here to download your file. $\times$

Figure 17-43. *Confirmation message*

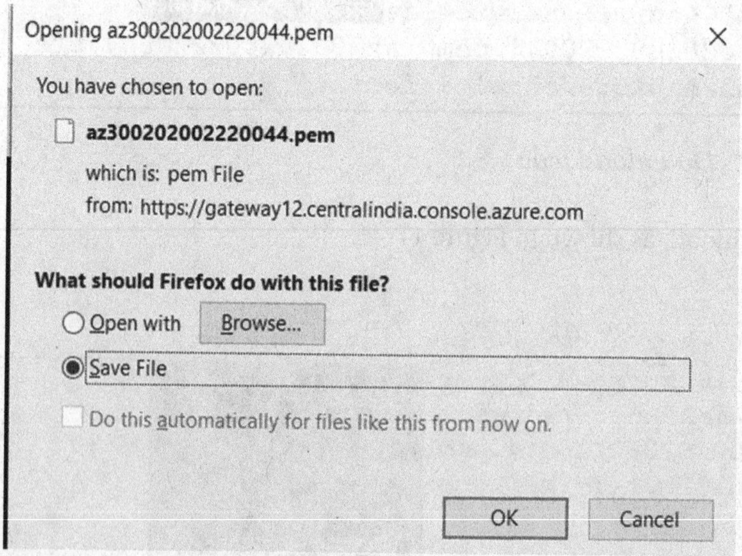

Opening az300202002220044.pem $\times$

You have chosen to open:

☐ **az300202002220044.pem**

which is: pem File
from: https://gateway12.centralindia.console.azure.com

What should Firefox do with this file?

○ Open with   Browse...

◉ Save File

☐ Do this automatically for files like this from now on.

OK   Cancel

Figure 17-44. *Saving the file*

You will need to follow these steps for other files as well. Let's go to the Firefox Options menu, as shown in Figure 17-45.

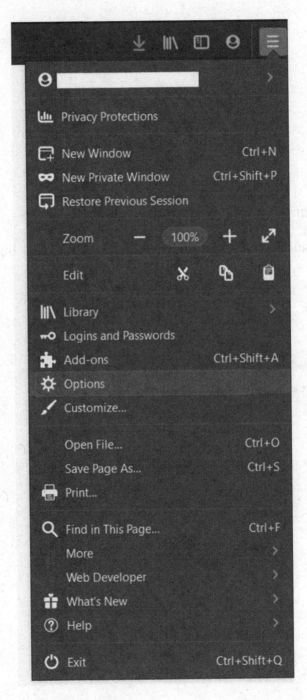

Figure 17-45. *Firefox Options menu*

Let's look for *view certificate* using the search box, as shown in Figure 17-46.

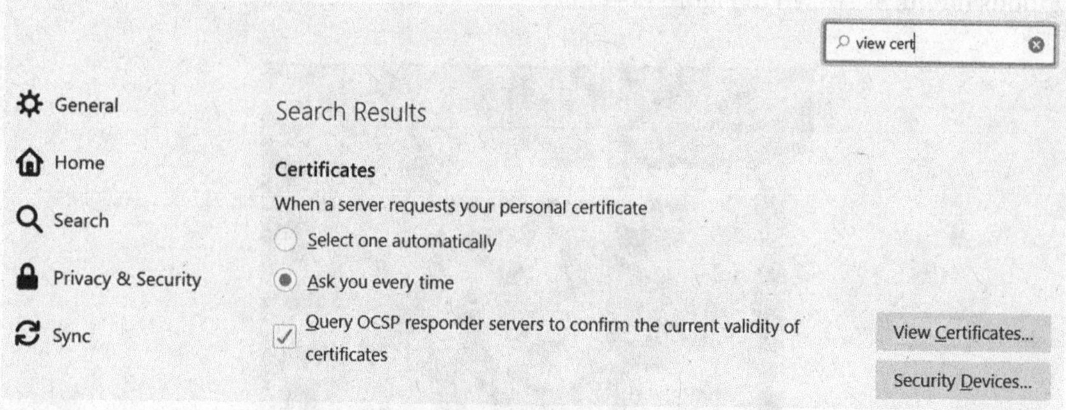

Figure 17-46. *Searching for view certificates*

Click View Certificates, click the Your Certificates tab, and click Import, as shown in Figure 17-47.

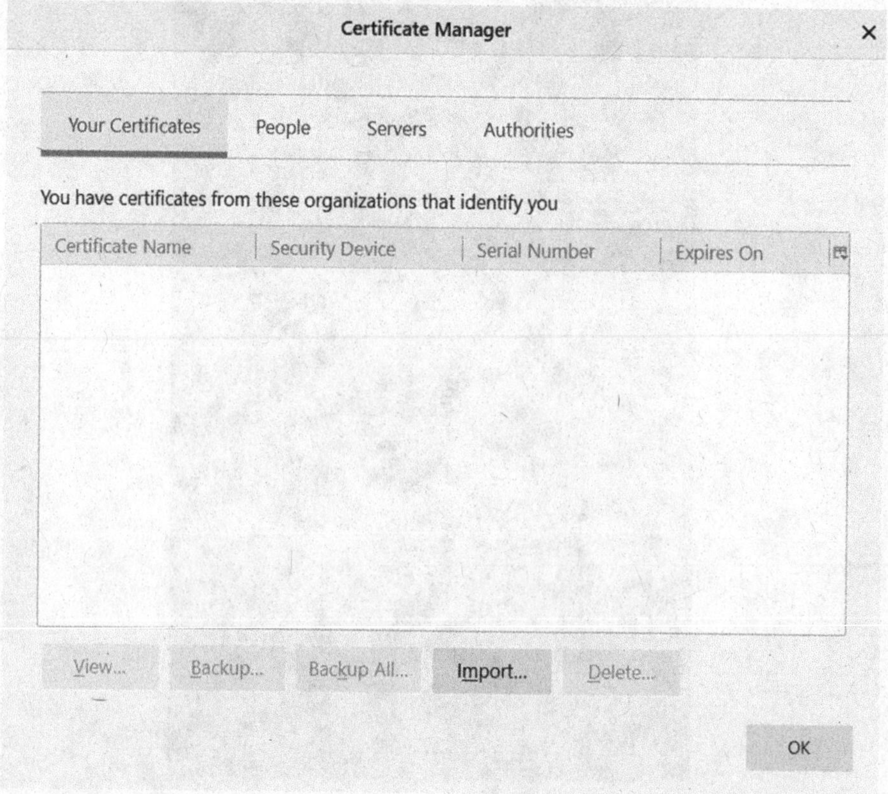

Figure 17-47. *Certificate Manager*

Once you select the certificate, it will ask for the password, which is used to encrypt the certificate backup. By default, there is no password for this, as shown in Figure 17-48.

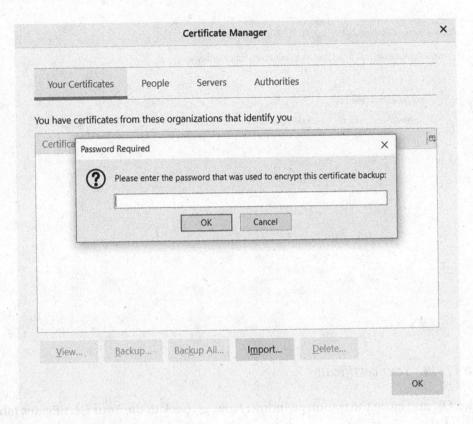

Figure 17-48. *Certificate password*

Hence, you can click OK. Your screen will look like Figure 17-49.

Figure 17-49. *Your certificates*

Click OK and close the options window. Now, go back to the Your Certificates tab and refresh the page. You'll see the dialog shown in Figure 17-50.

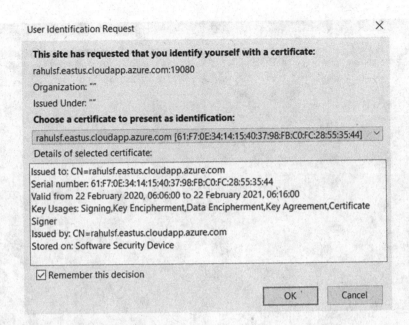

Figure 17-50. *User identification request*

This dialog box is saying that it's sending a user identification request, which is fine. You can click OK. It may again show the same failure message. But, refresh the screen again. It should eventually show the beautiful dashboard of the service fabric, as shown in Figure 17-51.

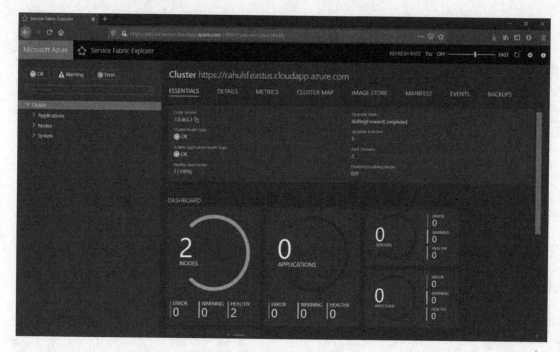

Figure 17-51. *Service Fabric Explorer dashboard*

You now have a console application that allows you to manage the service fabric cluster in a browser. This is the management console, and the only way to access it is via a security certificate.

You can see in Figure 17-52 that the Applications tab is blank as we haven't deployed any applications or microservices yet. But, that is fine.

Figure 17-52. *Applications tab*

You can deploy the app from the UI by clicking the Actions button highlighted in Figure 17-53.

Figure 17-53. *Composing an application*

You need to select the file in the Create Compose Application window, as shown in Figure 17-54.

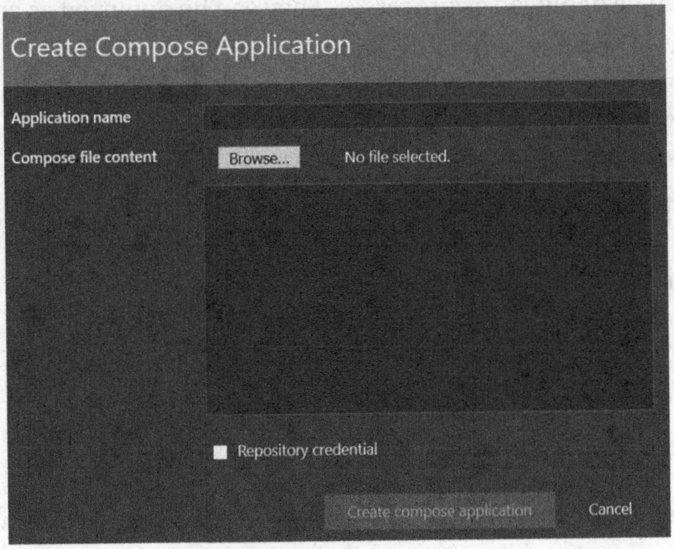

Figure 17-54. *Selecting an application*

The file should be in YML format. Or you can connect to it using Bash via the sfctl command, as shown here:

```
"sfctl cluster select --endpoint https://rahulsf.eastus.cloudapp.azure.
com:19080 --pem az300202002220044.pem --no-verify"
```

With this command, I am saying to connect the cluster with that endpoint having a PEM file in no-verify mode. As shown in Figure 17-55, it connects successfully.

```
rahul@Azure:~/service-fabric$ sfctl cluster select --endpoint https://rahulsf.eastus.cloudapp.azure.com:19080 --pem az300202002220044.pem --no-verify
/usr/local/lib/python3.5/dist-packages/urllib3/connectionpool.py:1004: InsecureRequestWarning: Unverified HTTPS request is being made to host 'rahulsf.
eastus.cloudapp.azure.com'. Adding certificate verification is strongly advised. See: https://urllib3.readthedocs.io/en/latest/advanced-usage.html#ssl-
warnings
  InsecureRequestWarning,
/usr/local/lib/python3.5/dist-packages/urllib3/connectionpool.py:1004: InsecureRequestWarning: Unverified HTTPS request is being made to host 'rahulsf.
eastus.cloudapp.azure.com'. Adding certificate verification is strongly advised. See: https://urllib3.readthedocs.io/en/latest/advanced-usage.html#ssl-
warnings
  InsecureRequestWarning,
rahul@Azure:~/service-fabric$
```

Figure 17-55. *sfctl options*

You can now go ahead and deploy apps here.

Deployment

Service fabrics can be deployed as processes. They can be deployed as containers, either Linux or Windows. They can be deployed as part of a CI/CD process.

You can refer to a working example at https://bit.ly/service-fabric-cluster.

Programming Models

Three types of service fabric can be developed.

- Guest executables
- Reliable services
- Reliable actors

Guest executables are pretty straightforward. For existing code that you have, you just need to deploy it in the service fabric. This means you haven't made any changes in the code specific to the service fabric. You will just deploy the regular .NET code, for example, inside the service fabric.

Creating this type of service fabric means you are not getting the full benefits of a service fabric. The service fabric will try to keep the code available and reliable, but the full suite of service fabric advantages won't be available.

The second option is to create a service fabric via reliable services. If you are developing code for a service fabric and you want to use the reliable services model, you need to call the reliable services APIs to set it up. This allows your application to interact with the service fabric.

The reliable services model is a service-oriented architecture (SOA), which means everything is designed around services. There are two kinds of states. The first is a stateless service. Stateless services can accept requests from anyone. Being stateless doesn't mean that it won't have any concept of state. Here, state will be stored elsewhere. Being stateful means the state is stored locally. Reliable services are basically reliable, available, scalable, and consistent.

The third type of programming model is reliable actors. Actors in service fabric models can only communicate through messages. Actors are similar to objects. For example, you can have actors like User, which can have properties like First Name, Last Name, etc. Users can perform actions like CRUD operations.

CHAPTER 18

Apps with Containers

Containers is one of the buzzwords used across the industry these days. Containers provide the flexibility to ship your code with the runtime so that it can run its own environment without any dependency on the OS. Basically, it makes your app cross-platform ready.

In this chapter, you will be using the Azure Kubernetes Service (AKS). Kubernetes is a container orchestration tool that simplifies the management of containers and also makes the process more efficient. The great thing about Kubernetes is that it is open source, invented by Google, so you can use Kubernetes with any cloud provider. Here are a few of its benefits:

- Automates various manual process

- Interacts with several group of containers

- Manages containers

- Self-monitoring

- Horizontal scaling

- Automatic rollouts and rollbacks

- Runs everywhere

Using the Azure Kubernetes Service

Let's get started. In the Azure portal, you can just search for *aks*, as shown in Figure 18-1.

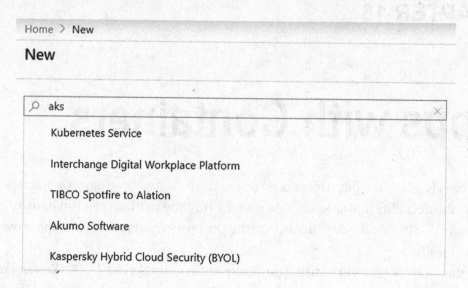

Figure 18-1. *Searching for aks*

Select Kubernetes Service from this list and then click Create. Figure 18-2 shows the screen that opens.

Figure 18-2. *"Kubernetes services" screen*

Fill in the required details, as shown in Figure 18-3.

Home > Kubernetes services > Create Kubernetes cluster

Create Kubernetes cluster

Basics   Scale   Authentication   Networking   Monitoring   Tags   Review + create

Azure Kubernetes Service (AKS) manages your hosted Kubernetes environment, making it quick and easy to deploy and manage containerized applications without container orchestration expertise. It also eliminates the burden of ongoing operations and maintenance by provisioning, upgrading, and scaling resources on demand, without taking your applications offline. Learn more about Azure Kubernetes Service

Project details

Select a subscription to manage deployed resources and costs. Use resource groups like folders to organize and manage all your resources.

Subscription * ⓘ	Visual Studio Enterprise with MSDN	∨
└─── Resource group * ⓘ	az300	∨
	Create new	

Cluster details

Kubernetes cluster name * ⓘ	rahulKubeCluster	✓
Region * ⓘ	(US) East US	∨
Kubernetes version * ⓘ	1.14.8 (default)	∨
DNS name prefix * ⓘ	rahulKubeCluster-dns	✓

Figure 18-3. *Kubernetes screen, Basics tab*

Clusters are pools of computers, starting with at least three. One is the orchestrator, and other two will act as the worker nodes.

On the Scale tab, you can select to use virtual nodes if required. Virtual nodes are useful when you are dealing with a serverless architecture. In this case, you can leave everything at the default settings, as shown in Figure 18-4.

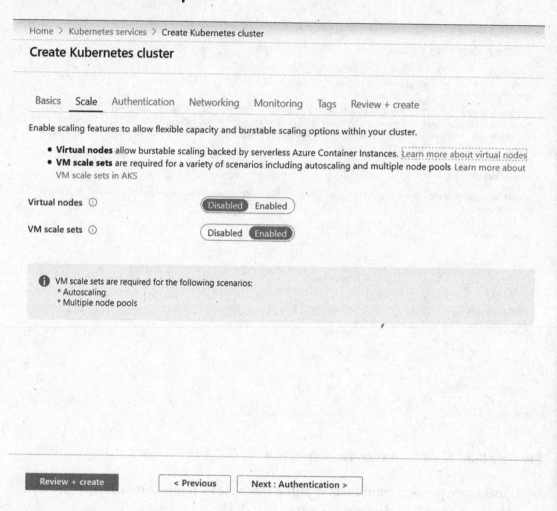

Figure 18-4. Scale tab

Next is the Authentication tab. Here, the service principle will be created. The service principle is the account under which the nodes will run. You can use the settings shown in Figure 18-5. We don't want role-based access control (RBAC) at the moment.

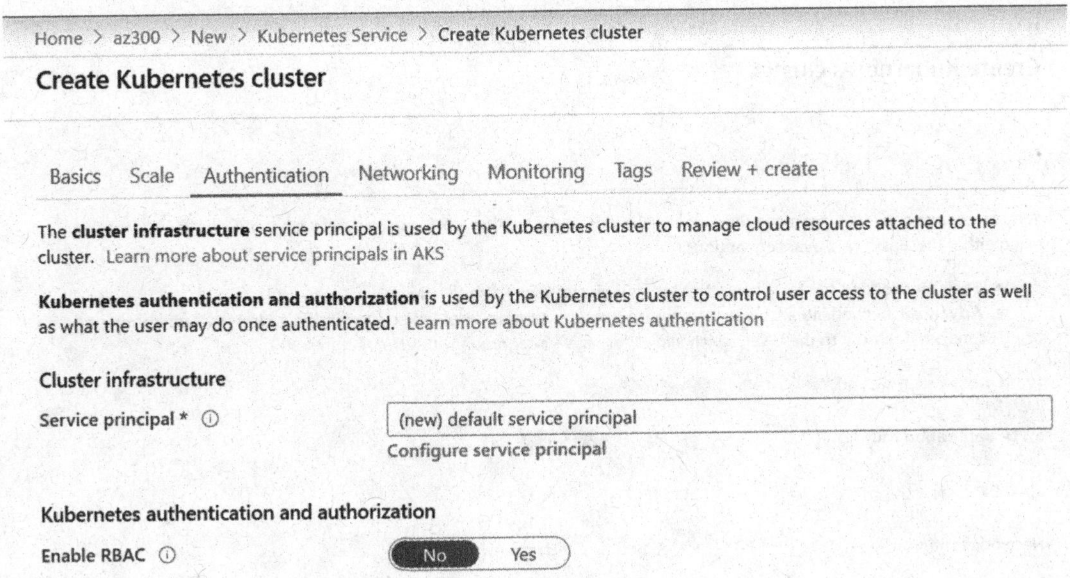

Home > az300 > New > Kubernetes Service > Create Kubernetes cluster

Create Kubernetes cluster

Basics   Scale   Authentication   Networking   Monitoring   Tags   Review + create

The **cluster infrastructure** service principal is used by the Kubernetes cluster to manage cloud resources attached to the cluster. Learn more about service principals in AKS

Kubernetes authentication and authorization is used by the Kubernetes cluster to control user access to the cluster as well as what the user may do once authenticated. Learn more about Kubernetes authentication

Cluster infrastructure

Service principal * ⓘ   (new) default service principal

                                          Configure service principal

Kubernetes authentication and authorization

Enable RBAC ⓘ   No   Yes

Figure 18-5. *Authentication tab*

Next is the Networking tab, as shown in Figure 18-6. Keep the default settings here.

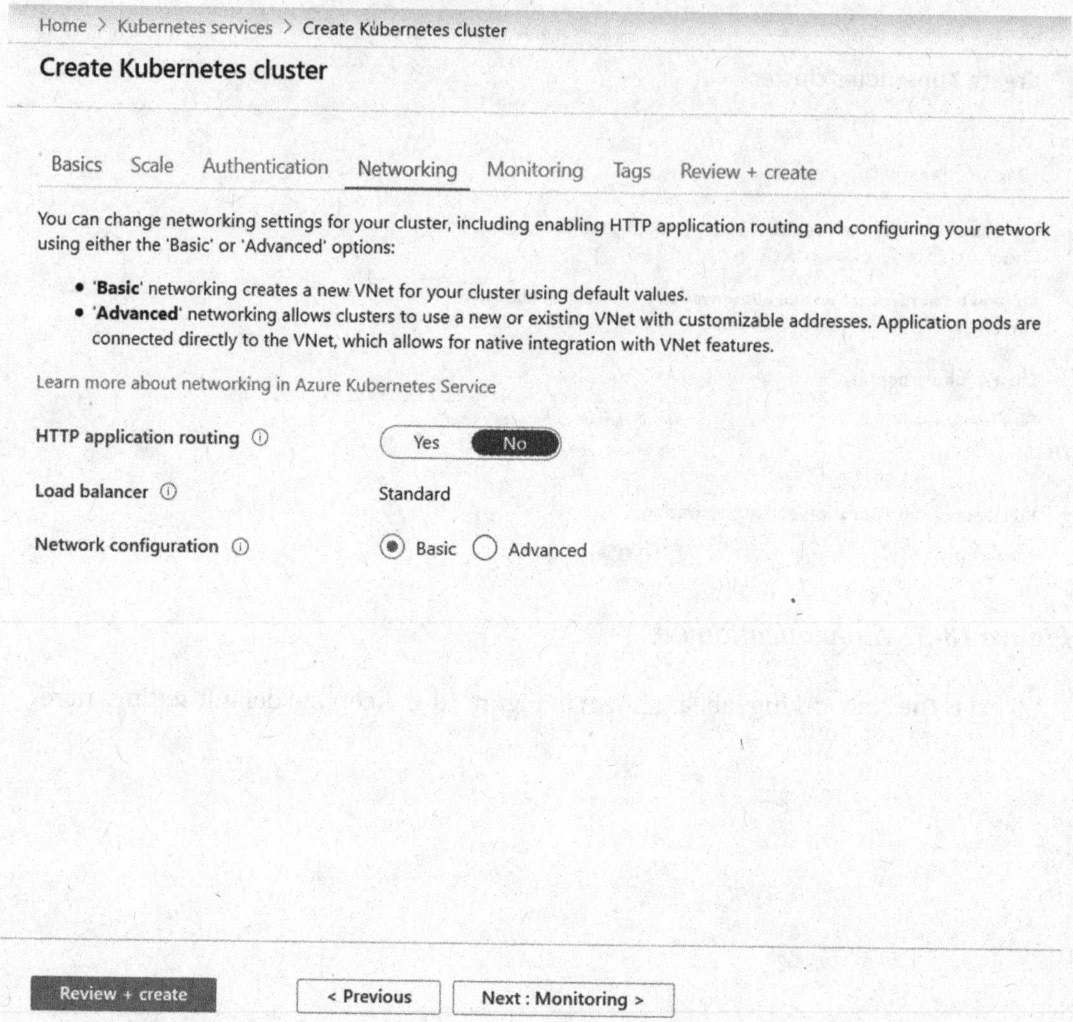

Home > Kubernetes services > Create Kubernetes cluster

Create Kubernetes cluster

Basics   Scale   Authentication   Networking   Monitoring   Tags   Review + create

You can change networking settings for your cluster, including enabling HTTP application routing and configuring your network using either the 'Basic' or 'Advanced' options:

- **'Basic'** networking creates a new VNet for your cluster using default values.
- **'Advanced'** networking allows clusters to use a new or existing VNet with customizable addresses. Application pods are connected directly to the VNet, which allows for native integration with VNet features.

Learn more about networking in Azure Kubernetes Service

HTTP application routing ⓘ   Yes   No

Load balancer ⓘ   Standard

Network configuration ⓘ   ● Basic ○ Advanced

Review + create   < Previous   Next : Monitoring >

Figure 18-6. *Networking tab*

Keep the default settings for the Monitoring tab, as shown in Figure 18-7.

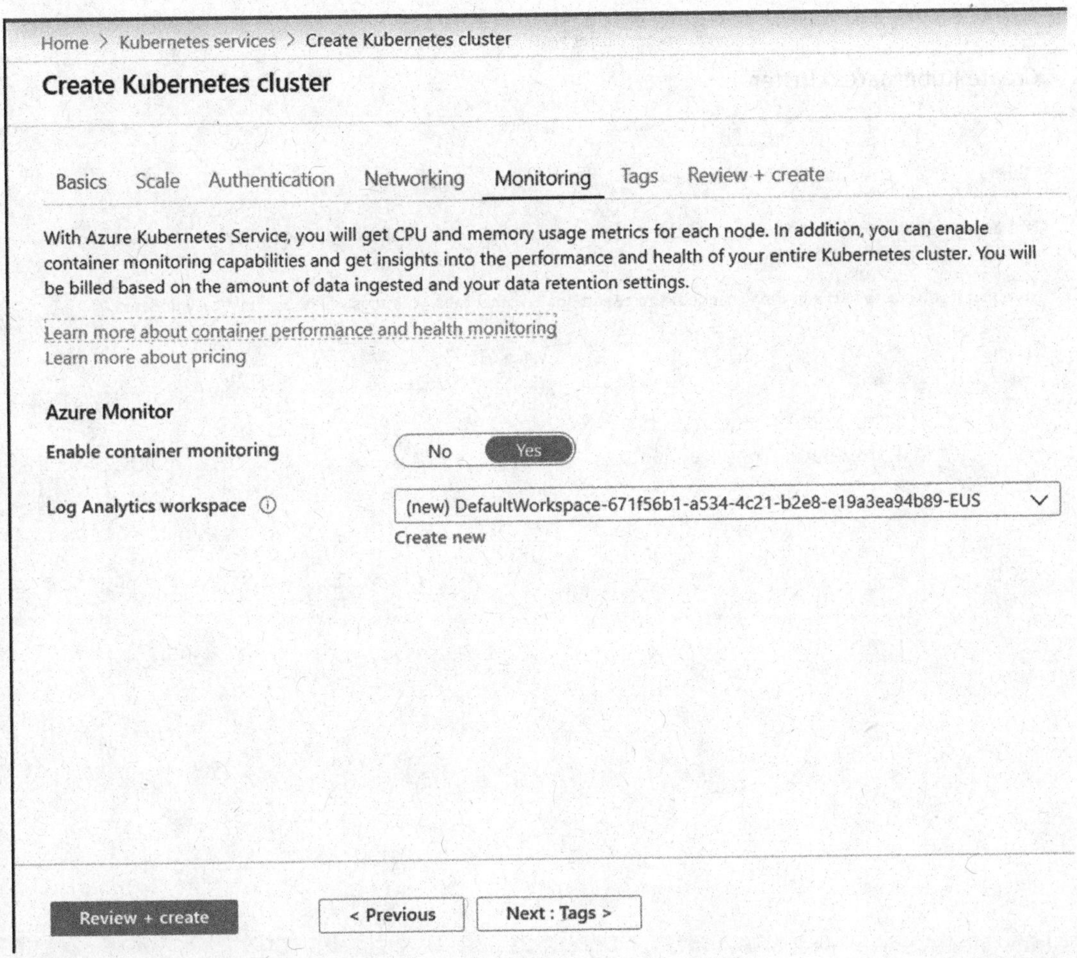

Figure 18-7. *Monitoring tab*

You can add tags as usual, as shown in Figure 18-8.

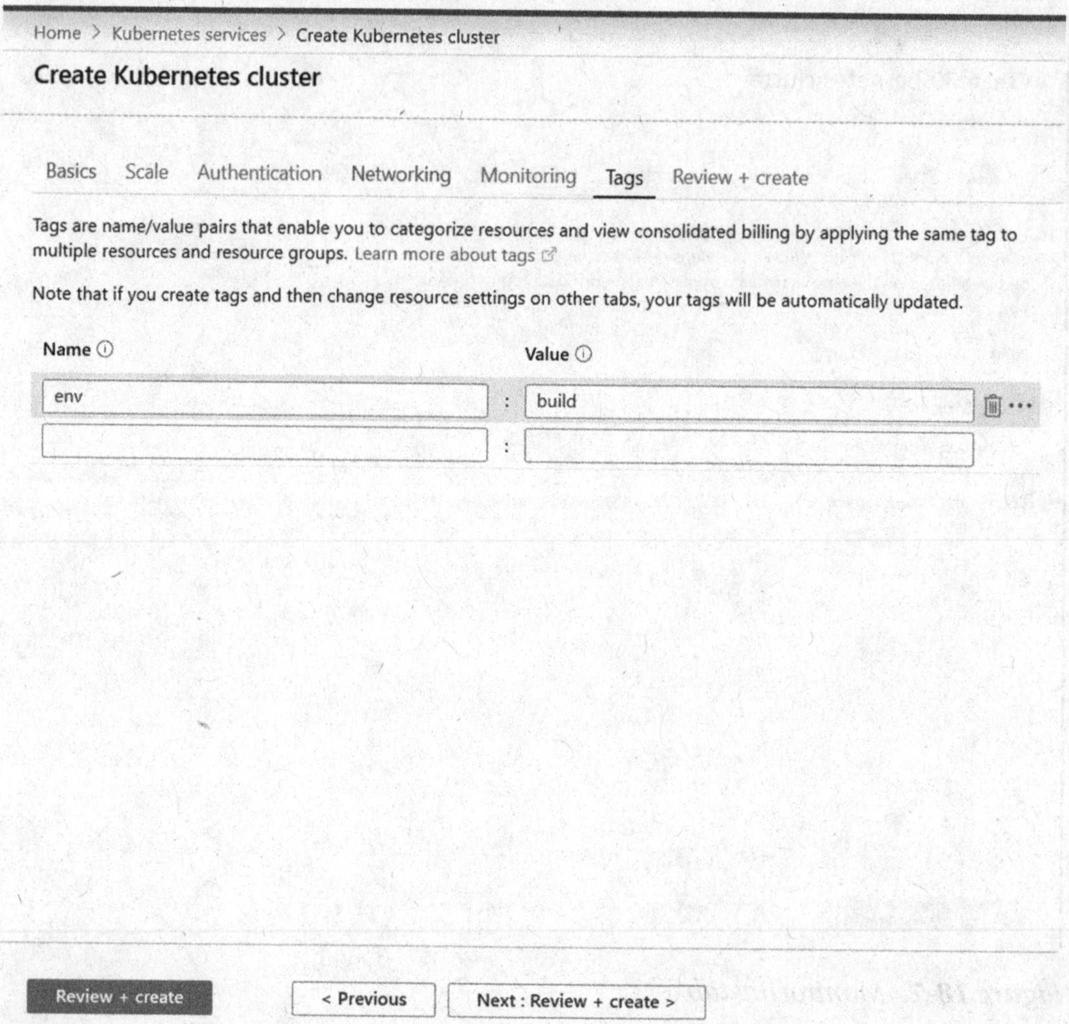

Home > Kubernetes services > Create Kubernetes cluster

Create Kubernetes cluster

Basics   Scale   Authentication   Networking   Monitoring   **Tags**   Review + create

Tags are name/value pairs that enable you to categorize resources and view consolidated billing by applying the same tag to multiple resources and resource groups. Learn more about tags ☑

Note that if you create tags and then change resource settings on other tabs, your tags will be automatically updated.

Name ⓘ   Value ⓘ

| env | : | build | 🗑 ••• |

| | : | | |

Review + create   < Previous   Next : Review + create >

Figure 18-8. Tags tab

Finally, click Next to go to the "Review + create" tab, as shown in Figure 18-9.

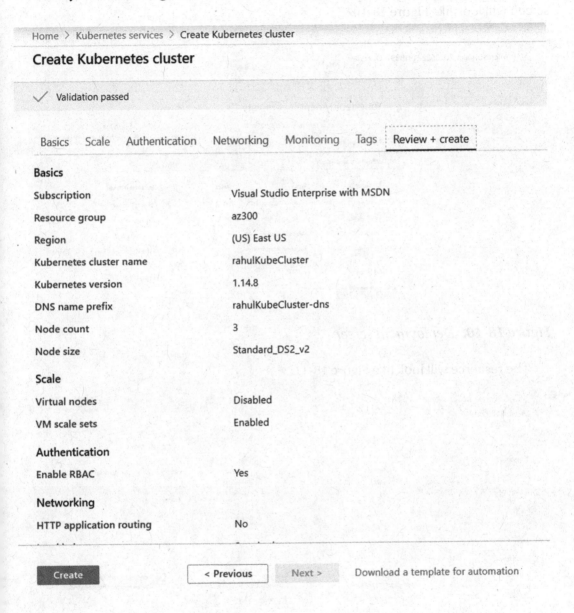

Figure 18-9. "Review + create" screen

The cluster will take some time to get created. After it's successfully created, your screen will look like Figure 18-10.

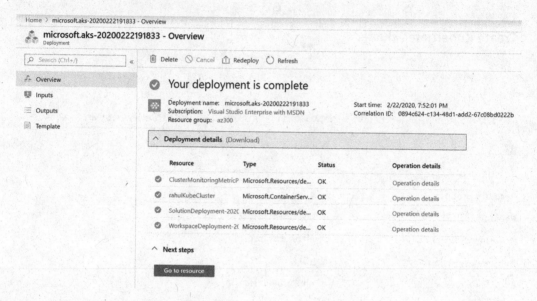

Figure 18-10. *Deployment screen*

The resource will look like Figure 18-11.

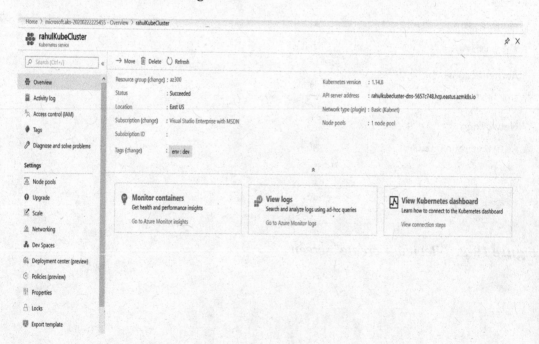

Figure 18-11. *Kubernetes Overview screen*

Deploying a Kubernetes Cluster

To deploy the cluster, let's use the CLI. In this case, you will use the kubectl command to interact with Kubernetes.

Before deploying it, you need to connect to the Kubernetes cluster. To do that, you will be using Azure AKS. Here is the command:

```
az aks get-credentials --resource-group az300 --name rahulKubeCluster
```

This command shows how to set up my cloud shell with the right context for my AKS cluster, as shown in Figure 18-12.

```
Bash      v  ⏻ ? ⚙ ⎘ ⎗ {} ⎆
rahul@Azure:~$ az aks get-credentials --resource-group az300 --name rahulKubeCluster
Merged "rahulKubeCluster" as current context in /home/rahul/.kube/config
rahul@Azure:~$
```

Figure 18-12. *Applied kubectl command*

Now, you can use kubectl. Let's check the nodes in the cloud shell, as shown in Figure 18-13.

```
Bash      v  ⏻ ? ⚙ ⎘ ⎗ {} ⎆
rahul@Azure:~$ kubectl get nodes
NAME                                STATUS   ROLES   AGE   VERSION
aks-agentpool-28526027-vmss000000   Ready    agent   13m   v1.14.8
aks-agentpool-28526027-vmss000001   Ready    agent   13m   v1.14.8
aks-agentpool-28526027-vmss000002   Ready    agent   14m   v1.14.8
rahul@Azure:~$
```

Figure 18-13. *Getting the nodes*

Next, you need to deploy some code into the cluster. Let's use the Microsoft sample for this. I have used the Azure vote bank sample from https://bit.ly/azure-voting-app.

I downloaded this file locally and then uploaded it in the cloud shell. Having said that, if I use dir in the shell, my screen will look like Figure 18-14.

Figure 18-14. *Checking the YML file*

You can now go ahead and type kubectl apply -f azure-vote-app.yml, as shown in Figure 18-15. This will push the deployments and service to these cluster nodes. The details of the YML file are beyond the scope of this book.

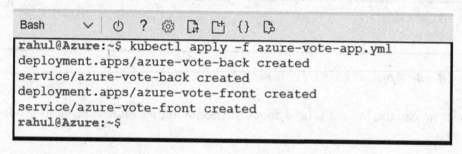

Figure 18-15. *Applying kubectl*

You can also get AKS service, as shown in Figure 18-16.

```
rahul@Azure:~$ kubectl get service
NAME                 TYPE            CLUSTER-IP       EXTERNAL-IP     PORT(S)         AGE
azure-vote-back      ClusterIP       10.0.39.197      <none>          6379/TCP        89s
azure-vote-front     LoadBalancer    10.0.84.240      40.88.23.230    80:31359/TCP    89s
kubernetes           ClusterIP       10.0.0.1         <none>          443/TCP         35m
rahul@Azure:~$
```

Figure 18-16. *Getting the service*

At this stage, when you paste 40.88.23.230 in browser, you can see the app running, as shown in Figure 18-17.

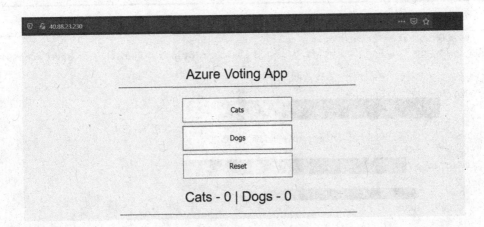

Figure 18-17. *App running*

Using the Kubernetes Dashboard

To run the Kubernetes dashboard locally, the first thing you need to do is install the Azure Command Line Interface. Get it here: `https://bit.ly/Azure-CLI`.

Now, log in with your Azure account in PowerShell with the `az login` command. This will open a browser with the Azure login. Select your account, and in ten seconds, it will redirect to PowerShell with the subscription, as shown in Figure 18-18.

```
Administrator: Windows PowerShell

PS C:\WINDOWS\system32> az login
You have logged in. Now let us find all the subscriptions to which you have access...
[
  {
    "cloudName": "AzureCloud",
    "id": "█████████████████████████",
    "isDefault": true,
    "name": "Visual Studio Enterprise with MSDN",
    "state": "Enabled",
    "tenantId": "██████████████████████████████",
    "user": {
      "name": "████████████████████████",
      "type": "user"
    }
  },
  {
    "cloudName": "AzureCloud",
    "id": "█████████████████████████",
    "isDefault": false,
    "name": "Microsoft Azure Sponsorship",
    "state": "Enabled",
    "tenantId": "██████████████████████████",
    "user": {
      "name": "███████████████████████",
      "type": "user"
    }
  }
]
PS C:\WINDOWS\system32>
```

Figure 18-18. *Azure login*

Once that is done, you need to install kubectl on the local machine with the command az aks install-cli.

Once this is done, you need to get the credentials of the AKS cluster and merge in the local machine. I will again use the same command, say, az aks get-credentials --resource-group az300 --name rahulKubeCluster.

You can access these commands directly from the "View dashboard" option, as shown in Figure 18-19.

Kubernetes dashboard ✕

To open your Kubernetes dashboard, complete the following steps:

(1)   Open Azure CLI version 2.0.27 or later. This will not work in cloud shell and must be running on your local machine. How to install the Azure CLI ⌐

(2)   If you do not already have kubectl installed in your CLI, run the following command:

```
az aks install-cli
```

(3)   Get the credentials for your cluster by running the following command:

```
az aks get-credentials --resource-group az300 --name rahulKubeCluster
```

(4)   Open the Kubernetes dashboard by running the following command:

```
az aks browse --resource-group az300 --name rahulKubeCluster
```

Useful links

What is Kubernetes dashboard? ⌐
Full instructions for opening the Kubernetes dashboard ⌐

Figure 18-19. *AKS commands in dashboard*

Once you execute one, the command line will look like Figure 18-20.

```
Administrator: Windows PowerShell                                    —    ☐    ✕
PS C:\WINDOWS\system32> az aks get-credentials --resource-group az300 --name rahulKubeCluster
Merged "rahulKubeCluster" as current context in C:\Users\rahuls\.kube\config
PS C:\WINDOWS\system32> ▪
```

Figure 18-20. *Getting credentials*

After this, you can browse the desktop with the command az aks browse --resource-group az300 --name rahulKubeCluster, as shown in Figure 18-21.

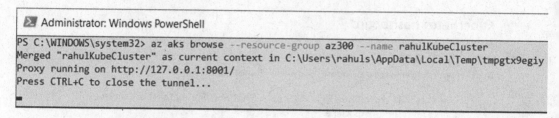

```
PS C:\WINDOWS\system32> az aks browse --resource-group az300 --name rahulKubeCluster
Merged "rahulKubeCluster" as current context in C:\Users\rahuls\AppData\Local\Temp\tmpgtx9egiy
Proxy running on http://127.0.0.1:8001/
Press CTRL+C to close the tunnel...
```

Figure 18-21. *AKS browse*

This will launch a browser, as shown in Figure 18-22.

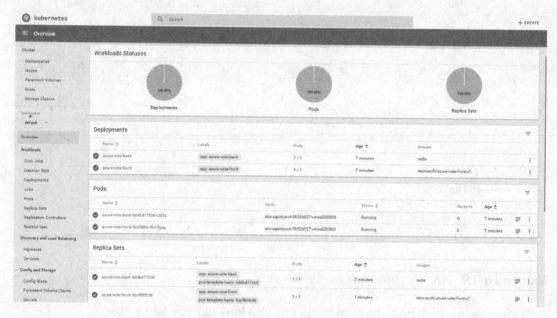

Figure 18-22. *Kubernetes dashboard in a browser*

This is very nice. You can control Kubernetes completely locally from the dashboard.

Running Containers Locally

To run containers locally, you need to install Docker first. Since I am on a Windows machine, I will install Docker for Windows from `https://bit.ly/win-docker-desktop`.

- Before installation, make sure to enable virtualization from the operating system level on the Windows machine. After that, you can go ahead and install Windows.

- Once Docker is installed and running, you will see the Docker icon in the system tray icon, as shown in Figure 18-23.

Figure 18-23. *Docker icon*

To demonstrate containers, I will clone the Azure vote app at `https://bit.ly/azure-sample-redis`. This file contains the `docker-compose` file as well, as shown in Figure 18-24.

```
 Windows PowerShell
PS D:\rahul\MyExperiments\azure\Azure Labs\azure-voting-app-redis> ls


    Directory: D:\rahul\MyExperiments\azure\Azure Labs\azure-voting-app-redis


Mode                LastWriteTime         Length Name
----                -------------         ------ ----
d-----        22-02-2020     23:33                azure-vote
d-----        22-02-2020     23:33                jenkins-tutorial
-a----        22-02-2020     23:33           1258 .gitignore
-a----        22-02-2020     23:33           1374 azure-vote-all-in-one-redis.yaml
-a----        22-02-2020     23:33            331 docker-compose.yaml
-a----        22-02-2020     23:33           1183 LICENSE
-a----        22-02-2020     23:33           1837 README.md


PS D:\rahul\MyExperiments\azure\Azure Labs\azure-voting-app-redis> ▂
```

Figure 18-24. *File listing*

The `docker-compose` file stitches together different Docker files running different services. I am not going into the details of containers here as it's beyond the scope of this book. Hence, I will simply execute `docker-compose up`, and it will start downloading the prerequisites and dependencies layer by layer, as shown in Figure 18-25.

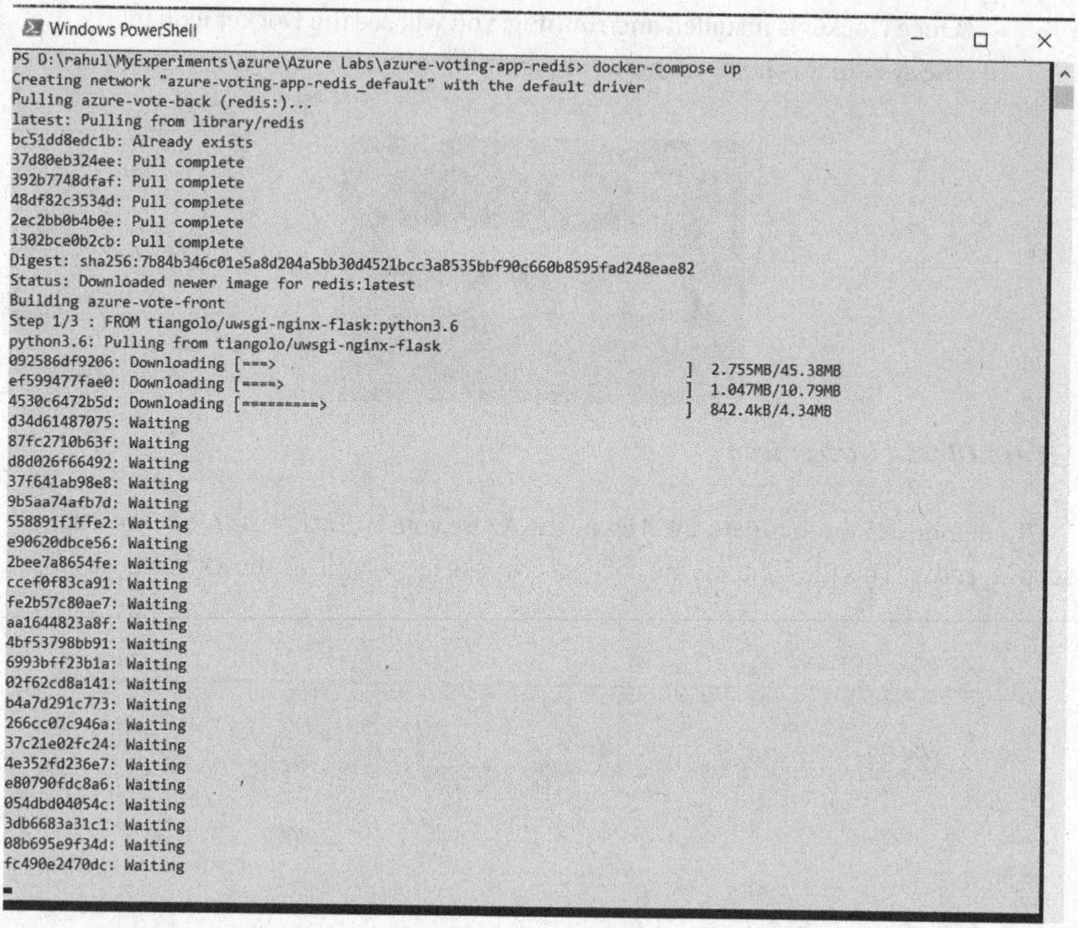

Figure 18-25. *Docker compose*

You may be asked to allow access, as shown in Figure 18-26.

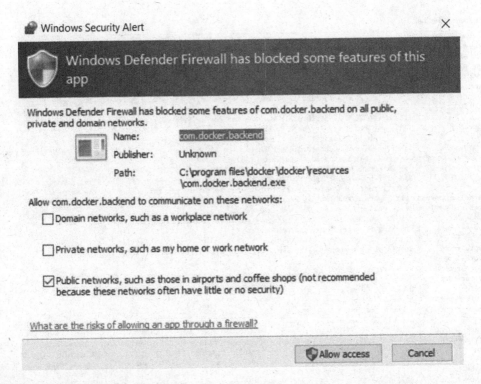

Figure 18-26. Allowing access

If you get a port already in use, then try to map the port to a different port. For example, I mapped port 80 to 8090. After it has been successfully executed, your screen will look like Figure 18-27.

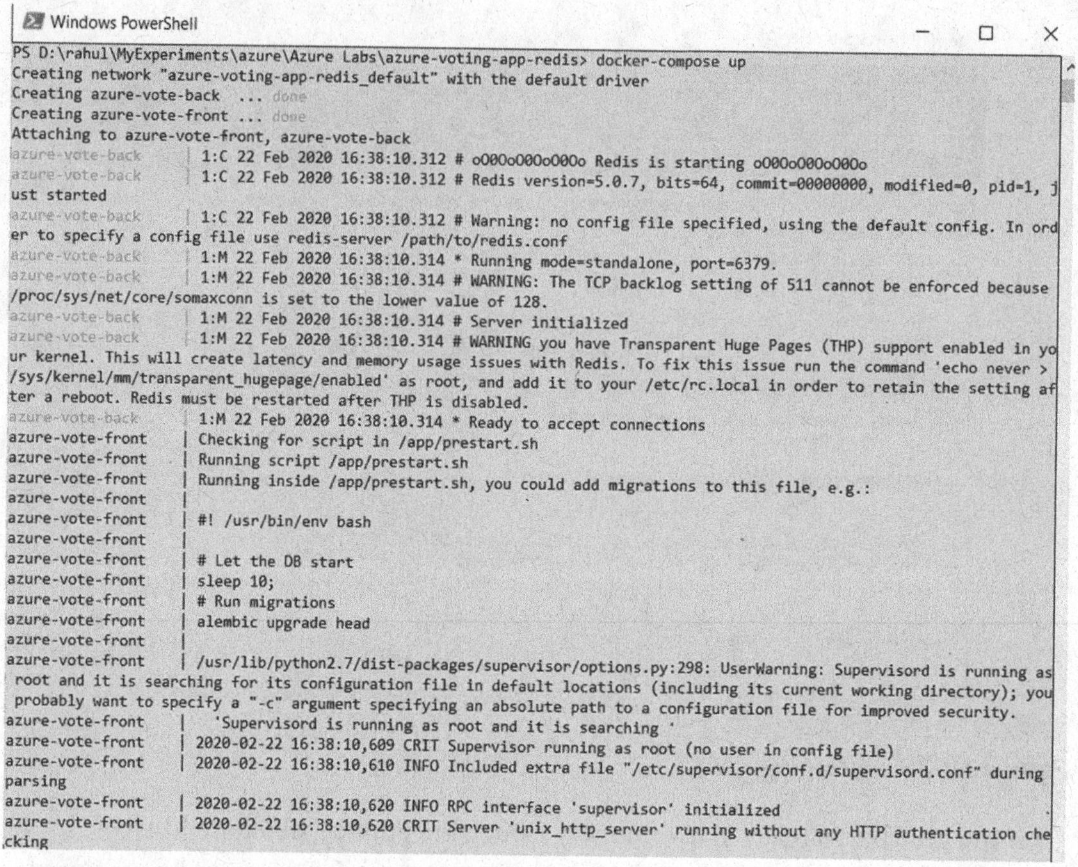

```
Windows PowerShell                                                                        —    □    ×

PS D:\rahul\MyExperiments\azure\Azure Labs\azure-voting-app-redis> docker-compose up
Creating network "azure-voting-app-redis_default" with the default driver
Creating azure-vote-back  ... done
Creating azure-vote-front ... done
Attaching to azure-vote-front, azure-vote-back
azure-vote-back    | 1:C 22 Feb 2020 16:38:10.312 # o000o000o000o Redis is starting o000o000o000o
azure-vote-back    | 1:C 22 Feb 2020 16:38:10.312 # Redis version=5.0.7, bits=64, commit=00000000, modified=0, pid=1, j
ust started
azure-vote-back    | 1:C 22 Feb 2020 16:38:10.312 # Warning: no config file specified, using the default config. In ord
er to specify a config file use redis-server /path/to/redis.conf
azure-vote-back    | 1:M 22 Feb 2020 16:38:10.314 * Running mode=standalone, port=6379.
azure-vote-back    | 1:M 22 Feb 2020 16:38:10.314 # WARNING: The TCP backlog setting of 511 cannot be enforced because
/proc/sys/net/core/somaxconn is set to the lower value of 128.
azure-vote-back    | 1:M 22 Feb 2020 16:38:10.314 # Server initialized
azure-vote-back    | 1:M 22 Feb 2020 16:38:10.314 # WARNING you have Transparent Huge Pages (THP) support enabled in yo
ur kernel. This will create latency and memory usage issues with Redis. To fix this issue run the command 'echo never >
/sys/kernel/mm/transparent_hugepage/enabled' as root, and add it to your /etc/rc.local in order to retain the setting af
ter a reboot. Redis must be restarted after THP is disabled.
azure-vote-back    | 1:M 22 Feb 2020 16:38:10.314 * Ready to accept connections
azure-vote-front   | Checking for script in /app/prestart.sh
azure-vote-front   | Running script /app/prestart.sh
azure-vote-front   | Running inside /app/prestart.sh, you could add migrations to this file, e.g.:
azure-vote-front   |
azure-vote-front   | #! /usr/bin/env bash
azure-vote-front   |
azure-vote-front   | # Let the DB start
azure-vote-front   | sleep 10;
azure-vote-front   | # Run migrations
azure-vote-front   | alembic upgrade head
azure-vote-front   |
azure-vote-front   | /usr/lib/python2.7/dist-packages/supervisor/options.py:298: UserWarning: Supervisord is running as
 root and it is searching for its configuration file in default locations (including its current working directory); you
 probably want to specify a "-c" argument specifying an absolute path to a configuration file for improved security.
azure-vote-front   |   'Supervisord is running as root and it is searching '
azure-vote-front   | 2020-02-22 16:38:10,609 CRIT Supervisor running as root (no user in config file)
azure-vote-front   | 2020-02-22 16:38:10,610 INFO Included extra file "/etc/supervisor/conf.d/supervisord.conf" during
parsing
azure-vote-front   | 2020-02-22 16:38:10,620 INFO RPC interface 'supervisor' initialized
azure-vote-front   | 2020-02-22 16:38:10,620 CRIT Server 'unix_http_server' running without any HTTP authentication che
cking
```

Figure 18-27. *App running inside Docker*

Therefore, when you navigate to `http://localhost:8090/`, you can see the app running from inside the container, as shown in Figure 18-28.

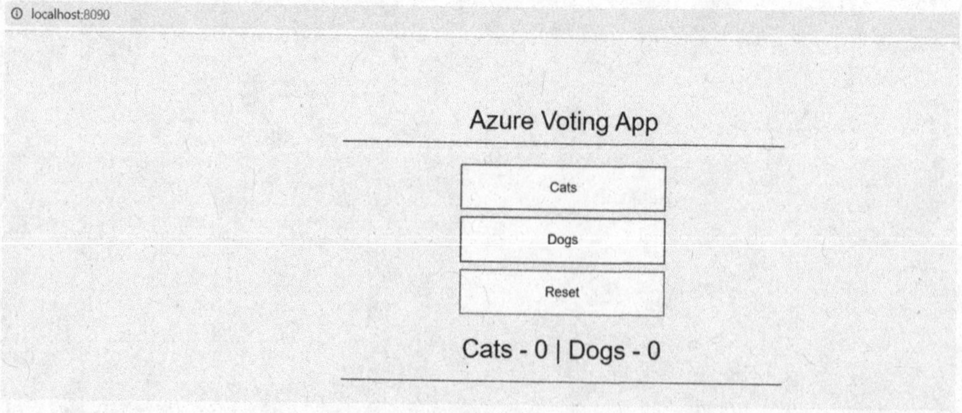

Figure 18-28. *App launched from Docker*

CHAPTER 19

Data Security

One of the best reasons to use Azure for your applications and services is to take advantage of its wide array of security tools and capabilities. These tools and capabilities help make it possible to create secure solutions on the secure Azure platform. Microsoft Azure provides confidentiality, integrity, and availability of customer data, while also enabling transparent accountability.

In this chapter, we will discuss data security. We already get tons of benefits when we store data in the cloud.

- Scaling

- Replication

- Tuning and optimization done for you

However, security becomes concern when your data becomes accessible from multitudes of devices. To rescue you from this, there are a variety of solutions.

- Encryption

- Firewall

- Virtual network service endpoints

- Private networks

Encryption

Let's start with encryption. Azure offers many kinds of databases.

- SQL Server

- Cosmos DB

© Rahul Sahay 2020
R. Sahay, *Microsoft Azure Architect Technologies Study Companion,*
https://doi.org/10.1007/978-1-4842-6200-9_19

- Azure Database for MySQL

- Azure Database for PostgreSQL

Microsoft Azure supports Transparent Data Encryption (TDE). This means data is stored on a physical disk in an encrypted state. But, when you read from that data and write to that data using databases, you are not dealing with encryption.

The following operations support TDE:

- Georestore

- Georeplication

- Copying a database

- Restoring a deleted database

When you export data from Azure, then that data is not encrypted. It will be in BACPAC format. Make sure not to keep the files in unencrypted locations; otherwise, you will have a security hole.

The other storage option is Storage Service Encryption (SSE). This is enabled by default on storage accounts and cannot be disabled.

Azure Key Vault

Azure Key Vault is a popular security solution in Azure. Secrets never get revealed to the developer or ops teams once a key vault is created. You can use the Azure Key Vault service to do the following:

- Protect encryption keys

- Protect certificates

- Protect passwords

Azure Key Vault follows the Federal Information Processing (FIPS) standards. This works based on the concept of centralized secrets. You can monitor when a secret was accessed and by whom.

Storing Azure Resource Manager Template Secrets

ARM templates are plain JSON files. However, you can store secrets using a vault and then reference the vault in template and parameter files.

Creating a Key Vault

Let's go ahead and create an Azure vault. Search for *key vault*, as shown in Figure 19-1.

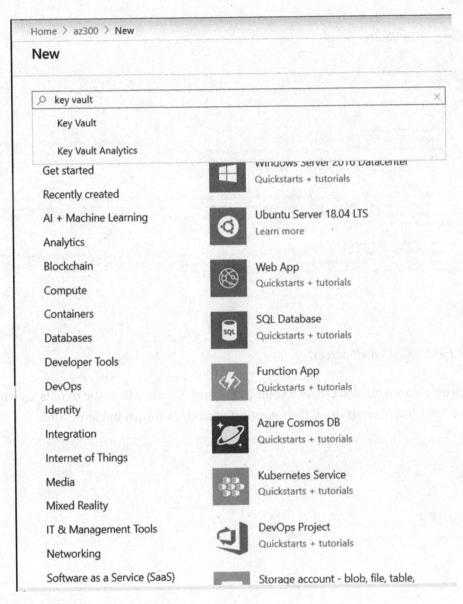

Figure 19-1. *Key vault search*

Clicking Key Vault will take you to the screen shown in Figure 19-2.

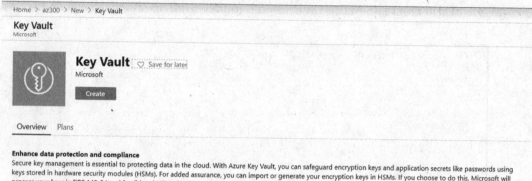

Figure 19-2. *Key Vault screen*

Let's now go ahead and create a vault by clicking Create. Fill in the details, as shown in Figure 19-3. You'll want to set the retention period, as shown in Figure 19-3.

Home > az300 > New > Key Vault > Create key vault

Create key vault

Basics   Access policy   Networking   Tags   Review + create

Azure Key Vault is a cloud service used to manage keys, secrets, and certificates. Key Vault eliminates the need for developers to store security information in their code. It allows you to centralize the storage of your application secrets which greatly reduces the chances that secrets may be leaked. Key Vault also allows you to securely store secrets and keys backed by Hardware Security Modules or HSMs. The HSMs used are Federal Information Processing Standards (FIPS) 140-2 Level 2 validated. In addition, key vault provides logs of all access and usage attempts of your secrets so you have a complete audit trail for compliance. Learn more

Project details

Select the subscription to manage deployed resources and costs. Use resource groups like folders to organize and manage all your resources.

Subscription *	Visual Studio Enterprise with MSDN
Resource group *	az300
	Create new

Instance details

Key vault name * ⓘ	rahul-key-vault
Region *	East US
Pricing tier * ⓘ	Standard
Soft delete ⓘ	Enable Disable

Figure 19-3. *Key vault creation*

Retention period (days) * ⓘ	90
Purge protection ⓘ	Enable Disable

Review + create   < Previous   Next : Access policy >

Figure 19-4. *Key vault retention period setting*

Click Next. On the "Access policy" tab, I have chosen all three settings listed, as shown in Figure 19-5.

Figure 19-5. *Key vault access policy*

You can also add an access policy if you want, as shown in Figure 19-6.

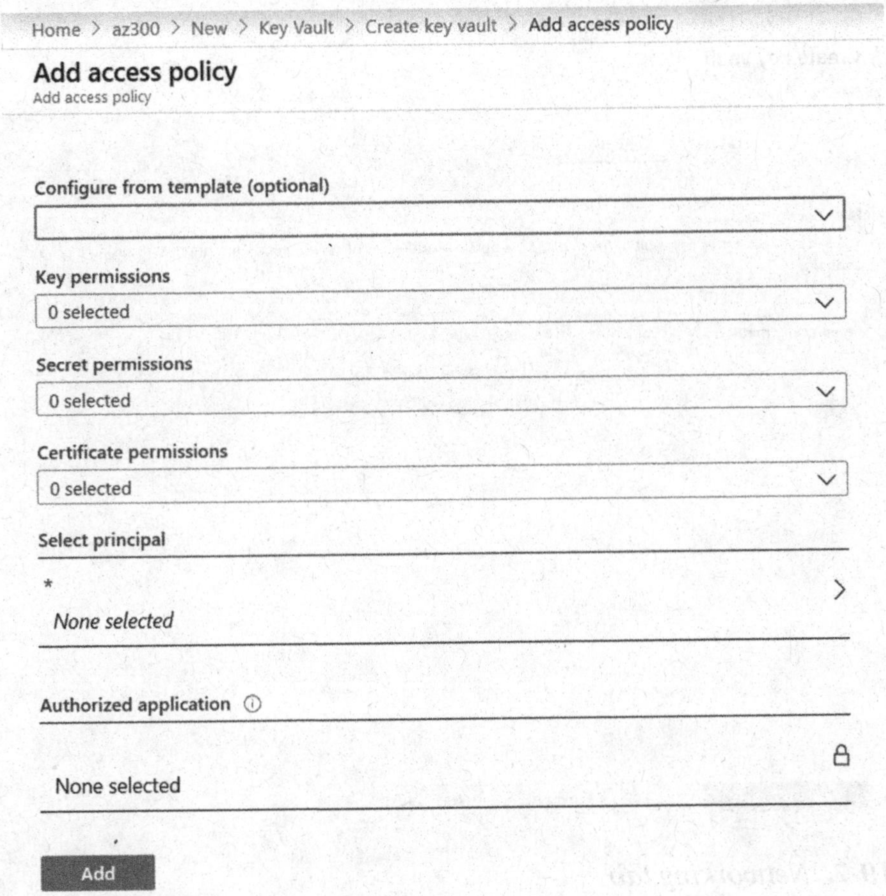

Home > az300 > New > Key Vault > Create key vault > Add access policy

Add access policy
Add access policy

Configure from template (optional)

[⌄]

Key permissions

[0 selected   ⌄]

Secret permissions

[0 selected   ⌄]

Certificate permissions

[0 selected   ⌄]

Select principal

*   >

None selected

Authorized application ⓘ

                                                                     🔒

None selected

[Add]

Figure 19-6. *Adding an access policy*

On the Networking tab, I have chosen the default settings, as shown in Figure 19-7.

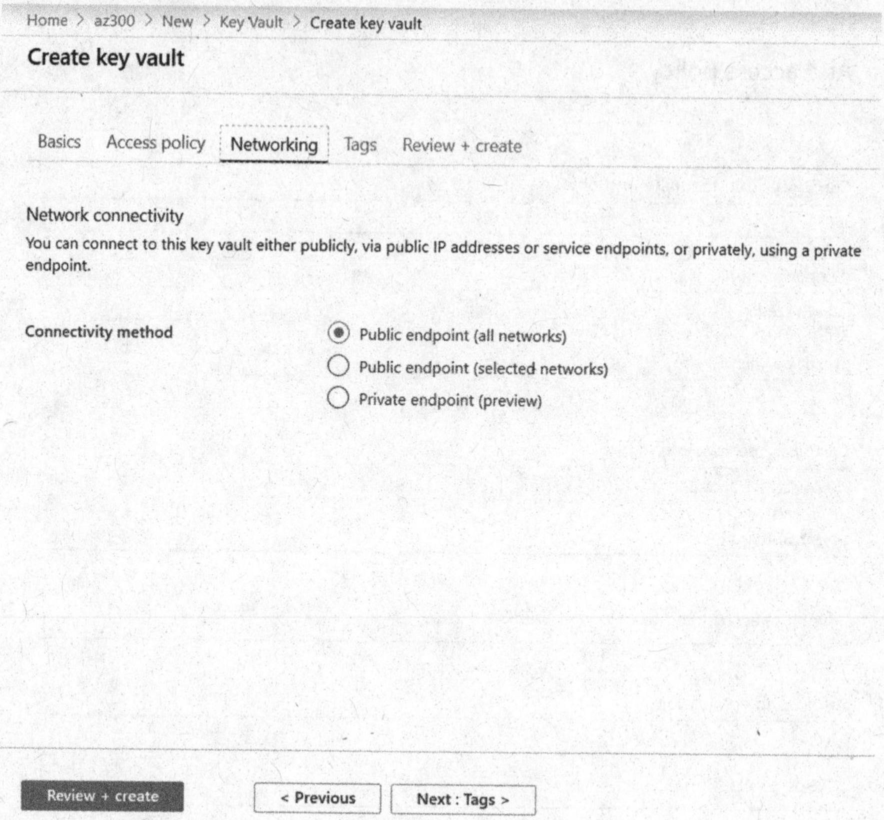

Figure 19-7. *Networking tab*

On the Tags tab, I have chosen the usual tag, as shown in Figure 19-8.

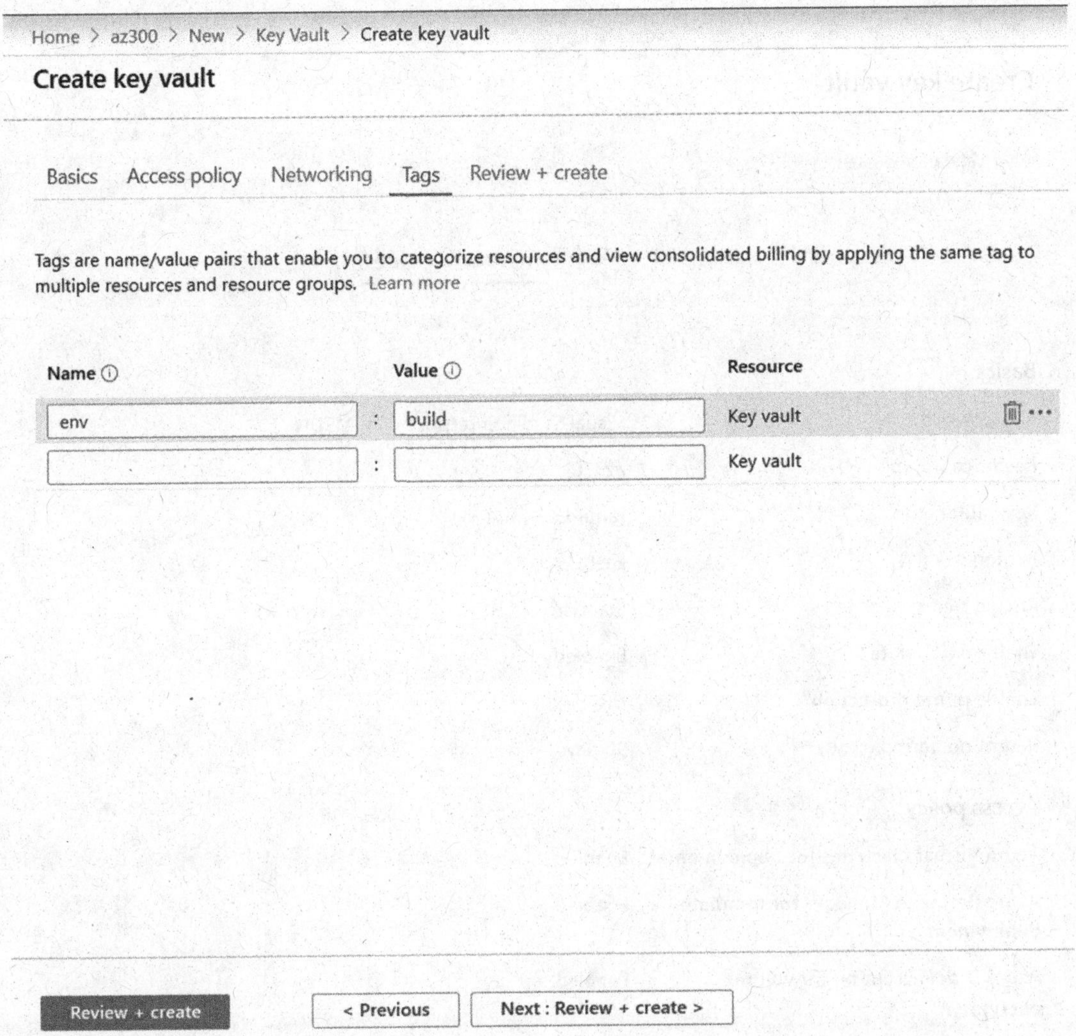

Home > az300 > New > Key Vault > Create key vault

Create key vault

Basics   Access policy   Networking   Tags   Review + create

Tags are name/value pairs that enable you to categorize resources and view consolidated billing by applying the same tag to multiple resources and resource groups. Learn more

Name ⓘ		Value ⓘ	Resource	
env	:	build	Key vault	🗑 •••
	:		Key vault	

Review + create   < Previous   Next : Review + create >

Figure 19-8. *Tags tab*

Finally, go to the "Review + create" tab, as shown in Figure 19-9.

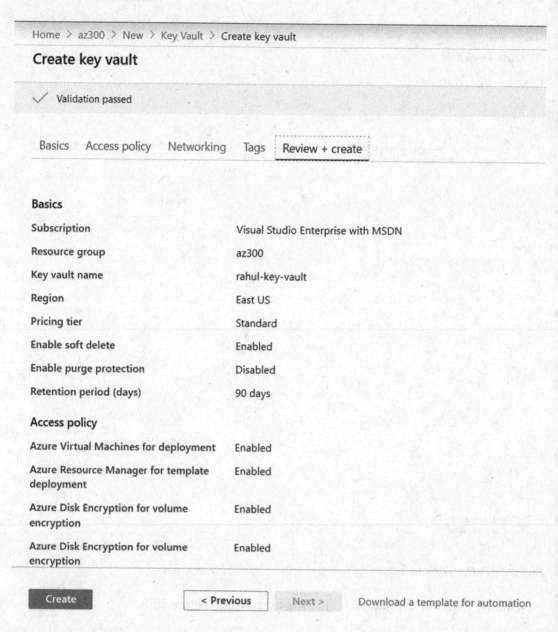

Figure 19-9. *"Review + create" tab*

It will take a couple of minutes to create a key vault. Once it is created, your screen will look like Figure 19-10.

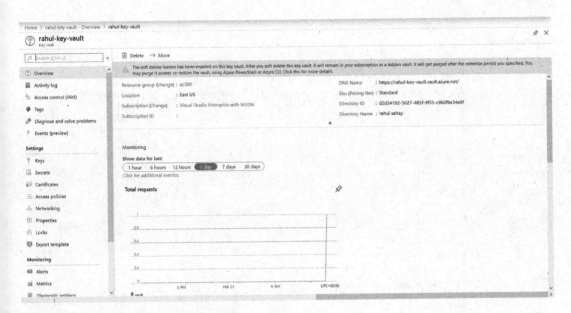

Figure 19-10. *Key vault Overview screen*

Creating a Secret

Let's now generate a secret by clicking the Secrets link and then the Generate/Import button, as shown in Figure 19-11.

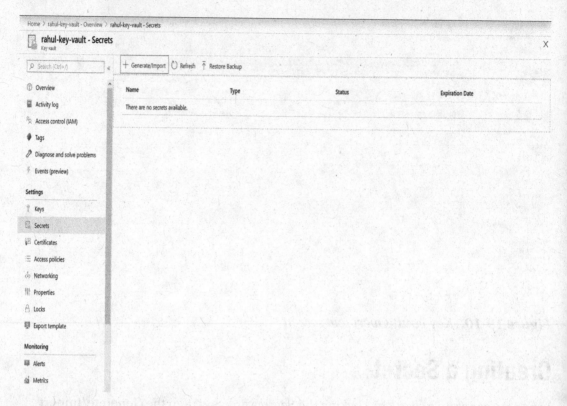

Figure 19-11. *Secrets link*

In Figure 19-12, I have chosen the Manual option.

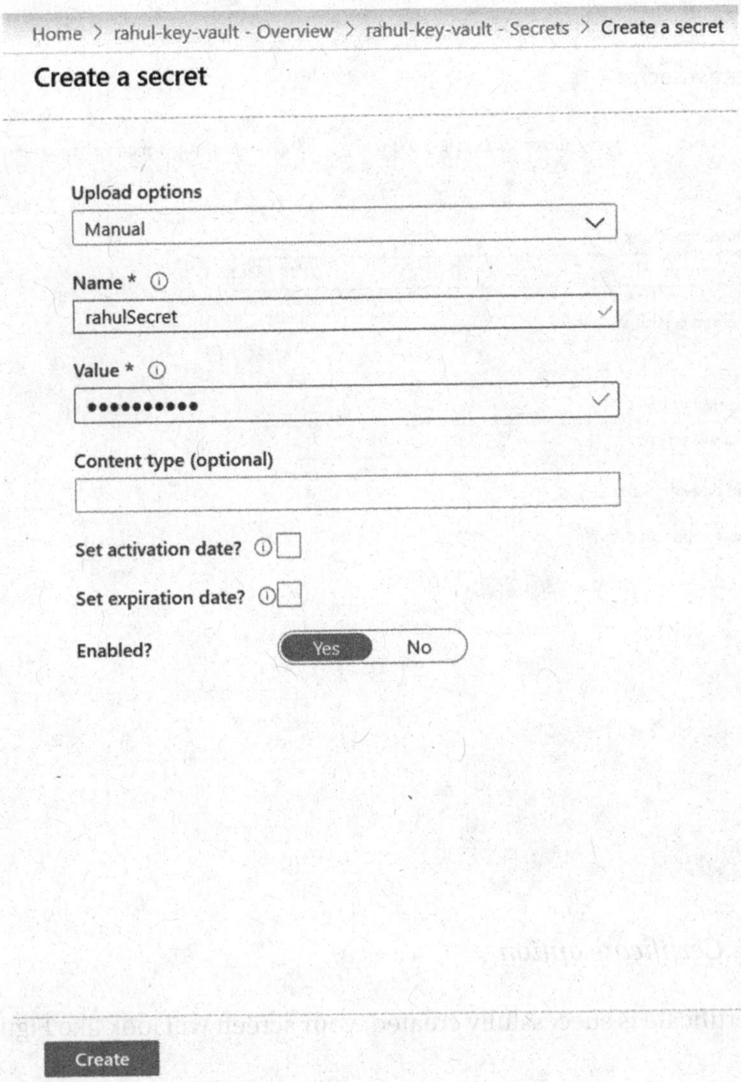

Home > rahul-key-vault - Overview > rahul-key-vault - Secrets > Create a secret

Create a secret

Upload options

Manual

Name * ⓘ

rahulSecret

Value * ⓘ

••••••••••

Content type (optional)

Set activation date? ⓘ☐

Set expiration date? ⓘ☐

Enabled?   Yes   No

Create

Figure 19-12. *Creating a secret*

Click the Create button. You can also upload a certificate to the vault, as shown in Figure 19-13.

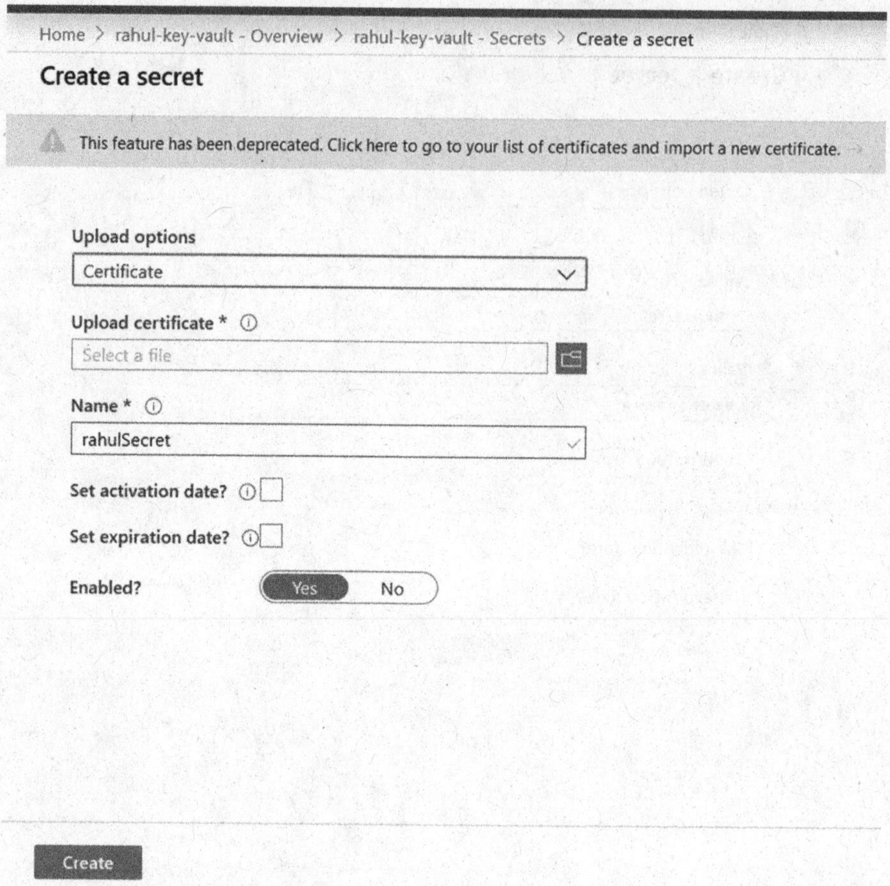

Figure 19-13. *Certificate option*

After the certificate is successfully created, your screen will look like Figure 19-14.

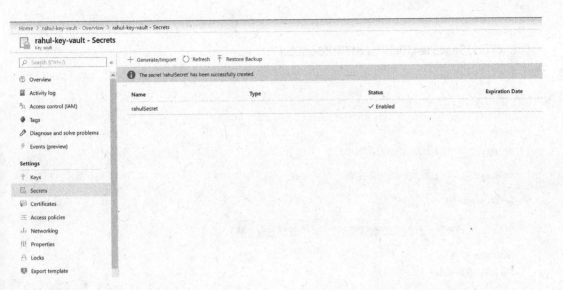

Figure 19-14. *Secrets screen*

When you click the secret, you can see the hash value applied to it, as shown in Figure 19-15.

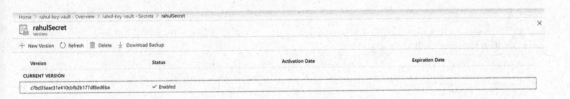

Figure 19-15. *Hash value*

After clicking the hash value, you can see its properties, as shown in Figure 19-16.

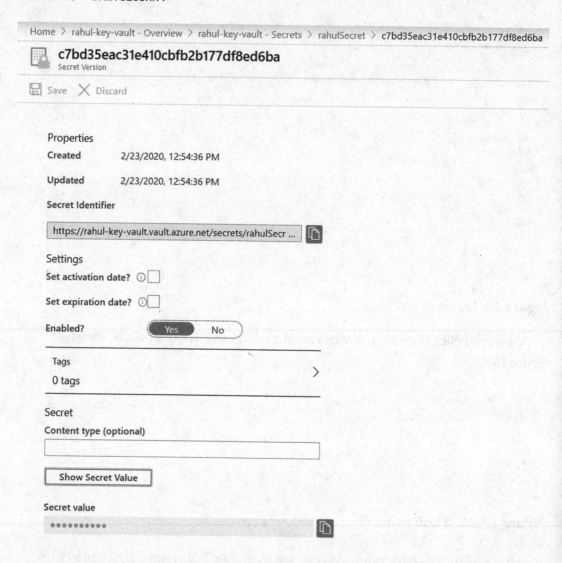

Figure 19-16. *Secret version*

You can use this URL for secret identification in your app or you can create a new version of it as well, as shown in Figure 19-17.

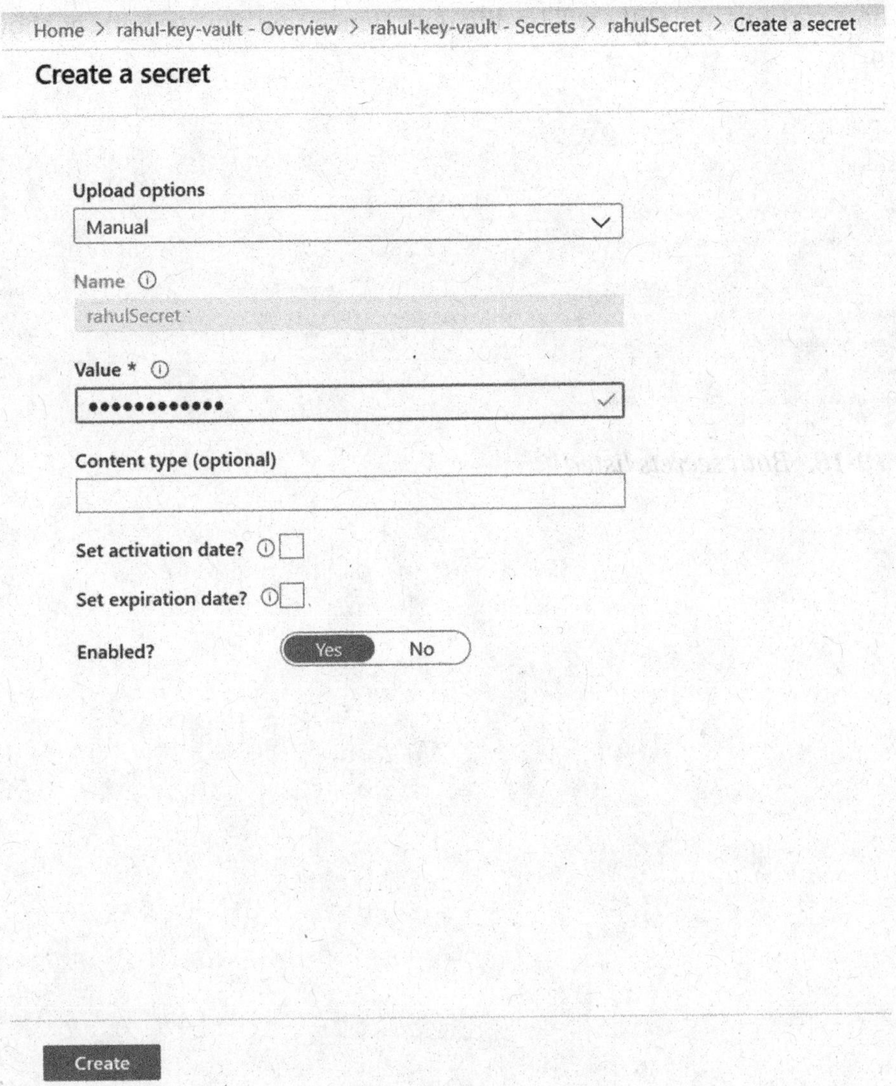

Home > rahul-key-vault - Overview > rahul-key-vault - Secrets > rahulSecret > **Create a secret**

Create a secret

Upload options

| Manual | ⌄ |

Name ⓘ

rahulSecret *

Value * ⓘ

| ●●●●●●●●●●●●● | ✓ |

Content type (optional)

Set activation date? ⓘ ☐

Set expiration date? ⓘ ☐

Enabled?   Yes   No

Create

***Figure 19-17.** Creating a second secret*

For both versions, the URLs will be different. Hence, you can use both, as shown in Figure 19-18.

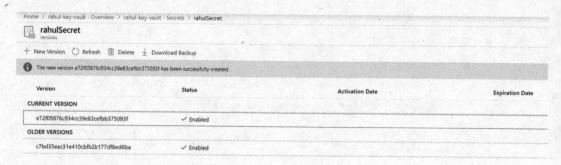

Figure 19-18. *Both secrets listed*

CHAPTER 20

Cosmos DB

Azure Cosmos DB is a fully managed database service with turnkey global distribution and transparent multimaster replication. In this chapter, you will explore Azure Cosmos DB in detail.

- Azure Cosmos DB can handle millions of transactions per second.

- Azure Cosmos DB is specifically designed for high performance. Therefore, if your app is using NoSQL and it has a requirement for high-performance and volume, then you should choose Cosmos DB.

NoSQL databases are referred to as nonrelational, NoSQL DBs, or non-SQL to highlight the fact that they can handle huge volumes of rapidly changing, unstructured data in a different way than a relational (SQL) database with rows and tables.

Creating a Cosmos DB

Search for *Cosmos DB*, as shown in Figure 20-1.

© Rahul Sahay 2020
R. Sahay, *Microsoft Azure Architect Technologies Study Companion*,
https://doi.org/10.1007/978-1-4842-6200-9_20

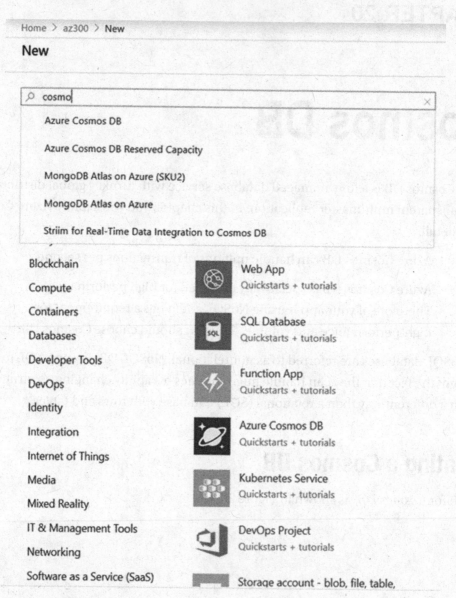

Figure 20-1. *Cosmos search*

Click Azure Cosmos DB, which will bring up the screen shown in Figure 20-2.

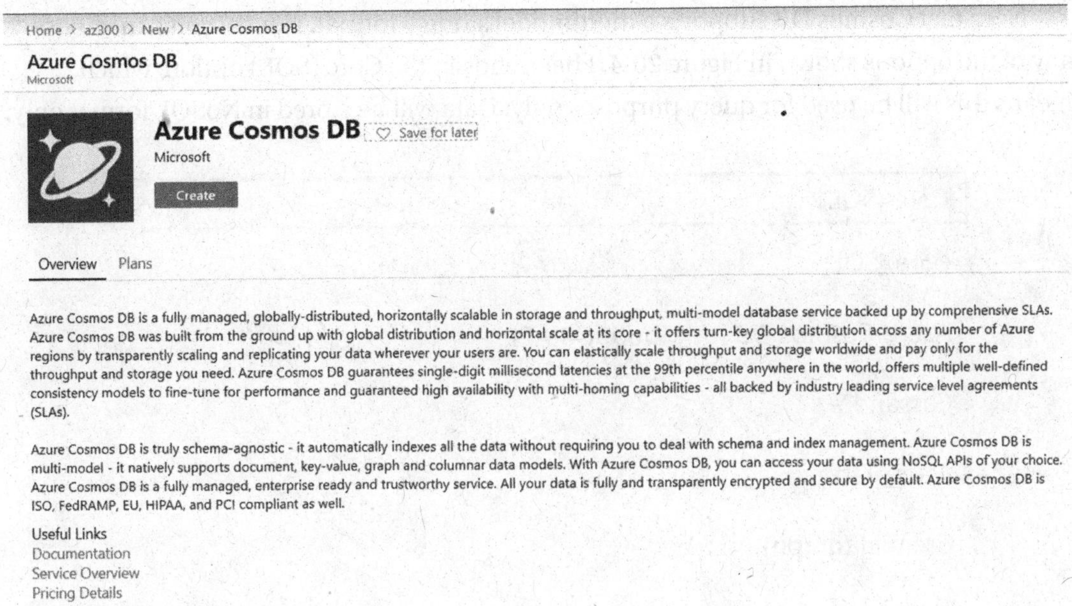

Home > az300 > New > Azure Cosmos DB

Azure Cosmos DB
Microsoft

Azure Cosmos DB ♡ Save for later
Microsoft

[Create]

Overview   Plans

Azure Cosmos DB is a fully managed, globally-distributed, horizontally scalable in storage and throughput, multi-model database service backed up by comprehensive SLAs. Azure Cosmos DB was built from the ground up with global distribution and horizontal scale at its core - it offers turn-key global distribution across any number of Azure regions by transparently scaling and replicating your data wherever your users are. You can elastically scale throughput and storage worldwide and pay only for the throughput and storage you need. Azure Cosmos DB guarantees single-digit millisecond latencies at the 99th percentile anywhere in the world, offers multiple well-defined consistency models to fine-tune for performance and guaranteed high availability with multi-homing capabilities - all backed by industry leading service level agreements (SLAs).

Azure Cosmos DB is truly schema-agnostic - it automatically indexes all the data without requiring you to deal with schema and index management. Azure Cosmos DB is multi-model - it natively supports document, key-value, graph and columnar data models. With Azure Cosmos DB, you can access your data using NoSQL APIs of your choice. Azure Cosmos DB is a fully managed, enterprise ready and trustworthy service. All your data is fully and transparently encrypted and secure by default. Azure Cosmos DB is ISO, FedRAMP, EU, HIPAA, and PCI compliant as well.

Useful Links
Documentation
Service Overview
Pricing Details

Figure 20-2. *Cosmos DB screen*

Let's click Create and provide the information shown in Figure 20-3.

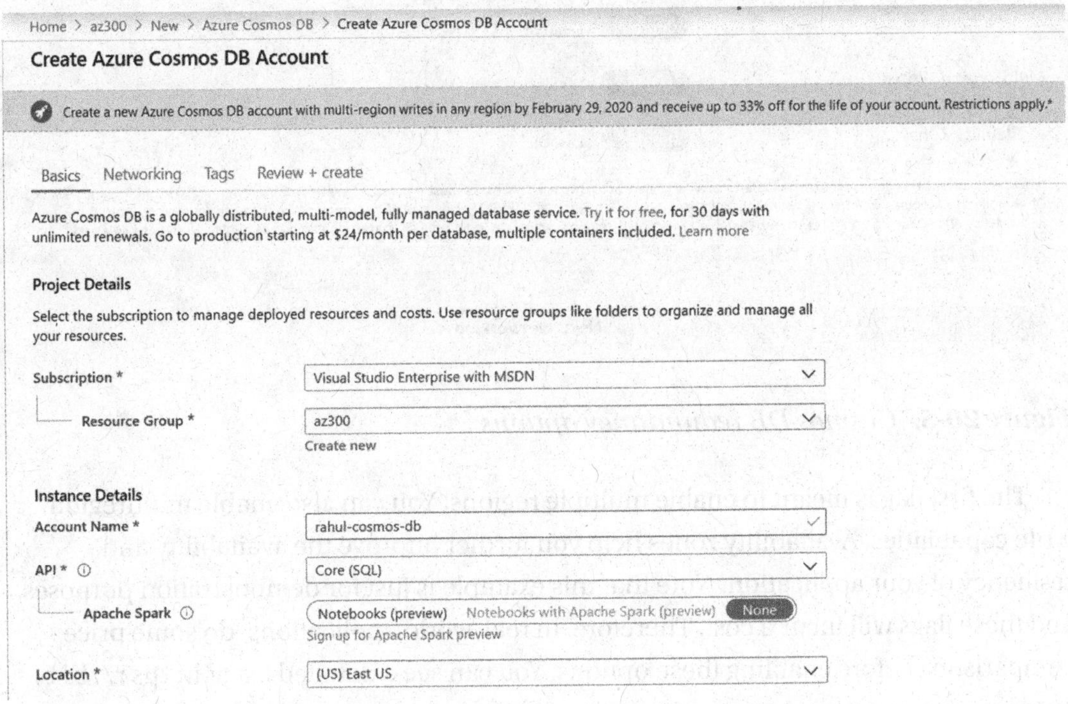

Home > az300 > New > Azure Cosmos DB > Create Azure Cosmos DB Account

Create Azure Cosmos DB Account

🚀 Create a new Azure Cosmos DB account with multi-region writes in any region by February 29, 2020 and receive up to 33% off for the life of your account. Restrictions apply.*

Basics   Networking   Tags   Review + create

Azure Cosmos DB is a globally distributed, multi-model, fully managed database service. Try it for free, for 30 days with unlimited renewals. Go to production starting at $24/month per database, multiple containers included. Learn more

Project Details

Select the subscription to manage deployed resources and costs. Use resource groups like folders to organize and manage all your resources.

Subscription * | Visual Studio Enterprise with MSDN   ∨ |

└─ Resource Group * | az300   ∨ |
                         Create new

Instance Details

Account Name * | rahul-cosmos-db   ∨ |

API * ⓘ | Core (SQL)   ∨ |

└─ Apache Spark ⓘ   (Notebooks (preview)   Notebooks with Apache Spark (preview)   None)
                         Sign up for Apache Spark preview

Location * | (US) East US   ∨ |

Figure 20-3. *Create Azure Cosmos DB Account screen, Basics tab*

701

Note that Cosmos DB supports a multimodel storage format. Hence, you can choose any of the options shown in Figure 20-4. I have chosen the Core (SQL) option, which means this will be used for query purposes only. Data will be stored in NoSQL format only.

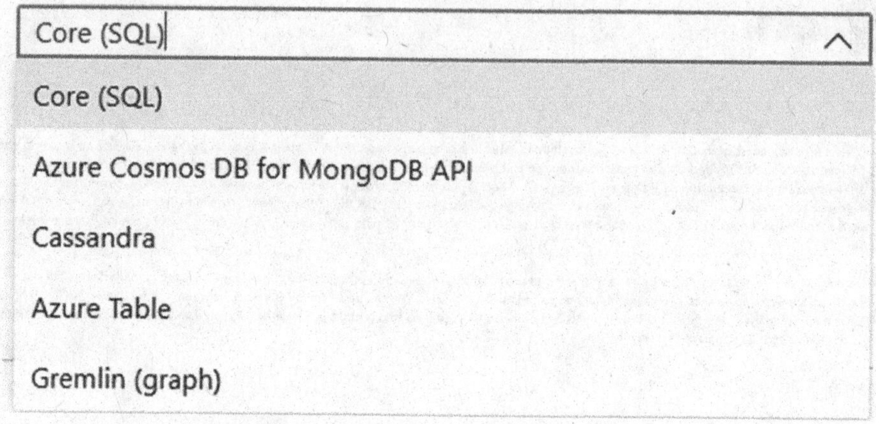

Figure 20-4. *Cosmos DB API options*

Next, you can enable all the options, as shown in Figure 20-5.

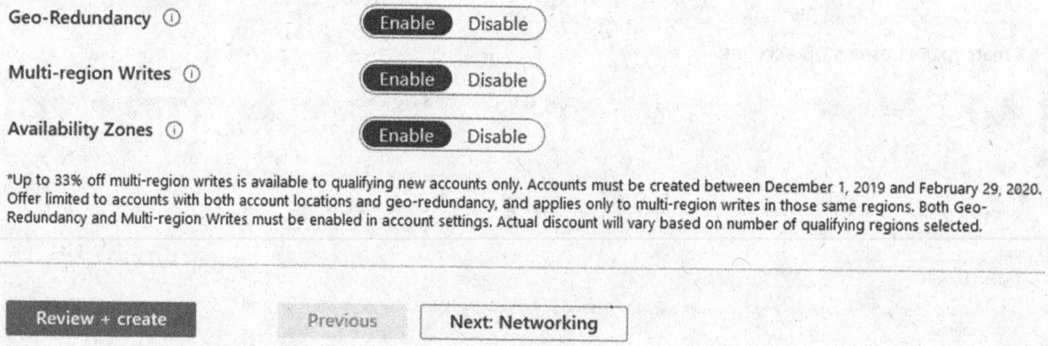

Figure 20-5. *Cosmos DB redundancy options*

The first flag is meant to enable multiple regions. You can also enable multiregion write capabilities. Availability zones help you further improve the availability and resiliency of your application. Note that this example is just for demonstration purposes, and these flags will incur a cost. Therefore, in real-world applications, do some price comparisons before enabling these options. You can see a detailed list at `https://bit.ly/azure-cosmos-pricing`.

On the Networking tab, you can go with the default settings, as shown in Figure 20-6.

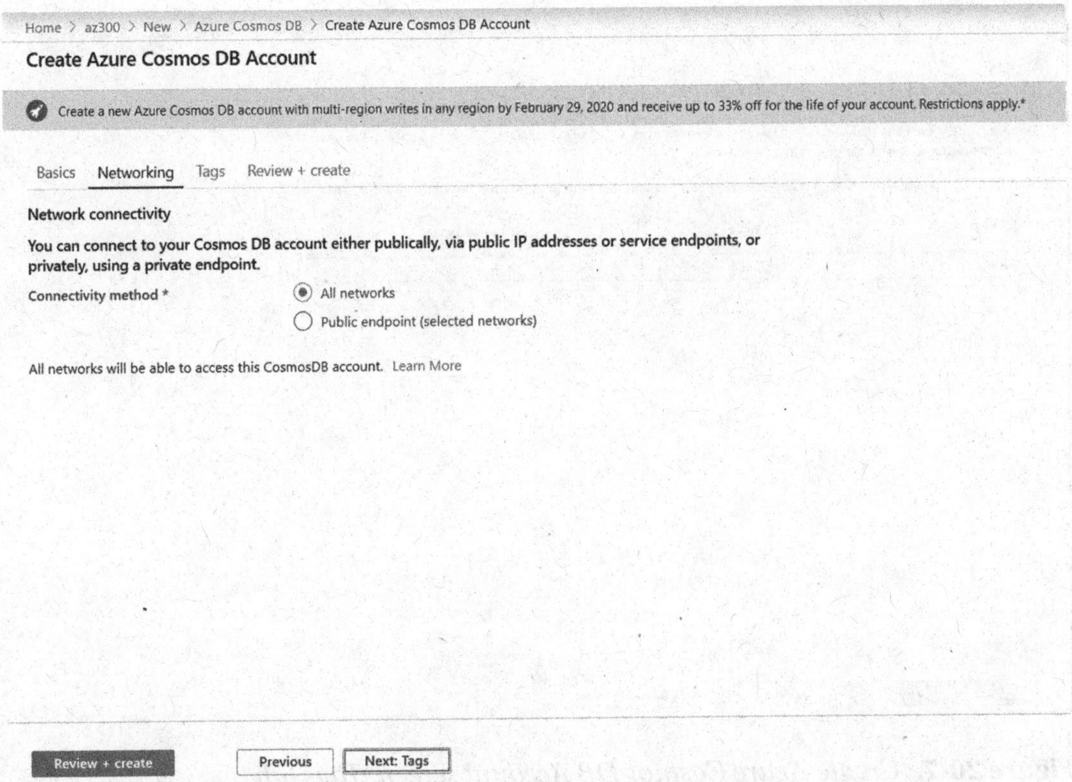

Figure 20-6. *Create Azure Cosmos DB Account screen, Networking tab*

Next comes the Tags tab, as shown in Figure 20-7.

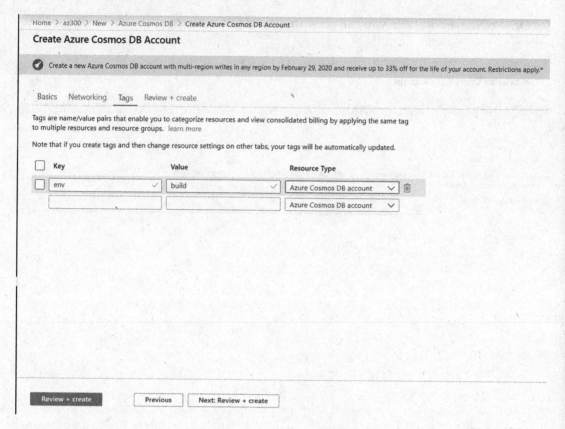

Figure 20-7. *Create Azure Cosmos DB Account screen, Tags tab*

Finally, the "Review + create" tab is shown in Figure 20-8.

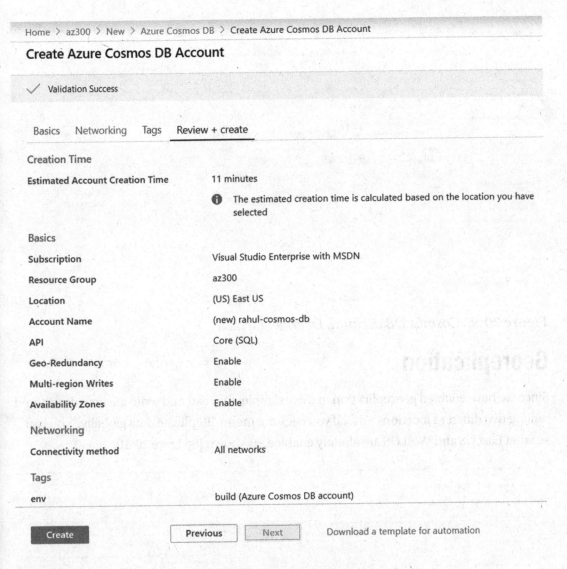

Home > az300 > New > Azure Cosmos DB > Create Azure Cosmos DB Account

Create Azure Cosmos DB Account

✓ Validation Success

Basics   Networking   Tags   **Review + create**

Creation Time

Estimated Account Creation Time   11 minutes

                                         ℹ️ The estimated creation time is calculated based on the location you have
                                             selected

Basics

Subscription   Visual Studio Enterprise with MSDN

Resource Group   az300

Location   (US) East US

Account Name   (new) rahul-cosmos-db

API   Core (SQL)

Geo-Redundancy   Enable

Multi-region Writes   Enable

Availability Zones   Enable

Networking

Connectivity method   All networks

Tags

env   build (Azure Cosmos DB account)

[Create]   [Previous] [Next]   Download a template for automation

Figure 20-8. Cosmos DB screen, "Review + create" tab

Click Create. This will take a couple of minutes. Once the Cosmos DB account is
created, you can go to the resource, as shown in Figure 20-9.

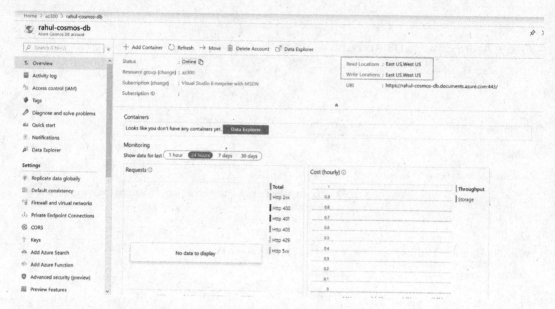

Figure 20-9. *Cosmos DB account, Overview screen*

Georeplication

Since we have enabled georeplication in this example, the read and write are now distributed among two different locations. Also, if you click the menu "Replicate data globally," you can see that East US and West US are already enabled, as shown in Figure 20-10.

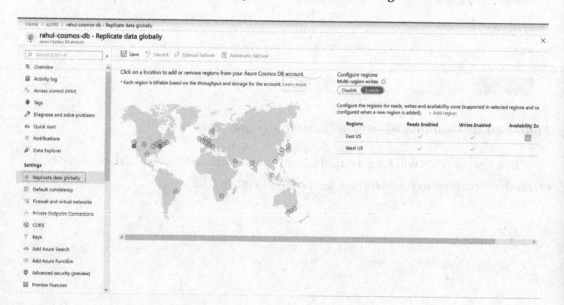

Figure 20-10. *Georeplication*

You can add other locations as well if you want that support here.

Creating an Items Container

Let's go to the "Quick start" section, where you can create some dummy data to get started, as shown in Figure 20-11. To do this, click "Create items container" and then download the sample if you want. One point to note here, these platform options keep changing. Hence, you need to select the right platform and look for Create Items container. Generally, its available with every platform.

Figure 20-11. *Create Items container*

From here, you can download the app and get started. You can also see the data online by clicking the Open Data Explorer option. This will open the screen shown in Figure 20-12.

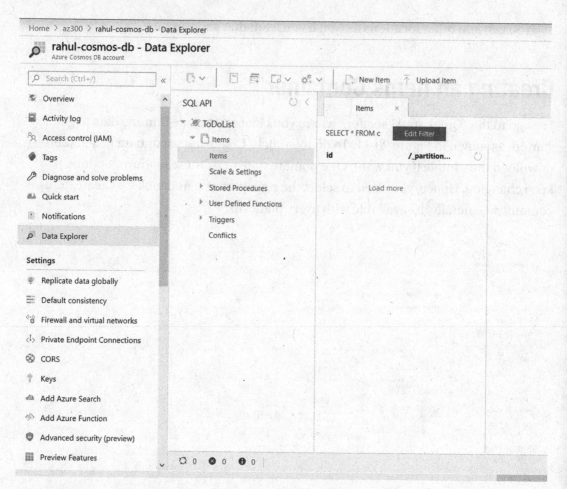

Figure 20-12. *Data Explorer*

Creating a Cosmos DB Collection

To create a new collection, click Browse in the left menu under Containers. This will bring up the screen shown in Figure 20-13.

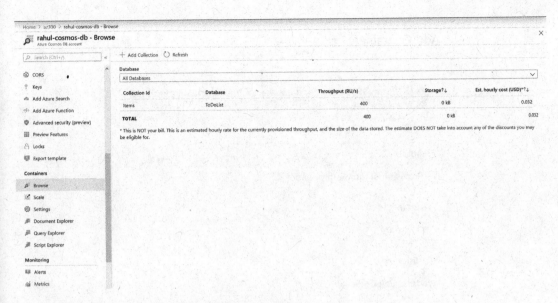

Figure 20-13. *Cosmos DB collection screen*

One collection is already there, which was just created. Now, you can click the Add Collection button and enter the details shown in Figure 20-14. I am just saying container id *employee* as an example. You are free to use whatever design you like.

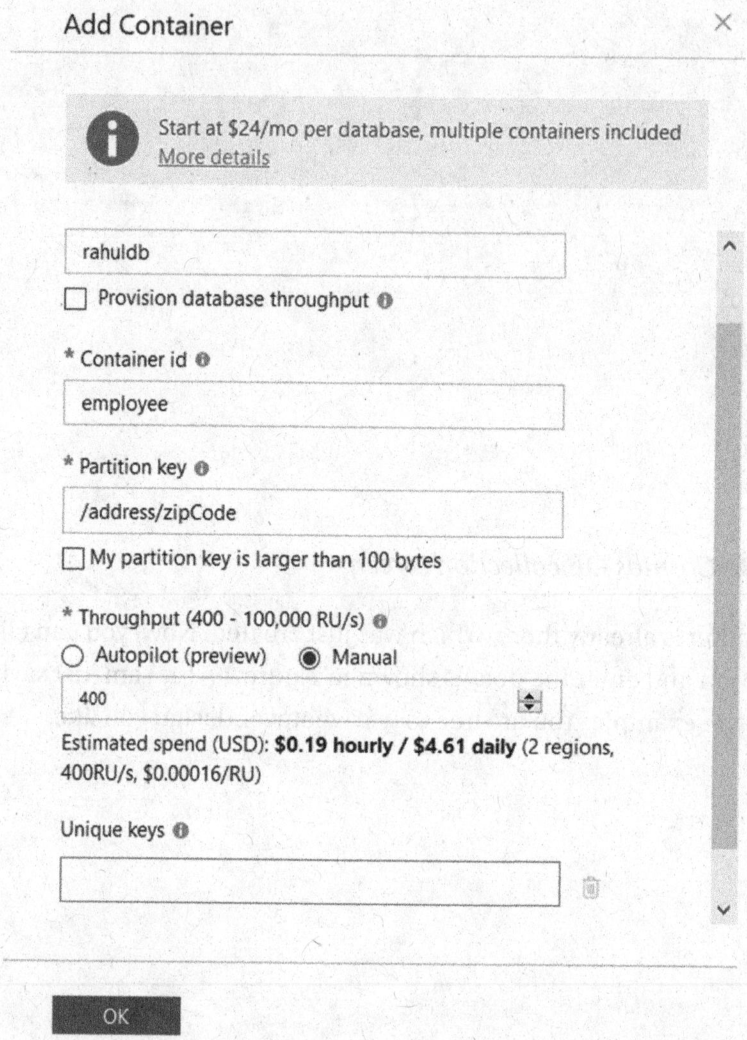

Add Container   ✕

ⓘ Start at $24/mo per database, multiple containers included
    More details

rahuldb

☐ Provision database throughput ❶

* Container id ❶

employee

* Partition key ❶

/address/zipCode

☐ My partition key is larger than 100 bytes

* Throughput (400 - 100,000 RU/s) ❶

◯ Autopilot (preview)   ⦿ Manual

400   ⬍

Estimated spend (USD): **$0.19 hourly / $4.61 daily** (2 regions,
400RU/s, $0.00016/RU)

Unique keys ❶

[   ] 🗑

OK

Figure 20-14. Adding a collection

As you can see in Figure 20-14, I have given rahuldb as the main database. Under one database, you can have multiple containers. Here, I have created an employee container underneath rahuldb.

The partition key is going to be used by Cosmos DB intelligently to divide the data between servers if the data becomes too big.

Lastly, you can choose to provide a unique key if you want. Click OK. Once the database is created, your screen will look like Figure 20-15.

Figure 20-15. SQL API screen

You can see that you have many options such as stored procedures, triggers, etc.

Adding Records to the Database

Let's start adding records to the Employee database that we just created, as shown in Figure 20-16.

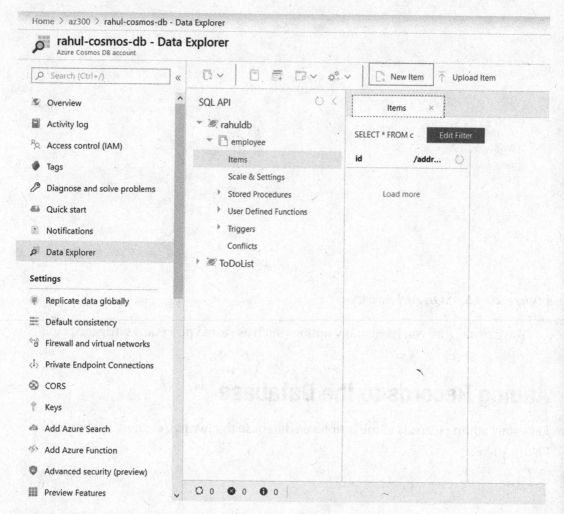

Figure 20-16. *New items*

Click New Item, enter the details shown in Figure 20-17 in JSON format, and then click Save.

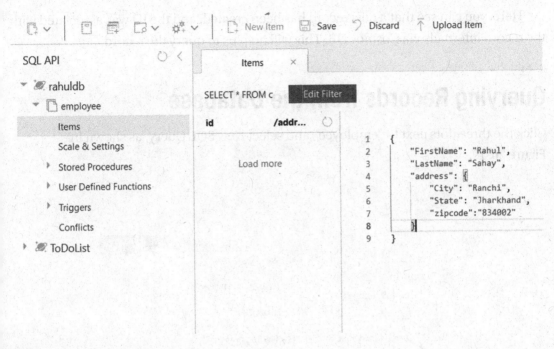

Figure 20-17. *Items collection*

Upon successful creation, your screen will look like Figure 20-18.

Figure 20-18. *Saved items*

Here, you can see that a new record has been created, and the ID was associated with the record internally via Cosmos DB. This will help us to query the record.

Querying Records from the Database

Click the three dots next to "employee" and select New SQL Query, as shown in Figure 20-19.

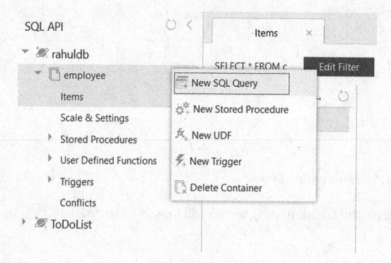

Figure 20-19. *New SQL Query menu item*

In the window that opens, you can type **SELECT * FROM c WHERE c.FirstName = 'Rahul'**. This will fetch the results, as shown in Figure 20-20.

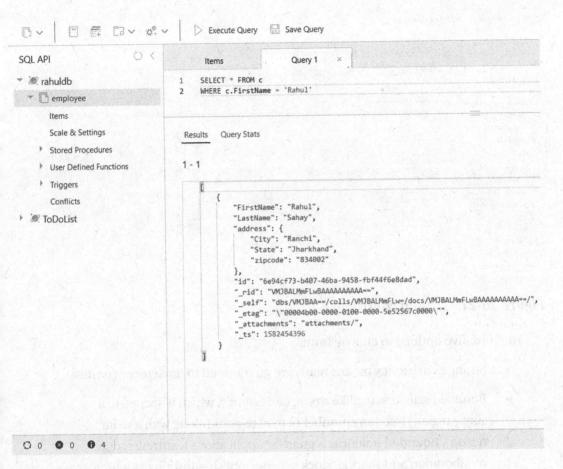

```
        □∨   |   □  □  □∨  ✱∨  |   ▷ Execute Query   □ Save Query

SQL API                    ○ <        Items              Query 1      ×

▼ ● rahuldb                        1   SELECT * FROM c
                                   2   WHERE c.FirstName = 'Rahul'
   ▼ □ employee

      Items
      Scale & Settings               Results   Query Stats
    ▶ Stored Procedures
    ▶ User Defined Functions         1 - 1
    ▶ Triggers
      Conflicts                      [
 ▶ ● ToDoList                            {
                                             "FirstName": "Rahul",
                                             "LastName": "Sahay",
                                             "address": {
                                                 "City": "Ranchi",
                                                 "State": "Jharkhand",
                                                 "zipcode": "834002"
                                             },
                                             "id": "6e94cf73-b407-46ba-9458-fbf44f6e8dad",
                                             "_rid": "VMJBALMmFLwBAAAAAAAAAA==",
                                             "_self": "dbs/VMJBAA==/colls/VMJBALMmFLw=/docs/VMJBALMmFLwBAAAAAAAAAA==/",
                                             "_etag": "\"00004b00-0000-0100-0000-5e52567c0000\"",
                                             "_attachments": "attachments/",
                                             "_ts": 1582454396
                                         }
                                     ]

 ○ 0   ● 0   ❶ 4
```

Figure 20-20. *Fetched results*

Default Consistency

Another benefit of using Cosmos DB is the consistency. If you go to Default Consistency under the Settings menu, you can see it's set to Session by default, as shown in Figure 20-21.

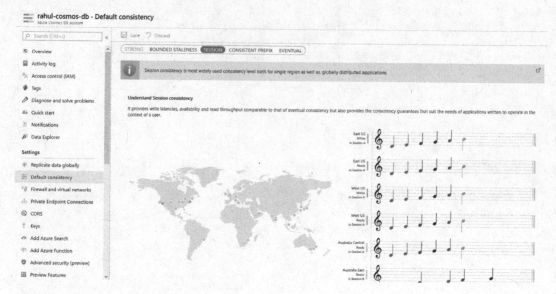

Figure 20-21. *Default consistency*

You have five options to choose from.

- Strong consistency means reads are guaranteed to most recent writes.

- Bounded staleness (unlike strong consistency, which is scoped to a single region) is for any number of read regions (along with a write region). Bounded staleness is great for applications featuring group collaboration and sharing, stock tickers, publish-subscribe/queuing, etc.

- Session consistency provides write latencies, availability, and read throughput comparable to that of eventual consistency but also provides the consistency guarantees that suit the needs of applications written to operate in the context of a user.

- Consistent prefix maintains order, meaning if writes are performed in the order A, B, C, then a client sees either A, A, B, or A, B, C, but never out of order like A, C or B, A, C. Consistent prefix provides write latencies, availability, and read throughput comparable to that of eventual consistency, but also provides the order guarantees that suit the needs of scenarios where order is important.

- Eventual consistency is the weakest form of consistency wherein a client may get the values that are older than the ones it has seen before, over time.

CHAPTER 21

Relational Databases

Azure SQL Database is a general-purpose relational database, provided as a managed service. With it, you can create a highly available and high-performance data storage layer for the applications and solutions in Azure. In this chapter, we will explore SQL Server on Azure. Select the Databases category in the left panel, as shown in Figure 21-1, and you'll see that a plethora of services are being offered.

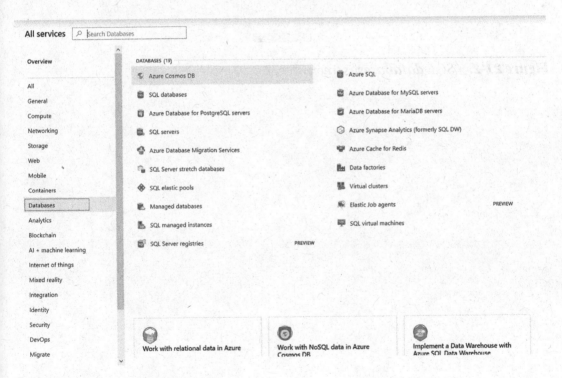

Figure 21-1. *Available databases*

From all these choices, select SQL database.

© Rahul Sahay 2020
R. Sahay, *Microsoft Azure Architect Technologies Study Companion,*
https://doi.org/10.1007/978-1-4842-6200-9_21

Creating a SQL Database

Click SQL Databases as shown in Figure 21-1 and add a new one, as shown in Figure 21-2.

Figure 21-2. *"SQL databases" screen*

Next, provide the details shown in Figure 21-3.

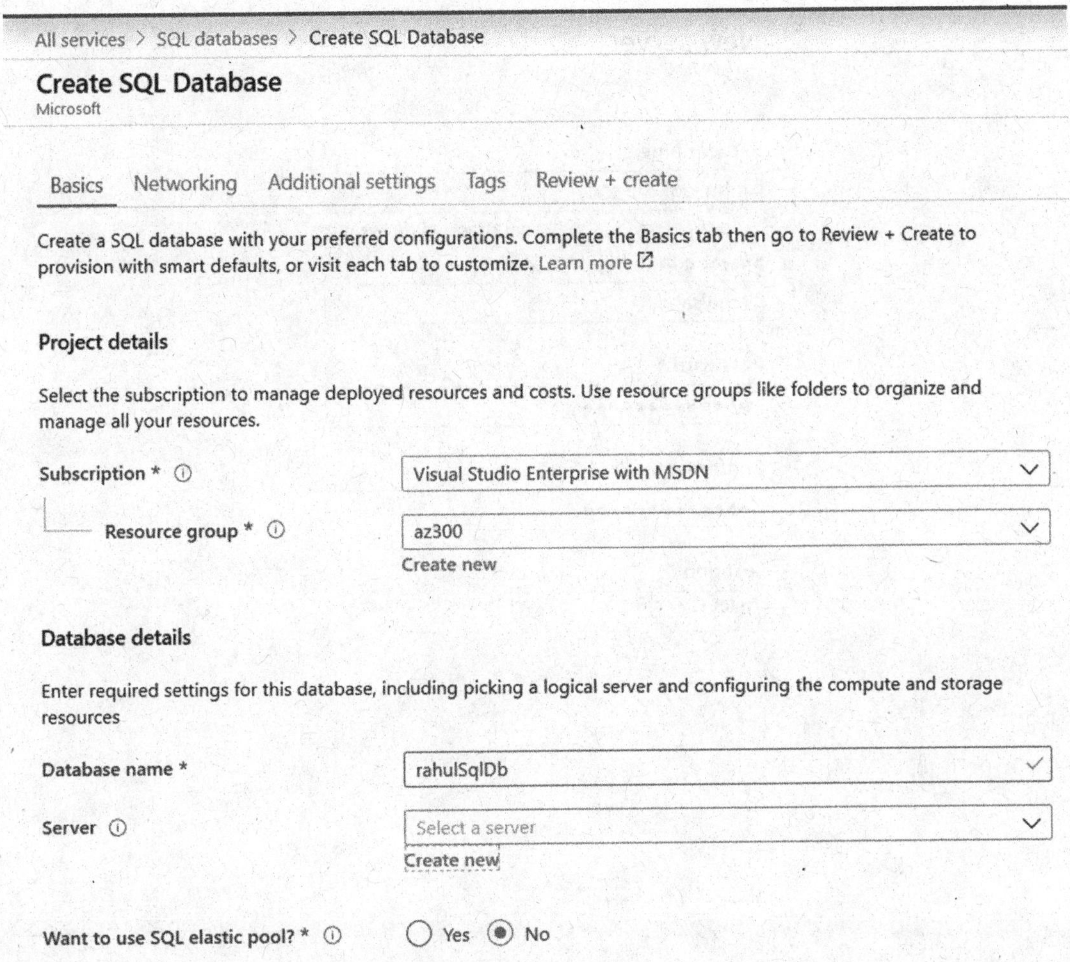

All services > SQL databases > Create SQL Database

Create SQL Database
Microsoft

Basics   Networking   Additional settings   Tags   Review + create

Create a SQL database with your preferred configurations. Complete the Basics tab then go to Review + Create to provision with smart defaults, or visit each tab to customize. Learn more ☒

Project details

Select the subscription to manage deployed resources and costs. Use resource groups like folders to organize and manage all your resources.

Subscription * ⓘ | Visual Studio Enterprise with MSDN   ⌄ |

└──── Resource group * ⓘ | az300   ⌄ |
                                     Create new

Database details

Enter required settings for this database, including picking a logical server and configuring the compute and storage resources

Database name * | rahulSqlDb   ✓ |

Server ⓘ | Select a server   ⌄ |
                                     Create new

Want to use SQL elastic pool? * ⓘ   ◯ Yes ◉ No

Figure 21-3. *"Create SQL Database" screen, Basics tab*

To create a new server, click "Create new" and enter the details shown in Figure 21-4.

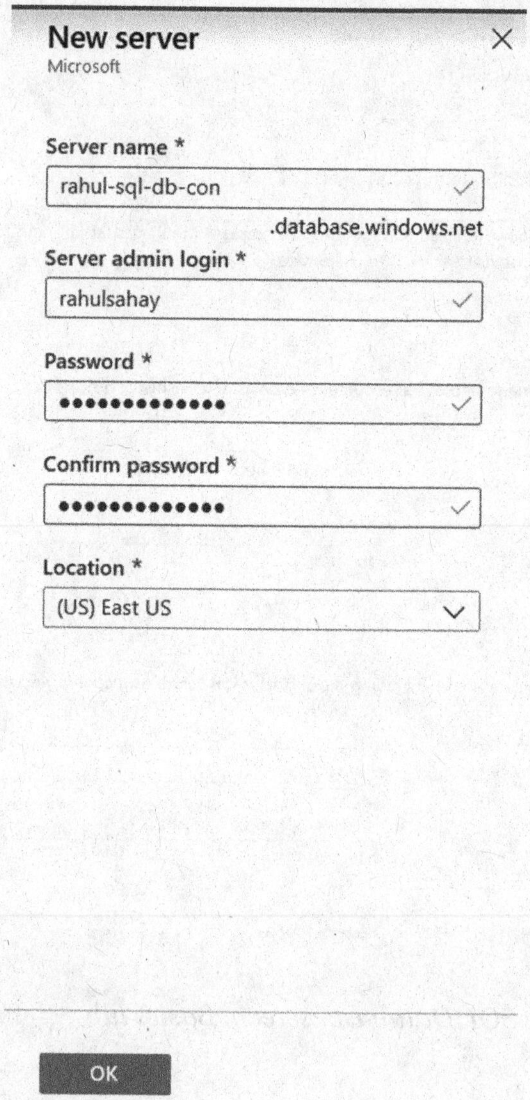

Figure 21-4. *Creating a new server*

Next you will see the elastic pool settings. This is going to come in handy when you have multiple databases. In that case, elastic pools provide a simple and cost-effective solution for managing the performance of multiple databases within a fixed budget.

An elastic pool provides compute *elastic data throughput units* (eDTUs) and storage resources that are shared between all the databases it contains. Databases within a pool use only the resources they need, when they need them, within configurable limits.

The price of a pool is based only on the amount of resources configured and is independent of the number of databases it contains. For now, we are not going to need it, so you can click No.

Then, in the Compute section, you will have various configuration options for the CPU. I will go with basic one, as shown in Figure 21-5.

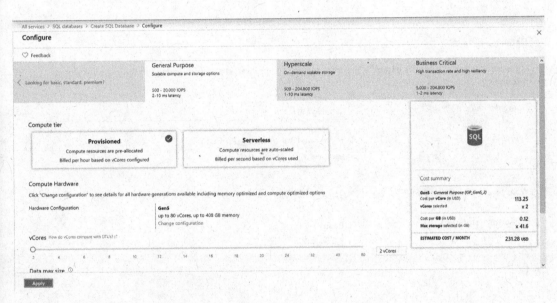

Figure 21-5. *SQL configuration screen*

Your screen will look like Figure 21-6. Note that if you need more compute power, you will need to pay more for extra cores.

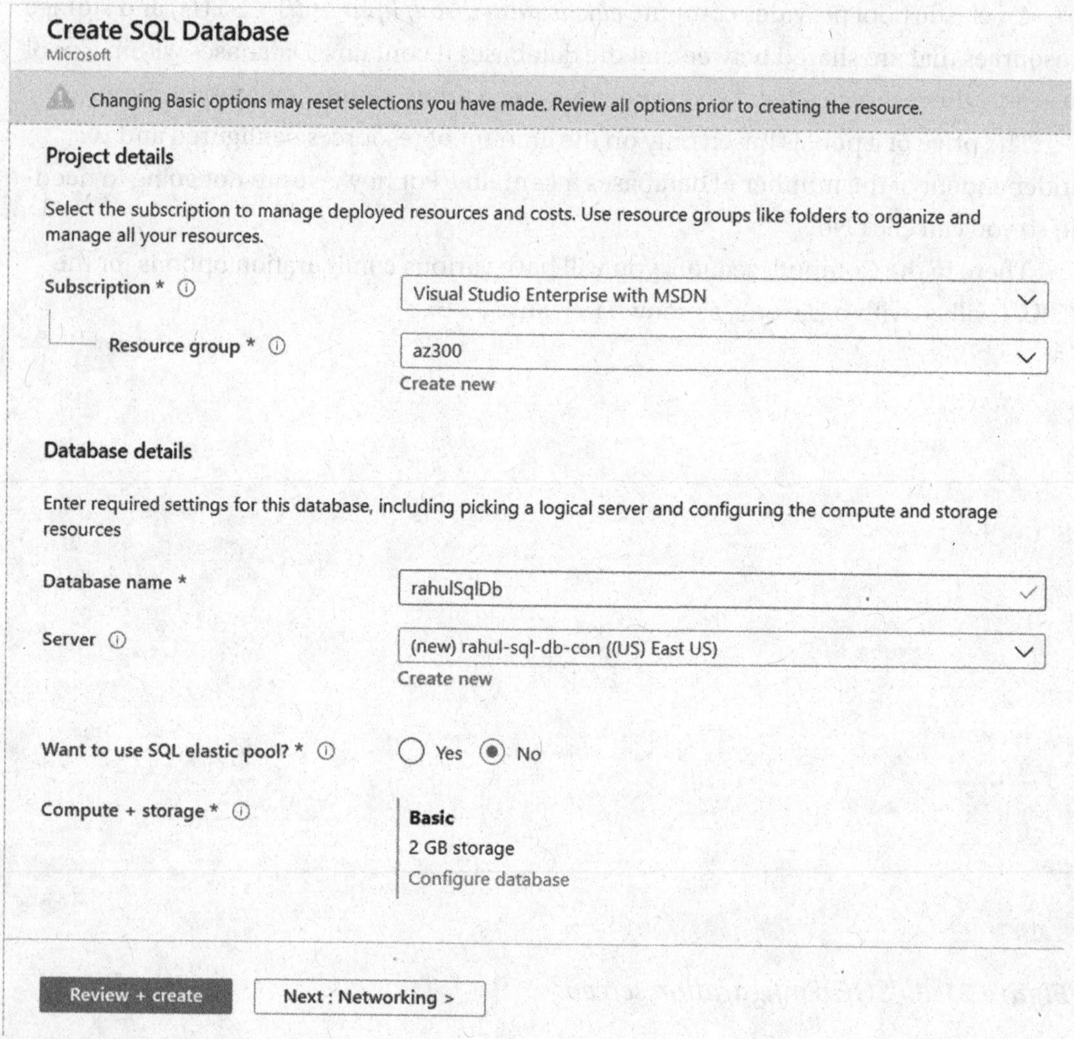

Create SQL Database
Microsoft

⚠ Changing Basic options may reset selections you have made. Review all options prior to creating the resource.

Project details

Select the subscription to manage deployed resources and costs. Use resource groups like folders to organize and manage all your resources.

Subscription * ⓘ

> Visual Studio Enterprise with MSDN   ⌄

⌙ Resource group * ⓘ

> az300   ⌄
>
> Create new

Database details

Enter required settings for this database, including picking a logical server and configuring the compute and storage resources

Database name *

> rahulSqlDb   ✓

Server ⓘ

> (new) rahul-sql-db-con ((US) East US)   ⌄
>
> Create new

Want to use SQL elastic pool? * ⓘ   ○ Yes ⦿ No

Compute + storage * ⓘ

> **Basic**
> 2 GB storage
> Configure database

[Review + create]   [Next : Networking >]

Figure 21-6. Project details

Figure 21-7 shows the Networking tab. Make sure you can access the server over a public network, and make sure that your current IP address is whitelisted by enabling Firewall rules as shown in Figure 21-7.

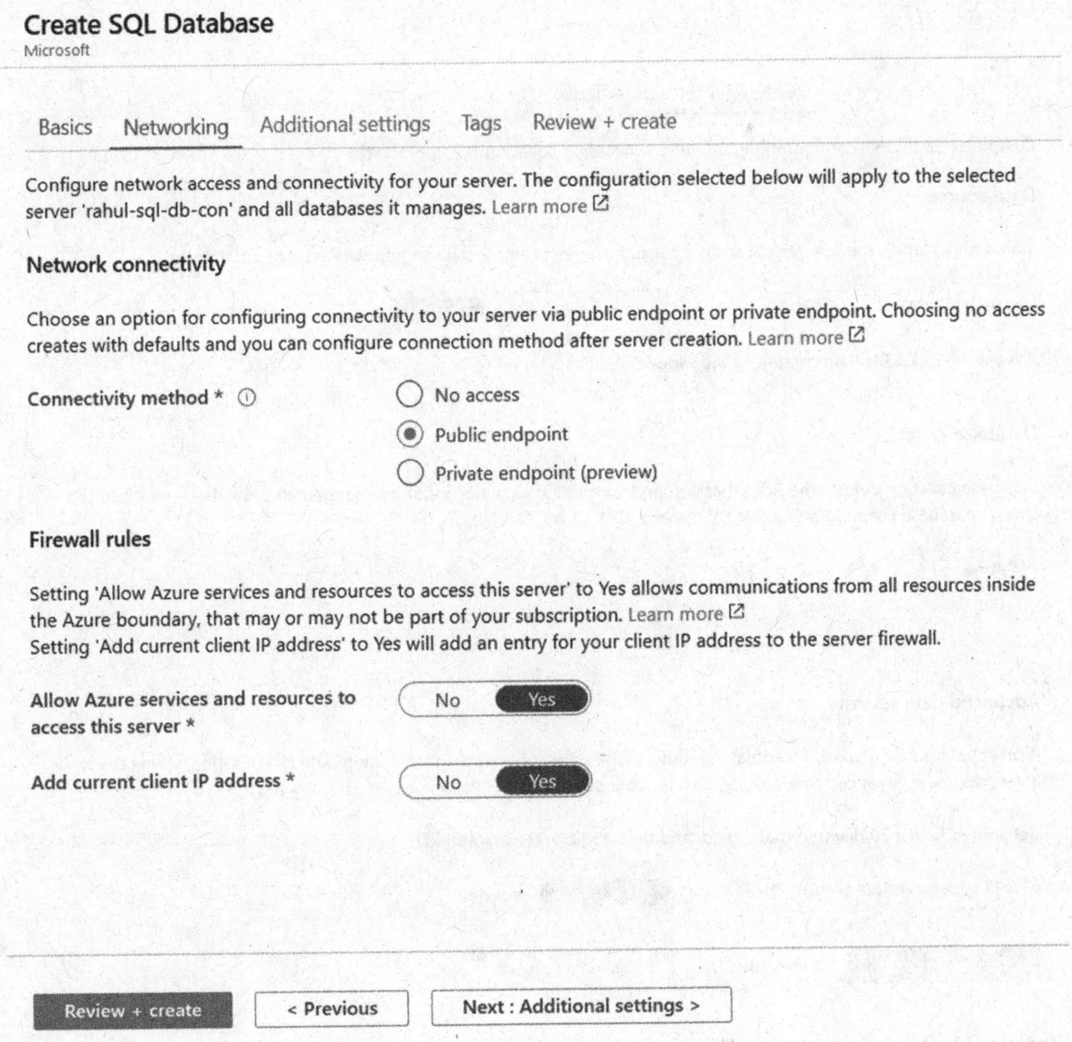

Create SQL Database
Microsoft

Basics   Networking   Additional settings   Tags   Review + create

Configure network access and connectivity for your server. The configuration selected below will apply to the selected server 'rahul-sql-db-con' and all databases it manages. Learn more ☑

Network connectivity

Choose an option for configuring connectivity to your server via public endpoint or private endpoint. Choosing no access creates with defaults and you can configure connection method after server creation. Learn more ☑

Connectivity method * ⓘ

    ◯ No access
    ◉ Public endpoint
    ◯ Private endpoint (preview)

Firewall rules

Setting 'Allow Azure services and resources to access this server' to Yes allows communications from all resources inside the Azure boundary, that may or may not be part of your subscription. Learn more ☑
Setting 'Add current client IP address' to Yes will add an entry for your client IP address to the server firewall.

Allow Azure services and resources to access this server *   (No   **Yes**)

Add current client IP address *   (No   **Yes**)

[Review + create]   [< Previous]   [Next : Additional settings >]

Figure 21-7. *Networking tab*

The next tab is "Additional settings." On this tab, you can select a sample database and enable advanced security, as shown in Figure 21-8.

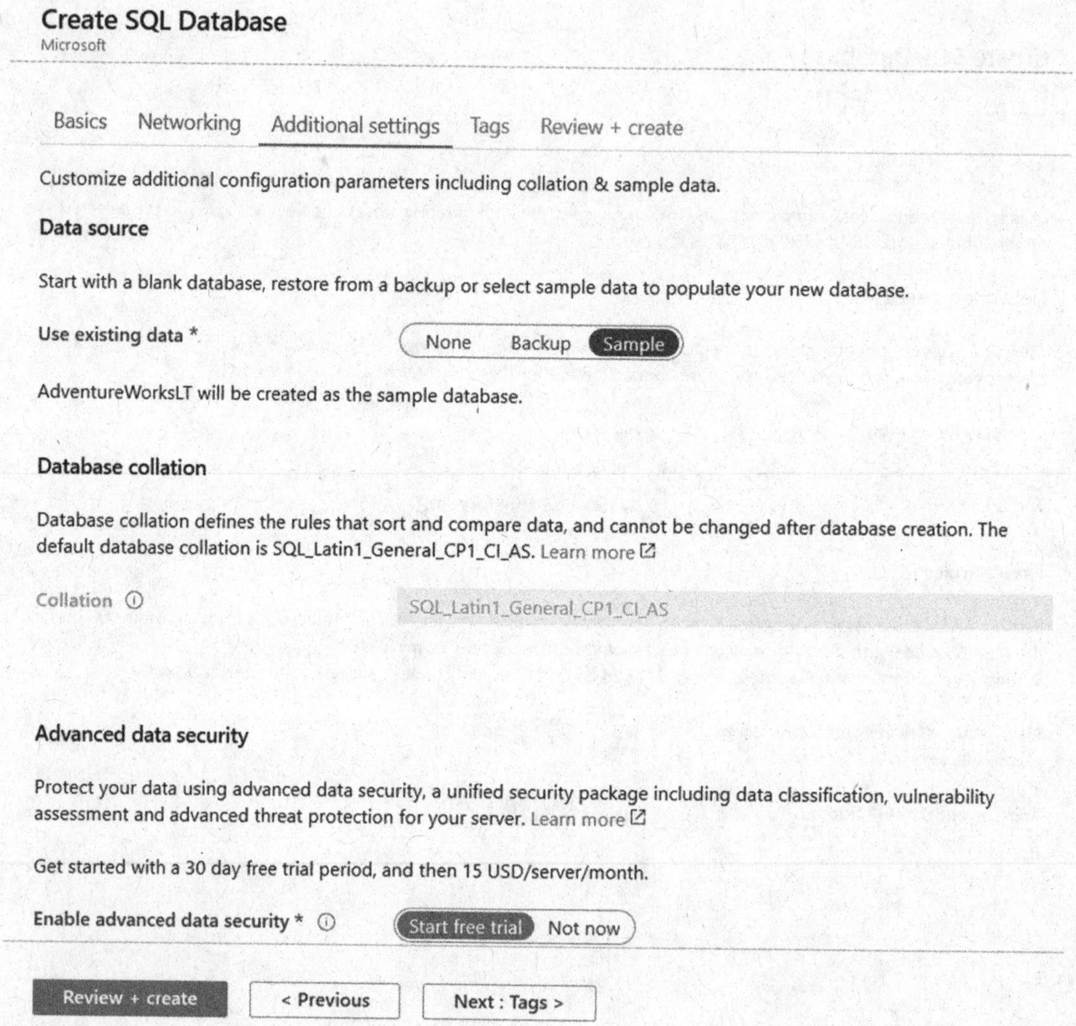

Create SQL Database
Microsoft

Basics   Networking   Additional settings   Tags   Review + create

Customize additional configuration parameters including collation & sample data.

Data source

Start with a blank database, restore from a backup or select sample data to populate your new database.

Use existing data *   None   Backup   Sample

AdventureWorksLT will be created as the sample database.

Database collation

Database collation defines the rules that sort and compare data, and cannot be changed after database creation. The default database collation is SQL_Latin1_General_CP1_CI_AS. Learn more ☒

Collation ⓘ   SQL_Latin1_General_CP1_CI_AS

Advanced data security

Protect your data using advanced data security, a unified security package including data classification, vulnerability assessment and advanced threat protection for your server. Learn more ☒

Get started with a 30 day free trial period, and then 15 USD/server/month.

Enable advanced data security * ⓘ   Start free trial   Not now

---

Review + create   < Previous   Next : Tags >

Figure 21-8. Advanced settings

Figure 21-9 shows the Tags tab.

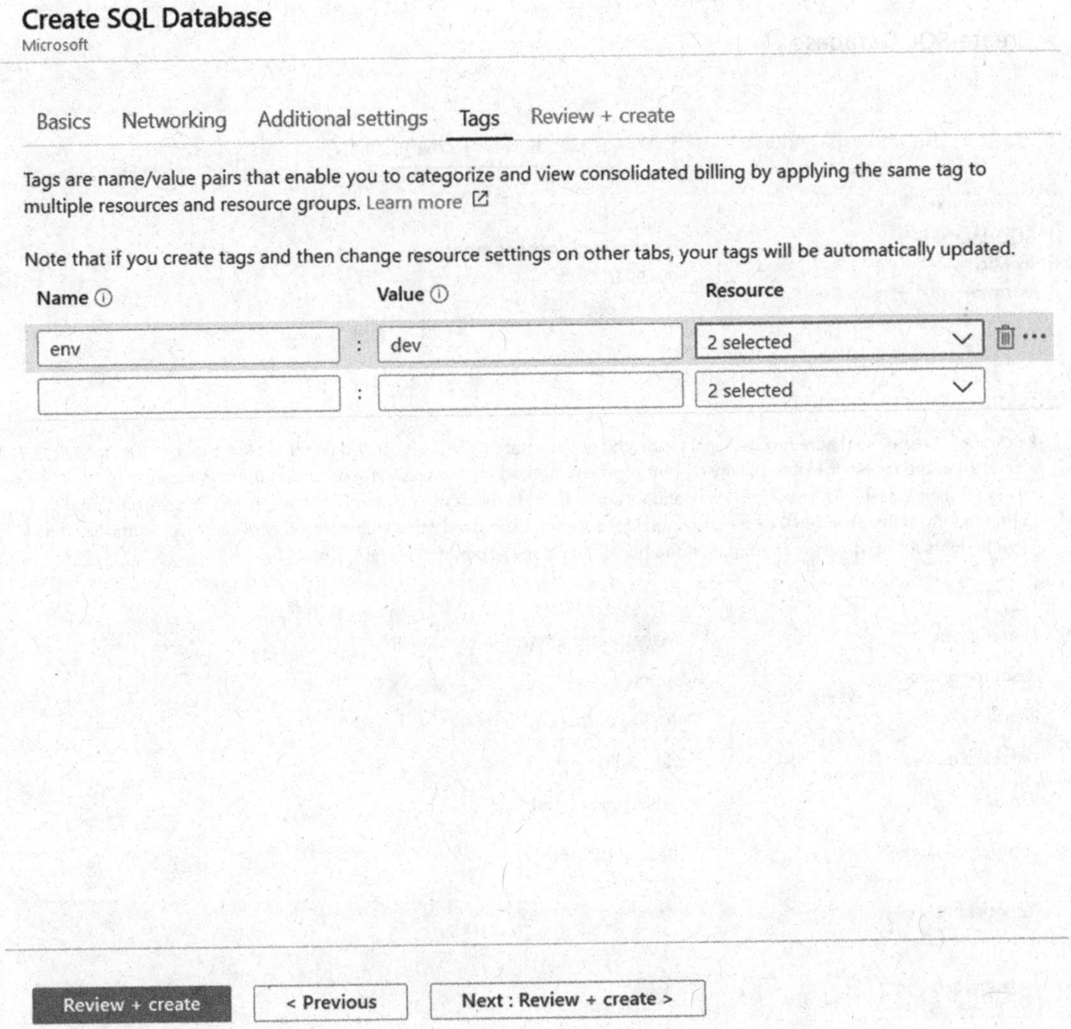

Create SQL Database
Microsoft

Basics   Networking   Additional settings   **Tags**   Review + create

Tags are name/value pairs that enable you to categorize and view consolidated billing by applying the same tag to multiple resources and resource groups. Learn more ⧉

Note that if you create tags and then change resource settings on other tabs, your tags will be automatically updated.

Name ⓘ		Value ⓘ	Resource		
env	:	dev	2 selected	⌄	🗑 ⋯
	:		2 selected	⌄	

Review + create   < Previous   Next : Review + create >

Figure 21-9. *Tags tab*

Figure 21-10 shows the "Review + create" tab.

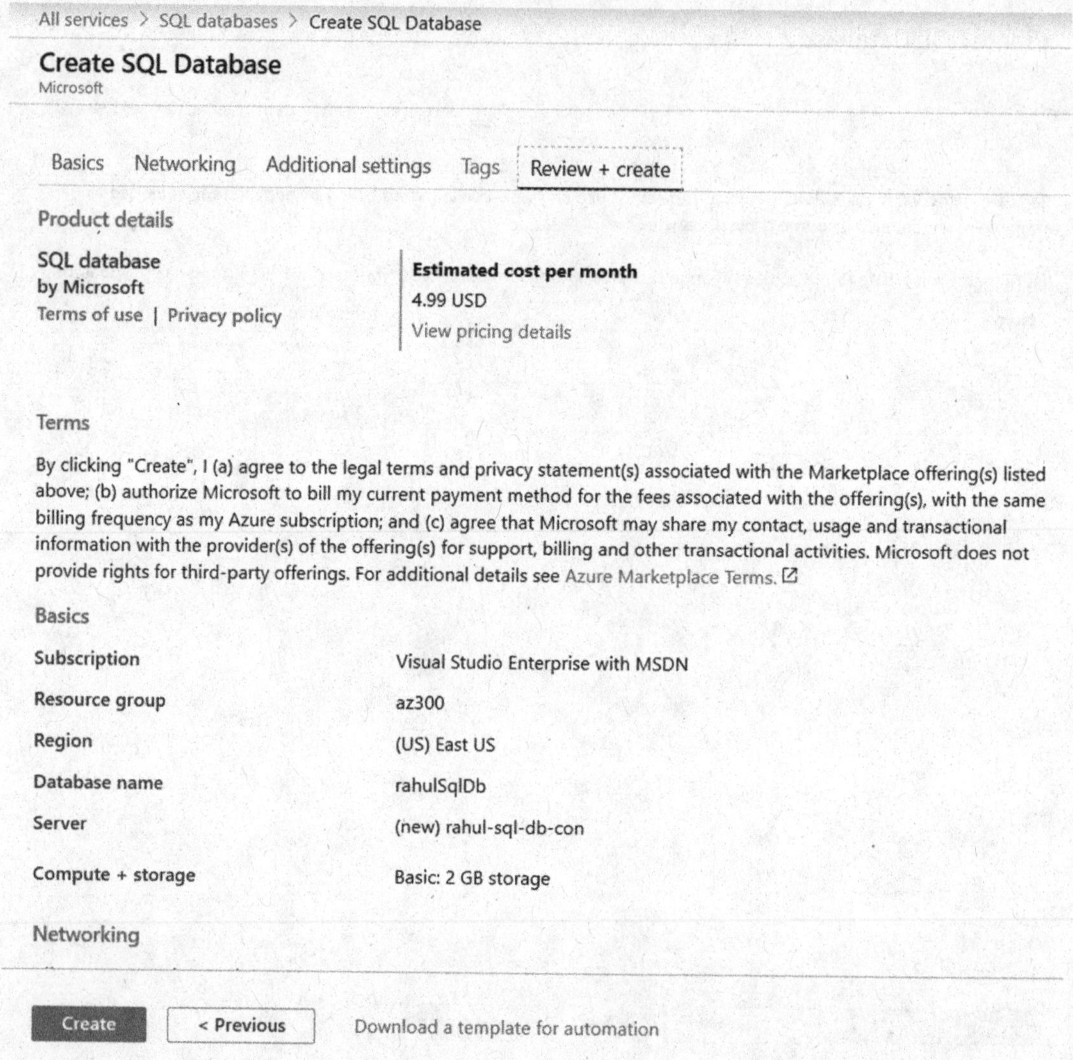

All services > SQL databases > Create SQL Database

Create SQL Database
Microsoft

Basics   Networking   Additional settings   Tags   Review + create

Product details

SQL database
by Microsoft
Terms of use | Privacy policy

Estimated cost per month
4.99 USD
View pricing details

Terms

By clicking "Create", I (a) agree to the legal terms and privacy statement(s) associated with the Marketplace offering(s) listed above; (b) authorize Microsoft to bill my current payment method for the fees associated with the offering(s), with the same billing frequency as my Azure subscription; and (c) agree that Microsoft may share my contact, usage and transactional information with the provider(s) of the offering(s) for support, billing and other transactional activities. Microsoft does not provide rights for third-party offerings. For additional details see Azure Marketplace Terms. ⧉

Basics

Subscription	Visual Studio Enterprise with MSDN
Resource group	az300
Region	(US) East US
Database name	rahulSqlDb
Server	(new) rahul-sql-db-con
Compute + storage	Basic: 2 GB storage

Networking

Create   < Previous   Download a template for automation

Figure 21-10. *"Review + create" tab*

Click Create. This will take some time. After the database is successfully created, your screen will look like Figure 21-11.

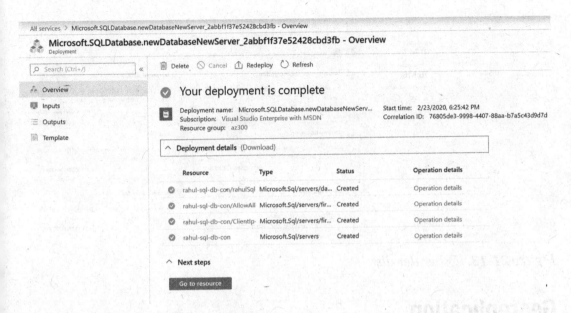

Figure 21-11. *SQL database deployed*

Now, you can go to the resource, as shown in Figure 21-12.

Figure 21-12. *"SQL database" screen, Overview*

You can see things like security, performance, etc., on the home screen itself, as shown in Figure 21-13.

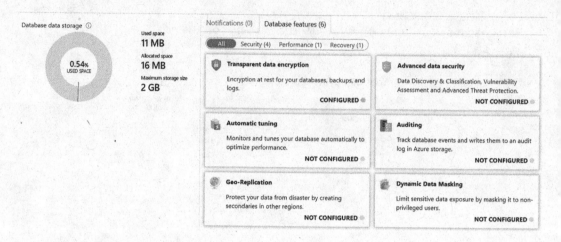

Figure 21-13. *Other details*

Georeplication

Like with Cosmos DB, you have the option to use georeplication in Azure SQL Database. After you click Geo-Replication, your screen will look like Figure 21-14.

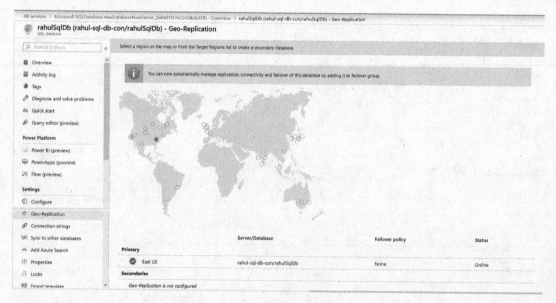

Figure 21-14. *Geo-Replication menu in left panel*

Right now, you can see that I have only one instance running in the East US region. There are no other backups. However, I can set up another replication instance, which will be another point from where data can be read. This location will be a read-only location.

On the map, the spots in purple show the locations that will be the highest-speed regions for replicas. If speed is not a concern, you can choose any green location.

You can select any of the regions from the list, as shown in Figure 21-15.

Select a region on the map or from the Target Regions list to create a secondary database.			
Primary			
✅ East US	rahul-sql-db-con/rahulSqlDb	None	Online
Secondaries			
Geo-Replication is not configured			
Target regions			
◯ West US 2			
◯ Central US			
◯ North Central US			
◯ Canada Central			
◯ East US			
◯ Canada East			
◯ East US 2			
◯ Brazil South			
◯ North Europe			
◯ France Central			
◯ Central India			
◯ East Asia			
◯ Korea South			
◯ Australia Southeast			
◯ Australia Central			

Figure 21-15. Selecting regions

As you can see in Figure 21-16, I have selected Central US as the secondary for this example.

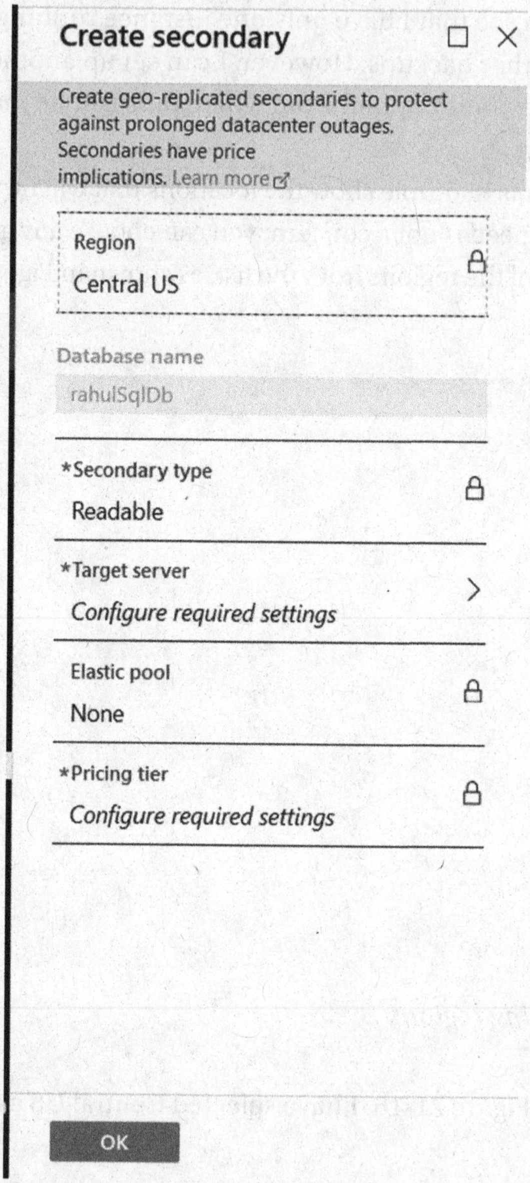

Figure 21-16. *Creating a secondary region*

Next you need to create a new server for this as well, as shown in Figure 21-17.

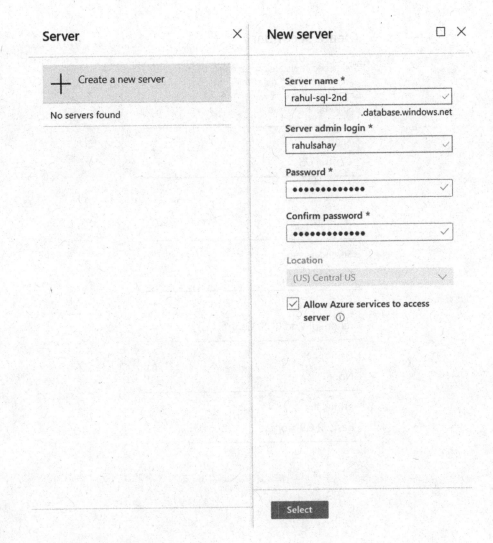

Figure 21-17. *Creating a new server*

Make sure to select "Allow Azure services to access server." This allows applications from Azure to connect to this server.

Finally, your screen will look like Figure 21-18.

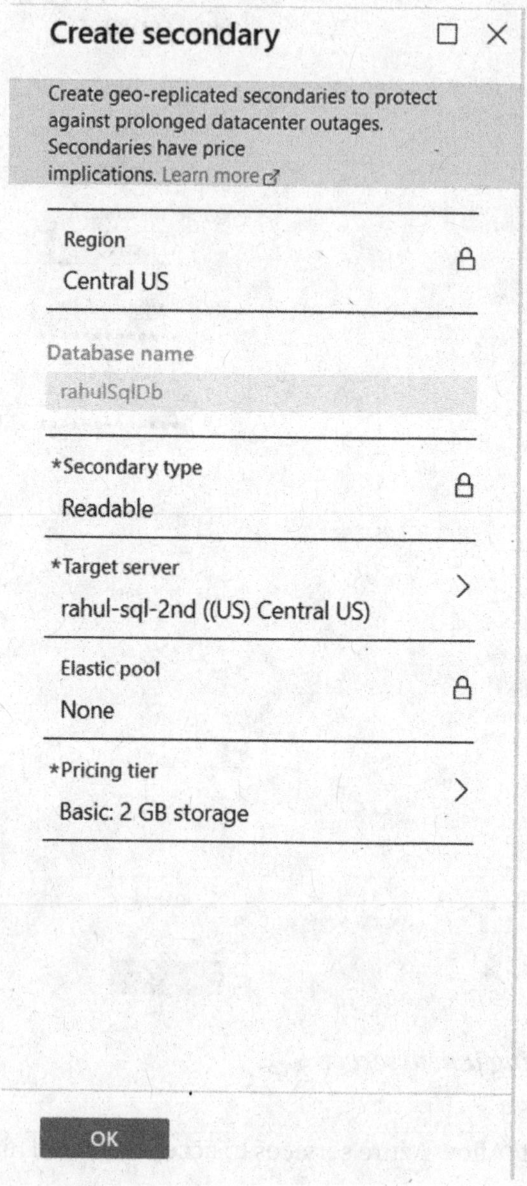

Create secondary

Create geo-replicated secondaries to protect against prolonged datacenter outages. Secondaries have price implications. Learn more

Region

Central US

Database name

rahulSqlDb

*Secondary type

Readable

*Target server

rahul-sql-2nd ((US) Central US)

Elastic pool

None

*Pricing tier

Basic: 2 GB storage

OK

Figure 21-18. *New server details*

Upon successful deployment, your screen will look like Figure 21-19.

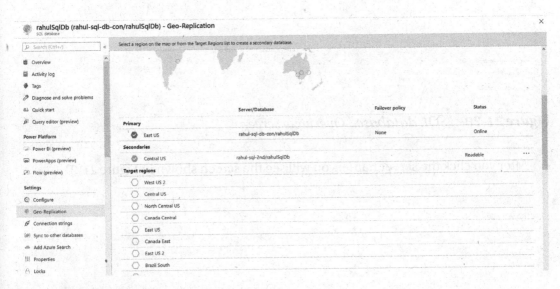

Figure 21-19. *Georeplication enabled*

This also means that once I write into my database, which is in the East US region, it will get replicated quickly to Central US for read-only purposes. This also means I will have to pay extra for extra servers.

Once the secondary location is up and running, you can force a failover. There is a way to basically instantiate the failover to Central US, and Central US will become the primary in that case. East US will be taken offline until it is repaired.

This also means georeplication is meant not only for performance but also for failover in terms of disaster.

For performance, application developers need to write APIs in such a way that they can identify the request location and, based on that, pick a nearby location to read data.

Database Firewalls

Database servers are protected by firewalls. You can set up a firewall for a server by clicking the server name on the Overview screen, as shown in Figure 21-20.

Figure 21-20. *"SQL database," Overview screen*

After you click the server name, you will see the screen shown in Figure 21-21.

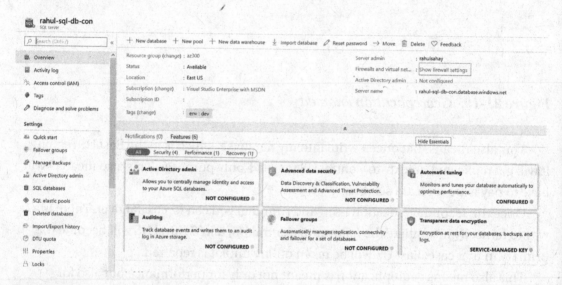

Figure 21-21. *"SQL server," Overview tab*

Click "Show firewall settings," and your screen will look like Figure 21-22.

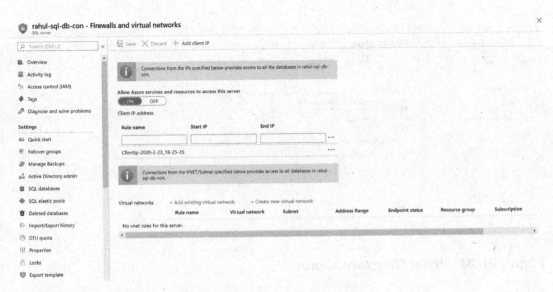

Figure 21-22. *Setting up a Firewall*

I already added my client IP address to the whitelist when I created the SQL database. If you did not add your IP address at that time, you will get an option to add your machine IP address. (I have masked mine in Figure 21-22.)

Setting Up an Active Directory Admin

Let's say you don't want users to use usernames and passwords to connect to a database. In that case, you can set up an Active Directory admin. On the Overview tab, click "Not configured," as shown in Figure 21-23.

Figure 21-23. *Setting up an admin*

The screen shown in Figure 21-24 will open.

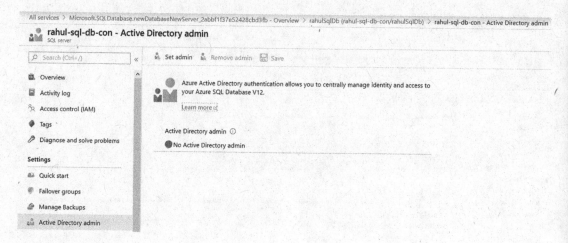

Figure 21-24. *Active Directory admin*

From here, you need to add the Active Directory and users from that directory and then use Azure SQL Database.

Query Editor

Let's say you want to see data in the Azure portal directly. You can certainly do that from the Query Editor, as shown in Figure 21-25.

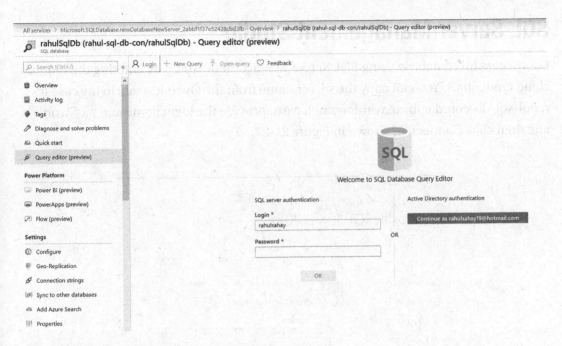

Figure 21-25. *Query Editor connection*

Here you can either provide the password you created earlier or use Active Directory authentication, explained previously. Figure 21-26 shows the Query Editor after logging in.

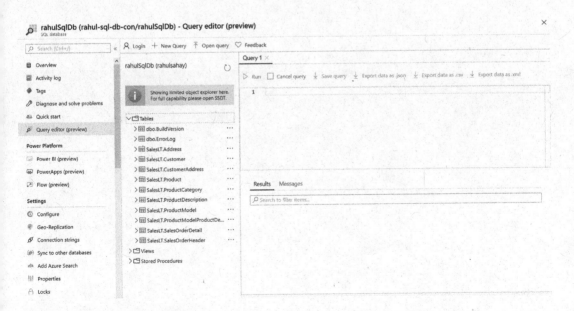

Figure 21-26. *Query Editor*

SQL Server Management Studio

Let's access this database using SQL Server Management Studio by entering the required cloud credentials. You can copy the server name from the Overview tab; in my case it's rahul-sql-db-con.database.windows.net. Next, provide the login name and password and then click Connect, as shown in Figure 21-27.

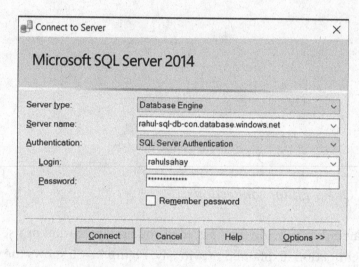

Figure 21-27. SQL connection

After you successfully connect, the screen will look like Figure 21-28.

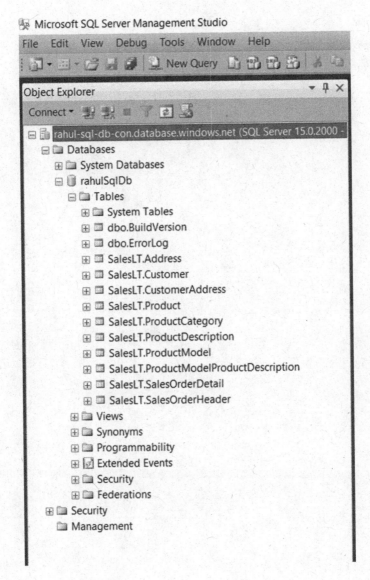

Figure 21-28. *Logged in locally*

CHAPTER 22

Exercises

This chapter contains nine examples of lab assignments that you can expect to be asked to complete during the exam. Let's go through the exercises one by one. You should be able to solve these exercises on your own after reading this book and studying the steps covered in the chapters.

Exercise 1

Create an Azure Functions app named *corplod1999* in the resource group named *corpupload1999* and integrate it with the output blob container. Write a function app to store a message in this blob container.

Exercise 2

Create an Azure Active Directory with a few test users. Create a group named Finance. Add users to this group. Create a web app and apply Active Directory authentication to it.

Exercise 3

Create a key vault named *corpup-keyvault* in the resource group you created in Exercise 1. Add a secret to the vault. Also, create another version of the secret in the vault. Verify their URLs.

Exercise 4

Create a SQL database in a resource group named *sqldb*. Create the database with a sample database attached to it. Use the online editor to log in to the database and query the table. Next connect to this database using SQL Server Management Studio. Apply georeplication to the database and set up a firewall.

741

© Rahul Sahay 2020
R. Sahay, *Microsoft Azure Architect Technologies Study Companion*,
https://doi.org/10.1007/978-1-4842-6200-9_22

Exercise 5

Create a Cosmos DB in a resource group named *cosmosdb*. Create a container with the employee collection. Add records to this collection and then retrieve it. Apply the default consistency to the database and enable georeplication.

Exercise 6

Create a virtual machine using an ARM template. Make sure to host the virtual machine in the East US region. Use AZVMDemo1 as the network interface name, and use AZVMDemo1-nsg as the network security group name.

Exercise 7

Create two virtual networks, VNet1 and VNet2. VNet1 should be in the East US region, and VNet2 should be in the West US region. Create VM1 in VNet1, and create VM2 in VNet2. Implement a cost-effective networking solution between these two networks.

Exercise 8

Create a storage account with a queue. Create a function app to write and read from the queue. Make sure the function app uses this queue during the integration process.

Exercise 9

Create a virtual machine scale set with Zone 2 as the availability zone and five fault domains. Also, make sure to set the autoscale rule with a minimum of 2 VMs and a maximum of 10 VMs. For scale-out, the CPU threshold should be 75%, then count can be increased by 1. For Scale in, CPU threshold should be 15%, then number of VMs can be decreased by 1.

CHAPTER 23

Practice Questions

In this chapter, you will find 50 multiple-choice questions. This will serve as a mock test. Select the best possible answer for each question. The answer key appears after the last question. Square checkboxes mean there are multiple answers; hence, you need to select more than one. Round radio buttons mean there is precisely one correct answer; hence, you should pick the best answer.

Questions

1. Let's say you have two virtual networks, VNet1 and VNet2, and you need to communicate between the two. How do you establish the connection?

   ○ Create a virtual network gateway

   ○ Use peering

   ○ Both

   ○ None

© Rahul Sahay 2020
R. Sahay, *Microsoft Azure Architect Technologies Study Companion*,
https://doi.org/10.1007/978-1-4842-6200-9_23

2. You need to connect both VNet1 and VNet2 without creating any additional resources. How do you achieve this?

    ○ Create a virtual network gateway

    ○ Use peering

    ○ Both

    ○ None

3. You need to make sure that remote engineers can connect securely to VNet1. What is the best possible solution?

    ○ Site-to-site access

    ○ Point-to-site access

    ○ Both

    ○ None

4. What type of storage account supports SMB 3.0?

    ☐ File storage

    ☐ Table storage

    ☐ Queue storage

    ☐ Blob storage

5. You need to configure Azure Backup for a Windows virtual machine that includes all files and the OS system states. What technique do you use?

    ☐ File backup

    ☐ Folder backup

    ☐ File and folder backup

    ☐ MARS agent

6. You need to configure Azure Backup for a Linux virtual machine. Which option will you select?

    ☐ File backup

    ☐ Folder backup

    ☐ Azure backup server

    ☐ MARS agent

7. You need to load balance the incoming web traffic using layer 7 load balancing capabilities. Which option best fits this scenario?

    ○ Load balancer

    ○ Application gateway

    ○ Both

    ○ None

8. You need to load balance traffic based on a path-based rule. Which option best fits this scenario?

   ○ Load balancer

   ○ Application gateway

   ○ Both

   ○ None

9. You have created an application gateway to protect the backend server from cyberattacks. Which option best fits this scenario?

   ☐ Load balancer

   ☐ WAF SKU

   ☐ Firewall

   ☐ None

10. You are the admin for the Contoso airline group. You notice an unusually high billing for one of the subscriptions. You need to find the root cause by checking the costs at the tag level. Which option best fits this scenario?

    ☐ Invoices

    ☐ Budgets

    ☐ Cost analysis

    ☐ None

11. You are responsible for designing a storage solution for the
     Contoso banking group. The storage needs to be accessed
     frequently. Which storage type should be used?

☐ General Purpose V2 hot tier

☐ Premium SSD

☐ General Purpose V1

☐ None

12. You need to design a scalable web application whose traffic varies
     heavily at any point of time. Suddenly you notice a spike in traffic
     ten times higher than usual that then goes back to normal. Which
     scalability option best fits this scenario?

☐ Availability sets

☐ Availability zones

☐ Virtual machine scale sets

☐ None

13. You need to connect two virtual networks, say VNet1 and VNet2, in such a way that they can send data back and forth to each other. Which technique will you use?

☐ Availability sets

☐ Load balancer

☐ VNet peering

☐ None

14. You need to create a storage solution and ensure that the storage solution is available all the time, even when the region goes offline. Which solution will you implement?

☐ LRS

☐ ZRS

☐ GRS

☐ None

15. You need to share read-only access to network storage. Which access will you select?

○ Access keys

○ Shared access signatures

○ Both

○ None

16. You need to report monthly risk events such as risky sign-ins. Which solution will you implement?

☐ Identity protection

☐ Conditional access

☐ Access reviews

☐ None

17. You need to bypass all employees from MFA who are logging in from the office. Which setting do you need to enable?

◯ Add the to remote IP addresses to MFA server

◯ Add the to office IP addresses to MFA server

◯ Both

◯ None

18. One of the legit users got stuck, and he is unable to authenticate via MFA. You need to make sure that he can log in at least once in the Azure portal. How do you enable this?

◯ Turn off MFA for his account

◯ One-time bypass

◯ Both

◯ None

19. When configuring an application gateway, you need to create a listener for subdomains. Which kind of listener will you implement?

   ○ Basic listener

   ○ Multisite listener

   ○ Both

   ○ None

20. You need to prevent fellow engineers from restarting the VM. He already has the Contributor role. Without changing his role, how do you achieve this?

   ☐ Use Deny assignments

   ☐ Apply a firewall

   ☐ Assign reader access

   ☐ None

21. You need to load balance layer 4 traffic coming to your web server. Which type of load balancer will you apply?

   ☐ Load balancer

   ☐ Application gateway

   ☐ Front Door

   ☐ None

22. You need to ensure the passwords are synced from your local Active Directory to Azure in a way that whenever users change their passwords locally, they get synced with Azure Active Directory. Which is the most cost-effective solution for this?

    ☐ Single sign-on

    ☐ Self-service reset portal

    ☐ AD Connect with P1 license

    ☐ AD Connect with P2 license

23. You need to analyze the cost graph of your subscription for the past two quarters. Which option best fits this scenario?

    ☐ Cost analysis

    ☐ Invoices

    ☐ Budget

    ☐ Cost overview

24. You need to configure the VM to automatically allow RDP traffic when your ARM template is used. Where will you provide the access rules?

   ☐ NetworkInterface

   ☐ NetworkSecurityGroupRules

   ☐ Image reference

   ☐ Cost overview

25. You accidentally deleted one of the important files kept on your VM. Which recovery method can retrieve files in the best possible way?

   ☐ Azure site recovery

   ☐ File recovery

   ☐ VM restore

   ☐ VHD restore

26. You need to create a new function app that will be running continuously and that requires dedicated compute power. Which app service plan will you be on?

        ○ Consumption plan

        ○ App service plan

        ○ Both

        ○ None

27. Which Azure load balancing solution can direct traffic to any internal or external IP address and is not restricted to apps hosted within Azure? (Select all that apply.)

        ☐ Azure Traffic Manager

        ☐ Azure Load Balancer

        ☐ Azure Application Gateway

        ☐ All

28. The system needs to automatically send mail whenever the pizza
delivery guy starts to deliver the order. If the delivery guy gets
stuck for some reason, the system should take care of that as well.
What technology will you choose?

☐ Event Grid

☐ Logic Apps

☐ Service Bus

☐ None

29. You need to automate the resource tagging process whenever any
resource gets created. Which option will you select?

☐ Event Grid

☐ Event Hub

☐ Service Bus

☐ None

30. You have a team of 12 remote developers who need access to one of the virtual networks, say VNet1. The connection should be secure without any hardware involvement, and it should be cost effective as well. Which solution is the best fit here?

   ○ Point to Site

   ○ Site to Site

   ○ Both

   ○ None

31. You are responsible for creating autoscaling solutions. You have a VM that runs once a month, and at its peak it utilizes 65% of CPU and memory. Which autoscaling option is the best fit here?

   ☐ Unpredictable

   ☐ Predictable

   ☐ Off and on

   ☐ None

32. You are responsible for creating autoscaling solutions. You have a scenario where the server runs most of the time at 90% of CPU. Which autoscaling pattern is the best fit here?

    ☐ Unpredictable

    ☐ Predictable

    ☐ Off and on

    ☐ Adding resources

33. You are responsible for designing a solution that will integrate an on-premises application with an application hosted on Azure. You need to make adjustments to the on-premises application so that it can talk to the Azure application securely. The solution also needs to be implemented in the least intrusive manner possible. Which technology is the best fit?

    ☐ Site to site

    ☐ Point to site

    ☐ Azure Relay Service

    ☐ All the above

34. You need to design a messaging system that can deliver messages reliably to different systems. This system should be capable of maintaining the message order as well. Which solution is the best fit here?

☐ Notification Hub

☐ Event Hub

☐ Event Grid

☐ Service Bus

35. You need to design a notification system that can send promotional content via push notifications to all the subscribed devices. Which option is the best fit here?

☐ Notification Hub

☐ Event Hub

☐ Event Grid

☐ Service Bus

36. You need to design a system that can handle data ingestion from
     IoT sensors. You expect millions of events per second. You need
     to select a technology that can handle a large volume of data
     ingestion. Which solution is the best fit here?

     ☐ Notification Hub

     ☐ Event Hub

     ☐ Event Grid

     ☐ Service Bus

37. You need to design a system that can handle event-based routing.
     For example, whenever any new file gets uploaded to the storage
     solution, you want to initiate a trigger to Logic App. Which
     solution is the best fit here?

     ☐ Notification Hub

     ☐ Event Hub

     ☐ Event Grid

     ☐ Service Bus

38. You need to design a scalable notification system that will be able to send and receive mail via REST API calls. Which solution is the best fit here?

☐ Notification Hub

☐ Event Hub

☐ Event Grid

☐ Send Grid

39. You need to design a secure solution that requires its secret to be updated monthly. At the same time, you need to keep in mind you won't be doing monthly deployments. Which solution is the best fit here?

☐ Access reviews

☐ Access keys

☐ Key vault

☐ Certificates

40. You need to create VMs using an ARM template. However, you need to make sure that passwords are stored as secure strings rather than in clear text. Which technology will you choose?

☐ Access reviews

☐ Access keys

☐ Key vault

☐ Certificates

41. You need to secure a database and make sure that it is encrypted at rest via encryption. Which encryption technology should be used?

☐ Transparent Data Encryption

☐ Always Encrypted

☐ None

☐ Certificates

42. As far as continuous deployment is concerned in Azure, which are the options that implement it?

☐ Azure DevOps

☐ GitHub

☐ BitBucket

☐ OneDrive

43. You need to deploy your web app to Azure. The web app needs to be connected with your company's custom domain, and manual scaling is required. Staging slots are not required. For this kind of requirement, which plan cost-effectively fits in?

☐ Free

☐ B1

☐ D1

☐ S1

44. You need to deploy your web app to Azure. The web app needs to be connected to your company's custom domain, with autoscaling, and staging slots are required. For these kinds of requirements, which plan cost-effectively fits in?

☐ Free

☐ B1

☐ D1

☐ S1

45. You need to secure your database in such a way that it is encrypted in transit and prevents database admins from viewing sensitive data in the database. Which option is the best fit here?

☐ Transparent Data Encryption

☐ Always Encrypted

☐ None

☐ Certificates

46. Is it possible to renew a certificate before its expiration is stored in Azure Key Vault?

○ True

○ False

47. You need to send a confirmation mail to users when they purchased a new product. Which technology option is the best fit here?

☐ SendGrid

☐ Notification Hub

☐ Event Hub

☐ None

48. You need to design an autoscaling platform for upcoming events, and you are not sure how this will affect the web servers running in full production mode 24/7. Which autoscaling pattern is best here?

☐ Adding resources

☐ On and off

☐ Predictable

☐ Unpredictable

49. Every time a new user customer is onboarded to the customer platform, you need to send a welcome message. Despite sending this message all the time manually, you need to automate the process. Which technology is the best fit here?

☐ Azure Functions

☐ Logic Apps

☐ Send Grid

☐ Notification Hub

50. You need to delegate a new responsibility to one IT support engineer to reset user passwords only in Azure AD. Which option is the best fit here?

○ Password administrator

○ Global administrator

○ Both

○ None

(Answer key provided on the next page.)

Answers

1. C. Both answers are valid.

2. B. Peering is correct. This doesn't require any additional resources.

3. B. Point-to-site access.

4. A. File storage supports.

5. D. MARS agent is correct.

6. C. Azure Backup server.

7. B. Application gateway. This supports layer 7 load balancing.

8. B. Application gateway. Path-based rules can be designed here.

9. B. WAF SKU. It helps to protect from SQL injection and other cyberattacks.

10. C. Cost analysis.

11. A. General Purpose V2 Hot Tier.

12. C. Virtual machine scale sets.

13. C. VNet peering.

14. C. GRS.

15. B. Shared access signatures.

16. C. Access reviews.

17. B. Add the Office IP addresses to the MFA server.

18. B. One-time bypass.

19. B. Multisite listener.

20. A. Use Deny assignments.

21. A. Load balancer.

22. C. AD Connect with P1 license. Option D is also correct, but it is not cost-effective.

23. B. Invoices.

24. B. NetworkSecurityGroupRules.

25. B. File recovery.

26. B. App service plan.

27. A and C. Traffic Manager and Application Gateway.

28.   B. Logic App.

29.   A. Event Grid.

30.   A. Point to site.

31.   C. Off and on.

32.   D. Adding resources.

33.   C. Azure Relay Service.

34.   D. Service Bus.

35.   A. Notification Hub.

36.   B. Event Hub.

37.   C. Event Grid.

38.   D. Send Grid.

39.   C. Key vault.

40.   C. Key vault.

41.   A. Transparent Data Encryption.

42.   A, B, and C. Azure DevOps, GitHub, and BitBucket.

43.   B. B1. S1 is also correct, but it's not a cost-effective solution.

44.   D. S1.

45.   B. Always Encrypted.

46.   A. True.

47.   A. SendGrid.

48.   D. Unpredictable.

49.   B. Logic Apps.

50.   A. Password administrator.

CHAPTER 24

Azure Architectural Practices

In this chapter, we will cover best practices to design scalable, resilient, and highly available applications based on proven practices. We will go through a set of recommended architectures for Azure. These days, instead of using monolithic designs, applications are decomposed into smaller fragments known as microservices. These trends also bring new challenges, such as the following:

- The application state is distributed.
- Operations are done in parallel and asynchronously.
- Resiliency.
- Deployments must be automated.
- Monitoring.
- Alerting.

Technology Choices

Once you know the type of architecture you are building, you need to make some decisions.

Compute Service

You need to choose a compute service. Azure offers a number of ways to host your application. The term *compute* refers to the hosting model for the computing resources that your application runs on. Figure 24-1 shows a flow chart that will help you choose the compute service for your application.

767

© Rahul Sahay 2020
R. Sahay, *Microsoft Azure Architect Technologies Study Companion*,
https://doi.org/10.1007/978-1-4842-6200-9_24

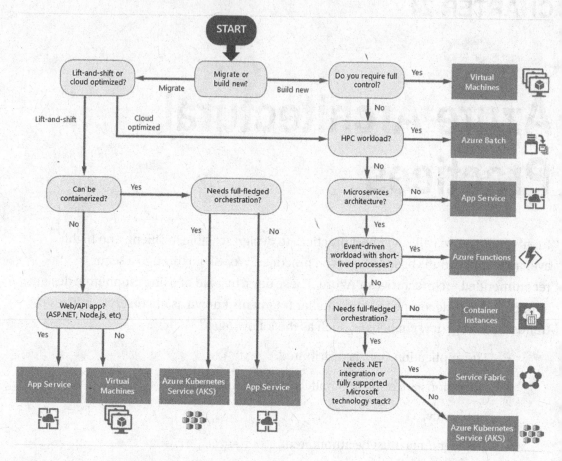

Figure 24-1. *Choosing a compute service*

- *Lift and shift* is a strategy for migrating a workload to the cloud without redesigning the application or making any code changes.

- *Cloud optimized* is a strategy for migrating to the cloud by changing the application implementation to take advantage of the cloud-native features.

Data Stores

Data stores were explained in earlier chapters of the book. For more details, you can refer to https://bit.ly/azure-data-store.

Data stores include databases but also storage for messages, queues, caches, logs, and anything that an application may need to store. Modern business systems manage increasingly large volumes of data. Data may be ingested from external services, generated by the system itself, or created by users. These data sets may have extremely varied characteristics and processing requirements. Businesses use data to assess trends, trigger business processes, analyze customer behavior, and do many other things. Choosing the right data store is really important before designing any application. This heterogeneity means that a single data store is usually not the best solution. Instead, it's often better to store different types of data in different data stores, each focused on a specific workload or usage pattern. The term *polyglot persistence* is used to describe solutions that use a mix of data store technologies. The following sections highlight types of data stores.

Relational Databases

Relational databases are one of the most common types of data store. A relational database organizes data as a series of two-dimensional tables with rows and columns. Each table has its own columns and rows. A relational database management system (RDBMS) implements a transactionally consistent mechanism that conforms to the ACID model for updating any information (ACID stands for atomic, consistent, isolated, and durable). Most key/value stores only support simple query, insert, and delete operations. To modify a value (either partially or completely), an application must overwrite the existing data for the entire value.

Here are some examples of relational databases:

- **SQL**: https://azure.microsoft.com/services/sql-database
- **MySQL**: https://azure.microsoft.com/services/mysql/
- **PostgreSQL**: https://azure.microsoft.com/services/postgresql/
- **Maria DB**: https://azure.microsoft.com/services/mariadb/

Key/Value Stores

A key/value store is essentially a large hash table. You associate each data value
with a unique key, and the key/value store uses this key to store the data by using an
appropriate hashing function. The hashing function is selected to provide an even
distribution of hashed keys across the data storage. The stored values are opaque to the
storage system software. Any schema information must be provided and interpreted by
the application. Essentially, values are blobs, and the key/value store simply retrieves or
stores the value by key.

Opaque to
data store

Key	Value
AAAAA	11010011110101001101011 11...
AABAB	1001100001011001101011110...
DFA766	0000000000101010110101010...
FABCC4	1110110110101010100101101...

Figure 24-2. *Key value*

Here are some examples:

- https://bit.ly/az-cosmos-db

- https://azure.microsoft.com/services/cache/

Document Databases

A document database is conceptually similar to a key/value store, except that it stores
a collection of named fields and data (known as *documents*), each of which could be
simple scalar items or compound elements such as lists and child collections. The data
in the fields of a document can be encoded in a variety of ways, including XML, YAML,
JSON, and BSON, or it can be stored as plain text. Unlike key/value stores, the fields in
documents are exposed to the storage management system, enabling an application
to query and filter data by using the values in these fields. A document store does not
require that all documents have the same structure. This free-form approach provides
a great deal of flexibility. Applications can store different data in documents as business
requirements change. Figure 24-3 shows a key document.

Key	Document
1001	```{ "CustomerID": 99, "OrderItems": [{ "ProductID": 2010, "Quantity": 2, "Cost": 520 }, { "ProductID": 4365, "Quantity": 1, "Cost": 18 }], "OrderDate": "04/01/2017" }```
1002	```{ "CustomerID": 220, "OrderItems": [{ "ProductID": 1285, "Quantity": 1, "Cost": 120 }], "OrderDate": "05/08/2017" }```

Figure 24-3. *Key document*

Here is an example: https://docs.microsoft.com/en-us/azure/cosmos-db/table-introduction/.

Graph Database

A graph database stores two types of information, nodes and edges. You can think of nodes as entities. Edges specify the relationships between the nodes. Both nodes and edges can have properties that provide information about that node or edge, similar to columns in a table. Edges can also have a direction indicating the nature of the relationship.

The purpose of a graph database is to allow an application to efficiently perform queries that traverse the network of nodes and edges and to analyze the relationships between entities. Figure 24-4 shows an organization's personnel database structured as a graph. The entities are employees and departments, and the edges indicate reporting relationships and the department in which employees work. In this graph, the arrows on the edges show the direction of the relationships.

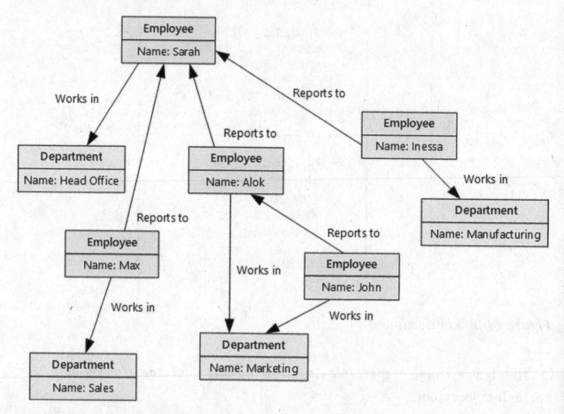

Figure 24-4. *Graph database*

Here is an example: https://docs.microsoft.com/en-us/azure/cosmos-db/table-introduction/.

Column-Family Databases

A column-family database organizes data into rows and columns. In its simplest form, a column-family database can appear similar to a relational database, at least conceptually. The real power of a column-family database lies in its denormalized approach to structuring sparse data.

You can think of a column-family database as holding tabular data with rows and columns, but the columns are divided into groups known as *column families*. Each column family holds a set of columns that are logically related together and are typically retrieved or manipulated as a unit. Other data that is accessed separately can be stored in separate column families. Within a column family, new columns can be added dynamically, and rows can be sparse (that is, a row doesn't need to have a value for every column). Figure 24-5 shows an example with two column families, Identity and Contact Info. The data for a single entity has the same row key in each column family. This structure, where the rows for any given object in a column family can vary dynamically, is an important benefit of the column-family approach, making this form of data store highly suited for storing structured, volatile data.

CustomerID	Column Family: Identity
001	First name: Mu Bae Last name: Min
002	First name: Francisco Last name: Vila Nova Suffix: Jr.
003	First name: Lena Last name: Adamcyz Title: Dr.

CustomerID	Column Family: Contact Info
001	Phone number: 555-0100 Email: someone@example.com
002	Email: vilanova@contoso.com
003	Phone number: 555-0120

Figure 24-5. Column-family database

Here's an example: `https://docs.microsoft.com/en-us/azure/hdinsight/hdinsight-hbase-overview`.

Data Analytics Stores

Data analytics stores provide massively parallel solutions for ingesting, storing, and analyzing data. This data is distributed across multiple servers using a share-nothing architecture to maximize scalability and minimize dependencies. The data is unlikely to be static, so these stores must be able to handle large quantities of information, arriving in a variety of formats from multiple streams, while continuing to process new queries.

Here are some examples:

- https://azure.microsoft.com/services/sql-data-warehouse/

- https://azure.microsoft.com/solutions/data-lake/

- https://azure.microsoft.com/services/data-explorer/

Search Engine Databases

A search engine database supports the ability to search for information held in external data stores and services. A search engine database can be used to index massive volumes of data and provide near-real-time access to these indexes. Although search engine databases are commonly thought of as being synonymous with the Web, many large-scale systems use them to provide structured and ad hoc search capabilities on top of their own databases.

The key characteristics of a search engine database are the ability to store and index information very quickly and the ability to provide fast response times for search requests. Indexes can be multidimensional and may support free-text searches across large volumes of text data. Indexing can be performed using a pull model, triggered by the search engine database, or using a push model, initiated by external application code.

Here is an example: https://azure.microsoft.com/services/search/.

Time-Series Databases

Time-series data is a set of values organized by time, and a time-series database is a database that is optimized for this type of data. Time-series databases must support a very high number of writes, as they typically collect large amounts of data in real time from a large number of sources. Updates are rare, and deletes are often done as bulk operations. Although the records written to a time-series database are generally small, there are often a large number of records, and the total data size can grow rapidly. Time-series databases are good for storing telemetry data. Scenarios include IoT sensors or application/system counters.

Here is an example: https://azure.microsoft.com/services/time-series-insights/.

Object Storage

Object storage is optimized for storing and retrieving large binary objects (images, files, video and audio streams, large application data objects and documents, and virtual machine disk images). Objects in these store types are composed of the stored data, some metadata, and a unique ID for accessing the object. Object stores enable the management of extremely large amounts of unstructured data.

Here is an example: `https://azure.microsoft.com/services/storage/blobs/`.

Shared Files

Sometimes using simple flat files can be the most effective means of storing and retrieving information. Using file shares enables files to be accessed across a network. Given the appropriate security and concurrent access control mechanisms, sharing data in this way can enable distributed services to provide highly scalable data access for performing basic, low-level operations such as simple read and write requests.

Here is an example: `https://azure.microsoft.com/services/storage/files/`.

Messaging Technology

Similarly, messaging technology holds high importance whenever designing any architecture. At an architecture level, a message is a datagram created by an entity (producer) to distribute information to other entities (consumers) so that they can act accordingly. See Figure 24-6.

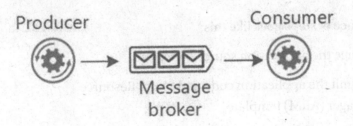

Figure 24-6. *Product consumer*

Messaging can be classified into two main categories. These are commands and events. To read the complete architecture of it, you can refer to `https://bit.ly/az-messaging`.

Design the Architecture

Once you have chosen the architecture style and the major technology components, you are ready to design your application. For example, let's consider the CI/CD cycle for Azure VMs. Figure 24-7 shows an architecture diagram.

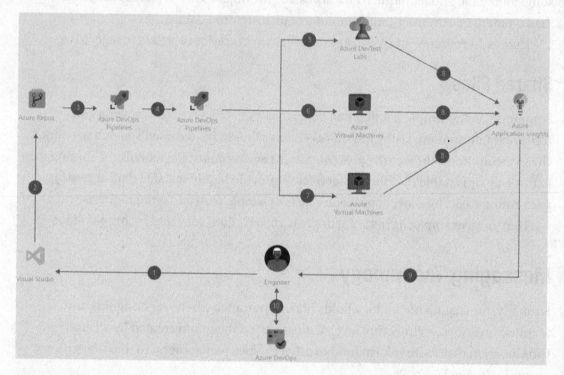

Figure 24-7. *Design architecture*

The sequence of steps goes like this:

1. Change the application source code.

2. Commit the application code and Azure Resource Manager (ARM) template.

3. Continuous integration triggers the application build and unit tests.

4. The continuous deployment trigger orchestrates the deployment of application artifacts with environment-specific parameters.

5. Deploy to the QA environment.

6.   Deploy to the staging environment.

7.   Deploy to the production environment.

8.   Application Insights collects and analyzes health, performance, and usage data.

9.   Review the health, performance, and usage information.

10. Update the backlog item.

These are the components involved:

- **Virtual machines**: Provision Windows and Linux virtual machines in seconds. You can read more about virtual machines at `https://azure.microsoft.com/services/virtual-machines`.

- **Azure DevTest labs**: Quickly create environments using reusable templates and artifacts. You can read more about this at `https://bit.ly/az-labs`.

- **Application Insights**: Detect, triage, and diagnose issues in your web apps and services. You can read more about Application Insights at `https://bit.ly/azure-monitor`.

- **Azure DevOps**: Build and deploy multiplatform apps to get the most from Azure services. You can read in detail about DevOps at `https://bit.ly/az-devops`.

You can see tons of solution ideas at `https://bit.ly/azure-architectures`.

Design Principles

Microsoft Azure recommends ten high-level design principles to make your application more scalable, resilient, and manageable. These design principles apply to any architecture style. They are as follows:

- Design for self-healing. In a distributed system, failures happen. Design your application to be self-healing when failures occur. You can read more about this at `https://bit.ly/azure-design-healing`.

- Make all things redundant. Build redundancy into your application to avoid having single points of failure. You can read more about this at `https://bit.ly/make-all-redundant`.

- Minimize coordination. Minimize coordination between application services to achieve scalability. You can read more about this at `https://bit.ly/Minimize-coordination`.

- Design to scale out. Design your application so that it can scale horizontally, adding or removing new instances as demand requires. You can read more about this at `https://bit.ly/scale-out-design`.

- Partition around limits. Use partitioning to work around database, network, and compute limits. You can read more about this at `https://bit.ly/Partition-around`.

- Design for operations. Design your application so that the operations team has the tools they need. You can read more about this at `https://bit.ly/Design-operations`.

- Use managed services. When possible, use platform as a service (PaaS) rather than infrastructure as a service (IaaS). You can read more about this at `https://bit.ly/paas-options`.

- Use the best data store for the job. Pick the storage technology that is the best fit for your data and how it will be used. You can read more about this at `https://bit.ly/az-data-store`.

- Design for evolution. All successful applications change over time. An evolutionary design is key for continuous innovation. You can read more about this at `https://bit.ly/design-for-evolution`.

- Build for the needs of business. Every design decision must be justified by a business requirement. You can read more about this at `https://bit.ly/build-for-business`.

Design Patterns

Software design patterns are nothing but proven industry practices to solve complex problems. Azure cloud design patterns address specific challenges around distributed systems. All aspects are listed with their references. You can take a look at the following pages for a detailed understanding:

- Availability: `https://bit.ly/availability-patterns`

- Data management: `https://bit.ly/data-management-patterns`

- Design and implementation: `https://bit.ly/design-and-implementation`

- Messaging: `https://bit.ly/messaging-patterns`

- Management and monitoring: `https://bit.ly/management-and-monitoring`

- Performance and scalability: `https://bit.ly/performance-and-scalability`

- Resiliency: `https://bit.ly/resiliency-patterns`

- Security: `https://bit.ly/security-patterns`

Best Practices

Azure best practices cover various design considerations including API design, auto-scaling, data partitioning, caching, and so on. You can find them at `https://docs.microsoft.com/en-us/azure/architecture/best-practices`.

Quality Pillars

A successful cloud application is based on five pillars of software quality.

- Cost

- DevOps

- Resiliency

- Scalability

- Security

You can visit `https://docs.microsoft.com/en-us/azure/architecture/framework/` to access your implementation.

References

You can use the following links for further practice:

- The Self-Paced Learning Program is available at `https://www.microsoft.com/handsonlabs/selfpacedlabs`.

- The Azure Code Samples are available at `https://docs.microsoft.com/en-us/samples/browse/?products=azure`.

- The Azure documentation is at `https://docs.microsoft.com/en-us/azure/?product=featured`.

- The Azure hands-on labs are at `https://azurecitadel.com/`.

- The Azure Architecture Center is at `https://docs.microsoft.com/en-us/azure/architecture/`.

Index

781

© Rahul Sahay 2020
R. Sahay, *Microsoft Azure Architect Technologies Study Companion*,
https://doi.org/10.1007/978-1-4842-6200-9

Printed in the United States
By Bookmasters